Grandmother's Hope Chest

French Sewing by Machine
Smocking
Shadowwork Embroidery
Embroidery

PRINTED BY *The C.J. Krehbiel Company*
Cincinnati, Ohio

PUBLISHED AND DISTRIBUTED BY
Martha Pullen Company, Inc.

518 Madison Street
Huntsville, Alabama 35801

(205) 533-9586

ISBN 1-878048-01-5

Grandmother's Hope Chest

French Sewing by Machine
Smocking
Shadowwork Embroidery
Embroidery

by Martha Campbell Pullen, Ph. D.

To Jackie

May God Bless You

Martha Pullen

10-23-99

Illustrations by *Angela Cataldo Pullen, Cynthia Handy, and Diane Zinser*
Photography by *Jack Cooper*
Editing and Photography Styling by *Amelia Johanson*
Book Design by *Joia Thompson*
Construction/Technical Editing by *Kathy McMakin*
Major Sewing Contributor: *Sue Pennington*
Other Contributors: *Bernina, Elna, Pfaff, and Viking*
Wendy Ragan

DEDICATION

IN HUNTSVILLE BUSINESS magazine, March 1987, Dr. Joe Pullen was the cover story in an article entitled "A Pioneer Of Implant Dentistry." The writer, Melissa Ford Thornton, began the piece like this, "Dr. Pullen's contributions have been recognized by many major dental organizations, but his real reward is the happiness he's been able to bring to people."

Since Joe has been bringing happiness, joy, encouragement, love, enthusiasm, excitement, direction, and guidance to my life and our children's lives for many years, it gives me great pleasure to tell you more about my husband, who also happens to be my best friend.

Joe was born on February 15, 1935 in Gadsden, Alabama, the only child of Dr. Joyce Buren Pullen and Emma Eileen Hodges Pullen. Mom, who had been a school teacher until Joe's birth, retired from the public schools permanently to raise her only child, a beautiful little blue-eyed blonde. Pop was a dentist in Boaz, Alabama. He came to this state directly from his Vanderbilt Dental School graduation in 1924, but he had difficulty earning a living in Boaz. Although this was prior to the depression, most of his patients still paid him in eggs, molasses, and cured hams. Not that the Pullen family wasn't grateful for these foods, but it was a little difficult to pay other bills with groceries. Pop's first "regularly paying job" was when he was named state dentist at Kilby Prison, and so when Joe was just a baby, the family moved to Montgomery. Pop used to tell our children that his salary was $3000 per year, and they thought they were rich. When Joe was in the second grade they moved to a growing and thriving Huntsville where Pop practiced until he was 78 years old. He would have loved to retire years earlier, but some of his patients told him that they simply would not go to another dentist.

Of course, Joe loved Huntsville from the very beginning. He began playing trumpet in the Huntsville High School band when he was in the fourth grade. It seems they were short of trumpet players, and he was very talented in band. He loved getting out of elementary school early every day and walking to the high school. The trumpet has continued to play an important role in Joe's life. He played in the University Of Alabama "Million Dollar Band" under the direction of Colonel Butler. Years later, one of his most enjoyable trumpet assignments was in the orchestra of Whitesburg Baptist Church and on mission trips to Jamaica and Israel. Despite his musical prowess, Joe never considered being anything other than a dentist. His undergraduate degree was from the University of Alabama, although he attended The University Of Alabama in Huntsville and Birmingham Southern College also. He graduated from The University of Alabama Dental School in 1961 after having won the honor of representing that school in a national dental student contest in California. He was busy from day one, since he entered Pop's practice upon graduation.

Shortly after he began practice, Joe heard of a brand new field of dentistry called implant dentistry. Since he had seen so many patients suffer because of missing teeth he began to look for courses to take. The rest is almost history because of what he has contributed to the highly specialized field of implant dentistry, which is an alternative to dentures. Joe began his study of implant dentistry almost three decades ago when the technique was in the experimental stages. He joined a small group of mostly New York dentists, The American Academy of Implant Dentistry. Since this group was in the forefront of developing important techniques, Joe began to attend their meetings and to travel to their offices to learn techniques. Since this particular technique was thriving in Europe Joe made arrangements to study with Dr. Orlay in England, Dr. Cherchev in France, and Dr. Mouritori in Italy. Joe has remained close friends with these men and considers it invaluable to have been personally taught by them early in the development of this type of dentistry. He also continued studying with American dentists who were expanding implant ideas here. Joe wanted to learn everything about this new type of dentistry.

After five years of nearly every weekend of travel and study, Joe began to teach implant dentistry to other dentists here and abroad. He has taught at dental schools from Harvard to the University of Alabama. He has taught at The Royal Academy of Medicine in London, The University of Zurich Dental School, and at Lariboisiere Hospital in Paris. He has also conducted seminars for dentists in Brazil, Japan, Singapore, and several other countries. I had the privilege of attending a reception in Paris, France at the Hotel de Ville (the town hall) where he was presented the Medal of the City of Paris by none other than the Mayor of Paris. The mayor stated that this honor was in recognition of his contribution to the international health community in the area of implant dentistry where he had helped to "alleviate pain and suffering of people the world over."

His contributions have been recognized by many major dental organizations. Over a period of 10 years, he has held the offices of president, treasurer, secretary, vice-president and president elect of the American Academy of Implant Dentistry. In 1983 he was elected President of the American Academy of Implant Dentistry and during that year traveled to eight different countries, representing this organization and teaching other dentists how to place implants. He has been president of

Grandmother's Hope Chest

the Alabama Academy of General Dentistry and holds membership in the American Dental Association. Dr. Pullen was named a fellow, an honor reserved for only 1 percent of the members, by the other fellows in the American Academy of Implant Dentistry. He is also a fellow of the American Academy of General Dentistry and of the Academy of Dentistry International. He was instrumental in founding The Alabama Implant Study Club, which has become one of the world's leading implant education groups. While the list of his honors and recognitions stretches beyond the limits of my imagination, his real message of implant dentistry, and other dentistry as well, lies in the patients he has treated right here in Huntsville. I might add that individuals have traveled from all over the United States for him to place implants.

I really cannot recall the number of dentists he has taught to do implants in this short passage. Many of them who flew from every part of the United States, have stayed in our home while Joe demonstrated and taught during the day and further taught in our living room at night. He has performed implants on closed circuit television at dental meetings for professionals worldwide. Until recently, I could truly say that dentistry was both his work and his hobby, but during the last three years, riding western pleasure horses has taken over the hobby aspect of his life. Dentistry will always be his number one love for work.

I am sure one of the most rewarding aspects of Joe's dental life has been mission trips sponsored by the Whitesburg Baptist Church in conjunction with the Foreign Missions Board of the Southern Baptist Convention. He has performed dentistry for people who had never had dental care available to them. The conditions were primitive to say the least since his surgical light was a hand held flashlight and the dental chair was a folding metal chair. He literally had to get on his knees on a concrete floor for upper extractions and lean over for lowers. God gave him the strength to see more than 500 patients on each trip. He simply said to them, "I come in the name of Jesus to relieve your pain."

I am very glad that Joe has always burned the midnight oil in his dental office. We met while I was on a consulting trip to Huntsville with the Army for graduate school. A very old crown fell off the front of my tooth, and I began desperately searching for an open dental office. After all, I was from out of town and didn't know a dentist in Huntsville. Wouldn't you know that his office was the only one in town open, and I begged his receptionist for an appointment. Joe and I married three months later.

We each had two wonderful boys when we married. I have always said that I wanted five children, which God blessed me to have. Many of you know that the birth of our daughter, Joanna, was the beginning of my heirloom sewing career! I guess I couldn't dedicate any book to Joe without thanking him for the role he has played in being a wonderful father to all five of our children. He has worked much longer than he should have to provide the finest private educations for them, he has counseled and taught them, has provided the finest of everything materially for them, and most importantly has loved them. He always told them, "There is absolutely no trouble that you can get into that I won't be there for you. Don't ever be afraid to come home when you need help."

Joe and I became Christians some 11 years ago. That walk with God is sweeter every day to Joe and to his whole family. His commitment to God's work was evident even before he became a Christian. Nearly every day of his dental life, he has done free dental work on either homeless individuals living in a shelter here in Huntsville or on kids living in another shelter, who are recovering from drug or alcohol abuse. I have seen him go out in the middle of the night again and again knowing full well that this trip would be unpaid. He has always said," I have a responsibility to alleviate pain if someone is hurting."

There would be no Martha Pullen Co., Inc, no Sew Beautiful Magazine, no books, no nothing I call my business if not for Joe. He gave me the courage to start the business, and he and God together have kept my strength going while we built this business. Ever since Joe and I married, I had made the statement that I was an entrepreneur at heart and that "I would rather try and fail than never to have tried at all." He kept reminding me of this statement when I would fantasize about starting my own business. I might add here, that he forced me to finish my Ph. D. after Joanna was born. I was enjoying her so much that I thought it really didn't matter whether I finished the dissertation or not. He insisted that I go the final mile, reminding me that winners don't quit.

He furnished, along with a significant contribution from Mama, my start up money for my first retail store. He has sold property on two occasions to pay my bills to keep this business going. As I have sat and cried saying, "It's not worth it—the business pressure isn't worth it," he has reminded me of the joy that I have brought to people. He literally supported the family, alone, for the first four years that I was in business. We were well into the fifth year before I could draw even a little salary out of the company. He has always reminded me that we won't starve if I lose all of the money and time that we have invested in this business. He reminds me that he values me just as much as a wife and a mother as he does as a businesswoman. I find fewer and fewer men in this day and age who value women as much without a paycheck as with one. Although Joe has enjoyed our success in this business, he certainly doesn't care about the money that I make.

Joe can be very proud of our children. Mark is a dentist practicing with Joe. Camp is in business with me. Jeff is in the restaurant business in Birmingham. John is a Baptist preacher in Mississippi while he finishes seminary. Later he will return to the mission field in Africa. The boys have all married precious Christian wives. Joanna is a very accomplished dancer, dance teacher, and volunteer worker. She studies and behaves herself like a sweet Christian young lady should. She continues to tell us that she will either be a dancing teacher or a first grade teacher. Joe's devotion to our children, our parents, our other relatives, and to me is the real cornerstone of his life. I see God's hand in his thoughts, actions, and deeds. He is a true joy bringer, a true helpmate, and a devoted man of God.

Joe, I will never be able to thank you enough for all you are, have been, and will be to me. I love you with all my heart, and I thank God for that day, 17 years ago, when the crown fell off my tooth. Looking at our lives as they unfold daily, I know it "didn't just happen." I need to thank God for you and for planning the rest of my life to be with you.

Martha

ACKNOWLEDGMENTS

Philippians 4: 6-9

6 Be careful (anxious) for nothing; but in every thing by prayer and supplication, with thanksgiving, let your requests be made known unto God.

7 And the peace of God, which passeth all understanding, shall keep your hearts and minds through Christ Jesus.

8 Finally, brethren, whatsoever things are true, whatsoever things are honest, whatsoever things are just, whatsoever things are pure, whatsoever things are lovely, whatsoever things are of good report; if there be any virtue, and if there be any praise, think on these things.

9 Those things, which ye have both learned, and received, and heard, and seen in me, do: and the God of peace shall be with you.

WRITING A BOOK this complicated and lengthy requires the help, dedication, and talents of many individuals. I have been very blessed with people who willingly help make my dreams a reality. Although my name appears on the cover of this book, each of these names certainly deserves cover billing also. The encouragement, help, suggestions, inspiration, work, ideas, and love of a number of people always will be a cornerstone for what success I may attain. To the following people, I will be eternally grateful.

My mother and father, Anna Ruth Dicus Campbell and Paul Jones Campbell were my first and greatest teachers. They taught me, among other things, that dreams are not impossible, stars are not unreachable, wrongs are not unrightable, and sorrows are not unbearable. The most important lesson that I learned from my parents was to turn to God first because He is unfailing.

My cousin, Christine Finch Jenkins, spent hours upon hours with me, teaching immature hands to make wonderful things, including Christmas stockings. My absolute joy of sewing first came from her when I was about 6 years old.

My high school home economics teacher, Mrs. Sarah Betty Ingram, instilled the love of sewing even further. She believed that we could sew anything!

My late mother- and father-in-law, Dr. Joyce Buren Pullen and Emma Hodges Pullen contributed hours upon hours of child care, cooking, and encouragement for all of my career ventures. Without their generous gift of time, I doubt that finishing my Ph.D. would have been possible.

My husband's aunt, Anna Mary McDonald, has been more like a mother to Joe and me. She is always there to support us and encourage us in all that we do. She is a very courageous lady who has handled arthritis and all of its problems with grace and dignity.

My friend, Mrs. Lili Jones, kept my home intact, and ironed millions of hours on these Swiss batiste clothes for our whole business. She went to be with the Lord last July. Joanna and I will always love her like a second mother (Joanna) and a sister (me).

My late nephew, Alex Walter Jackson, killed by a drunk driver. For all the joy one little, gorgeous, blonde boy could give a family in a short seven years. I would like to thank Mothers Against Drunk Driving for their untiring efforts to get drunk drivers off the highways.

My sister and brother-in-law, Mary and Rick Nixon, for encouraging me in the business, for hours of driving Anna and David to the photo shoots and for squealing over the clothes that I make for the children.

My sister, Dottie, my brothers Cliff and Robin, and their precious families for loving me and for always being proud of my accomplishments.

My son, William Campbell Crocker, for loving me and always putting up with me. Camp's interest in this business, sewing, publishing, people, and selling have earned him a place in the organizational structure of this business. I have always said that Camp could "sell snowballs in Alaska" because he loves people so much and because he has an uncanny zest and enthusiasm for living. He joined our firm upon graduation from Arizona State and his being here has enabled me to travel much more than I ever have had the opportunity.

My daughter-in-law, Charisse Fuentes Crocker, for loving Camp and for presenting us with our first grandchild, William Campbell Crocker, jr. Her enthusiasm for smocking and sewing has been a pure joy to me and I fully expect her to become a master seamstress. She is a wonderful Christian wife and mother who has her values in the proper order: God, family, and work. She has been so kind to me to always be available to run errands, to take care of Joanna while I traveled, and to cook dinners for Joe and Joanna while I am away from home so much. Her complete commitment of time and energy to the family is very Godly and appreciated.

My son, John Houston Crocker, for loving me and always putting up with me. John's complete love of the Lord and his unselfish missionary work in Africa continue to thrill me. I have never known any human being who had a more tender and giving heart towards those less fortunate than he. A lot of people will suffer less as a result of John and his wife, Suzanne's, work. I am also very glad that he has chosen to finish seminary at Mid America in Memphis. The joy of his pastoring Gray's Creek Baptist Church in Hernando, Mississippi is so wonderful. We love to hear the news of how the Lord is working in their ministry there. Their commitment to Africa is still present; if it is the Lord's will, they will be returning with the Southern Baptist Mission Board when they go back to Togo.

My daughter-in-law, Suzanne Laramore Crocker, for loving John and putting up with him. Sometimes you are so blessed from God to have a daughter who thinks only of the Lord's work and of her family. She has treated thousands of people in make-shift medical clinics in Togo. Her unselfishness and her devotion to God's work in Africa and to her family are terribly unusual. Not many wives would love living without electricity, running water, and the necessities of life to follow a husband to Africa to preach.

My son, Mark Edward Pullen, for loving me and always putting up with me. Mark is my great communicator, always counseling and putting things in the proper perspective. Mark's hard work and discipline have earned him a dental degree. Mark is not only a competent person but a caring person. It was a very exciting day in our family when Dr. Mark joined Dr. Joe in the dental practice here in Huntsville. He is the third generation Pullen dentist to practice in Huntsville.

My daughter-in-law Sherry Ann Green Pullen, for loving Mark and putting up with him. God blessed our family the day that Mark married Sherry Ann. Sherry Ann wrote the book on gentleness, unselfishness, kindness, hard work, consideration, and thoroughly spoiling a husband. When you have your priorities in the correct Christian order, as Sherry Ann does, I shouldn't be too surprised that the Lord would give her these qualities to share with others.

My son, Jeffrey David Pullen, for loving me and always putting up with me. Jeff has the extraordinary ability to love people and help them to understand how special and important they are. Jeff also works harder than anyone I have ever known to do his job and to help others do their jobs as well. My heart almost bursts with pride when Jeff's former employees nearly cry telling me that "Jeff was the most fair and best boss we ever had." We are so proud of the incredible success Jeff has had in several short years of restaurant management.

My daughter-in-law, Angela Cataldo Pullen, for loving Jeff and putting up with him. Our family received one of its greatest blessings the day that God gave us our "Angel." Angela is one of the artists for this book and what an artist she is. She is a wonderful Christian woman who will always put God first, her family second, and her work third. To get such a Godly daughter-in-law and such an outstanding artist in one person is a real blessing. Congratulations to Angela for graduating magna cum laude from the art department of Auburn University last March. Here is some last minute news: she has been hired as a designer by *Just Cross Stitch* magazine! She will love working with my dear friend, Phyllis Hoffman, and her wonderful staff.

Joanna Emma Joyce Pullen is the reason I became involved in the French sewing business in the first place. When my little girl was born after four boys, you can just imagine my excitement over my real live doll. All I wanted to do was hold her, tell her how wonderful she was, and dress her up in different dresses and lacy accessories. These clothes are love clothes for Joanna. Joanna is sweet, gentle, quiet, and caring. She loves people, especially children, and can't stand to see anyone cry or be lonely. Her volunteer efforts have been phenomenal for a young girl; she especially loves volunteering with children and senior citizens. Her talents in dance, gymnastics, drama, singing, and public speaking will take her far in life either professionally or in volunteer work. She is a champion for people less fortunate than she. She is a beautiful Christian, whom I believe God will use mightily in her teen years to influence other teens to stay away from drugs, alcohol, and immorality. She has been a joy every day of her life, and I thank God for entrusting her to us.

Within the heirloom sewing industry there are several people who not only help make this industry what it is today but who have also had a great influence on my life.

Margaret Boyles has always been there for me with her encouragement and creative ideas. She has taught in my schools, written for the magazine, and been one of my number-one supporters.

Wendy Lee Ragan has contributed so much to my life both in designing for the magazine and in personally doing just about everything else for me. I am especially appreciative to her for the delightfully elegant page of shadow embroidery designs she has contributed to this book.

Elizabeth Travis Johnson can be thanked for being the cornerstone in making this industry what it is today. Without her foundation through the last 40 years, I doubt that smocking and French sewing would have the same flavor and importance in today's international society. I would certainly call her the "Mother Of Heirloom Sewing."

Mildred Turner has been one of my closest friends from that first day she walked by my booth in her lavender ultra-suede suit and told me that she adored heirloom sewing as much as I did. She has written and written for the magazine, taught in my schools, and always been one of my best and most loyal customers.

Eunice Farmer, the mentor to my whole sewing business. She is a beautiful friend and a wonderful inspiration to all who love the sewing world.

Clotilde has become a very close personal and business colleague. She and Don have advised us on many matters, and I am very appreciative to them.

Gloria McKinnon brought Martha Pullen to Australia for the first time and has worked untiringly to spread our books and magazines to some of the most wonderful people in the world. I remember well her friendly teasing comments, "I think Australia and New Zealand are ready for heirloom sewing, but are they ready for Martha?"

I would like to thank each and every teacher who has ever traveled to Huntsville to teach at my School of Art Fashion during the past six years. Please accept my gratitude for all that they have meant and continue to mean to me.

It has been a great pleasure to work with the Bernina, Elna, Pfaff, and Viking companies in several chapters of this book. The lace making ideas will be appreciated by anyone who is fortunate enough to own one of these fabulous machines. Just wait until you make machine entredeux and pin stitching with a wing needle and these computer machines! I would like to thank each of these companies for sponsoring the traveling "Martha Pullen Schools of Art Fashion" and for sending machines and sergers out to these locations.

I would like to thank each and every student of mine, subscriber to *Sew Beautiful* magazine, shop owner who sells Martha Pullen products of any type, and customer of Martha Pullen Co., Inc. Without your loyalty over the years, this book wouldn't have been written because there wouldn't have been any Martha Pullen Company!

I would like to thank the Huntsville Botanical Gardens for allowing us to photograph part of this book on their grounds and Parisians of Huntsville for the loan of the antique baby carriage pictured on the dust jacket.

No business could be a reality without the talents of many people. This first set of individuals have "run" the business, while the others in the group wrote and produced this book. They are joys in my life and so appreciated for all that they do, day after day, year after year.

Kathy Pearce for loyalty, joy, steadfastness, and competency.

Yulanda Brazelton for perfection accuracy, extra errands, encouragement, and sweet words.

ACKNOWLEDGMENTS

Westa Chandler for efficiency, counseling with subscribers, and smiling even when two mailbags come in the door.
Donna King for sweetness, efficiency, and availability when needed.
Lakanjala Campbell for efficiency and extreme talent in the accounting and bookkeeping for the magazine.

There are individuals who physically worked on this book in particular. There are no words to express my complete gratitude to them for making this project a reality, not just a dream. I will attempt to thank these vital people for their efforts on this book.
Golden Rule Printing, with a special thanks to Larry Maxwell, has always been there to print anything. Their business really does follow the golden rule and I appreciate them.
Graphic Color always creates the most wonderful color separations. A very special thanks goes out to Phil Johnson and his staff.
C.J. Krehbiel is a wonderful printing company that receives large boxes of our work and turns them into books like this one. A very special thanks to their staff and Marvin Poenitske.

The next people that I would like to thank for their part in this book are my precious models and their mothers. They always wait so patiently and smile so beautifully. They deserve lots of credit for their outstanding performances. I love them, and I thank them.
Jack Cooper photographed this whole book in several locations. His patience with children is almost unbelievable. His keen eye for making a picture "happen" is very appreciated for this book and for our whole publishing business.
Without Sue Pennington, this book would have been several years longer in the making and it would not have been nearly as wonderful. Her original sewing designs in the Circa 1992 section are absolutely breathtaking. Her shark's teeth technique which she originally presented in the Summer 1991 Sew Beautiful magazine, has been a world wide favorite. Her ideas and sewing art are found throughout this book, and I appreciate her more than she will ever know. She is a very generous person in sharing her wonderful talent with the rest of the world.
Louise Baird was the creator of the recreation of the antique baby quilt. She also used the sewing machine to create the sewing machine quilting for the bears and the crib toy. We call on Louise for help on anything concerning the sewing machine. She seems to always be able to create what we thought wasn't possible.
Dottie Daniels' sewing and original smocking designs from only our ideas are absolutely wonderful. She has worked overtime making lots of the models from pattern pieces we just handed to her without even any labeling on them.
Patty Smith has sewn overtime for years to make all of our publications a success. Her design and sewing skills are known all over the world and she can make more dresses under pressure than anyone in the industry.
Becky Lambert and Diane Zinser for helping coordinate the photo shoots and other aspects of writing this book. Becky and Dianne are always willing to help with the whole business in any way possible.
Margaret Taylor for helping coordinate the photo shoots, helping write some of the technique sections, making a million phone calls, excellent paste up help, and writing lots of letters concerning details, details, and more details. I certainly can't forget her typing all of the orders into the computer.
Cynthia Handy for working with me several months to illustrate this book. Cynthia's lace absolutely dances, and her original shadow embroidery designs are breathtaking.
Diane Zinser for illustrating all of the pattern directions, lots of the book, and for helping write some of the technique instructions. Diane's sewing ability is invaluable since some of the illustrations she simply drew from my writing. Her drawings make construction easy to understand and stitch.
Angela Cataldo Pullen for her art work in illustrating my antique clothing collection, the Sue Pennington dresses, and most of the shadow embroidery designs. Just look for more "Pullen and Pullen." Angela's dresses seem to breathe, and the creativity for garment design in her head is almost unbelievable.
Kathy McMakin for designing, writing pattern directions, helping me with lots of the techniques, creating some of the techniques, proofing, sewing some of the garments, and always reminding me not to quit. Kathy has been writing with me for so long, that I cannot ever imagine days when she wasn't helping me do everything. She is a critical and vital link to any of my business endeavors from traveling and teaching to writing.
Scott Wright, who now works with me, took my original attempt (a box of photographs, homemade art, typed manuscript with lots of typos, and pretty color slides) at writing a book back in 1983 and put it together in book form. It became a best seller; I soon hired Scott! He has designed the layout on some of the color section of this book with his usual talent and creativity
Amelia Johanson has more journalistic and artistic talent in one finger than most of us ever acquire in a lifetime. I have renamed her "Ms. Magic Words" because her command of the English language is more delightful than any I have ever known. She can edit the most ordinary of words into lovely phrases, which seem to live and breathe. Her work in editing the new part in this book delights me. She has also planned and styled the photography.
Joia Thompson's book design was carefully researched and planned before she made her final decisions about the most wonderful and beautiful presentation. She researched new types to make this book have an image completely unique to this book. You know of course, that she also did the masterful layout of the *Antique Clothing* book. She has been working overtime for months executing exactly the right type of creativity for each section and perfectly placing hundreds of illustrations in the correct order, which is no small matter in a sewing/technique book. I love her design and layout of this book. I thank her for hundreds of hours in making this gorgeous book come alive.

Grandmother's Hope Chest

TABLE OF CONTENTS

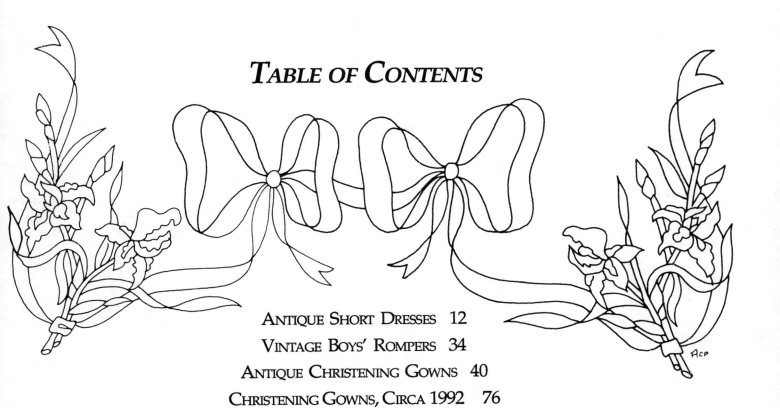

FOREWORD

A Note from Margaret Boyles

GRANDMOTHER'S HOPE CHEST, what wonderful pictures those words call to mind. Nearly everyone's grandmother has a trunk, box or drawer filled with carefully tended treasures from another time. It might be an old steamer trunk with graceful bowed top, ancient leather straps and time-blackened hinges. It could be a classic monogrammed canvas traveling case with elegant brass corners and time-softened painted letters like those we still choose today on our handbags and luggage. A fragrant cedar chest from the 20's or 30's might be your grandmother's choice of storage for the mementos she holds for you.

I REMEMBER ALL three treasure chests in my grandmother's attic plus an assortment of hat boxes and a huge carved golden oak dresser filled with all manner of Victorian baby clothes, ladies dresses, my grandmother's wedding dress and shoes, old letters and pictures, dolls and toys. There was one trunk filled with "dress-ups" saved for little girls and an old pier glass mirror which reflected familiar little faces under huge silk ribbon and ostrich feather trimmed hats. It was a wonderful place to spend the quiet afternoon of a rainy day.

MY GRANDMOTHER TREASURED most her collection of baby clothes. Since they had belonged either to her or my grandfather as babies or to her own children, she did not think of them as having any value other than sentimental. For her they held so many sweet memories that she could have written a book about them.

Martha Pullen has a grandmother's trunk too. Martha's antique collection fills myriad trunks with exquisite white clothing collected from all corners of this country, Great Britain, Europe, Australia and New Zealand. I've had the joy of traveling with her occasionally and watching in awe as her quick eye finds an elegant French child's dress in perfect condition or a less cherished christening robe that offers among its tatters good ideas for a technique that can be adapted for today or a lovely embroidery design still as beautiful as the day it was drawn.

THUS, OVER THE years, Martha's hope chests have filled to overflowing. The precious pieces tumble out in glorious profusion. Now Martha has opened her favorite trunk — the one that contains the baby collection for all of us to share! But we don't have to climb the dusty attic stairs to enjoy this collection. Martha has put the best of it between the covers of this book with the wonderful idea that those who do not have an grandmother's trunk collection can begin one in the form of a Hope Chest. If you begin now, grandbabies to come can wear and enjoy your beautiful adaptations, then they together with your memories of little ones in them can be packed away in your own trunk to be treasured by still another generation.

THIS BOOK IS more than a beautiful keepsake filled with inspiring pictures. It has those in lavish portions to be sure, but Martha has managed to add a treasure trove of new and useable sewing information and patterns to inspire us all to create the beauties with which she entices us! You will find delightful photographs and delicate line drawings of many of Martha's favorites of the antique baby dresses, christening gowns, coats and bonnets in her collection. From these she has adapted new patterns and techniques. There is a glorious collection of drawings and patterns for the best of the christening gowns with the details and measurements shown so you can recreate these old masterpieces. In addition there are many classic baby patterns for rompers and bubbles, precious day gowns, angelic smocked dresses, frilly bonnets, little boy suits, sweet bibs, a quilt — even adorable soft shoes and booties. When you begin to explore the new sewing techniques Martha has included, you will find many ways to make your own Heirloom sewing look more like the antiques. This book is a treasure that would fill many trunks with heirlooms for tomorrow.

MARTHA PULLEN IS a truly remarkable woman. She radiates the purity that begins with complete acceptance of her Christian faith and imbues every facet of both her personal and business life with it. She is gracious, giving and loving. She is loved and cherished by family and friends. She has the intellect, talent, vision and energy to dream an impossible task, then see it successfully completed. Her magazine, SEW BEAUTIFUL is such a project. Instead of being like most of us just wishing there was a good magazine interested in our passion for heirlooms, Martha found a way to bring it into being and to keep it beautiful, inspiring and useful. Its success is a tribute to Martha herself!

I KNOW YOU will love every page of this book and hope you will use it as a guide to making the beautiful things in it so your children and grandchildren will wear these lovely garments, then have their own Grandmother's Trunk to explore and cherish. I wish you many happy hours making what Martha calls "love clothes."

INTRODUCTION

Martha Campbell Pullen

Dear Friends,

Many of you have heard me quip that if I ever start looking at heirloom garments and don't well up with emotion, I'm going to look for a new line of work. Oh how I love smocking and French sewing. My husband accuses me of using the business as an excuse to purchase white antique garments for babies and adults. He's probably right! On my travels around the United States and to other countries, as well, the first thing I do is seek out the antique shops to try and satisfy my insatiable appetite for white heirloom clothing.

This book has several objectives. The first objective is try and convince you that now is the time to begin sewing for those future babies and grandbabies. Baby styles never change or rather haven't changed since the early 1800s, so I think it's safe to assume that these styles will remain constant for several years to come. Since I am a new grandmother, I have a baby for whom I can sew, and since we are expecting our second grandchild (and probably many more over the next few years), you can only imagine how excited I am about infant clothing. We only have one problem. Since all of our boys are about the same age, and all married within five years of each other, we find ourselves needing christening gowns, day gowns, bubbles, button on suits and hopefully bishop dresses and little girl bubbles all at one time. If only I'd started sewing things for these babies years ago. Mothers have long made garments and purchased treasures for their daughters' trousseaus. Why not do the same for future babies?

That question is really why I decided to write this book. I wanted to let all the future mothers and grandmothers know that it's perfectly alright to sew baby garments today and save them until the blessed occasion arrives. When I started jotting down ideas for this book's content, I didn't know I would be a grandmother before it got published. First, son Camp and his wife Charisse, announced that a little one was on the way, and shortly after, son Mark and his wife, Sherry Ann, announced that they were expecting. Little William Campbell Crocker, jr. arrived February 2, 1992 and our other precious child is due June 22, 1992. Needless to say, my mind has been swimming with thoughts of baby clothes since the day I learned of my impending grandmotherhood. How I wish I'd started a future baby trunk years ago.

The second reason I decided to write this book is because I've developed some really fun and ever-so-easy new ways to shape lace. I just couldn't wait to write another book to share with you these brand new, updated techniques. This is particularly exciting for me because I'm certain some of these techniques have never been published.

Third, I wanted to write a book that included complete geometric smocking instructions together with shadow embroidery instructions. The two go hand in hand in heirloom sewing, and I have yet to come across a book that includes instructions for both. Enjoy the six new geometric plates pictured in the color section.

Fourth, I wanted French sewing by machine instructions to be in that same book with smocking and shadow embroidery. Now you have a book that really has it all in heirloom sewing!

Fifth, I wanted to present my "new" antique clothing collection to you with infant clothing. I have found some garments with oodles of ideas to adapt for baby clothing, adult clothing, and doll attire also. Some of the christening dress ideas and skirt patterns are just as useful for adult clothing as they are for infant clothing. Please feel free to make a size four or larger using the ideas from these antique christening skirts, bodices, and sleeves. Your imagination is your only limitation.

Sixth, I wanted a basic baby clothing book with all of the basic baby clothing patterns included. I sometimes have trouble finding all of the infant daygowns, bubbles, and christening gowns I like in individual patterns. You will be able to make almost any variation of infant garment from the patterns we have included in this book.

Seventh, I wanted to offer some new christening patterns and ideas, which I believe you will find in the American-circa 1992 gowns by Sue Pennington. These outstanding designs are a combination of her creativity and techniques found on my antique garments.

Eighth, I wanted patterns not only for the infants, but also for the older baby. With so many children coming into this world weighing more than 10 pounds, we need larger sizes in infant styles.

I started making heirloom clothing years ago as "love" clothes for our daughter, Joanna. I rediscovered that warm feeling in making clothes for Campbell and for our new grandchild who hasn't yet arrived. Making and stitching clothes for our little ones has been the great joy of my sewing life. Oh, how I want each stitch to be perfect. But to be quite honest, the stitches don't have to be perfect to be beautiful. These clothes are made with love; that's what makes them treasures.

Mothers and grandmothers have always loved dressing their children, and these clothes, in particular, seem to say, "You are the most perfect child who was ever born. You are loved and I want to make beautiful clothing for you to wear." Some of these clothes, of course, will be passed down to other generations. The memories we are making through these garments, will, I think, be remembered long after the clothes are gone. I have so many happy memories of Mama and Aunt Chris making beautiful things for me to wear. I'm not sure that many of these things were saved carefully and put away. I am sure, however, that those wonderful memories are saved and stored in my heart. I can still hear Gramps Pullen telling of the happy times when Aunt Emma and her mother made gorgeous clothes for them when they were children. There were stories of the Christmas visits when Aunt Emma would bring all the girls in the family a new dress and then she would take them to the photographer to have their pictures made.

This book has been written for you to enjoy and to treasure. I wish that I could meet each of you personally and that we could talk about loving our children and grandchildren. Be sure to send me pictures after you make these beautiful clothes. I will enjoy looking at your children, nieces, nephews, Godchildren and of course, GRANDCHILDREN!

May God Bless Each Of You,
Martha

Antique Short Dresses

A LITTLE GIRL *toddling around in her Sunday dress, it's difficult to imagine anything sweeter. I know a 2-year-old who calls every pretty dress she has her "cute" because when she wears one people ooh and aah and tell her how cute she looks. Never underestimate the logic of a child.*

LITTLE GIRLS ADORE *dresses. If their mother's would permit it, some would chose to wear a dress to the playground, to the backyard barbecue, and even to the grocery store — the more lace, the better. Just try convincing a little girl to take off a French sewn dress the first time she tries it on; balancing the national budget might be easier.*

IT MAY NOT *have been like this centuries ago, when children wore dresses all the time. There were no Gap Kids or Osh Kosh® back then. Babies started out in daygowns and worked their way up to short dresses, and it wasn't only the girl babies. Toddler boys wore dresses, too.*

THE SHORT DRESSES *in my antique collection were purchased in England and America. All were worn around the turn of the century. They're full of details you could reproduce in a present day dress. Some are middy styles; others fall from a high yoke. With very little background information on some of these pieces, I'd be hard pressed to find out whether they were made for a boy or a girl. Today's versions would obviously be made for the latter.*

MARINDA,
RUE DES CAPUCINE
Dress One
French - circa 1880

This magnificent baby dress is one of four that I purchased from the same estate in Cheltenham. The garment, including the embroidery and the faggoting between the delicate puffing, is made completely by hand. The embroidery appears to be tamboured chain stitch. The tag in the garment reads: Marinda, Rue Des Capucine. I fantasize that a shop which specialized in baby and young children's elegant clothing made these garments. Since there are four of these dresses, either the family had two children or the mother loved the dresses so much, she bought two which were very similar. Remember, short dresses like these were used for girls as well as boys during this period.

The first two dresses have squared yokes and sleeves, which are exactly alike. On this first puffing dress, there is a sweet batiste casing around the waistline to hold a wide ribbon. This casing is 7 inches long and 1-1/4 inches wide. Gathered French edging encircles the casing, which is on the outside of the dress. On the skirt, there are rows of the tiniest puffing alternating with straight netting, attached by hand faggoting. Each puffing strip and each netting strip is 1 inch wide. There is a ruffle on the bottom with more of the tamboured chain stitch embellishment. Two rows of 1-inch gathered netting make two ruffles on the bottom of the dress; one about 1 inch above the bottom of the dress and one is actually the bottom of the dress.

The back of the dress has the same batiste casing through which ribbon can be run. The dress closes right over left with five loops and five flat buttons. The total circumference of the skirt is 56 inches; the center back length is 19 inches.

Rompers, Bibs, Aprons, and a Dress

"The average mother feels that if she makes the children's dresses dainty and attractive and finds time to make rompers, bibs, and aprons to wear over them, that the latter must go unadorned, much as she would enjoy decorating them with bright colors or odd little animals and figures that children love. A delightful solution of the problem is offered by the items that are to be made up with the edges finished by binding, lace, or hem, so that each garment may have its individual touch of embroidery with little expenditure of time. The fond aunt or older sister who is looking for practical gifts will enjoy this."

Author unknown, "Rompers, Bibs, Aprons, and a Dress," The Modern Priscilla, (November, 1916), p. 16.

MARINDA, RUE DES CAPUCINE
Dress Two
French - circa 1880

This second dress has exactly the same embroidery and sleeves as the first one. The skirt has rows of tamboured chain stitch running around the circumference at five places. The tamboured chain stitch embroidery is placed at 2-inch intervals and has gathered lace netting stitched below each row of embroidery. The bottom of the dress is finished with this gathered lace netting as is the other dress. The circumference of this dress is 54 inches. The total back length is 17 inches. The back of the dress laps right over left and is closed with four flat buttons and four loops.

Marinda, Rue Des Capucine III

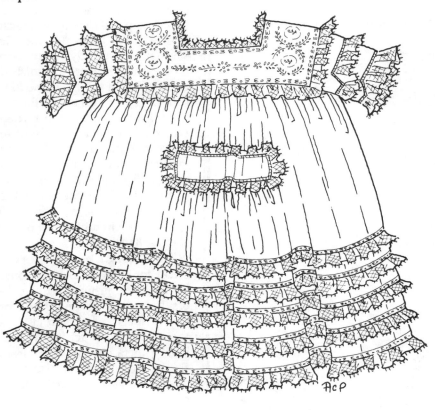

Marinda, Rue Des Capucine II

MARINDA, RUE DES CAPUCINE
Dress Three
French - circa 1880

The second two of the Marinda dresses feature puffing, faggoting and ruffles. There are the sweetest rows of 1-inch wide puffing on each sleeve with precious 1-inch wide ruffles on the edge. Faggoting is found between each row of trim. The round collar has one row of batiste, one row of puffing, and one ruffle, each connected with faggoting. The skirt consists of three rows of puffing with an equal strip of batiste between the rows; another 1-inch ruffle finishes the bottom. The puffing is rolled and whipped by hand and the faggoting is by hand also.

The circumference of the skirt is 56 inches; the back length is 17 inches. The back closes with a drawstring within a casing and a tiny round button with a button loop. Two more tiny buttons and button loops close the collar.

MARINDA,
RUE DES CAPUCINE
Dress Four
French - circa 1880

The second puffing dress has a round yoke with two rows of puffing and a 3/8-inch ruffle around the neckline. This design has a few more details than the first dress in that it has 3/4-inch wide ruffles below each row of puffing on the skirt. Once again, hand faggoting bridges each row of trims. The sleeves have a 1-inch row of puffing and a 3/4-inch ruffle of fabric trims the edge of the dress. Each row of puffing on the skirt measures 1-1/8 inch wide. The finished back dress length is 20 inches; the circumference of the skirt is 56 inches. The back laps right over left and is closed with three tiny, round buttons and button loops. The sleeves on all four of the Marinda dresses are set in with faggoting.

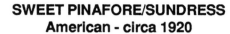

Sweet Pinafore/Sundress

**Marinda, Rue Des Capucine
Dress Four**

SWEET PINAFORE/SUNDRESS
American - circa 1920

This very thin batiste pinafore is completely handmade. The gathering along the front and back is simply hand stitches drawing up the fabric. A stabilizer is stitched along the back of the neckline to hold the stitches in place. These stitches aren't uniform, such as hand drawn-up dots for smocking; they are tiny and randomly placed and the effect is very sweet. The neckline is finished with a wide bias binding, which extends to form the stabilizer for the gathered portion of the neckline. The finished, bias-bound width across the front and the back is 10 inches. The four, decorative, French knot balls on the very tip top of the shoulder stretch over 1 inch. One-half inch is stitched permanently; then a snap is on each side where the finished closed portion is 1 inch. The four balls are composed of one French knot after another and then wrapped around something to make a ball shape. They are purely decorative. There is a batiste binding around the armhole. The hem is 4-1/4 inches wide. The total length of the pinafore is 20 inches; the circumference of the skirt is 58 inches.

This design would be very sweet for today. Smocking would be an option instead of the gathers. If you use quilting thread or elastic thread, you could just use the smocking machine, run in your gathers, and stabilize it from the back. You could also back smock the garment for the same effect.

CURVED/MITERED SWISS EMBROIDERED DRESS
English - circa 1930

The bodice on this dress is so sweet. Two strips of 1/2-inch lace are shaped into a slight curve from the shoulder seam of the dress and mitered into another curve to fit into the seam. A delicate embroidery design fits nicely in between these lace miters. The miters on this antique dress are exactly like those I call "folded back miters," and the technique for making them will be described later in this book. I would like to believe that this dress was embroidered by hand, but it was not. A bias binding, topstitched on both the top and the bottom, finishes the neckline, the sleeves, and the seam where the bodice joins the gathered skirt. The skirt is a purchased Swiss eyelet. The underarm sleeve length is 5-1/4 inches. The total dress back length is 30 inches. The circumference is 46 inches. Two buttons close the dress right over left.

Sensible Wear

"Baby's comfort is the first and only thing to consider in making these first garments. Make them as simply as possible, to avoid every unnecessary seam and also save your own time in making and laundering them. Many fresh, clean dresses, not beautiful ones, will be Baby's first requirements. Make them of soft, fine cloth and sew them by hand, to avoid hard, irritating edges. Save your fine elaborate embroidery and lovely lace edges for later public appearances."1

"A very sensible idea which many mothers advocate is to keep the little girls in wash dresses and bloomers throughout the winter, with heavy outer coats to protect them. Scotch plaid gingham is about the nicest material for this purpose, and it comes in a variety of color-combinations. The one-piece dresses with loose belts are very good for small girls. Heavy linen or jersey may be used for these."2

1. Ethel D Hayden, "Outfitting the Newest Baby," The Modern Priscilla, (August, 1920), p. 25.
2. Mary E. Fitch, "Winter Styles for Small Folks," Needlecraft, (December, 1917), p. 20.

✳

CONVERTIBLE MIDDY SWISS DRESS
English-circa 1915

What a creative grandmother to add the conversion package to this dress! Originally made by machine, it is a high yoke dress with a Swiss embroidered, sailor-type collar. At a later date, a 3/4-inch casing plus drawstring was added by hand on the inside of the dress to make it not only a high yoke dress but also an adorable middy, when the drawstring is pulled. What a wonderful idea to adapt for today! The little casing looks like a tuck from a distance, so no one would ever suspect it houses a drawstring. I would make the dress so long that it would be used as a middy the first year, and after the child grew a couple of inches, she could wear the high yoke version.

The casing is 11 inches from the center front of the dress. The total back length of the dress is 21-1/2 inches. The circumference of the skirt is 56 inches. The sailor-type collar is out of this world and would be easy to reproduce. Five strips of Swiss insertion are stitched together for the top of the collar; the center strip is 1 inch wide Swiss insertion, and the four outer strips are of the 1-3/4 inch. Mitered around the bottom of this created piece is another strip of the 1-inch wide insertion. Gathered, rather fully, so it is extra beautiful, is a Swiss edging 4 inches wide. I love the way the seamstress eased lots of fullness in the corner areas where it hangs just right and doesn't cup.

The long sleeves have four sets of two 1/8-inch tucks with 1/8 inch between the two. The sets of tucks are spaced 3/4 of an inch apart. The cuffs consist of the 1-3/4-inch wide Swiss insertion with gathered French lace at the bottom. The underarm sleeve measurement is 7 inches. The elegant skirt has two 1/8-inch tucks spaced 1/8 inch apart followed by two strips of the 1-3/4-inch Swiss insertion. An adorable gathered ruffle is made by placing two 1/8-inch tucks at the top of the 4-inch wide Swiss edging. Then the whole piece of Swiss edging is gathered for the ruffle at the bottom of the dress.

The Sailor Suit

A prime example of British royal influence on civilian dress is the popularity of sailor suits. The children of the royal family adopted a sailor style of dress in the mid 1800s, and soon every child's wardrobe included either a sailor suit or sailor dress. The boy's version consisted of a sailor blouse with a square collar worn with knickerbockers and a sailor hat. By 1880, the style was being adapted to suit girls' wardrobes. The feminine variation was basically a sailor blouse with a pleated skirt in navy serge or white drill (twill). At first, this informal style was thought only appropriate for seaside apparel. However, it soon became part of a little girl's basic wardrobe. The sailor style could easily be transformed to a more formal look by adding a pleated skirt and double breasted jacket.

Color combinations for nautical clothing have deviated little in the past 140 years. Even in the mid 1800s, sailor costumes were primarily white and blue or navy blue and pale blue embellished with gold or silver braid. [3]

3. Buck, Anne and Cunnington, Phillis, Children's Costume in England, 1300 - 1900, (London, Adam and Charles Black Limited, 1965) pgs. 214-215.

UNUSUAL PUFFING DRESS
English-circa 1880

The treatment on this handmade dress really is, yet really isn't, puffing. At first glance, one might notice a puffing strip right above the slightly raised waistline. A closer examination reveals that this puffing strip, which is 2 inches wide, has tiny tucks on the top and gathering on the bottom. The tucks are 1/16 inch wide and spaced 1/16 inch apart. The bottom of the strip is gathered like typical puffing.

The squared neckline is a lovely combination of Swiss insertion and French insertion. Gathered French edging finishes the neckline; entredeux is used in the armholes and around the neckline. The Swiss edging has three rows of entredeux stitched into the trim. On the bodice of the dress, the seam allowance of this entredeux trim is left untouched and treated as fabric. In the sleeves and skirt, the seam allowance is trimmed away and entredeux edges serve as the edge. The sleeve cuff is a piece of 5/8-inch Swiss trim with the entredeux used as the edge. Gathered French edging is the trim for the bottom of the sleeve. The sleeve underarm seam measures 6 inches.

The waistline of this dress uses the Swiss strip with a fabric casing behind it so that ribbon can be run through the dress to tie in the back. Another clever construction feature is the unusual grow tuck. The top two inches of the skirt were folded down; then the hand rolling, whipping, and gathering to gather the skirt to attach to the bodice of the dress were done at the fold line. Later the skirt could be removed, more gathering done at the top of the 2-inch fold over piece and 2 inches added to the length.

The total back length is 19 inches. The circumference of the skirt is 54 inches. The skirt is simple and ever so sweet. Three sets of 1/16-inch tucks, spaced 1/4 inch apart, are placed at 3/4-inch intervals. Two rows of the Swiss insertion follow with a 3/4-inch strip of batiste between the two rows. A double hem, measuring 2-1/2 inches, finishes the bottom of the skirt.

EYELET MIDDY
English–circa 1900

This dress is wearable today, yet aptly fit into the 1900s. Two strips of Swiss eyelet travel horizontally across the bodice; two strips of the same insertion run vertically up and down the dropped waistline of the dress. A beautiful Swiss beading is found at the waistline and at the sleeves. The bouncy skirt has three rows of machine-made pintucks on the top and three rows on the bottom. Since there were no double needles in 1900s, these were made by folding the fabric and running a row of straight stitches as closely to the edge as possible. Aren't we glad that we have double needles and pintuck feet for today's sewing machines? Another row of insertion is used between the double-pintucked trim. A closer look reveals that the second set of three pintucks is stitched onto a wide Swiss edging, which is really the ruffle of the skirt. This is a great idea for using today's wide Swiss pieces, which are technically edgings but commonly called "collar pieces." The patterns in the beading, the insertion, and the wide edging do not match. Once again, this lends credibility to my theory that heirloom dresses are just as beautiful when lace patterns don't match. In nearly all of my antique garments, there are at least two patterns of Swiss trims or French laces used. Please use what you have or what you can find on sale, or just choose from the fabric store laces which don't match. They are wonderful together and make the garment much more interesting.

The sleeves have another three rows of pintucks about midway down the 3/4-inch sleeve. Gathered, narrow French edging trims the top and the bottom of the beading of the sleeves and the neckline. The back length of the dress is 20 inches; the circumference of the skirt is 68 inches. The dress laps right over left and has a back casing that hides the three buttonholes. One other noteworthy back detail are the pintucks placed in sets of two instead of three as on the rest of the dress.

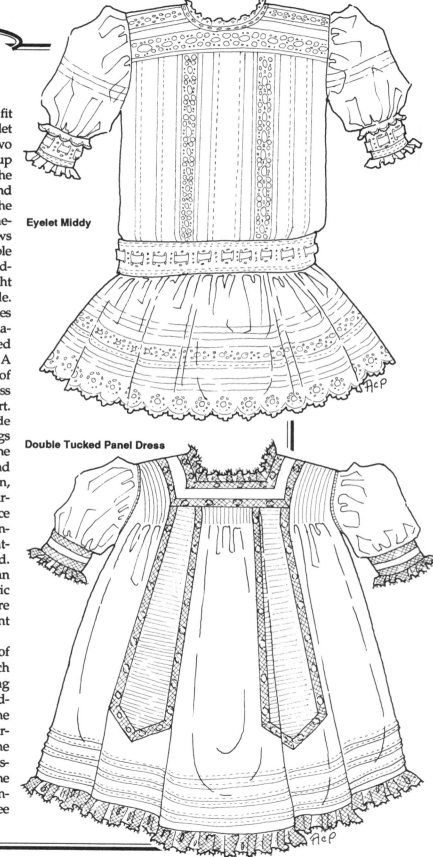

Eyelet Middy

Double Tucked Panel Dress

Grandmother's Hope Chest

DOUBLE TUCKED PANEL DRESS
English - circa 1890

Double tucked panels gracefully flow at an angle down the skirt of this baby dress. The entire dress is stitched by hand. Can you even imagine the time it took to make 1/16-inch tucks spaced 1/16 inch apart? Today, with modern sewing machines and the magical double needles, we can get the same effect with almost no effort!

Each side panel of the dress has 14 whipped tucks spaced 1/8 inch apart. The center section has 28 more of these whipped tucks. Lace insertion is mitered around the neckline and at the bottom of the tucked panels. The sleeves are set in with entredeux and have two rows of 3/8-inch lace insertion with a 3/8-inch strip of batiste in between the two strips of insertion. Gathered, French, 1/4-inch edging finishes the neckline and the sleeves. The skirt has two rows of 1/16-inch tucks, spaced 1/4 inch apart; there is 3/8-inch spacing between the three sets of tucks. Flat lace edging 5/8-inch wide is stitched at the bottom of the skirt. The dress laps right over left and is closed with three tiny buttons and button loops.

The finished dress length is 16 inches; the circumference of the skirt is 52 inches. Sweet 1/8-inch tucks travel all the way across the back of the bodice. I think these tucked panels would be elegant not only on this short baby dress but also on the skirt of a christening gown.

UNUSUAL TUCKING DRESS
English - circa 1920

This entire dress, including the whipping of all the tiny tucks, is handmade. Oh, the patience that this English grandmother must have had! This is the first time I have ever seen a tucked Peter Pan collar. Three sets of three 1/16-inch tucks embellish the skirt. The sets of tucks are spaced 3/4 inch apart. The bodice has the same 1/16-inch tucks in sets of three spaced 3/8-inch apart. The tucks on the collar are 1/8 inch apart, and there is 1/4-inch spacing between each set of three tucks. The beauty of this dress centers around the various sizes and placement of tucks. The total length of the dress is 18 inches. The fullness of the skirt measures 60 inches. The hem measures 2 inches deep.

The collar is finished with entredeux and gathered 1/2-inch French lace, which is also used on the bottom of the sleeve. Below the front and back bodice is a little Swiss beading with entredeux on the top and bottom, which carries only 1/8-inch ribbon. The same Swiss beading is used on the bottom of the sleeves with French edging gathered for the final sleeve treatment. The dress is closed with two pearl buttons and button loops; it laps right over left. The center back placket on the skirt measures 4 inches. One of the features that I love the most about antique clothing is the creativity grandmothers used to lengthen or enlarge clothing. On this dress, the underarm of the sleeve has been opened about an inch and finished very carefully. Either the child grew in the arms or it was passed to another child whose arms were a bit chubbier. A little tag in the back of the dress has the initials V.B. Since I love to fantasize, I will pretend that this dress belonged to Victoria Baker.

HEAVY TATTED BOY DRESS
English - circa 1850

On Kings Road in Chelsea there are a number of antique malls. After browsing though all that I could find, I surmised that none of them carried any white clothing. Only after traveling to the far back of one of the malls did I see this beauty hanging high from a ceiling. The dealer informed me that it was a boy dress and asked if I would like to look at it. The "lace" is really a very heavy tatting done with a heavy cord. The work is exquisite and every stitch of the dress — lace making to interior French seams — is done by hand. The triple featherstitch hems the dress and embellishes the top and bottom of the 3/4-inch waistline banding, which is wide for banding. There is a little cutwork in the form of flower-type medallions on the skirt. The trim around the neckline is cutwork with tatting attached for the scalloped edging. The work is magnificent although the fabric and the threads are very heavy. I could certainly appreciate that this dress was made for a male child after looking at it closely.

The same little shoestring ties run through this garment as is true of most of my pre-1890 garments. Of course, all the interior seams are French and that beautiful, heavy-threaded, triple featherstitch is used to embellish anywhere the laces are attached. The garment laps right over left and actually has two handmade buttonholes and two pearl buttons in addition to the drawstrings. The total back length of the dress is 18 inches; the circumference of the skirt is 64 inches. It is really mind boggling for me to hold this dress and know that it is probably older than 140 years. I am sure it has been through washing and more washing. It probably has been lost in a trunk somewhere for no telling how long. Oh how I wish I knew the place and date that it was made and the name of the grandmother who made it.

Please use the new machines with their built-in monogramming to put information on the hem or inside the back facing. I recommend several things, 1. The name of the child. 2. The date. 3. The name of the seamstress. 4. The city and country where it was made. 5. The special occasion (fifth birthday suit or dress, a christening or first communion dress, or a Christmas outfit).

Caps

Until about 1850, babies wore caps both indoors and outdoors. Those from well-to-do families were sometimes overwhelmed by trims on their lawn caps, which included lace edgings, muslin frills, embroidery, and even feathers. Caps for "less fortunate" babies were notably more simple and thus more practical. They were usually a rectangle of soft muslin or calico shaped with a drawstring.

Newborn babies wore "day-caps," which were then covered with hoods for protection. As a result, the sex of a child was not always easy to determine. To save onlookers embarrassment, a simple rosette embellishing the hood offered some help. If the rosette were worn on the left side, the baby was a boy. If it embellished the front, the baby was a girl. [5]

5. Buck and Cunnington, pgs. 150-151.

GENUINE ENGLISH SMOCK
WITH GROW TUCKS
English - circa 1880

One of my favorite things to do is haunt the London flea markets with a "torch," the English word for flashlight. Usually it is cold, and there are wonderful stands with hot potatoes, hot coffee, and, of course, marvelous sweets available to warm the body.

On my last trip to London, I was looking in the outside stalls with my torch, and I spotted this little smock. The price was, of course, too high; however, I rationalized that this book was to include smocking directions and I really needed to include a smock as part of my collection. Upon examining the garment, I realized that it was smocked with string. Looking on the back of the smock, I realized that the dots had probably been drawn up because the pleats on the back were very uniform. There is smocking on both the front and back; the sleeves are smocked also. The smocking stitches used on this particular garment are stem stitch on the top and bottom rows, cable rows, two-step wave rows, and more cable rows. Featherstitching in this very coarse string trims the collar and the shoulder seams.

There are two grow tucks, one on the skirt and one on the sleeves. These grow tucks are put in with hand stitching. The other seams are by machine. The garment laps right over left and is closed with three buttons and handmade buttonholes. The hem is closed with machine stitching and measures 2-5/8 inches wide. The total dress length is 20 inches; the circumference of the skirt is 55 inches. The underarm sleeve measurement is 11 inches. All in all, I'm glad I purchased this smock. Actually, most of the antique children's smocks that I have seen have been made from a coarser fabric, far too worn out to be very pretty. This one, in its heavy batiste, is really quite lovely.

Lawn Tennis Pinafore

Children's fashion often reflects current adult trends. In the late 1870s, the lawn tennis pinafore was a prime example. The decorative embellishments associated with the smocked frocks of English rural workers were first thought fashionable as tennis apparel. The style soon made its way into children's wardrobes.

In 1884, Weldon's, an instructor of home dressmakers, published several booklets on the subject of practical smocking. These included examples of country smocks with decorative embroidery and gathering.

Smocking was used as embellishment for not only everyday dresses of linen or cotton, but also for dresses of silk and fine wool.[6]

6. Ibid. pgs. 217-218.

LACY V YOKE DRESS
English - circa 1890

I purchased this dress in Cheltenham. It is made by hand and by straight stitch on a sewing machine. There is a tiny laundry mark in the back facing which reads "Betty Clarke." The rolling, whipping, and gathering on the skirt and sleeves are done by hand. The tucks and lace attachment everywhere else are straight machine stitching. The high yoke style of the bodice is slightly scooped at the neckline. I love the way this seamstress shaped the laces into a V in the front and at angles on the side of the bodice. Double entredeux was used to attach each piece of lace. Three miters were necessary to shape the V lace design on the bottom of the bodice. The magnificent, round thread, French lace insertion is 1-1/4 inch wide; it is used on the bodice, the sleeves, and the fancy band of the skirt. The matching edging on the bottom of the dress is 1-1/2 inch wide. The matching French edging around the neckline and on the bottom of the sleeves is 3/8 inch wide.

The fancy band strip is straight except for the gathered lace edging on the bottom. The total width of the fancy band is 7 inches. It consists of lace insertion, tucking strip, lace insertion, tucking strip and gathered edging. The tucking strips are 1-5/8 inch wide, featuring five 1/16-inch tucks spaced 1/8 inch apart. There is a 1/4-inch space at the bottom and the top of each tucking panel which joins the lace. On the sleeve, the gathers are rolled and whipped directly to the lace insertion; double entredeux is found at the bottom of the lace insertion between the insertion and the flat lace edging.

The back closes right over left and has three pearl buttons with hand worked buttonholes. The placket in the center back of the skirt measures 7 inches. The total dress back length is 23 inches. The circumference of the skirt is 73 inches.

Scooped Neck Middy

SCOOPED NECK MIDDY
American - circa 1880

Since I purchased this dress at a doll show in California, I suspect that it might be a California piece. The dress is in rather bad condition, with several tiny holes throughout the batiste. The design, however, is one you might like to copy for your little girl. The middy style, popularized in the late 1880s, is one of my favorites. The scooped neck of this dress is finished with a tiny bias binding. Gathered French edging finishes the neckline. A very pretty, self-fabric ruffle 3-3/4 inches wide travels from the back of the neckline down to the dropped waist middy line. The ruffle decreases gradually to a width of 2 inches when it is stitched into the waistline of the front of the dress. The same ruffle treatment travels down the back of the dress. Flat French edging is stitched at the bottom of this ruffle. A bias binding finishes the bottom of the sleeve with very full French edging gathered and hand whipped to the bottom of the bias binding. A row of machine gathers covers about half of the front of the dress approximately 3/4 inch above the waistline. The waist band is of Swiss insertion with entredeux on both sides. Since a straight stitch sewing machine was used, some of each side of the seam allowance on the Swiss insertion attaches both the top of the garment and the skirt. Fleur de lis is the design on the Swiss insertion. There is a bias binding at the bottom of the skirt, which was used to attach a gathered Swiss trim repeating this same fleur de lis design. Then French edging is stitched on underneath this Swiss insertion. The total back length of the dress is 24 inches; the circumference of the skirt (not including the ruffle) is 78 inches. The skirt has three panels to give it this much fullness. It is very unusual for a child's dress this old to have this much fullness in it.

SIMPLE FRENCH KNOT DRESS
English - circa 1870

The lowered square neckline and the front panel with a sash tie reveal the approximate year this dress was begun. French knots are placed on the batiste seam allowance of the entredeux. Sashes, measuring 4-1/4 inches wide, are gathered at the front, French knot area and tie in the back. Each side of the seam has been rolled and whipped. The bottom of each sash has a 1-1/4-inch hem. Entredeux and mitered laces travel around the squared neckline; narrow French edging is used above the insertion. Entredeux, insertion, and gathered edging finish the sleeves. The back is one piece with a placket measuring 5-1/2 inches down the center back. It closes with two buttons and two hand worked buttonholes. The bottom of the dress has two 5/8-inch tucks spaced 3/8 inch apart; entredeux and slightly gathered edging finish the bottom of the dress. The total length of the dress is 18-1/2 inches. The fullness of the skirt is 52 inches.

THE V DRESS
English - circa 1860-1870

This is the second dress in my collection with these double triangular points on the sleeves. The first is featured in *Antique Clothing: French Sewing By Machine*, and it is called "Rouching Baby Dress." This dress has the drawstring closing at the neckline and at the waistline. The longer waistline also indicates an early origin. The casings measure 1/4 inch wide and have a delicate shoestring type tie run through them. These two string ties are the only visible fastening on the back of the dress.

The V shaping on the front of the dress features both hand embroidery and Swiss embroidery. The dress had to have been made sometime after 1850 because the first Swiss embroideries made on the machine came out of Switzerland around 1850. Hand featherstitching trims the casing around the neckline, the waistline, and the sleeves. The tiny pleats feature delicate, precise pleating, which looks as if it were pleated on a smocking machine. My guess would be that dots were placed on the skirt and it was gathered up much like we used to gather pleats before pleaters. The finished, pleated edge is folded over about 1 inch on the back. It is butted to the finished casing edge and whipped on by hand.

The two triangles extending over the sleeve measure 1-3/4 inches wide at the neckline edge and 1 inch at the point. Each triangle point also has handfeather stitching all around the edges. Gathered 1/2-inch French edging finishes the edges. This same edging is used around the neckline and the edges of the sleeves.

I tend to wonder if this dress weren't a christening dress which was later shortened for a child's dress. The bodice of this type of dress could be drawn up to fit a tiny infant, then extended to fit a 2-year-old child. The skirt has five pleats; four are 3/8 inch wide and one is 1 inch wide. The skirt has a hem measuring 2 inches. The total length of this dress is 19-1/2 inches. The fullness of the skirt is 63 inches.

PEACH SILK DRESS
English- circa 1910

It is so unusual to find a silk dress in good repair. This peach silk dress simply slips on over the head and has no buttons. The front and back of the dress are exactly the same. Sixty two tucks measuring 1/8 inch each with 1/8-inch spacing between each tuck make up the bodice of the dress. What is unusual about the tucking in the neckline area is that four sets of seven tucks extend the full length of the dress. The pattern is as follows: five released tucks measuring 3-1/2 inches long begin the series; seven tucks are next, which go to the hemline of the dress; eight released tucks are next with the same 3-1/2-inch measurement, then seven more full tucks, eight short ones, seven long ones, eight more short, seven more long, and finally five more short ones to finish the front. Three sets of seven long tucks are on the side of the dress, the underarm, and the other side of the underarm. There is a tuck centered under the armhole, which folds the set of seven tucks into a tuck which releases 2-1/2 inches down from the center of the armhole. In other words, the fullness of this panel of seven tucks is tucked over under the armhole. There is 2-3/8 inches in between each set of seven long tucks.

The collars are the same on the front and the back. Each echoes the seven tuck treatment; the top of the silk tucked portion of the collar is 8-1/4 inches; the bottom is 12-1/2 inches. Hemstitching and 3/8-inch French edging finish three sides of each collar. The collar is attached to the dress with hemstitching.

The neckline opening is 19 inches; exactly 1 inch in on both front sides is a tiny pearl button. One inch in on both of the back sides is a button loop. When closed, this button and loop treatment takes 4 inches off the neckline opening to better fit a child. The hemline is finished with hemstitching and flat lace edging. The length of the garment is 20 inches. The fullness in the skirt is 46 inches.

DIVIDED COLLAR
HEMSTITCHED DRESS
English - circa 1900

This garment of hand hemstitching is simply a work of art! Actually the whole dress is made by hand. The long sleeves are rolled and whipped to a simple band of entredeux with gathered lace. The handmade beading is 1-1/4 inch wide; the buttonholes made for ribbon are 1 inch wide. Entredeux attaches the bodice to the skirt on the front and back of the dress. The hand hemstitched collar has a 2-3/4-inch spacing between the fronts of the collar. My guess would be that if the collar had been a traditional one, meeting in the front, it would have hidden the hand work on the bodice. The design statement is absolutely lovely with this divided collar. The skirt features the same hemstitching pattern of one row of hemstitching and five rows of hemstitching right together. There are three single rows and two sets of five rows spaced 3/8 inch apart. The hem is 2-1/2 inches deep. The underarm sleeve measurement is 7 inches. The back of the dress is fastened with three pearl buttons and loops; it laps right over left. The back placket in the skirt is 3 inches long. The back dress length is 15-1/2 inches. The circumference of the skirt is 63 inches.

27

HEAVY FABRIC MIDDY
WITH ADDITIONS
English - circa 1860

What an interesting dress to decipher! I felt a little like Sherlock Holmes trying to unlock the mystery of this dress in an antique store in Cheltenham. This certainly cannot be called a museum piece in its quality of stitching or design; however, it is very old, which makes it valuable to me and my research.

The original garment, made of a decoratively woven, white, heavy fabric, was scoop-necked and had a plain straight sleeve. Decorative featherstitching trimmed the original center panel and the sleeves. Probably about 30 years later as the scoop neckline became less fashionable, the seamstress decided to alter the dress. Handmade eyelet of a different fabric was made to go around the neckline, the sleeves, and the bottom of the dress. My guess is that some length was taken from the hemline in order to fill in the neck. This method of filling in the neck is seen on so many garments both in museums and in antique stores. The featherstitching, which embellishes the present "doctored" dress, is of the same coarse thread; however, the stitches aren't from the same embroiderer because they are very different. There is also a gusset to increase the size of the middy band which is 2-1/2 inches wide. Probably at the time of the alteration, whomever was to wear the dress was heavier than its original owner.

The puffed sleeves may also have been an alteration. The original sleeve lining in this dress is the straight sleeve as is so often found on the scooped neck dresses of the mid 1800s. The puffed sleeve is stitched on in a peculiar manner and it is almost straight in its design. The eyelet trim is very wide on the bottom, which adds about 3-1/2 inches in length. There are still three usable tucks, which could be let out to add even more length.

The back closes right over left, and the original part of the dress is closed with six buttons. The altered upper portion closes with a drawstring. The total back length of the dress is 22 inches. The circumference of the skirt is 55 inches.

Bibs

"Mothers who wish to make pretty, serviceable bibs for the baby will find that a guest-towel, narrow but long, will provide two. Just cut the towel in halves, cut the opening for the neck in each, bind the edges that are cut or have no selvage with narrow tape, and add strings of the same for tying. A design of chickens, geese, or other bird or animal can easily be outlined or cross-stitched on the front and will please the little ones. These bibs are cheap, easily made and washed, and look very attractive; they make nice gifts at Christmas.

Needlecraft (December, 1917) p. 17.

———— ✳ ————

TUCKED SWISS DRESS
English - circa 1860

This Swiss dress is another one of my London flea market treasures. Not only is the original dress made completely by hand, but the altered sleeve is stitched by hand as well. The eyelet in the dress is Swiss machine made. This dress has lovely rows of six, hand-stitched, 1/8-inch tucks carefully and perfectly placed 1/8 inch apart on both the bodice and the skirt. The Swiss trim is attached to the tucking strips with uniformly-placed French knots. Again and again in my antique collections, I find these gorgeous French knots used as a construction aide. They are lovely, for sure, but on a more practical note, they stitch together parts of a garment or sometimes even act as staystitching to hold down gathers. French knots finish the neckline and the waistline of this dress. The puffed sleeve is an alteration. The bias binding on the edge of this puffed sleeve, which is carefully stitched underneath the straight Swiss eyelet one, is finished with a featherstitch. I did not find any featherstitching anywhere else on the dress. One might wonder why more French knots weren't used to trim the cuff of the puffed sleeve. I suppose this grandmother preferred to featherstitch.

The back laps right over left and is closed with narrow bias bindings with that shoestring-type draw cord. Something of note is the single button right in the middle of the back with a single handmade buttonhole. I tend to wonder if that button and buttonhole weren't added at the same time as the puffed sleeve. The back length measurement of the dress is 23 inches. The circumference of the skirt (not the ruffle fullness) is 64 inches.

Baby Lingerie

"For the new baby, a coat and bonnet should be fashioned of soft wool cashmere, silk crepe faille, or crepe de Chine in white, light pink, or blue. The coat might have a fitted yoke, which achieves smoothness at the top. Below, the combination with straight smooth front may be trimmed with lace and embroidery. Fresh, blue, and orchid are dainty.

For a little older child, narrow lace edging always gives an effect of daintiness and femininity, and little floral sprays of embroidery add interesting bits of color. These colors used on underwear should always be soft and delicate. Cotton crepe, nainsook, rayon, or voile are the choice for the simple lingerie of the girl from 4 to 14 years of age. Crepe de Chine and radium are desirable for her dressier types. Lace in two widths may combine effectively to trim a little girl's petticoat. Tiny monogram in white or in a soft color gives interest and individuality to children's lingerie for ages 1 to 6.

Author unknown, "Lingerie for Various Ages," Pictorial Review, (February, 1928), p. 124.

PLAIN IMPORTED
HANDMADE DAYGOWN
English - circa 1940

This Swiss batiste daygown has a tag in the neckline which reads "Lantone, Reg'd, Handmade" and it is obviously completely made by hand. Probably it was made in the Philippines. Even the embroidery on the circular yoke is done by hand. In short, it is simple and beautiful. All interior seams are French and properly done. The underarm sleeve measurement is about 2-1/2 inches. The bottom of the sleeve is rolled and whipped and has straight French edging attached. There is a tiny piece of French edging finishing the neckline. The bottom has a tiny strip of French insertion rolled and whipped to the bottom of the gown and a tiny ruffle rolled and whipped to the bottom of the insertion. The width of this ruffle is 3/4 inch. The total length of this daygown is 20 inches; the fullness measures 38 inches. Oh how I would love to be able to purchase at the department store a daygown like this. Since I love to sew, I will just have to make my elegant little daygowns; this type of quality has long since left the stores. Sewing is one way to assure quality which isn't available today at any price.

ALMOST STRAIGHT DRESS
English - circa 1920

Doctoring, lengthening, and fixing clothing for longer wear almost seems to be a mother's destiny. This unusual dress has been lengthened at both the sleeve line and the hemline. The original dress consisted of four tucks, then two rows of laces, which curved at the bottom of the dress and 14 tucks in the center front of the dress. The tucks are 1/8-inch, machine-made tucks and are spaced 1/4 inch apart. The lace edging was slightly gathered and shaped in a very pretty elongated "U" shape in three different sections of the front of the garment. A bias binding finishes the neckline and the original sleeve of the dress. Gathered edging trimmed the neckline bias and the sleeve bias. At the bottom of the original dress were three rows of gathered lace edging with three tucks on the batiste strip in between the edging. The last row of lace edging was the bottom of the dress.

Later, as the child grew or as it was passed along to another child, another row of tucks with gathered lace was added and two rows of tucking and gathered lace were added to the bottom of the sleeve making it a 3/4-inch sleeve. Since the tucked material and the laces are the same as the original dress, this smart mother must have saved material and lace. Something that I think is of interest is that the stitching doesn't appear to be the same length or done with the same size needle when the tucks were made on the last band of tucking. The holes are larger and the thread is whiter and the machine doesn't appear to be the same. This makes me think that we mothers and grandmothers ought to make an extra "fancy band" to put away when we finish each dress so that it will be handy when the child grows or when, maybe years later, the dress is needed for another size child entirely. On second thought, where would I find the extra fancy band if the next child came along 20 years later? Only if I put it in my lock box would I be able to find it in my world. Super organized people who never lose or misplace anything might want to keep scraps of the materials for future use. The total length of the altered dress is 25-1/2 inches; the circumference of the dress is 36 inches. This is the "slimmest" in my collection of antique children's clothing!

Almost Straight Dress

Wonderful Round Yoke Dress

WONDERFUL ROUND YOKE DRESS
American - circa 1910

I purchased this little dress in Huntsville, so perhaps it is an Alabama piece. The yoke in front is round; in back it is square. The back features two sets of four handmade tucks and a back placket measuring 6 inches into the skirt. The front is very unusual in that it is in one piece with the round yoke scooped out and the gathers made in the center front of the bottom of the yoke. Entredeux joins the round yoke body of the dress; the yoke is made of Swiss insertion attached with a straight stitch on the sewing machine to round thread French lace insertion. The neckline binding is another piece of this Swiss insertion finished with gathered French edging. This same treatment finishes the long sleeves. The underarm sleeve length is 5-1/2 inches.

The fancy band on this dress appears to be 9 inches long; however, there is a fancy band and then an adorable ruffle, which looks very much like the fancy band. The fancy band is 4-1/2 inches wide and features three strips of 3/8-inch French round thread insertion with 1-inch plain strips of batiste in between. The ruffle consists of three strips of 1-inch plain batiste with two strips of 3/8-inch lace insertion between them and a row of 1/2-inch round thread French edging stitched straight on the bottom of the ruffle. The total length of the dress is 20-1/2 inches; the circumference of the dress (not the ruffle) is 61 inches. As usual, on this type of antique dress, all of the inside seams, including the armhole seam, are French.

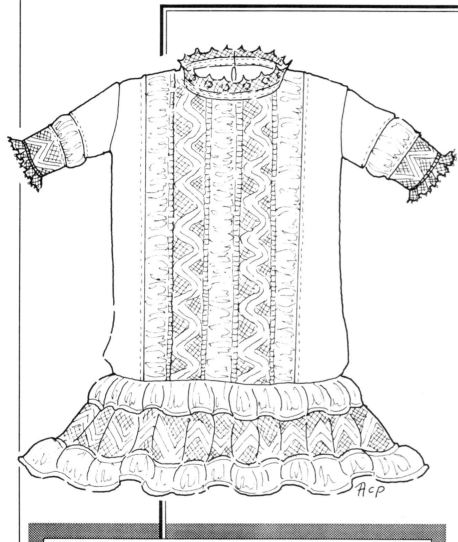

HAND WOVEN NETTING LACE MIDDY DRESS
American - Circa 1900

I overlooked this dress when I saw it in an antique store here in Huntsville. From a distance the dress looked very coarse and crudely made. Its fabric is a very heavy batiste of a questionable quality. The puffing is heavy and I really didn't like the lace. Upon more careful inspection, I came to appreciate the creativity of the dress. This grandmother has taken netting and woven thread through the netting to make her own lace insertion. The threads are even tied off at points throughout the wide netting lace. Since she only had a straight stitch on her sewing machine, she used a bias binding to finish all of the sides of the puffing. That makes perfect sense especially if you are using a heavy fabric. Thank heaven for today's wonderful sewing machines and sergers! I think the edging she used at the neckline and at the bottom of the sleeve might have been made at home also. Since the puffing on the bottom has no lace at all, I think she ran out of lace. Her bias binding serves the purpose just as well. The whole back is strips of puffing with the handmade netting lace. The front is three strips of puffing and lace. A puffing band is gathered for the ruffle with more of this lace and the puffing band on the bottom has no lace at all to finish it. She has added a puffing band at the bottom of the sleeve along with her handmade lace and the little bit of edging which I believe she made, also. This is one of the few garments from my collection which doesn't have French seams on the interior. The seams are simply stitched and I might add, they have ravelled quite badly. The back is closed with six pearl buttons and six handmade buttonholes. It laps left over right, which is unusual also. The total back length of the dress is 17 inches. The fullness at the bottom of the ruffle is 56 inches. This is certainly one of my most interesting pieces although I don't include it among my finest.

Summer Bonnet

"And for the 'littlest one,' who must never be forgotten nor, indeed, can be, there is a bonnet of handkerchief-linen, embroidered in delicate pattern, eyelet and solid. The round crown, the closing at the back, edge of neck and turnover are buttonholed in tiny scallops, and the hemstitched ties are fastened on by means of ribbon rosettes, easily removed when the bonnet requires laundering. Many mothers have adopted the plan of making several sets of ties for the same bonnet so there are always fresh ones to put on; the idea is a good one, and to be heartily recommended."

Martha Dean Wallace, "For the Children's Summer Outfits," Needlecraft, (July, 1917), p. 20.

MACHINE HEMSTITCHED WRAPAROUND SLIP
English - Circa 1890

Since the first machine hemstitcher was made in the mid 1880s, it makes sense to me that it would have been commonly used in the home by 1890. This precious slip would be darling as a wrap-around sundress today. The scooped neckline clues me in on its date. The lace is absolutely gorgeous and a lot of lace has been used. I certainly wouldn't put this much lace on a slip. Machine hemstitching is used to join the very wide and heavy lace insertions at the bodice area and on the skirt. If you are fortunate enough to have one of today's modern computer sewing machines and a wing needle, you can make gorgeous hemstitching on your sewing machine. By the way, a few of the old hemstitchers are available today. I bought one for $1500 and never was able to get even 12 inches of pretty hemstitching from it. It now catches dust. Please don't fool with one of the old ones unless you are a real sewing machine mechanic! Just buy a new top-of-the-line computer sewing machine and you are in for the treat of your life!

The wrap-around part of the slip ends with buttons and buttonholes right in the front of the slip. The lace insertion used is 2-1/2 inches wide; the edging is 3-1/2 inches wide. The slip has a little straight machine sewing on the back panels of the wrap strips; the rest is either hemstitched or stitched by hand. The large buttonhole in the back through which the wrap panel runs is stitched by hand also. The two tiny tucks on the skirt are stitched by machine. They appear to be whipped by hand; however upon closer examination, I notice that this grandmother simply folded in the tuck and straight stitched it as closely to the edge as possible making it appear to be a hand tuck. This is a very interesting idea. Now, aren't you glad that we have double needle pintucking available on our machines? I certainly am since I love pintucks—the easy way.

Nursery Heresy

"Emboldened by the opinion of one of the leading New York physicians, I offer a comfortable summer clothing suggestion for the baby in short clothes. If hygienic for summer, why not for winter? There sometimes crops out an opinion that "fresh" diapers are not necessary, but are to be dried and used again. The real danger lies in using squares at all; the body and loins are sweltered and that is bad for kidneys, therefore for the whole body. Short and loose infant bloomers are so much better in every way, and a quantity of them for frequent change will cost no more than the squares. Where diapers are used at all, the oftener they are changed for fresh ones the better; after one use, they should be washed and rinsed free of soap. To quote a doctor, 'the most hygienic diapers are those that are always dropping off.'"

Maude Kent, M.D. "Mother Problems," *The Modern Priscilla*, (June, 1914), p. 45. ———— ✳ ————

Vintage Boys' Rompers

LITTLE BOYS' SUITS *from vintage stock are difficult to find. I suppose that boys have always worn out their clothing faster than girls. Just go to any Sunday school class and see who is tearing down the slide or scooting across the floor. You guessed it, the boys. As a mother of four boys, I also know that I didn't have as many fancy things for them as I had for our one daughter, Joanna. Our culture dictates that we don't dress up boys as much as we do girls. It's a shame really. The only time boys will consent to wearing pretty things is when they're young. I guess that's not really consent; they're just too little to mind. Please do dress your little boys up in lace or embroidery as long as it is appropriate.*

WHAT WAS ONCE *called a crawler is more commonly called a bubble or romper today. It is actually a one-piece garment which opens at the crotch and at the back neckline. It sometimes features a belt. Hand embroidery decorates nearly all the rompers that I have seen. Rompers were first introduced as playclothes for young children. They were soon adapted for infant wear. My entire collection of boy rompers was purchased from a dealer in Phoenix, Arizona. It stands to reason that these rompers belonged to one child; all but one were commercially produced and have tags that read "handmade." One is from Feltman Brothers and the others are from a company unfamiliar to me. Some of them are handmade completely, including the side seams and the French seams in the interior of the garment. They are laden with details, which can be adapted to current bubble patterns.*

ROMPERS WERE MADE *of heavier fabric than many garments so the underclothing could not show through. In a fine batiste dress, for instance, a slip could be used to curtain the body. For today's bubbles, I think broadcloth, linen, gingham, chambray, and other heavier fabrics are best. Several of the rompers in my collection are, of course, blue for boys.*

THE BOY ROMPERS *in my collection did not have elastic in the legs as do bubbles dated post 1940. Because of the absence of elastic, I have dated these garments circa 1920. In the '20s pattern catalogues, boy rompers do not have elastic in the legs. Instead, the leg openings lay away from the child's leg as do those on button-on suits or "bobby suits," which is what they were called in the 1940s and 1950s.*

THERE ARE SEVERAL *bubble patterns in the pattern section of this book that you can use for adaptations. Or try another Martha Pullen pattern ,"Drew's and Erin's Bubble." Please also enjoy using the precious embroidery designs included in this book to embellish bubbles for your little boys. I have another hint; with a simple change in sleeve treatment, these bubbles would be darling for your little girl also.*

WHITE BELTED ROMPER
American - circa 1920

Although this romper has no tag in the neckline, I believe it to be a commercially-imported garment. The delicate embroidery on the shaped, Peter Pan collar is finished with bias binding, faggoting, and bias tubing. Eight 1/8-inch tucks embellish the front of the suit with French knots down the center of the sets of tucks. A button-on belt, which goes all the way around the suit, is attached with belt loops. Three buttons fasten the crotch of the suit; two buttons fasten the back, which laps right over left. A separate cuff is stitched to the sleeve and folded up. A tiny bit of faggoting and bias binding treatment are found on the center of the cuff.

DUSTY BLUE EMBROIDERED ROMPER
American - circa 1920

This dusty blue romper has white cuffs, a white collar, and white buttons on the belt. The pointed effect on the collar and the sleeves is a nice touch. Blue embroidery decorates the collar and white embroidery dances down the front. Four 1/4-inch tucks are on the front of the garment. The tag in the neckline reads "Handmade Embroidery, Size 3." The back closes right over left and is fastened with only one button at the neckline. The belt goes all the way around the suit, which is closed at the crotch with three buttons.

BLUE SHEEP ROMPER
American - circa 1920

This white romper features lots of handmade details. The tag in the neckline reads, "Handmade, imported, FB." I think this would be a Feltman Brothers design. There are two sets of side tucks with six tucks in each set. A non-functional blue pocket with the same diamond pattern as is on the collar, is positioned at the bottom of each set of side tucks. A blue lamb is embroidered on the center front of the garment. Blue cuffs and a blue collar embroidered in white complete the garment. The back fastens with two buttons and the suit laps right over left.

SCALLOPED ROMPER
American - circa 1920

The scallops on this suit are edged in a handmade buttonhole stitch. You can achieve this same effect using a scallop stitch on a computer sewing machine. This scalloped edge is a lovely way to finish collars, sleeves, and bottoms of garments including boy bubbles. Delicate embroidery adds to the detailing on this suit. The cuffs and collars are blue fabric with white embroidery. The body of the suit is white (with the exception of the blue trim on the legs) with blue embroidery. The collar consists of a scalloped curved part and a small square part also trimmed with machine scallops at the center front. Three bars of blue fabric are attached to the garment with hand faggoting. Six 1/4-inch tucks are stitched in by hand. The suit is closed at the crotch with three buttons. Pretty flowers, French knots and stem embroidery is placed vertically on the front of the garment. The tag inside the collar on this romper reads "Handmade, imported, 3."

✳

WHITE AND BLUE BELTED ROMPER
American - circa 1920

This white romper features blue cuffs, blue collar, and blue embroidery on the front. Four sets of two 1/8-inch tucks and blue embroidery embellish the front. White embroidery is sprayed across the blue collar. Outline stitch, lazy daisies, and French knots are the primary embroidery stitches. Turned-up, matching blue cuffs and a little, white double-button belt are the finishing details. Three buttons close the crotch opening. The back laps right over left and is closed with two buttons. "Handmade embroidery, size 2" reads the neckline tag.

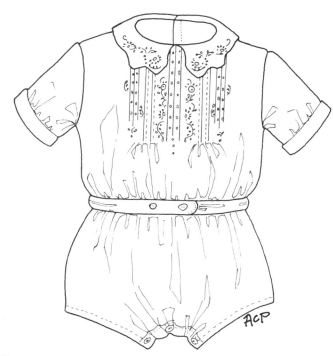

MEDIUM BLUE FRENCH KNOT ROMPER
American - circa 1920

Simple French knots are the embroidery of choice on the front of this romper as well as on the sleeves. Eight 1/4-inch tucks — four on each side of center — travel down the front. Two rows of hand hemstitching fall in between the tucks. Additional embellishment on the bodice include French knots in white embroidery thread. The white cuffs piped in blue feature more French knots, this time in blue. The pointed collar is white fabric bound in blue bias strips with faggoting between the two strips. Blue satin stitch daisies are located in each point of the collar. More French knots are above the satin stitched daisies. Three buttons close the crotch; the back is lapped right over left and is closed with two buttons. The tag in the neckline reads "Handmade, Baby Craft."

BLUE SHANTUNG
EMBROIDERED ROMPER
American - circa 1940

It appears to me that this suit was made at home rather than purchased. The seams are flat felled and there is an attempt at machine buttonholes on the crotch and the back closings of the garment. I think the buttonholes are those made when using an attachment applied to a straight stitch sewing machine. The little suit has sweet embroidery and a hand hemstitch running down the front panel of the garment. Eight 1/8-inch tucks are also on the front of the garment. The turned-up cuff is stitched down with a straight stitch and the collar features curved scallops with lazy daisies and a French knot in the center of each little flower. The embroidery is of white and navy blue; the suit is a pastel blue. It laps right over left in the back with two buttons. The crotch has three buttons to close it.

BLUE INSET WHITE ROMPER
American - circa 1940

This adorable suit has a combination of blue embroidery on the white suit, white embroidery on the blue collar and blue cuffs. Blue insets shaped like bars with white embroidery are shaped on the front of the garment. Hand hemstitching attaches the bars to the front of the suit. Eight tucks grace the front of the romper. The blue collar has white squares hemstitched in a similar fashion as the blue bars were attached to the suit front. There is a tag in the neckline which says, "Hand Embroidered, 6 months." My guess would be that the suit was made in the Philippines. Three buttons close the crotch of the suit. The back has two buttons and laps right over left. What a precious suit for today's boys.

❋

Antique Christening Gowns

PERHAPS NO OTHER *garment is handed down from generation to generation like a christening dress or baptismal robe, as they were called in England before the turn of the century. Often, those who have no interest in antique clothing will cherish the family christening gown for the sentimental value woven into every stitch. Grandmothers or mothers who aren't fortunate enough to have inherited a family gown will plan and stitch an heirloom christening gown for a newly born infant, one on the way, or even for a "someday" child who has yet to be conceived. Since this book is a hope chest for grandmothers-to-be, it seems likely that many mothers reading this book will begin to plan christening gowns for their future grandchildren.*

TRADITIONAL CHRISTENING GOWNS *are appropriate for baby dedications, which is the practice at some churches, as well as for more formal baptismal services. Although worn just briefly, these dresses mark one of the most important events in a child's life, so it seems only natural that parents have a formal portrait made of their child in the gown. Imagine the pleasure future generations will derive from a picture of their great grandfather in the same christening dress the most recent descendant will wear.*

CHRISTENING GOWNS CAN *be elaborate with yards and yards of lace and intricate embroidery. Or they can be sweet and simple with very little lace or perhaps embroideries rather than lace. Traditionally, a family gown is worn by both boys and girls. A christening is one occasion when few would question a boy baby's wearing a fancy lace gown. Machine embroidery using today's modern machines is absolutely gorgeous; don't hesitate to decorate a gown with this type of embroidery. Although, I have to admit, hand work is most elegant if you have the time. Shadowwork embroidery is a quick and easy alternative! There is always the option of working a Swiss handloom into the dress design if you do not have the skills, the time, or the inclination to embroider. Another decorative option, which can be just as exquisite, is the use of lace bands or lace shaping.*

FOR THOSE PLANNING *to make a christening gown, this book offers endless ideas. Included are the basic patterns of nearly all popular designs from 1880 to the present. Enjoy the sketches of the antique designs and begin to let the imagination run wild. Remember, the fun of heirloom sewing is that you are the designer. It is perfectly acceptable to use any idea from any history book or from this book to make a garment, which is entirely yours. I like to believe that the women who made the antique dresses illustrated here would be very flattered at the thought of someone's using design elements from their garments to make a christening gown in this century. Isn't that what the sisterhood of sewing is all about?*

CORDED SMOCKING TUCKED
CHRISTENING GOWN
English-circa 1880

This dress was purchased in the Cheltenham area of England. Swiss eyelet embellishes the curved neckline and sleeves. Entredeux flanks both side of the eyelet on the sleeves. Slightly gathered French lace edges the bottom of each sleeve and the top of the neckline.

The "corded smocking" technique on this dress is absolutely fabulous. Upon first examining it, I noticed what appears to be a smocked stem stitch holding the tiny batiste gathers. Looking through a magnifying glass I find that the gathers are held by the placement of a fine twisted cord (similar to Pearl cotton) right on top of the gathers. The hand stitching is done from the back of the garment. Three of these rows of "corded smocking" are found at the top center neckline, at the top of the sleeves, and at the bottom of the bodice at the waistline. A tiny row of featherstitching is found at the top of the neckline curved Swiss trim and at the bottom of this trim.

The total gown length is 39 inches. The fullness of the skirt is 71 inches. From the top of the tucking panel to the bottom of the skirt is 7-1/2 inches. The skirt tucking pattern consists of one 1/2-inch tuck, 1/4-inch space, and 3-1/8-inch tucks (separated by 1/8-inch spaces). This pattern is repeated four times and finished with a 2-inch hem. The dress meets in the center back and was fitted to the baby with casings into which cording was run to act as a drawstring. This cording looks like a very skinny and very fine shoe string.

The tucks on the skirt and the hem are by machine. The hem is straight stitched by machine. The bodice of this dress is stitched completely by hand. The Swiss embroidery is by machine but every other stitch is by hand, including the featherstitching around the neckline and the attachment of the gathered lace around the neckline and the sleeves. The cording of the "corded smocking" is stitched by hand. The skirt is one piece of fabric with only one side seam; therefore, fabric to make this skirt, which at that time would have been purchased at the dry goods store, would have had to have been wider than 72 inches. I don't think fabrics that wide were made in the 1800s. Nor do I believe this needlewoman would have put a hem in with a straight stitch like topstitching, which is what I have found on this gown. What I believe is that a mother used a gorgeous sheet from her hope chest to make the christening gown. I'm assuming she either had no money to buy materials for the christening dress for her baby or, more likely, she was too frugal to sleep on such a beautiful, tucked sheet. She had a better use for it.

There are no rules as to how long or how full a christening gown should be. Study the measurements in this book concerning length and fullness to help you decide the dimensions of your dress. The longest dress from my antique collection measures 46 inches from the back neck to the bottom of the skirt. The shortest from my collection measures 29 inches. My suggestion for length is from 26 inches for a shorter dress to 46 inches for a longer one. Quite honestly, I prefer the latter. I also like a fuller dress because when the pastor or priest holds the infant, a fuller dress will lie prettier. At First United Methodist Church in Huntsville, Alabama, the pastor walks the full length of the church holding the infant for everyone to see after the baptism. The fuller dresses don't get twisted quite as easily when the pastor in his robe tries to turn the baby around.

In some countries, Australia included, the christening gown is sometimes left open in the back, and fastened just at the yoke/bodice area. Obviously, the slip plays an important part in this style gown. With this back open, it is easy to hold the infant and have the dress drape over the pastor's or priest's arm.

Grandmother's Hope Chest

ELEGANT SIMPLICITY CHRISTENING GOWN
English-circa 1900

The Swiss handloom on this gown is the tiniest that I think I have ever seen. The total width of the handloom, with entredeux on either side, is just a hair wider than 1/4 inch. The French round thread lace is 1/2 inch wide. I love the way the lace and Swiss alternate diagonally across the bodice; then about 2 inches from the center front of the garment a horizontal band begins. The Swiss trim connects the first part of the bodice, then French lace, then another Swiss trim, which is wide enough to carry ribbon. So sweet! The tiny sleeve fancy band has lace, Swiss trim, lace, and lace edging. The neckline features a dainty bias band trimmed with featherstitching, which also acts as a casing for the cording to pull to fit the baby. Slightly gathered French lace edging is stitched at the top of this bias band.

From the back, this gown laps right over left. It closes with two handmade fabric-covered buttons. The pull cord is found at the neckline only because ribbon must have been run through the Swiss ribbon, beading-type trim. The skirt placket measures 9 inches, which is reasonably long for a back placket. The total dress length is 34 inches and the circumference of the skirt is 64 inches. The underarm total length measurement of the sleeve is 6-1/2 inches.

The dress is made totally by hand including the inside seams, the five tiny 1/16-inch tucks on the skirt, and the hem, which is 2-1/2 inches wide.

SWISS SHAPED INSET CHRISTENING GOWN
English-circa 1910

Among the details on this dress is a Swiss inset, which I feel certain was made specifically for infant dresses. This seamstress used a bias casing topstitched on the top and the bottom to attach the Swiss strip and the gathered bodice. My thinking is that the bodice was gathered then the Swiss piece was placed on top of the wide gathered piece, then the bias tubing was stitched right on top of both pieces. After that, the excess gathered fabric was cut away from the back. The sleeves and the skirt feature three tucks. A bias binding and gathered French edging finish the sleeves and the neck.

The total back length of the dress is 33 inches; the circumference of the dress is 58 inches. The finished underarm sleeve length is 4-1/2 inches. The skirt has a 2-inch hem. From the back, the dress laps right over left with fabric-covered, flat buttons. A drawstring runs through the casing around the neckline.

SWEET CLUNY
CHRISTENING GOWN
English-circa 1915

Sweet and simple aptly describe this precious christening gown. Upon closer inspection of the dress, which I purchased in Cheltenham, I discovered that every inch of it was stitched by hand. The lace is a very delicate Cluny type; the hand embroidered handloom in the high-yoked bodice of this gown is the most delicate triple featherstitch that I have ever seen. The neckline is finished with a tiny bias binding and the featherstitch is repeated again around the neckline and at the bottom of the bodice. The skirt has two sets of 1/16-inch tucks spaced 1/8 inch apart; a 5/8-inch space separates the two sets of tucks.

Swiss trim and gathered, tiny Cluny edging grace the bottom of the sleeves. The same Swiss trim is used as "entredeux" to join the gathered ruffle on the bottom of the gown. English, flat, Cluny edging finishes the bottom of the ruffle. From the back, the gown laps right over left with two pearl buttons. The finished underarm sleeve length is 5-1/4 inches. The circumference of the skirt is 60 inches. The placket in the back of the gown is 3-1/2 inches long.

Grandmother's Hope Chest

SCALLOPED V-SASH TIED BABY GOWN
English-circa 1915

The front of this garment has sets of three tucks sandwiched in between lovely Swiss trim. The scalloped V design on the front is further embellished with Swiss trim outlining the shape on the front of this gown. The total underarm sleeve measurement is 6 inches. The Swiss trim at a slightly raised waistline is 1 inch wide by 4-3/8 inches long. A sash joins each side of this Swiss band treatment; each sash measures 1-5/8 inches by 16 inches long. Needless to say, this sash wasn't meant to tie into a large bow in the back. The total back length of this gown is 33 inches.

The coarseness of the material and the back design indicate this is a night dress rather than a christening dress. The back is a one-piece A-line instead of a typical yoke design. A bias casing finishes the neckline. It houses a cord which can be drawn up to fit the baby's neck. The gown laps right over left. The total circumference of the gown is 52 inches. A narrow, gathered lace finishes the sleeves and the neckline. Gathered Swiss trim follows the scalloped V treatment of the front of the gown. A hemstitch is stitched on each side of each of the tucks, which measure a little less than 1/4 inch each. Using today's modern hemstitches built into our machines and a wing needle, we could reproduce this effect.

NETTING EMBROIDERED CHRISTENING GOWN
English-circa 1930

The focal point of this ecru netting gown is the embroidery on the skirt. Five rows of Swiss netting insertion are stitched vertically on the high bodice of the garment. The short sleeves have faggoting and French lace at the bottom. The back laps right over left and closes with two pearl buttons. The total back length of the gown is 29 inches; the circumference is 49 inches.

My excitement mounted after purchasing this gown because I realized that all of the embroidery could be reproduced on a sewing machine. Using cotton netting fabric (or even netting with some man made fibers in it) and the large, built-in stitches on the new computer machines, you can make your own lace with little expense. What excitement!

Materials For The Christening Gown

The ultimate christening gown fabric, which should last through the ages, is Swiss batiste. Cotton simply holds up better than other fibers. Of course, the royal gowns are made of silk. Silk is a lovely and elegant fabric; however, it is not as strong as cotton. Both are fabulous for christening gowns. Wash after each wear. Don't starch or iron. Wrap the garment in low acid tissue paper and store in your bottom drawer.

French or English cotton laces would be my only choice in trimmings. They will hold up through the centuries with ease if they are cared for and stored in any decent fashion. Looking through some of my antique garments, I am almost convinced that they will last without any care whatsoever. Synthetic fiber laces not only turn yellow with age, they aren't nearly as beautiful as their cotton counterparts. Do use French or English cotton laces. By the way, all laces being made today in France and England have a 10 percent nylon fiber content. This is still considered cotton lace. The 10 percent nylon has been added for strength. They still dye and wear like 100 percent cotton laces, which, to my knowledge, are no longer being made.

PUFFING EYELET CHRISTENING GOWN
English-circa 1900

This gown highlights one of the most beautiful sewing treatments for the high yoke bodice. The top of the bodice is constructed of Swiss insertion stitched vertically and attached to entredeux on both sides. Below this strip, which is about 1 inch wide right below the center neckline, is a horizontal strip of the same Swiss insertion. Below that is a strip of very full puffing. Below this is another strip of the Swiss insertion. The high neckline is finished with a bias strip embellished with French knots on the bias binding. Gathered French edging is stitched above this bias binding. The sweet sleeves feature Swiss insertion at the bottom with gathered French edging at the top and the bottom. The top gathered sleeve edging was simply gathered and stitched on after the sleeve was finished.

Drawstrings run through casings at the neckline and waistline to close the back, right over left. The back placket descends 8 inches into the skirt. The total length of the gown is 41 inches; the circumference of the skirt is 70 inches. The total underarm length of the sleeve is 6-1/2 inches. Three 1/8-inch tucks with a 1/2-inch tuck covering another piece of Swiss edging 1-1/2 inches wide decorates the skirt. Tiny piping is used around the armhole. This may be the only dress in my collection on which tiny piping is used as the upper sleeve finish.

TUCKS AND MITERS CHRISTENING GOWN
English-circa 1900

One of the most beautiful garments in my collection is this delicate Swiss batiste gown laden with detail. It would be a fabulous creation for today's baby. Every inch of this dress is stitched by hand. The trims are Swiss machine made. The first step in making this bodice would be to create a strip of released pintucks. The tucks descend to 2 inches below the exact center front of the garment. They extend to the shoulders on the rest of the front yokes. A 1/4-inch- wide Swiss trim, with the tiniest entredeux on either side, is attached to French edging to make the strip, which is mitered on both sides of the bodice. The center front of the bodice is a tiny trim with French edging on both sides of the strip. Traditional miters are used on this garment; however, I would use folded back miters in a reproduction. After the miters are made, the center piece should be stitched down right on top of the whole garment. The excess tucked fabric can then be cut away from behind the mitered sections and from the center section. Below this lovely treatment is a piece of Swiss beading with entredeux on both sides; the beading is 1/4 inch wide. A tiny 3/8 inch wide beading is used around the neckline of this garment. What is unusual is that no bias binding was stitched around the neckline. Beading around the neckline is a more modern treatment. Narrow French edging is gathered and stitched to the top of this Swiss beading as a finishing touch.

The underarm finished sleeve length is 6-1/2 inches. The bottom of the sleeve is finished with the 1/4-inch Swiss beading that was used on the neckline; gathered French edging is on the bottom of this trim. The back of the dress is very similar to the front with released tucks and the mitered trim. The dress laps right over left and is closed with two pearl buttons and button loops. The total gown length is 40 inches. The skirt circumference is 62 inches.

The delicate fancy band on the skirt is simple but elegant! The tucking strip consists of two sets of three tucks, one band of Swiss insertion, French edging, Swiss insertion, and three more tiny tucks. Each tuck is 1/16 inch wide and is spaced 1/8 inch from the next. Entredeux is at the bottom of this tucking strip and a gorgeous ruffle follows. The total ruffle is 3 inches wide and consists of three tucks, a strip of the tiny Swiss insertion, and French, 1-inch, round thread edging stitched straight at the bottom.

Color Of The Christening Gown
Tradition dictates the color of most christening gowns to be white or off-white with matching laces and trims. Other elegant choices are white fabric with ecru lace, or ecru fabric with ecru lace. I have seen sheer white gowns with a pale pink or a pale blue slip underneath for a shadow of color. Although most embroidery is done in the same color as the dress, it is not unusual to see pastel embroidery on christening gowns today. There are no rules. If you would prefer a pale pink gown for a girl and a pale blue one for a boy, then by all means, make it. If you want pale pink ribbon run through beading on a girl's gown or pale blue for a boy, do so. Pale yellow and pale peach increase your field of options. My personal favorites are all white, white with ecru laces, or all ecru. But remember, this is an heirloom to be passed down to future generations of your loved ones. You are the designer.

Sleeves Of The Christening Gown
Once again, make it to suit you. A short, puffed sleeve is fine for boys or girls. A long, puffed sleeve seems to be the sleeve of choice for this decade, however. I personally love the sleeve bottom gathered to entredeux, a strip of beading, another strip of entredeux, and a piece of gathered lace attached to the bottom of the entredeux. Sleeves smocked at the bottom are pretty. You might also finish the sleeve with a bias binding and a little gathered lace attached to the bottom.

Another lovely sleeve finish is the Swiss embroidered beading which has entredeux on both sides. For the bottom finish, you can use a tiny Swiss edging or gathered French or English lace.

THIRTEEN TUCKS SWISS CHRISTENING GOWN
English-circa 1870

This gown has a lowered neckline, short sleeves and a bodice longer than most. I know the dress was made later than the mid 1850s because the eyelet trims are Swiss, rather than handmade. The earliest Swiss eyelets date back to the late 1850s. The bodice features Swiss insertions and Swiss edgings for an elegant touch. A bias casing encircles the scooped neckline as well as the waistline; both are closed and fitted with a drawstring. Gathered French edging is whipped, by straight machine stitch, to the neckline of the dress.

The skirt has 13 beautiful tucks, each 1/4 inch wide and 1/4 inch from the next. The gathered Swiss, 4-inch ruffle on the bottom is attached in a most unusual way. On the top, unfinished edge of this Swiss edging, about 1/2 inch is turned under to make a finished edge to the Swiss edging. This Swiss ruffle was attached to the skirt by the seamstress placing it directly on top of the skirt (wrong side of the ruffle to right side of the skirt), then placing a straight piece of Swiss trim (1/4 inch wide) on top of the ruffle and stitching through all three layers on top and bottom. The little foldback ruffle peaks above the Swiss trim about 1/4 inch. This is the first and only time that I have ever seen a ruffle attached in this manner, and I find it quite elegant. The total length of the dress is 46 inches. The total circumference of the skirt is 72 inches.

UNIQUE OLD PUFFED SLEEVED TUCKED GOWN
English-circa 1890

Upon first examination, I assumed this garment had been made prior to 1890. The skirt is similar to those popular in the 1850s, and there are drawstrings around the waistline and the neckline. The skirt, with its front panel and tucks around the bottom, in combination with the front panel design, was borrowed from an earlier period, as well. If it weren't for the puffed sleeves with the bias binding and slightly gathered French lace edging, I would date this dress much earlier; however, I tend to think that whomever created this gown adored older-looking styles, but preferred a contemporary puffed sleeve treatment.

The total back length of the dress is 42 inches; the circumference is 72 inches. Swiss trims embellish the front panel and the skirt. The tucks on the skirt are 1/4 inch and are placed 1/4 inch apart. The first section has 24 tucks; the center section has 10 tucks and the bottom section has 10 tucks. There are four tucks which travel around the rest of the skirt. The Swiss insertion in the garment is 1-1/4 inches wide; the Swiss edging is 2 inches wide.

MAGNIFICENT AYRSHIRE
CHRISTENING GOWN
English-circa 1840

I completely fell in love with this gown when I purchased it in Cheltenham. Although there are some tears in the fabric, it is still in wonderful condition. There are so many things I love about this dress. First, it is an altered gown. Originally, this dress featured short sleeves and a low neckline, typical of the mid 1800s style. Every inch of the embroidery is by hand. Some people speculate that the Ayrshire garments of this era were probably embroidered by the nuns in convents. I think that even in 1840 no mother would have had the time to put thousands of hours of embroidery into one christening gown. The embroidery is absolutely unbelievable with its eyelets — little lacy holes around satin stitches. All of the hemstitching is so perfect that you would think it was made on Swiss machines. Oh, how I do love Ayrshire embroidery.

As I looked at the designs of this embroidery, the daisies, lily of the valley, diamonds, leaf shapes, leaves, oblong flowers, and on and on, I dreamed that you would be able to create, by hand or machine, a pattern similar to this. Cynthia sketched this embroidery design, full size, so that you can use shadow embroidery, satin stitches, or whatever stitches you prefer on your hand-embroidered gown. You might want to use one of today's modern machines to reproduce the exquisite all-over embroidery.

I think the neckline and sleeves on this dress were altered about 1890 when necklines became higher on christening gowns. You can see that this mother has added long sleeves and a plain fabric piece in the neckline with a casing and a drawstring. The original dress was closed with a drawstring also. This gown now has three drawstring casings; one on the new section at the top of the neckline, one at the original neckline, and one at the waistline. The gown laps right over left and closes with loops and flat buttons covered with the batiste fabric of the original gown. Every stitch in this gown, even the modification, is by hand. The sleeve is sweet in that it features two rows of gathered French laces stitched down on top of the sleeve. A gathered French edging is also stitched at the top of the modified neckline treatment. Satin stitches embellish the casing of the original gown at the waistline. The original gown was 45 inches long. With the neckline modification, it is 48 inches long. The total underarm sleeve length is 5-3/4 inches. The circumference of the skirt is 76 inches. The beautiful Ayrshire panel is 6 inches wide at the top, 26 inches wide at the bottom, and 38 inches long.

A Baby's Hands

"Like crumpled blossom petals, moving slowly,
  Upon the wind's frail, sighing lullaby;
And yet as high and wonderful and holy,
  As God's great love that reaches from the sky!
A helpless as a bit of thistle blowing,
  Across a meadow filled with lovely things,
And yet as strong—aws subtle and as glowing,
  As a white bird that flies on golden wings...
A baby's hands — weak, tiny fingers, groping
  To find a place of tenderness and rest
They are the answer to the wistful hoping,
  The prayer that lives in every woman's breast
A baby's hands—as shy as April weather,
  Yet strong enough to hold the world together."

Margaret Sangster, "A Baby's Hands," The Delineator, (October, 1926) p. 5.

Grandmother's Hope Chest

DAISY HAND EMBROIDERED CHRISTENING GOWN
English-circa 1900

I spotted this gown at an antique mall in London. I love the style; however, it is the lacy-type hand embroidery design filled with dancing daisies that I adore most. I just had to bring it back to my readers. The embroidery isn't as difficult to do today. It doesn't require 3,000 hours of handwork because it could be recreated on today's sewing machines.

The garment features a panel of embroidery on the almost to-the-waistline bodice and a panel on the skirt. Both panels are attached to the garment with faggoting, by hand, of course. The neckline is finished with entredeux and gathered lace. The waistline features a tiny Swiss beading with ribbon run through. The puffed sleeves have entredeux and gathered French edging on the bottom. The back of the gown laps right over left and is closed with two buttonholes, two flat pearl buttons and the ribbons, which run all the way around the waistline of the gown. The placket extends 7 inches into the back of the skirt.

The total length of the gown is 35 inches. The underarm sleeve length is 5 inches. The circumference of the skirt is 60 inches. The bottom of the skirt has a strip of French insertion 1 inch wide stitched flat to the skirt. A 2-inch-wide strip of French edging is slightly gathered and stitched to the insertion. There is a little laundry marking in the back of the gown which reads "Fisher."

The embroidery pattern can be found in the pattern envelope.

OVER-THE-WAIST RUFFLE CHRISTENING GOWN
English-circa 1890

Using a "torch" (flashlight) for my only lighting, I first discovered this little beauty in an early morning market trip in London. With this inadequate light, I really didn't think it was spectacular. Once the sun was up, I returned to inspect the gown again, and realized its appeal. The lines of the neckline are gorgeous; the bodice is almost to the waistline. The V-shaped embellishment on the front extends 1 inch past the waistline, and the gathered 2-inch eyelet ruffle drops below the waistline

The dress length is 39 inches. The circumference of the gown is 104 inches. This very full gown consists of three skirt panels; two measure 38-1/2 inches and one measures 27 inches. The small panel is in the back of the garment. The underarm sleeve length is 6 inches. The gown laps right over left and the back placket extends 9 inches into the skirt. The back closes with drawstrings at the lowered neckline and at the waist. Featherstitches embellish the bias casing, which joins the waistline of the gown to the skirt. Narrow French edging is used two places on this gown. First, it is gathered and stitched to the Swiss trim around the bodice of the dress. Second, it is slightly gathered and stitched to the bottom of the sleeve. The sleeve fullness is held in place with about 1 inch of gathers similar to the ones you put in a smocked sleeve before you smock the small portion of the sleeve. The skirt has a 3-inch hem with a 2-inch piece of Swiss edging stitched underneath.

DUAL EMBROIDERY PERSONALITY GOWN
English-circa 1850

I have given this gown an unusual name for a specific reason. Let me elaborate. The gown is made completely by hand, including the tiny embroidered trim around the neckline. I am certain that the sleeves were added at a later date because of the style of the gown. Originally, the gown would have sported a scooped neck and short sleeves. The long sleeves were added when styles changed. I have seen this type of alteration on christening gowns so many times. The reason for calling this dress a "Dual Embroidery Personality Gown" is that I don't think the embroidery on the original bodice could have possibly been done by the same person who did the hand embroidery on the skirt. The skirt embroidery is lovely but very rough compared to the embroidery on the bodice. The patterns don't even blend and even the stitching to attach the garment is not as fine as that found on the skirt. While the predominant pattern on the bottom of the skirt is a little daisy; there are no daisies on any of the trims at the top of the skirt.

Another theory that I have is that the original skirt might have been beautifully embroidered in an elegant panel from the waist down to the skirt. After styles changed from scooped neck to high neck and from short sleeves to long, the family might have taken the gorgeous skirt and made a new, more modern bodice for it. Perhaps later, someone else in the family found the original bodice, added the sleeves, and made another skirt to go on the original bodice.

The total length of the gown is 40 inches; the circumference of the skirt is 84 inches. The original bodice is embroidered in one piece with a hand embroidered ruffle which also goes into a V down and over the skirt about 1 inch. The added sleeves have a bias cuff with French edging stitched to them. The total underarm sleeve length is 4-1/2 inches. The gown is closed with drawstrings run through casings at the neckline and at the waistline. The placket is stitched 5 inches into the skirt. The bottom of the skirt features two sets of three tucks 1/4 wide, spaced 1/4 inch apart. Between the two sets of tucks is a hand embroidered strip of eyelets. The hand embroidered edging on the bottom is 1-1/2 inches wide and has eyelets on the bottom in the shape of a scallop.

Hand-work

"Every mother wants her children to be well dressed and she knows that the hall-mark of attractive clothes for both grownups and children, but especially for the little people, is hand-work. And yet, how can I spend time embroidering when there is such need in the world? is the very next thought. But that difficulty is quickly settled by choosing either garments that are made up all ready to put on when the hand-work has been done, or by taking the utmost advantage of the simplicity that now marks fashionable attire for big and little people. Few seams, straight lines, frank and simple closings all conspire to take the dread out of dressmaking.

Another element of efficiency and hence of thrift is to be found in anticipating our needs. If summer sewing is started early enough there need be no rush just when we should be packing for a trip to cooler climates."

Eveyln Desguin, "For Kiddies All the Way from One to Ten," The Modern Priscilla, (March, 1918), p. 28.

Grandmother's Hope Chest

NEW YORK CITY CHRISTENING GOWN
American-circa 1900

Halfway out on Pier 49, at an antique show on a cold November day, I purchased this gown. I'm assuming it has New York roots; however, New England wouldn't be a bad guess either. One has to look under the gathered lace edging trim to see that what at first glance appears to be a rounded bodice is actually a squared, high-yoke bodice. The rounded look is caused by the placement of the 1-1/2 inch wide lace edging, which is stitched down with a small bias strip, trimmed with featherstitching. The bodice consists of sets of three tucks with 1-1/4-inch insertion between the tucks.

The skirt treatment is unusual in that the fabric strips are all doubled. For the top band, a 1-5/8-inch hem is turned up and straight stitched. Insertion is straight stitched between the turned-up hem, the next fabric band, and the last one; these bands are doubled strips of fabric as well. Gathered lace edging 2-1/2 inches wide finishes the bottom of the gown. A bias band with featherstitching and gathered lace edging trim the bottom of the sleeve.

The underarm sleeve measurement is 7-1/2 inches; the back length of the gown is 38 inches. The circumference of the skirt is 70 inches.

FOLD OVER NECKLINE CHRISTENING GOWN
English-circa 1880

I believe this handmade gown is a daygown rather than a christening gown. Around the neckline, the top is simply gathered and folded over. It has the drawstring, a treatment used frequently on earlier baby dresses. A bias strip stabilizes the neck area into a scooped neckline. The straight sleeves can be folded up for a little baby or lengthened for a larger baby. Narrow lace edging finishes the neckline and the sleeves. The hem is simply folded up and hemmed. The front gathers are held in place by little cords, which are whipped by hand.

The gown laps right over left in the back and the only visible method of closing is the drawstring in the neckline. My guess would be that beauty pins were used at the waistline and perhaps at one point in between the neckline and the waist. The back length is 33 inches; the underarm sleeve measurement is 6-3/4 inches. The circumference of the gown is 71 inches. The little sash that ties the gown is 23-1/2 inches long and 1-5/8 inches wide.

MARTHA'S FAVORITE CHRISTENING GOWN
English, circa 1900

I simply couldn't wait to buy this gown when I saw it in a London antique shop and get this book written so you could copy the design for your baby! The bodice is a combination of two rows of 2-inch Swiss embroidered insertion (without entredeux on the sides) with 5/8-inch, round thread, French lace in between. Swiss beading with entredeux on each side is stitched right on top of the created piece at the shoulders and at the bodice center. The double V on the bodice front is 3 inches wide and 1-1/2 inches deep. A piece of tape type trim is sewn on at the side of the bodice and down into this V on both sides.

If I were reproducing this design, I would make the bodice in a square, gather the skirt, pin the V bodice on this straight gathered skirt, stitch the bottom of the V bodice onto the gathered skirt, and trim away the excess skirt from the back. The back bodice is made from the same piece as the front bodice except that it is stitched on straight in the back.

The V panel in the skirt front is 4 inches wide. It has a 1-3/8-inch piece of French round thread lace on either side of the 2-inch Swiss insertion, which is the same as on the bodice. It is mitered in the center front skirt and the trim begins under the arm. The measurement from the center front of the gown to the bottom of the miter is 21 inches. On the bottom of the skirt, before the fancy band begins, there are three 1/16-inch tucks positioned 1/2 inch apart, one row of the 1-1/4-inch French, round thread lace, and one row of the 2-inch Swiss embroidered insertion.

There are really two ruffle sections to this gown or two fancy bands. The first fancy band is gathered to the bottom of the Swiss insertion. It measures 9 inches. The top of the fancy band has a 3-inch section of batiste with three 1/16-inch tucks near the bottom. A row of 1-1/4-inch French, round thread lace follows. The tucked strip and lace row repeat, followed by a strip of the Swiss 2-inch embroidered trim.

The second ruffle section or second fancy band consists of a gathered, 4-inch-wide, Swiss eyelet edging.

The underarm sleeve measurement is 6 inches. The puffed sleeves have three rows of tucks, one row of 3/4-inch French insertion and three more tucks. The sleeve band is simply beading with entredeux on each side; gathered narrow French edging finishes the sleeve.

The fullness of the main part of the skirt, before the fancy band, is 65 inches. The fullness of the bottom of the dress is 104 inches. The back placket is 9 inches deep into the skirt. The dress laps right over left and is closed with two button loops and little flat, handmade, fabric-covered buttons. Gathered lace edging finishes the neckline. The total length of the dress is 41 inches.

The dress is made entirely by machine, and the Swiss insertion in the dress and that on the skirt are not of a matching pattern. The laces in the dress are different patterns as well.

Clothing for Boys

"Little suits planned for contrasting fabrics are particularly becoming to the very small boy. A new model has an interesting tab arrangement on the straight trousers and the body and sleeve cut in one. Use linen madras, galatea, chambray, cotton poplin or shantung; or use dimity with poplin or linen. The latter combination is particularly cool for summer."1

"The small man who has just graduated to the dignity of trousers will look well in one of the new suits with a sailor-blouse of wash-material, such as linen or galatea, and with a detachable collar and straight trousers of heavy flannel, serge or cheviot which are buttoned on to the blouse at the waistline. This is very convenient and economical, because the blouse usually soils quickest, and in this way it is an easy matter to replace it.

For outdoor wear until he is about five or six years old, he may be dressed in one of the good-looking double-breasted overcoats with a warm turnover collar and cuffs of beaver, nutria, or some of the fur fabrics which wear so well."2

1. Author unknown, "Good-Looking Clothes for The Small Boy's Active Summer Days," The Delineator, (June, 1921), p. 96.

2. Mary E. Fitch, "Winter Styles for Small Folks," Needlecraft, (December, 1917), p. 20.

Grandmother's Hope Chest

INDIAN AYRSHIRE EMBROIDERY CHRISTENING GOWN
English- circa 1880

Because of the difficulty in obtaining Ayrshire embroidered garments, which were so beloved in 19th century England, English women took their ideas to India where embroidery was readily available at affordable prices. The work on this gown is entirely done by hand. You will notice that it is larger and has an Indian flavor but is still in keeping with the lovely Ayrshire work, which was being produced in England.

This gown is unusual because it is open down the back; an underdress or slip was made to complete the ensemble. The French lace attached around the neckline is round thread. The neckline and waistline of the garment are closed with drawstrings as is so typical on garments of this era. The total back length of the dress is 39 inches; the circumference of the garment is 59 inches.

Cynthia Handy reproduced the embroidery on this dress for you to re-create by hand or machine. This design is in the pattern envelope.

Grandmother's ... Chest

LACE OVER THE SLEEVES
SIMPLE BABY DAYGOWN
American-circa 1910

This Swiss batiste daygown is so simple, yet absolutely elegant. The only embellishments are five tucks at the bottom of the gown, lace edging at the bottom of the bias-bound sleeve, lace edging at the neckline above the bias neckband, and little strips of edging inserted over the top of the sleeve. The idea I love so much on this garment is the 1-1/4-inch lace edging inserted over the top of the sleeve. The basic garment is an A-line with fullness gathered at the neckline in both the front and back of the garment. The total back length of the garment is 32 inches; the fullness is 70 inches. The back placket is 14 inches long and the garment laps right over left in the back. When I purchased this dress, it had a gold beauty pin on the neckline. Since there are no buttonholes or buttons, I tend to think that one beauty pin is all that was used to close the back of the dress. There is a sweet little ribbon tied into a flat bow at the sleeves where the lace edging begins in the front and where it ends at the back.

MAGNIFICENT STRIPES AND LACE CHRISTENING GOWN
English-circa 1880

When I spotted this gown in an antique shop in London, my initial reaction was to buy it to put on the cover of this book. It's so unusual. Every stitch is by hand. What appear to be tucks on the skirt, bodice, and sleeves are really woven-in stripes on a Swiss fabric. Each strip has seven of these woven-in tucks. The gorgeous round thread French lace is 1-3/4 inches wide; each tucking strip is also 1-3/4 inches wide.

The scooped neckline is finished with a drawstring and a fabulous 5-1/4-inch gathered strip of French edging. This neckline edging matches the strips in the rest of the gown. The bodice has a strip of this tucked fabric inserted with lace. Entredeux is found on both sides of the lace in the bodice; however, no entredeux is used with each strip in the gown. At the bottom of the bodice, a strip of the tucked fabric is gathered with six rows of pleating; this looks as if it were run through a smocking pleater and left unsmocked. The tiny puffed sleeves have three more rows of this type of gathering held in place by a bias strip sewn in under the sleeve. The back closes with three buttonholes and three handmade, fabric-covered flat buttons. The total back length is 37 inches. The circumference of the skirt, not counting the wide, French, gathered edging, which makes the ruffle at the bottom of the gown, is 74 inches. Entredeux and gathered wide edging finish the bottom.

ROUND YOKE
BABY NIGHTGOWN
English-circa, 1880

Every stitch on this nightgown was put in by hand. And although it is not museum quality, I don't suppose I would put a masterpiece on my babies for sleeping either. The neckline is rounded and trimmed with featherstitching. Swiss trim travels around the neckline and across the front panel to which the sashes attach. The back of the garment is one piece with a placket down the center back, which laps right over left. The neckline closes with a drawstring for the purpose of fitting a large baby or a small baby. The use of a drawstring is really quite practical. I remember that my husband's father was in the hospital for three months right after Joanna was born. Of course, we waited until after he was released for her christening, and in that time, she grew too big for the neckline of her dress; we had to leave the top button unbuttoned. The gown that we made for my nephew David's christening was also too small at the neckline because he had such a big neck. Be careful to make your necklines big enough. That is why I think mothers of another century were so smart. They had to use their garments for months and later pass them down for other generations. They couldn't take a chance on the neckline's being too small.

The back length of this nightgown is 33 inches; the underarm sleeve measurement is 7-1/4 inches. The circumference of the gown is 64 inches.

V-SLEEVE CHRISTENING GOWN
English-circa 1820

Determining the time period of these garments is sometimes difficult, as was the case with this handmade gown. I went to the history books with the details of the garment. Its neckline is extremely low and it has puffed sleeves, which lead me to believe the garment is early 1820s. I've dated it at least this early because in the drawstring around the neckline and the waist, there is a tiny little cord unlike all of the rest of the cords in the drawstrings of my garments. I have never seen it before. The sleeve has a drawstring in it also hidden underneath the V treatment of the cuff. All of the interior seams are French, of course, and the embroidery is by hand, including the Swiss look trims. The back length of the gown is 45 inches; the underarm sleeve length is 5 inches. The circumference of the skirt is 58 inches. The gown is of a heavy cotton, which has the weave of a lightweight linen. The fabric is unlike any that I have seen.

Grandmother's Hope Chest

HAND EMBROIDERED CHRISTENING COAT
English-circa 1890

Christening coats traditionally had three sections; the long one, which was the basic coat portion, the cape portion, and the collar. I was told by one antique dealer in London that it is all the rage for women to buy the larger ones to use as theatre capes today. My christening coat is quite a vision of hand embroidery. Nearly all of the capes that I have seen are a dark ecru. I am assuming this is because most are made of wool challis and the wool couldn't have been dyed a stark white prior to the turn of the century. Elaborate embroidery decorates the collar, the cape, and the coat. The neckline closes with a silk ribbon tie which means that it could have been used for a baby coat the whole time the infant was carried in arms.

The back length of this coat is 41 inches. The length of the cape is 28 inches. The collar is 4 inches wide. The finished neck measurement of the cape is 13 inches. The basic design of the garment is a circular skirt attached to a bodice round yoke. This garment is lined in silk also and has a fabric interfacing to provide warmth.

Outdoor Wear

    For most of the 19th century, the garment of choice for children was the pelisse, or coat with a cape. Outer garments of that era have been found with both attached and removeable capes. Earlier pelisses were shaped like traditional capes with the addition of sleeves. Later pelisses were cut more like frocks, but contrary to frocks of this period, had a high neck, long sleeves, and front fastenings. Although merino wools in winter and cottons in summer were most often used in the construction of the pelisse, is was not unusual to see pelisses made of dimity, fine muslin, velveteen, or pique'. Trims for the pelisses included silk fringe, embroidery and or braid in the mid 1800s. Ruffles and insertions of embroidery or lace and borders of silk embroidery were used in the latter part of the century. The pelisses were as beautifully embellished as some of the frocks they covered.[15]

15. Buck and Cunnington, pgs. 169-170.

EYELET CHRISTENING COAT
English-circa 1900

This beautiful wool challis christening coat has gathered eyelet for its trim and a lovely 1/4-inch tucked collar for added interest. The tucked collar is 3-1/2 inches wide and has gathered 4-inch eyelet trim attached to the collar. The total length of the coat is 38 inches; the length of the cape is 20 inches. The coat closes with a silk tie, which measures 6 inches by 22 inches. The yoke of the coat is rounded, and the skirt is cut in a circle but also has lots of gathers to attach around the yoke. This is a very full coat. The same embroidered eyelet is used around the cape and the bottom. The eyelet is embroidered on the same wool challis from which the coat is made. I'm inclined to think that the coat maker contracted with a Swiss embroiderer to make the trims for this coat. There is a matching little Swiss guipure which trims the bottom of the tucking on the collar and the place on the cape where the gathered trim joins the cape.

Careful Mothers

"Careful mothers are giving thoughtful consideration to the clothing of their children this year more than ever before, and the woman who has learned that quality is the very foundation of conservation is looking carefully at material, style, and make.

The rapidity with which American women are grasping the lesson of thrift is one of the big encouraging elements of the war. Thrift is not meaning to the women of the country, simply going without. It has its root in that much abused and, until now, hardly used word efficiency."

Evelyn Desguin, "For Kiddies All The Way from One to Ten," The Modern Priscilla, (March, 1918), p. 28.

CURVED PRINCESS FRONT PANEL EMBROIDERED GOWN
American-circa 1900

This lovely curved princess front dress is the actual antique, copied here for the curved panel adaptation also featured in this book. This delicately-embroidered gown is embellished with double-bullion wrapped daisies, made in sets of five around an eyelet hole. Along the front of the front panel is 3/4-inch wide French insertion with double featherstitch along the side. A gathered Swiss batiste ruffle is gathered along the front of this panel and finished with flat French edging. The total width of this side ruffle is 1-1/2 inches. Around the neckline is a tiny Swiss beading with entredeux on both sides; gathered 1/2-inch French edging finishes the neckline. The long sleeve measures 4-1/2 inches under the arm. The actual bottom sleeve finish was gone when I purchased it, and the sleeves look exactly like this picture. My guess would be that the same Swiss beading and gathered lace edging would have finished the sleeves. The back of the gown is princess lined also and has 19 released 1/8-inch tucks spaced 1/8 inch across the back. It laps right over left with three buttons for the closure of the back placket. The total back length of this dress is 34 inches; the circumference in the fullest part of the skirt is 68 inches.

Diane Zinser re-created this embroidery design for you to make either by hand or machine. It is included in the pattern envelope with this book.

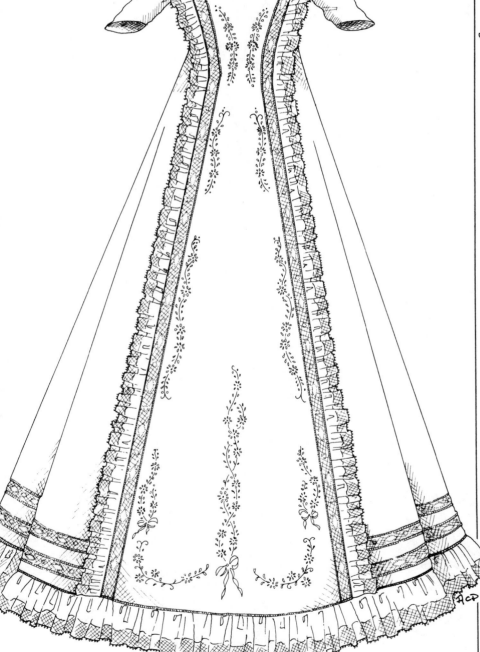

CURVED PRINCESS DIAGONAL TUCKED GOWN
English-circa 1900

This gown was in such bad condition when I found it that I considered not purchasing it. Actually, the front tucking panel is in great condition; the fabric in the rest of the garment is rotten in places. Upon careful consideration I decided that it had enough lovely features to include it in my collection. The garment is close enough to the design of the Curved Princess Front Panel Embroidered Dress that one could use the pattern in this book and actually make this very tailored gown. The front curved panel features several sets of diagonal folded tucks, 1/8 inch wide and spaced 1/8 inch apart. One-inch-wide Swiss embroidered insertion fits between the diagonally tucked panels. Swiss edging in a narrow width, 1/2-inch wide, finishes the neckline and the sleeves. The same tucked panels are also used on the bottom of each sleeve. The length of the sleeve is a bit longer than usual, 6 inches. The total back length of the gown is 38 inches. The skirt circumference is 48 inches, is finished with a gathered Swiss edging 4-1/2 inches wide. The back is plain and features a to-the-waist yoke. Five buttons close the gown, lapping left over right.

SIMPLE LACE V FRONT
FRENCH KNOT DAISY GOWN
American-circa 1920

This gown contains some very simple and sweet ideas you can incorporate into a christening gown, a skirt, or yoke of any heirloom garment. Two strips of lace and two strips of Swiss embroidered insertions stitched at angles offer an interesting effect at the yoke. The high yoke bodice features Swiss embroidered insertion stitched around with the French edging gathered all the way around the bodice. Only Swiss insertion highlights the neckline. The plain long sleeve has a 1/2-inch wide cuff. The total underarm sleeve length is 5-1/2 inches. The total back length is 32 inches; the circumference of the skirt is 48 inches.

The V design on the front of the gown is a combination of Swiss insertion and flat lace edging stitched onto the skirt and mitered in the center front. A lace edging flower has been shaped at the top of the V. Around the skirt, 3 inches above the bottom of the garment, is another row of embroidered Swiss insertion with the flat lace. A 1-3/4-inch hem has been straight stitched on the sewing machine. The back is closed with two buttons and laps right over left.

The design on the Swiss embroidered insertion which is only 1/2 inch wide is very sweet and unusual. A serpentine-shaped cording is stitched at the top and bottom of the daisy designs only. The rest of the cord hangs loose. Each daisy consists of five French knots with one French knot in the middle.

ROYAL CHRISTENING DRESS
Australian - circa 1880

I love this dress so much! As a matter of fact, this is the only dress from my Antique Clothing book that I have "redone" a little and brought forward to this book. In the original dress, all of the trims were Swiss. I have asked Angela to redo this dress showing the use of French or English laces in combination with the Swiss for one more adaptation of my favorite christening dress that I have ever owned!

Among my collection of Australian garments it his gorgeous christening gown. The scooped neckline style leads me to believe it was constructed between 1850 and 1880; however, the machine work, including the eyelet places the piece closer to 1880. Swiss-manufactured eyelets first began coming out of Switzerland about 1850. They were commonly used in fine, baby garments by 1880. machine sewing of tucks began to appear around 1870. Before this time, the garments were usually made entirely by hand. A combination of tucks and insertions was used in the 1870s and 1880s. These tucked front gowns remained very popular until 1900. Another sign that the dress was made closer to 1880 is the triangular panel in the front.

The whole front panel is one piece of fabric, tucked completely across. It is 34 inches long, 9 inches wide at the very top and 18 inches wide at the bottom. The 1/8 inch tucks are placed 1/2 inch apart. There are 41 tucks on the panel. On the bodice, the center panel of French lace is straight; the others are placed at angles, tucked under this one straight piece of lace. Swiss 2 1/4 inch embroidered edging is used for the sleeves, bodice trim, skirt trim and skirt panel trim. The bias binding around the neckline is 1/4 inch wide; it is made like a casing and a drawstring is run through it to adjust the neckline for individual fit for infants. The total back length of the dress is 39 inches; the circumference is 72 inches.

EMBROIDERY AND SQUARES
YOKE GOWN
English-circa 1900

Absolutely exquisite is the yoke embroidered design on this bodice. The gown is totally made by hand. There are so many unique features on this gown that I probably should start with the bodice and continue to the skirt. The squares, or half squares to be exact, on either corner of the bodice are mitered and surrounded by two rows of triple featherstitch. The lace edging around the neckline is mitered and finished into squares. Delicate hand embroidery, which includes eyelets, travels around the neckline and around the back. This would be an excellent place to use those wonderful new sewing machines with the incredible embroidery capacity. Of course, you would use very delicate thread in white on white. On the back bodice the half squares only have the double row of triple featherstitching, not the lace insertion as the front has. Entredeux finishes the neck edge, the bodice edges, and the sleeve edges. Gathered lace edging finishes the neck and the sleeves. The skirt is absolutely precious also. Three folded tucks, 1/8 inch wide spaced 1/8 inch apart are on either side of a pretty dot French insertion only 1/4 inch wide. A four inch hem has been stitched to the dress by a row of triple featherstitch instead of a traditional hem. The back length of the dress is 32 inches; the circumference of the skirt is 60 inches.

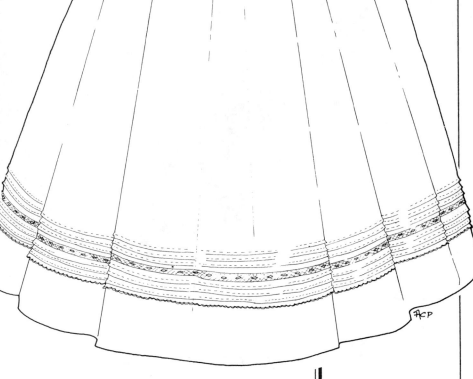

Christening Gowns

circa 1992

WHEN IT COMES *to heirloom sewing, very little is new. Lace shaping, tucks, puffing, and portrait collars have been around forever. However, combining these steadfast techniques with individual design and creativity heirloom sewing will continue to be fresh. I have always told my students that if there ever comes a day when I don't get a major thrill over each new heirloom garment that I see, I will probably look for a new line of work.*

ADAPTATIONS OF ANTIQUE *christening gown designs continue to thrill me the most. The designs here originated in so many different places, I could go on for hours... I'll attempt to be brief. I bought the curved front panel gown at a flea market in Nashville. Several of the ideas came from older garments purchased in Australia. Adaptations of my collection of antique garments always serve as inspiration for sleeves, skirts, yokes, collars, or other parts of the garments. The high yoke dress has been used from my second book for more than seven years. The idea to use a lowered yoke dress for a pattern was inspired by a Brazilian garment I purchased. The christening coat or overdress style was one I found on a garment made in the Philippines. Notice I use the word "idea" for all these garments. With the exception of the antique curved panel front dress, none of the gowns or patterns here are exact copies of antique or newly purchased garments. Sometimes we used a sleeve idea from an antique clothing book, the bodice treatment from an antique garment, and two or three skirt ideas from other books of mine. Occasionally we took ideas from garments featured in Sew Beautiful.*

I COMMISSIONED SUE PENNINGTON *and gave her complete artistic freedom to put idea to fabric. You have to understand how easy it is to work with Sue. There is no doubt that when her dresses arrive they will be magnificent. The following 16 pages feature the stunning results. With a few of my ideas and a lot of her adaptations, Sue Pennington created this section for you. I must confess that some of these designs are entirely hers. She's a seamstress of unlimited talent; her skills at the sewing machine are superb. How she combines heirloom sewing techniques is pure art, as you are about to discover.*

SUE WROTE THE *original directions for the Shark's Teeth technique in Sew Beautiful magazine after I sent her an antique petticoat featuring this treatment. This technique appears again in the center curved panel of one of the christening gowns. She originated the Australian Organdy Windowpane technique, which combines machine applique and embroidery into a lovely heirloom look. It was her idea to use Celtic quilting designs to shape laces into something absolutely new and unique in the heirloom sewing field. She thought to shape three lace circles into the front of our first grandson's christening dress. These three circles stand for the Father, the Son, and the Holy Spirit. Having "three" of anything is not new on clothing such as christening dresses and communion dresses. Often, in my antique collection, I will find three tucks. I like to believe that they stand for the Trinity on clothing created for religious occasions, not to overlook that elements placed in three's make for a lovely design statement.*

CHRISTENING GOWNS AND *first communion dresses are among the happiest of garments created in heirloom sewing. Some families choose to make only one dress to be worn by every relative at his or her religious event. I, as you might suspect, am having one made for each grandchild so that his/her family will not have to share the dress with other siblings. I am using the built-in alphabets in my sewing machine to put something similar to the following in the slip or ruffle of the dress. "William Campbell Crocker, jr., February 2, 1992, Son of Charisse Fuentes Crocker and William Campbell Crocker. Christened, Holy Spirit Church, Huntsville, Alabama, February 16, 1992. Grandson of Mr. and Mrs. Albert Fuentes (Guymon, Oklahoma), Drs. Martha Campbell Pullen and Joseph Ross Pullen (Huntsville, Alabama), and William Wynn Crocker (Phoenix, Arizona)." It is so easy to use these alphabets that you could go even further and put the names of the great grandparents, for whom the child was named, who made the dress, any history of laces or antique bits and pieces that were added to the dress.*

I TALKED WITH *one grandmother in Louisiana who shared that she had had a relatively short christening dress. When her grandchildren came along, she wanted to use her dress, but she preferred a longer and more elaborate version. She began to gather family treasures such as handkerchiefs, bits of old laces, and other handmade pieces. Commissioning a designer in New Orleans, she presented the short dress plus other family treasures and gave her permission to add other things to the garment in order to lengthen it. It was a magnificent gown. I am giving myself and you permission to add family treasures including handkerchiefs, doilies, other crochet items, tatted items even if it is just a tatted cross, or old laces to an old dress or to be incorporated into a new dress. There is nothing more rich in tradition than a family christening gown.*

ELONGATED DIAMONDS AND ZIGZAGS GOWN
AMERICAN - CIRCA 1992

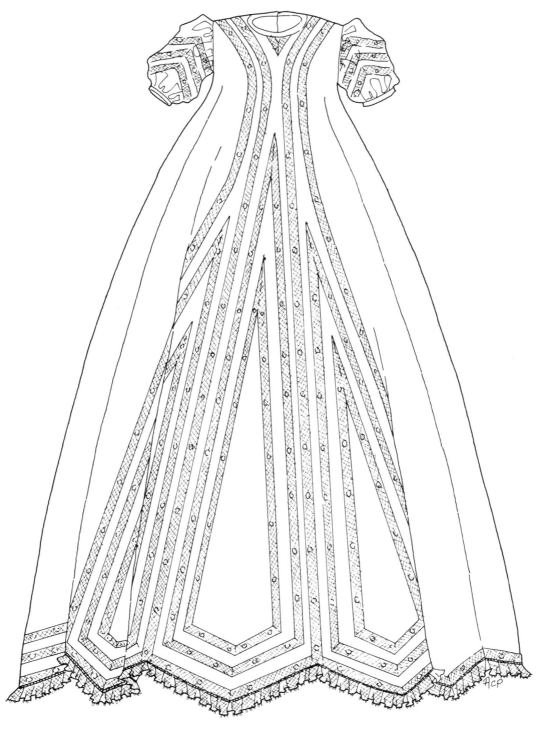

Pattern Pieces Used:
Antique Curved Panel Front, Side, Back Yoke, Back Skirt, Long Puffed Sleeve. Lace templates for the bottom and front of the dress are also included in the pattern envelope.

Supplies and Gown Description

- 2-1/2 yards white Nelona
- 22 yards insertion
- 3 yards entredeux
- 4-1/2 yards of 1-inch or wider edging

Note: Extend all skirt pieces 10 inches at lower edge

———— ✳ ————

This elegant dress is easy to make and features the antique curved front panel pattern. The fabric is a white Nelona. The strips of 1/2-inch lace insertion, which travel ever so elegantly down the front of the dress and around the bottom of the zigzags on the skirt, are in a cross pattern. I think this lace is especially nice for baptismal gowns; in addition to the religious symbolism, this lace is also a reasonably inexpensive one. Sue used a very narrow and tiny featherstitch in a rayon embroidery thread (Sulky) to attach the laces to the garment. The zigzag shapes of the lace insertion on the skirt are especially elegant when repeated on the sleeves. Notice the diamond type shapes into which the garment insertions end on the front panel. A tiny bias binding finishes the sleeves and neck edge of the garment. The back of the dress is a high yoke style and has two buttons and a placket. Entredeux and gathered lace edging finish the bottom of the dress.

The total back length of the dress is 38 inches; the fullness of the skirt is 80 inches. The lace edging on the bottom of the dress is 1-1/2 inches wide.

All seams are 1/4 inch.

Step 1. Trace the dress front onto a block of fabric

Step 2. Transfer all lace placement lines (fig. 1).

Step 3. Pin lace as indicated. The inner edge of a strip of insertion is placed along the side front stitching line (1/4 inch in from pattern cutting line).

Step 4. Carefully miter the upper points of the elongated diamonds.

Step 5. Baste lace in place with a short straight stitch.

Step 6. Starch and press front so that it is fairly stiff.

Step 7. With white rayon machine embroidery thread in the needle and fine cotton thread in the bobbin, stitch over the headings of the basted lace with a machine featherstitch (W=2.5, L=1.5) or as desired. Trim fabric from behind lace and cut out front (fig. 2).

Step 8. Cut out dress sides, skirt back, and sleeves.

Step 9. Transfer lace placement lines and attach lace as for front (fig. 3).

Step 10. Pin dress front to side fronts. The unstitched heading of the lace along the princess seam line should overlap the edge of the side front by 1/4 of an inch so that the lace heading is on the stitching line.

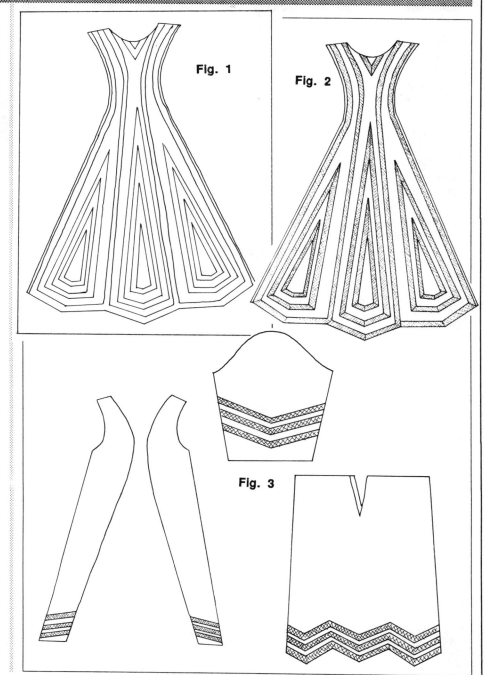

Fig. 1

Fig. 2

Fig. 3

79

Elongated Diamonds and Zigzags Gown

American - circa 1992

Step 11. Baste in place and featherstitch. Trim fabric from behind lace **(fig. 4)**.

Step 12. Cut out yoke backs and enough bias strips (1-1/4 inches wide) to go around neck and cuffs.

Step 13. Press under facings on yoke backs, and stitch to front at shoulder seams **(fig. 5)**.

Step 14. Press seams toward back.

Step 15. Press bias strip in half lengthwise. Stitch bias strip to neck edge with a 1/4 inch seam line and raw edges even. Be careful not to stretch neck edge **(fig. 6)**.

NOTE: If you think you might have a problem with this, stay stitch the neck edge first. Stitch again very close to first stitching and trim seam allowance to 1/8 inch. Fold the folded edge of the bias strip up and over the seam allowance. Stitch in the ditch from the right side to secure the bias band or stitch by hand.

Step 16. Make a 4-1/2-inch placket in the center of the skirt back **(fig. 7)**.

Step 17. Gather the upper edges of the skirt back, and stitch to the back yokes **(fig. 8)**.

Step 18. Press seam toward yokes.

Step 19. Gather the lower edges of the sleeves, and finish with a bias band 6-1/2 inches long in the same manner as the neck edge. Do not secure the bias band to the inside of the cuff for 1 inch at each end.

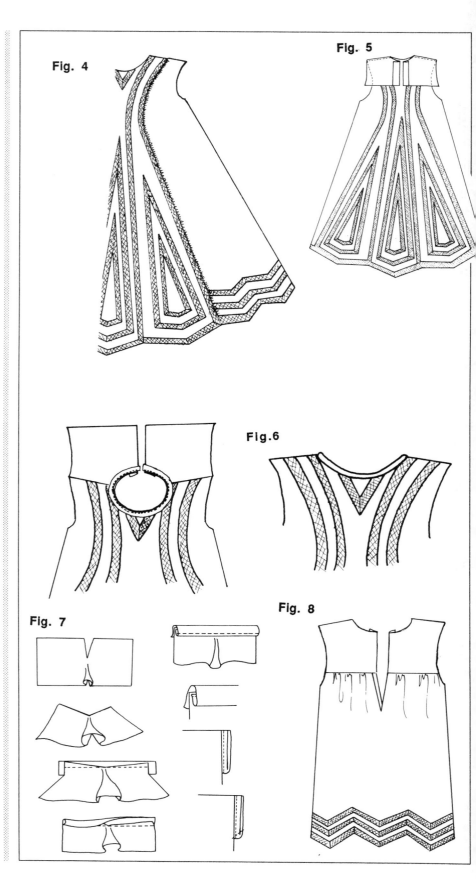

Fig. 4

Fig. 5

Fig. 6

Fig. 7

Fig. 8

Step 20. Gather sleeve caps and stitch sleeves to dress **(fig. 9).**

Step 21. Stitch one side seam, matching lace at hem, underarm seam, and cuff seam.

Step 22. Fold bias strip out as you stitch this seam **(fig. 10).**

Step 23. Finish seam allowance and press toward back.

Step 24. Turn the remaining section of bias binding to the inside and stitch.

Step 25. Trim one batiste edge from entredeux.

Step 26. Zigzag entredeux to insertion at lower edge of dress. Do not try to bend the entredeux around the corners. Instead, cut the entredeux as you stitch to the end of each straight section and overlap the entredeux one hole at the corner as you continue stitching the next straight section **(fig. 11).**

Step 27. Trim the other batiste edge from the entredeux.

Step 28. Attach slightly gathered edging to entredeux, gathering lace more at points to prevent cupping.

Step 29. Stitch other side seam **(fig. 12).**

Step 30. Close back yoke with buttons and buttonholes or beauty pins.

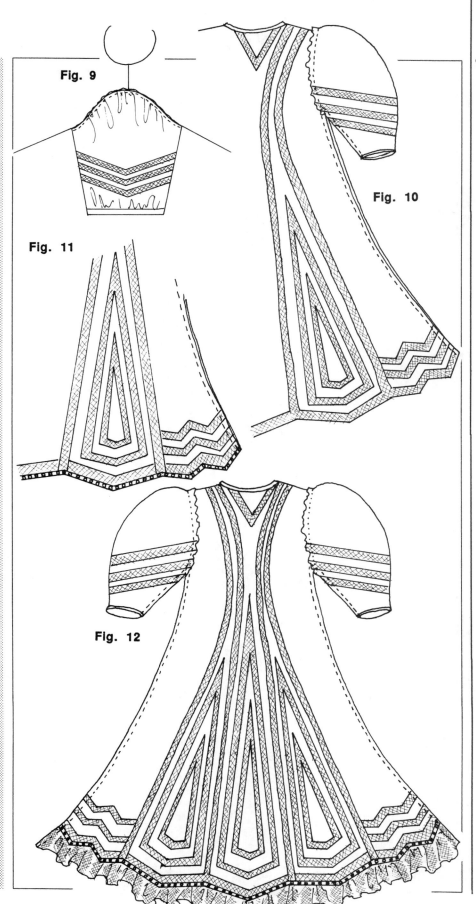

Fig. 9

Fig. 10

Fig. 11

Fig. 12

ANTIQUE CURVED PANEL DRESS
WITH SMOCKED RUFFLE
AMERICAN - CIRCA 1992

Pattern Pieces Used:
Antique Curved Panel Front, Side, Back Yoke, Back Skirt, Short Puffed Sleeve.

Supplies and Gown Description

- 1-2/3 yards Nelona
- 8-1/2 yards 6-1/2-inch wide Swiss edging
- 3-2/3 yards entredeux
- 1-2/3 yards tiny piping (optional)

- 2-1/4 yards 2-inch wide embroidered Swiss insertions
- 2 yards narrow Swiss edging with entredeux

- 9-1/2 yards 1/4-inch ribbon (Not required if Swiss edging does not have beading slots and a different smocking design is used.)

Sue adapted this pattern from an elegant curved panel pattern, an exact copy of an antique dress I have had for years. She smocked 6-1/2 inch wide ruffles to go on top of the panel. The bottom of the dress has Swiss white-on-white embroidered insertion with entredeux at the bottom and the top; a gathered 6-1/2 inch wide Swiss edging makes the ruffle at the bottom. The smocking has little buttonholes worked in the smocking in order that ribbon can be run through the actual smocking. The Swiss insertion is mitered to make the neckline of the dress. Another piece of the Swiss 6-1/2 inch wide edging is used for the sleeves; elastic is run through the sleeve very close to the point where the embroidery begins. The back of the dress is a high yoke bodice, which is closed with buttons. The total dress is 33 inches long. A piece of Swiss trim with tiny piping finishes the sides of the panels going down the front.

All seams are 1/4 inch

Step 1. Cut four strips of 6-1/2-inch wide Swiss edging 15 inches, 20 inches, 32 inches, and 45 inches.

Step 2. Pleat seven rows in all four pieces. Tie off one piece to 4 inches. Tie off another piece to 5-1/2 inches. Tie off another to 9 inches. And tie the last one to 13 inches.

Step 3. Smock five rows in desired pattern. Block to widths in Step 2 **(fig. 1)**.

Step 4. Cut a piece of batiste 17 inches wide and 7 inches long.

Step 5. Place the 13-inch smocked piece, right side up, on top of this fabric so that the upper raw edges are even and the smocked piece is centered.

Step 6. Baste in place, 1/2 space above top smocked row **(fig. 2)**.

Step 7. Cut a piece of batiste 13 inches wide by 6-3/4 inches long.

Step 8. Turn the basted smocking upside down, centered, over this piece of batiste so that the smocked Swiss is sandwiched between the two batiste layers. Stitch on top of basting stitching **(fig. 3)**.

Step 9. Finish seam and press up **(fig. 4)**.

Step 10. Baste the 9-inch smocked strip to the top of this 14-inch piece of batiste, matching centers **(fig. 5)**.

Step 11. Cut a piece of batiste 9 inches wide by 6-3/4 inches long.

Step 12. Turn the basted smocking upside down over this piece of batiste so that the smocked Swiss is sandwiched between the two batiste layers.

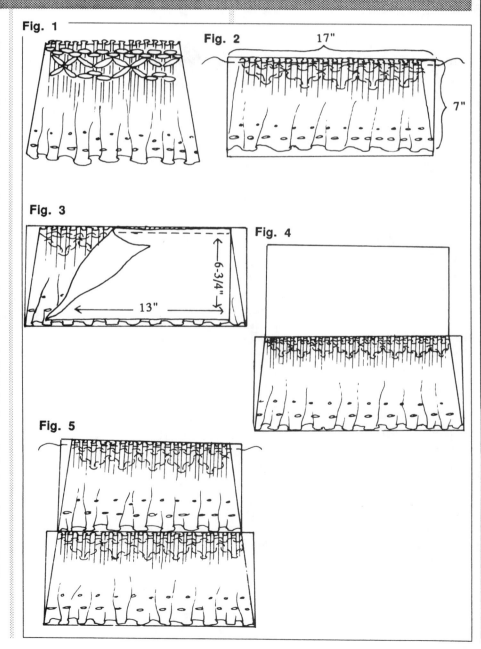

Fig. 1 Fig. 2 17" 7" Fig. 3 13" 6-3/4" Fig. 4 Fig. 5

ANTIQUE CURVED PANEL DRESS WITH SMOCKED RUFFLES

AMERICAN - CIRCA 1992

Step 13. Stitch on top of basting stitching **(fig. 6)**.

Step 14. Finish seam and press up **(fig. 7)**.

Step 15. Baste the 5-1/2-inch smocked strip to the top of this 9-inch piece of batiste and baste **(fig. 8)**.

Step 16. Cut a piece of batiste 5-1/2 inches wide by 6-3/4 inches long and stitch to smocking as before **(figs. 9 and 10)**.

Step 17. Baste 4-inch piece of smocked Swiss to top of 5-1/2-inch batiste **(fig. 11)**.

Front yoke

Step 18. Cut three pieces of 2-1/4-inch wide Swiss insertion, each 4 inches long.

Step 19. On one piece, make a dot on the long side 1-1/8-inch from each end. Draw a line to connect this dot with the corner on the other side **(fig. 12)**. Do the same thing on one end of the other two pieces of insertion.

Step 20. Lay the pieces of insertion, right sides together, so that the lines match up. Stitch along the lines to miter the corners of the yoke.

Step 21. Finish seam by serging or zig-zagging and press toward center **(fig. 13)**.

Step 22. Stitch mini-piping to lower edge of yoke with 1/4-inch seam **(fig. 14)**.

Step 23. Stitch yoke to upper row of smocked Swiss, right sides together **(fig. 15)**, matching stitching lines.

Step 24. Finish seam and press toward yoke.

Step 25. Mark center of front panel.

Step 26. Lay front pattern on wrong side of panel, matching marked center front with pattern fold line. Do not try to fold the front panel - the smocking makes it too bulky to mark accurately.

Step 27. Trace the shoulder and hem cutting lines.

Step 28. On the side front seam, extend the seam allowance 1/4 inch beyond pattern cutting line. Flip pattern over to mark the other side of the front.

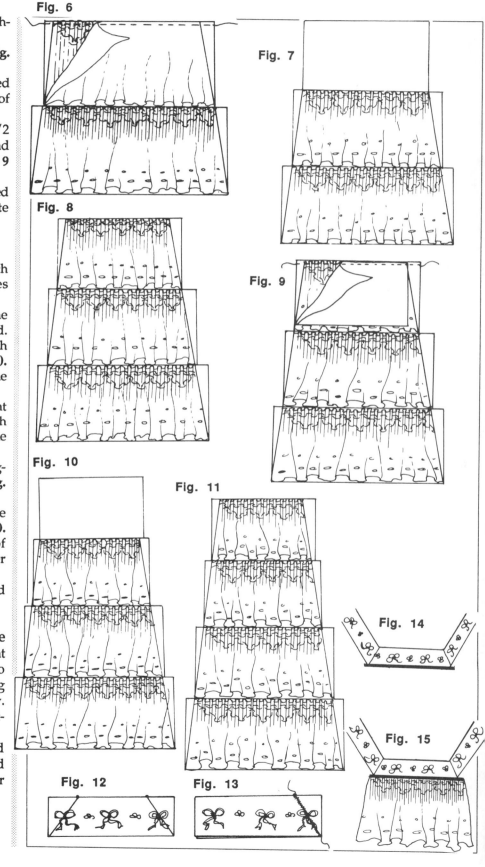

Fig. 6

Fig. 7

Fig. 8

Fig. 9

Fig. 10

Fig. 11

Fig. 12

Fig. 13

Fig. 14

Fig. 15

Step 29. On the right side, stitch the smocked Swiss pieces to the batiste underlayer just inside the marked cutting lines. Use a short zigzag when stitching smocked sections to hold smocking stitches in place if the knots are cut away.

Step 30. Cut dress front along cutting lines (fig. 16).

Step 31. Cut out side fronts, extending the side front seam allowance 1/4 inch and cutting the lower edge 2 inches shorter than the pattern.

Step 32. Attach entredeux to the lower edge of the side front pieces with a 1/4 inch seam.

Step 33. Attach Swiss insertion to entredeux (fig. 17).

Step 34. Stitch piping to princess seam of side fronts with a 1/4-inch seam.

Step 35. Place side front over front, with raw edges of side front seam even, and stitch seam right on top of piping stitching. This piping is optional; just stitch a plain seam if you decide not to use it. Finish seam and press away from center (fig. 18).

Step 36. Cut the batiste edge from narrow Swiss edging with entredeux. Place the edging so the entredeux of the edging is right along the piping.

Step 37. Stitch the edging in place with a very narrow zigzag, stitching into the ditch of the piping seam (fig. 19).

Step 38. Cut out the back yokes and press under the facings.

Step 39. Stitch to front at the shoulder seams. Press seam toward back (fig. 20).

NOTE: The narrow Swiss edging around the neck was attached differently than usual so that the miters at the corners of the square neck would be more precise.

Step 40. Trim the batiste edge off the narrow Swiss edging.

Step 41. With the facings folded open, and the scalloped edge of the edging even with the cut edge of the neckline, stitch the entredeux to the fabric with a very narrow zigzag (W=1 or 1-1/2, L=1).

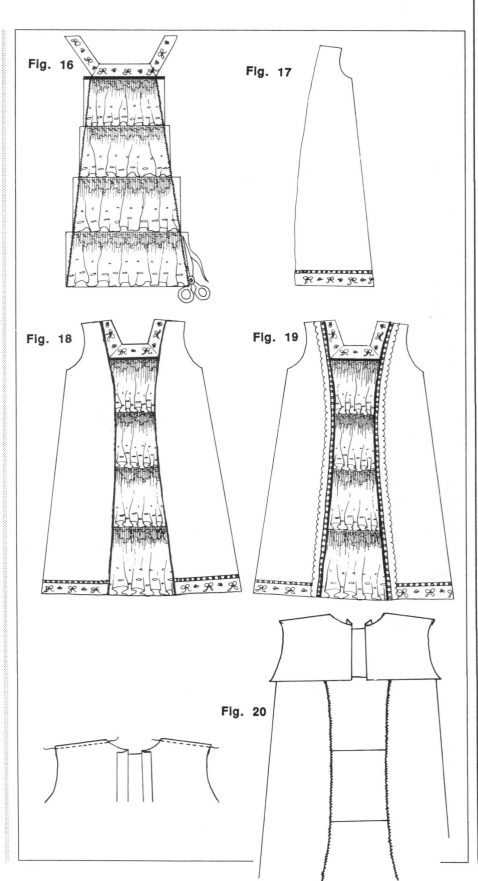

Fig. 16

Fig. 17

Fig. 18

Fig. 19

Fig. 20

Antique Curved Panel Dress with Smocked Ruffles

American - circa 1992

Step 42. Fold the insertion into neat miters at the corners. Press the fabric under the insertion back toward the yoke, clipping curves if necessary.

Step 43. Now, from the right side, zigzag again through the entredeux and the folded edge of the fabric, with the same machine settings. Trim excess fabric from the wrong side.

Step 44. Press the corners into sharp, even miters, and zigzag on the right side right on top of the fold, backstitching at both ends.

Step 45. Trim point on wrong side.

Step 46. Fold back facings into place, and stitch (**fig. 21**).

Step 47. Cut back skirt 2 inches shorter than pattern.

Step 48. Stitch entredeux to lower edge of skirt and Swiss insertion to entredeux both with 1/4-inch seams.

Step 49. Make 4-1/2-inch placket in center of skirt back. Gather top edges of skirt back and stitch to yokes. Press seams up (**fig. 22**).

Step 50. Cut short puffed sleeves out of 6-1/2-inch Swiss edging so that top of sleeve cap is at the raw edge of the edging. In other words, make the sleeve as long as possible.

Step 51. Attach elastic (see *Lily of the Valley Christening Gown*). Stitch 1/8- inch elastic 1-1/2 inches from lower edge of sleeve, or just above the heavily embroidered portion of the edging (**fig. 23**).

Step 52. Gather sleeve cap and stitch to dress (**fig. 24**).

Step 53. Stitch one side seam, matching all seams (**fig. 25**).

Step 54. Attach entredeux all around lower edge of dress, being careful not to catch the smocked Swiss edging in the stitching (**fig. 26**).

Step 55. Attach gathered Swiss edging to the entredeux and stitch remaining side seam (**fig. 27**).

Step 56. Close back yoke with buttons and buttonholes or beauty pins.

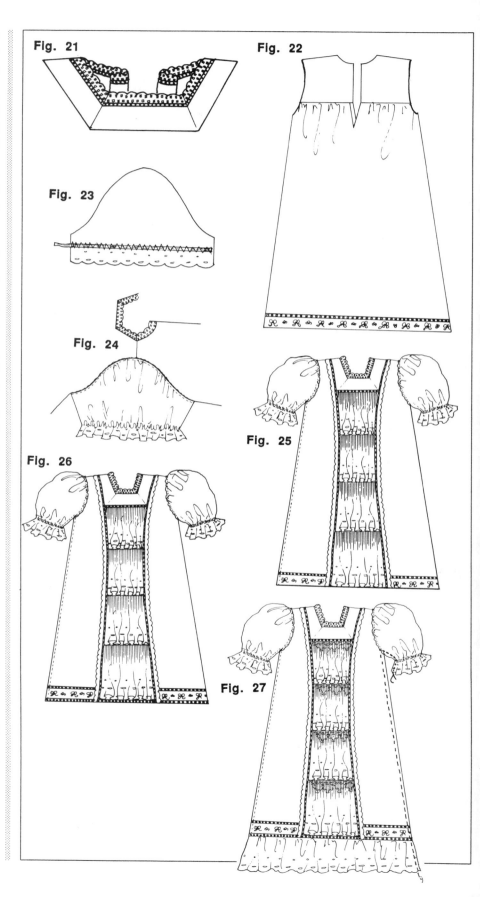

Fig. 21

Fig. 22

Fig. 23

Fig. 24

Fig. 25

Fig. 26

Fig. 27

PRINCESS SEAM GOWN WITH ORGANDY SCALLOPS AND INSERTS
AMERICAN - CIRCA 1992

Pattern Pieces Used:
Antique Curved Panel Front, Side, Back Yoke, Back Skirt, Short Puffed Sleeve. Lace templates for Organdy Scallop, Front and Bottom, are also included in the pattern envelope.

Supplies and Gown Description

- 2-1/2 yards Nelona
- 3/4 yard cotton organdy
- 4 yards entredeux
- 19 yards insertion (#1) 5/8-inch wide
- 5 yards insertion (#2) 5/8-inch wide
- 8 yards 3/4-inch wide edging
- 6 yards 2-1/4 inch wide edging

This gown combines traditional heirloom sewing with applique, built in stitch embroidery, Australian Windowpane Organdy Motifs, and lace shaping on organdy. Using the princess seam front panel, which is adapted from our antique dress, Sue let her sewing machine become a machine embroiderer's dream. The antique princess panel is outlined on both sides with purchased entredeux; purchased entredeux also encircles the neckline with gathered lace. A wide piece of French lace is gathered into a little ruffle at the shoulders of this dress, and the bottom of the sleeves have entredeux and gathered lace edging. Two different patterns of lace are used in this dress. The lace shaping on either side of the princess panel is almost in the shape of a pineapple. An Australian Windowpane Organdy motif comes out of the top of the pineapple as well as built in stitches from the sewing machine, which resemble flowers and leaves. All the stitching is done white on white. The appliqued windowpane flowers are stitched on organdy as well as the lace shaping. The ruffle on the bottom of this dress is shaped scallops on organdy. Machine entredeux is stitched to the bottom of these scallops on the organdy and gathered lace finishes the ruffle. The back length of the dress is 42 inches; the circumference is 80 inches. The beauty and details of this dress call for one of the newest computer machines. If you don't own one of these, you can still make this dress using free hand embroidery stitches.

Step 1. Extend lower edge of gown fronts and back pattern pieces by 10 inches, retaining the curve at the bottom.

Step 2. Tear one width of organdy 18 inches wide for the skirt front, leaving the other 9 inches for the skirt back.

Step 3. Place the skirt pattern pieces over the organdy so that the new, extended hemline is 4 inches above the lower edge of the organdy. Place the front and side front so that the cutting lines for the side front seams just meet.

Step 4. Trace the hemlines on the organdy. On the front, draw in the line for the side front seam (fig. 1).

Step 5. Center the side front motifs over the lines drawn for the side front seam lines, and trace all the lace placement lines on the organdy.

Step 6. Use the scalloped hem design to draw scallops all across the front and back organdy pieces. Shape lace insertion as indicated on all the lace placement lines (fig. 2).

Step 7. Zigzag in place along all headings except the outer most edges.

Step 8. Along the lower scalloped edge use an entredeux stitch to attach the lace to the organdy (fig. 3). Do not stitch the outer edges of the pineapples or the top of the slightly curved lace above the scallops to the organdy.

Step 9. Trim the organdy from behind the lace of these sections. It is not necessary to trim the organdy from behind all the insertions because of the sheerness of the organdy.

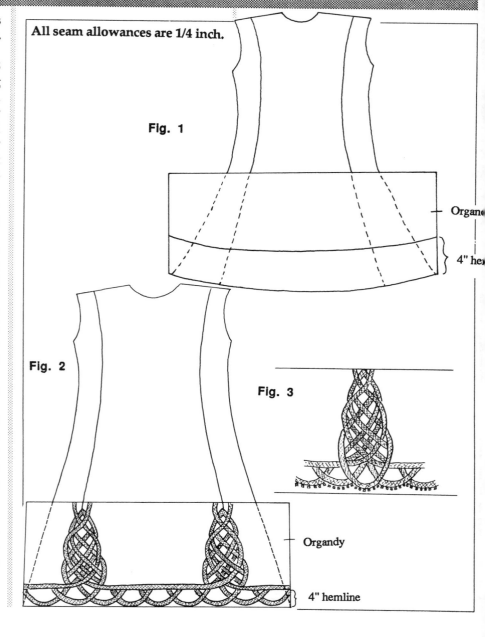

All seam allowances are 1/4 inch.

Fig. 1

Organdy

4" hemline

Fig. 2

Fig. 3

Organdy

4" hemline

PRINCESS SEAM GOWN WITH ORGANDY SCALLOPS AND INSERTS

AMERICAN - CIRCA 1992

Step 10. Rinse these lace-organdy pieces in water to remove all the marking lines. Press.

Step 11. Trim the organdy just below the entredeux stitching **(fig. 4)**.

Step 12. Cut out remaining pieces.

Step 13. Make a mark 10 inches from the bottom of each front and side front seam allowance.

Step 14. Stitch entredeux to both sides of side front seams with a 3/8 inch seam allowance **(fig. 5)**.

Step 15. Stitch insertion(#2) to the entredeux on both sides of the center front.

Step 16. Ease the lace on the curve at the waistline so it will lay flat.

Step 17. Stitch the entredeux on the side fronts to the insertion **(fig. 6)**.

Step 18. Shape insertion (#1) at the neckline (front and back) so that the inner edge of the insertion is along the cut neckline edge.

Step 19. Zigzag the lower edge of the insertion and trim fabric from behind, except at the back placket edges.

Step 20. Leave fabric behind the lace to support buttons and buttonholes **(fig. 7)**.

Step 21. Zigzag gathered 3/4-inch edging to the entredeux on both sides of the side front seams **(fig. 8)**.

Step 22. Place the lace-organdy hemline panels on the skirt so that the lower edge of the slightly curved insertion at the top of the scallops is even with the lower cut edge of the skirt.

Step 23. The pineapples on the front will be centered over the lower raw edge of the side front seams and should extend just past the bottom of the insertion-entredeux edging treatment on the side front seams **(fig. 9)**.

Step 24. Zigzag the lace-organdy section in place along all unstitched lace headings. The raw edges at the intersection of the pineapples and the side front seams will be covered by the organdy cutwork flower.

Step 25. Trim all fabric away from behind the lace-organdy sections **(fig. 10)**.

Step 26. Trace the organdy cutwork flower on a double layer of organdy (reverse the pattern for the right side front).

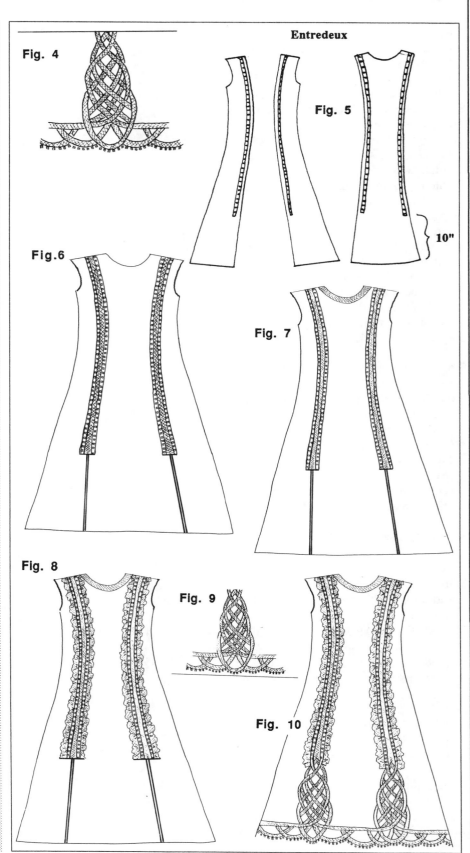

Entredeux

Fig. 4

Fig. 5

10"

Fig.6

Fig. 7

Fig. 8

Fig. 9

Fig. 10

Princess Seam Gown with Organdy Scallops and Inserts
American - circa 1992

Step 27. Place this double layer of organdy over the top of the pineapple so that the stem extends down into the pineapple and all raw fabric and lace edges are covered by the flower motif.

Step 28. Stitch the flower using the technique for organdy cutwork found in *Australian Windowpane Motif Christening Gown.* Use decorative machine stitching to add leaves and small satin stitch flowers as desired after cutwork is complete (**fig. 11**).

Step 29. Stitch shoulder seams, matching the insertions at the neckline, and catching the ends of the gathered edging in the seams.

Step 30. Attach entredeux to the insertion at the neck edge, and then stitch gathered 3/4-inch edging to the entredeux to finish the neckline (**fig. 12**).

Step 31. Make a 4-1/2-inch placket in the skirt center back.

Step 32. Gather the skirt back and stitch to the back yokes (**fig 13**).

Step 33. Cut two 14-inch lengths of 2-1/4-inch wide edging. Gather slightly to fit ungathered sleeve caps.

Step 34. Place edging on top of sleeve caps so that the heading of lace and raw edges at ends of lace will be caught in sleeve seam, and run gathering threads through both fabric and lace (**fig. 14**).

Step 35. Cut two 7-inch lengths of entredeux, gather lower edges of sleeves to fit entredeux, and stitch.

Step 36. Trim other side of entredeux, and attach gathered 3/4-inch edging (**fig. 15**).

Step 37. Gather sleeve caps and stitch sleeves to dress (**fig. 16**).

Step 38. Stitch one side seam, matching all seams and lace intersections (**fig. 17**).

Step 39. Attach slightly gathered 2-1/4-inch edging to the entredeux stitching.

Step 40. Stitch the remaining side seam (**fig. 18**).

Step 41. Fasten back opening with buttons and buttonholes or beauty pins.

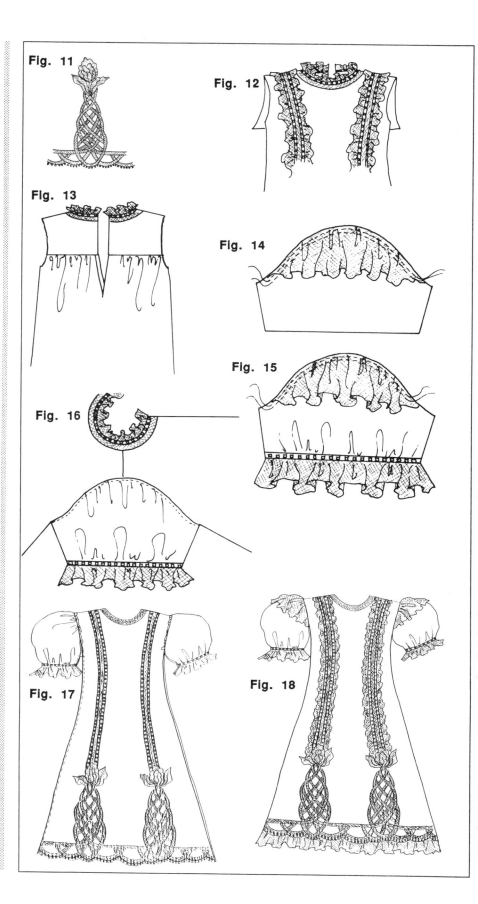

Fig. 11

Fig. 12

Fig. 13

Fig. 14

Fig. 15

Fig. 16

Fig. 17

Fig. 18

GODET CURVED PUFFING CHRISTENING DRESS
AMERICAN – CIRCA *1992*

Pattern Pieces Used: Curved Puffing Front Yoke, Curved Puffing Back Yoke, Armhole Template, Gore with Puffing and Lace Template, Short Puffed Sleeve, Godet with Lace Loop Template. Cutting guide also included in pattern envelope.

Step 1. Cut out pattern pieces as indicated on layout diagram as seen on Gore Pattern piece.

Godets

Step 2. Trace lace design on the eight godet pieces. Shape lace as indicated turning under the cut edges of the lace. Starch and press.

Step 3. Stitch with a narrow zigzag or a pin stitch and wing needle **(fig. 1)**.

Step 4. Shape a piece of lace along lower curved edge of godet, so that lower edge and cut edge of fabric are even.

Step 5. Stitch upper edge of lace to fabric with a zigzag or pin stitch. Trim all fabric from behind lace **(fig. 2)**.

Gores

Step 6. Trace gores on tissue paper.

Step 7. Cut 12 to 14 strips of fabric 1-3/4 inches wide and 45 inches long. Seam the short ends of four or five pieces together to make several long strips.

Step 8. Using quilting thread for gathering the puffing, create the curved puffing and place at the bottom of each tissue gore. NOTE: Use puffing portrait collar directions found in this book to create puffing.

Step 9. Cut the puffing and lace to extend slightly past the sides of the tissue pattern.

Step 10. Build and shape the skirt panels from the bottom up in this order: puffing, insertion, beading, insertion, puffing and insertion. Stitch together through the tissue creating a curved band. Remove from the tissue.

Step 11. Place curved band on gore fabric. Stitch in place along the top of the insertion piece.

Step 12. Trace the sides of the gore pattern on the curved band. Cut away fabric under the curved band but do not trim the excess laces from the sides yet **(fig. 3)**.

Step 13. Place lace insertion along the side of the gore so that the outer edge of the lace and cut edge of the fabric are even, down to the lower strip of puffing.

Step 14. Miter the corner, and shape the lace along the puffing strip, just as the previous strips of lace were attached to the curved puffing.

Step 15. Miter at the other corner, and continue up the other side.

Step 16. Stitch along inner edge of lace and trim fabric and excess puffing and lace, from behind the insertion **(fig. 4)**.

Supplies and Gown Description

- 4 yards white Nelona
- 36 yards 5/8-inch lace insertion
- 3-1/2 yards beading
- 2 yards 5/8-inch edging
- 10 yards 1-1/2-inch edging
- 1-1/2 yards entredeux
- 1 yard 1/4-inch satin ribbon
- white quilting thread & tissue paper

The curved puffing/lace insertion on the bodice is attached to a square bodice. In other words, the bodice is square; the skirt is just gathered to the bodice in both the front and the back. The skirt has eight gores and eight godets. The godets are inserted into the gores of the skirt about 10-1/2 inches from the bottom of the bodice yoke. The curved godets have an unusual loop design with curved ends inserted between the gores of the skirt. I call this type of lace shaping, free standing shapes. Curved lace makes scallops at the bottom of the godets and at the bottom of the dress panels. The curved puffing strips are sandwiched between rows of curved insertion and beading. Gathered lace edging zigzagged right to the curved lace finishes the bottom of the dress. The total back length of the dress is 36 inches; the circumference is 170 inches. I have to mention here that this skirt would be just as pretty in an older child's dress, an adult dress, a wedding dress, a debutante dress, or a mother of the bride dress. None of these heirloom ideas are limited to christening gowns.

Note: All seam allowances are 1/4 inch.

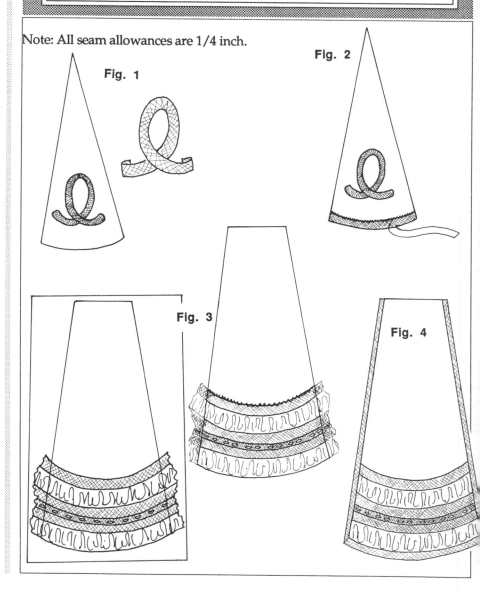

Fig. 1

Fig. 2

Fig. 3

Fig. 4

GODET CURVED PUFFING CHRISTENING DRESS

AMERICAN - CIRCA 1992

Assembling the skirt

Step 17. Join one skirt gore to one godet piece.

Step 18. Place the lace insertion running up the side of the gore over the side of the godet so that the lace overlaps the fabric about 1/2 inch and the laces at the lower curved edges meet.

Step 19. Stitch from bottom to about 1/2 inch from point of godet **(fig. 5)**.

Step 20. Trim fabric from behind lace. Similarly, place another gore on the other side of the godet and stitch in place, making the insertions meet at the point of the godet **(fig. 6)**.

Step 21. Zigzag the insertion on the sides of the gores together above the point of the godet **(fig. 7)**.

Step 22. Stitch another godet to the other side of the gore, and continue around skirt, alternating gores and godets, until all pieces are joined.

Step 23. Attach slightly gathered 1-1/2-inch edging to lower edge of skirt **(fig. 8)**.

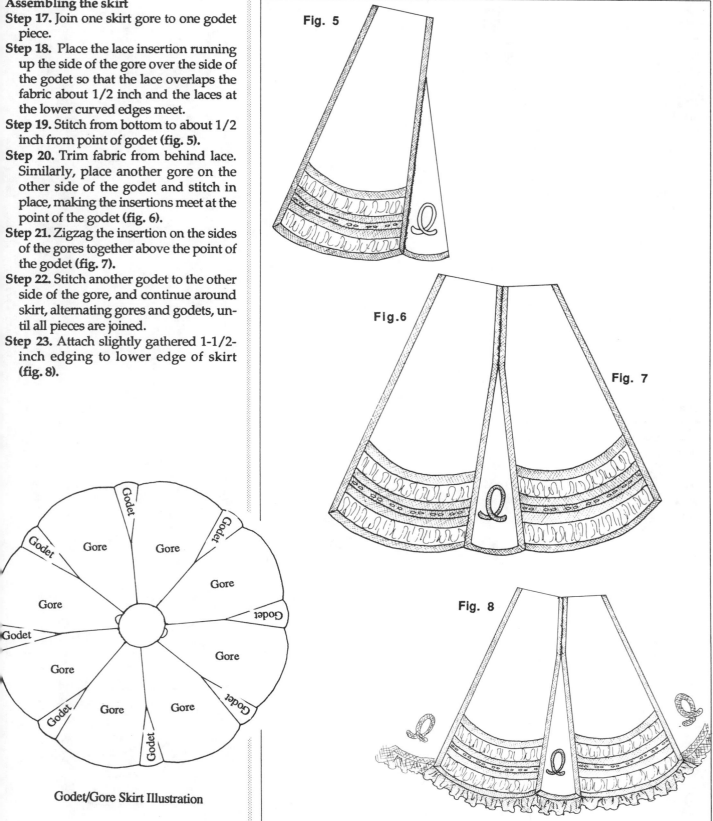

Godet/Gore Skirt Illustration

GODET CURVED PUFFING CHRISTENING DRESS
AMERICAN - CIRCA 1992

Step 24. Lay the skirt so that the upper edges are even and the sides are folded in the center of two gores.

Step 25. Cut armholes using the armhole template **(fig. 9)**.

Step 26. Mark center front and back.

Step 27. Fold at center front, matching armholes. Make a mark at the center front fold 1-1/4-inch below the raw edge, and draw a smooth, gradual curve from this point tapering to the upper raw edge of the skirt at the armhole **(fig. 10)**. Cut along this line.

Step 28. Make a 4-1/2-inch placket at the center back **(fig. 11)**.

Yoke

Step 29. Shape lace insertion along indicated line on front yoke.

Step 30. Stitch along upper edge of lace.

Step 31. Trim away fabric behind lace, and save this lower part of the yoke **(fig. 12)**.

Step 32. Cut a 45-inch strip of fabric 1 inch wide, and make puffing using quilting thread to pull up gathers as before.

Step 33. Shape and stitch to curved insertion, and stitch another piece of insertion below puffing **(fig. 13)**.

Step 34. Place this upper yoke over the reserved lower yoke that was trimmed away. Match the curved cut edges together, then pin the lower row of insertion to the lower yoke **(fig. 14)**.

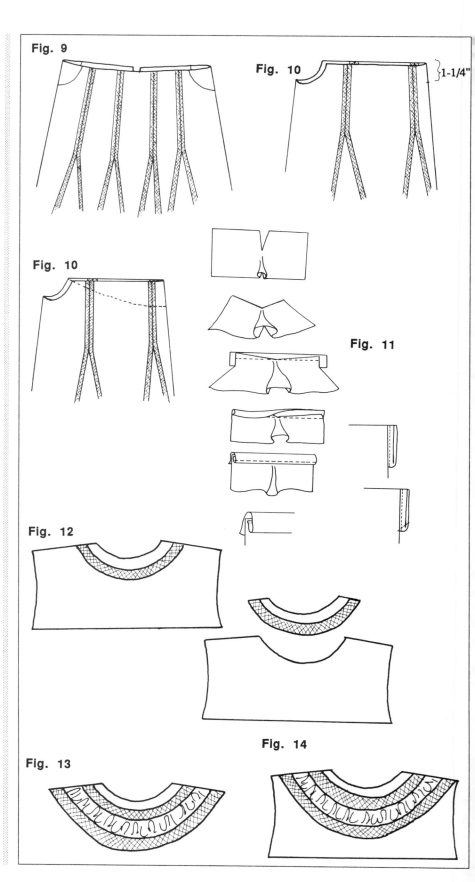

Fig. 9

Fig. 10

1-1/4"

Fig. 10

Fig. 11

Fig. 12

Fig. 13

Fig. 14

Step 35. Stitch, and trim away excess fabric behind the lace/puffing. Trim shoulders to fit pattern.

Step 36. Stitch shoulder seams (**fig. 15**).

Step 37. Attach entredeux to neck edge, then stitch gathered 5/8-inch edging to entredeux (**fig. 16**).

Step 38. Stitch gathered 1-1/2-inch lace along lower edge of curved insertion; folding the lace under and stitching a hem at both shoulder seams (**fig. 17**).

Step 39. Gather the front and back skirts and attach to front and back yokes, being careful not to catch gathered lace edging on front yoke in this stitching (**fig. 18**).

Sleeves

Step 40. Cut two 16-inch pieces of entredeux, and one 16-inch piece of beading.

Step 41. Zigzag a strip of entredeux on both sides of the beading.

Step 42. Stitch gathered 5/8-inch edging to the other side of the one of the strips of entredeux.

Step 43. Cut this 16-inch strip in half to make two armbands (**fig. 19**).

Step 44. Gather the sleeves to fit the armbands. Stitch (**fig. 20**).

Step 45. Run gathering threads in the sleeve caps and stitch the sleeve under-arm seams (**fig. 21**).

Setting in the sleeves

NOTE: These sleeves must be set in, they cannot be put in flat before the dress side seams are sewn, because there are no side seams!

Step 46. Turn the dress inside out, and the sleeves right side out.

Step 47. Pin the sleeve inside the armhole, matching the sleeve underarm seam with the center of the armhole cutout, and the top of the sleeve with the shoulder seam.

Step 47. Stitch this seam with the dress still inside out, stitching from the inside of the sleeve (**fig. 22**).

Step 48. Close the dress with buttons and buttonholes or beauty pins.

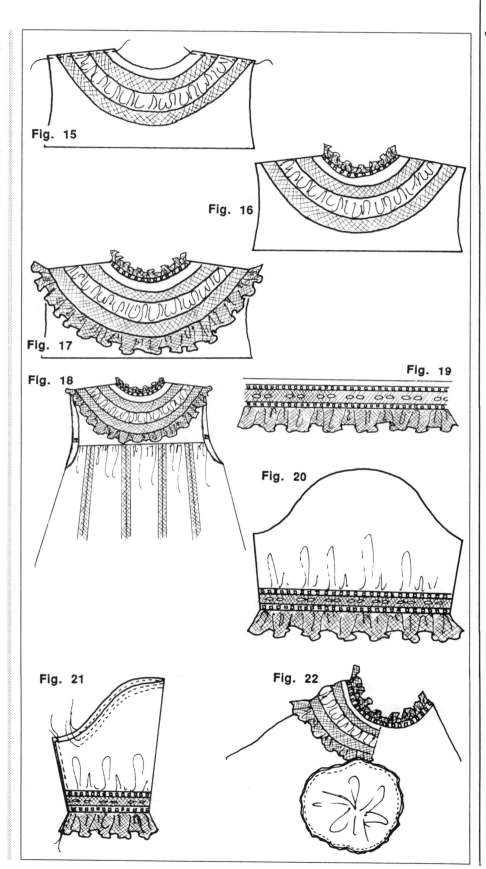

Fig. 15

Fig. 16

Fig. 17

Fig. 18

Fig. 19

Fig. 20

Fig. 21

Fig. 22

LILY OF THE VALLEY SWISS NETTING
PANEL CHRISTENING GOWN
AMERICAN – CIRCA 1992

Pattern Pieces Used: High Yoke Front and Back, Long Puffed Sleeve, Armhole Template.

Supplies and Gown Description

- 2-1/4 yards cotton netting
- 7-1/2 yards 6-inch wide lily of the valley netting edging
- 10 yards lily of the valley netting insertion
- 1/2 yard 1/8-inch elastic
- small remnant of cotton organdy

The body of this dress is made of polyester/cotton blend Swiss netting and the trims of 100 percent cotton Swiss trims embroidered on netting. The high yoke bodice has a double bodice; one of netting fabric and an over bodice of the netting 6-inch trim. The scallops of the trim are stitched down on the gathers of the skirt to give the appearance of having a scalloped bodice. The front panel measures 10-1/2 inches at the top and 19 inches at the bottom. The panel consists of netting, puffing, insertion, netting with gathered lace edging on top of the netting panel; this is repeated down the skirt. Swiss insertion is stitched down either side of this center panel. The fancy band on the bottom has insertion, puffing, and insertion. Gathered Swiss edging finishes the bottom of the skirt. Swiss insertion is stitched about midway on the netting sleeves. In actuality, the sleeve is a short sleeve with insertion stitched to it and then a piece of the 6-1/2 inch wide edging is stitched to that insertion. Elastic is then inserted at the bottom of the netting portion of the 6-1/2 inch wide Swiss edging. This is a really unusual way to make a long sleeve using wide Swiss embroidered trim. The dress is 38 inches long and 90 inches around.

Puffing

Step 1. Cut two pieces of lily of the valley insertion each 3-7/8 yards long.

Step 2. Trim the netting off the edges right along the sides of the straight, heavy embroidered cord on each side of the insertion (just like trimming the batiste from entredeux) **fig. 1**.

Step 3. Cut enough 2-3/4-inch strips of netting to equal 8 yards. This equals five strips of 60-inch wide netting.

Step 4. Seam these pieces together to form one long strip. To sew seams in netting, stitch with a narrow zigzag (W=1, L=1), to allow for the stretchiness of the netting - a straight stitch will break easily.

Step 5. Trim the seam allowance to 1/8 inch from the stitching **(fig. 2)**. The netting will not ravel, so no additional seam finish is necessary. The netting is so transparent that serging would be visible from the right side.

Step 6. Gather both long edges of this strip, allowing for a 1/2-inch seam. Arrange the gathers so the folds are perpendicular to the gathering threads **(fig. 3)**.

Step 7. Place the trimmed insertion right side up on top of the puffing so that the corded edge is on the 1/2-inch seam line.

Step 8. Use a narrow zigzag (W=1.5, L=1) to stitch right on top of the heavy embroidery **(fig. 4)**.

Step 9. Stitch insertion along both sides of the puffing **(fig. 5)**.

Step 10. On the wrong side, trim the seam allowance of the puffing to about 1/8-inch from the stitching line.

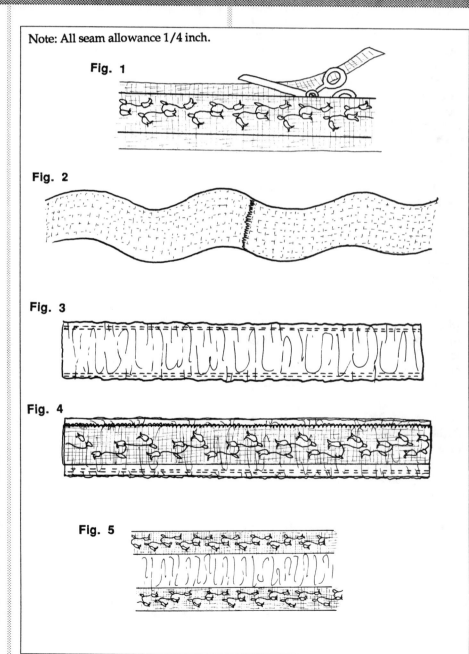

Note: All seam allowance 1/4 inch.

Fig. 1

Fig. 2

Fig. 3

Fig. 4

Fig. 5

LILY OF THE VALLEY SWISS NETTING PANEL CHRISTENING GOWN

AMERICAN - CIRCA 1992

Skirt

Step 11. Cut two skirt pieces 45 inches by 29 inches.

Step 12. At the top of the center back, make a 4-1/2-inch long continuous lap placket **(fig. 6).**

Step 13. Fold the skirt front in half and mark the center front at top and bottom. At the top edge, make a mark 3-1/2 inches on each side of center front.

Step 14. At the bottom, make a mark 10-1/2 inches on each side of the center front. Connect the marks with a straight line to make a wedge shape on the front of the skirt **(fig. 7).**

Step 15. Stitch skirt front to back halfway up one side seam. (This will allow you to stitch sleeves in using the flat method.) **Fig. 8.**

Step 16. Place a strip of insertion-puffing-insertion around the lower edge of the skirt so that the lower edge of the insertion is even with the lower raw edge of the skirt. Cut out arm opening using the armhole template.

Step 17. Zigzag, with narrow stitch, on top of the corded edges of the insertion on both sides of the puffing, and along the top edge of the upper row of insertion. This puffing strip will be stitched to the netting of the skirt in three places. Trim the netting of the skirt away below the lower row of insertion **(fig. 9).**

Step 18. Measure up 4-1/2 inches from the top of the upper row of insertion on the skirt and draw a line parallel to the insertion between the two marked "wedge" lines.

Step 19. Measure this line. Cut a piece of the puffing-insertion strip to this measurement plus 1/2 inch **(fig. 10).**

Step 20. Cut a piece of wide netting edging 3/4-yard long and trim the top unembroidered edge so that the width of the edging is 5 inches. Gather this edging to fit the puffing insertion strip you just cut.

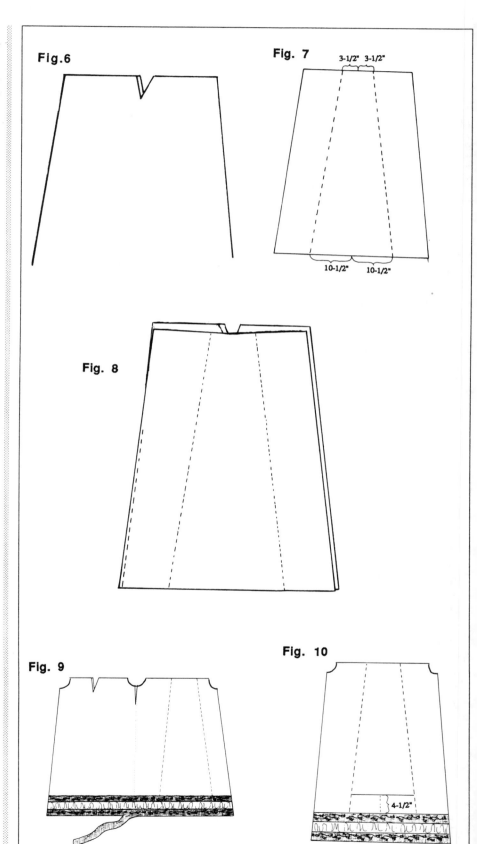

Step 21. Attach the edging to the bottom of the puffing-insertion strip in the same manner as the puffing was to the insertion. Trim the edging seam allowance to 1/8 inch **(fig. 11)**.

Step 22. Place this puffing insertion edging piece on the dress front, matching up the insertion edging seam line and horizontal line drawn on the dress front. Stitch with a narrow zigzag over both edges of both rows of insertion **(fig. 12)**.

Step 23. Measure up 3-1/2 inches from the top of the upper row of insertion and draw a line as before. Measure this line and cut a piece of the puffing--insertion strip to this measurement plus 1/2 inch.

Step 24. Cut a piece of wide netting edging 22 inches long and trim the top edge so that the width of the edging is 4 inches. Gather, stitch to the puffing-insertion strip, and trim as before. Place on the dress so that the insertion edging seam line is right on top of the marked line. Stitch over both edges of both rows of insertion **(fig. 13)**.

Step 25. Measure up 2-1/2 inches from the top of the upper row of insertion and draw a line. Cut a piece of the puffing insertion strip to this measurement plus 1/2 inch.

Step 26. Cut a piece of edging 18 inches long, and trim to a width of 3 inches.

Step 27. Attach the edging to the insertion, and attach the puffing insertion edging to the dress in the same manner as the two previous sections **(fig. 14)**.

Step 28. Place a strip of insertion on top of the dress front so that the inner border of the insertion is along the marked "wedge" line. Zigzag over the inner border only of the insertion.

Step 29. Lift the insertion up and trim away any excess insertion, puffing, and edging from behind the insertion.

Step 30. Now lay the "wedge" insertion flat, and zigzag over the outer border.

Step 31. Fold the ends under diagonally at the lower edge to look as if the insertion has been mitered. **(fig. 15)**.

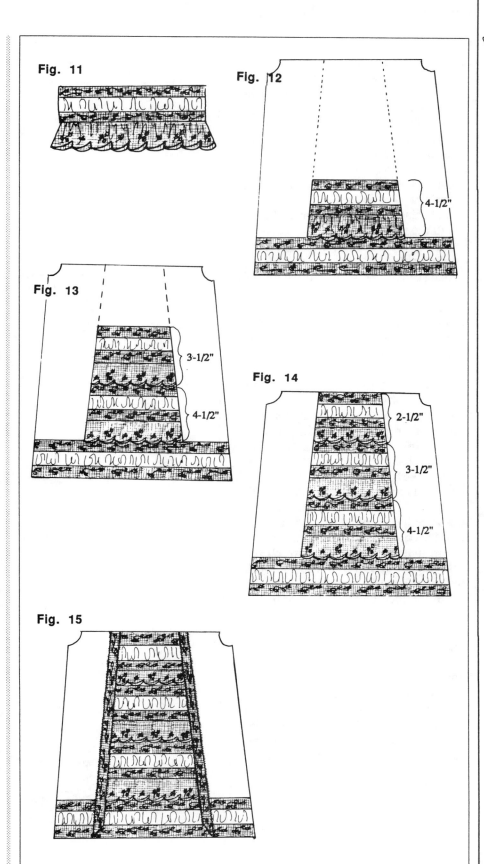

Fig. 11

Fig. 12

Fig. 13

Fig. 14

Fig. 15

LILY OF THE VALLEY SWISS NETTING PANEL CHRISTENING GOWN
AMERICAN - CIRCA 1992

Yoke

Step 32. Cut one yoke front and two yoke backs from the netting for the yoke lining. Cut one front and two backs from netting edging (**fig. 16**).

Step 33. Place the scalloped edge of the edging just slightly below the seam line on the pattern.

Step 34. Cut a bias strip of netting 1-1/4 inches wide and 13 inches long for the neck binding.

Step 35. Gather the skirt front and back to fit the yokes.

Step 36. Place the netting yokes on the wrong side of the skirt, and stitch the yoke seams. The seam will be on the right side of the dress. Stitch this seam again very close to the first stitching.

Step 37. Trim seam to 1/8 inch (**fig. 17**).

Step 38. Lay the edging yokes right side up on top of the netting yokes so that the cut edges are even and scalloped edge just covers the stitching line. The raw seam will be hidden.

Step 39. Stitch with a tiny zigzag through all layers, right on top of the previous seam line. Or, stitch over the scalloped edge of the border. Now, treat both yoke layers as one.

Step 40. Interface the back facings with a double layer of cotton organdy.

Step 41. Stitch shoulder seams (**fig. 18**).

Step 42. Fold the bias binding in half lengthwise. Press. Don't stretch the binding. (**fig. 19**). Stitch to the neck edge with a 1/4 inch seam, with the facings folded under at the fold line.

Step 43. Let the binding extend 1/4 inch past each end. Trim excess (**fig. 20**).

Step 44. Stitch again close to the first stitching, and trim seam to 1/8 inch.

Step 45. Fold under the 1/4 inch extensions of the binding at the center back. Wrap the binding around the seam allowance. From the right side, stitch in the ditch of the binding, catching the folded under edge on the wrong side (**fig. 21**).

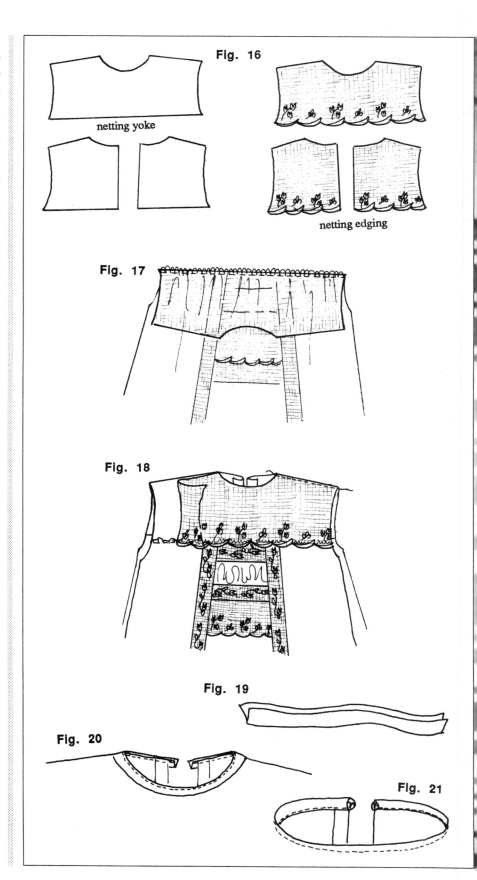

Fig. 16

netting yoke

netting edging

Fig. 17

Fig. 18

Fig. 19

Fig. 20

Fig. 21

Sleeves

Step 46. Cut two pieces of edging and two pieces of insertion each 12 inches long. Trim the netting borders from the insertion.

Step 47. Place the insertion on top of the upper edge of the edging, overlapping about 1/2 inch. Zigzag the lower edge of the insertion to the edging, and trim the excess netting on the back side to about 1/8 inch (**fig. 22**).

Step 48. Cut two pieces of netting 12 inches wide and 6 inches long.

Step 49. Place the upper edge of the insertion about 1/2 inch over the 12 inch edge of the netting. Zigzag in place and trim (**fig. 23**).

Step 50. Use these blocks of fabric to cut the sleeves (**fig. 24**).

Step 51. Mark a long piece of 1/8-inch elastic the wrist measurement plus 1 inch. Do not cut!

Step 52. Place the end of the elastic on the wrong side of the sleeve, just above the embroidered portion of the edging. Anchor in place with a few straight stitches.

Step 53. Change to a wide zigzag (W=5, L=2) and zigzag over the elastic, being careful not to catch the elastic in the stitching. Stitch to within 1/2 inch from the end of the sleeve.

Step 54. With the needle in the fabric, lift the presser foot, and gently pull the elastic until the mark on the elastic is at the seam line.

Step 55. Lower the presser foot, switch back to a straight stitch, and anchor this end of the elastic.

Step 56. Cut the elastic (**fig. 25**). Repeat for the other sleeve.

Step 57. Gather the sleeve cap and stitch the sleeve to the dress (**fig. 26**).

Step 58. Trim the seam allowance to 1/8 inch.

Step 59. Stitch the side seams (**fig. 27**).

Step 60. Gather remaining edging and stitch to insertion at lower edge of skirt (**fig. 27**).

Step 61. Close the back yoke with buttons and buttonholes, or use beauty pins.

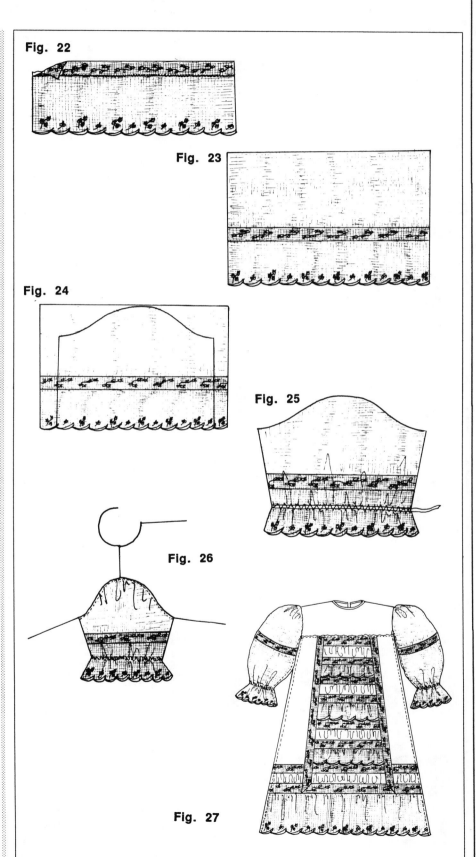

Fig. 22

Fig. 23

Fig. 24

Fig. 25

Fig. 26

Fig. 27

Wool Challis Christening Coat

American - circa 1992

Supplies
• 2 yards 60-inch wide wool challis
• 2-1/2 yards 45-inch wide lining fabric

Pattern Pieces Used: Coatdress Front Yoke, Coatdress Back Yoke, Armhole Template, Long Puffed Sleeve. Directions for altering yoke pattern pieces for coat collar given on page 104.

Note: All seam allowances 1/4 inch.

Skirt

Step 1. Tear a strip of wool challis several inches longer than desired coat skirt length. Finished coat length should be about 1 inch longer than gown.

Step 2. Using a 3.0/90 double needle and starting 1 inch above the lower edge, stitch rows of tucks the width of the fabric until the tucked section measures about 5 inches wide.

Step 3. Press down and steam well.

Step 4. Allow for 1/2-inch seams at yoke and hem. Cut off top of skirt to measure 1 inch shorter than the desired length **(fig. 1)**.

Step 5. Fold fabric in half, matching selvages, then in half again. Mark quarter points.

Step 6. At the top edge, at these 1/4 and 3/4 folds, cut armholes using the armhole template.

Step 7. At the center front lower edge, cut off the corners at a 45 degree angle across the tucked section **(fig. 2)**.

Step 8. Using the skirt as a pattern, cut a facing for the front and lower edges.

Step 9. This facing should be 3-1/4 inches wide down the fronts and 4-3/4 inches deep at the hem **(fig. 3)**.

Step 10. Cut the lining 2-1/4 inches shorter than the skirt and 5-1/2 inches narrower **(fig. 3)**. Seam the lining together as required to get the necessary width.

Step 11. Using the skirt as a pattern, cut the armholes in the lining.

Step 12. Fold the skirt fronts into thirds and the back into sixths. Stitch released tucks as directed in *Tucked Christening Gown with Swiss Handloom* **(fig. 4)**.

Step 13. Right sides together, stitch lower edge of the lining to upper edge of the facing with 1/2-inch seam.

Step 14. Right sides together, stitch the lining to the facing, down the center fronts to several inches from the lower edge. There will be a bulge of extra lining fabric at this lower edge **(fig. 5)**.

Step 15. Turn lining and facing right sides out. Press the center front seam allowances toward the lining. Press the extra lining fabric into a pleat at the lower edge.

Step 16. By hand, slip stitch the remainder of the center front lining seam in place **(fig. 6)**.

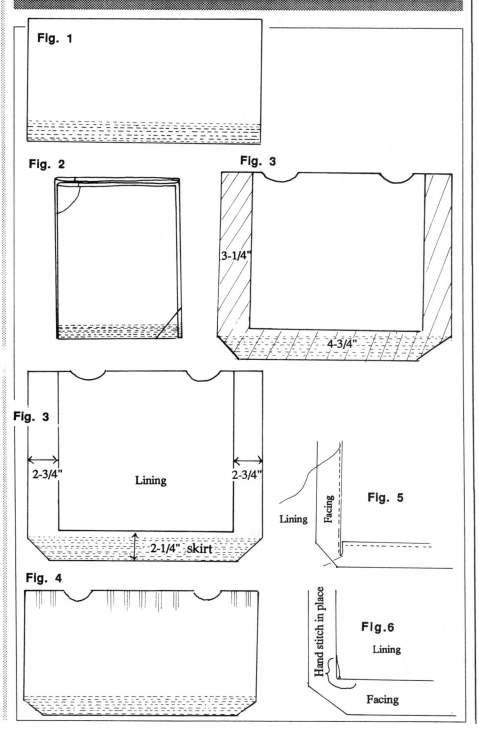

Coat Description

This christening coat made of off-white wool challis would be the perfect choice to complement a gown in cooler weather. There are two sets of triple pintucks on either side of the coat; five more sets are spaced across the back. The coat is fully lined and the sleeves are finished with a bias binding and a double challis ruffle below the binding. The sailor collar has 13 double needle tucks on the front and back collars; it also is finished with a double challis ruffle. This same double challis ruffle travels down the front and across the bottom of the coat. Twenty five double needle pintucks are found at the bottom of this coat. It is fully lined with silk. The total back length of the coat is 36 inches. The circumference is 53 inches.

Fig. 1

Fig. 2

Fig. 3

3-1/4"

4-3/4"

Fig. 3

2-3/4"   Lining   2-3/4"

2-1/4" skirt

Fig. 4

Lining   Facing

Lining

Fig. 5

Hand stitch in place

Fig. 6

Lining

Facing

WOOL CHALLIS CHRISTENING COAT

AMERICAN - CIRCA 1992

Step 17. Cut eight yards of 3-inch-wide ruffle strips for skirt, collar, and cuffs. Seam short ends together and press in half lengthwise, right sides together.

Step 18. Stitch two rows of gathering threads along raw edges, allowing for a 1/2-inch seam (**fig. 7**).

Step 19. Place facing and skirt right sides together with gathered ruffle sandwiched in between and all row edges even. Gather extra fullness in the ruffle at the corners to prevent cupping.

Step 20. Stitch through all layers in a 1/2-inch seam. Trim seam allowance and turn right sides out. Understitch facing. Press well.

Step 21. Lay the skirt and skirt lining on a flat surface and trim upper edges. Run gathering threads through both layers at top of skirt (**fig. 8**).

Yokes

Step 22. Cut one yoke back and two fronts from challis and from lining.

Step 23. Mark center fronts and fold lines.

Step 24. Stitch shoulder seams in wool yokes and in lining yokes.

Step 25. Place wool back yoke (right side up) with gathered skirt back (right side down) on top of yoke.

Step 26. Place lining back yoke (right side up) over wrong side of skirt, with all raw edges even.

Step 27. Stitch, trim, and press seam (**fig. 9**). Do the same for the skirt fronts and front yokes, with the edge of the ruffle extending just to the center front marks.

Step 28. Turn right sides out. Press, and finish yoke and lining facing edges.

Step 29. Press under both layers of facing at fold line. Baste yoke and facing together at neckline close to raw edges (**fig. 10**).

Collar

Step 30. Cut fabric 6 inches long and 20 inches wide.

Step 31. Beginning 1 inch from one long edge, stitch tucks the same as on skirt until tucked section is 2-1/4 inches wide (**fig. 11**).

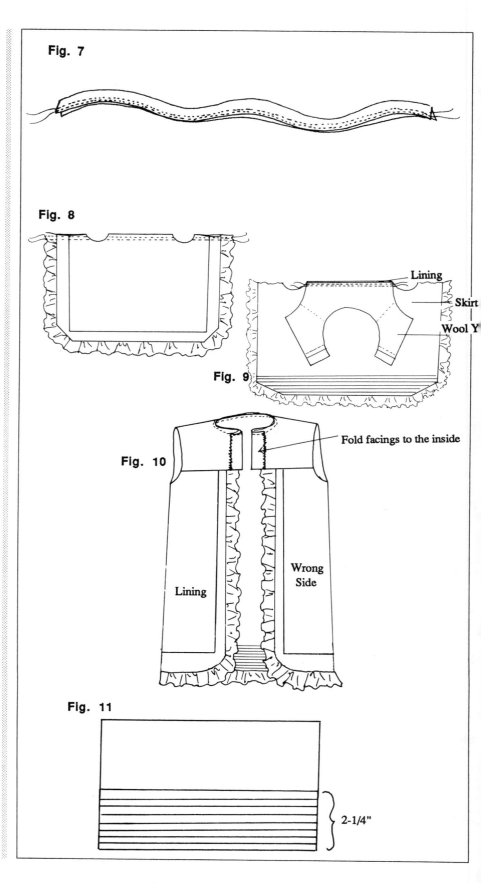

Fig. 7

Fig. 8

Fig. 9

Lining

Skirt

Wool Y

Fig. 10

Fold facings to the inside

Lining

Wrong Side

Fig. 11

2-1/4"

Step 32. Press tucks down and steam.

Step 33. Use yoke pattern to cut collar pieces from tucked fabric and lining.

Step 34. Cut off 1-1/2 inches from center fronts of collar and lining **(fig. 12).**

Step 35. Stitch shoulder seams. Stitch together collar and lining, right sides together with ruffle sandwiched in between and with all raw edges even.

Step 36. Trim seam allowance, turn right sides out, and press well **(fig. 13).**

Step 37. Baste collar to neck edge.

Step 38. Cut a bias strip of lining fabric 1-1/4-inches wide and 14 inches long.

Step 39. Press in half lengthwise.

Step 40. Use bias strip as a facing and stitch neckline seam with a 1/4-inch seam allowance, with front facings folded to wrong side.

Step 41. Stitch again close to first stitching. Trim seam allowance, clip curves, and understitch bias strip.

Step 42. Fold bias strip down and stitch to yoke by hand or machine **(fig. 14).**

Sleeves

Step 43. Cut sleeve linings as on pattern, and cut sleeves 1/2 inch shorter than pattern.

Step 44. Cut sleeve cuffs 1-1/2 inches wide and 7 inches long **(fig. 15).**

Step 45. Gather sleeves to fit cuffs and stitch with 1/2- inch seam. Trim seam and press toward cuff.

Step 46. Gather ruffle and lower edge of lining to fit cuff. Sandwich ruffle between cuff and lining, right sides together. Stitch with 1/2-inch seam.

Step 47. Trim seam, press toward lining. Understitch. Press lining up **(fig. 16).**

Step 48. Run gathering threads through both layers - wool and lining - of sleeve cap.

Step 49. Stitch sleeve seam, matching cuff seams and edge of ruffle. Press.

Step 50. Gather sleeve cap, and set sleeve into coat. Stitch armscye seam **(fig. 17).**

Step 51. Make two buttonholes in right front yoke. Sew buttons to corresponding positions on left yoke.

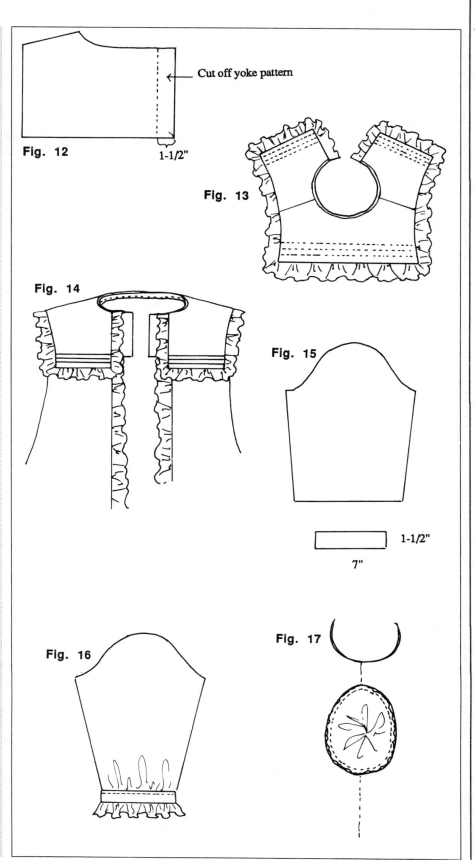

Cut off yoke pattern

Fig. 12

1-1/2"

Fig. 13

Fig. 14

Fig. 15

1-1/2"

7"

Fig. 16

Fig. 17

SCALLOPED COLLAR NETTING DRESS AND BONNET
AMERICAN - CIRCA 1992

Pattern Pieces Used: Mid Yoke Front, Mid Yoke Back, Short Puffed Sleeve, Scalloped Collar Front, Scalloped Collar.

Supplies and Gown Description

- 2-1/4 yards cotton netting
- 2-1/4 yards Nelona or other batiste for underlining
- 11 yards 1-inch wide lace edging
- 2-1/4 yards 5/8-inch wide lace edging

- 2 yards 2-1/4-inch wide lace pointed edging
- 8 yards 3/4-inch wide lace edging
- 1 yard 3/8-inch wide lace edging
- 1/2 yards lace beading

- 5 yards 1-inch wide lace insertion
- 3-1/2 yards 5/8-inch wide lace insertion
- 2 yards 3/8-inch wide insertion
- 1-1/2 yards entredeux

This idea came from a European magazine. The laces are stitched down to the netting dress, which is a polyester/cotton blend netting from Switzerland. Lace puffing rosettes embellish both the points of lace on the skirt and the center points of the sleeves. The low waisted pattern in this book was used. The bodice extends 1 inch below the sleeve edge under the arm. The scalloped collar has insertion plus gathered edging on the edge. The collar has edging stitched flat into a V shape plus another row of insertion echoing that shape. Below the insertion V is gathered edging. One of the wonderful things about this dress is the use of seven different patterns of lace. The sleeves have entredeux plus beading with gathered lace at the bottom of the beading. Two rows of gathered lace edging finish the entredeux finished neckline. One row of neckline edging is on the top of the entredeux; one row is gathered on the bottom. The skirt has one row of edging, three rows of insertion and a wide row of edging all shaped into a V. The bottom of the skirt is one row of flat insertion finished with gathered lace edging butted to it and zigzagged together. There is no entredeux at the bottom of the dress. The total dress length is 37 inches; the circumference of the skirt is 90 inches. Choose heavily textured laces. Delicate and airy laces will get lost in the netting.

All seam allowances are 1/4 inch.
Skirt

Step 1. Cut two pieces of netting 45 inches wide and 31 inches long for the skirt front and back.

Step 2. Make a 4-1/2-inch continuous lap placket in the center of one piece for the back opening **(fig. 1)**. On the other piece make a mark in the center, 6 inches from the lower edge.

Step 3. Make two marks at the top edge, 6 inches from each side edge. Connect marks to make a large "V" **(fig. 2)**.

Step 4. Place 1-inch wide lace insertion so that the outer edge of the insertion is along the line, mitering the insertion at the point of the "V". Zigzag in place (W=1.5, L=1) **fig. 3**. There is no need to trim the netting from behind the lace.

Step 5. Place the 2-1/4-inch wide pointed lace so that heading is along the drawn line, right next to the 1-inch insertion. Miter neatly at the point of the "V".

Step 6. Zigzag along heading and along the pointed edge of the lace **(fig. 4)**.

Step 7. Draw lines inside the "V" 1-1/4 inches, 2-1/4 inches and 3-3/4 inches from the inner edge of the 1-inch insertion **(fig. 5)**.

Step 8. Place the inner heading of the 3/8-inch insertion along the 1-1/4-inch lines and stitch.

Step 9. Place the inner heading of the 5/8-inch insertion along the 2-1/4-inch lines and stitch.

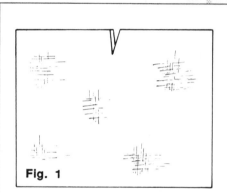

Fig. 1

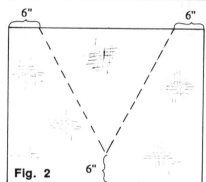

6"   6"

6"

Fig. 2

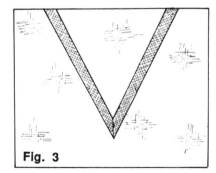

Fig. 3

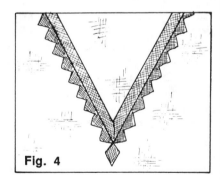

Fig. 4

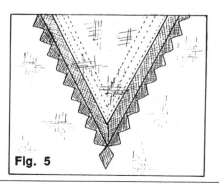

Fig. 5

SCALLOPED COLLAR NETTING DRESS

AMERICAN - CIRCA 1992

Step 10. Place the inner edge of the 5/8 inch edging along the 3-3/4-inch lines and stitch along both the heading and the scalloped edge (**fig. 6**).

Step 11. To stitch seams in netting, simply stitch along the seam line with a tiny zigzag and trim 1/8-inch from the stitching.

Step 12. Stitch the skirt front to the back at one side seam, right sides together (**fig. 7**).

Step 13. Place 1-inch insertion along the lower edge and stitch the upper heading of the insertion to the netting.

Step 14. Trim the netting away from behind this insertion close to stitching.

Step 15. Gather 1-inch edging and zigzag to the lower edge of the insertion (**fig. 8**). Stitch the remaining side seam.

Step 16. Measure the length of the netting skirt and cut two 15-inch lengths of Nelona 1-1/2 inches less than this measurement.

Step 17. Make a placket in the center back as in the netting. Stitch one side seam (**fig. 9**).

Step 18. Zigzag flat 1-inch edging to the bottom of the Nelona underlining. Stitch the remaining side seam (**fig. 10**).

Step 19. Place the underlining, right side out, inside the netting skirt, also right side out. Align the top raw edges. Match the plackets, side seams, and center fronts.

Step 20. Run gathering threads through both layers (the netting skirt and underlining) and treat as one from here on in the construction (**fig. 11**).

Collar

Step 21. Cut one netting collar from scalloped collar pattern, and mark lace placement lines.

Step 22. Stitch insertions and flat edgings as indicated (**fig. 12**).

Step 23. Stitch gathered 3/4-inch edging along the outer edge of the 3/8-inch insertion (**fig. 13**).

Step 24. Shape 5/8-inch insertion along the scalloped edge of the collar so that the outer edge of the insertion is even with the cut edge of the collar. Do not turn insertion up the center back of the collar. Edges remain raw for now.

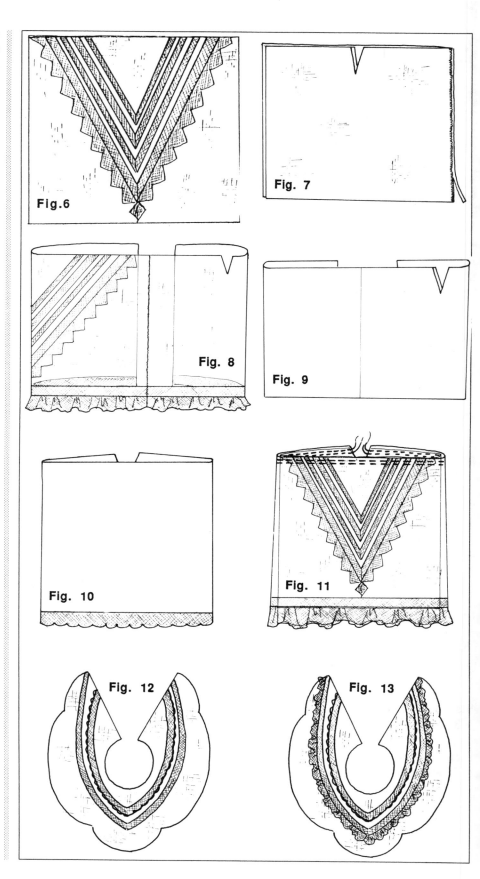

Fig.6

Fig. 7

Fig. 8

Fig. 9

Fig. 10

Fig. 11

Fig. 12

Fig. 13

Step 25. Trim netting from behind the 5/8-inch insertion **(fig. 14)**.

Step 26. Attach gathered 1-inch edging to the outer edge of the 5/8-inch insertion. The center back edges should be left flat, not gathered, and the scalloped edge of the insertion even with the cut edge of the netting. Gather extra fullness into the back corners **(fig. 15)**.

Bodice

Step 27. Use the mid yoke front and back patterns to cut bodices out of netting and Nelona.

Step 28. Stitch the shoulder seams in the netting and in the Nelona bodices.

Step 29. Place the netting bodice over the underlining bodice, wrong sides together. Pin or baste all edges together. Treat the two layers as one **(fig. 16)**.

Step 30. Fold back and press the back facings.

Step 31. Place the collar, right side up, over the bodice, matching center fronts and backs. Baste or pin collar in place.

Step 32. Attach entredeux to neck edge (to all three layers - collar, netting bodice, and Nelona underlining) **fig. 17**.

Step 33. Trim the remaining entredeux edge. Attach gathered 3/8-inch edging to the trimmed entredeux edge **(fig. 18)**.

Step 34. Now attach gathered 3/4-inch edging just below the entredeux. The heading of the gathered lace will be right along the entredeux - fabric seam line, and the zigzag will go into the ditch of the entredeux and through the edging into collar and bodice **(fig. 19)**.

Step 35. Fold under the raw ends of this edging so the folds are even with the 1-inch edging up the center back **(fig. 20)**.

Sleeves

Step 36. Cut two short puffed sleeves from netting **(fig. 21)**.

Step 37. Cut a piece of entredeux 16 inches long, trim one side, and zigzag to lace beading.

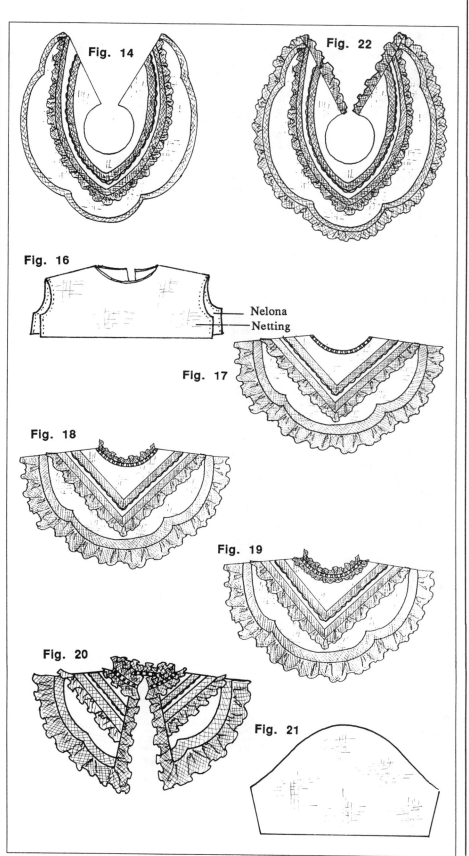

Fig. 14

Fig. 22

Fig. 16
— Nelona
— Netting

Fig. 17

Fig. 18

Fig. 19

Fig. 20

Fig. 21

SCALLOPED COLLAR NETTING DRESS

AMERICAN - CIRCA 1992

Step 38. Stitch gathered 1-inch edging to the other edge of the beading. Cut this strip in half to form two sleeve bands **(fig. 22).**

Step 39. Gather the sleeves to fit the bands and stitch to the entredeux **(fig. 23).**

Step 40. Gather the sleeve caps. Stitch the sleeves to the bodice **(fig. 24).**

Step 41. Stitch the side seams. Match the sleeve bands, underarm seams, and lower edges of the bodice **(fig. 25).**

Step 42. Gather the skirt to fit the bodice and stitch. Finish the seam and press toward the bodice **(fig. 26).**

Lace Rosettes

Step 43. Cut six lengths of 3/4-inch edging each 13 inches long.

Step 44. Stitch the cut ends together in a tiny seam. Pull the heavy gathering threads from both cut ends at once, gathering the lace as tightly as possible. Be careful not to gather the edging **(fig. 27).**

Step 45. By hand, with a needle and double thread, stitch together the base of the rosette **(fig. 28).**

Step 46. Stitch one rosette to the entredeux at the center of each sleeve band. Stitch four rosettes at the point of the lace "V" on the skirt as shown on the dress **(fig. 29).**

Step 47. Run ribbon through the beading on the sleeves.

Step 48. Close the back with buttons and buttonholes or beauty pins.

Bonnet

Step 49. Cut a rectangle of netting 13 inches wide and 14 inches long.

Step 50. Fold in half lengthwise and stitch the short raw edges with a 1/2-inch seam **(fig. 30)**

Step 51. Trim seams and turn right side out and press.

Step 52. Turn the folded long edge under 1/4-inch and press.

Step 53. Stitch very close to the folded under edge to form a casing **(fig. 31).**

Step 54. On the right side, stitch flat 3/4-inch edging so that the heading of the lace is just along the stitching line **(fig. 32).**

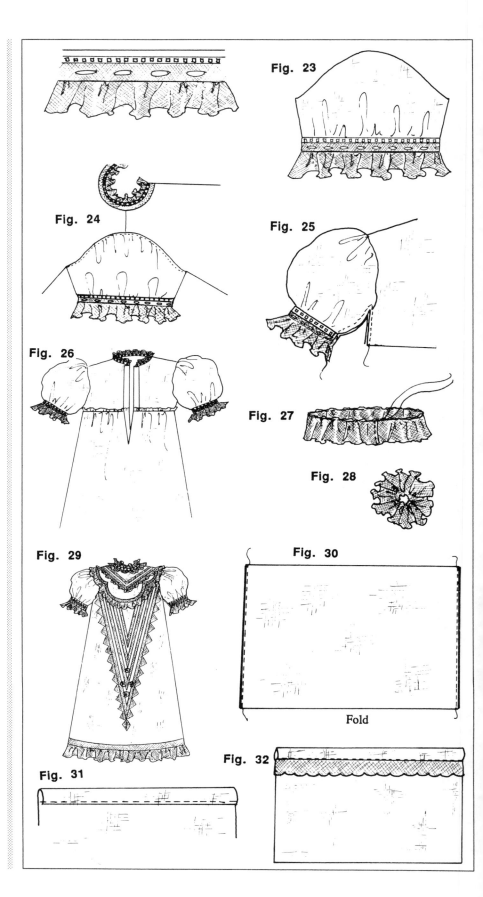

Fig. 23

Fig. 24

Fig. 25

Fig. 26

Fig. 27

Fig. 28

Fig. 29

Fig. 30

Fold

Fig. 31

Fig. 32

Step 55. On the long raw edge, make two marks 2-1/2inches from the short ends.

Step 56. Make another mark in the center 1-1/2 inches from the folded edge of the casing.

Step 57. Connect the marks to form a "v".

Step 58. Draw another "V" 7/8 inch inside the first one. (**fig. 33**).

Step 59. Stitch 5/8-inch insertion along the outer "V" so that the outer edge of the insertion is along the marked line.

Step 60. Similarly stitch 3/8-inch insertion along the inner "V".

Step 61. Stitch gathered 3/4-inch edging to the outer edge of the 5/8-inch insertion (**fig. 34**).

Step 62. Place 1-inch insertion along the long raw edge, folding under 1/2 inch on each end even with the netting, and stitch along the inner heading.

Step 63. Trim netting from behind the insertion. Attach entredeux to insertion (**fig. 35**).

Step 64. Cut a piece of netting 23 inches wide and 2-1/2 inches long. Fold in half lengthwise.

Step 65. Place slightly gathered 1-inch edging 3/8-inch over the long raw edge and zigzag in place.

Step 66. Trim netting from behind lace.

Step 67. Run gathering threads very close to the long folded edge and gather to fit entredeux (**fig. 36**).

Step 68. Right sides up, butt the gathered, folded edge up to the entredeux and zigzag in place.

Step 69. Fold under small hems on each end (**fig. 37**).

Step 70. On the underside of the ruffle, zigzag gathered 1-inch insertion right along the seam line of the ruffle and entredeux (**fig. 38**).

Step 71. Cut two streamers of 1-inch ribbon 18 inches long and stitch to bonnet at ends of entredeux.

Step 72. Make two lace rosettes as for gown and stitch over ends of ribbon.

Step 73. Cut a 20-inch length of 1/8-inch ribbon and run it through the casing.

Step 74. Pull the ribbon up and tie in a bow (**fig. 39**).

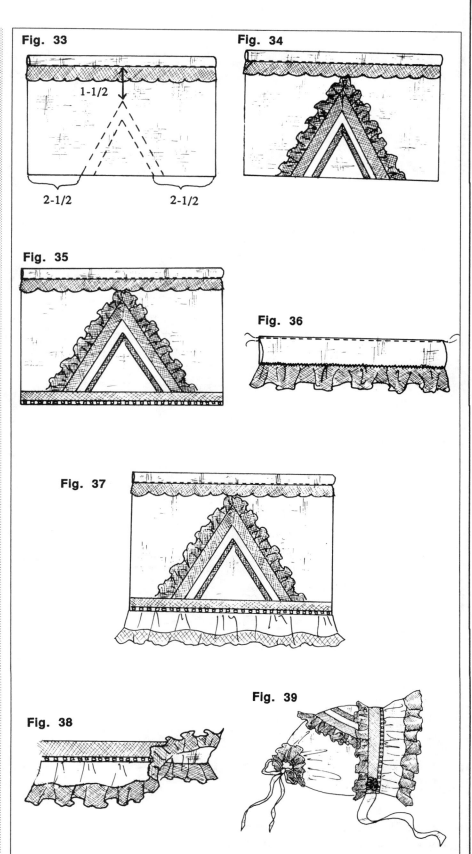

Fig. 33

Fig. 34

Fig. 35

Fig. 36

Fig. 37

Fig. 38

Fig. 39

1-1/2

2-1/2   2-1/2

PRINCESS SEAM GOWN WITH SHARK'S TEETH AND SLIP
AMERICAN - CIRCA 1992

Pattern Pieces Used: Antique Curved Panel Front, Side, Back Yoke, Back Skirt, Short Puffed Sleeve. Shark's Teeth Template is also included in the pattern envelope.

Supplies and Gown Description

- 4 yards Nelona, other batiste or silk
- 5 yards 5/8-inch lace insertion
- 16 yards entredeux
- 16 yards 2-1/4-inch wide lace edging
- 1 yard 1-1/2-inch wide lace edging
- 1 yard 3/8-inch wide lace edging
- 1/2 yard beading

This curved panel has rows of shark's teeth, finished on either side with entredeux and lace insertion. It is made of Swiss batiste called Nelona. Entredeux, insertion, and entredeux travel vertically along the center panel. Wide lace edging of 2-1/2 inches is gathered to go along the center panels. The bottom of the dress has entredeux and a wide batiste ruffle with the wide edging stitched straight along the bottom of the batiste ruffle. Straight edging is stitched on the ruffle at the top. When the ruffle is gathered, it appears to have gathered lace edging at the top. The sleeves are short, puffed ones with entredeux, beading, entredeux and gathered lace on the edge. Entredeux and gathered lace finish the neckline of the dress. The length of the dress is 33 inches.

All seam allowances are 1/4 inch.

Step 1. Tear two strips of fabric 6 inches wide by 45 inches long.

Step 2. Press, starch, and stitch three rows of shark's teeth using directions found on page 192 Shark's Teeth techniques. **Note:** When stitching the zigzag that holds the folded-under corners in place, use a zigzag stitch width of 1.5 instead of 1.0 (**fig. 1**).

Step 3. Stitch entredeux to both sides of shark's teeth strips. Leave about 1/4-inch fabric between entredeux and shark's teeth (**fig. 2**).

Step 4. Cut a piece of the shark's teeth strip 5 inches long. Center one of the triangle motifs.

Step 5. Zigzag a piece of insertion to the entredeux on the upper edge of the strip. Stitch the entredeux to the upper edge of the insertion.

Step 6. Cut a piece of plain fabric 8-inches wide and 4 inches long. Center the 8-inch width above the insertion-shark's teeth strip and stitch the fabric to the strip. This is the top part of the princess seam panel (**fig. 3**).

Step 7. Build the panel, alternating the shark's teeth-entredeux strip with insertion. Use the pattern piece to determine the length to cut the strips. Be sure to center the triangular motifs of the shark's teeth strips. Continue in this manner until there are nine shark's teeth strips alternating with ten strips of insertion (**fig. 4**).

Step 8. Stitch entredeux to the bottom of the lower strip of insertion.

Step 9. Stitch a strip of plain fabric 2-1/2 inches wide to the entredeux with a 1/4-inch seam. Stitch entredeux to the bottom of the fabric. Stitch another 2-1/2-inch wide strip of fabric to the bottom of this entredeux (**fig. 5**).

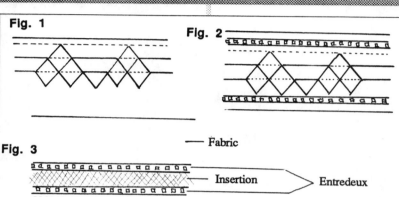

Fig. 1

Fig. 2

Fig. 3

— Fabric

— Insertion

> Entredeux

— Shark's Tooth Insert

— Entredeux

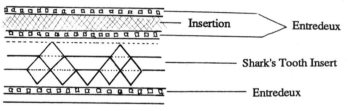

Fig. 4

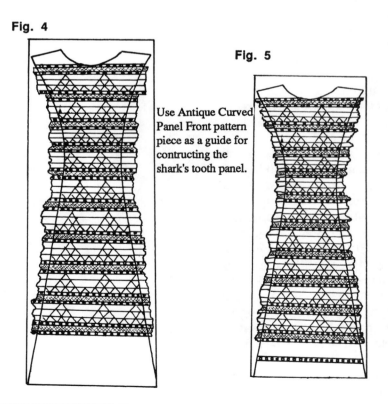

Fig. 5

Use Antique Curved Panel Front pattern piece as a guide for contructing the shark's tooth panel.

PRINCESS SEAM GOWN WITH SHARK'S TEETH AND SLIP

AMERICAN - CIRCA 1992

Step 10. The front panel should now be as long as the front pattern piece. If it is not, adjust the front, side front, and back skirt pattern pieces to fit this front panel. Any difference in length can be adjusted for in the depth of the ruffle.

Step 11. Cut out the gown curved center front from this shark's teeth - insertion-entredeux panel (**fig. 6**).

Step 12. Cut out the remaining pattern pieces: Antique Curved Side Panel, Curved Back Skirt, Curved Back Yoke and Short Sleeves.

Step 13. Stitch entredeux to the sides of the curved front panel, and to the long curved edges of the side front panels, using 3/8-inch seams.

Step 14. Trim the batiste from the remaining edges of the entredeux on both sides of the center front panel.

Step 15. Pull the thread in the heading of the insertion to make the lace lie flat at the waistline curves.

Step 16. Zigzag one side of the insertion to the front panel and the other side of the insertion to the side panel (**fig. 7**).

Step 17. Make a 4-1/2-inch placket in the center skirt back. Gather the skirt back to fit the back yokes, and stitch (**fig. 8**).

Step 18. Stitch the back yoke to the front at the shoulder seams (**fig. 9**).

Step 19. Stitch entredeux to the neck edge, then attach 3/8-inch gathered edging to the entredeux (**fig. 10**).

Step 20. Cut two strips of entredeux and one strip of beading 14 inches long.

Step 21. Trim one side of each strip of entredeux. Zigzag entredeux to both sides of beading. Trim remaining side of one of the strips of entredeux and attach gathered 1-1/2-inch edging.

Step 22. Cut this sleeve band strip in half.

Step 23. Gather the lower edges of the sleeves to fit the sleeve bands, and stitch (**fig. 11**). Gather the sleeve caps and stitch the armscye seam (**fig. 12**).

Step 24. Stitch gathered 2-1/4-inch gathered edging to entredeux joining the side front panels to vertical insertion.

Step 25. Fold under a narrow hem on the lace at the shoulder seams.

Step 26. Stitch the narrow hem, keeping the edging free from the fabric where it extends past the sleeve seam (**fig. 13**).

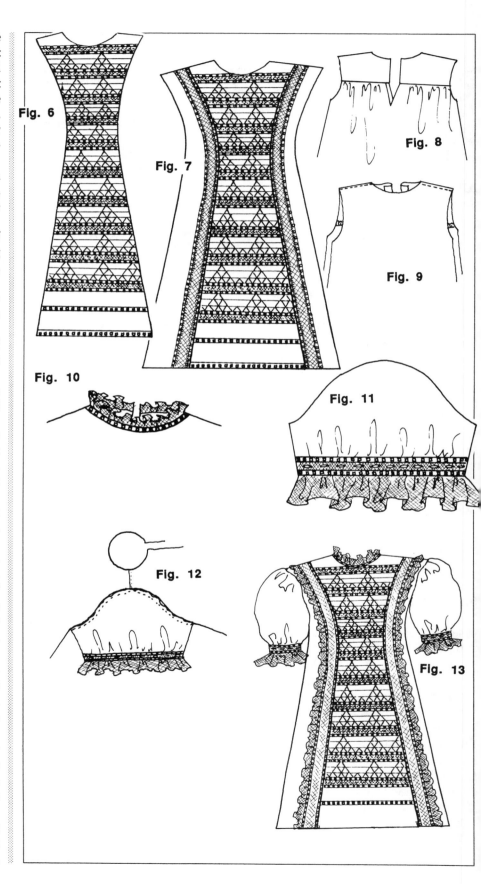

Fig. 6
Fig. 7
Fig. 8
Fig. 9
Fig. 10
Fig. 11
Fig. 12
Fig. 13

Step 27. Stitch one side seam, matching underarm seams **(fig. 14)**.

Step 28. Stitch entredeux around lower edge of skirt **(fig. 15)**.

Step 29. Cut three strips of fabric 45 inches wide and 5-1/4 inches long or desired width for ruffle.

Step 30. Stitch together into one long strip, and attach flat wide edging to one long edge **(fig 16)**.

Step 31. Gather the ruffle and attach to the entredeux at the lower edge of the skirt **(fig. 17)**. Stitch gathered wide edging on top of the ruffle right on top of the ruffle-entredeux seam line.

Step 32. Stitch gathered wide edging to the two rows of entredeux at lower edge of the center front panel, so that the edging covers the plain fabric.

Step 33. Fold under the ends of the lace even with the entredeux of the side front seams, and stitch **(fig. 18)**.

Step 34. Stitch the remaining side seams **(fig. 19)**. Close the back with buttons and buttonholes or beauty pins.

Slip

Step 35. Cut out slip. Place center front on fold, and the center back 1/2 inch from the selvage. Do not cut out the neck and armholes yet, just mark seam lines. The length of the slip pieces should be 3 inches shorter than the finished gown.

Step 36. Stitch a 1/2-inch seam at the center back, trim and finish the seam **(fig. 20)**. Stitch the right shoulder seam **(fig. 21)**.

Step 37. Using tear away stabilizer or two layers of water-soluble stabilizer, stitch a machine satin-stitch scallop along the lines marking the neck and armholes.

Step 38. Tear or dissolve the stabilizer, and trim the fabric very close to the scallops.

Step 39. Stitch one side seam **(fig. 22)**.

Step 40. Attach entredeux to the lower edge of the slip. Attach gathered wide edging to the entredeux.

Step 41. Stitch the other side seam.

Step 42. Make two buttonholes on the left back shoulder overlap. Use stabilizer when stitching these buttonholes through one layer of fabric.

Step 43. Stitch buttons under buttonholes on left front shoulder underlap.

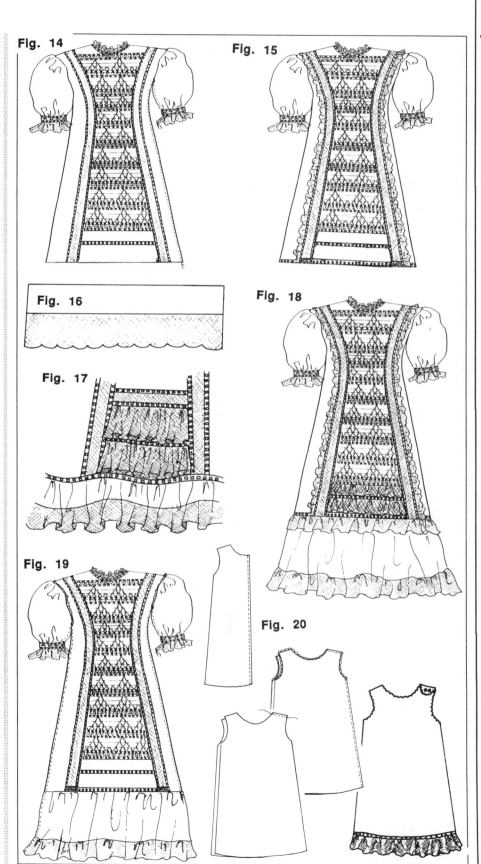

Fig. 14   Fig. 15   Fig. 16   Fig. 17   Fig. 18   Fig. 19   Fig. 20

CAMPBELL'S CHRISTENING GOWN AND SLIP

AMERICAN - CIRCA 1992

Pattern Pieces Used: Campbell's Skirt Gore, Campbell's Skirt Godet, High Yoke Front, High Yoke Back, Long Puffed Sleeve, Slip Front and Back, Campbell's Celtic Lace Template. **Note:** *Directions for Celtic Lace Designing - page 245

Supplies and Gown Description

- 6 yards Nelona
- 17-1/2 yards 1/4-inch or 3/8-inch wide insertion
- 6-1/2-inch yards beading
- 9-1/2 yards entredeux
- 13 yards 3-1/2" wide edging
- 10 yards 2-inch wide edging
- 1-1/2 yards 3/8-inch wide edging
- 7 yards 1/8-inch wide satin ribbon

I purchased this pinkish ecru lace about four years ago in Australia from an antique dealer who informed me that this crown lace had been made in 1936 in England in anticipation of the coronation of Edward VIII. Edward became king upon the death of his father, George V, on January 20, 1936 He abdicated the throne on December 11 of the same year to marry an American, Wallace Warfield Simpson. I also purchased a companion lace with the same dark pinkish color with robin's egg blue stitching intertwined with the ecru lace. When I arrived home from Australia, Joe looked at this lace and declared that all of our grandsons had to be christened in this lace since it was boy lace. I'm not sure that the crowns on the lace imply that only a male could wear the lace; however, Joe had his own opinion on the subject. When an ultrasound indicated that Charisse and Camp's baby was to be a boy, I called Sue Pennington and ask her to help in designing and creating this gown. As usual, her answer was enthusiastic and very positive.

Sue not only knew how to use the unusually colored lace, she figured a formula to dye the rest of the laces and the entredeux a close match! She even dyed the Swiss batiste fabric of the dress in a rosy off white. The design has four large godets, which feature two rows of 2-inch curved puffing connected with beading laced with robin's egg blue ribbon. Lace, 3/8 inch wide, is formed in a Celtic quilting shape about 13 inches high and 11 inches wide. Inside the center of this beautiful quilted lace shape are three circles representing The Father, The Son, and The Holy Spirit. This tiny 3/8-inch lace is shaped between each godet and again in a graceful loop on the parts of the skirt between the godets. This same tiny lace travels in a scalloped manner around portions of the skirt; purchased entredeux, dyed the same dark ecru as the crown antique lace, finishes the scalloped portion of the skirt. At the top of the fabric ruffle is a row of gathered crown ecru edging which is the same fullness of the fabric ruffle. A beautiful 5 inch wide fabric ruffle is gathered along the bottom of the scalloped skirt to which the 3-1/2 inch wide ecru and robin's egg combination lace edging is stitched flat. In other words, the ruffle is a total of 8-1/2 inches wide.

The bodice of the dress is a high yoke square bodice; although it appears to be a round yoke bodice because of the rows of circular puffing, laces, and entredeux. Beginning 3/4 inch below the center neckline is a rounded row of ecru entredeux, 3/8 inch wide lace insertion, 1 inch wide row of puffing, 3/8 inch wide insertion, entredeux, and gathered wide lace trim of robin's egg blue and ecru. The neckline has a row of the king lace with a bias binding at the top. The long sleeves are gathered at the bottom to a row of entredeux, beading, entredeux, and gathered king lace edging. Robin's egg blue ribbon is run through the beading.

The matching slip is a masterpiece also. It has tiny lace zigzagged around the arms and the neckline. The slip buttons down the back and has a placket. The bottom of the slip has seven double needle, wide pintucks, and a row of purchased, dyed entredeux is below these pintucks. A wide fabric ruffle (8 inches) has the beautiful ecru and robin's egg blue lace (3-1/2 inches) stitched straight to the bottom of the ruffle.

The total length of the dress is 43 inches. The fullness of the dress is 120 inches. The beauty of the dress still completely overwhelms me and most who have seen it. Of course, the dress pales in comparison to the tiny little boy who wore it to be christened at Holy Spirit Church, Sunday, February 16, 1992.

Skirt

Step 1. Cut six Campbell's gore panels.

Step 2. Notice the bottoms are gently curved arcs (fig. 1).

Step 3. On one panel, trace Campbell's Celtic lace design, from the pattern envelope, near the bottom of the panel. Follow the directions in this book for Celtic Lace Shaping and stitching the insertion. This is the center front panel.

Step 4. Trim fabric from behind insertion (fig. 2). Place insertion along the long side edges and the lower curved edge of this panel so that the outer edge of the insertion is even with the cut edge of the fabric. Miter the lace at the lower corners.

Step 5. Stitch the inner edge of the lace to the fabric.

Step 6. Trim fabric from behind the insertion (fig. 3).

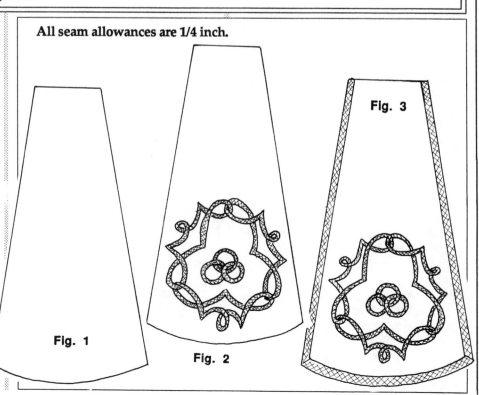

All seam allowances are 1/4 inch.

Fig. 1

Fig. 2

Fig. 3

CAMPBELL'S CHRISTENING GOWN AND SLIP

AMERICAN - CIRCA 1992

Step 7. On one other panel (for the center back), make a 4-1/2-inch continuous lap placket at the center top.

Step 8. Shape insertion around the side and lower edges as for the front panel.

Step 9. Stitch in place, and trim **(fig. 4)**.

Step 10. On the four remaining panels, trace the loop design, centered, 7 inches above the lower curved edge.

Step 11. Shape insertion along these lines, folding under the raw ends.

Step 12. Shape insertion along the lower curved edge. Stitch in place, and trim **(fig. 5)**.

Step 13. Cut four Campbell's Godets **(fig. 6)**.

Step 14. Cut or tear 7 strips of fabric 2-1/4 inches wide and 45 inches long for the puffing. Stitch the short ends together to form one long strip. Press. Zigzag over quilting thread or use a gathering foot to create puffing.

Step 15. Trace godet on tissue paper.

Step 16. Place tissue pattern on a fabric board and shape the following starting at the bottom of the tissue pattern: beading, puffing, beading, puffing, and beading **(fig. 7)**.

Step 17. Zigzag the strips together through the tissue. Remove from tissue.

Step 18. Place the beading/puffing section on the fabric godet with the beading meeting the curved edge of the godet.

Step 19. Stitch the upper edge of the top row of beading to the fabric godet.

Step 20. Trim the fabric away under the beading-puffing section **(fig. 8)**.

Step 21. Run 1/8-inch ribbon through the beading. Make sure ribbon is loose enough to prevent the godet from distorting.

Step 22. Stitch insertion to the left long edge of two of the godets, and to the right long edge of the other two godets.

Step 23. Let the insertion extend 1/4-inch past the beading at the lower edge.

Step 24. Trim fabric, lace, and puffing from behind insertion **(fig. 9)**.

Step 25. Stitch a godet to each side of the front and back panels. On the left sides, stitch a godet which has insertion on

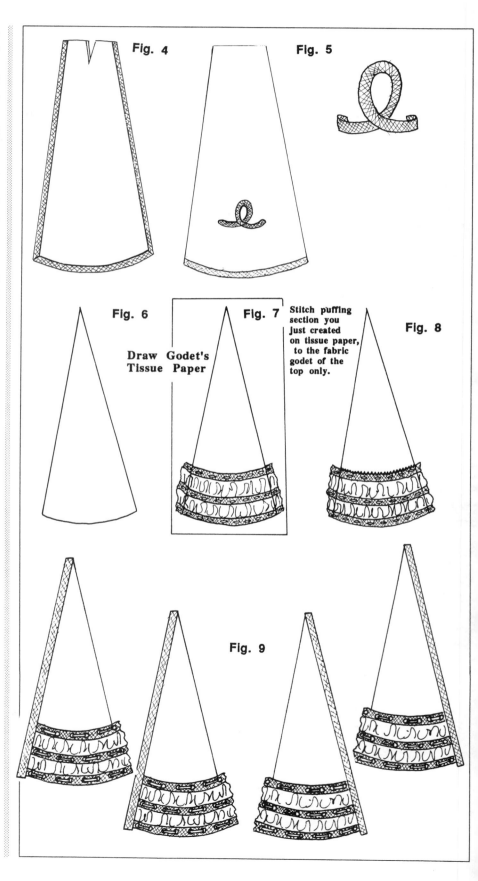

Fig. 4

Fig. 5

Fig. 6

Fig. 7

Draw Godet's Tissue Paper

Stitch puffing section you just created on tissue paper, to the fabric godet of the top only.

Fig. 8

Fig. 9

the left side. Also for the right side, stitch a godet which has insertion on the right side.

Step 26. Start with the lower edges even and the insertion of the center panels 1/4 inch over the raw edge of the godets. Stitch in place and trim.

Step 27. Now attach a side panel (with a loop design and insertion along the lower edge only) to both sides of the center panel with godets attached.

Step 28. Line up the lower edges. Remember, the insertion along the side of the godet extends 1/4-inch beyond the insertion and beading at the lower curves with the insertion 1/4-inch over the raw edges of the side panels. Stitch in place and trim (**fig. 10**).

Step 29. Trim the upper edge of the skirt to even them if necessary. Use the armhole templates from the high yoke pattern to cut armholes.

Step 30. Repeat **steps 25 - 29** for skirt back (**fig. 11**).

Yoke

Step 31. Believe it or not, this round yoke look is actually a square yoke in disguise. Cut front and back yokes from the high yoke pattern.

Step 32. Stitch the shoulder seams. Press under the back facings (**fig. 12**).

Step 33. Cut fabric strip 1-1/8 inches wide and 45 inches long for puffing.

Step 34. Zigzag over quilting thread as for the curved puffing on the skirt.

Step 35. Using the yoke as a guide, with the back facings opened, make a tissue paper guide and shape the insertion, on both sides of the puffing, to fit the yoke. Use a fabric board to shape lace and puffing.

Step 36. The bottom of the insertion should come to 3/4 inch from the cut edge at the center front and shoulders. Follow the neckline curve.

Step 37. Stitch insertions and puffing through the tissue pattern, then stitch trimmed entredeux to inner and outer edges of the insertion/puffing piece (**fig. 13**).

Step 38. Tear away tissue paper.

Step 39. Place puffing/insertion/entredeux semicircle on top of yoke.

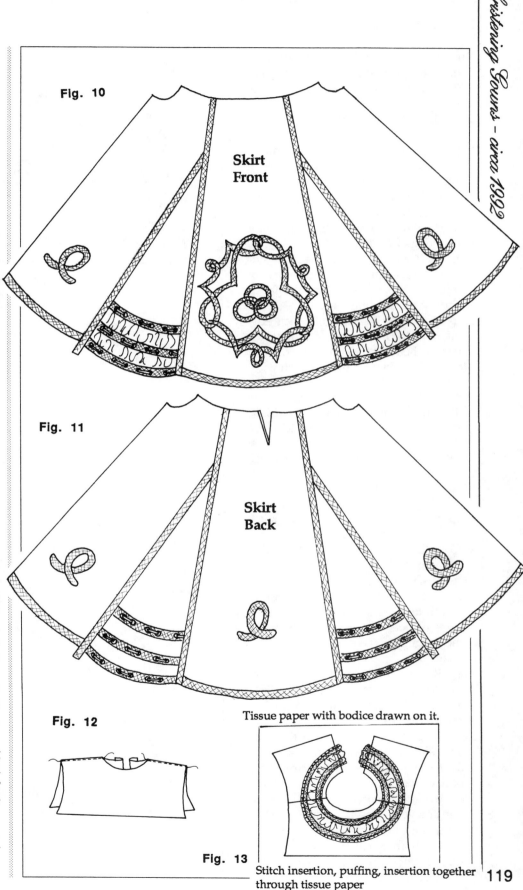

Fig. 10

Skirt Front

Fig. 11

Skirt Back

Fig. 12

Tissue paper with bodice drawn on it.

Fig. 13

Stitch insertion, puffing, insertion together through tissue paper

CAMPBELL'S CHRISTENING GOWN AND SLIP

AMERICAN - CIRCA 1992

Step 40. With narrow zigzag, stitch the outer edge of both rows of entredeux (the edge which is not stitch to insertion) to the yoke **(fig. 14)**.

Step 41. On the underside, trim away the center of the yoke fabric under the puffing, and clip remaining fabric every 1/2 inch or so all the way to the zigzag stitching line.

Step 42. Fold and press the fabric away from the puffing/insertion, pulling the fabric slightly to reveal the holes in the entredeux **(fig. 15)**.

Step 43. Zigzag again on the right side over the previous zigzag to secure the folded under fabric. Trim the fabric close to the stitching line.

Step 44. Gather 20 inches of 2-inch edging to fit the neck edge, folding under narrow hems at the center back.

Step 45. Cut a bias strip 1-1/4 inch wide. Press in half lengthwise. Stitch to the neck edge with a 1/4-inch seam, with the back facings folded under. Make sure to catch edging in this stitching.

Step 46. Stitch again close to the first stitching, and trim seam to 1/8 inch **(fig. 16)**.

Step 47. Fold bias over seam allowance, tucking under 1/4-inch at back openings. Stitch in the ditch or stitch by hand to secure **(fig. 17)**.

Step 48. Gather skirt front and back to fit yokes and stitch yoke seams **(fig. 18)**.

Step 49. Cut long sleeves, two pieces of entredeux and one piece of beading 15 inches long. Stitch entredeux to both sides of beading. Stitch gathered 2-inch edging to one side of entredeux to form cuffs.

Step 50. Cut this band in half, gather sleeves to fit cuffs, and stitch **(fig. 19)**.

Step 51. Gather sleeve caps and stitch to gown **(fig. 20)**.

Step 52. Cut 1-1/8 yards (for 6 month size, slightly more for larger sizes) of 3-1/2 inch edging and narrow hem both cut edges.

Step 53. Gather to fit outer row of entredeux on yoke. Check to make sure lace does not cup. Look for a cape-like, rather than a ruffly, effect. Use a longer length of lace if a ruffly look is desired.

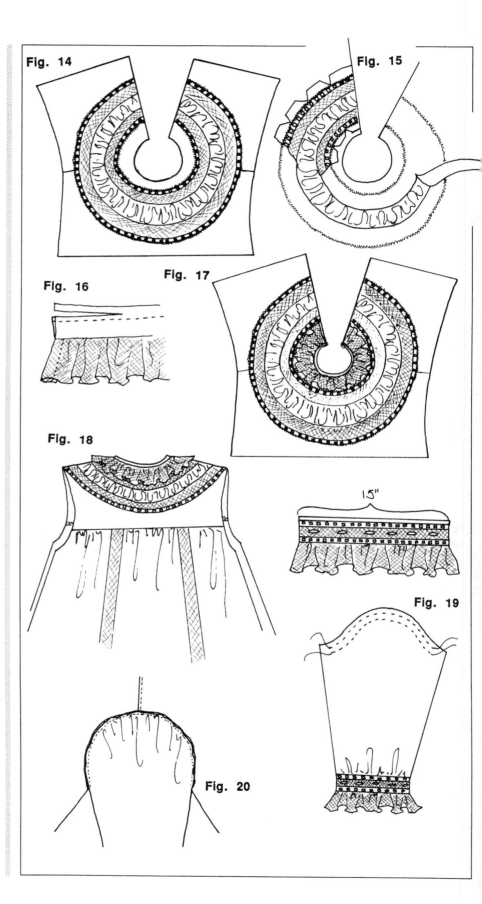

Fig. 14

Fig. 15

Fig. 16

Fig. 17

Fig. 18

15"

Fig. 19

Fig. 20

Step 54. Zigzag the edging to the outer edge of the curved entredeux around the yoke. Lace should extend to folded edge on right back, and 3/4 inch from folded edge on left back, to allow fro placement of button **(fig. 21)**.

Step 55. Stitch one side seam from hem to cuff **(fig. 22)**.

Step 56. Fold under the little 1/4 inch extensions of insertion along the side skirt panels to the inside of the dress. Stitch entredeux around the dress bottom. Trim away the excess 1/4 inch lace tabs **(fig. 23)**.

Ruffle

Step 57. Cut or tear 6-1/2 strips of fabric 5-3/4 inches wide and 45 inches long.

Step 58. Stitch short ends together into one long strip. Stitch flat 3-1/2 inch edging to one long edge.

Step 59. Gather ruffle to fit entredeux at lower edge of skirt, and stitch **(fig. 24)**.

Step 60. Gather 2-inch wide edging. Stitch to entredeux at top of ruffle **(fig. 25)**.

Step 61. Stitch remaining side seam **(fig. 26)**.

Step 62. Cut two 18-inch lengths of ribbon and run through beading at wrists.

Step 63. Close back with buttons and buttonholes or beauty pins.

Slip

Step 64. Cut out and construct slip as for *Christening Puffing Coat and Underdress.* Allow for an 11-1/2-inch ruffle and several rows of pintucks.

Step 65. Finish armholes, neckline, and placket as in directions.

Step 66. Stitch one side seam.

Step 67. With a 3.0 double needle, stitch seven rows of pintucks 1-inch above lower edge. Press down.

Step 68. Stitch entredeux to lower edge.

Step 69. Cut 2-1/2 strips of fabric 8-1/2 inches wide and 45 inches long.

Step 70. Stitch together to form one long strip, and attach 3-1/2-inch wide edging to one long edge.

Step 71. Gather ruffle to fit entredeux and stitch.

Step 72. Stitch remaining side seam, and close back placket with two tiny buttons.

Fig. 21

Fig. 22

Fig. 23

Fig. 24

Fig. 25

Fig. 26

Pattern Pieces Used: Australian Windowpane Front Yoke, Back Yoke; Short Puffed Sleeve; Armhole Template; Lace Shaping Templates for yoke and dress bottom, windowpane embroidery motif for yoke and dress bottom.

Supplies and Gown Description

- 2-1/4 yards white Nelona
- 1 yard ecru entredeux
- 9 yards ecru 1/2-inch insertion
- 1/2 yard ecru beading
- 11 yards ecru 1/2-inch edging
- 4 yards ecru 1-inch edging
- 1/4 yard white cotton organdy
- ecru rayon embroidery thread
- 1 yard 1/4- inch satin ribbon

Using a technique for peek-a-boo organdy motifs, which I first saw on a blouse in Australia, this lovely garment illustrates just how elegant machine embroidery and applique can be on a museum-quality heirloom garment. The white dress features ecru laces and machine embroidery, which includes lots of ecru machine entredeux stitched in shapes into various places in the dress. The curved laces attached with the wing needle pin stitch on the sewing machine, of course, are really on a square high yoke bodice. They just appear to be on a curved bodice. The skirt has three loops, which have been machine pin stitched and entredeux stitched. The gathered lace edging is zigzagged around the shapes. Roses, leaves, and wispy shapes of machine entredeux comprise the design statement. The hem of the skirt has wing needle/entredeux stitched in at the bottom. The only place on the dress where "real" Swiss purchased entredeux has been used is around the neckline and the sleeves. The neckline is finished with an entredeux and gathered lace finish; the puffed sleeves have entredeux, beading, and gathered lace as a finishing treatment. The total back length of the dress is 36 inches; the circumference is 84 inches.

Organdy Cutwork Motifs - General Directions

Step 1. Trace cutwork motif onto a piece of organdy large enough to fit into a machine embroidery hoop.

Step 2. Place a second piece of organdy under this traced one, matching grainlines. Treat the two layers of organdy as one.

Step 3. Position the organdy on the right side of the Nelona in the appropriate position (refer to pattern piece), and place all three layers in a machine embroidery hoop **(fig. 1)**.

Step 4. Thread your machine with fine white thread in the bobbin and ecru rayon machine embroidery thread in the needle.

Step 5. Using a small zigzag (L=1, W=1), stitch around outer edges of the design.

Step 6. With a sharp scissors, trim the organdy from the outside of the design on the right side of the fabric **(fig. 2)**.

Step 7. Turn the fabric over, and trim the Nelona away from the inside of the design **(fig. 3)**.

Step 8. Work on the right side and continue to use the machine embroidery hoop. With a medium width satin stitch (L=0.35, W=2), or whatever gives you a smooth satin stitch on your machine, stitch around all petals and leaves, working from the background to the foreground **(fig. 4)**. The veins in the petals and leaves are made with a stitch width of 1 at both ends, increasing gradually to a width of two in the center. Be sure to secure the threads at both ends.

Step 9. The stem of the bud is made with a stitch width of 3, increasing to 5 or 6 right at the base of the bud.

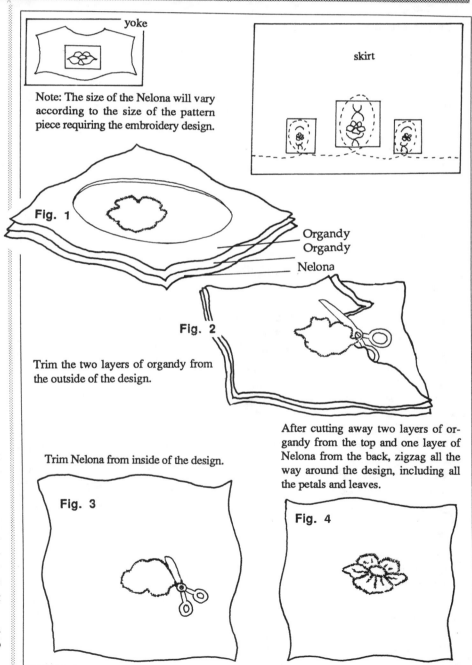

yoke

Note: The size of the Nelona will vary according to the size of the pattern piece requiring the embroidery design.

skirt

Fig. 1

Organdy
Organdy
Nelona

Fig. 2

Trim the two layers of organdy from the outside of the design.

After cutting away two layers of organdy from the top and one layer of Nelona from the back, zigzag all the way around the design, including all the petals and leaves.

Trim Nelona from inside of the design.

Fig. 3

Fig. 4

AUSTRALIAN WINDOWPANE MOTIF CHRISTENING GOWN
AMERICAN - CIRCA 1992

Step 10. Cut or tear two strips of fabric for skirt, each 33 inches long, or desired length.

Step 11. Cut blocks of fabric for front and back yokes several inches larger than pattern.

Step 12. Trace all lace placement lines, dots, and entredeux stitch lines on skirt (**fig. 5**) and yoke (**fig. 6**).

Step 13. Stitch organdy cutwork motifs following steps 1-9. Stitch an entredeux stitch along the indicated lines with the rayon machine embroidery thread and a wing needle (**fig. 7**).

Step 14. With the rayon thread and a regular needle, stitch tiny satin stitch dots (W=2.5), securing thread at beginning and end of each dot.

Step 15. Shape lace insertion along indicated lines, except at neckline, and stitch in place with fine ecru thread, a wing needle, and an entredeux or pin stitch (**fig. 8**).

Step 16. Rinse all pieces in warm water. Roll in a towel to remove excess water, and press dry, right side down.

Step 17. Trim batiste from behind lace, except on back opening underlap (this stays so you have something in which to make a buttonhole (**fig. 9**).

Step 18. Trim batiste just below entredeux stitching at lower edge of skirt.

Step 19. Attach slightly gathered 1/2-inch edging as shown on skirt and yokes with entredeux stitch as you would to regular entredeux (**fig. 10**).

Step 20. Stitch shoulder seams. Press

Step 21. Shape 1/2-inch insertion around neckline, with inner edge of insertion 1/4 inch below raw neckline edge (**fig. 11**).

Step 22. Attach lower edge only of insertion with pin stitch or entredeux stitch (**fig. 12**).

Step 23. Trim fabric from behind lace (except on back underlap). Attach trimmed entredeux to neckline edge of insertion, and attach gathered 1/2-inch edging to remaining edge of entredeux (**fig. 13**).

Step 24. Use the armhole templates to cut armholes in the upper corners of the skirt pieces (**fig. 14**).

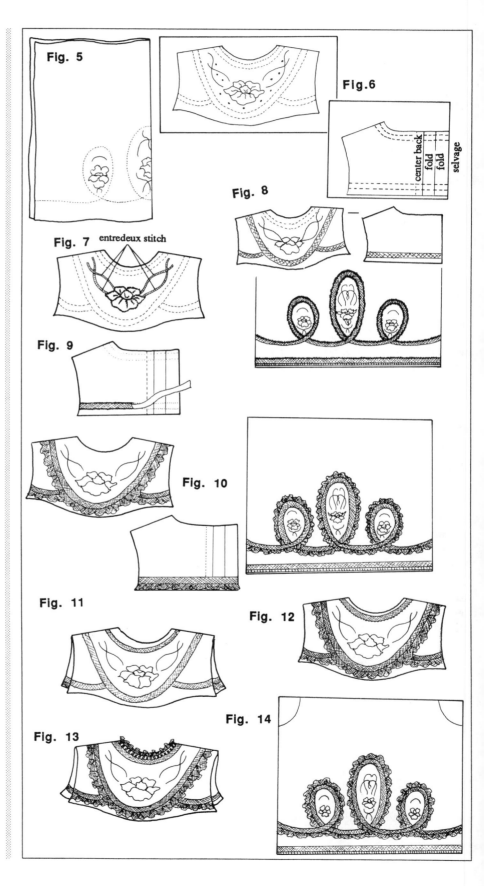

Fig. 5

Fig. 6

Fig. 7   entredeux stitch

Fig. 8

Fig. 9

Fig. 10

Fig. 11

Fig. 12

Fig. 13

Fig. 14

Step 25. Fold skirt front at center, with upper edges even. Make a mark at the fold 1-1/4 inch below upper raw edges.

Step 26. Draw a smooth, gradual curve from this mark, tapering to the upper raw edges at the armholes **(fig. 15)**.

Step 27. Cut along this line.

Step 28. Make a 4-1/2-inch placket at center of back skirt **(fig. 16)**.

Step 29. Gather front and back skirts to fit yokes, and stitch skirts to yokes, being careful to avoid catching lace edging in this stitching. Finish seams and press toward yokes **(fig. 17)**.

Step 30. Cut two pieces of entredeux each 8 inches long.

Step 31. Trim one side, and attach to beading.

Step 32. Attach gathered 1/2-inch edging to the other side of beading **(fig. 18)**.

Step 33. Gather sleeve to fit entredeux and stitch **(fig. 19)**.

Step 34. Gather cap of sleeve to fit armscye, and stitch **(fig. 20)**.

Step 35. Stitch one side seam, matching armbands, underarm seams, and lace on skirt **(fig. 21)**.

Step 36. Attach gathered 1-inch edging to lower edge of skirt **(fig. 22)**.

Step 37. Stitch remaining side seam **(fig. 23)**.

Step 38. Run ribbon through beading on sleeves.

Step 39. Close back with buttons and buttonholes, or use beauty pins.

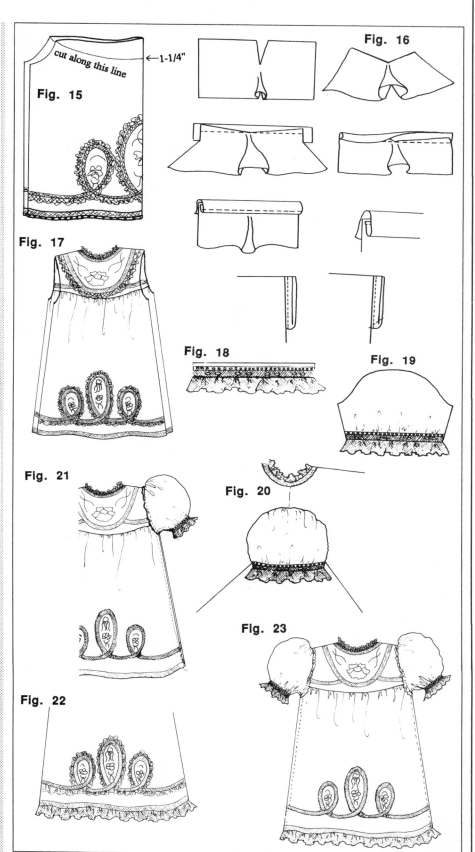

Fig. 15
Fig. 16
Fig. 17
Fig. 18
Fig. 19
Fig. 20
Fig. 21
Fig. 22
Fig. 23

cut along this line
←1-1/4"

PORTRAIT COLLAR TRIPLE RUFFLE
CHRISTENING GOWN
AMERICAN - CIRCA 1992

Pattern Pieces Used: High Yoke Front and Back, Armhole Template, Short Puffed Sleeve. Directions for Portrait Collar found on page 227.

Grandmother's Hope Chest

Supplies and Gown Description

- 3 yards white Nelona
- 7-1/2 yards dove motif Swiss handloom

- 27 yards lace insertion (#1)
- 3 yards each of two different lace insertions (#2, #3)

- 2-1/2 yards each of four different lace insertions (#4,#5,#6,#7)
- 14 yards lace edging
- 3 yards entredeux

This gown is actually beginning French sewing at its easiest. The dress consists of a wide, straight fancy band, which is 19 inches long. The fancy band has three rows of insertion stitched together, a 1-1/2 inch wide tucking strip with five 1/4 inch wide tucks, and a Swiss insertion from Martha Pullen Co., Inc, which is embroidered, white on white, with a dove. The dove strip is alternated with the tucked strip. The finished length on each ruffle strip is 4-1/2 inches and it consists of three tucks on the bottom with flat edging stitched below that. The total back length of the dress is 39 inches; the circumference of the skirt portion of the dress is 82 inches. This is a beginning French sewing project with the only round lace work being the portrait collar, which is shaped and stitched right through tissue paper. The sleeves of the dress are finished with entredeux and gathered lace edging. Several different patterns of French lace are used in this garment. I encourage grandmothers to mix and match laces for an elegant look.

Fancy band

Step 1. Lightly starch and press the Swiss handloom and the lace insertions.

Step 2. Cut the dove handloom into three equal 2-1/2-yard pieces. Cut or tear four strips of fabric 2-1/2 inches wide.

Step 3. Stitch the short ends to form two 90-inch strips.

Step 4. Using a wide (4.0) double needle, stitch five rows of pintucks on both strips. Press the tucks down.

Step 5. Each strip of handloom is 2-1/2 yards long. Using the techniques of lace-to-lace and lace-to-fabric, stitch together the fancy band like this (**fig. 1**):
Insertion #1, Insertion #2, Insertion #1
Swiss Handloom
Insertion #1, Insertion #3, Insertion #1
Tucked Fabric Strip
Insertion #1, Insertion #4, Insertion #1
Swiss Handloom
Insertion #1, Insertion #5, Insertion #1
Tucked Fabric Strip
Insertion #1, Insertion #6, Insertion #1
Swiss Handloom
Insertion #1, Insertion #7, Insertion #1

Step 6. Stitch entredeux to the lower edge of the fancy band (**fig. 2**).

Triple Ruffle

Step 7. Cut nine 45-inch strips of fabric each 5 inches wide. Seam three strips together for each ruffle. Now you have three long strips.

Step 8. Using the lace-to-fabric technique, stitch lace edging to one long edge of each strip (**fig. 3**).

Step 9. Using the 4.0 double needle, stitch 3 pintucks the length of each strip, just above the edging. Press the tucks down (**fig. 4**).

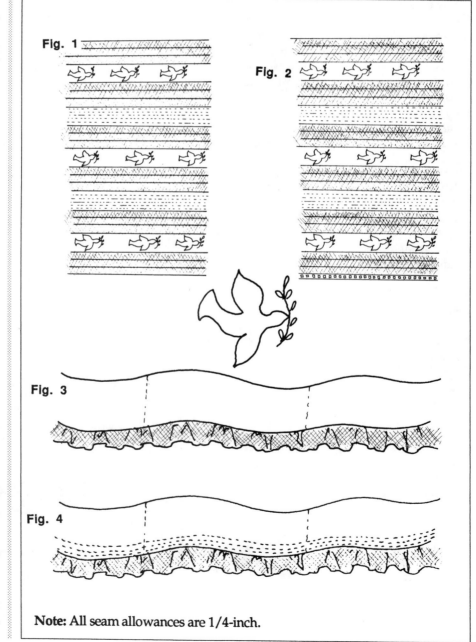

Fig. 1

Fig. 2

Fig. 3

Fig. 4

Note: All seam allowances are 1/4-inch.

PORTRAIT COLLAR TRIPLE RUFFLE CHRISTENING GOWN

AMERICAN - CIRCA 1992

Step 10. Cut or tear four strips of fabric each 4 inches wide. Seam the short ends to form two 90-inch strips. These are the flat pieces under your ruffles.

Step 11. Gather one ruffle strip to fit the 4-inch wide strip, stitch with a 1/2 inch seam. Finish this seam (**fig. 5**).

Step 12. Press this seam allowance away from the ruffle.

Step 13. Gather another ruffle strip. Place it right side up on top of the first ruffle strip with the raw edge even with the raw edge of the flat 4-inch strip.

Step 14. Place the second 4-inch strip right side down on top of the ruffle - the second ruffle is sandwiched between the two flat 4-inch strips (**fig. 6**).

Step 15. Stitch and finish this seam. Press ruffle down and the top flat strip up.

Step 16. Gather the third ruffle strip and place it right side up on top of the second flat strip with the raw edges even (**fig. 7**). Pin.

Step 17. Attaching The Skirt To The Ruffle: Place the entredeux of the skirt fancy band right side down on top of this third ruffle.

Step 18. Using the technique Entredeux to Gathered Fabric, attach the skirt fancy band to the ruffle (**fig. 8**).

Yoke and Collar

Step 19. Cut two high yoke fronts and four high yoke backs.

Step 20. Stitch shoulder seams to make one bodice and one lining (**fig. 9**).

Step 21. Follow the Portrait Collar directions found in this book. Use (from the neckline) insertion #2, insertion #1, insertion #3, insertion #1 (**fig. 10**).

Step 22. Trim away excess insertion at center back, allowing for edging to go up the center back edges, and for 1/4 inch to be turned under.

Step 23. Overcast the back edges, and fold under 1/4 inch (**fig. 11**).

Step 24. Stitch gathered lace edging around lace portrait collar and along folded under center back edges (**fig. 12**). Entredeux can be used around the collar. I wanted a softer look.

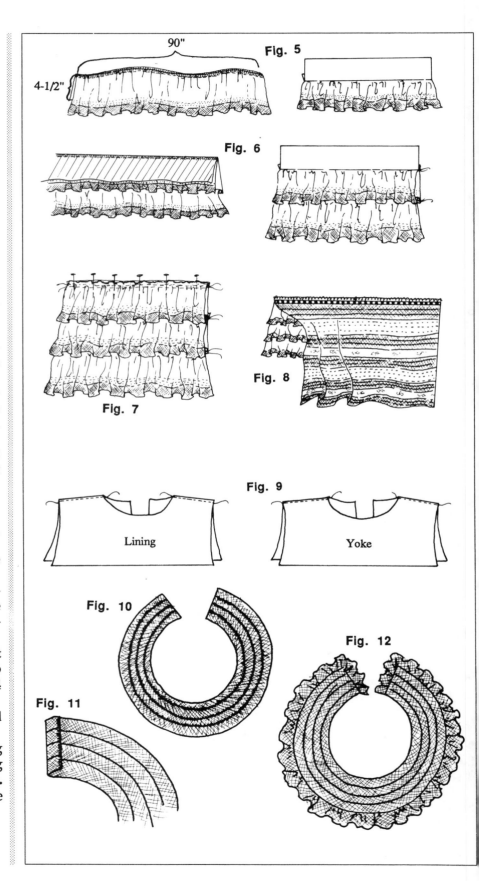

Fig. 5

Fig. 6

Fig. 7

Fig. 8

Lining   Fig. 9   Yoke

Fig. 10

Fig. 11   Fig. 12

Grandmother's Hope Chest

Step 25. Place the collar right side up on top of the yoke, also right side up.

Step 26. Place the heading of the inner row of insertion right on the seam line. Stitch through this heading with a very narrow zigzag (W=1, L=1) (**fig. 13**).

Step 27. Place the yoke lining right side down over the collar, raw edges even. Turn the whole thing over, and straight stitch right on top of the tiny zigzag, through all layers (**fig. 14**).

Step 28. Trim and clip the seam allowance. Turn right sides out, and press. From here on out, treat both yoke and lining as one (**fig. 15**).

Step 29 Cut or tear two strips each 8 inches wide for the skirt front and back.

Step 30. Use the armhole guides to make the armhole cutouts (**fig. 16**).

Step 31. In the center of the back, make a 4-1/2-inch long continuous lap placket.

Step 32. Gather the skirt front and back to fit the yoke front and back, stitch, finish the seam, and press the seam allowance toward the yoke (**fig. 17**).

Step 33. Cut out short puffed sleeves.

Step 34. Cut two 9-inch lengths of entredeux. Trim one batiste edge, and zigzag gathered edging to the entredeux (**fig. 18**).

Step 35. Gather the lower sleeve edge to 9 inches. Stitch to the entredeux (**fig. 19**).

Step 36. Finish the seam. Press the seam toward the sleeve, and secure with a tiny zigzag.

Step 37. Gather the sleeve caps, and stitch the armhole seams (**fig. 20**).

Step 38. Stitch one side seam, matching underarm seams and entredeux and edging on sleeve (**fig. 21**).

Step 39. Using the Lace-to-Fabric technique (Martha's Magic) stitch the "fancy band/ruffle" part of the skirt to the "bodice/sleeve/upper skirt" part of the dress. Stitch around to the unstitched side. Then, finish stitching from outer sleeve underarm to the end of the ruffle at dress bottom (**fig. 22**).

Step 40. Close the back opening with buttons and buttonholes or beauty pins.

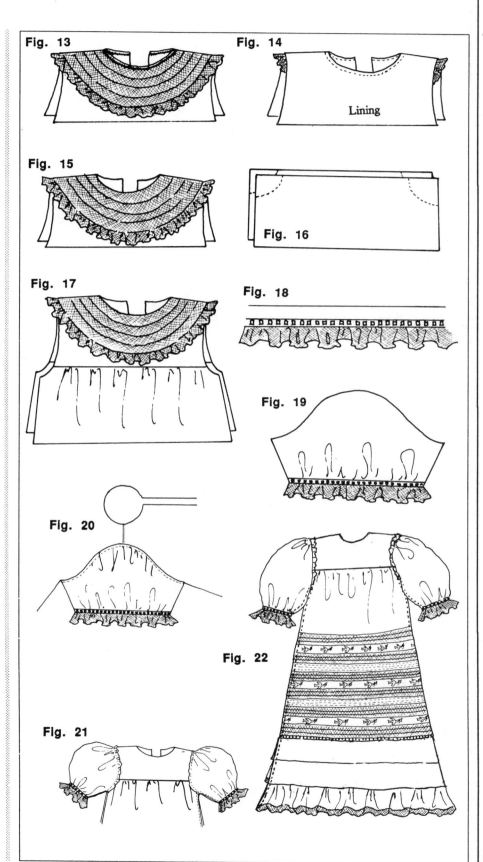

Fig. 13
Fig. 14 — Lining
Fig. 15
Fig. 16
Fig. 17
Fig. 18
Fig. 19
Fig. 20
Fig. 21
Fig. 22

TUCKED CHRISTENING GOWN WITH GUIPURE LACE
AMERICAN - CIRCA 1992

Pattern Pieces Used: Low Yoke Front and Back (Adaptations given in gown directions.), Short Puffed Sleeve.

Supplies and Gown Description

- 2-13/4 yards Nelona
- 4 yards 2-inch wide Guipure lace insertion

- 3 yards 3-1/2-inch wide Guipure lace edging
- 11 yards entredeux

This tucked bodice has pintucks, which appear to be folded but in reality are made with a 3.0/80 double needle and a five groove pintuck foot. The machine tucks are stitched two grooves apart with a 1.5 straight stitch length. The pintucks measure about 1/16 inch wide and they are about 1/32 inch apart. With double needles and today's fabulous computer sewing machines, uniform pintucks can be had without a light year of folding and pressing. The pintucks are pressed to each side with the division in the middle. The pintucks travel in a slight V in the front up to the sleeve line. The 2-inch-wide tucked skirt panels consist of seven rows of pintucks all pressed toward the bottom of the dress. The short puffed sleeves have a ruffle of fabric finished with a bias binding. The neckline is finished the same. The skirt fancy band is quite unusual. The top row of the fancy band has 2- inch wide Swiss Guipure insertions with entredeux and a 2-inch-wide tucked panel, entredeux, Swiss Guipure, and entredeux. The fullness of the first panel is the same as the bottom of the bodice of the dress, 36 inches. The second portion of the panel is 11 inches long and 66 inches full. A 9-inch ruffle is pintucked in the same double needle fashion with nine pintucks. Entredeux, Swiss Guipure, and entredeux complete this portion of the fancy band. The bottom portion of the fancy band consists of a 9 inch wide pintucked fabric ruffle with 11 pintucks on the bottom, entredeux, and flat Swiss Guipure 3-1/2 inch wide edging zigzagged to the bottom of this ruffle. The circumference of this ruffle is 106 inches. The total length of the dress is 40 inches.

Tucked bodice

Step 1. On a block of fabric 24 inches wide and 14 inches long, draw a "V."

Step 2. In the center of the fabric make a mark 6-1/2 inches down from the top and on each side of the fabric, mark 4-1/2 inches from the top.

Step 3. Connect the dots with a straight line to make a very shallow "V."

Step 4. Stitch pintucks from the top of the fabric down to the line (fig. 1). Do not backstitch to secure the threads, but pull the threads to the wrong side and tie off.

Step 5. Stitch released tucks across the width of the fabric. Press the tucks away from the center.

Step 6. Use the pattern for the *Low Yoke Dress.* Fold the tucked piece in half at the center front. Keep the lengthwise grain at the edges of the piece parallel with the center front fold line. There will be some fullness below the tucks that will not lay flat - that's ok.

Step 7. Place the low yoke front on the tucked fabric, matching center fronts. The shoulder seams should be near the top of the tucked edges.

Step 8. Trace the pattern except for the lower edge.

Step 9. From the bottom of the armhole, draw a line to the bottom of the fabric angling out about 1 inch.

Step 10. Measure down 11-1/2 inches from the highest point of the shoulder seam at the neckline and draw across the bottom of the tucked piece, curving up slightly at the side seam.

Step 11. Cut out the front. (fig. 2).

Note: All seam allowances 1/4 inch.

Fig. 1

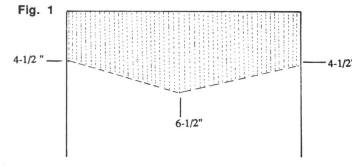

4-1/2 " —   — 4-1/2"

6-1/2"

Fig. 2

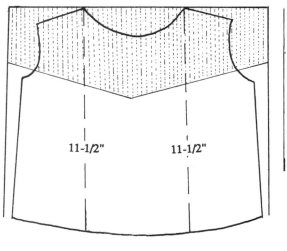

11-1/2"   11-1/2"

Tucked Christening Gown with Guipure Lace
American - circa 1992

Step 12. Cut the back in the same way as the front, from an untucked piece of fabric, using the low yoke back pattern, and placing the center back on a fold.

Step 13. Make a 9-inch long continuous lap placket in the center back (fig 3).

Step 14. Stitch the shoulder seams (fig. 4).

Step 15. For ruffles on the neck and sleeve, cut three pieces of batiste 1-3/4 inches by 24 inches. Also cut enough 1-1/4 inches bias strips to bind the neck and sleeves.

Step 16. Press the ruffles and bias strips in half lengthwise.

Step 17. Run gathering threads in the ruffle strips 1/8-inch and 3/8-inch from the raw edges (fig. 5).

Step 18. Pull up one ruffle strip to fit the neck edge. Fold the ruffle under diagonally at the center back, so that the raw edge will be caught in the binding stitch.

Step 19. Place a folded bias strip on top of the ruffle, all raw edges even.

Step 20. Stitch with a 1/4-inch seam. Stitch again close to the first stitching, and trim to 1/8-inch (fig. 6).

Step 21. Fold the bias strip over to the inside, encasing the raw edges.

Step 22. Stitch in the ditch, or stitch by hand to secure (fig. 7).

Step 23. Cut out short puffed sleeves, and run gathering threads in the sleeve cap and sleeve bottom (fig. 8).

Step 24. Pull up the sleeve bottom to measure 7 inches. Gather a ruffle to measure 7 inches and place the ruffle along the bottom of the sleeve.

Step 25. Place a folded bias strip over the ruffle, all raw edges even, and stitch and finish like the neck edge (fig. 9). Stitch sleeve in place (fig. 10).

Step 26. Stitch one side seam, folding the bias strip open at the sleeve (fig. 11).

Step 27. Finish securing the bias sleeve binding by machine or hand.

Step 28. Trim one side of the entire 11 yards of entredeux. Zigzag entredeux to both sides of 4 yards of Guipure insertion, and to the top edge of 3 yards of Guipure edging (fig. 12).

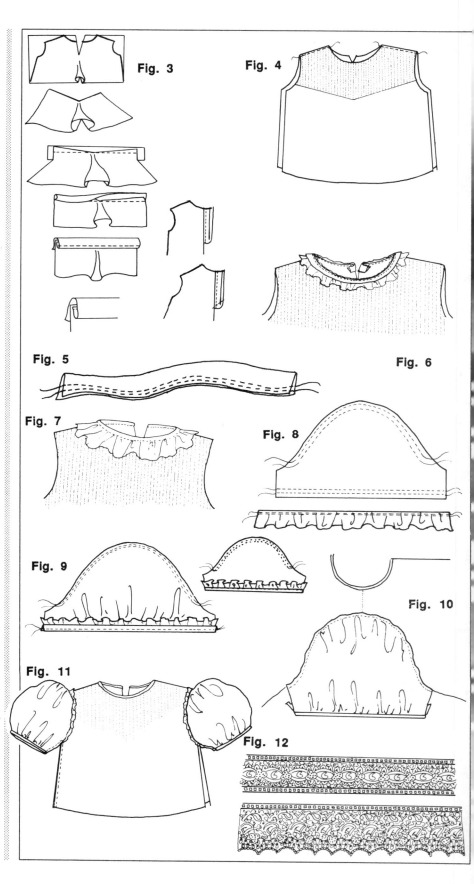

Fig. 3
Fig. 4
Fig. 5
Fig. 6
Fig. 7
Fig. 8
Fig. 9
Fig. 10
Fig. 11
Fig. 12

Step 29. Measure around the bottom edge of the tucked dress top (the circumference). It should be approximately 1 yard around.

Step 30. Cut or tear a strip of fabric 5 inches wide by 36 inches long.

Step 31. Stitch seven rows of pintucks. Press the tucks down, and trim the strip so the pintucks are centered and the strip is 2-1/4 inches wide **(fig. 13)**.

Step 32. Stitch a strip of entredeux-trimmed insertion to both sides of this strip, and then stitch this insertion - tucking - insertion strip to the top tucked part of the gown **(fig. 14)**.

Step 33. Cut or tear four strips of fabric 12 inches by 45 inches. Seam two of these strips together making a piece which is 90 inches long. Cut off 18 inches from one side leaving a strip which is about 72 inches long.

Step 34. Stitch nine rows of tucks, starting 3/4 inch from the lower edge.

Step 35. Press down and attach the remaining 2 yards of entredeux trimmed insertion just below the tucks **(fig. 15)**.

Step 36. Gather the upper edge of this second tier of the skirt and attach to the upper portion of the gown **(fig. 16)**.

Step 37. Stitch the remaining two 12-inch strips together, and also the 18-inch strip that was cut off of the second tier. The strip should measure about 3 yards.

Step 38. Stitch 11 rows of tucks at the lower edge. Press, and attach the entredeux edging strip **(fig. 17)**.

Step 39. Gather the upper edge and stitch this third tier to the entredeux of the one above **(fig. 17)**.

Step 40. Stitch the remaining side seam, and finish the bias binding of the sleeve like the other sleeve **(fig. 18)**.

Step 41. Make buttonholes on the back placket, through the dress right back and folded under continuous lap placket. They should be vertical and about 1/4-inch from the folded edge. Lap the right side over the left, and stitch buttons in corresponding positions on the placket only - the placket is not turned under on the left side **(fig. 19)**.

36" Fig. 13 2-1/4"

Fig. 15

Fig. 14

Fig. 16

Fig. 17

Fig. 18

Fig. 19

TUCKED COATDRESS AND SLIP WITH HANDLOOM
AMERICAN - CIRCA 1992

Pattern Pieces Used: Coatdress Front Yoke and Back Yoke, Armhole Template, Long Puffed Sleeve, Slip Front and Back, Hexagonal Lace Shaping Template.

Supplies and Gown Description

- 4 -1/2 yards Nelona
- 5 yards all white embroidered 2-1/4 inch wide Swiss handloom
- 14 yards 1/2-inch wide lace insertion

- 1/2 yard beading
- 2-1/2 yards entredeux
- 11 yards 1-inch wide lace edging
- 2-1/2 yards 1/2-inch wide lace edging

This coat has those perennial favorites of mine, machine pintucks made with the 3.0/80 double needle. These are the machine pintucks that look like folded tucks! Two sets of three tucks 11-1/2 inches long extend down the front of the coat on either side. Five sets of matching tucks, 11-1/2 long, are spaced evenly on the back of the coat. The bodice is lined and the neckline is finished with entredeux and gathered lace edging. The long, puffed sleeves have entredeux, beading and gathered lace zig-zagged right to the bottom of the beading without any entredeux at the bottom. Each hexagon is 5 inches long and 2 inches wide. White-on-white Swiss handloom is the base for the hexagonal lace shaped figures which are joined to each other with a lovely cross-over lace shaping. The same hexagonal lace figures travel in two rows around the bottom of the coat and above the bottom of the tucking strip on the coat. Double needle tucks, 25 to be exact, are nestled between those beautiful figures. The slip is precious! Twenty-two tucks travel down the front of it. Entredeux and a gathered 3-1/4-inch-wide ruffle finish the bottom of the slip. The slip has an opening on one shoulder, a fold-over tab with a tiny button and buttonhole. The total back length of the dress is 36 inches. The total fullness of the coat is 64 inches. The circumference of the slip is 52 inches.

Step 1. Dye all materials off white according to page 267, if desired.

Step 2. Cut a strip of fabric measuring 10 inches wide and 31 inches long. Cut two strips measuring 10 inches wide and 15 inches long. Seam the 10-inch sides together, with one 15-inch strip on each side of the 31 inch strip.

Step 3. Using a 3.0 double needle, stitch tucks the length of the strip until the tucked area is at least 5-1/2 inches wide. Starch lightly and press tucks down (**fig. 1**).

Step 4. Cut a piece of Swiss handloom 52 inches long.

Step 5. Using the template, mark 10 hexagons on the handloom.

Step 6. Shape lace along marked lines, mitering corners and forming finished, mitered corners at both ends.

Step 7. Stitch the insides of the lace hexagons, and trim handloom fabric away from behind the lace (**fig. 2**).

Step 8. Center this lace-handloom strip along the lower edge of the tucked strip so that the lowest tuck is almost at the bottom of the "V's" between hexagons.

Step 9. Stitch the upper edge of the lace hexagons to the tucked fabric. Trim fabric away from behind lace (**fig. 3**).

Step 10. Cut another strip of handloom 60 inches long.

Step 11. Mark 12 hexagons and shape and stitch lace the the first strip.

Step 12. Center this along the top of the tucked strip. Stitch the lower edge of the lace hexagons to the tucked fabric. Trim fabric from behind lace (**fig. 4**).

All Seam Allowances are 1/4 inch.

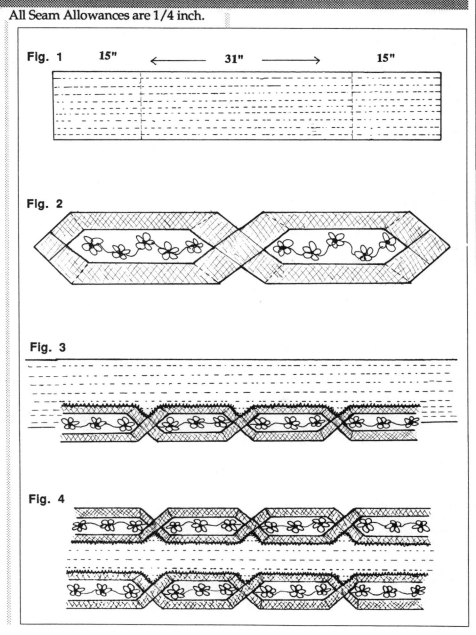

Fig. 1 15" ← 31" → 15"

Fig. 2

Fig. 3

Fig. 4

TUCKED COATDRESS AND SLIP WITH SWISS HANDLOOM

AMERICAN - CIRCA 1992

Step 13. Cut two strips of handloom each 28 inches long for the skirt center front. Make hexagons as before. There will be five complete hexagons, and a partial hexagon at the top of each strip.

Step 14. Cut two pieces of handloom, each 6 inches long. Mark one hexagon on each. Shape lace, stitch and trim.

Step 15. Cut one skirt back 26 inches long, 31 inches wide. Cut two skirt fronts 15 inches wide, 26 inches long.

Step 16. Use the armhole templates to mark and cut the armholes.

Step 17. Stitch lower half of the side seams (fig. 5).

Step 18. Place the fancy band over the skirt. Match side seams and center back so that the skirt fabric comes just below the bottom of the "V" and on the top row of lace.

Step 19. Zigzag upper edge of lace hexagons to the plain skirt fabric, and trim fabric from behind lace (fig. 6).

Step 20. Place the center front hexagon strips down the skirt center front. Place the single hexagons at an angle so that the points connect the lowest row of hexagons with the row of hexagons down the fronts (fig. 7).

Step 21. Zigzag the lace to the skirt. Trim fabric from behind the lace.

Step 22. Attach gathered 1-inch edging to the lace hexagons down the center fronts and around the bottom of the skirt (fig. 8).

Step 23. Divide the skirt back into sixths and press creases to mark (fig. 9). Divide each skirt front into thirds and press to mark.

Step 24. At each pressed fold line, stitch three released pintucks (with a 3.0 twin needle) from the upper edge of the skirt down 12 inches (fig. 10).

Step 25. Pull threads to the wrong side and tie off.

Step 26. Cut two yoke backs, 4 yoke fronts and two long sleeves.

Step 27. Using directions from *Scalloped Coatdress with Embroidered Slip* construct a yoke.

Step 28. Stitch skirt to yoke.

Step 29. Trim batiste from entredeux long enough to fit around neck edge.

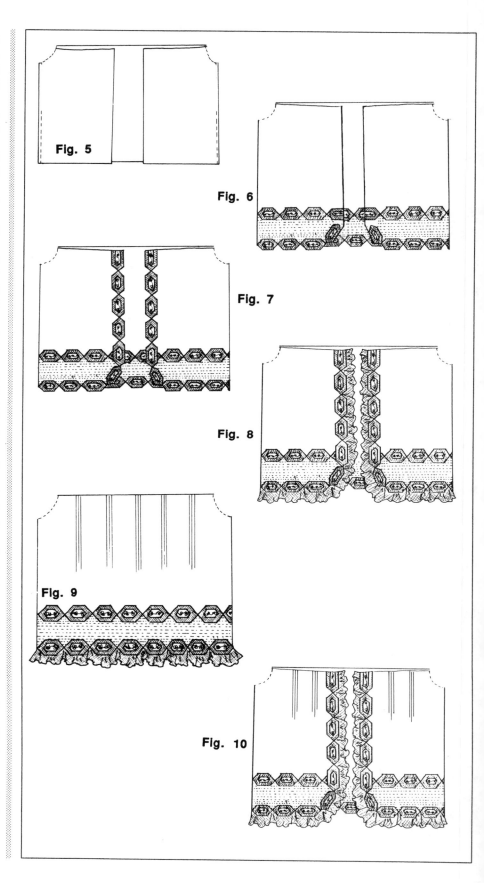

Fig. 5

Fig. 6

Fig. 7

Fig. 8

Fig. 9

Fig. 10

Step 30. Butt entredeux to finished neck edge. Zigzag, just barely catching the lined fabric edge. Extend the entredeux 1/2 inch past front openings.

Step 31. Stitch gathered 1/2-inch edging to entredeux. Turn under entredeux and edging at front edges and stitch **(fig. 11)**.

Step 32. Cut a piece of entredeux 13 inches long. Trim one side.

Step 33. Stitch beading to entredeux. Stitch gathered 1 inch edging to beading. Cut in half to form one wrist band **(fig. 12)**

Step 34. Gather lower edge of sleeves to fit wrist bands and stitch **(fig. 13)**.

Step 35. Gather sleeve caps. Stitch sleeves to dress **(fig. 14)**.

Step 36. Stitch remainder of both side seams to wrists, matching underarm seam and lace at wrists **(fig. 15)**.

Step 37. Run ribbon through beading and tie in bows.

Step 38. Close front yoke with two buttons and buttonholes.

Slip

Step 39. Cut slip back 4 inches shorter than finished dress length. Cut a block of fabric slightly longer than this length for the slip front.

Step 40. Stitch vertical pintucks (3.0 twin needle) down center fabric. The strip of tucks in the center of the fabric should be about 4 inches wide or wider.

Step 41. Press tucks to one side. Fold in the center, and cut the slip front from this tucked fabric **(fig. 16)**.

Step 42. Construct shoulder seam and attaching lace around neckline and armholes as in *Scalloped Coatdress with Embroidered Slip*.

Step 43. Stitch one side seam **(fig. 17)**.

Step 44. Attach entredeux to lower edge.

Step 45. Cut two strips of fabric 3 inches wide and 45 inches long. Stitch to make one long strip.

Step 46. Attach flat 1-inch edging to one long edge.

Step 47. Gather ruffle to fit skirt. Stitch ruffle to entredeux **(fig. 18)**.

Step 48. Stitch remaining side seam. Fasten left shoulder with one or two tiny buttons and buttonholes **(fig. 19)**.

Fig. 11

Fig. 12

Fig. 13

Fig. 14

Fig. 15

Fig. 16

Fig. 17

Fig. 18

Fig. 19

CHRISTENING PUFFING COAT AND UNDERDRESS
AMERICAN - CIRCA 1992

Pattern Pieces Used: Coatdress Front Yoke, Coatdress Back Yoke, Armhole Template, Long Puffed Sleeve, Slip Front and Back

Supplies and Gown Description

- 3-1/3 yards ecru Nelona
- 17-1/2 yards entredeux
- 8 yards 1-inch wide Cluny or tatted edging
- 4 3/8-inch pearl buttons
- 1 yard 3/8-inch lace edging
- ecru rayon machine embroidery thread

The idea of a christening coat and underdress isn't new. Although the coat is called a coat, it is actually an overdress, which only buttons at the front bodice. It is open all the way down the front. Cluny laces trim this ecru Nelona dress; three panels of 2-inch puffing are sandwiched between 1-1/8 inch panels of three double needle pintucks with machine featherstitching between the sets of three pintucks. The sleeves have a straight panel of the featherstitching/pintuck strips with entredeux on both sides. Straight Cluny lace finishes the edges of the sleeves. The front bodice features the pintuck/featherstitching panels with entredeux between each panel. Two buttons close the coat. The bodice is lined.

The underdress looks like a little slip with lace edging around the neckline and the sleeves. The 5 inch wide ruffle on the bottom of the slip is attached to entredeux at the top and has straight Cluny lace on the bottom. The back is closed with two buttons and buttonholes. The total length of the coat is 30 inches. The circumference is 51 inches.

Note: All seam allowances 1/4 inch.

Puffing Strips

Step 1. Starch and press entredeux.

Step 2. Cut or tear eight or nine strips of fabric 2-1/2 inches wide and 45 inches long. Seam the narrow ends together to form a long strip.

Step 3. Run gathering threads 1/8-inch and 3/8-inch from both long edges, using all purpose cotton-covered polyester thread in the bobbin and a loosened top tension (fig. 1).

Step 4. Cut two strips of entredeux, each 4-1/2 yards long.

Step 5. Pull up the gathering threads on the puffing strip, and stitch entredeux to both gathered sides of the strip making sure gathers are evenly distributed, and that the gathers remain perpendicular to the entredeux.

Step 6. Using the technique "Entredeux to Gathered Fabric" attach the entredeux to both sides of this puffing strip (fig. 2).

Step 7. If desired you can topstitch the zigzagged under portion of the seam (fig. 3).

Step 8. Cut this long puffing strip into thirds (fig. 4).

Pintucked Strips

Step 9. Cut or tear two pieces of fabric 26 inches wide and 12 inches long (fig. 5).

Step 10. Press but do not starch this fabric.

Step 11. With a water-soluble marker, draw five lines, 2 inches apart, the entire length of the strip (fig. 6).

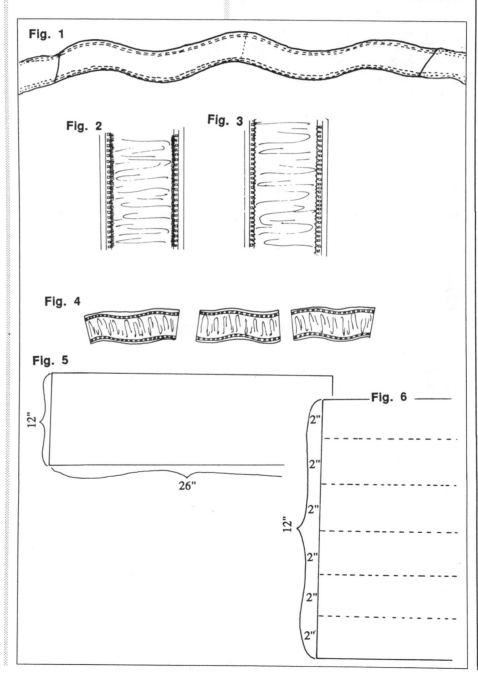

Fig. 1 Fig. 2 Fig. 3 Fig. 4 Fig. 5 Fig. 6

CHRISTENING PUFFING COAT AND UNDERDRESS

AMERICAN - CIRCA 1992

Step 12. Set up your machine for double needle pintuck, using a 1.6 or 2.0 double needle, a 7 or 9 groove pintuck foot, fine thread, and a tightened top tension.

Step 13. Using the drawn lines as a guide, stitch three pintucks very close together (I used adjacent grooves in a 7-groove foot). Leave a 1/4-inch or 3/8-inch space, and stitch three more pintucks (fig. 7).

Step 14. Rinse the fabric to remove the marker lines, and press to block.

Step 15. Now starch the fabric. (If you want to keep the pintucks from getting too flat, do the pressing on the wrong side of the fabric, on top of a velour bath towel.)

Step 16. With rayon machine embroidery thread in the machine, stitch a feather stitch (w=2.5, L=2) in the center of the area between the trios of pintucks (fig. 8)

Step 17. Cut the strips apart, making sure to leave adequate seam allowances. Then, cut four of the 26 inch strips in half (13 inches and 13 inches) and stitch to each side of a 26-inch strip, using a 1/4-inch seam allowance (fig. 9).

Step 18. Stitch together the fancy band, alternating three puffing strips with four pintucked strips. This fancy band will be 51 inches long after stitching.

Step 19. Stitch entredeux on the top and bottom raw edges of the pintucked strips. Your skirt fancy band should consist of: entredeux, pintucked strip, entredeux, puffing, entredeux, pintucked strip, entredeux, puffing, entredeux, pintucked strip, entredeux, puffing, entredeux, pintucked strip, entredeux (fig. 10).

Step 20. For the ruffle, cut or tear two 5-inch by 45-inch strips of fabric and seam the short ends together.

Step 21. Run gathering threads along one long edge and attach 1 inch wide edging to other long edge. Gather to fit fancy band and stitch (fig. 11).

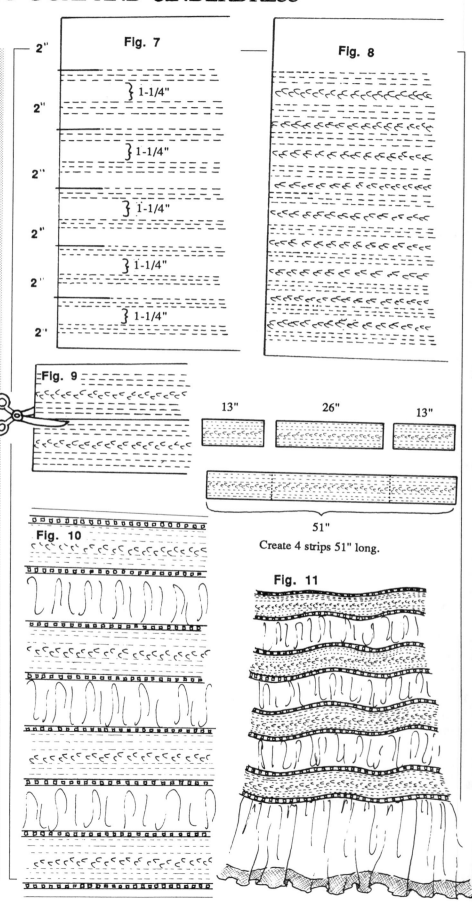

Fig. 7

2"

2"

} 1-1/4"

2"

} 1-1/4"

2"

} 1-1/4"

2"

} 1-1/4"

2"

} 1-1/4"

2"

Fig. 8

Fig. 9

13"   26"   13"

51"

Create 4 strips 51" long.

Fig. 10

Fig. 11

Step 22. Cut two skirt fronts 12 inches long by 13 inches wide and one skirt back 12 inches long by 26 inches wide. Cut out arm holes.

Step 23. Stitch side seams, leaving 6 to 8 inches open under the arms (**fig. 12**). This is done so that the sleeves can be put in flat instead of set in. Set-in sleeves this tiny are difficult to work with.

Step 24. Stitch the fancy band to the skirt (**fig. 13**).

Step 25. Trim the front opening edges straight and even, and attach entredeux down both front edges and trim batiste from entredeux (**fig. 14**).

Step 26. Attach edging to entredeux.

Step 27. Fold edging under 1/4 inch at lower edge and stitch (**fig. 15**).

Yoke

Step 28. Create fabric for front yoke by cutting 4-inch pieces from the remaining pintucked strip and stitching entredeux between them until the block is large enough for the front yoke pattern pieces (**fig. 16**).

Step 29. Cut a right and left yoke out of this block and cut a right and left yoke out of plain batiste for the yoke lining.

Step 30. Cut two back yokes from plain batiste (**fig. 17**).

Step 31. Stitch the pintucked fronts to a back yoke at the shoulder seams, and stitch the lining fronts to back yoke at the shoulders (**fig. 18**).

Step 32. Trim these seams and press open.

Step 33. Place the yoke and the lining right sides together, with all edges even.

Step 34. Stitch with a 1/4-inch seam around the neck, down the center fronts, and across the bottom of the center overlap to the center front mark (**fig. 19**).

Step 35. Trim seams to 1/8 inch. Clip curves, turn right side out, and press (**fig. 20**).

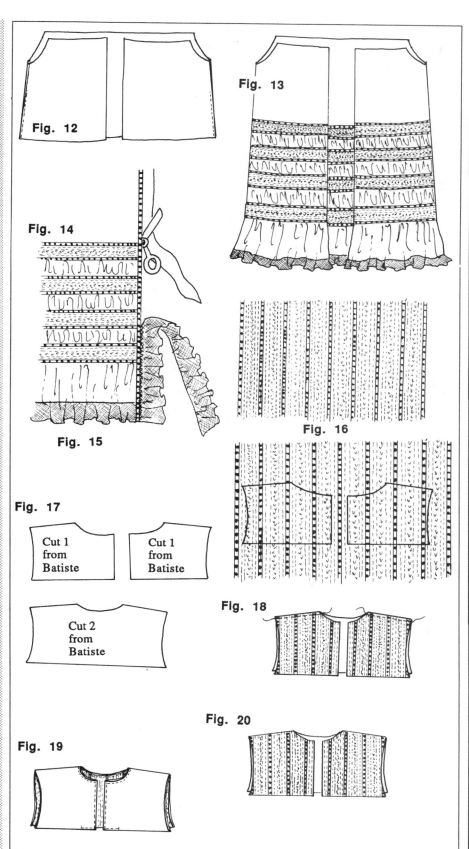

Fig. 12

Fig. 13

Fig. 14

Fig. 15

Fig. 16

Fig. 17

Cut 1 from Batiste

Cut 1 from Batiste

Cut 2 from Batiste

Fig. 18

Fig. 19

Fig. 20

CHRISTENING PUFFING COAT AND UNDERDRESS
American - circa 1992

Step 36. Gather skirt fronts to fit lower edges of front yokes.

Step 37. Right sides together, stitch skirt to yoke, with edging at center front. Be careful not to catch lining in this stitching **(fig. 21)**.

Step 38. Stitch again close to first stitching. Trim seam and press.

Step 39. Turn under seam allowance on lining and slip stitch by hand **(fig. 22)**.

Step 40. Gather skirt back to fit back yoke, and stitch right sides together, treating back yoke and lining as one.

Step 41. Finish seam and press toward yoke **(fig. 23)**.

Sleeves

Step 42. Cut sleeves from pattern, 1-1/4-inch shorter than pattern.

Step 43. To make cuff, cut two strips of pintucked fabric 6-1/2 inches long, or long enough to fit around baby's fist, plus seam allowances.

Step 44. Attach entredeux to both sides of pintucked strips and attach edging to one of the entredeux strips.

Step 45. Gather sleeve to fit cuff and stitch. Run two gathering rows in sleeve cap **(fig. 24)**.

Step 46. Gather sleeve cap to fit armscye, and stitch **(fig. 25)**.

Step 47. Stitch side seams, from previous stitching on skirt all the way up to the cuffs, matching underarm and cuff seams **(fig. 26)**.

Step 48. Make two buttonholes in right front, and sew buttons on left front **(fig. 27)**.

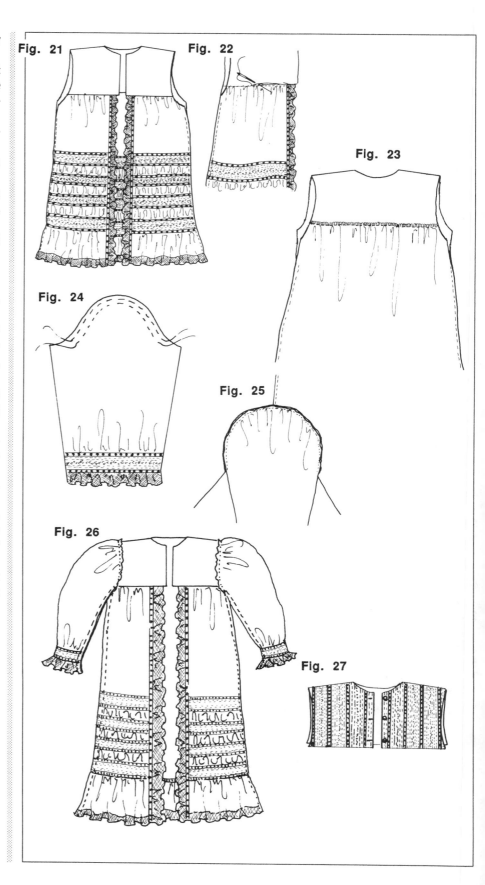

Fig. 21 Fig. 22 Fig. 23 Fig. 24 Fig. 25 Fig. 26 Fig. 27

Slip

Step 49. Cut out slip.

Step 50. Place slip center back 1/2-inch from selvage instead of on fold, and cut both shoulders at shoulder seam cutting line (no extensions).

Step 51. Cut slip to a length that will be about 1 inch shorter than puffing coat, allowing for a 5-inch ruffle. Approximate length is 29 inches.

Step 52. Stitch and finish shoulder seams (fig. 28).

Step 53. Starch and press neck and armhole edges.

Step 54. Place 3/8-inch edging around neck and armhole edges so that the scalloped edge of the lace is even with the cut edges of the slip.

Step 55. Stretch the lace slightly on the curves. Allow the lace to extend 1/2-inch past selvage edges at center back.

Step 56. Zigzag heading of lace to fabric.

Step 57. Lightly starch and press lace so it will lay flat, then trim fabric from behind lace (fig. 29).

Step 58. Stitch side seams (fig. 30).

Step 59. Attach entredeux to lower edge of slip (fig. 31).

Step 60. Cut or tear two strips of fabric 5 inches wide and 45 inches long.

Step 61. Stitch to make one long strip, and attach 1-inch edging to one long edge (fig. 32).

Step 62. Gather other long edge to fit entredeux, and stitch (fig. 33).

Step 63. Stitch center back in a 1/2-inch seam to 7 inches from lace at neck edge. (fig. 34).

Step 64. Press seam to the right, pressing under 1/2 inch on the right back all the way up to the neck edge.

Step 65. Stitch diagonally through the seam allowance just below this placket opening.

Step 66. Fold under the 1/2 inch lace extensions and stitch in place (fig. 35).

Step 67. Make two vertical buttonholes in the right back, one just below the lace at the neck edge, and another about 2 inches below the first.

Step 68. Stitch buttons on left back.

Fig. 28   Fig. 29   Fig. 30

Fig. 31

45"   45"   5"

Fig. 32

Fig. 33

Fig. 34

Fig. 35

143

CHRISTENING GOWN WITH GODETS, PINTUCKS, AND SWISS MOTIFS

AMERICAN - CIRCA 1992

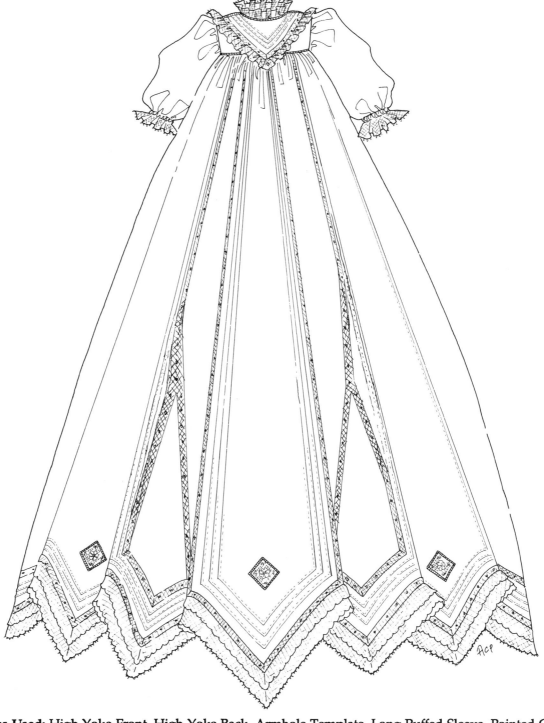

Pattern Pieces Used: High Yoke Front, High Yoke Back, Armhole Template, Long Puffed Sleeve, Pointed Gore, and Pointed Godet.

Supplies and Gown Description

- 4-3/4 yards Nelona (gown and slip)
- 23 yards 5/8-inch wide lace insertion
- 18 yards 1-inch wide lace edging
- 2-1/2 yards 1/2-inch wide lace edging
- 1 yard entredeux
- 2 yards Swiss beading
- 8 Swiss motifs
  2 inches by 2 inches
- 1/2 yard 1/8-inch elastic

The skirt of this gown is made up entirely of eight gores and eight godets joined together with lace insertion and attached to the yoke with entreduex. Sue embellished each gore with three rows of pintucks, placed about 3/4 inch from the edge; they start at the top and go around the two long sides and the pointed bottom. She placed a square Swiss motif at an angle near the bottom of each gore to echo the pointed line of the skirt. A row of insertion outlines each gore. Between the gores are godets, inserted about halfway down the skirt, and trimmed with mitered insertion and three rows of wide V-shaped pintucks. Two rows of mitered edging travel around the skirt in a zigzag pattern to finish.

The basic bodice of the gown has lace insertion, edging, and pintucks, which Sue fashioned in a wide "V" on the front and back. She joined the shoulders with entredeux and finished the neck opening with entreduex and gathered edging. The long sleeves of the gown are decorated at the shoulder with V-shaped pintucks and mitered insertion. They are gathered at the wrist with elastic and finished with edging.

All seams are 1/4 inch.

Step 1. Cut front and back yokes from high yoke pattern. Cut long sleeves, eight pointed gores, and eight pointed godets.

Step 2. Lightly starch and press fabric, lace insertion, and Swiss motifs.

Skirt panels

Step 3. Pin lace insertion along long edges and bottom "V" of all skirt gores so that the outer edge of insertion is even with the cut edge of the fabric.

Step 4. Miter corners.

Step 5. Using a narrow zigzag (w=1.5 or 2.0, L=0.6), stitch along the inner heading of the insertion.

Step 6. Trim fabric away from behind lace (fig. 1).

Step 7. With 1.6 mm twin needles, stitch three rows of pintucks just inside the insertion.

Step 8. Run the edge of the presser foot along the zigzag to position the first pintuck row. Use the grooves in the pintuck foot as a guide for stitching the two inner rows (fig. 2).

Step 9. Place the square Swiss motifs diagonally (so that they are diamonds instead of squares) about 1-1/4 inches above the inner pintuck.

Step 10. Zigzag around the motifs and trim the fabric away from behind them close to the stitching (fig. 3).

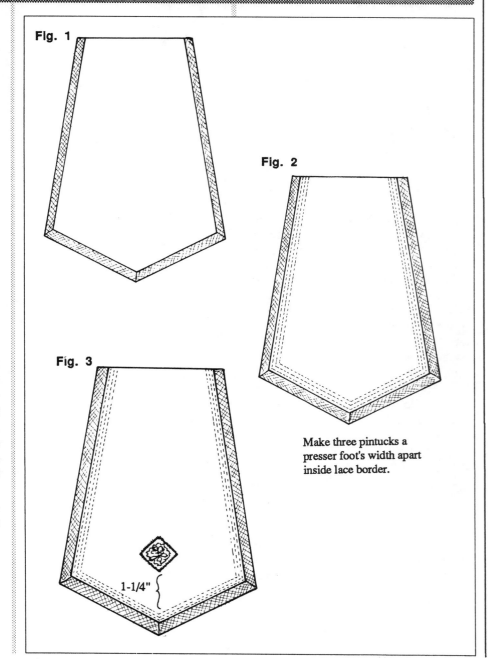

Fig. 1

Fig. 2

Make three pintucks a presser foot's width apart inside lace border.

Fig. 3

1-1/4"

CHRISTENING GOWN WITH GODETS, PINTUCKS, AND SWISS MOTIFS
AMERICAN - CIRCA 1992

Godets

Step 11. Pin lace insertion along "V" of godets (not along sides) so that the outer edge of insertion is even with cut edge of the fabric, mitering corner.

Step 12. Zigzag inner heading of lace.

Step 13. Stitch three rows of pintucks above insertion as on skirt panels.

Step 14. Place another row of insertion above pintucks, spaced the same distance from the pintucks as the first row of insertion. Miter corner.

Step 15. Zigzag along both edges of lace.

Step 16. Trim all fabric from behind insertions (fig. 4).

Joining skirt gores and godets

Step 17. Starch and press panels and godets.

Step 18. Join one gore and one godet.

Step 19. Place the lace insertion running up the side of the panel over the side of the godet so that the lace overlaps the fabric about 1/2 inch and the insertions meet at the lower edge.

Step 20. Zigzag along the edge of the insertion from the bottom to about 1/2 inch from the point of the godet.

Step 21. Trim fabric from behind lace (fig. 5). Similarly, place another panel on the other side of the godet and stitch in place, making the insertions meet at the point of the godet.

Step 22. Zigzag the insertions on the sides of the panels together above the point of the godet (fig. 6).

Step 23. Stitch another godet to the other side of the panel, then another panel, etc., until all the pieces are joined.

Step 24. Cut two lengths of 1-inch wide edging each 6-1/4 yards long.

Step 25. Place the scalloped edge of one piece just over the heading of the other piece. Stitch together with a straight stitch or a tiny zigzag (W=1, L=1) to form a wide edging (fig. 7).

Step 26. Zigzag this wide edging to the lace insertion on the bottom of the skirt, mitering all the corners (fig. 8).

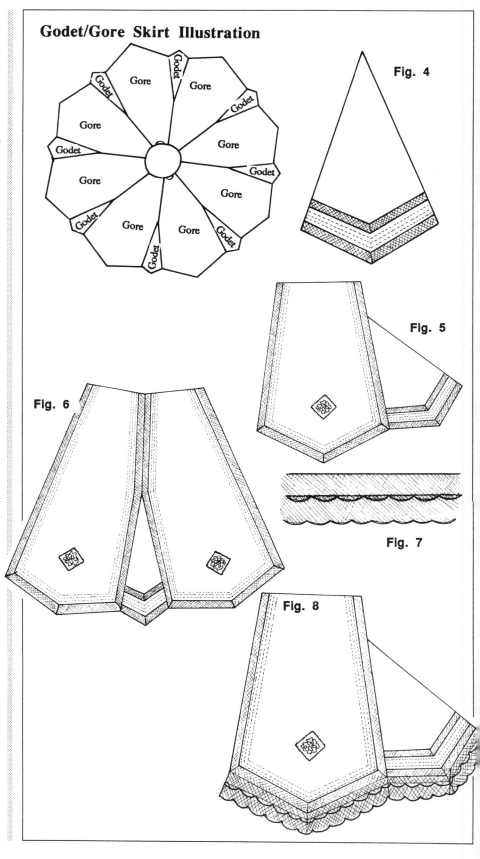

Godet/Gore Skirt Illustration

Fig. 4

Fig. 5

Fig. 6

Fig. 7

Fig. 8

Step 27. Stitch the skirt into a circle. Lay the skirt so that the upper edges are even and the sides are folded in the center of two panels.

Step 28. Cut the armholes using the armhole template. Mark center front and center back (fig. 9).

Step 29. Make a 4-1/2-inch long placket at the center back (fig. 10).

Yoke

Step 30. On the yoke front, make a mark at the center front 5/8 inch above the lower edge. Make another mark on the shoulder seam 1 inch in from the armhole cut edge.

Step 31. Connect these dots to form a "V" (fig. 11).

Step 32. Place the outer edge of insertion along this line. Miter at the "V", and zigzag both headings to the fabric.

Step 33. Trim fabric from behind lace, and stitch three rows of double needle pintucks within the "V" (fig. 12).

Step 34. On the back yokes, make a mark on the shoulder seam 1 inch in from the armhole edge, and another mark at the lower edge 1-1/2 inches to the side of the facing fold line.

Step 35. Connect the dots and place the outer heading of insertion along line.

Step 36. Stitch lace to fabric. Trim and stitch pintucks as for front (fig. 13).

Step 37. Stitch shoulder seams together with entredeux (fig. 14).

Step 38. Place a flat piece of 1-inch wide lace edging along the outer edge of the insertion and zigzag along the heading. Miter the lace at the front "V" and ease it to fit the angles at the shoulder seams without cupping.

Step 39. Attach entredeux to the neck edge, and zigzag 1/2 inches gathered edging to the entredeux (fig. 15).

Step 40. Attach entredeux to lower edges of front and back yokes, folding up the edging at the point of the front "V" to avoid catching the edging in the stitching. The edging on the back yoke will be secured in the seam.

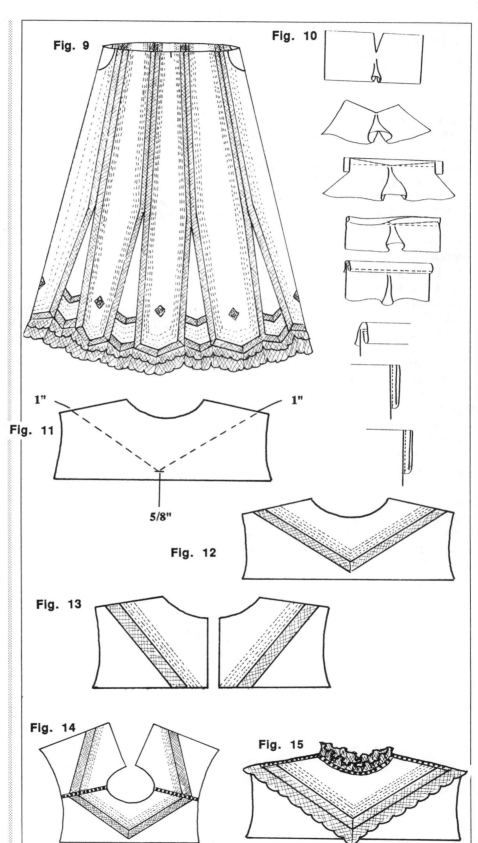

Fig. 9

Fig. 10

Fig. 11

1"   1"

5/8"

Fig. 12

Fig. 13

Fig. 14

Fig. 15

Christening Gown with Godets, Pintucks, and Swiss motifs
American - circa 1992

Step 41. Gather the skirt front and back to fit the yokes, and stitch to the entredeux, again taking care not to catch the edging on the front yoke (fig. 16).

Sleeves

Step 42. Draw a "V" on the cap of the sleeves 4-1/2 inches deep and 6 inches wide (fig. 17).

Step 43. Attach insertion and stitch pintucks as on yoke front (fig. 18).

Step 44. Press under 1/4 inch on the lower edge of the sleeves.

Step 45. Place the folded edge over the heading of 1 inch edging and straight stitch in place close to fold (fig. 19).

Step 46. Attach elastic as described in the *Lily of the Valley Christening Gown*, stitching 1/8 inch elastic over the folded-under raw edge. The zigzag over the elastic will encase the raw edge (fig. 20).

Step 47. Run gathering threads in the sleeve caps and stitch the underarm seams (fig. 21).

Step 48. Set the sleeves in using the directions given for the *Godet Curved Puffing Christening Dress* (fig. 22).

Step 49. Close the dress with buttons and buttonholes or beauty pins.

Slip

Make slip using directions for *Christening Puffing Coat and Underdress* substituting Swiss beading for the entredeux above the ruffle.

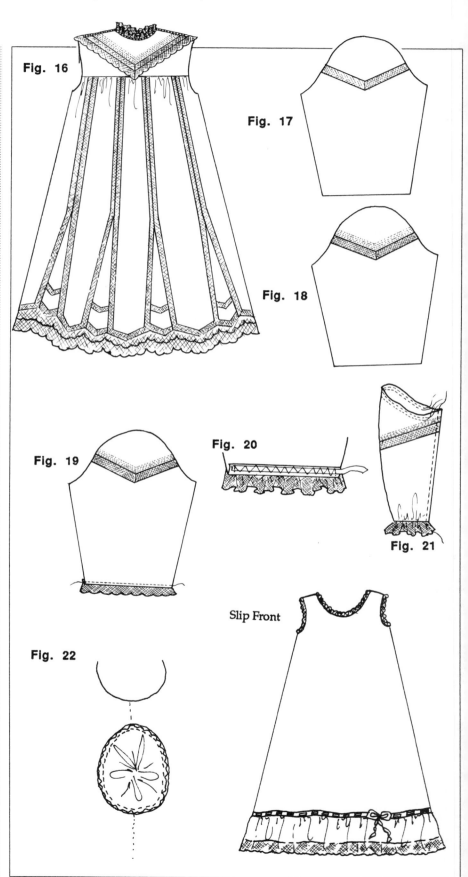

Fig. 16

Fig. 17

Fig. 18

Fig. 19

Fig. 20

Fig. 21

Fig. 22

Slip Front

SCALLOPED COATDRESS WITH EMBROIDERED SLIP

AMERICAN - CIRCA 1992

Pattern Pieces Used: Coatdress Yoke Front, Coatdress Yoke Back, Armhole Template, Long Puffed Sleeve, Slip Front (with Lace Template and Embroidery Design), Slip Back. Lace Scalloped Template for coat is also included in pattern envelope.

Scalloped Coatdress with Embroidered Slip

American - circa 1992

Slip

Step 1. Trace slip back and slip front with embroidery design and lace placement designs on blocks of fabric large enough for slip front and back. Do not cut out. Do all embroidery and press.

Step 2. Pin lace along lace placement lines, turning under cut ends in a rounded shape on the scroll sections of the lace design.

Step 3. Starch and press, being careful not to press embroidery design flat.

Step 4. Pin stitch or zigzag along all edges of the center front lace motif **(fig. 1).**

Step 5. Pinstitch or zigzag the upper edge of the scallops around the bottom of the slip.

Step 6. Stitch an entredeux stitch along the lower edge of the scallops **(fig. 2).** Optional - use entredeux.

Step 7. Rinse fabric to remove marking lines, and press.

Step 8. Trim fabric from behind all lace and below the hemstitching on the scallops. Leave just a tiny strip of fabric with "holes" in it attached to the lace **(fig. 3).**

Step 9. Stitch right shoulder seam **(fig. 4).**

Step 10. Starch and press neck and armhole edges.

Grandmother's Hope Chest

*Note: All seams 1/4"

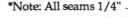

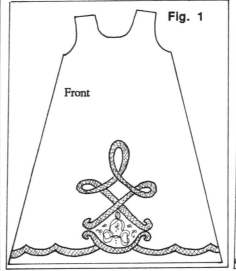

Fig. 1

Front

Back

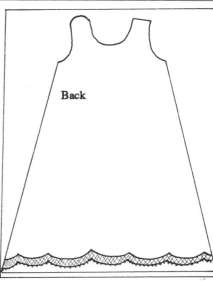

Fig. 4

Fig. 3

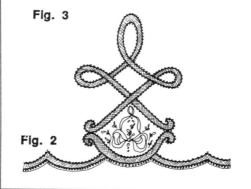

Fig. 2

Step 11. Cut two squares of fabric 2 inches wide and 2 inches long, with one edge along the selvage.

Step 12. Place these squares under the shoulder laps, with the selvage toward the bottom of the dress. This acts as a facing and stabilizes the buttons and buttonholes.

Step 13. Pin in place, and treat as one layer from here on (**fig. 5**).

Step 14. Place 3/8-inch edging so that the scalloped edge is even with the cut edge of the neck and armholes.

Step 15. Stretch lace slightly along the neck and armhole edges, and pull the gathering thread in the heading to ease the lace around the curved shoulder lap. Zigzag the heading of the lace to the fabric (**fig. 6**).

Step 16. Trim excess fabric from behind edging. Stitch one side seam, finish and press (**fig. 7**).

Ruffle

Step 17. Approximately 26 yards of 1-inch wide edging will be used for the ruffle. Cut a 3-yard piece of edging.

Step 18. Place the scalloped edge of the cut piece just over the heading of another long piece of edging.

Step 19. Stretch the 3-yard piece slightly and zigzag (W=1, L=1) along the scalloped edge so that the heading of the other piece of lace is caught in the stitching (**fig. 8**). The second row of lace will be slightly longer than the first and will cause the strip to curve.

Step 20. Now place the scalloped edge of the second strip of lace over the heading of the third strip, and zigzag, stretching the second strip (or the top layer)(**fig. 9**). Continue, stretching each strip of lace as you stitch, until there are seven strips of lace joined together.

Step 21. Gather the top of this lace flounce slightly and stitch to the hemstitching along the bottom of the scallops just as you would to entredeux (**fig. 10**).

Step 22. Stitch the remaining side seam, finish and press (**fig. 11**).

Step 23. Stitch two buttonholes in the back shoulder lap, and stitch buttons in corresponding positions on front shoulder underlap (**fig. 12**).

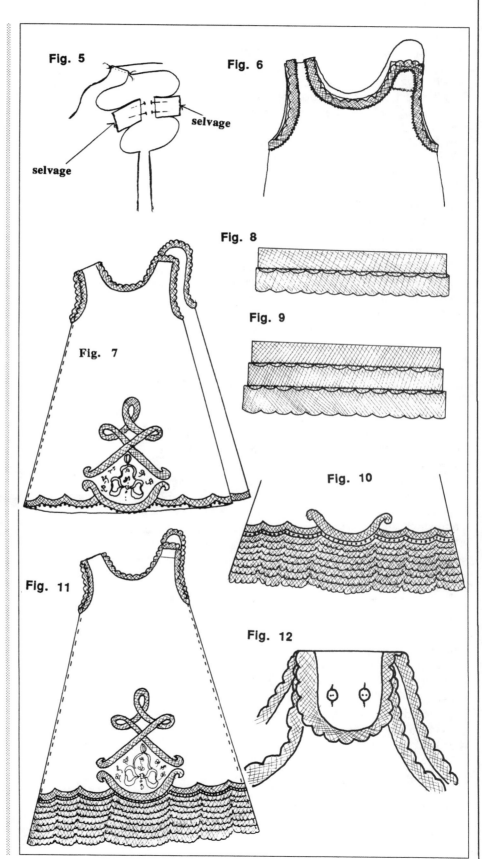

Fig. 5

selvage

selvage

Fig. 6

Fig. 7

Fig. 8

Fig. 9

Fig. 10

Fig. 11

Fig. 12

SCALLOPED COATDRESS WITH EMBROIDERED SLIP

AMERICAN - CIRCA 1992

Coatdress

Step 1. Cut one skirt back 25 inches wide by 31 inches long, and two fronts 12 inches wide by 31 inches long.

Step 2. Use the armhole templates to cut out the armholes in the upper corners.

Step 3. Stitch the side seams to within 10 inches of the armholes. This seam is left open so the sleeves can be stitched in flat rather than set in (**fig. 13**).

Step 4. Use the pattern to trace the scallops on the skirt (**fig. 14**).

Step 5. Shape lace along the lace placement lines. Starch and press.

Step 6. Pinstitch or zigzag along all headings of the lace except the bottom of the outer row of scallops. Use an entredeux stitch or Venetian hemstitch to secure this lace edge.

Step 7. Rinse fabric to remove marker lines. Press.

Step 8. Trim fabric from behind all lace and to just below hemstitching.

Step 9. Gather 1-inch wide lace edging and zigzag to the "holes" of the hemstitching along the lace scallops just as you would do entredeux (**fig. 15**).

Step 10. Cut out two back and four front yokes.

Step 11. Stitch each back to two fronts at shoulder seams and press (**fig. 16**).

Step 12. Place yokes right sides together, and stitch with 1/4-inch seam around neck edge, down fronts, and along lower edge of yoke to center front marks (**fig. 17**).

Step 13. Trim seams to 1/8-inch. Clip curves, turn right sides out, and press.

Step 14. Gather skirt fronts to fit yoke fronts.

Step 15. Right sides together, stitch skirt to yoke with edging at center front. Be careful not to catch lining in stitching.

Step 16. Stitch again close to stitching and trim seam allowance.

Step 17. Press. Fold under lining seam allowance and slip stitch in place by hand (**fig. 18**).

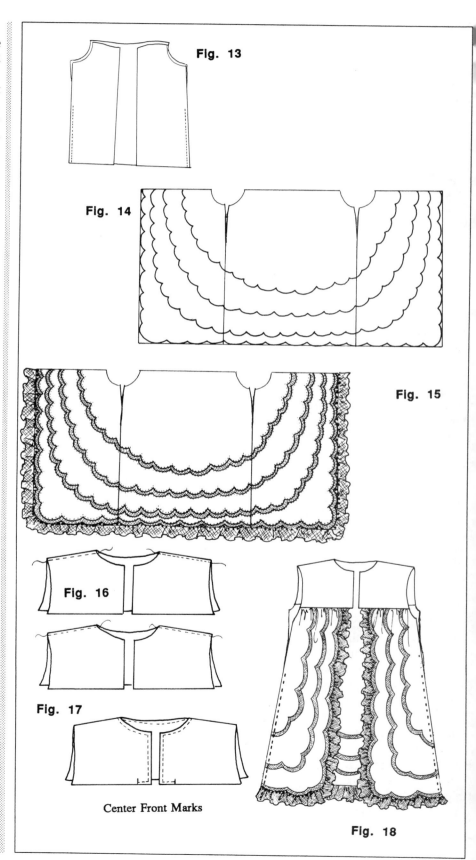

Fig. 13

Fig. 14

Fig. 15

Fig. 16

Fig. 17

Center Front Marks

Fig. 18

Step 18. Gather back skirt to fit back yoke and stitch, treating back yoke and lining as one.

Step 19. Finish seam and press up (**fig. 19**).

Step 20. Cut out sleeves.

Step 21. Cut two pieces of entredeux, each 14 inches long.

Step 22. Trim batiste from one side of each, and stitch entredeux to both sides of 14-inch piece of beading.

Step 23. Trim batiste from other side of one of the entredeux edges and attach gathered 1-inch edging.

Step 24. Cut this entredeux, beading, entredeux, edging strip in half to form two cuffs.

Step 25. Gather lower edge of sleeve and attach entredeux edge of cuff (**fig. 20**).

Step 26. Gather sleeve cap and stitch armscye seam (**fig. 21**).

Step 27. Stitch side seams from previous side seam stitching up to cuff, matching all seams (**fig. 22**).

Step 28. Cut a piece or entredeux 1-1/4 yards long. Trim one batiste edge.

Step 29. Gather 1-inch edging and zigzag to entredeux.

Step 30. Trim the other side of the entredeux to form a lace-entredeux "string" (**fig. 23**).

Step 31. Stitch this "string" all around the yoke and neckline. Start at the lower edge of the yoke on the underlap side, leaving 1/2 inch to turn under.

Step 32. Butt the entredeux up against the yoke fabric and zigzag, one stitch into the fabric, one stitch into a hole of the entredeux. Continue along the yoke seam stitching on top of the skirt right at the seam.

Step 33. Make a square corner at the sleeve seam. Continue over the shoulder, across the back yoke, over the other shoulder, across the other front yoke, up the front overlap and around the neck.

Step 34. Turn under 1/2 inch at each end and stitch (**fig. 24**).

Step 35. Close with two buttons and buttonholes.

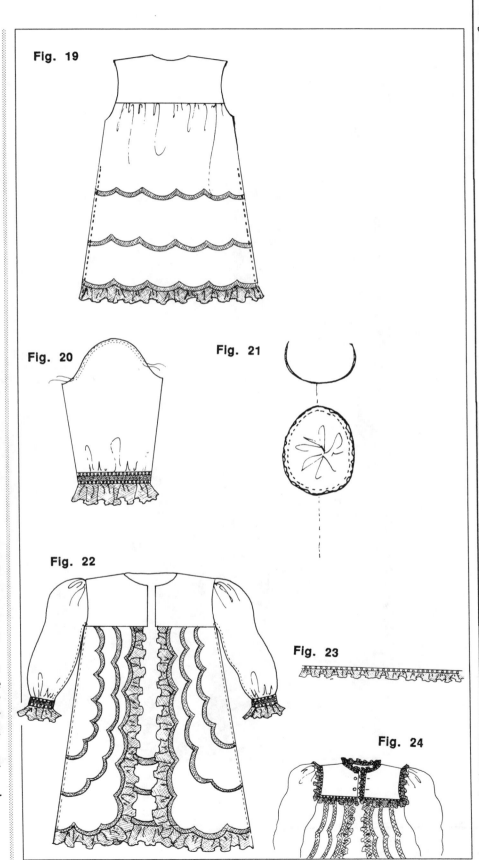

Fig. 19

Fig. 20

Fig. 21

Fig. 22

Fig. 23

Fig. 24

154

Gifts

ANGEL WRIST RATTLE

Angel Supplies
Ecru satin (face and wrist strap)
Yellow broadcloth (wings)
Lightweight fusible interfacing
Machine embroidery thread
  pink, flesh, yellow
DMC floss Choose several different colors
  of yellow (2 yards of each color) to give
  hair a shaded color. Separate strands of
  each color and then place back together.
Scrap of lace (7-1/2 inches long)
Batting or fleece
Spring tension hoop
Water soluble stabilizer
1-inch velcro
Open-toe applique foot
Open darning foot or darning spring
Bell (slightly flattened with a hammer)

Angel Pattern

CONSTRUCTION

Step 1. Interface square of satin. Place square of fabric right side up in hoop with two layers of water soluble stabilizer on wrong side. Trace outside of design and facial features onto right side with water soluble pen or pencil **(fig. 1)**.

Step 2. Use free motion embroidery with a straight stitch to outline eye, nose, and mouth. Straight stitch, just outside edge of outline, two times with a stitch length of about one **(fig. 2)**.

Step 3. Place three to five strands of different colors of DMC embroidery floss together as one thick strand. Use a matching yellow machine embroidery thread in needle. Take a few stitches to anchor (or tie on).

Step 4. Still using free motion techniques, anchor strand of floss in seam allowance by stitching over floss several times with a straight stitch. Remember to lower presser foot bar and move the hoop since there is no presser foot or feed dogs. Use a long slender firm object such as a bodkin, shish kabob stick or knitting needle to loop floss. Stitch loop in place, stitching back and forth over the loop end by moving the hoop **(fig. 3)**. Be careful not to stitch on the bodkin or knitting needle. Repeat the looping and stitching as desired. Start a second row next to first row, pushing the completed loops aside with the bodkin while forming new loops **(fig. 4)**. Finish by anchoring well in the seam allowance, and trimming excess floss. Keep loop height consistent for a smoother look.

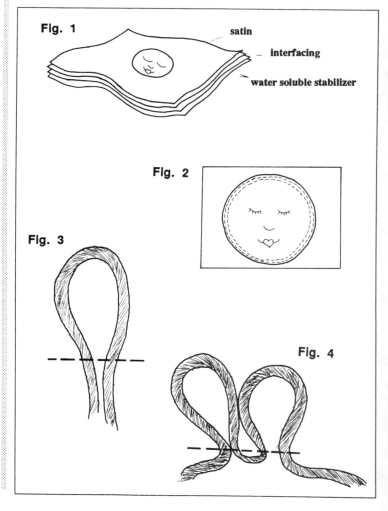

Fig. 1

satin

interfacing

water soluble stabilizer

Fig. 2

Fig. 3

Fig. 4

Step 5. Trace wing design onto wrong side of interfaced square of wing fabric (large enough for both wings). Layer as follows: batting or fleece, interfaced wing fabric without design (right side up), and wing fabric with design facing up (right side down). Stitch on design line using a short, narrow zigzag stitch (W=1, L= 1/2 to 1) **fig. 5.**

Step 6. Trim close to stitching and clip curves. Turn and press wings. Pin finished wings into position to wrong side of face fabric, keeping seam allowances of wings inside seam allowance of face. (You still have a square of fabric with facial features and hair stitched, and outline of head.) **Fig. 6.**

Step 7. Layer: square of interfaced satin for back (right side down), a layer of batting, and square for front with wings pinned or basted in place. Straight stitch on drawn line. Straight stitch a second time just to outside of first stitching. Zigzag, encasing these rows of parallel stitching (not a satin stitch) **fig. 7.** Trim close to zigzag stitching. Be careful not to cut stitching. Satin stitch over edge using a wide enough stitch to go completely off the edge to encase raw edges **(fig. 8).**

Step 8. In center of back, place a line of FRAY CHECK or other seam sealant. Let dry. Slit in the middle of the FRAY CHECK line with a seam ripper and stuff with extra batting and bell. Slip stitch the opening closed.

Step 9. Cut a 2-1/2- inch by 8-inch strip of satin for wrist band and a 1-inch by 8-inch of batting. Stitch long edge of fabric with a 1/4-inch seam allowance, leaving an opening in center for turning. Press seam open with seam in center **(fig. 9).** Lay batting under wristband and stitch short edges of band and batting together **(fig. 10).** Trim the corners and turn band to right side. This will cover the batting. Press and slip stitch opening closed.

Step 10. Position wrist band on back of face. Hand stitch in place. Stitch velcro in place **(fig. 11).**

Step 11. Finish short edges of lace. Gather to fit placement of lace on front. Zigzag lace to edge **(fig. 12).**

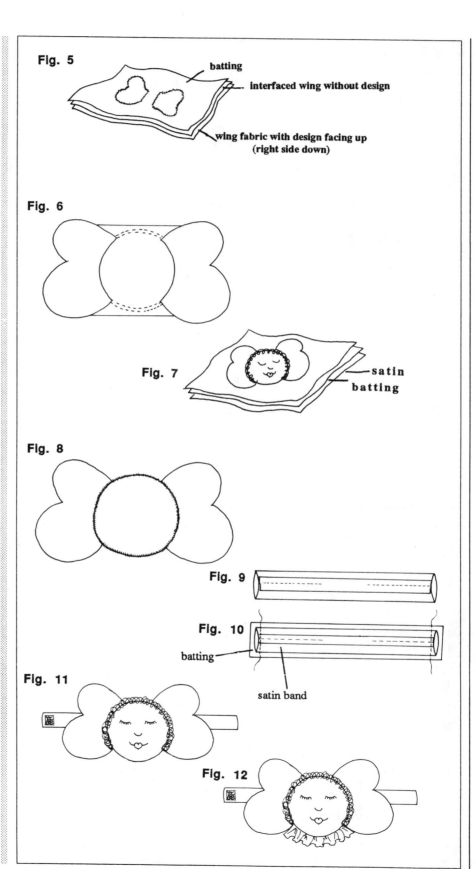

Fig. 5

batting

interfaced wing without design

wing fabric with design facing up (right side down)

Fig. 6

Fig. 7

satin
batting

Fig. 8

Fig. 9

Fig. 10

batting

satin band

Fig. 11

Fig. 12

157

BUNNY WRIST RATTLE

Bunny Supplies

Pink fabric (face and wrist strap)
Light pink fabric (ears)
Machine embroidery thread
  white, dark pink
DMC floss (ears)
Light weight fusible interfacing
Batting or fleece

Spring tension hoop
Water soluble stabilizer
1-inch velcro
Open-toe applique foot
Open darning foot or darning spring
Bell (slightly flattened with hammer)

CONSTRUCTION

Follow angel directions replacing ears for wings. Use free motion embroidery for facial features and looping technique of floss for ear centers.

Bunny Pattern

CRAZY STITCH BEARS

Supplies

- Variety of machine embroidery threads, different colors and kinds (Sulky, DMC, Mettler)
- 3 pieces broadcloth or other medium to heavy-weight fabric (2 inches larger around design).
- 1 piece batting same size as front
- Polyfill
- Water soluble pen or pencil
- Scraps of ribbon and lace and lace motifs
- 1/4-inch ribbon to seperate areas after stitching
- Ruler
- Water soluble stabilizer (Several layers to be placed under broadcloth or batiste. Tear away or stitch and tear away products can be used, but excessive tearing away after delicate stitching can damage stitches. Wide zigzag stitches will require more stabilizing.)
- Bear Pattern From Pattern Envelope

CONSTRUCTION

Step 1. Spray starch fabric

Step 2. Using a water-soluble pen or pencil divide square into random sections **(fig. 1)**.

Step 3. Layer: Water soluble stabilizer and fabric right side up. Pin together.

Step 4. Position lace motifs and lace and ribbon scraps as desired in different areas. Pin in place.

Step 5. Choose different threads and automatic decorative stitches at random to stitch each area, stopping and starting at the drawn lines. Stitch in different directions and angles to give a quilted look **(fig. 2)**.

Step 6. After completing all sections, place 1/4-inch ribbon on drawn lines, covering the lines and the ends of the stitching in each area. Be careful not to have raw edges of the ribbon exposed. Stitch ribbon on each side with a straight stitch **(fig. 3)**.

Step 7. Wash fabric to remove all markings and water soluble stabilizer.

Step 8. Press right side down on terry cloth towel.

Step 9. Trace outline of pattern on crazy stitched fabric with water soluble pen or pencil **(fig. 4)**.

Step 10. Using a narrow, short zigzag stitch, stitch 1/8 to 1/4 inch in from drawn line **(fig. 5)**.

Step 11. Layer: plain fabric (right side down), batting, fabric and top decorative layer (right side up). Pin together in several places.

Step 12. Using a small zigzag, stitch 1/2 inch in from around drawn edge, leaving a 2-inch opening **(fig. 6)**.

Step 13. Cut out, on drawn line, through all layers **(fig. 7)**.

Step 14. Stuff to desired fullness.

Step 15. Stitch opening closed.

NOTE: For string of three bears, place ribbon at ends of arms between layers before final stitching.

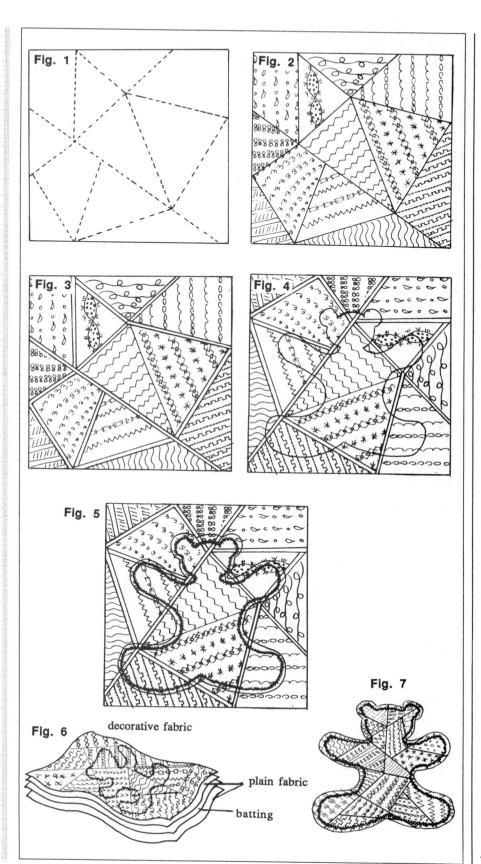

Fig. 1 Fig. 2 Fig. 3 Fig. 4 Fig. 5

Fig. 6 decorative fabric plain fabric batting

Fig. 7

BIB

Supplies
1/3 yard fabric
1-1/2 yards lace edging
  (1/2 inch to 5/8 inch wide)
Optional: Floss for embroidery,
  lace strips, embroidery strips etc.
Inner Bib pattern from envelope
Outer Bib pattern from envelope

▓ CONSTRUCTION

Step 1. Cut two inner bibs of fabric. (Optional: one piece of thin batting.) Place the two pieces right sides together **(fig. 1)** with the batting on top of the two pieces of fabric **(fig. 2).**

Step 2. Stitch around the outer edge of the bib using a 1/4-inch seam **(fig. 3).** Turn to right side through the neck opening **(fig. 4).** (The batting will be inside the two layers of fabric.)

Step 3. Cut one bib from the outer bib pattern. This layer of fabric can be cut from created fabric of laces, embroideries, etc **(fig. 5).** Or, embroidery can be stitched on a square of fabric and this layer of bib can be cut from this **(fig. 6).**

Step 4. Using Martha's Magic, attach gathered lace to the outer edge of this bib layer **(fig. 7).**

Step 5. Place the outer layer to the inner layer, right side together. Stitch around the neck edge, using a 1/4-inch seam. Trim to 1/8-inch and overcast using a zigzag or serger **(fig. 8).** Flip the outer layer of the bib to the front hiding the neck seam.

Step 6. Create a buttonloop on the edge of the bib neck. Attach a button to the other side for closure **(fig. 9).**

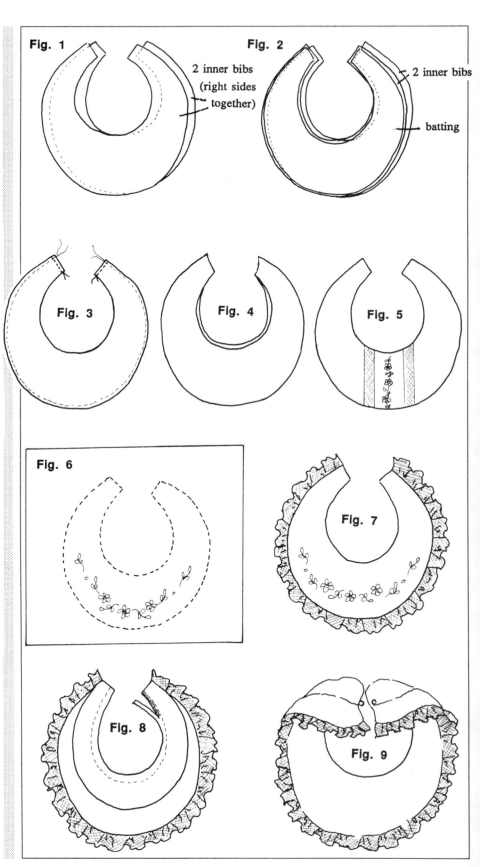

Fig. 1

Fig. 2 — 2 inner bibs (right sides together) — 2 inner bibs — batting

Fig. 3

Fig. 4

Fig. 5

Fig. 6

Fig. 7

Fig. 8

Fig. 9

Grandmother's Hope Chest

Supplies
One piece of organdy to pintuck 4 inches wide
by 20 inches long.
1 yard 1/2-inch or 5/8-inch lace insertion
2-3/4 yards 1-inch lace edging
1 yard 1/2-inch ribbon
1-1/3 yards 1/4-inch ribbon

CONSTRUCTION

This precious bonnet is easy to make on the sewing machine and will fit a tiny baby as well as an older child by simply tying the ribbons differently. Made as a gift, this bonnet would only cost about $10.

Step 1. Pintuck the organdy at 1/4-inch intervals.
Note: Pintucking is optional. Any fabric or decorative material can be used. For example, embroidered insertion, machine-made embroidery on organdy or batiste, or ribbon can be used instead of pintucked organdy.

Step 2. Cut one piece of pintucked organdy 14 inches by 1 inch. This is the strip for across the head (**fig. 1**).

Step 3. Cut one piece of pintucked organdy 6-3/4 inches by 1 inch. This is the center back strip (**fig. 2**).

Step 4. Using the technique, "Martha's Magic" zigzag the insertion to both sides of both pieces. Do not carry the insertion around the ends of the pieces. Leave them raw (**fig. 3**).

Step 5. Cut two 4-1/2-inch pieces of lace edging. Put these aside. They will later be used for making lace medallions where the ribbon attaches to tie under the chin.

Step 6. Using the rest of the lace insertion, gather and distribute it to go around all sides of the 14-inch piece and to go around three sides of the 6-3/4-inch piece. Be sure to put extra fullness of the gathered lace edging as you travel around the corners. Zigzag the gathered lace edging to the lace insertion on both pieces. When you travel around the unfinished corners on the 14-inch piece, simply place the gathered edging on top of the unfinished organdy and zigzag on top of the lace edging. If there is any excess organdy underneath the zigzagged lace, trim it away. You can probably stitch closely enough to the edge that this trimming won't be necessary (**fig. 4**).

Step 7. Center the unfinished edge of the 6-3/4-inch piece under the 14-inch piece, creating the "T." Zigzag the back strip to the front strip where the insertion joins the edging of the front strip (**fig. 5**).

Construction Instructions continued on next page.

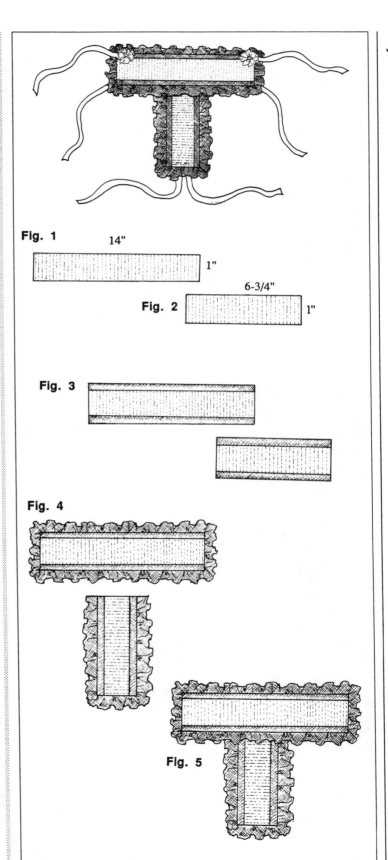

Fig. 1   14"
1"

Fig. 2   6-3/4"
1"

Fig. 3

Fig. 4

Fig. 5

LACY TUCKED BONNET

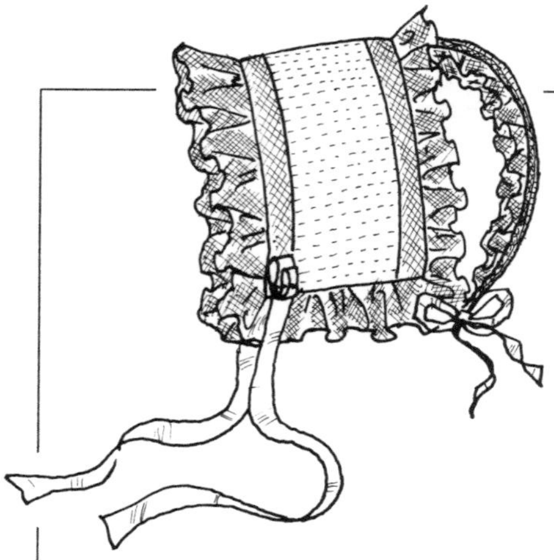

Step 8. Cut the 1-yard-piece of 1/2-inch ribbon in half. These are the ties for the 14-inch piece of the bonnet which will tie under the chin. To create ribbon folds, mark (with straight pins) the ribbon from one end as follows: 1-1/4 inches, 2-1/4 inches, and 3-1/2 inches. Fold the ribbon at the 1-1/4-inch mark. Fold the ribbon in the opposite direction at the 2-1/4-inch mark and again in the opposite direction at the 3-1/3-inch mark. Fold the 1/4-inch extension under the first fold. Stitch along the lower edge by hand or machine. Place along the front corner of the bonnet and stitch in place by hand or machine. Repeat for other side of bonnet **(fig. 6)**.

Step 9. Cut the 1/4-inch ribbon into four, 12-inch pieces. Fold one end of the ribbon to the inside 1/4 inch and stitch to each remaining corner of the bonnet **(fig. 7)**.

Step 10. Using one of the 4-1/2-inch pieces of lace edging, place right sides together and stitch ends together using a tight zigzag. Pull the gathering thread in the top of the lace at the cut ends. Tie the pull threads together. Place lace flowerette over ribbon and stitch in place by hand. Repeat for other side of bonnet **(fig. 8)**.

Fig. 6

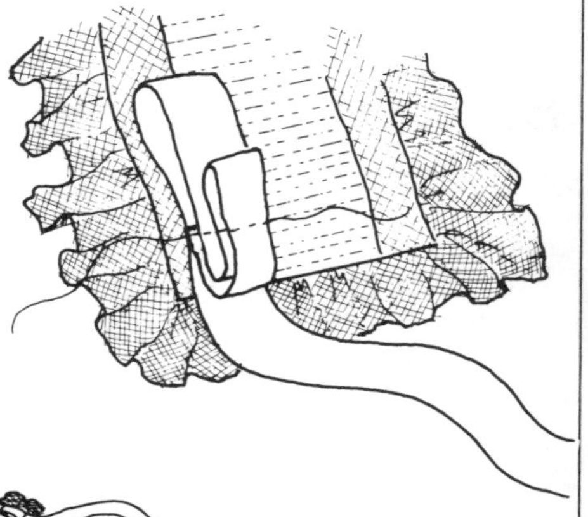

Fig. 7

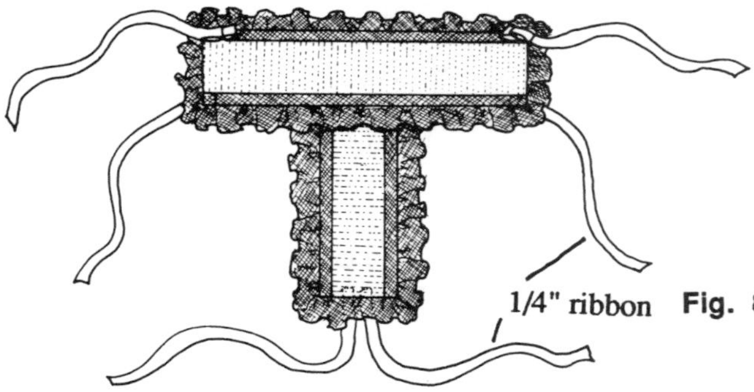

1/2" ribbon

1/4" ribbon   **Fig. 8**

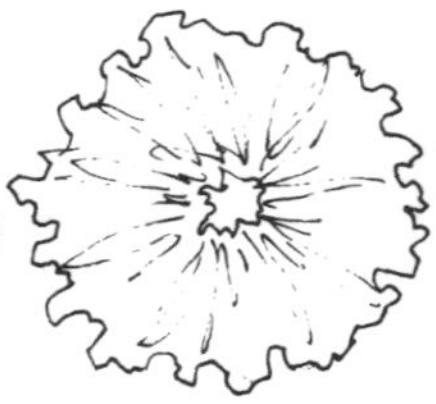

FANCY FRENCH BONNET

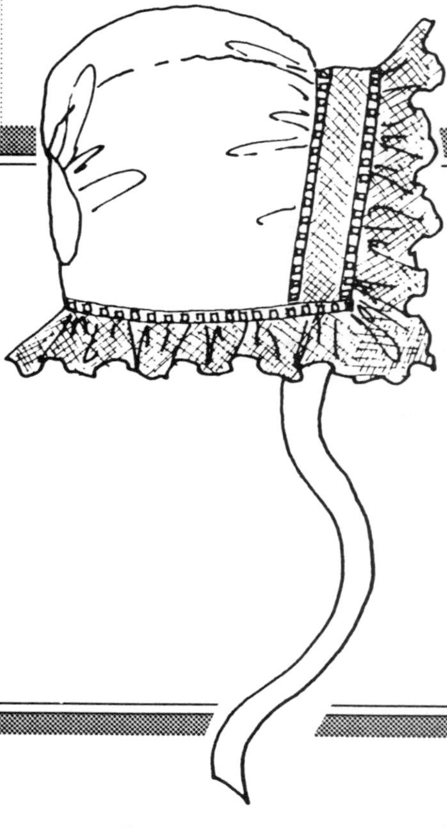

Supplies
- 1/4 yard Organdy
- 2 yards of 1/2-inch edging
- 1 yard 7/8-inch or 5/8-inch ribbon
- *Newborn:* 10-1/2 inches of 1-1/4-inch lace insertion and 1 yard entredeux
- *Small:* 12 inches of 1/2-inch lace insertion and 1 yard entredeux
- *Medium:* 13 inches of 1-3/4 yards and 1-1/8 yards entredeux
- *Large:* 14 inches of 2-inch lace insertion and 1-1/8 yards entredeux

Pattern can be found in accompanying envelope.

FANCY FRENCH BONNET

CONSTRUCTION

Step 1. Cut bonnet, bonnet lining, and circle using the pattern for Fancy French Bonnet. Run two gathering rows, 1/4 inch and 1/8 inch, in the front of the bonnet and the back of the bonnet. Stop 1/2 inch from the ends. Do the same in the lining **(fig. 1)**.

Step 2. Place center backs of the bonnet right sides together and stitch using a 1/4-inch seam. Repeat for the bonnet lining **(fig. 2)**.

Step 3. Place the wrong side of the bonnet to the wrong side of the lining. Pin center back bonnet to center back lining and back fold of bonnet to back fold of lining. Gather bonnet to fit lining. Pin front fold line of bonnet to front fold line of lining. Gather bonnet to fit lining **(fig. 3)**.

Step 4. Mark the four points on the back circular hole of the bonnet, top center back, bottom center back and the sides. Divide the fabric circle into four equal points. Place the right side of the circle to the right side of the bonnet opening and stitch using a 1/4-inch seam. Overcast seam allowance with a zigzag **(fig. 4)**.

Step 5. Attach entredeux to each side of the lace insertion strip, using the method entredeux to fabric. This is the band for the bonnet front.

Step 6. Attach band to bonnet front (stitch through both lining and bonnet) using the method entredeux to gathered fabric. Trim band ends even with the ends of the bonnet **(fig. 5)**.

Step 7. Attach a piece of entredeux to the lower edge of the bonnet using the method entredeux to fabric.

Step 8. Starting at the center back, gather lace edging and attach to the entredeux around the bonnet using the method entredeux to gathered lace **(fig. 6)**.

Step 9. Cut ribbon in half and stitch under lace edging to the upper and lower edge of the entredeux **(fig. 7)**.

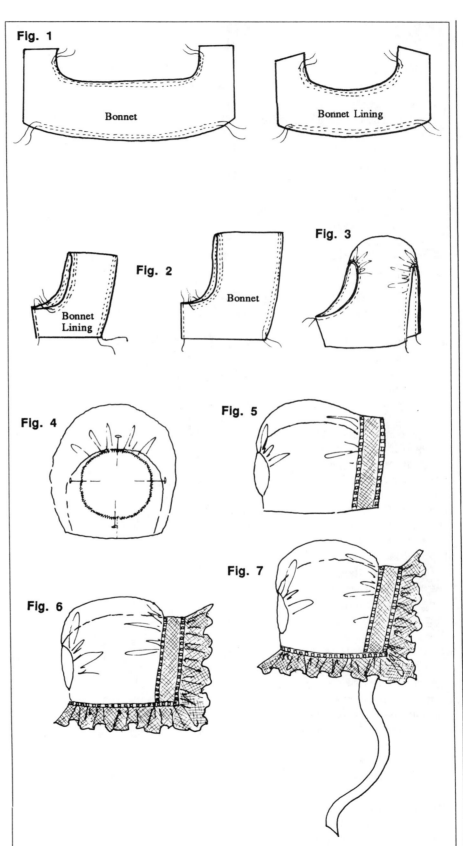

NETTING BONNET

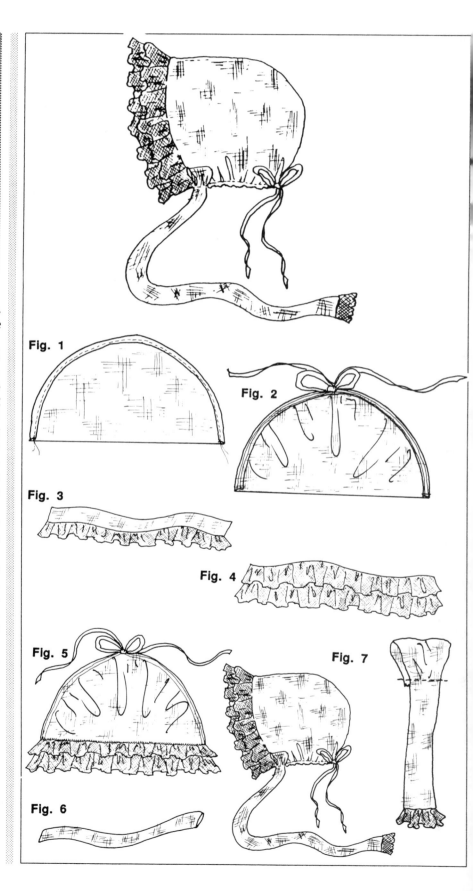

◼ CONSTRUCTION

Step 1. Cut pattern from netting square. Serge or zigzag the outer curved edge of the bonnet.

Step 2. Turn this edge under 1/4 inch and stitch in place to create a casing **(fig. 1)**.

Step 3. Cut two piece of ribbon 18 inches long. Run a ribbon through the casing starting at the front of the bonnet and pushing the ribbon through the netting at the center back. Tack the end of the ribbon in place along the front edge. Repeat for the other side. Tie ribbon to measurement given on pattern piece **(fig. 2)**.

Step 4. Ruffle: Attach one lace piece to netting strip, using Martha's Magic method **(fig. 3)**.

Step 5. Place the second piece of lace 1/4-inch from the cut end of the netting, wrong side of lace to right side on netting/lace. Stitch in place using a gathering stitch. Gather to fit the front edge of the bonnet **(fig. 4)**.

Step 6. Place the ruffle to the bonnet, right sides together. Stitch using a 1/4-inch seam. Overcast or serge the seam allowance. Stitch the seam allowance to the bonnet using a tiny zigzag **(fig. 5)**.

Step 7. Place the long sides of one netting tie piece right side. Stitch using a 1/4-inch seam. Repeat for the other tie. Turn ties to the right side **(fig. 6)**.

Step 8. Zigzag edging lace to the ends of the ties. Place a 1-inch loop in the other end of the tie. Zigzag loop in place along front side of the bonnet **(fig. 7)**.

Fig. 1

Fig. 2

Fig. 3

Fig. 4

Fig. 5

Fig. 6

Fig. 7

Grandmother's Hope Chest

SMOCKED BONNET

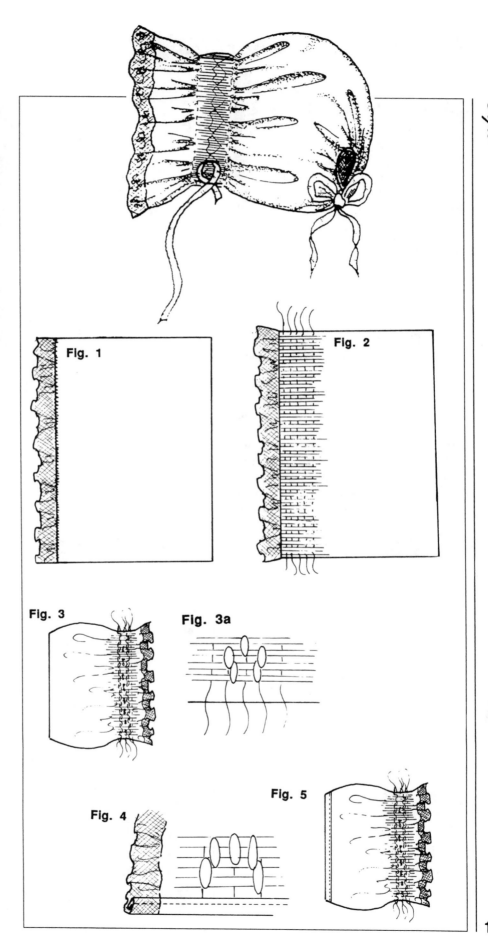

Fig. 8

Supplies
- 1/4 yard fabric (P - 6 months)
  1/3 yard fabric (6 months -18 months)
- 1 yard of 1/2-inch ribbon
- 1/3 yard of 1/4-inch ribbon
- 1-1/4 yard of 1/2-inch lace edging

Cut or tear fabric to desired size:
Preemie-0: 8 inches by 36 inches
0-6 months: 9 inches by 40 inches
6-12 months: 9-1/2 inches by 45 inches
12-18 months: 10 inches by 45 inches

CONSTRUCTION

Step 1. Attach lace to one long side of the bonnet using the lace-to-fabric method **(fig. 1).**

Step 2. Pleating - Measure from the edge of the lace 3/4 inch for a 0-6 months and 1-1/4 inch for the other sizes. Run your first pleating row at this measurement. Pleat 5 rows; you will smock 3 (more or less rows can be run if desired) **fig. 2.**

Step 3. Smock on the middle three rows leaving 1/4 inch along the short sides unsmocked **(fig. 3).** Pull out pleating threads **(fig. 3a).**

Step 4. Finish these short edges by turning under 1/8 inch and 1/8 inch again. Stitch **(fig. 4).**

Step 5. Turn back edge under 1/8 inch and again 3/8 inch. Press in place. Stitch along the inside edge creating a casing **(fig. 5).**

Step 6. Thread smaller ribbon through the casing. Pull ends to form a circle and tie in a bow. Attach ribbons to the sides of the bonnet at the smocking.

Fig. 1

Fig. 2

Fig. 3

Fig. 3a

Fig. 4

Fig. 5

BATTENBERG PLACEMAT BONNET

▨ CONSTRUCTION

Step 1. Fold placemat in half or almost in half creating a rectangle 18 inches by 7 inches.

Step 2. Stitch 3/8 inch from the folded edge of the rectangle creating a casing **(fig. 1)**.

Step 3. Run two gathering rows at the front of the bonnet, 4-5/8-inches from the back fold and 5 inches from the back fold **(fig. 2)**.

Step 4. Gather to 11 inches for newborn size or 12 inches for 3 to 6 month size.

Step 5. Center 1/2 inch ribbon over gathering threads. Zigzag in place over outer edges of ribbon. Fold ribbon on the sides of the bonnet to create a loop. Stitch in place **(fig. 3)**.

Step 6. Run the 1/4-inch ribbon through the back of the bonnet. Pull bonnet back into a circle and tie in a bow.

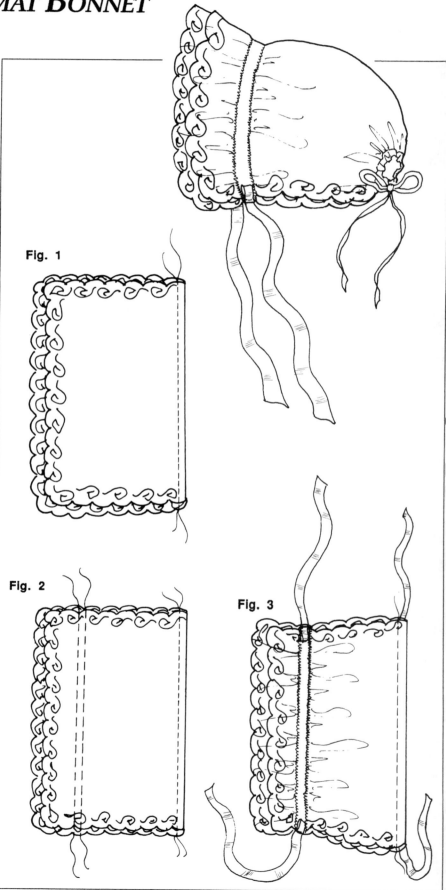

Fig. 1

Fig. 2

Fig. 3

Grandmother's Hope Chest

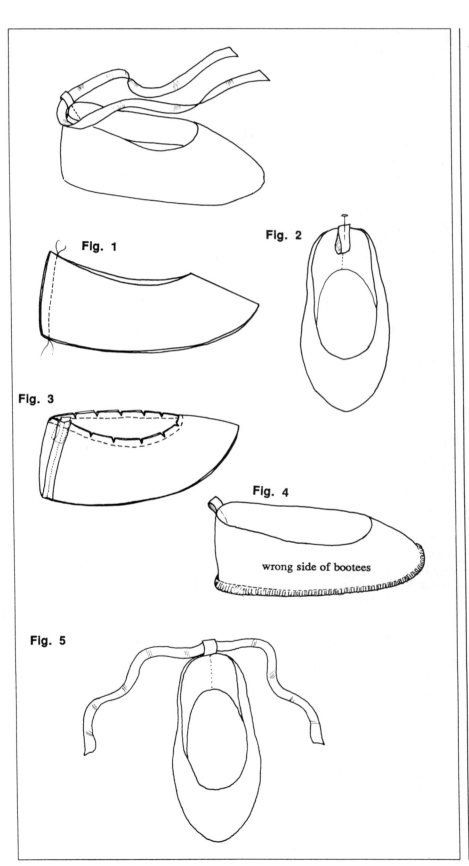

Fig. 1

Fig. 2

Fig. 3

Fig. 4

wrong side of bootees

Fig. 5

Bootee Supplies
- 1/4 yard of fabric
- 1/4 yard medium or light weight interfacing (optional)
- Thread
- 1 yard 1/4-inch ribbon (Ballet, Scalloped or Tied Bootees Only)
- Two tiny baby buttons (Buttoned Bootees Only)

*Additional notions listed in decorating directions
*All bootee patterns found in pattern envelope.

* Note for all bootees: For a stiffer bootee, place interfacing along the wrong side of the bootee lining and treat as one layer.

CONSTRUCTION

Step 1. Place back of bootee right sides together and stitch using a 1/4-inch seam allowance **(fig. 1)**. Repeat for lining piece.

Step 2. Cut a piece of 1/4-inch ribbon 1-1/2 inches long, loop and pin to the right side of the top of the bootee at the back seam **(fig. 2)**.

Step 3. Place the lining to bootee, right sides together, and stitch around top edge using a 1/4-inch seam. Clip the curves of the seam allowance **(fig. 3)**.

Step 4. Turn the bootee right side out and press. Flip bootee lining over bootee so seam is between lining and bootee.

Step 5. Run two easing rows around lower edge at 1/8 inch and 1/4 inch.

Step 6. Place right side of the bootee to the right side of the sole (two layers of fabric treated as one layer). Match the center back of the sole to the back seam of the bootee and the center front of the sole to the center front of the bootee. Gather bootee to fit the sole. Stitch in place using a 1/4-inch seam. Overcast the seam using a zigzag **(fig. 4)**.

Step 7. Turn bootee to the right side. Thread 17 inches of ribbon through the ribbon loop **(fig. 5)**.

Step 8. Repeat steps 1-7 for other bootee.

BOOTEES - TIED AND BUTTONED

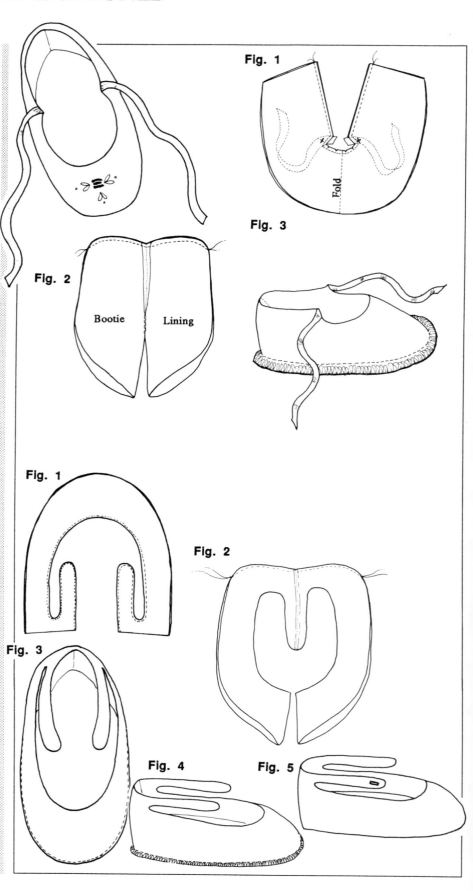

▨ TIED BOOTEES

Step 1. Cut two pieces of ribbon 7 inches long. Place ribbon to bootee at the x. Pin in place.

Step 2. Place the right side of the bootee to the right side of the lining. Stitch inside using a 1/4-inch seam **(fig. 1)**.

Step 3. Place the linings right sides together and the bootees right sides together. Stitch along the back using a 1/4-inch seam **(fig. 2)**.

Step 4. Flip bootee over lining, turning the bootee to the right side.

Step 5. Place right side of the bootee to the right side of the sole (two layers of fabric treated as one layer). Match the center back of the sole to the back seam of the bootee and the center front of the sole to the center front of the bootee. Stitch in place using a 1/4-inch seam. Overcast the seam using a zigzag **(fig. 3)**. Turn to right side.

▨ BUTTONED BOOTEES

Step 1. Place the right side of the bootee to the right side of the lining. Stitch inside edges using a 1/8-inch seam **(fig. 1)**.

Step 2. Place the linings right sides together and the bootees right sides together. Stitch along the back using a 1/4-inch seam **(fig. 2)**.

Step 3. Flip bootee over lining, turning bootee and straps to right side.

Step 4. Run two gathering rows around lower edge of bootee at 1/8 inch and 1/4 inch **(fig. 3)**.

Step 5. Place right side of the bootee to the right side of the sole (two layers of fabric treated as one layer). Match the center back of the sole to the back seam of the bootee and the center front of the sole to the center front of the bootee. Gather the bootee to fit the sole. Stitch in place using a 1/4-inch seam. Overcast the seam using a zigzag **(fig. 4)**.

Step 6. Turn bootee to the right side. Work a tiny buttonhole in the bootee strap **(fig. 5)** or use floss to make a button loop.

▨ SCALLOPED BOOTEES

Step 1. Draw bootee pattern on fabric rectangle (**fig. 1**).

Step 2. Scallop around the inside edge of bootee and outside edge of the toe (**fig. 2**).

Step 3. Trim scallops and cut out bootee. Pin toe in place (**fig. 3**).

Step 4. Place bootee backs right sides together. Stitch using a 1/4-inch seam. Overcast using a zigzag (**fig. 4**).

Step 5. Follow steps 4 - 6 of *Buttoned Bootee* to complete bootee. Stitch ties in place on each side (**fig. 5**).

▨ BOOTEES EMBELLISHMENTS

Lace Strips (fig. 6)
***Additional Notion Requirements:**
5 inches lace insertion
10 inches entredeux
20 inches of lace edging

Step 1. Trace bootee pattern on fabric to be decorated.

Step 2. Create a 5-inch fancy band of lace insertion, entredeux and edging lace.

Step 3. Cut this band in half and place the center of the lace insertion along the center front of the bootee. Zigzag in place along the entredeux.

Step 4. Cut bootee from created fabric. Cut bootee linings from remaining fabric.

Step 5. Construct as Tied Bootee.

Embroidered (fig. 7)
***Additional Notion Requirements:**
Embriodery floss
Embroidery hoop
Embroidery needles

Step 1. Trace bootee pattern on fabric to be embroidered.

Step 2. Mark the 1/4-inch seam allowance to achieve correct placement for the embroidery.

Step 3. Place bootee in hoop and embroider.

Step 4. Cut bootees from created fabric and bootee linings from remaining fabric.

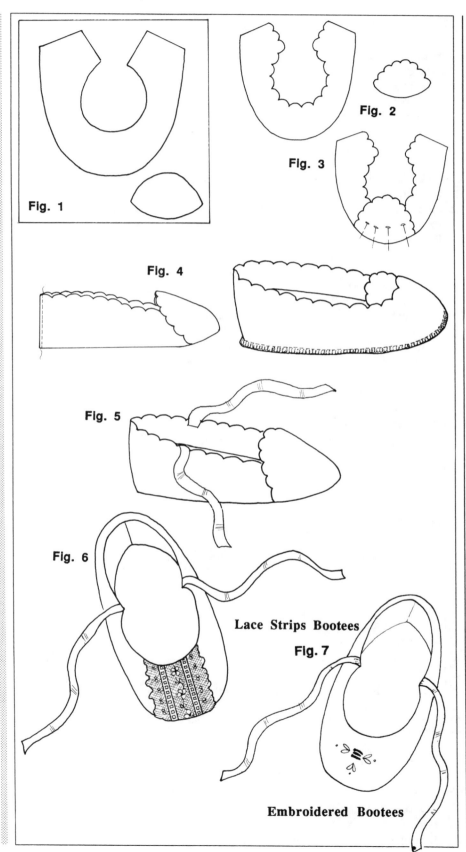

Fig. 1

Fig. 2

Fig. 3

Fig. 4

Fig. 5

Fig. 6

Fig. 7

Lace Strips Bootees

Embroidered Bootees

169

BOOTEES

![img](BOTTEES EMBELLISHMENTS)

▦ BOTTEES EMBELLISHMENTS

Pintucking (fig. 8)
* Additional Notions Requirement:
Pintuck foot
Double Needle
Two spools of lightweight cotton thread

Step 1. Pintuck two fabric pieces to a 6-inch by 6-inch square.
Step 2. Starch and press. Trace pattern on pintucked fabric. Stitch just inside the cutting lines.
Step 3. Cut out bootees from created fabric and bootee linings from remaining fabric. Construct as Tied Bootees.

All Lace Bootees (fig. 9)
*Additional Notion Requirements
Approximately 4-2/3 yards of 1/2-inch lace insertion

Step 1. Create two squares of lace 6 inches by 6 inches. These lace pieces should be created using identical lace strips in the center of the squares and additional strips along each side of the center strip. The square will be folded down the center, on top of the bootee.
Step 2. Starch very heavily and press!
Step 3. Trace the bootee pattern on the lace square.
Step 4. Stitch just inside the cutting lines.
Step 5. Cut and construct. Use netting or fabric as lining.

HOPPY THE RABBIT

> ### Supplies
> - 2/3 yards fabric
> - 3-1/2 yards of 5/8-inch or 7/8-inch double face satin ribbon
> - 1 yard of 1/4-inch ribbon
> - One bag of poly-fil
> - Two 1/2-inch buttons
> - Ribbon floss or embroidery floss for the nose
> *Pattern found in pattern envelope.

▦ CUTTING GUIDES

Cut one of the following - Back body (on fold), Front body (on fold), Bottom (on fold) and Tail
Cut two of the following - Head, Top leg and Back leg
Cut four of the following - Ears and arms

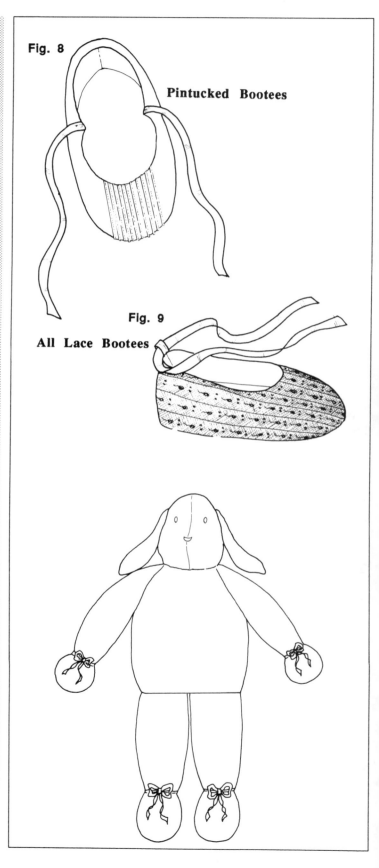

Fig. 8

Pintucked Bootees

Fig. 9

All Lace Bootees

Step 1. Place two arm pieces right sides together and stitch using a 1/4-inch seam **(fig. 1)**. Repeat for other arm. Turn arms to right side and stuff leaving 1-inch free from stuffing at the top of the arm.

Step 2. Run a gathering stitch in the foot of the back leg **(fig. 2)**. Stitch a dart in the foot of the top leg by folding the foot to the leg and stitching **(fig. 3)**.

Step 3. Place the back leg to the front leg, gather the back leg at the foot to fit the top leg. Pin in place and stitch using a 1/4-inch seam **(fig. 4)**. Turn to the right side and stuff stopping the stuffing 1 inch from the top of the leg.

Step 4. Place bottom to lower back, right sides together and stitch using a 1/4-inch seam **(fig. 5)**.

Step 5. Place front to back along the sides and stitch using a 1/4-inch seam **(fig. 6)**.

Step 6. Place the legs between the right side of the bodice back and right side of the bodice front. Pin in place and stitch using a 1/4-inch seam **(fig. 7)**. Stitch lower edge of back opening into a dart **(fig. 8)**. Turn to right side.

Step 7. Place the ears right sides together and stitch at 1/4-inch seams **(fig. 9)**. Clip curves and turn to the right side. Repeat for other ear. Place the ear to right side of one head piece along placement line and stitch using a 1/8-inch seam **(fig. 10)**. Flip ear toward top of head and stitch enclosing the seam allowance of the first seam **(fig. 11)**.

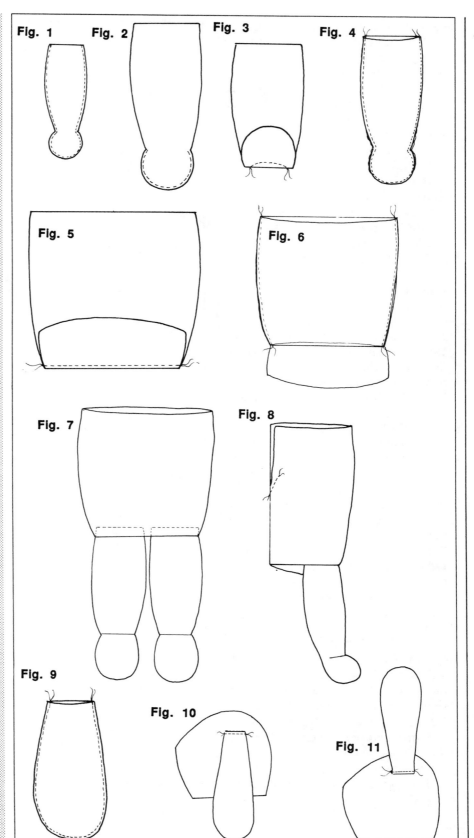

Fig. 1 Fig. 2 Fig. 3 Fig. 4 Fig. 5 Fig. 6 Fig. 7 Fig. 8 Fig. 9 Fig. 10 Fig. 11

HOPPY THE RABBIT

Step 8. Place head pieces right sides together and stitch using a 1/4-inch seam, stopping 3-inch from the lower edge of the head **(fig. 12)**.

Step 9. Place arms to body centering arms on side seams of body at the neck edge. Pin in place. Run a gathering stitch 1/4-inch from the neck edge **(fig. 13)**. Gather neck/arms to fit the head match the center of the head with the center of the body and arms to side of head. Turn the edges of the back opening and the edges of the head opening to the inside 1/4-inch. Match these folds. Stitch using a 1/4-inch seam **(fig. 14)**.

Step 10. Stuff the head (tight) and body. Stitch, with floss or silk ribbon, the nose using a satin stitch. Close the back with hand stitching.

Step 11. Tail - Run a gathering thread 1/4 inch from the edge of the circle **(fig. 15)**. Gather slightly and stuff with batting. Pull gathers tight and tie the two gathering threads together **(fig. 16)**. Hand stitch tail to the back of the bunny **(fig. 17)**.

Step 12. Tie 15 inches of ribbon on each leg in a bow and 13 inches of ribbon on each arm in a bow. Tie 10 inches of ribbon in a bow for each ear. Tack bow to the top of the ear **(fig. 18)**.

Step 13. Dress: Create a strip of fabric 12 inches wide by 36 inches long. Finish the short end of the strip by turning the edge to the inside 1/4 inch and 1/4 inch again and straight stitching in place. Stitch a gathering row 1/4 inch from the top edge and gather to 10 inches. Center this 10 inch piece to the center of a ribbon 1-1/4 yards long **(Fig. 19)**. Tie under the arms.

Step 14. Collar: Create a strip of fabric 28 inches long by 4 inches wide. Finish the sides of the strip as described in step 12. Fold under the top edge 1/4 inch and press or serge. Fold under 1/4 inch and press to create a casing. Stitch along the lower edge. Run a 1 yard piece of 1/4 inch ribbon in this casing, gather and tie around the neck **(fig. 20)**.

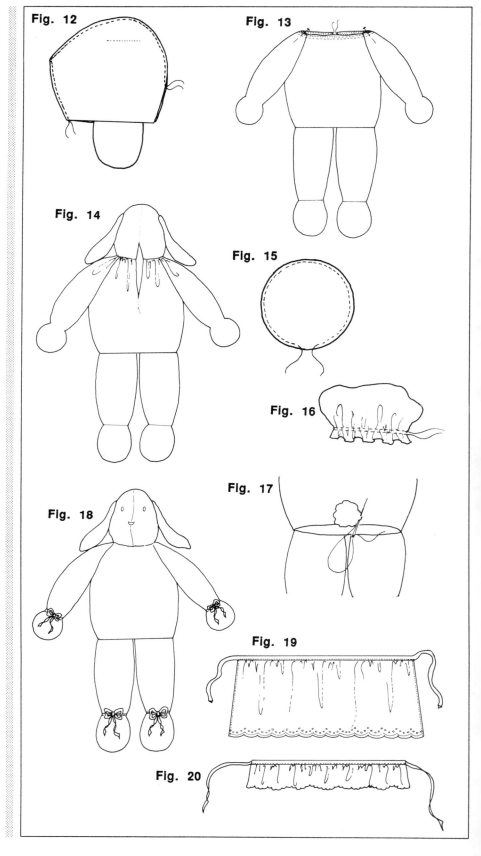

Fig. 12

Fig. 13

Fig. 14

Fig. 15

Fig. 16

Fig. 17

Fig. 18

Fig. 19

Fig. 20

Supplies

- Nainsook (very light weight "see through" fabric), Swiss Batiste, or any "see through" fabric 2-1/2 yards
- White American broadcloth, 1-1/2 yards
- Quilt batting, 2 pieces 27 inches by 36 inches
- Edging lace, 9-1/2 yards
- Scraps of yellow broadcloth
- Water soluble pen or pencil
- Piece of water soluble stabilizer for monogram

- Clean sewing machine in good working order
- Applique foot
- Darning foot (preferably open) or Darning spring
- Safety pins
- DMC Pearl cotton #8 in colors below and Machine Embroidery Thread in colors:
  pink - 605 , blue - 809 , green - 954, yellow - 727
  light grey - 415, flesh - 754, dark grey - 413, white
- Patterns In Pattern Envelope

Step 1. Cut or tear two pieces of nainsook and broadcloth crosswise to 27 inches by 36 inches. The 27 inches is on the selvage edge.

Step 2. Cut out two pieces of extra soft batting , 27 inches by 36 inches **(fig. 1)**.

Step 3. Trace design onto one piece of the nainsook with water soluble pen or pencil. Trace in the center of the fabric and include the cutting as well as the stitching lines **(fig. 2)**.

Step 4. Place yellow broadcloth under (wrong side) of hair area, making sure fabric extends beyond edges of the hair outline. This can be placed in a hoop if desired, with the yellow fabric held in the hoop also. Set sewing machine up with a narrow zigzag (1/2 to 1 stitch width and a 1/2 to 1 stitch length) and open-toe applique foot. Thread with white machine embroidery thread in bobbin and yellow machine embroidery thread in size 70(10) needle on top.

Step 5. Zigzag on traced line **(fig. 3)**. Carefully trim excess yellow fabric from wrong side, close to stitching without cutting the stitching. Repeat for each shadow appliqued area: Stars and boat **(fig. 4)**.

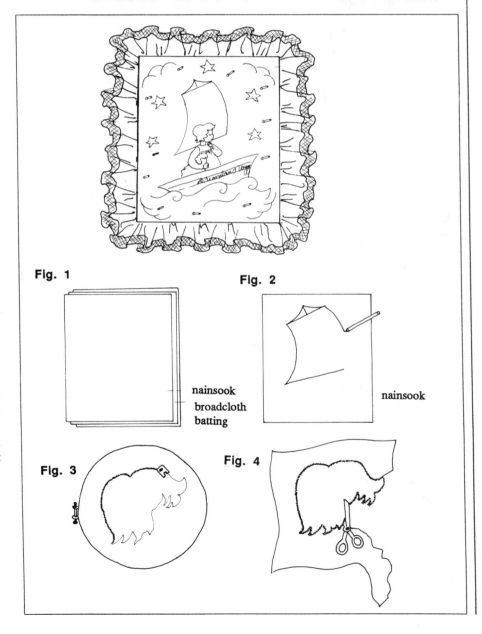

Fig. 1

Fig. 2

nainsook
broadcloth
batting

nainsook

Fig. 3

Fig. 4

DREAMLAND VOYAGE QUILT

Step 6. Layer one piece of batting, broadcloth and nainsook with design right side up, being careful not to have any folds or creases. Use plenty of safety pins to hold layers together, placing them away from stitching lines (**fig. 5**).

Step 7. Starting with the sail, stitch through all layers while guiding the pearl cotton along the marked line. White thread should be in the bobbin and matching pink in the needle. Use an open-toe applique foot or applique foot with hole for pearl cotton to be threaded through. Use a zigzag stitch with a width wide enough to cover pearl cotton (1-1/2 to 2 width, length of 2 to 3). Leave a 4-inch tail of thread and pearl cotton at beginning and end of all lines (**fig. 6**).

Step 8. Work background to foreground (sail first, outside "lattice" next, clouds next, etc). This stitching will anchor the pearl cotton and "quilt" at the same time. Safety pins can be removed as needed.

Step 9. Free motion embroidery was used for dress. Drop feed dogs, lower top thread tension slightly and use darning foot or spring. Straight stitch on lines drawn several times in the blue thead.

Step 10. A machine decorative stitch was used at the neck edge, wrists and yoke with white machine embroidery thread through all layers. The eyes and the mouth of the child and the eyes of the lamb are free motion also.

Step 11. Trace "DREAMLAND VOYAGE" onto piece of water soluble stabilizer. Position and pin in place. Using blue machine embroidery thread and free motion embroidery, stitch over lines with a width of 1 to 1-1/2 one time (in other words monogram). Tear away excess stabilizer (**fig. 7**).

Step 12. After all lines are stitched over with pearl cotton, the tails of thread should be brought to the wrong side. Thread tails into hand sewing needle and draw to wrong side, working the thread into the batting for an inch or more (**fig. 8**). Trim excess thread. Round corners of quilt and stitch all layers together on outside edge with multiple zigzag stitch (**fig. 9**).

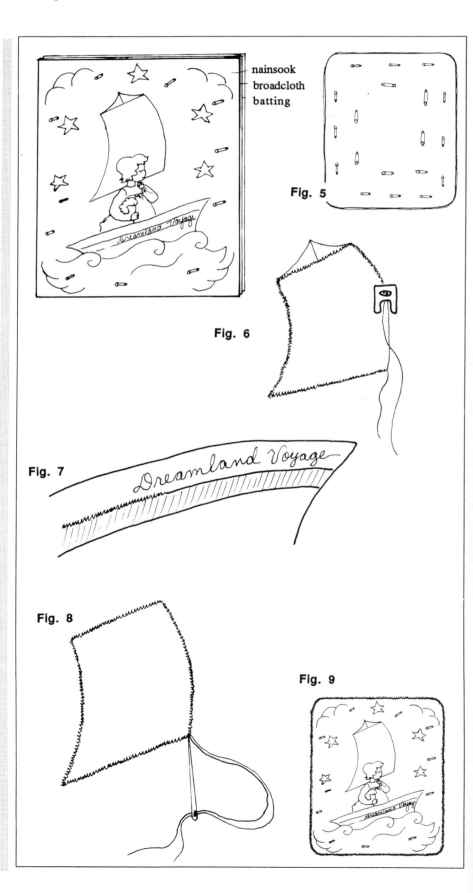

nainsook
broadcloth
batting

Fig. 5

Fig. 6

Fig. 7

Dreamland Voyage

Fig. 8

Fig. 9

Step 13. Cut or tear eight crosswise lengths of nainsook 4-inches wide. The length of the ruffle can be changed to make less full. Stitch 4-inch edges together, making one long strip. Apply lace edging (right sides together) to long edge of nainsook using lace-to-fabric technique. Press open. Stitch edges together to form a circle. Mark ruffle and quilt top at 1/8ths or 1/16ths.

Step 14. Zigzag over a cord (white pearl cotton used here), at seam allowance of ruffle, with a width of approximately 2 and length of 2-3, being careful not to stitch through cord. This cord will be used to gather ruffle to fit quilt top. Pin ruffle to quilt at marks, right sides together. Pull cord to fit quilt between marks and gathers to be evenly spaced.

Step 15. Stitch right side of ruffle to right side of quilt top **(fig. 10).**

Step 16. Layer other pieces of batting, broadcloth and nainsook. Be careful that all is flat without creases. Use safety pins to hold together **(fig. 11).**

Step 17. Place completed top on pinned together back, right sides together. The ruffle will be between the two layers. Stitch around quilt leaving a 6-inch to 8-inch opening in the bottom edge of the quilt for turning. Trim and grade seam allowances after making sure ruffle is not caught in seams. Turn to right side, **(fig. 12),** slip stitch opening closed.

Step 18. Free motion outline quilt the sailboat to hold the front and back together **(fig. 13).** More quilting can be done if desired.

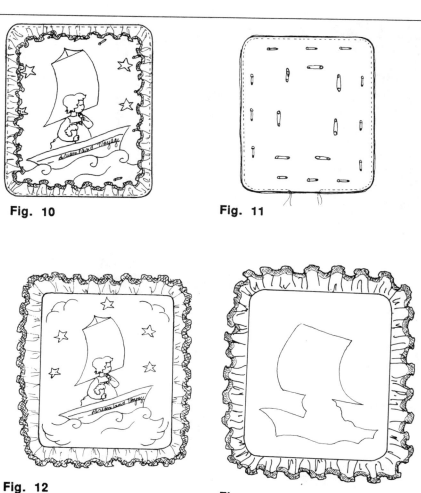

Fig. 10

Fig. 11

Fig. 12

Fig. 13

MEMORABILIA HOOP

Supplies

- 10-inch to 15-inch wooden hoop
- Netting - two pieces to fit hoop
- 2-1/2 to 3 yards lace edging
- Glue gun
- Knick knacks - rattle, birth announcement, lace scraps, etc.
- Wax paper
- Ribbon

Step 1. Place bottom of hoop on wax paper and a layer of netting on top of the bottom hoop.

Step 2. Place the knick knacks on the netting arranging as desired.

Step 3. Glue in place using a glue gun.

Step 4. Place layer of netting on top of knick knacks.

Step 5. Place several dots of glue along the inside of the top hoop. Clamp top of hoop in place. Trim excess netting from the back of the hoop.

Step 6. Gather the lace edging and glue along the edge of the hoop.

Step 7. Tie ribbon into a bow and place over the lace edging where the edging overlaps.

Antique children's coat.

Tucked Swiss Dress.

1

(From left) Wonderful Round Yoke Dress and Unusual Puffing Dress.

(From left) Magnificent Strips and Lace Christening Gown and Martha's Favorite Christening Gown.

**Convertible Middy Dress
and Eyelet Middy.
Inset: Divided Collar
Hemstitch Dress.**

Variation of Williamsburg Daygown with front lace shaping and handkerchief insert.

Inset: Hoppy the Bunny

Top Left: **Back button Bishop Daygown with only front pleated and smocked with "Baby Rattle."**
Top Right: **Button front daygown/bubble with entredeux and ruffle.**
Bottom: **French Daygown with antique insertion.**

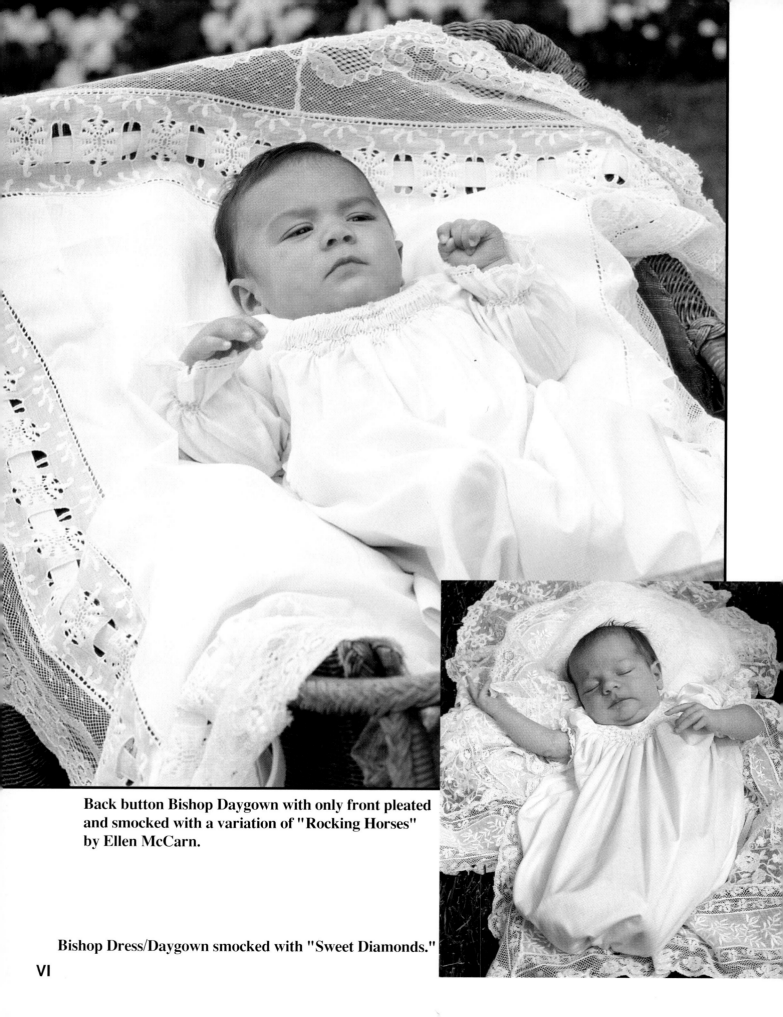

Back button Bishop Daygown with only front pleated and smocked with a variation of "Rocking Horses" by Ellen McCarn.

Bishop Dress/Daygown smocked with "Sweet Diamonds."

High Yoke Dress with Diaper Cover smocked with "Summer Gardens."

Dresses are Bishop Dress/Daygown pattern smocked with (from left) "Sweet Diamonds," "Wistful Waves," and "Baby Kisses."

(From left) Button Front Bubble/Daygown and Bishop Dress/Daygown smocked with "Sweet Diamonds."

High Yoke Dress smocked with "Daisy Row."

(From left) **High Yoke Dress and Diaper Cover smocked with "Summer Garden" and High Yoke Dress with lace overlay.**

Top, left: **Button Bootees**

Center: **Heirloom bibs**

Bottom: **(From left) Tied Bootees with embroidery, Ballet Bootees, all lace Ballet Bootees, Tied Bootees with lace, and Scalloped Bootees.**

IX

Top: Antique daygown with reproduction using French Daygown pattern.

Bottom: Antique Apron with Baby Shadow Diamonds.

x

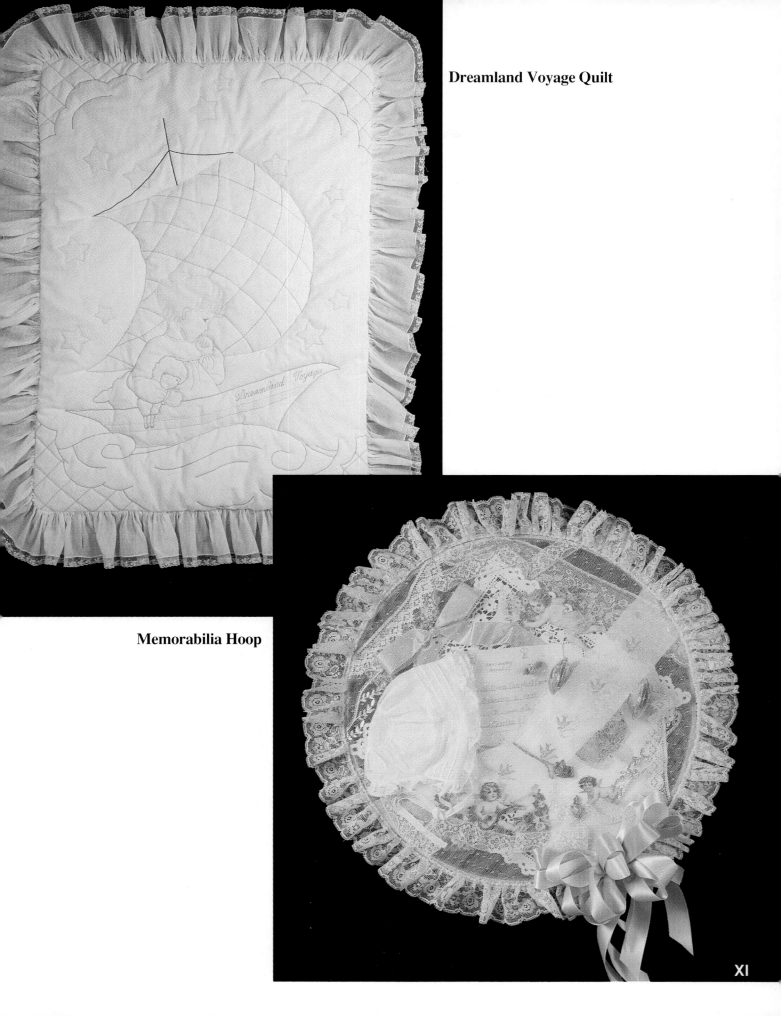

Dreamland Voyage Quilt

Memorabilia Hoop

XI

Top: **Crazy Stitch Bear**

Center: **Crazy Stitch Fabric**

Bottom: **Crazy Stitch String of Bears**

Top: **Williamsburg Daygown with embroidery design included in pattern.** *Bottom:* **(From left) Low Yoke Dress with smocked collar smocked with "First Spring Buds" and French sewn version of the Mid Yoke Dress.**

High Yoke Dress with square collar embellished with antique motifs.

Bishop Dress/Daygown and T Bonnet.

T Bonnets

xv

(From left) **Double Breasted Daygown and Button Front Daygown/Bubble.**

Double Breasted Bubbles

Rabbit and Angel Wrist Rattles.

XVI

Top: (From left) **Smocked yoke dress using a variation of the Mid Yoke pattern and smocked with "Diamonds of Joy" and French sewn version of the Mid Yoke Dress.** *Bottom:* **Pleated Front Daygown and Bubble.**

Variation of the High Yoke Dress with shark's teeth technique.

Godet Curved Puffing Christening Dress

High Yoke Dress with collar
embellished with Madeira
applique.

Lace shaping from quilting template
on variation of the High Yoke Dress.

XIX

(From left) Battenberg Lace Bonnet, Fancy French Bonnet, Smocked Bonnet, and Netting Bonnet.

Scalloped Collar Netting Dress and Bonnet.

XX

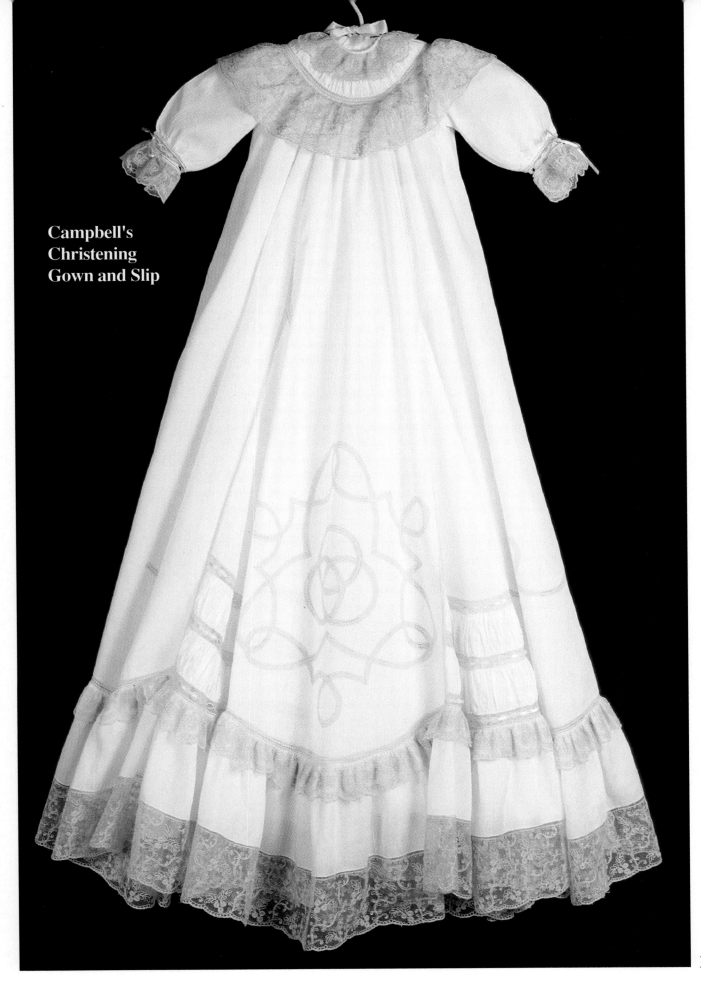

Campbell's
Christening
Gown and Slip

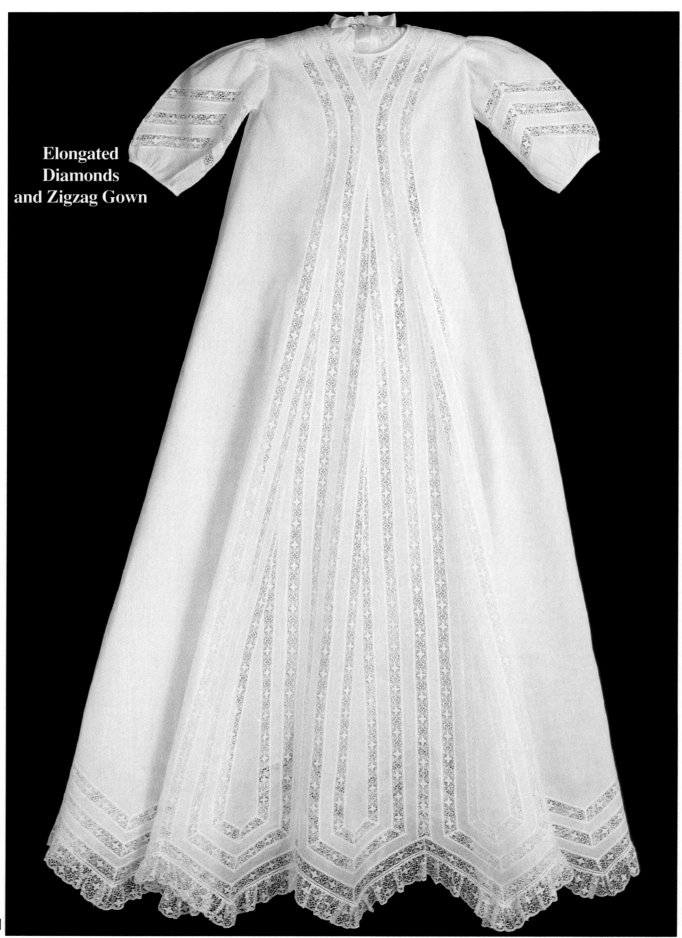

Elongated
Diamonds
and Zigzag Gown

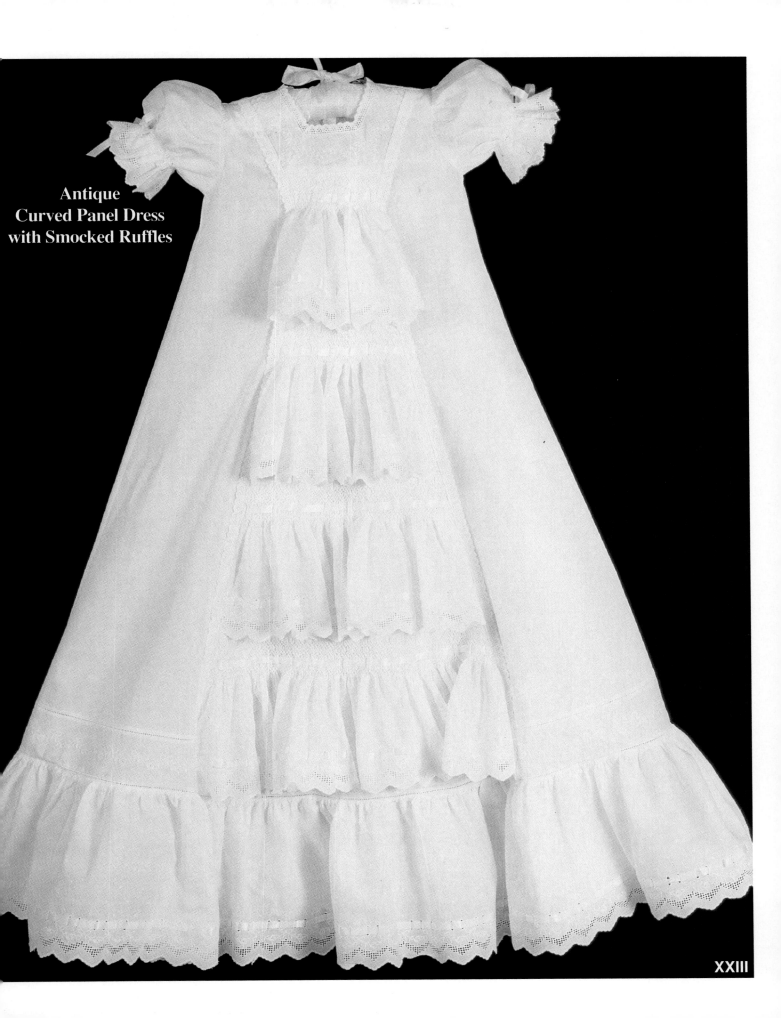

Antique
Curved Panel Dress
with Smocked Ruffles

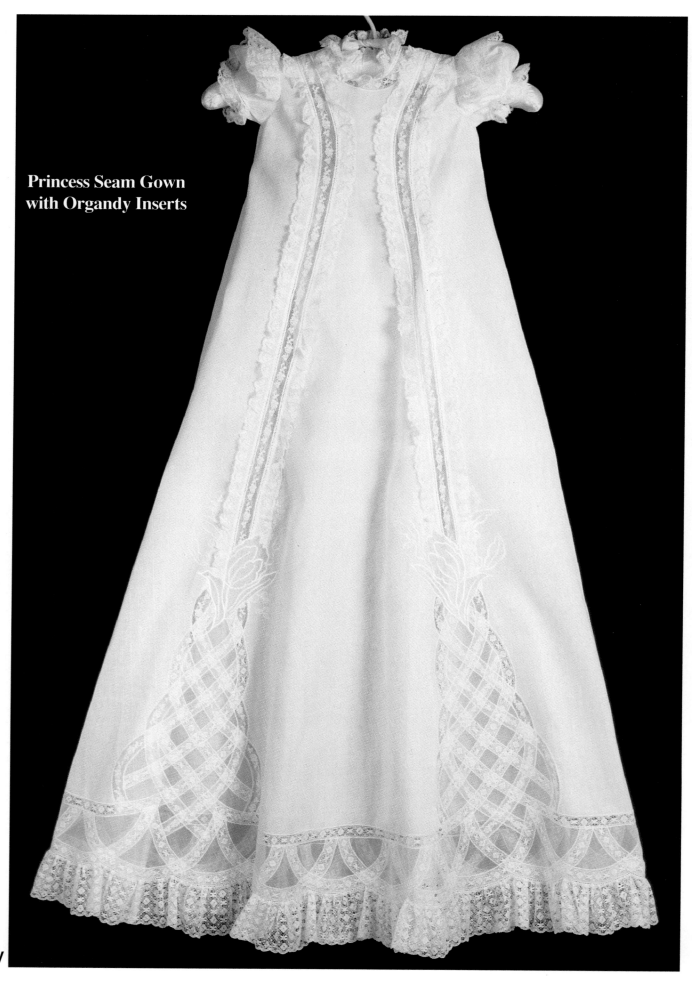

Princess Seam Gown with Organdy Inserts

**Godet Curved Puffing
Christening Dress**

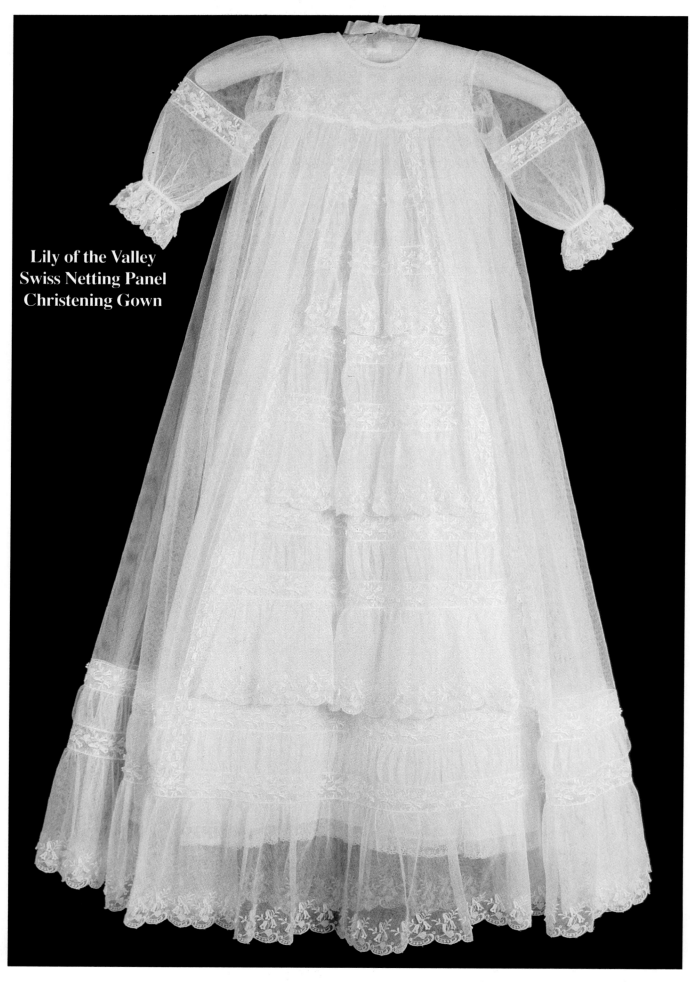

Lily of the Valley
Swiss Netting Panel
Christening Gown

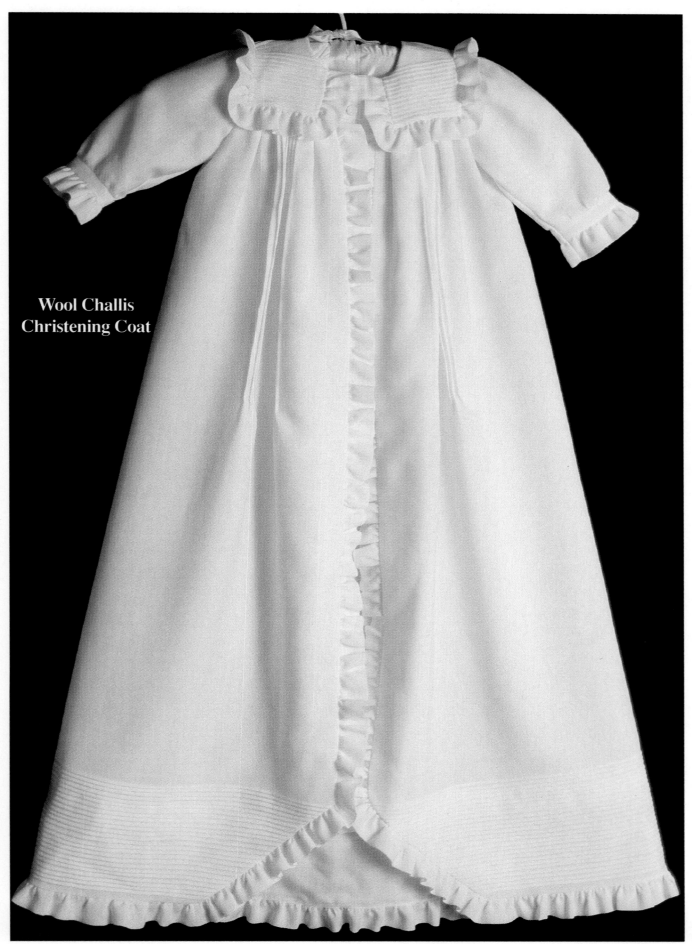

Wool Challis
Christening Coat

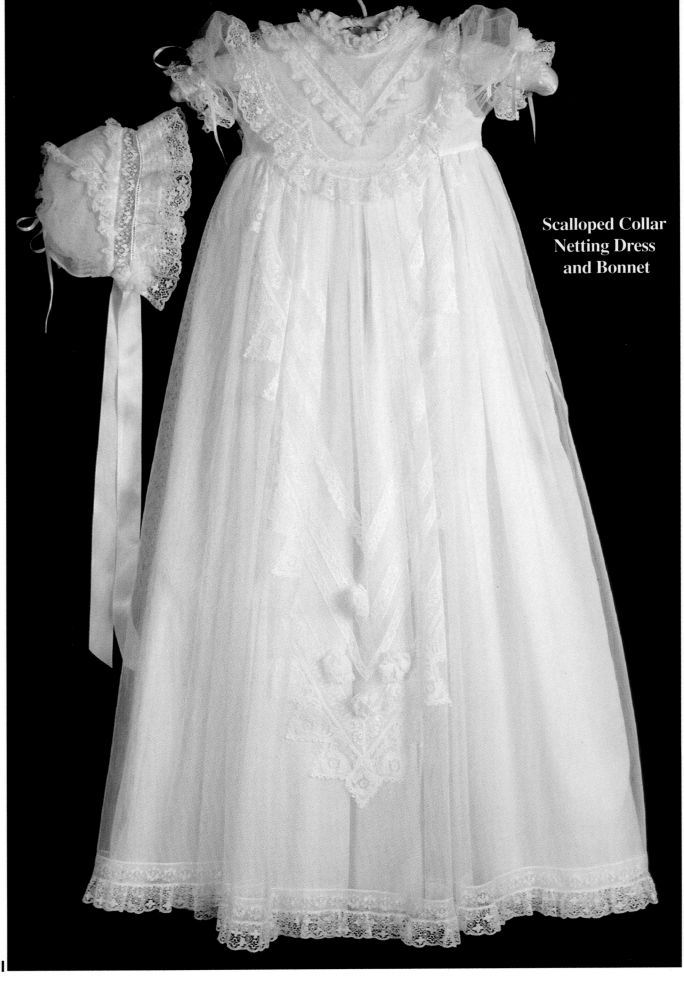

**Scalloped Collar
Netting Dress
and Bonnet**

**Princess Seam Gown
with Shark's Teeth
and Slip**

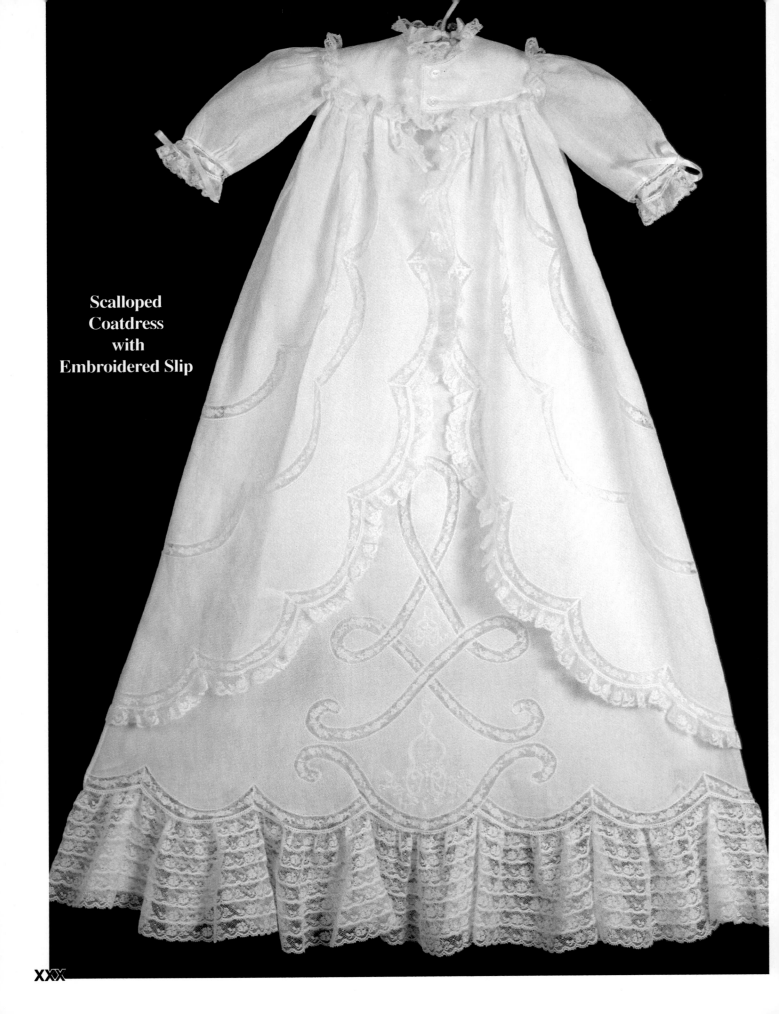

**Scalloped
Coatdress
with
Embroidered Slip**

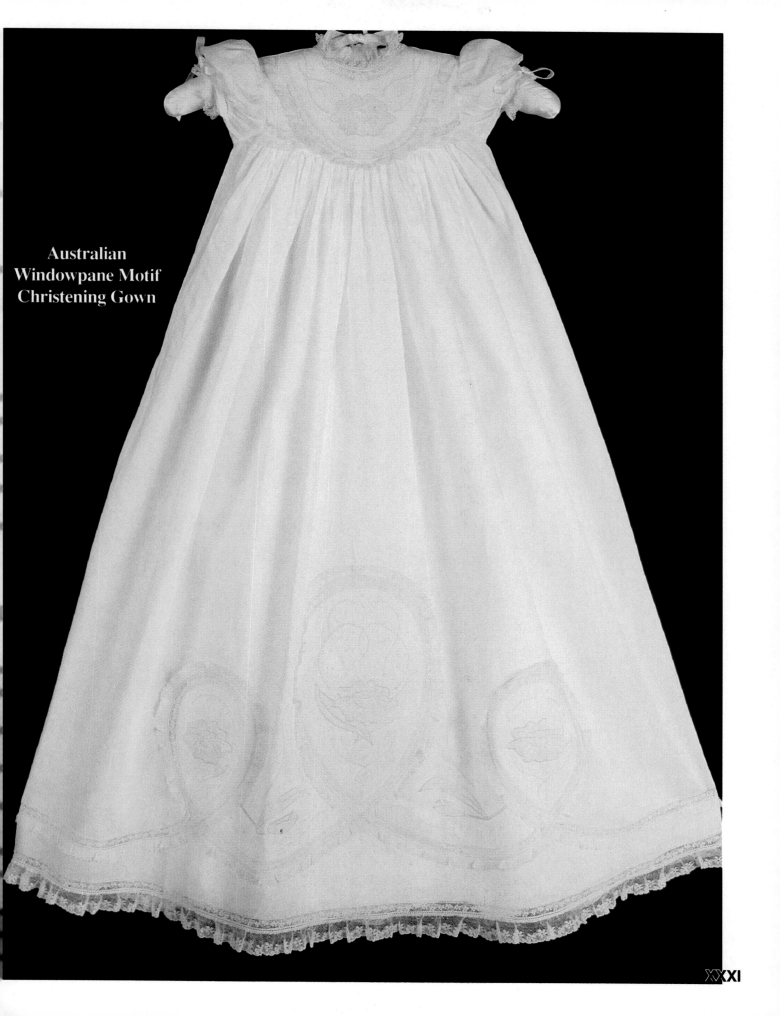

Australian
Windowpane Motif
Christening Gown

**Portrait Collar
Triple Ruffle
Christening Gown**

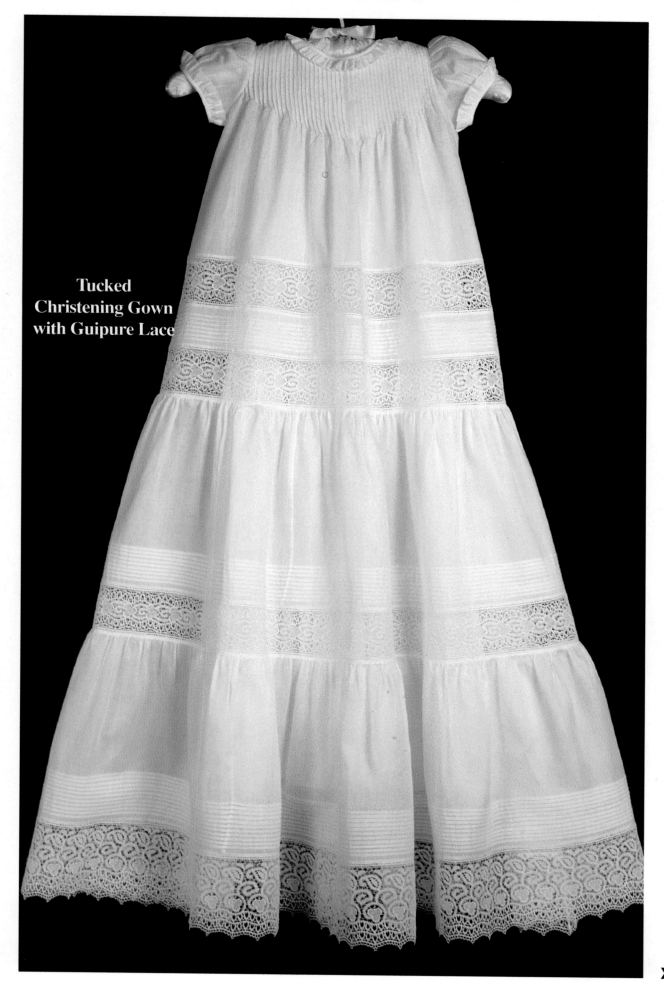

**Tucked
Christening Gown
with Guipure Lace**

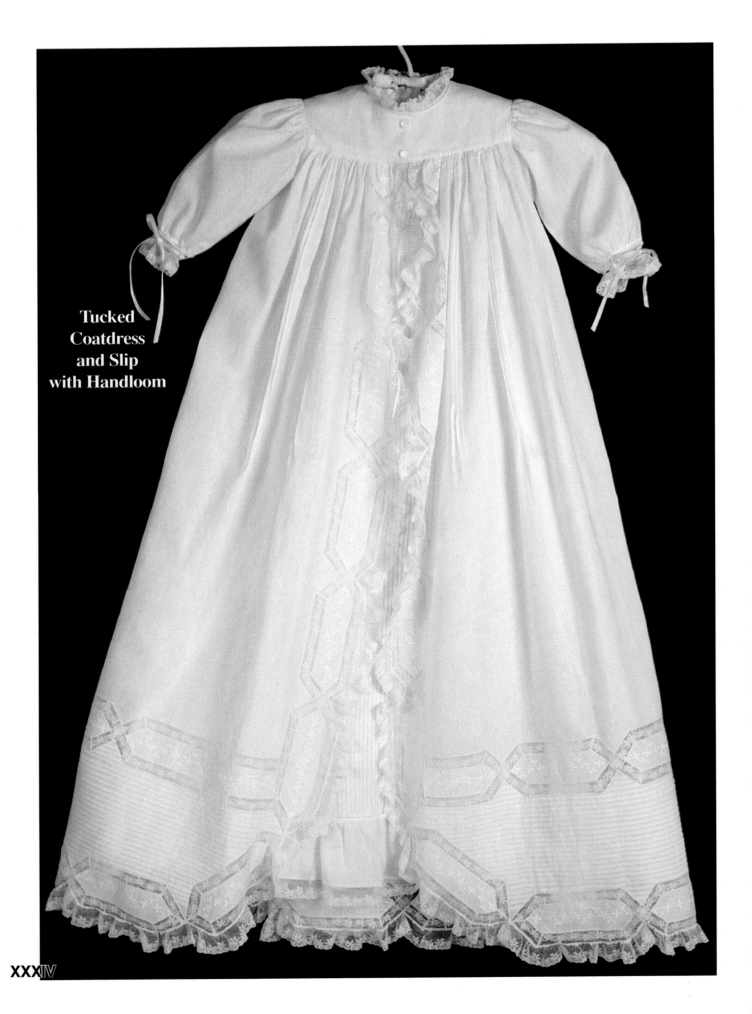

**Tucked
Coatdress
and Slip
with Handloom**

Christening Puffing Coat and Underdress

**Christening Gown
with Godets,
Pintucks,
and Swiss Motifs**

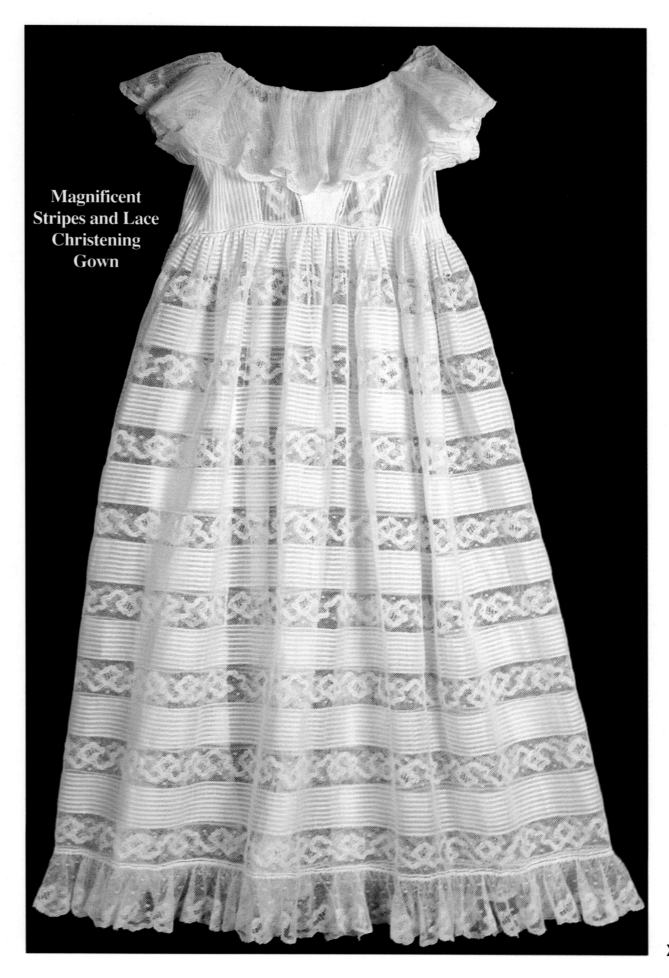

Magnificent
Stripes and Lace
Christening
Gown

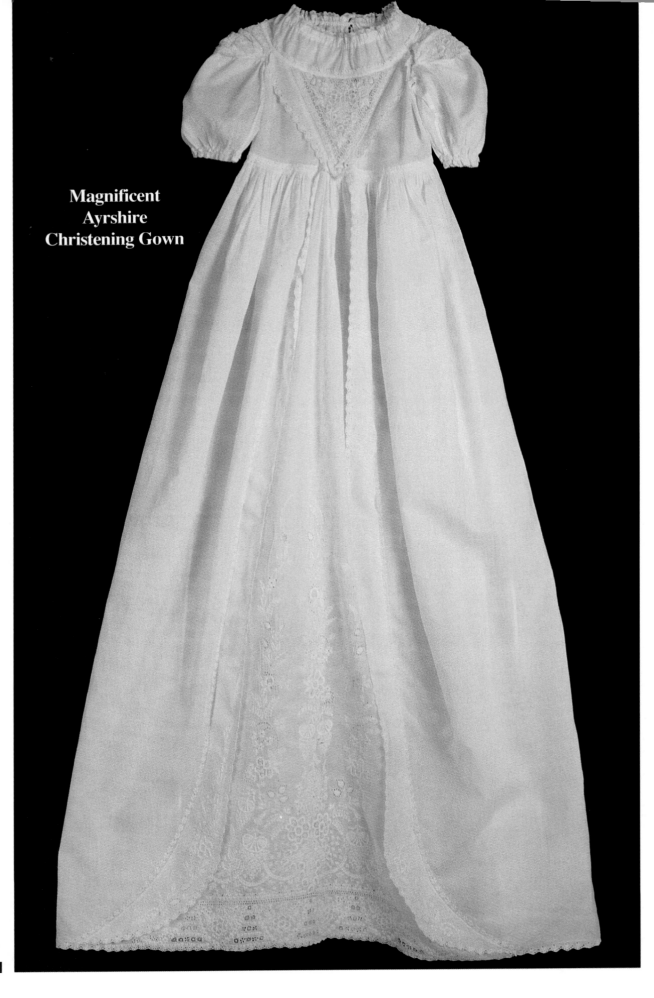

Magnificent Ayrshire Christening Gown

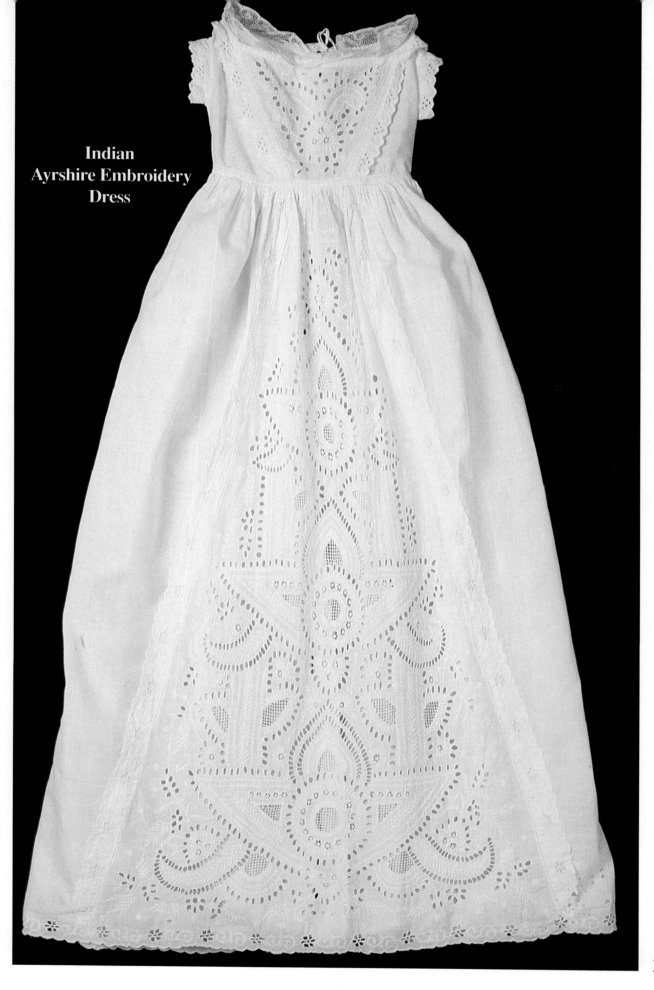

Indian
Ayrshire Embroidery
Dress

Martha's
Favorite
Christening
Gown

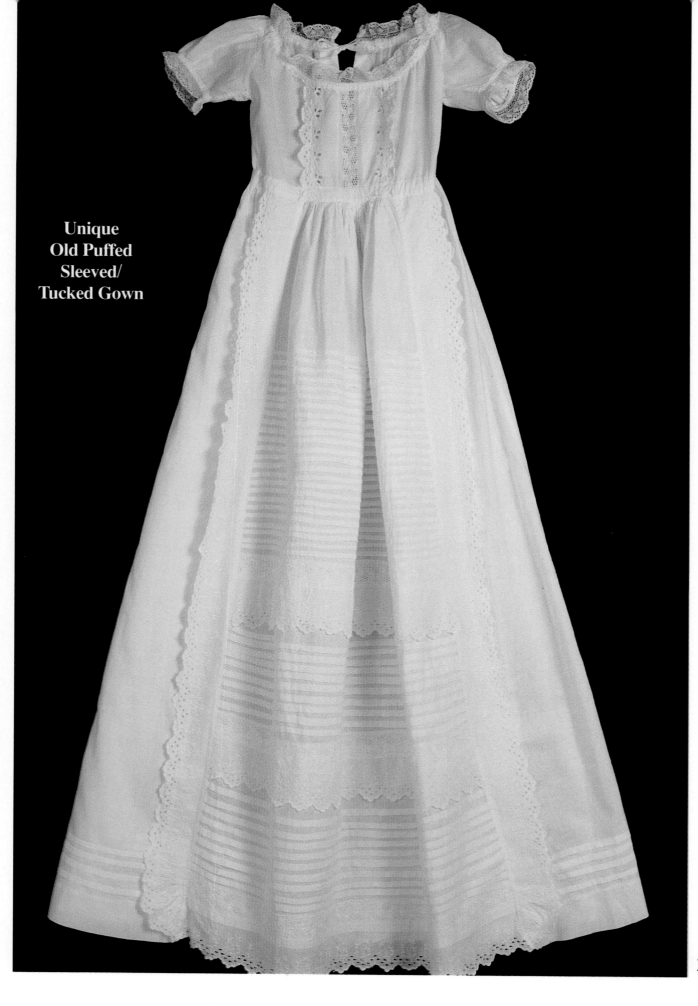

**Unique
Old Puffed
Sleeved/
Tucked Gown**

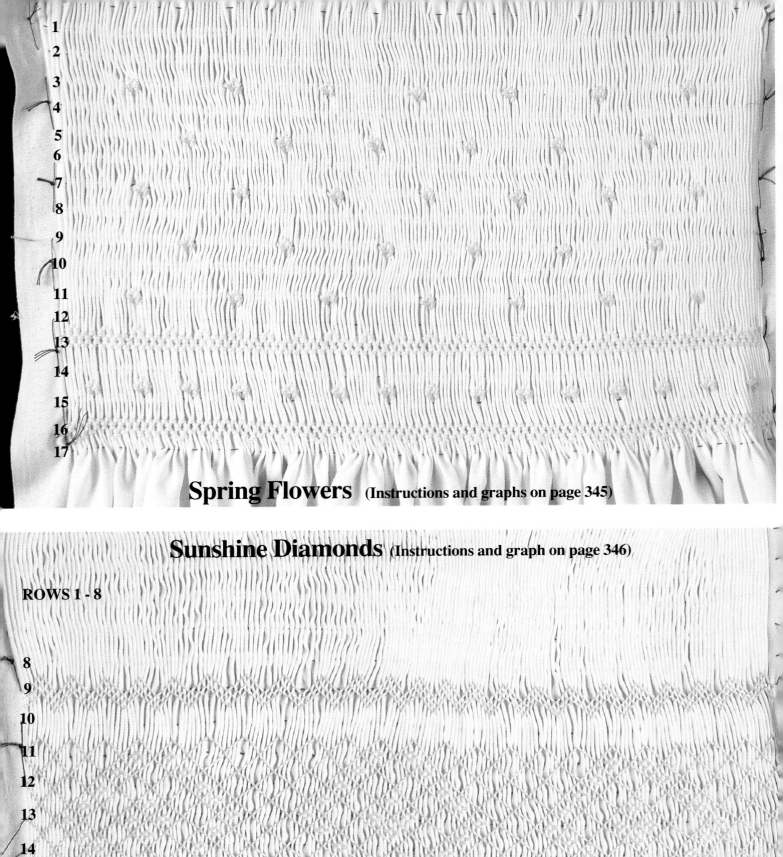

1
2
3
4
5
6
7
8
9
10
11
12
13
14
15
16
17

Spring Flowers (Instructions and graphs on page 345)

Sunshine Diamonds (Instructions and graph on page 346)

ROWS 1 - 8

8
9
10
11
12
13
14
15
16
17
18 XLII

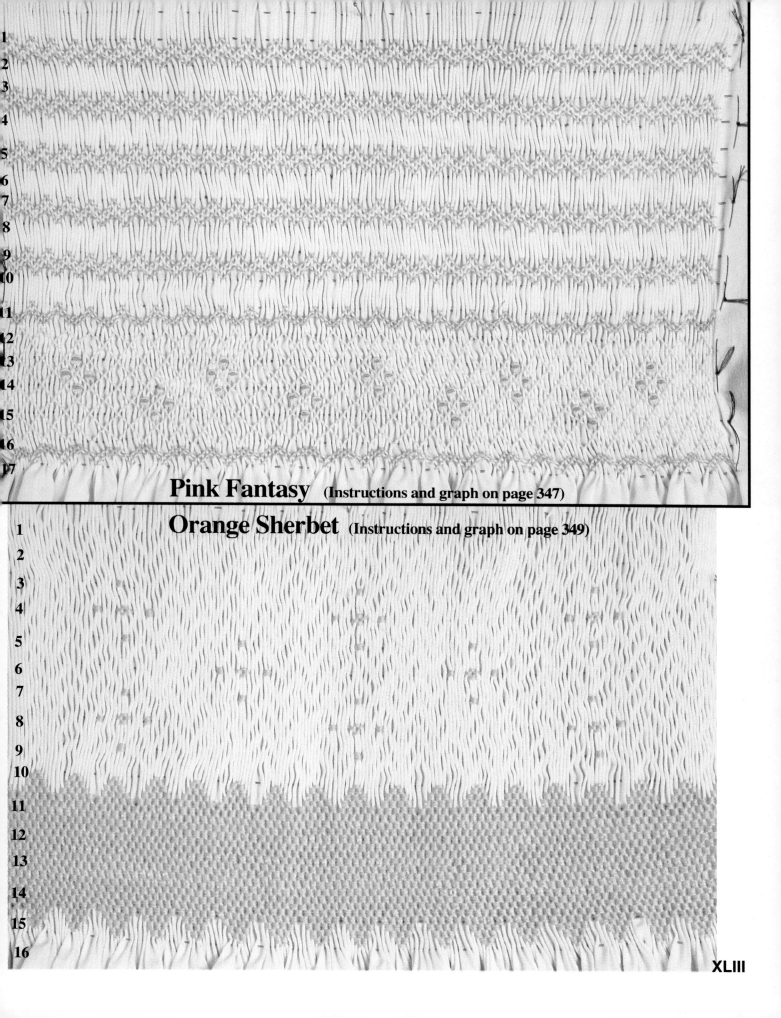

Pink Fantasy   (Instructions and graph on page 347)

Orange Sherbet   (Instructions and graph on page 349)

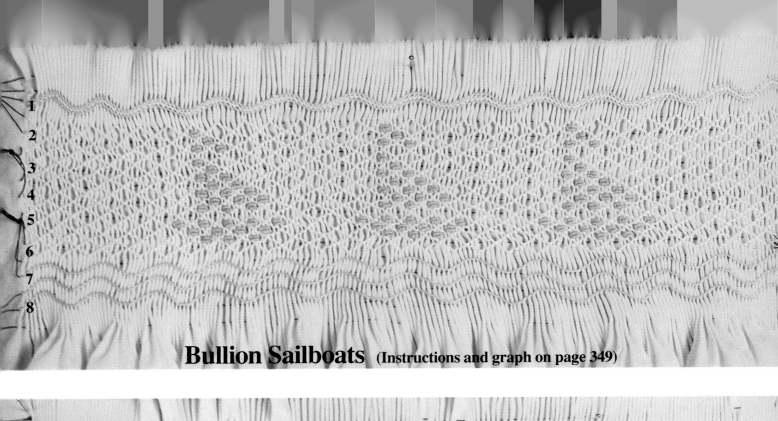

1
2
3
4
5
6
7
8

Bullion Sailboats (Instructions and graph on page 349)

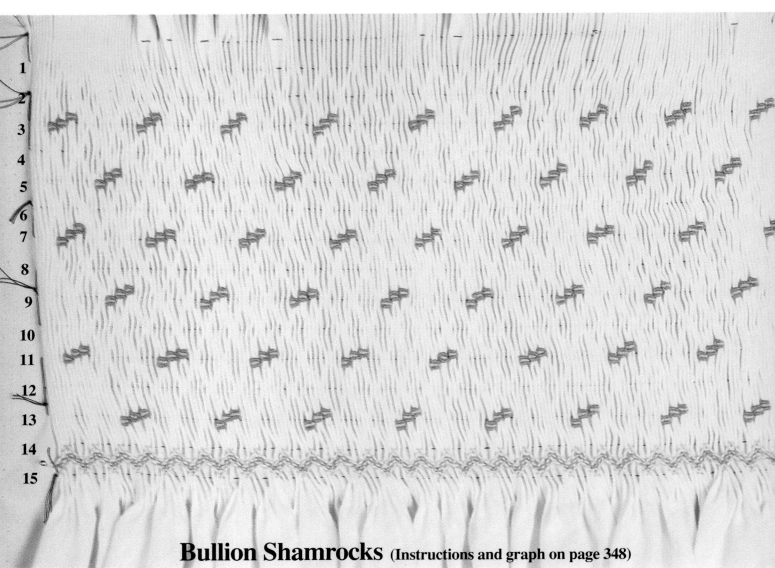

1
2
3
4
5
6
7
8
9
10
11
12
13
14
15

Bullion Shamrocks (Instructions and graph on page 348)

Lace Making on the
Pfaff 1475 CD

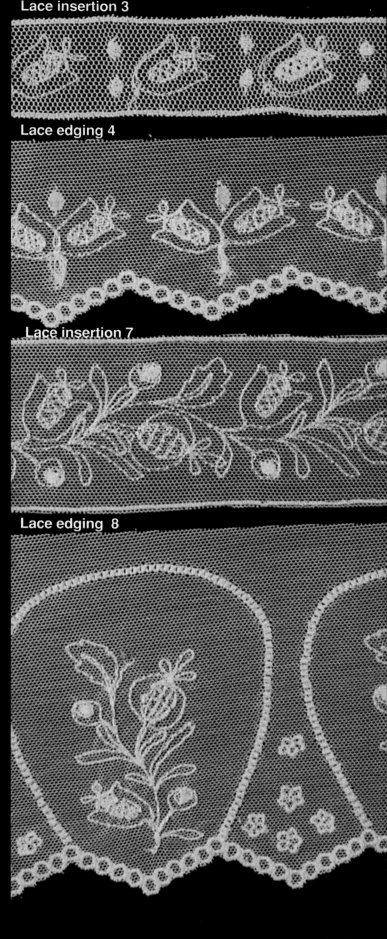

Lace edging 4

Lace insertion 7

Lace edging 8

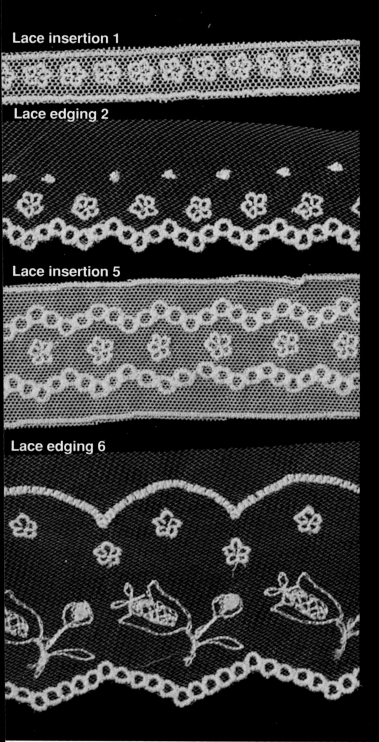

Lace insertion 1

Lace edging 2

Lace insertion 5

Lace edging 6

Lace Making on the
Bernina 1530

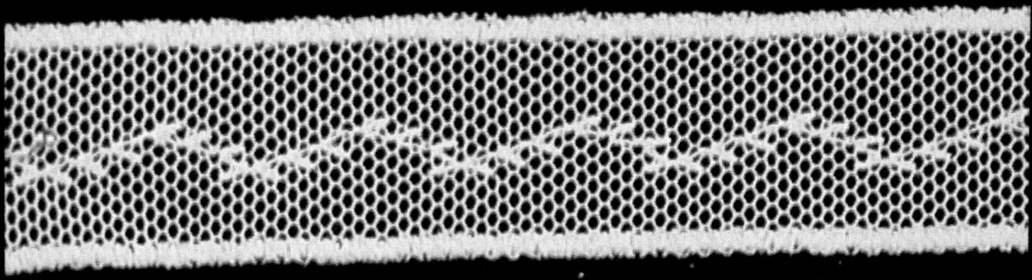

Lace insertion 1

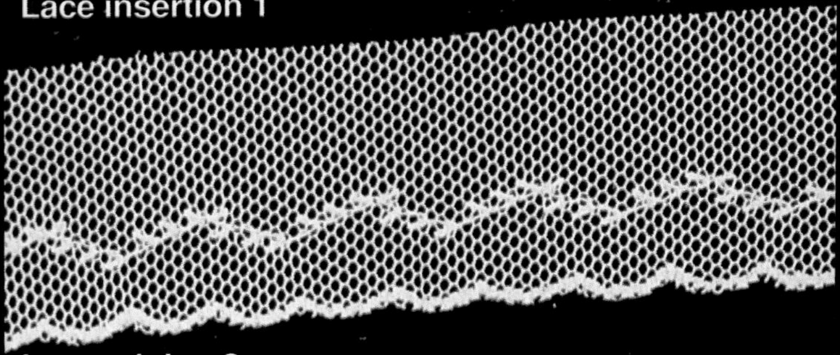

Lace insertion 3

Lace edging 2

Lace edging 4

Lace insertion 5

Lace insertion 7

Lace edging 6

Lace insertion 5

Lace edging 8

Lace Making on the
Elna 9000

Lace insertion 3

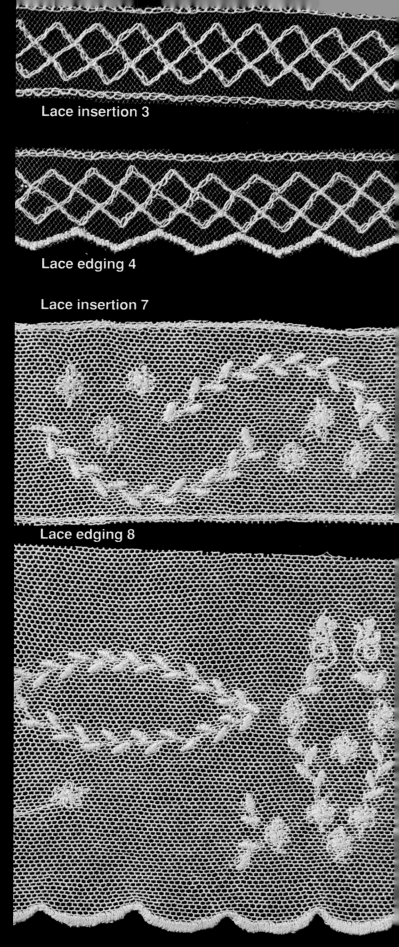

Lace insertion 1

Lace edging 2

Lace edging 4

Lace insertion 7

Lace insertion 5

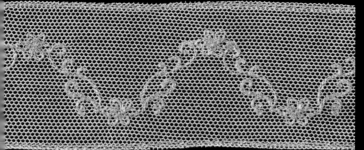

Lace edging 8

Lace edging 6

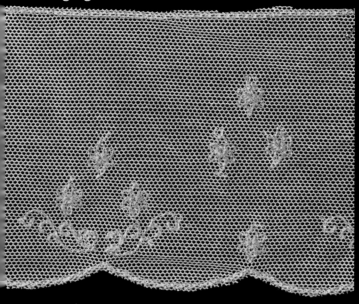

Lace Making on the
Viking #1

Lace insertion 1

Lace edging 2

Lace insertion 5

Lace edging 6

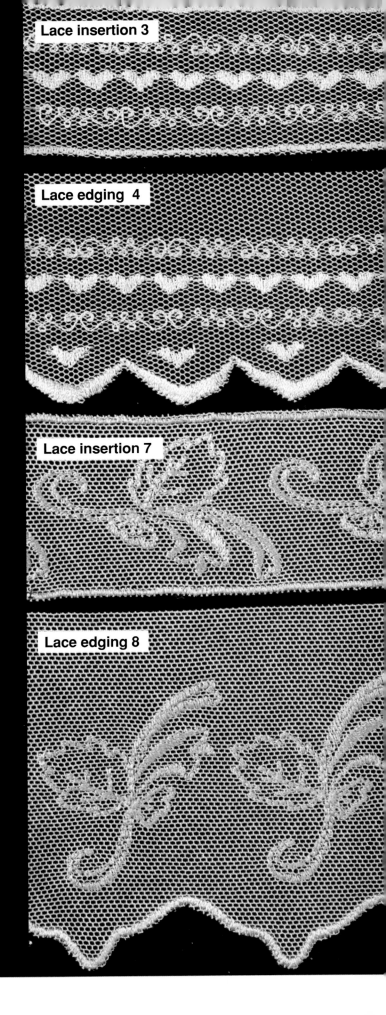

Lace insertion 3

Lace edging 4

Lace insertion 7

Lace edging 8

Original French Sewing Techniques

WORKING WITH LACE

LACE STRAIGHT EDGE TO LACE STRAIGHT EDGE

Use this technique when applying: lace insertion to lace insertion; lace insertion to lace beading; lace insertion or lace beading to non-gathered straight edge of lace edging; and Swiss embroidered trims to entredeux edgings

Step 1. Spray starch and press each piece.
Step 2. Place the two pieces, side by side, butting them together, but not overlapping. It is important to match patterns in the lace **(fig. 1).**
Step 3. Begin 1/4 inch or 3/8 inch from the ends of the pieces to be joined. This keeps the ends from digging into the sewing machine **(fig. 2).**
Step 4. Zigzag the two edges together. Zigzag again if spaces are missed.
Step 5. Stitch just widely enough to catch the two headings of the pieces of lace (or embroidery). Laces vary greatly in the widths of the headings. The stitch widths will vary according to the lace heading placement and your preference.
Step 6. Stitch the length as tightly or as loosely as you wish. You don't want a satin-stitch; however, you don't want the dress to fall apart either. Work with your trims and your sewing machine to determine the length and width you want. Suggested stitch width and length:
Width=2 to 3 — I prefer 2-1/2
Length=1 to 1/12 — I prefer 1

LACE EDGING TO LACE EDGING

Use this technique when you need a wider piece of lace edging.

Step 1. Spray starch and press the two edgings to be joined.
Step 2. Lay one piece of edging on the table, right side up.
Step 3. Lay the next piece of edging, right side up, on top of the first one.
Step 4. Check to be sure that the scallops of the second piece overlap the heading of the straight side of the first piece by at least 1/8 inch.
Step 5. Straight stitch inside the heading of the bottom straight edge **(fig. 1).**
Step 6. Suggested stitch length:
Length=1-1/2 to 2-1/2

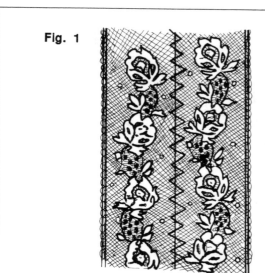

Fig. 1

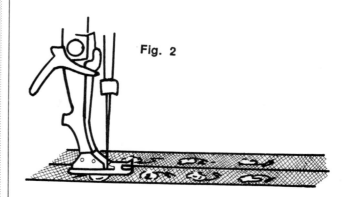

Fig. 2

Fig. 1

Grandmother's Hope Chest

LACE FLAT EDGE TO FABRIC

Use this technique when applying lace edging to ruffle or skirt; embroidered insertion to straight edge of lace; lace edging to sleeve edge, as on smocked sleeve or bottom of sleeve with elastic casing; and Swiss edging (with scallops trimmed) to a flat surface to fabric edge, as on ruffles, sleeves, or collars.

MARTHA'S MAGIC

Step 1. Spray starch and press both the lace and the fabric.

Step 2. Place right sides to right sides.

Step 3. NOTE: Leave 1/8 inch to 1/4 inch of fabric edge before placing the lace to be joined **(fig. 1)**.

Step 4. Zigzag with a satin stitch, going into the heading of the lace and all the way off the fabric edge **(fig. 2)**.

Step 5. Suggested stitch length: Width=3-1/2 to 4 Length=1/2 or as short as possible

NOTE: 1/8 inch to 1/4 inch of the fabric is exposed before the lace flat edge is put into place. The fabric edge will completely fold into the stitch when you are finished.

Step 6. Why shouldn't you just place the edge of the lace and the edges of the fabric together and zigzag? They will come apart. There is not enough strength in the edge of the fabric without the extra 1/8 inch or 1/4 inch folded into the zigzag.

Step 7. Press the lace and fabric open. A common question is, "Which way do I press this roll?" Press the seam however it wants to lie. Naturally, it will fold toward the lace.

TOP STITCHING LACE

Step 1. Work from the right side, after the lace has been pressed open.

Step 2. Zigzag on top of the little roll which is on the back of the garment. Your width should be very narrow — just wide enough to go from one side of the roll to the other side. It should not be too short. You want it to be as invisible as possible **(fig. 3)**.

Step 3. This zigzag holds the lace down and gives added strength to the seam. Its main purpose, however, is to hold the lace down.

Step 4. Stitch width and length:
Width=1/2 to 1-1/2, Length=1 to 2

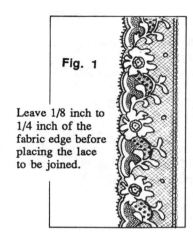

Fig. 1

Leave 1/8 inch to 1/4 inch of the fabric edge before placing the lace to be joined.

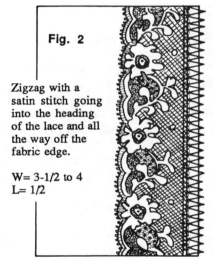

Fig. 2

Zigzag with a satin stitch going into the heading of the lace and all the way off the fabric edge.

W= 3-1/2 to 4
L= 1/2

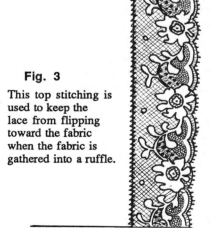

Fig. 3

This top stitching is used to keep the lace from flipping toward the fabric when the fabric is gathered into a ruffle.

WORKING WITH LACE

CUTTING FABRIC FROM BEHIND LACE
That Has Been Shaped and Zigzagged

I recommend two pairs of Gingher scissors for cutting away fabric from behind stitched laces. One is the "Duck Bill" or applique scissors. The "Duck Bill" on the scissors allows you to hold the laces in safety while clipping the fabric from behind. For years, that was the only kind of scissor I recommended.

Now, Gingher has another pair suited for this task. They are called Pocket Scissors and look much like kindergarten scissors because of the blunt ends. But don't be fooled by appearances; the blades on Gingher Pocket Scissors cut fabric from behind lace with ease.

PATCHING LACES

Trimming fabric away from behind stitched-down lace can be difficult. It is not uncommon to slip, thus cutting a hole in your lace work. How do you repair this lace with the least visible repair? It is really quite simple.

Step 1. Look at the pattern in the lace where you have cut the hole. Is it in a flower, in a dot series, or in the netting part of the lace? **(fig. 1)**

Step 2. After you identify the pattern where the hole was cut, cut another piece of lace 1/4 inch longer than each side of the hole in the lace.

Step 3. On the bottom side of the lace in the garment, place the lace patch **(fig. 2)**.

Step 4. Match the design of the patch with the design of the lace around the hole where it was cut.

Step 5. Zigzag around the cut edges of the lace hole, trying to catch the edges of the hole in your zigzag **(fig. 3)**.

Step 6 . Now, you have a patched and zigzagged pattern.

Step 7. Trim away the leftover ends underneath the lace you have just patched **(fig. 3)**.

Step 8. And don't worry about a piece of patched lace. My grandmother used to say, "Don't worry about that. You'll never notice it on a galloping horse."

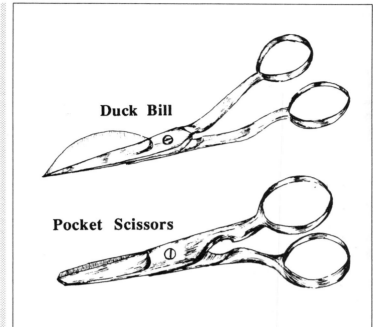

Duck Bill

Pocket Scissors

Fig. 1

Fig. 2

Fig. 3
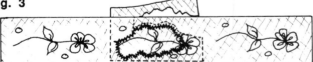

PIECING LACE NOT LONG ENOUGH FOR YOUR NEEDS

From my sewing experience, sometimes you will need longer piece of lace than you have. Perhaps you cut the lace incorrectly or bought less than you needed and had to go back for more. Whatever the reason, if you need to make a lace strip longer, it is easy to do.

Step 1. Match your pattern with two strips that will be joined later (**figs. 1 and 3**).

Step 2. Is your pattern a definite flower? Is it a definite diamond or some other pattern that is relatively large?

Step 3. If you have a definite design in the pattern, you can join pieces by zigzagging around that design and then down through the heading of the lace (**fig. 2**).

Step 4. If your pattern is tiny, you can zigzag at an angle joining the two pieces (**fig. 2**). Trim away excess laces close to the zigzagged seam (**Fig. 4**).

Step 5. Forget that you have patched laces and complete the dress. If you discover that the lace is too short before you begin stitching, you can plan to place the pieced section in an inconspicuous place.

Step 6. If you were already into making the garment when you discovered the short lace, simply join the laces and continue stitching as if nothing had happened

STITCHING FANCY BANDS FROM FIRST ONE END AND THEN THE OTHER

Sometimes fancy bands curve after you have sewn all of the laces and trims together. Usually, you can spray starch and iron the curve to straighten it out. According to Kathy McMakin, the way to stitch long pieces of laces together without resulting in a curve is to begin zigzagging your laces together at one end. To zigzag the next row, begin sewing from the end you just finished. Bi-directional stitching of these laces will help tremendously in avoiding curved fancy bands. If you still end up with a slight curve in your fancy band, let the curved part face the ruffle.

MATCHING LACE PATTERNS

Do you match lace patterns as you stitch around your fancy band? For intricate patterns with small designs, the answer is "no." For very large patterns in round-thread laces, as in a huge flower every 1 inch or so, the answer is "yes." If you are stitching along on your fancy band and your pattern begins to fall out of design sequence, pull on the other side of the lace until the pattern matches again. Lace is a very forgiving textile which will allow itself to be pulled and pinched for various techniques. Pull it or pinch it until it lines back up.

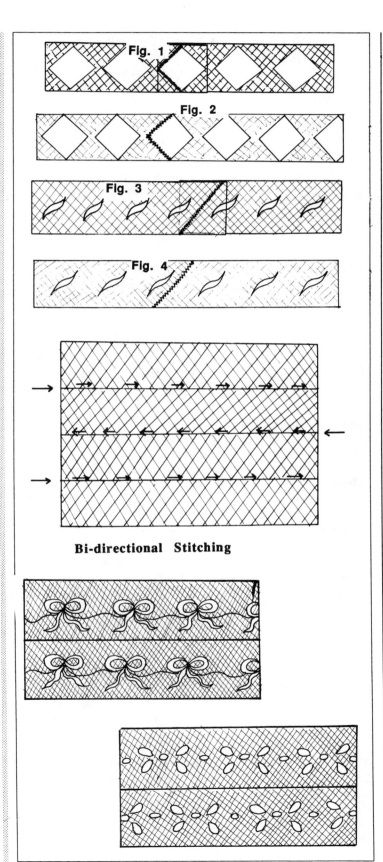

Fig. 1

Fig. 2

Fig. 3

Fig. 4

Bi-directional Stitching

WORKING WITH LACE

▨ IF YOUR FANCY BAND IS TOO SHORT

Not to worry; cut down the width of your skirt. Always make your skirt adapt to your lace shapes, not the lace shapes to your skirt.

▨ MAKING DIAMONDS, HEARTS, TEAR-DROPS, OR CIRCLES FIT SKIRT BOTTOM

How do you make sure that you engineer your diamonds, hearts, teardrops, or circles to exactly fit the width skirt that you are planning? The good news is that you don't. Make your shapes any size that you want. Stitch them onto your skirt, front and back, and cut away the excess skirt width. Or, you can stitch up one side seam, and zig-zag your shapes onto the skirt, and cut away the excess on the other side before you make your other side seam.

▨ PLANNING THE WIDTH OF SKIRT FOR FANCY SHAPED BOTTOM

Please don't make a 90-inch skirt circumference when you are going to make intricate lace shapes on the bottom. The lace shapes will be lost in the fullness. I recommend a 60-inch to 72-inch total circumference; that's 30 inches to 36 inches of fullness in both the front and the back.

▨ RIBBON TO LACE INSERTION

This is tricky! Lace has give and ribbon doesn't. After much practice, I have decided that for long bands of lace to ribbon, as in a skirt, it is better to place the lace on top of the ribbon and straight-stitch (Length 2 to 2-1/2). For short strips of lace to ribbon, it is perfectly OK to butt to-gether and zigzag.

Directions for Straight-Stitch Attachment (fig. 1):
Step 1. Press and starch your ribbon and lace.
Step 2. Place the heading of the insertion just over the heading of the ribbon and straight-stitch (Length=2 to 2-1/2).

Directions for Zigzag-Stitch Attachment (fig. 2):
Step 1. Press and starch your ribbon and lace.
Step 2. Place the two side by side and zigzag (Width=1-1/2 to 2-1/2, Length 1-2).

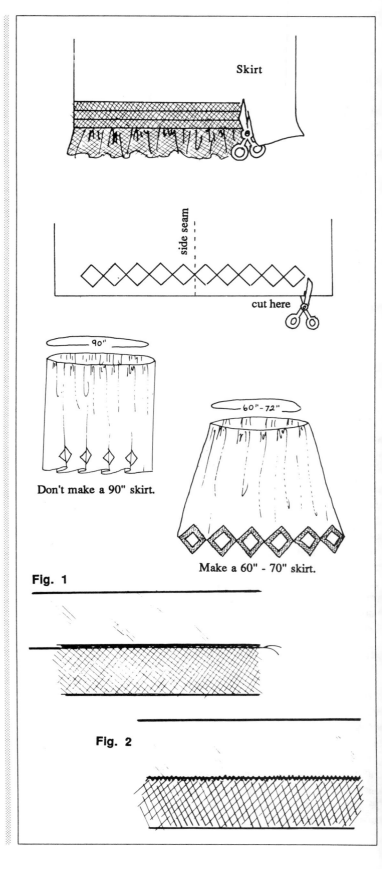

Don't make a 90" skirt.

Make a 60" - 70" skirt.

Fig. 1

Fig. 2

Grandmother's Hope Chest

WORKING WITH ENTREDEUX

▨ FLAT LACE TO ENTREDEUX

Step 1. Trim one batiste side of the entredeux.

Step 2. Spray starch and press entredeux and lace.

Step 3. Lay trimmed edge of entredeux beside the flat side of the lace. These should be right sides up. Butt them together; they should not overlap. In other words, zigzag, side by side, right sides up.

Step 4. Zigzag them together, trying to make one stitch of the machine go into one hole of the entredeux and over, just catching the heading of the lace **(Figs. 1 and 2).**

Step 5. SuggestedWidth=2-1/2 to 3-1/2, Length=2-1/2

▨ ENTREDEUX TO FLAT FABRIC

Method 1 - Stitch-In-The-Ditch

Step 1. Do not trim entredeux.

Step 2. Spray starch and press fabric and entredeux.

Step 3. Place together batiste edge of untrimmed entredeux and edge of the fabric. (This is similar to the sewing of any two seams of a dress. Place the edges and sew the seam.)

Step 4. Sew in straight, short stitches along the right hand side of the entredeux (the side of the entredeux that is next to the body of the sewing machine.) This is called "stitch-in-the-ditch" because it is just that — you stitch in the ditch of the entredeux (Length= 2-1/2) **Fig. 1**

Step 5. Trim the seam, leaving about a 1/8-inch seam allowance **(fig. 2).**

Step 6. Zigzag a tight stitch (not a satin) to go over the stitch-in-the-ditch and all the way off the edge of the fabric edge. This zigzag will completely encase the fabric left on the entredeux and the straight stitch you just made (Width=2-1/2 to 3, Length=1) **Fig. 3.**

Step 7. Press the zigzagged seam toward the fabric. All of the holes of the entredeux should be showing perfectly.

Step 8. This top stitching step is not necessary if you are using entredeux to flat fabric; however, you may choose to make this stitching. When you make the top stitch, zigzag on top of the fabric. As close as possible, zigzag into one hole of the entredeux and into the fabric. Barely catch the fabric in this top zigzag stitch. Adjust your machine length and width to fit each situation **(fig. 4).**

Step 9. My machine width and length:
> Width=1-1/2 to 2
> Length=2

Step 10. You can choose to do top stitching from the back of the fabric. If you work from the back, you can hold the seam down and see a little better. On entredeux to flat fabric, the choice of top stitching from the top or from the bottom is yours.

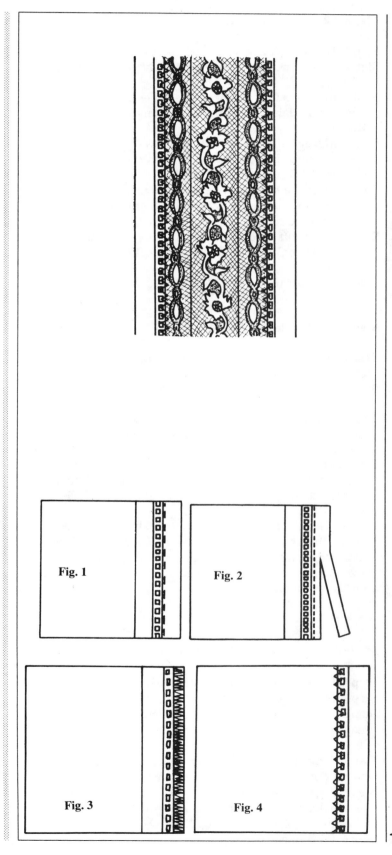

Fig. 1

Fig. 2

Fig. 3

Fig. 4

Original French Sewing Techniques

183

WORKING WITH ENTREDEUX

Method 2 - Trimmed Entredeux

Step 1. Trim one side of the entredeux **(fig. 1)**.

Step 2. Spray starch and press both the entredeux and the fabric edge.

Step 3. Run a straight row of short stitches as close to the edge of the fabric as is possible (Length=1-1/2 to 2) **(fig. 2)**.

Step 4. Zigzag a tiny zigzag over this row of stitches. The zigzag should enclose the first row of stitching (Width=2-1/2, Length=1/2) **(fig. 3)**.

Step 5. Place the trimmed entredeux edge into the ditch made by the previous two steps. The fabric and the entredeux are right sides to right sides **(fig. 4)**.

Step 6. Zigzag off the edge of the fabric and into one hole of entredeux (Width=3, Length=1-1/2) **(Fig. 5)**. Sew carefully.

Step 7. Press open.

Method 3 - Quick, But Not As Strong

Step 1. Trim one side of the entredeux **(fig. 1)**.

Step 2. Press and spray starch fabric edge and entredeux.

Step 3. Lay trimmed edge of entredeux to fabric edge, right sides together.

Step 4. Leave 1/8 inch to 1/4 inch of fabric edge before placing the entredeux edge to be stitched on the fabric **(fig. 2)**.

Step 5. Zigzag with a satin stitch, going into one hole of the entredeux and off the fabric edge. This will be a short, wide zigzag (Width=3 to 4, Length=1 to 1-1/2) **Fig. 3**.

Step 6. The 1/8 inch to 1/4 inch of the fabric is exposed before the zigzag is sewn, attaching the entredeux. The fabric edge will roll into the entredeux completely when the zigzag stitches are completed.

Step 7. Press open.

Method 4 - Entredeux to Flat Fabric

Step 1. Do not trim border off entredeux.

Step 2. Place edge of entredeux to edge of fabric.

Step 3. Stitch in the ditch of the entredeux as close to the edge of the entredeux as possible (Length=2-1/2) **(fig. 1)**.

Step 4. Trim the border of both the entredeux and the fabric down to a width of 1/8 inch **(fig. 2)**.

Step 5. Zigzag, going all the way off of the fabric and into one hole. The batiste border will roll into the seam (Width=3-1/2, Length=1) **Fig. 3**.

Step 6. Press open.

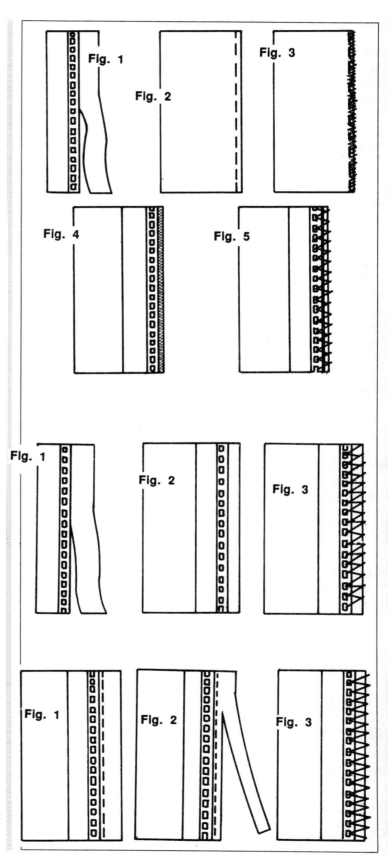

■ ENTREDEUX TO GATHERED FABRIC

Method 1

Step 1. Press, don't spray starch the fabric.

Step 2. Do not cut off the edges of the entredeux.

Step 3. Run two rows of long gathering stitches on the fabric (Length=4). There are two methods for running these gathering stitches.

    a. Sew the first gathering row 1/4 inch from the edge of the fabric. Sew the second gathering row 3/4 inch from the edge of the fabric (**fig.1**).

    b. Sew the first gathering row 1/4 inch from the edge of the fabric. Sew the second gathering row 1/4 inch below the first row. This is the more traditional method of running two gathering rows (**fig. 2**).

Step 4. Gather by hand to adjust the gathers to fit the entredeux.

Step 5. Lay right side of the entredeux to right side of the gathered fabric. This step reminds me of the days when we put waistbands on very full gathered skirts. This step is basic dressmaking.

    a. If you gathered with the first method (1/4-inch and 3/4-inch gathering rows), place the ditch of the entredeux below the first gathering line. The ditch of the entredeux would be about 3/8 inch from unfinished edge.

    b. If you used the second method (1/4-inch and 1/2-inch gathering rows), place the entredeux on or a little below the second gathering row.

Step 6. Stitch in the ditch of the entredeux, using a short straight stitch. This stitch is on the right side of the entredeux. This side is closest to the body of the sewing machine (Length=2) **Fig. 3**

Step 7. Move over just a little and straight stitch the second time. This holds down the gathers under the entredeux (**fig. 4**).

Step 8. Trim away both layers as close to the straight stitch as you can trim (**fig. 5**).

Step 9. Zigzag to finish the process. This zigzag is not a satin stitch but close to a satin stitch. This zigzag stitch encloses the stitch-in-the-ditch seam, the second seam and goes off the side to catch the raw edges (Width=3, Length=3/4 to 1) **Fig. 6**

Step 10. Press the satin stitched roll toward the fabric.

Step 11. Scotch tape stitch on the wrong side of the fabric. Zigzag into one hole of the entredeux and off into the zigzagged seam. This should be as narrow a seam a possible (Width=1-1/2 to 2-1/2, Length=2) **Fig. 7**.

Step 12. This last step can be zig-zagged from the top also. It is easier to zigzag it from the bottom if the step is "entredeux to gathered fabric" because of the bulk of the zigzagged seam. When zigzagging entredeux to flat edge (as given in the section just preceding this one) it seems easier to zigzag the final step from the top.

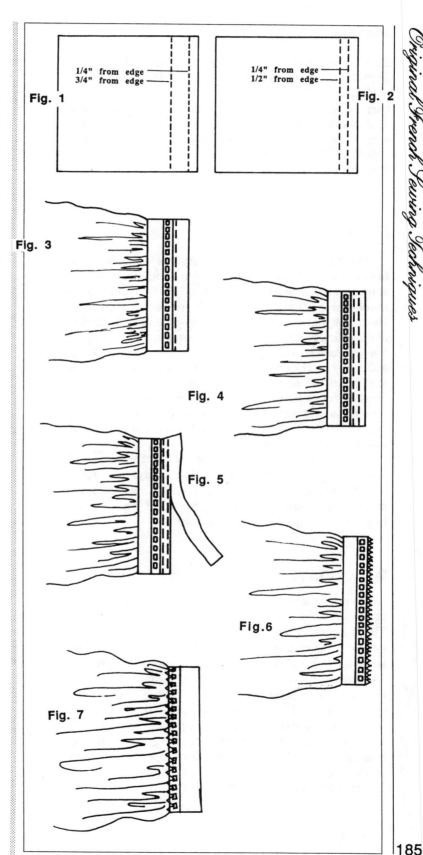

Fig. 1   1/4" from edge   3/4" from edge

Fig. 2   1/4" from edge   1/2" from edge

Fig. 3

Fig. 4

Fig. 5

Fig.6

Fig. 7

WORKING WITH ENTREDEUX

Method 2

Step 1. Follow steps 1 through 6 of Method 1 (**fig. 1**).

Step 2. Trim to within 1/8 inch of the stitch-in-the-ditch (**fig. 2**).

Step 3. Zigzag, going into one hole of the entredeux and all the way off of the edge of the fabric. This will roll the fabric/entredeux border right into the entredeux (Width=3 to 4, Length=1-1/2) **Fig. 3.**

▓ SERGER FEVER

Oh what a wonderful tool the serger is for French sewing by machine! I cannot say enough about how this machine has simplified the "Entredeux To Flat Fabric" technique and the "Entredeux To Gathered Fabric" technique. First of all, the serger does three things at once. It stitches in the ditch, zigzags, and trims. Secondly, the serger goes twice as fast as your conventional sewing machine. Probably you can eliminate two sewing steps and do that one step twice as fast. Kathy McMakin has written a how-to book, "French Sewing By Serger." It gives complete instructions and settings on how to do these wonderful French sewing techniques by serger. It is available from Martha Pullen Company.

Another way to use the serger is for French seams. I always did hate those little things. Now, I serge my French seams. I serge in my sleeves! I serge the sleeves in my smocked bishops; you will not believe the improvement in getting bishops through the pleater!

▓ HOLIDAYS AND VACATIONS

It's not uncommon to find a hole in the seam of laces, or between the laces and fabrics that have been joined. This occurs when both pieces of lace do not get sewn together in the zigzag or the laces do not get caught in the lace-to-fabric, zigzagged seam. This is not a mistake. I refer to this as a holiday or vacation. Sometimes we take long vacations (long holes) and sometimes we are only gone for a few hours (very tiny holes). These vacations and holidays are easily fixed by simply starting above the hole and zigzagging past the hole, being careful to catch both sides of lace or fabric to repair the opening. No backstitching is necessary. Clip the excess threads and no one will ever know about your vacation.

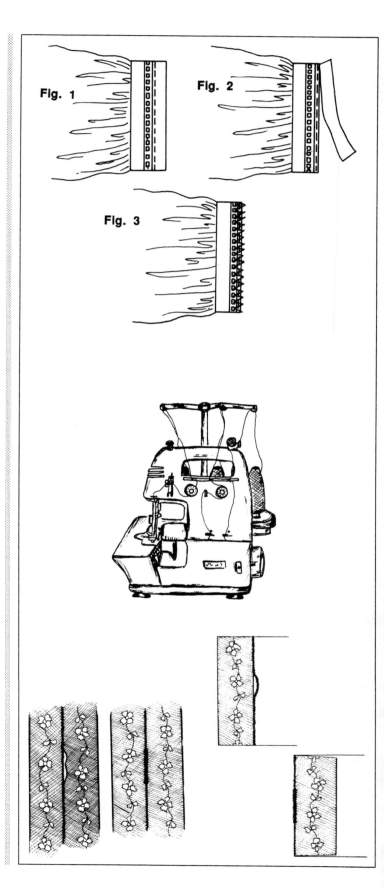

Fig. 1   Fig. 2

Fig. 3

▨ LACE INSERTION PLACKET

Step 1. Cut a slit in the garment the desired length of the placket opening **(fig. 1)**. Cut a piece of 1/2-inch insertion or edging twice this measurement.

Step 2. Pull the skirt apart so that the fabric slit is in a V-shape **(fig. 2)**.

Step 3. Place the right side of the lace to the right side of the V, allowing 1/8 inch of the fabric to extend past the lace **(fig. 3)**.

Step 4. Zigzag the lace to the fabric, using the method "Lace to Fabric" **(fig. 4)**.

Step 5. Press the seam allowance to the fabric.

Step 6. Pull lace to the inside at the point of the V. Sew a dart, starting 1/2 inch from the fold in the lace and stitching to the point **(fig. 5)**. **Optional:** Zigzag over the stitching line and trim away excess lace **(fig. 6)**.

Step 7. Turn back the side of the placket that will be on top when overlapped **(fig. 7)**.

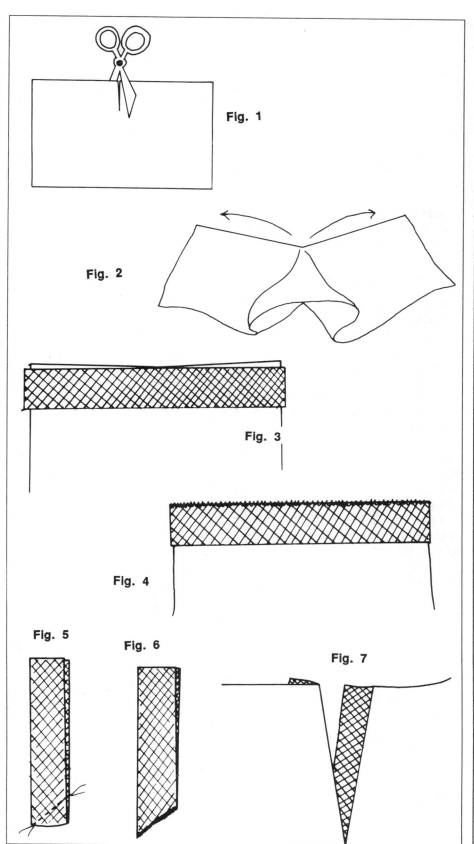

Fig. 1

Fig. 2

Fig. 3

Fig. 4

Fig. 5

Fig. 6

Fig. 7

PLACKETS

▨ CONTINUOUS LAP PLACKET

Step 1. Cut a slit in the garment piece the length needed for the placket (**fig. 1**). Cut a placket strip from the fabric along the selvage 3/4 inch wide and 1/2 inch longer than twice the length of the slit (**fig. 2**). Make the placket, using the following directions.

Step 2. Pull the slit apart in a V-shape (**fig. 3**).

Step 3. Place the placket to the slit, right sides together. The slit is on the top and the placket is on the bottom. Note that the raw edge of the placket meets the V in the slit.

Step 4. Stitch, using a 1/4-inch seam allowance only catching a few fibers at the point. The placket strip will be straight. The skirt will form a V (**fig. 4**).

Step 5. Press the seam toward the selvage edge of the placket strip. Fold the selvage edge to the inside (**fig. 5**). Whip by hand (**fig. 6**) or finish by machine, using the following directions.

Step 6. Pin placket in place. From the right side of the fabric, top stitch ON THE PLACKET 1/16 inch away from the original seam (**fig. 7**).

Step 7. Pulling the placket to the inside of the garment, fold the placket in half, allowing the top edges of the garment to meet (**fig. 8**). Sew a dart, starting 1/2 inch up from the outside bottom edge of the placket to the seam (**fig. 9**).

Step 8. Turn back the side of the placket that will be on top when overlapped (**fig. 10**).

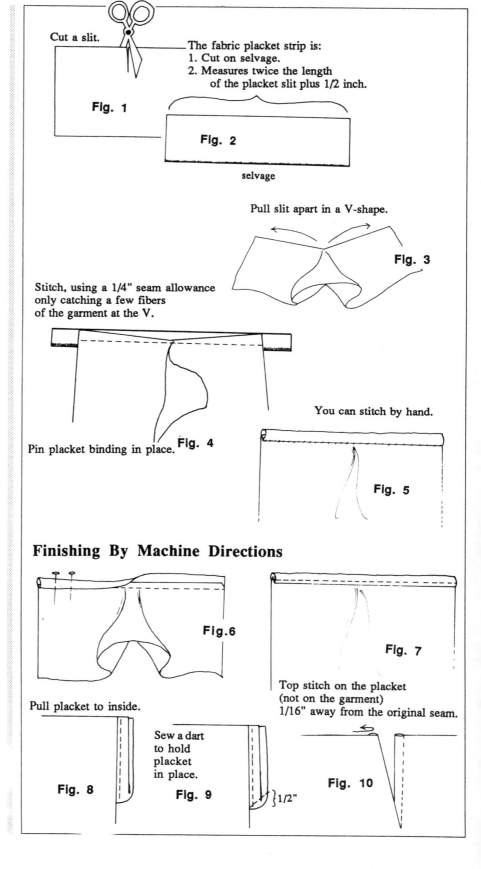

Cut a slit.

The fabric placket strip is:
1. Cut on selvage.
2. Measures twice the length of the placket slit plus 1/2 inch.

Fig. 1

Fig. 2

selvage

Pull slit apart in a V-shape.

Fig. 3

Stitch, using a 1/4" seam allowance only catching a few fibers of the garment at the V.

You can stitch by hand.

Pin placket binding in place. **Fig. 4**

Fig. 5

Finishing By Machine Directions

Fig.6

Pull placket to inside.

Fig. 7

Top stitch on the placket (not on the garment) 1/16" away from the original seam.

Sew a dart to hold placket in place.

Fig. 8

Fig. 9 }1/2"

Fig. 10

▓ DOUBLE-LACE BACK PLACKET

This back placket is a pretty as well as strong way to make a back placket when you don't want a double fold back of fabric.

Step 1. Trim the center-back bodice, dress edge evenly. Trim away the fold backs.

Step 2. Place a piece of lace insertion on both the front and the back of this raw, center-back edge (**fig. 1**).

Step 3. Stitch, using a tiny straight-stitch through both headings and the dress.

Step 4. Fold both pieces of lace insertion over to the center back edges. Press.

Step 5. Stitch both pieces of lace insertion together (through the heading), using a straight-stitch at the center-back line.

Step 6. Now, you have a back placket in which to make your buttonholes.

▓ SNAPS

Snaps are used to fasten two parts of a garment together at points where there is little strain and where the closing must remain smooth and inconspicuous. Snaps come in various sizes. Number 4/0 snap size is for sheer fabrics; plastic snaps are good for heirloom sewing. A single, strong thread is used to sew on the snaps. This is one place where a synthetic thread might be better than cotton thread. The snaps should be concealed but placed near enough to the edge of the lap so that the edge does not roll back, and near enough together so the material will not gap.

Step 1. Take a back stitch in the center of the mark, and place the needle through one of the holes in the snap.

Step 2. The snap is sewn in place with buttonhole stitches in each of the four holes by sliding the needle from hole to hole underneath the strip.

Step 3. Care should be taken that the stitches are not allowed to pass through the batiste or other heirloom material so that they show on the right side of the garment.

Step 4. Sew on the ball part of the snap first.

Step 5. To correctly locate the position for the socket portion of the snap, the ball part of the snap is placed over the under closing and the spot marked with a pin.

Step 6. After finding the correct point, stitch the socket part on firmly.

Step 7. To fasten the thread, two or three small stitches should be taken.

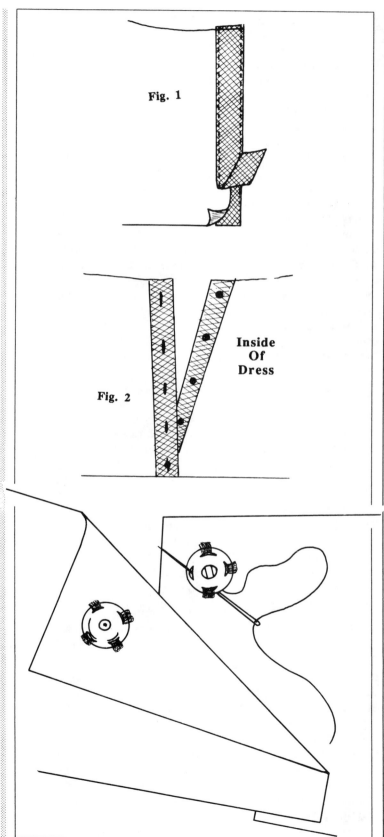

Fig. 1

Fig. 2

Inside Of Dress

BUTTONS

▓ BUTTONS, BUTTONS, BUTTONS

Buttons may be used for function or fashion. They may fasten with buttonholes or loops. The preferred button for heirloom sewing is pearl. Plastic is not acceptable for true heirloom sewing. There are two basic types of buttons: those with shanks and those with two or more holes (**fig. 1**).When purchasing pearl buttons, check carefully for smoothness of finish and strong construction. Some antique pearl buttons might have cracks. These won't hold up well. Rough, sharp places anywhere on the button could tear up your buttonholes or the threads attaching the buttons. A weak shank could easily pull out, especially on a boy's button-on pants.

If buttons are used only as decoration, the location of each should be determined and marked by a water-soluble pen, a pencil, or straight pins. If buttons are to be used to fasten the garment, they should be sewed on after the buttonholes to determine proper placement. The opening of the garment should be lapped correctly, and the buttonhole position should be at the outer end of the buttonhole (**fig. 2**). The position for all of the buttons should be marked before any of them are sewed on.

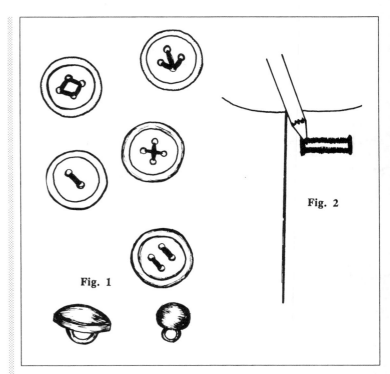

Fig. 1

Fig. 2

▓ SEWING ON BUTTONS

Directions for Button-Stitching Foot:

The method of sewing on buttons varies somewhat with the type of button. Sewing machines usually have a button stitching foot available, which will hold the button flat.

Step 1. Turn off your feed dogs if you are going to sew the button on with this foot.

Step 2. Place a pin on top of the button to create a shank that will allow space for the overlapped layer of fabric to be buttoned (**fig. 3**).

Step 3. Carefully turn your zigzag width to the proper width to go in and out the two holes.

Step 4. Turn the fabric slightly when you get ready to go in and out the other two holes — if it is a four-hole button.

Step 5. To tie off, take several stitches in the same hole, after the button is stitched down. Turn off the zigzag when you make this stitch. Use Scotch tape to hold the button down while you are sewing it on.

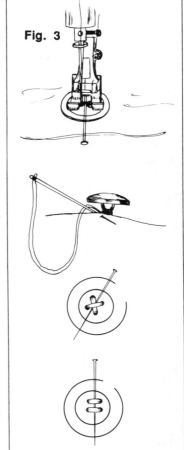

Fig. 3

▓ ATTACHING BUTTONS BY HAND

If the button is a flat button, a shank needs to be made. The shank must be added so that the buttonhole side of the garment may lie flat against the button side of the garment. A heavy single, medium double, or a heavy double thread is satisfactory for sewing on buttons.

Step 1. A small stitch on the right side of the garment, which will be covered by the button, is used to fasten the thread.

Step 2. Pass the needle up through a hole in the button and down through the other hole to the wrong side of the button. Slip a pin or a toothpick under the stitch. If a two-hole button is used, stitches should be parallel with the buttonhole to prevent it from spreading.

Step 3. Continue stitching until the button is secure.

Step 4. Bring the needle out between the button and fabric.

Step 5. Remove pin and pull the button to the top of the loop.

Step 6. Wind the thread around the loose stitches to make a firm shank. With several small stitches, fasten on the wrong side of the fabric.

New Techniques

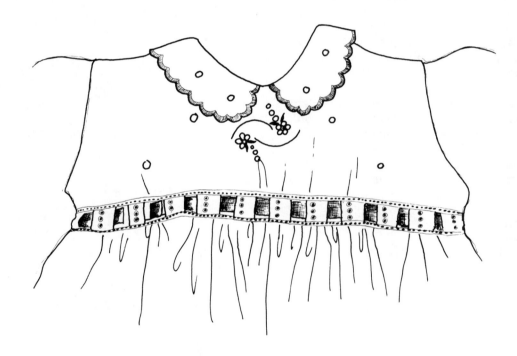

SHARK'S TEETH TECHNIQUE

One afternoon while browsing in an antique store here in Huntsville, I saw a petticoat which absolutely winked at me. I had to take it home. Later that day I called my incredibly talented friend, Sue Pennington, to ask her if she could unravel the techniques which were used in making this breathtaking petticoat. Sue and her family began to call this petticoat, the shark's teeth garment because sharks have rows and rows of white triangular teeth. For an example of the Shark's Teeth technique see the Antique Curved Panel Shark's Teeth Dress in the Christening Gown, circa 1992 section.

Since the technique and the original Sue Pennington garments appeared in *Sew Beautiful*, Summer 1991 magazine, the response has been unbelievable. Most readers love the tailored look of this type of French sewing. Don't be afraid of making shark's teeth. They are very easy to make especially if you use glue stick to hold the points into place while you sew. By the way, you can make a shark's teeth panel to insert into any portion of any garment. Just make the panel larger than your pattern piece, and after completing the shark's teeth treatment, cut out your garment.

The fabric used to make shark's teeth must be lightweight and closely woven. Polyester-cotton blends would be difficult to work with because they do not hold a sharp crease. Heavily starched light weight cottons work beautifully. This technique is not difficult, although accuracy in marking, pressing, cutting and stitching is necessary. The results are well worth the effort.

Materials Needed
- 100% cotton fabric
- Dixon pencil or quilter's pencil (Nancy's Notions)
- Fabric glue stick
- Sharp scissors

Pattern Envelope Pieces Needed
- Template
- Tucking Guide

Step 1. Using the tucking guide from the pattern envelope mark tucking lines across fabric using a Dixon pencil or quilter's pencil. The marking device must be easily removed after ironing. I usually mark tucking lines using dots or short lines. Mark tucks lightly, just enough for you to see. These tucking lines are 1-5/8 inch apart (**fig. 1**).

Step 2. Fold fabric along these lines, wrong sides together and press (**fig. 2**).

Step 3. Stitch 1/2 inch from the fold of the fabric. This creates a tuck (**fig. 3**).

Step 4. Place the tucked piece on the ironing board, tuck side up, and slide the iron over the tucks in one direction.

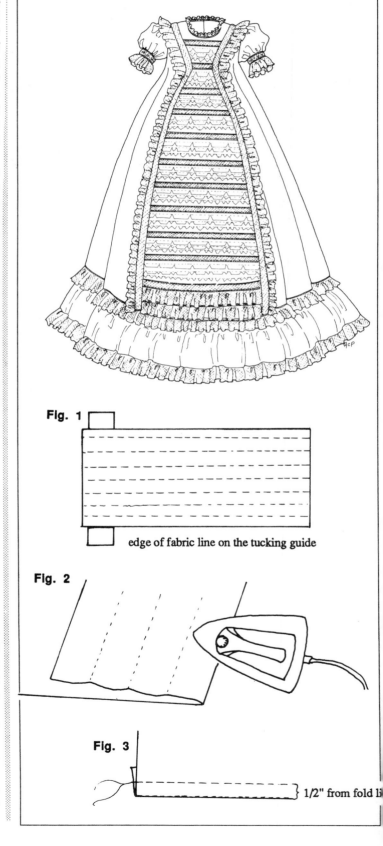

Fig. 1

edge of fabric line on the tucking guide

Fig. 2

Fig. 3

{ 1/2" from fold l

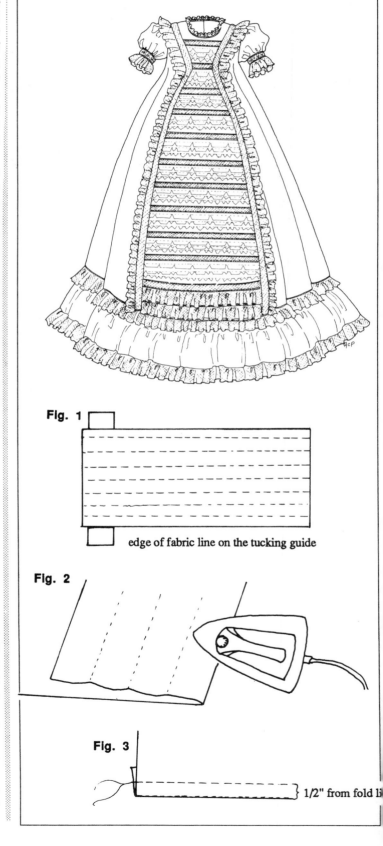

Step 5. Turn the piece over, tucked side down, starch and press again. Now starch and press one more time with the tucks right side up. The tucks should almost touch (**fig. 4**).

Step 6. With the tucks pointing at you, place the Shark's Teeth template (pyramid) centered under the tucked panel with the widest part of the template (pyramid) closest to you and the top of the template (pyramid) at the first tuck. Transferring the marks to the top of the tucks can be done using three different methods, all methods will have the same end results.

I. WINDOW METHOD

To see the marks through three fabric layers hold the template and tucked fabric to a window and transfer the marks of the pyramid to each tuck. The first tuck will have one mark, the second tuck - two marks, the third tuck - three marks, etc. Once marking is started be careful not to let the template slip. Template marks are equally spaced on each side of the mark above (**Fig. 5**).

II. LIFT AND MARK METHOD

Lift the tuck to allow you to see the template through one fabric layer but transfer the mark to the fold of the tuck with a dot (**fig. 6**). Repeat transfer for the other pleats.

III. FOLDING THE TEMPLATE METHOD

Step 7. Mark the first tuck in the center. This represents the first mark of the template (**Fig. 7**).

Step 8. Fold the template so that the second row of marks is at the top of the paper (**fig. 8**).

Step 9. Place template under the second tuck and center these two marks with the first mark of the first tuck. Transfer these two marks on the second tuck (**fig. 9**).

Step 10. Fold the template so that the third row of marks is at the top of the paper.

Step 11. Place the template under the third tuck and center these three marks with the two marks of the tuck above (**fig. 10**).

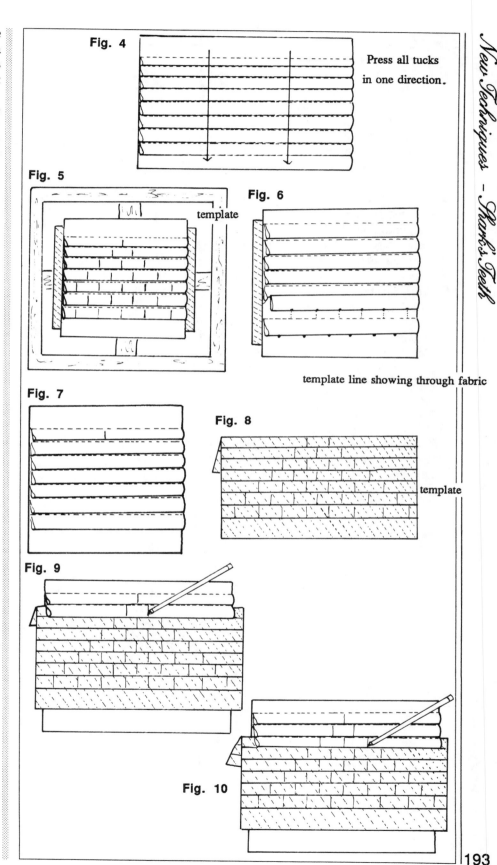

Fig. 4   Press all tucks in one direction.

Fig. 5

Fig. 6   template

template line showing through fabric

Fig. 7

Fig. 8   template

Fig. 9

Fig. 10

193

SHARK'S TEETH TECHNIQUE

Step 12. Transfer all marks using the preferred transfer technique **(fig. 11)**.

Step 13. Clip perpendicular to the fold of the tuck, through the two layers of the tuck. Clip to, but not through the stitching line of the tucks **(fig. 12)**.

Step 14. Flip the first tuck up, at the clip, so that you can see the underside and place a small amount of fabric glue on each side of the clip **(fig. 13)**.

Step 15. Fold the cut edges of the clip to the underside of the tuck just over the stitching line **(fig. 14)**. These fabric angles should hide the stitching line of the tuck and create the angular opening in the first tuck **(fig. 15)**.

Step 16. Repeat for all clips.

Step 17. Starch and press tucks back toward you hiding all the folded corners **(fig. 16)**.

Step 18. Top stitch just under the stitching line of the tuck with a tiny zigzag (3/4 length and 1 width). This stitching will be made through the two layers of the tuck and the base fabric **(fig. 17)**. Instead of a zigzag, a decorative stitch can be used **(fig. 18)**. This zigzag or decorative stitch should catch all the clipped edges of fabric **(fig. 19)**.

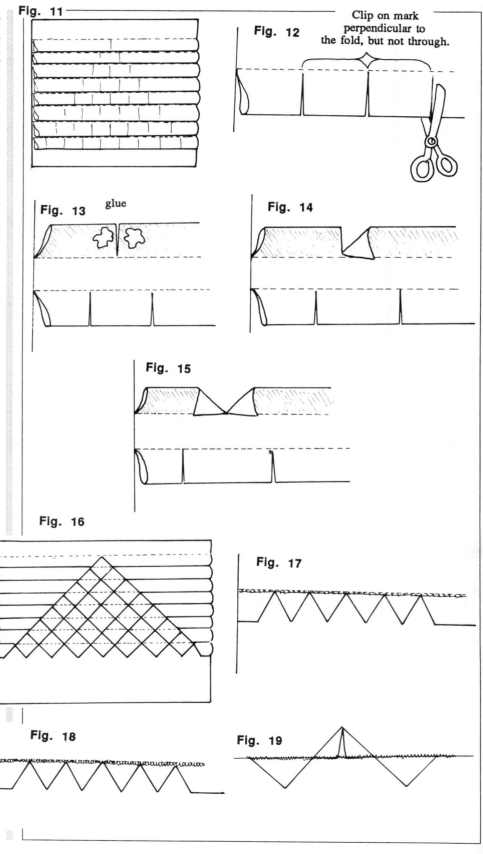

Fig. 11

Fig. 12 Clip on mark perpendicular to the fold, but not through.

Fig. 13 glue

Fig. 14

Fig. 15

Fig. 16

Fig. 17

Fig. 18

Fig. 19

▦ ADDING SHARK'S TEETH TO YOUR PATTERN

Shark's teeth can be added to a pattern by working with a block of tucks the length and width of the pattern piece. Cutting lines for the open angles of the sharks teeth can then be placed appropriately and construction of the sharks teeth completed as stated above.

Step 1. Measure the pattern piece for your shark's teeth at the widest point and the longest point **(fig. 20)**.

Step 2. Using the longest length, multiply this measurement by two. This will give you the number of 1/2-inch tucks required for this pattern piece. Each of these tuck will take up 1 inch of the fabric. Now to find the length to cut the fabric, add the length of the pattern plus the number of tucks required. The width will remain the same. Cut a piece of fabric to this measurement plus 2 inches extra in length and width (to be on the safe side) **Fig. 21**.

Step 3. Mark for the tucks by starting 1-1/2 inch from the bottom edge of your fabric with your first fold mark. Mark the entire piece **(fig. 22)**.

Step 4. Tuck the fabric as described in Step 2 and 3. Starch and press tucked piece as described in Step 4. Trace pattern piece on tucked piece using a fabric marker **(fig. 23)**.

Step 5. Decide where to put the open angles of the shark's teeth design. The pyramid shape is the most common design but others may be used. Mark tucks for cutting **(fig. 24)**.

Step 6. Follow Steps 5 through 11 to complete shark's teeth. Cut out along pattern lines and construct garment according to directions.

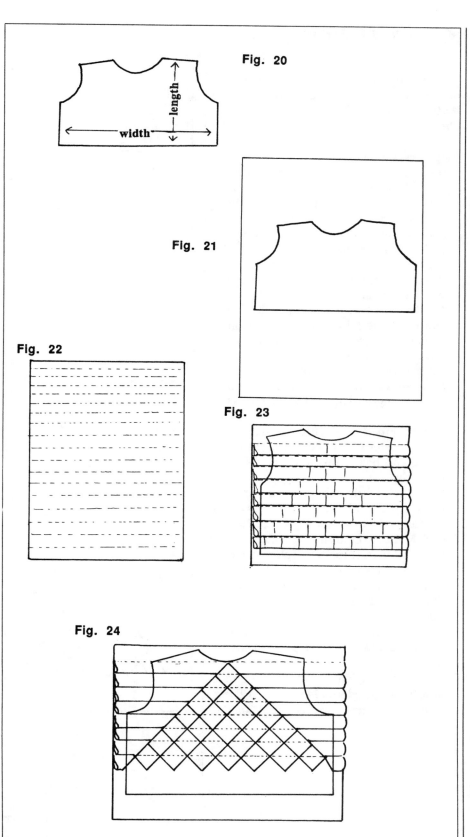

Fig. 20

Fig. 21

Fig. 22

Fig. 23

Fig. 24

SHARK'S TEETH TECHNIQUE

▓ SHARK'S TEETH INSERTION

An example of sharks teeth insertion is on the front panel of Sue Pennington's Antique Curved Panel Shark's Teeth Dress.

Step 1. When making a shark's teeth insertion, decide on the number of tucks desired. Use the following formula for cutting the width of the insertion fabric: 1-5/8 inch multiplied by the number of tucks plus 1 inch (extra fabric top and bottom for space and seam allowance). For Sue's dress, three tucks were used. Therefore the formula for the width of the fabric is 1-5/8 inch x 3 = 4-3/4 inch +1 inch = 5-3/4 inch. The length of the fabric will depend on where the insertion is used. Sue's dress took approximately two 45-inch lengths for the front panel. Dress bottoms would take approximately two 45-inch lengths. Cut fabric for tucked piece.

Step 2. Start marking the first tucking line in the center of the fabric. Measure above and below this fold line 1-5/8 inch (fig. 25).

Step 3. Tuck fabric using general directions step 2 and 3. Starch and press using General Directions step 4 (fig. 26).

Step 4. Mark the bottom tuck with parallel lines 7/8 inch apart. Cut along these lines for open angles of the teeth (fig. 27). Place the template under the remaining tucks to complete the pyramids (fig. 28). Mark the cutting lines and complete the shark's teeth using the General Directions steps 5 - 11 (fig. 29).

Step 5. Use completed strip as insertion attaching entredeux, laces, etc to the shark's teeth insertion piece (fig. 30).

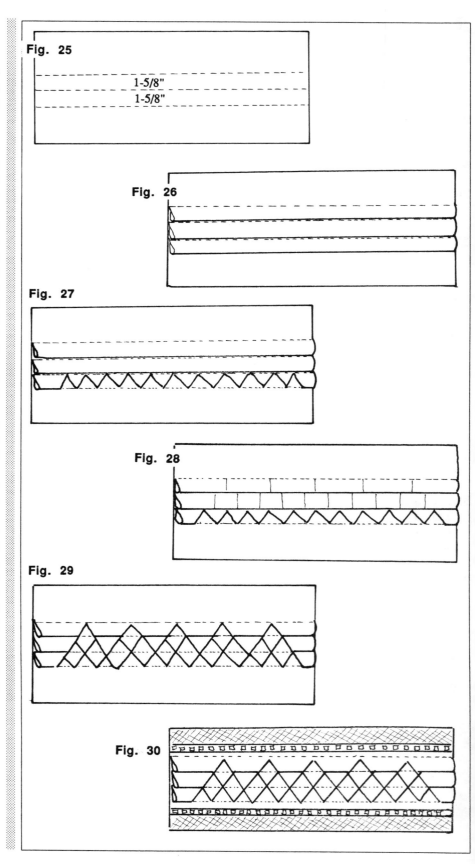

Fig. 25

1-5/8"
1-5/8"

Fig. 26

Fig. 27

Fig. 28

Fig. 29

Fig. 30

BABY SHADOW DIAMONDS

I fell in love with shadow diamonds with the purchase of the Ladies Shadow Diamond Skirt, featured in my *Antique Clothing, French Sewing by Machine* book. From all over the world ladies have enjoyed making shadow diamonds for collars, skirts, bodices and sleeves. One morning as we were working on this book in the studio, our friend Gail Settle came up the stairs. She had a bag with a real surprise in it which she felt we would want to see.

It was the sweetest antique apron that I have ever seen with these baby shadow diamonds on the front of the skirt of the apron and on the ties. What an incredible amount of work for an apron! Immediately we asked if we could include this template and technique for baby diamonds in the new book. Gail agreed. This technique would be so sweet in the princess curved front christening gown or on a high yoke bodice of another gown. Enjoy this technique. Please work slowly because it is tedious!

Materials Needed
- X-acto knife and cutting mat or small pair of very sharp scissors
- Suggested fabrics: Linen, Swiss Batiste, Victorian batiste or any other fabric that holds a crease.
- Dixon pencil or regular pencil
- Thread, iron, ironing board and starch
- Baby Shadow Diamond Template (page 198)

GENERAL DIRECTIONS

Two pieces of fabric will be required to complete this technique. The top layer will have the diamond shapes cut into the fabric. This cut layer will be the outside of the garment. The second layer will be placed behind the diamond cut outs to shadow through.

Step Trace lightly, using a Dixon pencil or pencil, the shadow diamond template on the wrong side of the fabric (**fig. 1**). The template can be extended to cover more area or squares can be arranged to form shape.

Step 2. Using and X-acto knife and cutting mat or small pointed scissors cut, very carefully, along solid lines of the + (**fig. 2**).

Step 3. Working from the wrong side of the fabric, pull the center points at the middle of the "X's" that you have just cut, to the back creating an open diamond (**fig. 3**). Finger press in place. This should hold the fold back pieces enough for you to then press it with an iron.

Step 4. Press folds in place.

Step 5. Place second layer of fabric over the folded angles. The second layer of fabric will show through the holes. Pin the two layers of fabric together and straight stitch along the folds in a diagonal pattern (**figs. 4 and 5**) or straight stitch around the edges of the square to hold the fabric angles in place (**fig. 6**). This stitching will hold folded edges in place.

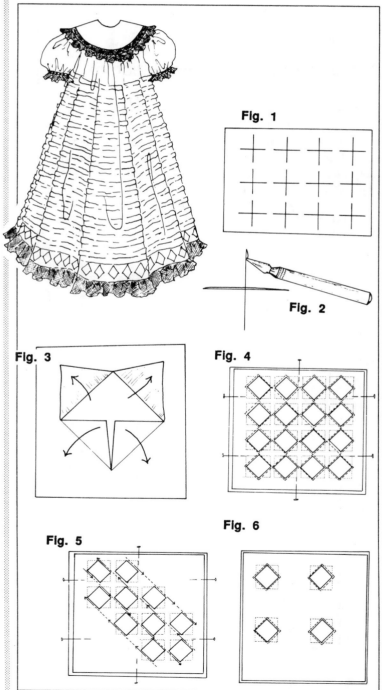

Fig. 1

Fig. 2

Fig. 3

Fig. 4

Fig. 5

Fig. 6

BABY SHADOW DIAMONDS

▨ SHADOW DIAMOND INSERTION

Cut a strip of the fabric the length and width of the desired insertion piece. Trace, cut and press open diamonds. Place second layer of fabric cut the same width and length as the first. Place on top of the cut diamonds and stitch in place as described in step 5 of the General Directions. Continue adding laces, entredeux, etc. to the shadow diamond insertion treating the two layers of fabric as one layer **(fig. 7)**.

▨ SHADOW DIAMOND YOKE OR BODICE

Cut two rectangles of fabric larger than the yoke or bodice. Trace the pattern on the top rectangle using a fabric marker. Trace the shadow diamond template in desired position. Cut and press folds of diamonds in place. Place second layer of fabric which is cut the same width and length as the first on top of the diamonds and stitch in place as described in step 5 of the General Directions. Straight stitch just inside the pattern line **(fig. 8)**. Cut pattern from fabric and stitch two layers of fabric as one layer **(fig. 9)**.

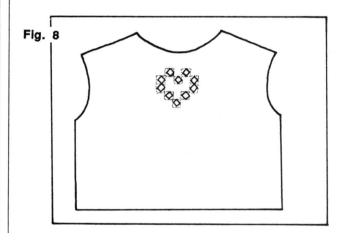

Fig. 7

Fig. 8

Fig. 9

Baby Shadow Diamond Template

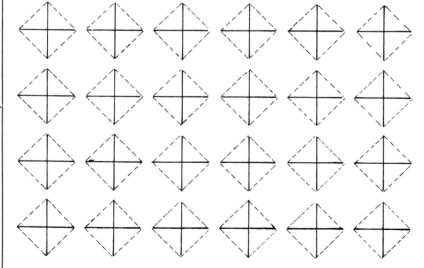

MAKING LACE ON THE MACHINE
BERNINA, ELNA, PFAFF, AND VIKING

*With today's new sewing machines there is absolutely no reason that you can't make your own laces on netting using built-in stitches. The vines and flowers, large stitch capabilities, scalloped stitches and other **built-in stitches**, are perfect for this new technique - lace making on the sewing machine. We consulted with the educational directors of my favorite sewing machine companies-Bernina, Elna, Pfaff and Viking-and asked them to develop the best technique for lace making on their top-of-the-line computerized machines. They did and we are reporting the actual stitches used, the techniques used, and the other ideas which they wanted you to know. Machine embroiderers have been making laces on the machine for a long time using free-motion embroidery. Since that is another skill altogether, I wanted this section to be "fool-proof;" therefore we required that the stitches that were to be provided here for you to be those built in - you just choose and stitch. We would like to thank our favorite sewing machine companies for their contribution to the whole heirloom sewing industry and most specifically, for taking the time to stitch the lace and to write the directions for this section. Please look in the color section of this book to see actual lace samples described on the next pages.*

▓ GENERAL DIRECTIONS

Lace making by machine is simply decorative stitches or machine embroidery stitches made on netting.

Insertion - To make a piece of insertion lace, simply stabilize the netting using one of the methods listed below in **Step 2**. Run two parallel rows of satin stitching the desired width apart to border the insertion. Fill in the netting between the parallel rows of stitching with decorative stitches to create lace.

Edging - To make a piece of edging, finish one edge of the netting using a scallop or other decorative satin stitch in which the fabric along the lower edge of the stitch can be totally trimmed away. Decorative stitches can then be placed above this edging stitch to create lace edging.

Step 1. Cut netting strip to the width and length desired plus 2 inches extra in length and width. If cotton netting is used, starch and press the netting before cutting because the netting will shrink.

Step 2. Stablize the netting using one of the following methods:

A. Solvy or Aqua Sol - This water soluable stabilizer can be placed under the netting, on top of the netting or the netting can be placed between two pieces of the water soluable stabilizer. More than one layer of stabilizer can be used if desired. This stabilizer can either be pinned in place or secured by placing teflon pressing sheets on the top and bottom of the stabilizer/netting/stabilizer and pressing. Remove the pressing sheet. The netting and stabilizer are secure. After stitching, rinse the fabric in cold water to remove stabilizer.

B. Liquid Stabilizer - "Perfect Sew" is a product distributed by Pati Palmer. This is a liquid that can be painted on the fabric or the fabric can be dipped into the stabilizer. After drying, the fabric is very stiff. Stitches can then be placed on the stiffened fabric with a minimal amount of puckering. "Perfect Sew" works best with 100% cotton fabric. After stitching, rinse the fabric in cold water to remove stabilizer.

C. Making Liquid Stabilizer
To make your own liquid stabilizer - Place 1 yard of Solvy or Aqua Sol into 1/2 to 3/4 cup of water. The mixture will be the consistancy of egg yokes. Paint or dip the netting with the mixture. Let the netting dry. It will be very stiff. Stitch in desired manner. After stitching, rinse the fabric in cold water to remove stabilizer.

D. Tear Away or Stitch and Tear - If satin stitching is used, a tear away stabilizer will work. However, the stabilizer must be torn away very gently or you may distort the more delicate stitches. When making lace on netting, the delicate straight decorative stitches were done using stabilizing method A, B or C. For the heavier decorative stitching, such as the edging scallop or other edging satin stitches, a tear away stabilizer could be used to hold the netting.

Step 3. Use the decorative stitches on your sewing machine to create lace insertions, lace edgings or lace fabric. Clip excess threads. Rinse fabric with water to remove stabilizer. Press. This technique will let you experiment with what your sewing machine can do while creating the most beautiful and unique lace designs.

LACE MAKING ON THE BERNINA 1530

All of the lace samples were prepared as follows:
1. Netting Used: cotton/polyester or all cotton
2. Spray starch and press netting
3. Each sample was stitched using 4 layers of Solvy underneath the netting.
4. After sewing Solvy was rinsed from the netting. Let dry.
5. Starch and press.

#1 1/2-inch Lace Insertion (cotton/polyester)
Foot #20 Open Embroidery
Thread Used: Mettler/Swiss Metrosene #30 cotton embroidery (color 703) top, Mettler/Swiss Metrosene #60 cotton embroidery (color 02) bobbin
Needle: #70 or #80 universal needle
Step 1. Stitch parallel satin stitch rows 1/2 inch apart.
Step 2. menu G2, pattern #8, double stitch pattern x 3

#2 1/2-inch Lace Edging
Foot #20 Open Embroidery
Thread Used: Mettler/Swiss Metrosene #30 cotton embroidery (color 703) top, Mettler/Swiss Metrosene #60 cotton embroidery (color 02) bobbin
Needle: #70 or #80 universal needle
Step 1. menu G2, pattern #8, double stitch pattern x 3.
Step 2. Stitch the following scallop pattern 1/2-inch below the decorative completed in Step 1: menu H, pattern #9, width 3, mirror image, double needle limitation x 2

#3 1-inch Lace Insertion (cotton/polyester)
Foot #20 Open Embroidery
Thread Used: Madeira #30 rayon embroidery (color 1082) top, Madeira Decor 6 (color 1450) bobbin
Needle: #80 universal needle
Step 1. Stitch parallel satin stitch rows 1 inch apart.
Step 2. Stitch center design from the reverse side. Solvy will be next to the presser foot.
Right row: menu I1, pattern #6
Left row: I1, pattern #6, mirror image, pattern begin
Sewing instructions: stitch right row; return to top of stitching. Select mirror image and pattern begin; sew left row 3/8 inch from right row), matching patterns.
Center row: menu G1, pattern #11, double needle limitation x 2

#4 1-inch Lace Edging
Step 1. Use instruction #3 for the decorative stitching omitting parallel stitching lines.
Step 2. Scallop (stitch 1/4" from decorative stitching) - menu H, pattern #9, stitch width 2, mirror image, pattern extension x 4.

#5 2-inch double or 4-inch Old McDonald Insertion (cotton/polyester)
Foot #20 Open Embroidery
Thread Used: Mettler/Swiss Metrosene #30 cotton embroidery (colors #498, #805, #501) top, Mettler/Swiss Metrosene #60 cotton embroidery bobbin
Needle: #70 or #80 universal needle
Step 1. Animals - MR + menu K - pattern #4 + pattern #6 + menu L - pattern #1 + menu K - pattern #2 + pattern #1
Sewing instructions: stitch right side of center row; pivot and stitch left row, matching stitching at center; stitch outer right row top to bottom (1 inch from center rows), turn fabric then stitch outer left row top to bottom (1 inch from center rows).
Step 2. Letters - MR menu D
O+L+D+space+M+C+D+O+N+A+L+D+space+H+A+D+space A+space+F+A+R+M+space
Sewing instruction - stitch "OLD MCDONALD HAD A FARM" along outer edge, 1 inch from outer row.

#6 4-inch Old McDonald Edging
Step 1. Follow directions for Insertion#5
Step 2. Make one row animals in yellow thread; one row in pink thread; and another row in yellow, then make row of letters spelling "OLD MCDONALD HAD A FARM" 1 inch from outer edge.

#7 2-inch Lace Insertion (cotton/polyester)
Foot #20 Open Embroidery
Thread Used: Madeira #30 rayon embroidery (color 1082) top, Mettler/Swiss Metrosene #60 cotton embroidery (color 02) bobbin
Needle: #70 or #80 universal needle
Step 1. Stitch parallel satin stitch rows 2 inches apart.
Step 2. Center row (left side - menu G1, pattern #9 extension x 2
Center row (right side - menu G1, pattern #9 extension x 2, mirror image, pattern begin. Stitch with 2 threads through one needle (#30 rayon embroidery thread), sew right side of center row first; return to top of stitching; select mirror image and pattern begin function; stitch left side of center, matching patterns.
Step 3. left row - menu - G1, pattern #9
Right row - menu G1, mirror image, pattern begin
Sew with two threads through one needle (#30 rayon embroidery thread), stitch right and left rows, 1/2 inch from center rows.

#8 Lace Edging (cotton/polyester)
Step 1. Follow directions for lace design using #7 lace insertion step 2 - 3.
Step 2. Sew edging stitch using menu H, pattern #9, mirror image, soluble stitch pattern x 2. This stitch is placed 5/8 inch from last row of decorative stitching.

All of the lace samples were prepared as follows:
1. Pre-shrink netting with cotton content.
2. Layer aqua solve, netting and aqua solve.
3. Transfer template lines on aqua solve with washable markers.
4. To remove aqua solve - Tear away excess and wash remainder under cool running water.

Machine Preparation
Use the following unless otherwise indicated.
1. Needle: #80/12
2. Needle tension: 2-1/2
3. Bobbin: 50 weight cotton DMC
4. Foot: "b" for twin needle and satin scalloped edges
   "a" for all other decorative stitches

Seam Allowances 1/2-inch width easily defined with one row twin needle (1.6/70) straight stitch. No aqua solve required. Needle tension: 5. Stitch: #1.

#1 Lace Insertion (nylon)
Thread: Top 40 weight rayon (Sulky)
Floral pattern: Cassette 2
Memory: Stitch # 852, Stitch # 125, Stitch #852, +face to face + mirror image key.

#2 Lace Edging (nylon)
Floral pattern: (same as #1 lace insertion)
Scallop Edge: Cassette 6 - Stitch #800
Dot: Stitch #92 (Width 4.4, Length 0.3)

#3 Lace Insertion (nylon)
No aqua solve required.
Thread: top and bobbin 30 weight cotton DMC
Needle: twin needle (1.6/70)
Needle Tension: 5
Stitch: #5 (width 6.2, length 1.8)
Stitch three rows

#4 Lace Edging (nylon)
Prepare and sew same as Insertion #3.
Satin Edge: Tension 3.5, Cassette 2
In memory: Stitch #867, Stitch #867 + mirror

#5 Lace Insertion (cotton/polyester)
Thread: Top 30 weight cotton DMC
Decorative pattern: Cassette 6
In memory Stitch #811, Stitch #807 + face to face, Stitch #811, Stitch #807

#6 Lace Edging (cotton/polyester)
Scallop Edge: Aqua solve on top only, bobbin pearl rayon cord.
Needle tension: 5
Needle: Twin 1.6/70, Stitch #90 (length 3.1)
Scroll Pattern: Cassette 6
A - #807 mirror
B - #807
Flower: Cassette 6   C - #811

Placement for Lace #6

#7 Lace Insertion (cotton netting)
Thread: Top 30 weight cotton DMC
Ivy: Cassette 2   Stitch #852
Flowers: Cassette 6   Stitch #811

#8 Lace Edging (cotton netting)
Thread same as Insertion #7
A. Ivy: Cassette 2   Stitch #852
B. Ivy Mirrored: Cassette 2   Stitch #852 + mirror image key
C. Flowers: Cassette 6   Stitch #811
D. Motif: Cassette 6   Stitch #808
E. Motif: Cassette 6   Stitch #808 + mirror image key

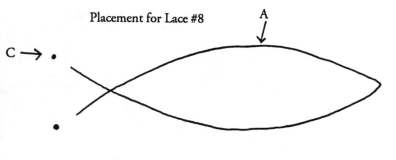

Placement for Lace #8

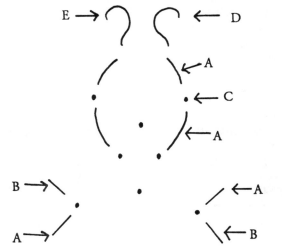

LACE MAKING ON THE PFAFF 1475CD

All of the lace samples were prepared as follows:

1. Universal needles, size 70, unless otherwise stated.
2. Press together: one layer presser cloth, next two layers of Wash Away or Solvy, one layer of netting and one layer presser cloth.
3. Used only Pfaff's Mez Alcazar Rayon Thread #485 as both upper and lower threads.
4. All stitches were secured with Fray Chek.
5. Tension was loosened to the buttonhole range.
6. Since the same machine was used, it was not necessary to program each stitch into the machine for each piece. They were programed once and used again and again.
7. When finished, run the piece under cold running water until water soluable stabilizer is gone. Press.

#1 1/2-inch Lace Insertion (50% cotton, 50% polyester) Foot #2

Step 1. Stitch parallel satin stitch rows 1/2 inch apart.
Step 2. Sew stitch #137 in the middle of the netting strip.

#2 1-inch Lace Edging - Foot #2

Step 1. Program the following into an empty M-memory. 156(1x),217(3x),156(1x),217(3x),156(1x),215(3x),156(1x), 215(3x)
Step 2. Stitch 1 inch from the edge the above program.
Step 3. Center one stitch #137 in arch.
Step 4. Place random stitch #127 made as small as possible 1/2 inch above the flowers.

#3 1-inch Lace Insertion (50% cotton, 50% polyester) Foot #8

Step 1. Stitch parallel satin stitch rows 1-inch apart.
Step 2. Thread eye of single needle with two spools of thread. Sew at right angles wth your strip. Begin with stitch #204 wth the red hash mark in foot #8 even with the satin stitch. Stitch until the stem of the tulip comes back to the beginning of the stem. Stop. Press pattern start key to reset stitch #204.
Step 3. Move the presser foot 1/4 inch away from the top of the first tulip and repeat **step 2.** Continue until your strip of lace netting is completely full of tulips.
Step 4. Program into an M-memory the following:
127 - 5.0 width, 0.3-length, 5.0 pattern length
00- 6.0 length
127 - 5.0 width, 0.3-length, 5.0 pattern length
With single pattern key on, sew a row in between each tulip. **Note:** This entire insertion is sewn crosswise.

#4 2-inch Lace Edging (100% cotton) - Foot #8

Step 1. Program the following into an empty M-memory. 156(1x),217(3x),156(1x),217(3x),156(1x),217(3x),156(1x), 217(3x),156(1x),217(3x),156(1x),215(3x),156(1x),215(3x), 156(1x), 215(3x),156(1x), 215(3x), 156(1x) 215(3x)
Step 2. Stitch the above program 1-inch away from the edge of the netting.
Step 3. Select stitch #204. Stitch one tulip beginning in the

center of the V. Stop sewing after the tulip's stem is complete. Press pattern start and continue sewing until all of the tulips in one dirtection are sewn
Step 4. Press pattern mirror. Beginning in the same spot, sew another tulip facing the opposite direction.
Step 5. Select stitch #127, 6.0 width , 0.3 length, 6.0 pattern length. Single pattern and sew one ball between each set of tulips.

#5 1-1/2-inch Lace Insertion (100% cotton) - Foot #2

Step 1. Stitch parallel satin stitch rows 1-1/2 inches apart.
Step 2. Use program in Lace Edging #2, Step 1.
Step 3. Sew the above memory beginning with the needle 1/2 inch away from each parallel satin stitch line.
Step 4. Using stitch #137 and single pattern, stitch centering one in each arch.

#6 3-inch Lace Edging (50% polyester, 50% nylon) - Foot #8

Step 1. Use program in Lace Edging #4, Step 1.
Step 2. Stitch the above program 1 inch from netting edge.
Step 3. Select stitch #204. Center stitch beginning in each V point and stitch #204 until the stem of the ball flower is complete. Stop and press the pattern start key. Repeat until a flower is in each of the V points.
Step 4. Measure up 2-1/2 inches from the top of the V on each side and mark using a washout pen or pencil. Use the template and mark the scallop.
Step 5. Change foot to #2 and a 120 wing needle. Select stitch #169, 3.0 width, 2.5 length and stitch following the scalloped line.
Step 6. Change back to a size 70 universal needle. Select stitch #137, single pattern. Sew one flower in the center of each scallop and one at each scallop point.
Step 7. Fill in each ball flower with stitch #127, 5.0 width, 0.3 length, 5.0 pattern length. Be sure to use single pattern.

#7 2-inch Lace Insertion (100% cotton) - Foot #8

Step 1. Stitch parallel satin stitch rows 2 inches apart.
Step 2. Stitch #204 down the center of the parallel satin stitch lines. Change to foot #2.
Step 3. Using stitch #127, 5.0 width, 0.3 length, and 5.0 pattern length, stitch one ball in each of the circle flowers.

#8 4-inch Lace Edging (100% cotton) - Foot #8

Step 1. Use program in Lace Edging #4, Step 1.
Step 2. Stitch the above program 1 inch from netting edge.
Step 3. Select stitch #204. Single pattern. Sew one pattern in every other V.
Step 4. Fill in each ball flower with stitch #127, 5.0 width, 0.3 length, 5.0 pattern length. Be sure to use single pattern.
Step 5. Using template, mark around each flower with a water disappearing marker.
Step 6. Change foot to #2 and a 120 wing needle. Select stitch #169, 3.0 width, 2.5 length and stitch following the drawn line.
Step 7. Change back to a size 70 universal needle. Select stitch #137, single pattern. Sew five flowers randomly in the center between each loop where you do not have #204.

Grandmother's Hope Chest

All of the lace samples were prepared as follows:
1. Netting Used: cotton/polyester or all cotton
2. Solvy or Aqua-Solv used as stabilizer
3. Sandwich netting between two layers of Aqua-Solv or Solvy. Using a press cloth on top and bottom press using a dry iron.
4. Before sewing, snap on correct presser foot as recommended on infodisplay.
5. After sewing Solvy was rinsed from the netting. Let dry.
6. Starch and press.

#1 Lace Insertion (cotton)
Thread - Sulky 30 weight - Top tension 2 to 2-1/2
Fine embroidery cotton in bobbin
Step 1. Stitch two parallel satin stitch rows (A14) 1 inch apart.
Step 2. Stitch L 5 (daisy stitch) in the center of the rows of satin stitches.

#2 Lace Edging (Cotton)
Thread - Sulky 30 weight - Top tension 2 to 2-1/2
Fine embroidery cotton in bobbin
Step 1. Scallop L 34 4.0 twin needle (touch twin needle safety)
Step 2. Stitch L 5 (daisy stitch) Stop. Place stitch at the top of the scallop.

#3 Lace Insertion (polyester)
Thread - Sulky (variegated pastels)
Step 1. Stitch two rows of parallel satin stitching (A14) 1-1/2 inches apart.
Step 2. Stitch D 24 (hearts) in the center of the rows of satin stitches
Step 3. Stitch E 36 on both sides of the hearts, mirror one side

#4 Lace Edging (polyester)
Thread - Sulky
Step 1. Stitch L 34 (scallop) along bottom of netting
Step 2. Stitch D 24 - single hearts in each scallop

Step 3. Stitch E 36 1/4 inch from hearts
Step 4. Stitch D 24 (heart) 1/4 inch from E 36
Step 5. Stitch E 36 mirror image 1/4 inch above hearts

#5 Lace Insertion (cotton)
Thread - Sulky 30 weight - Top tension 2 to 2-1/2
Fine embroidery cotton in bobbin
Step 1. Stitch two rows of parallel satin stitching (A14) 1-1/2 inches apart.
Step 2. Stitch Woven Stitch E 15, stitch length - 6.0, stitch width - 6.0
Touch stop for single pattern
Touch needle down to pivot at right angles

#6 Lace Edging (cotton)
Thread - Sulky 30 weight - Top tension 2 to 2-1/2
Fine embroidery cotton in bobbin
Step 1. Scallop - L 44, 4.0 twin needle, (touch twin needle safety)
Step 2. Stitch Woven Stitch E 15, stitch length - 6.0, stitch width   - 6.0
Touch stop for single pattern
Touch needle down to pivot at right angles

#7 Lace Insertion (cotton)
Thread - Sulky 30 weight , Top tension 2 to 2-1/2
Fine embroidery cotton in bobbin
Step 1. Stitch two rows of parallel satin stitching (A14) 2 inches apart.
Step 2. Stitch L 6 (flower design) in the center of the two rows of satin stitching.

#8 Lace Edging (cotton)
Thread - Sulky 30 weight - Top tension 2 to 2-1/2
Fine embroidery cotton in bobbin
Step 1. Program L 4 ◈ → L 4 stitch length 0.1 → Repeat (touch twin needle safety for 1/2 width)
Step 2. Stitch flower design L 6 above scallop

Lace Shaping

What I love about learning is that it is never over and that it seems to change constantly! With the publication of my first hard cover book, Antique Clothing: French Sewing By Machine, I thought I had delivered to my readers the absolute easiest method of lace shaping those wonderful diamonds, hearts, bows, scalloped skirts, ovals and so forth. Two years later, and many hundreds of hours of teaching all over the world, I have some new methods which will make some of the old ones seem obsolete. When I finished the Antique Clothing book, I simply wondered what I would write about next. Little did I know that I would change and improve those same techniques which seemed so wonderful at the time, to make them even simpler for our readers.

One of the funniest things that I have to relate is that this fold-back method was actually featured in my very first book written in 1983. Why on earth I didn't apply that fold- back method of mitering to lace shaping in addition to traveling around a square collar, I don't know. Recently, while on one of the teaching tours, the fold-back method once again popped into my mind. I tried it on several shapes and it is unbelievable how easy miters became. The best news of all is that you don't ever have to take mitered laces off of the garment after you have shaped them on the board. Just pin them flat and go to the sewing machine.

Another thing that has changed in my teaching of lace shaping is our method of attaching the wonderful lace shapes. We have discovered the fabulous entredeux stitches and wing needle of today's modern sewing machines. If you haven't invested in one of these machines, this is the perfect time for you to considerate it. Refer to the section "Making Entredeux (Or Hemstitching) On Your Sewing Machine" for more information. If your machine doesn't have these wonderful stitches built in, try using a 100 wing needle and a zigzag on your sewing machine for a "sort of" look of hemstitching. Better still, go to your sewing machine dealer and request a demonstration of a new machine.

If you do have the ability to make these wonderful stitches which really are like entredeux, then you probably won't ever buy entredeux again. Just remember, when you use those heavy entredeux stitches, use stabilizer underneath them and stitch through fabric. What I am really trying to say is that you can't stitch this wonderful entredeux stitch through

two pieces of lace, for instance. Using the stabilizer makes it appear that it is alright to butt two pieces of lace together and join them with those beautiful entredeux stitches; however, when you pull the stabilizer away, the stitches won't hold their perfect shape in between just the two pieces of lace. What do you do if you would like to stitch entredeux in between two pieces of lace? Simply   put a strip of fabric right under the point where you have butted the two pieces of lace together. Put your stabilizer underneath that and you can stitch machine-entredeux to your heart's content. After completing the stitching, pull away the stabilizer and trim the fabric from both sides of the stitching. Completing a garment this way will look as if you put $50 worth of entredeux on your dress. Just remember to use fabric underneath two pieces of lace when you want to stitch the machine entredeux directly onto laces.

When you are stitching machine-entredeux around lace shapes such as hearts, diamonds, ovals, or bows, you will just use stabilizer underneath the stitching since you already have fabric ready to stitch through. You do not need to zigzag first before you machine-entredeux stitch. Just shape your laces, spray starch and pin them, place your stabilizer underneath the lace shape and machine-entredeux stitch. After you stitch your entredeux on both sides of the lace shaping, cut your fabric away from behind the lace.

There are two ways to finish the bottom of a garment when using lace shapes such as hearts, circles, bows, ovals, or diamonds on the bottom. Remember, first of all, that you stitch those shapes onto a plain, square skirt bottom. Later that straight skirt bottom will be cut away. The first method of finishing the skirt bottom when you machine entredeux stitch is to stitch the tops of the shapes all the way across the skirt first. When you get ready to finish the bottom of the skirt, gather your lace edging and butt it up to the shaped lace insertion. Put your stabilizer underneath the fabric and machine entredeux stitch, attaching the lace insertion and the gathered lace edging at the same time you are stitching.

The second method is to stitch your entredeux on the bottom of a scalloped, heart, or diamond skirt. Stitch your entredeux on both sides before cutting away any of the skirt. Trim the fabric from behind the lace shapes and trim the bottom almost to the edge of the machine-entredeux stitching. Be careful not to trim to the stitching but give yourself several threads of fabric. Then, you can butt your gathered laces right up to the stitched in entredeux and zigzag on your gathered laces. Be very careful of the width setting when stitching the gathered laces to the trimmed entredeux so that you won't smush the entredeux when you are zigzagging. Please don't be afraid of scalloped skirts, hearts, diamonds, or flip flopping lace bows. With the improved techniques in this book, you really will find that they are easy. Before long, you'll be stitching shapes with ease.

LACE SHAPING TECHNIQUES

MY PHILOSOPHY OF EDUCATION

I would like to share with you a life changing philosophy of education that was taught to me by Dr. Bill Purkey, one of my most important mentors, while I was in graduate school at the University of Florida. Since learning to sew is education, perhaps you will enjoy reading this section. He told us that he was going to blow an old American adage (or Australian, New Zealand, English, Canadian, or whatever). Everybody in your life taught you "When something is worth doing, it is worth doing right! or well." I'm telling you that there is no truth at all in that statement. Does that blow your mind? Well, I would like for each person reading this book to think of one thing that you do extremely well! I mean you are really good at this something. Then I would like for you to raise your hand if you did this thing well the very first time you ever did it. Isn't that funny? I bet 99% of you didn't raise your hand, did you? If you will let me rephrase the old American adage to read another way, I think it will make more sense for my life, and possibly for yours. "When something is worth doing, it is worth doing very poorly at first or very awkwardly. Only then, do you ever have a chance of doing it over and over again to make it better and perhaps eventually as perfect as it can be." Please think of something you really do well and think to yourself how long it took you to learn how to do that thing well. Then, please have patience with yourself and your family when you or they begin something new. I wish every teacher in the world working with children, would tell the class this adage. I think self concepts would be raised and little people would think that their first and awkward work was just the beginning of something wonderful after they practiced.

PURCHASING GLASS HEAD PINS

I have something very important and a little bit funny to interject here. Before you begin any lace shaping and poking pins into boards and pulling strings and other things associated with making these fabulous heirlooms, purchase yourself a goodly number of **GLASS HEAD PINS. All of this type of work has to be spray starched and pressed right on top of the pins.** Since plastic head pins melt, obviously they won't do. All metal pins such as the iris pins with the skinny little metal heads won't melt; however, when you pin hundreds of these little pins into cardboard, your finger will have one heck of a hole poked into it. Please purchase glass head pins and throw away your plastic head pins. How many

times have I heard the question,"Martha, can you tell which are plastic and which are glass?" Well, I have to answer, "No, I can't until I put an iron to them. Then it is too late!" Get the proper pins, please. I also find that it is easier to get the pins one at a time if you have a wrist pin holder. Please don't stick your hands into a pin box. More than one time I have brought my hand out with a pin stuck in my finger when I have attempted to do this. If you don't have a wrist holder, then scatter some pins out on your fabric board so you can see where you are picking them up. This might seem a little trite for me to be telling you this; however, you really don't know how many pins you will work with when you begin shaping laces.

DRAWING SHAPES WITH DOTS RATHER THAN A SOLID LINE

Margaret Boyles taught me years ago that it is simpler to draw your shapes on fabric by making dots about one half inch apart than it is to draw a solid line. This also means less pencil or marker to get out of the fabric when your lace shaping is finished (fig. 1).

Please mark the turn around areas such as the center top and center bottom of the heart in a solid line. Also, make a solid line when marking the insides (bottom and top) of the heart where you will fold back your laces to make your fold back miter. When I am marking diamonds, I also make a solid line at the four angles of the diamonds. I make little dots as I travel around the straight sides. I also make a solid line into the center of the diamonds where I will pin at the top and at the bottom for my fold back miter.

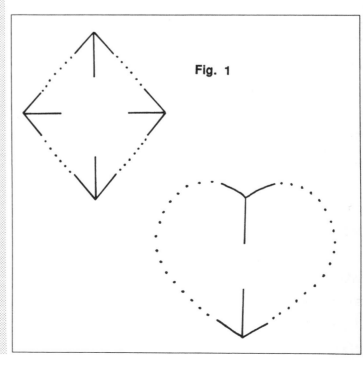

Fig. 1

▨ Shish Kabob Sticks For Pushing And Holding Everything

When we teach in Australia we learn so much from the women there who are expert seamstresses. Actually we learn so much from students we teach all over the world. I have always said that learning from my students is the most exciting part of our education no matter where we go. I first learned about shish kabob sticks from some of the technical school sewing teachers in Australia.

Nearly every woman in Australia uses a shish kabob stick (about 5 or 6 inches long, not the super long ones) to push and to hold with her right hand as sewing goes into the sewing machine. These sticks are used instead of the usual long pin or worse still, seam ripper that I

have used so often. The sticks are wonderful for holding all fabrics, are inexpensive, have no sharp point to damage fabric or sewing machine needles and really are easy to hang on to. At several of our sewing seminars, we have handed out the shish kabob sticks and the ladies have loved using them. The idea is that you can have something to hold your fabric or shaped lace on fabric as it feeds through the sewing machine which won't damage anything. Also, it keeps fingers away from the actual needle. Although I have never run a needle through my hand, I have certainly known of others who have done this. Using this stick is a safety technique as well as an efficient technique.

▨ MAKING A FABRIC BOARD

Fabric boards have become a must for lace shaping or any kind of working-in-the-round in heirloom sewing. They double as portable ironing boards also. At my School of Art Fashion in Huntsville, we make these boards in the double-wide version for collar classes and in the single-wide version for single lace shaping of hearts, diamonds, ovals, loops, and other shapes. Instructions for the double board follow, since it is the most convenient to have. You can also purchase a June Taylor Quilting Board for lace shaping also. We recommend that you make a little "sheet" just like a fitted sheet on your bed if you purchase this type of quilting board for your lace shaping. Since we use so much starch, the little sheet can be removed and washed and not ruin the surface of your quilting board. If you don't want to make this little sheet, then simply use a pillowcase over your June Taylor Board. Cardboard cake boards, covered with one layer of fabric or paper, also work well. You can also use just a sheet of cardboard. Another alternative is to go to any store which has old shipping boxes to throw away and cut the side out of a cardboard box. Cover the cardboard with paper or fabric and use this as your fabric board.

One thing I don't particularly like in lace shaping is a padded board with a lot of bounce. I think it is easier to get the laces shaped properly without a lot of padding such as quilt batting. The simpler the better is my philosophy.

Materials Needed
1. Two fabric rolling boards from the fabric store
2. Wide duck tape
3. Double thickness of fabric or butcher paper to cover the board

Step 1. Place two fabric boards (the kind that batiste or broadcloth is rolled on) side by side **(fig. 1)**.

Step 2. Tape the boards together, lengthwise **(fig. 2)**. Apply plenty of tape to make the boards sturdy.

Step 3. Cover the board with a double thickness of fabric or butcher paper. This hides the tape and makes the board look nicer. This also protects the garment from possibly getting ruined by having the tape melt or glue come out as you starch and press the lace Safety pin or staple the fabric to the back of the boards. Both methods work wonderfully.

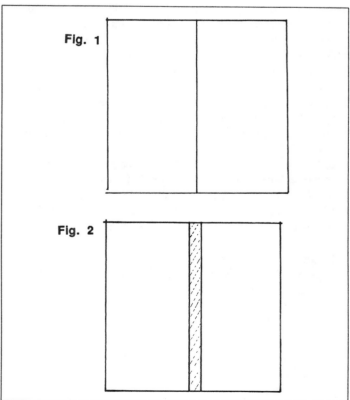

Fig. 1

Fig. 2

Making A Scalloped Skirt, Martha's New Way

Fold Back Miters

Those of you who have been sewing with me for the past 10 years know that my philosophy is to make the prettiest dress possible with the least amount of frustration. In my first hard cover book, *Antique Clothing, French Sewing by Machine*, I shared with you the easiest way that I had found, at that point, to make a scalloped skirt. Two years later, I am ready to share with you a brand new method of making a scalloped skirt which makes it even easier. **You don't have to take the shaped laces off of the skirt for your miter!** You are going to love this new method of "fold-back miters."

▓ TEARING AND MARKING YOUR SKIRT

Step 1. Pull a thread and cut or either tear your skirt. I usually put 88 inches in my skirt, two 44-inch widths - one for the front and one for the back. Make the skirt length the proper one for your garment **(fig. 1)**.

Step 2. Put in a French seam (or serge) one side seam only. You now have a flat skirt, which is approximately 88 inches wide **(fig. 1)**. Probably by now you know that I really don't make French seams anymore; I use the rolled hem finish on the serger. It is beautiful, strong, and prettier than most French seams.

Step 3. Fold the skirt in half at the seam line **(fig. 2)**. Press. Fold it again **(fig. 3)**. Press. Fold it again **(fig. 4)**. Press. Fold it again **(fig. 5)**. Press. When you open up your skirt, you have 16 equal sections **(fig. 6)**. This is your guideline for your scallops. Each section is 5-1/2 inches wide.

Step 4. You can make a template which fits between your folds by using a saucer, a dinner plate, an artist's flex-i-curve® or whatever has a curved edge. Make one template which has only one full sized scallop and the points of two more. Draw a straight line bisecting each top point of the scallop; make this line extend at least 2 inches above and below the point of the scallop **(fig. 7)**. Make this template on a piece of paper so you can slip the bottom of the piece of paper along the bottom of the fabric and draw only one scallop at a time. You will slip this template between the folds that you made earlier by folding and pressing. This is the simplest way to get those scallops drawn on the whole skirt.

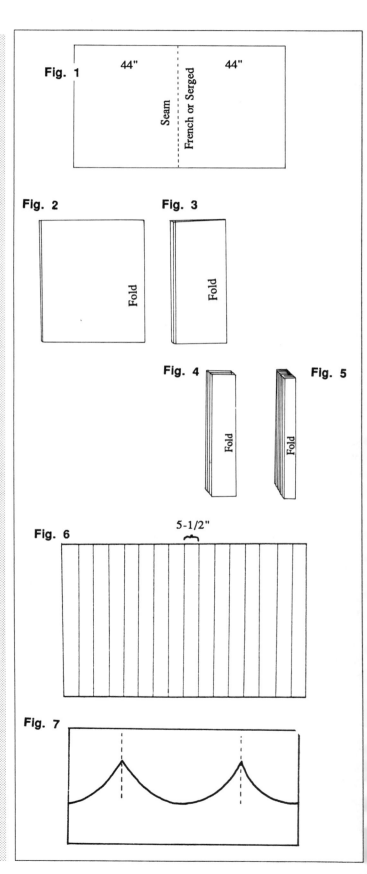

Grandmother's Hope Chest

Step 5. Draw your scallops between these folds or pressed in creases (fig. 8). You can place the scallops anywhere on the skirt bottom that you want to place them. For maximum use of the fabric, use the following guidelines for placing the scallops near the bottom of the skirt fabric. The bottom of the scallop (**Line A to B**) is at least 1-1/2 inches from the bottom of the skirt fabric (**fig. 9**).

Step 6. Draw a line at the top of each scallop, bisecting the top of the scallop, approximately 2 inches tall. On **figure 9** the top of each scallop is **point C**; this 2-inch line extending above the scallop is **point D (fig. 9)**. These bisecting lines going out of the top of each scallop are very important in the new fold back method of miters which follow.

▓ PREPARING SKIRT FOR LACE SHAPING

Step 1. Get a fabric board. This board is approximately 23 inches, which will allow you to work effectively with four scallops at one time. It does not matter how many scallops you work with at one time. The size of your board determines that.

Step 2. Working from the left side of your skirt, place the left side of the skirt on the fabric board, right side up (**fig. 8**). If you are right handed, it is easier to work from left to right. You can also work from the right of the skirt or from the center of the skirt which has been French seamed or serged together.

▓ PINNING THE LACE INSERTION
To The Skirt Portion On The Fabric Board

Step 1. Cut enough lace insertion to go around all of the scallops on the skirt. Allow at least 16 inches more than you measured. You can later use the excess lace insertion in another area of the dress. If you do not have a piece of insertion this long, remember to piece your laces where the pieced section will go into the miter at the top of the scallop. Refer to the section, "Piecing Lace That Is Not Long Enough For Your Needs." This way the pieced lace will not show at all.

Step 2. Pin the lace insertion to the skirt (one scallop at a time only) by poking pins all the way into the fabric board, through the bottom lace heading and the fabric of the skirt. Notice on **figure 10** that the bottom of the lace is straight with the pins poked into the board. The top of the lace is rather "curvy" because it hasn't been shaped to lay flat yet.

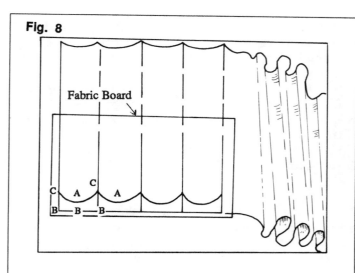

Fig. 8

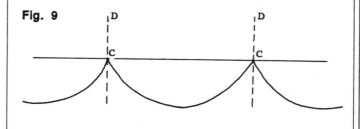

Fig. 9

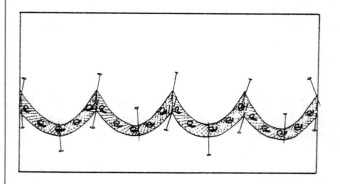

Step 3. As you take the lace into the top of the first scallop, carefully place a pin into the lace and the board at **points C and D**. Pinning the D point is very important. That is why you drew the line bisecting the top of each scallop **(fig. 10)**. Pin the B point at exactly the place where the flat lace crosses the line you drew to bisect the scallop.

Step 4. Fold back the whole piece of lace onto the other side **(fig. 11)**. Remove the pin at **C** and repin it to go through both layers of lace. Leave the pin at point **D** just as it is.

Step 5. Then fold over the lace to place the next section of the lace to travel into the next part of the scallop **(fig. 12)**.

NOTE: If a little bit of that folded point is exposed after you place the lace into the next scallop, just push it underneath the miter until the miter looks perfect **(Fig. 13)**. I lovingly call this "mushing" the miter into place.

Step 6. To shape the excess fullness of the top of the scallop, simply pull a gathering thread at the center point of each scallop until the lace becomes flat and pretty **(fig. 14)**.

Step 7. Place a pin in the lace loop you just pulled until you spray starch and press the scallop flat. Remember, it is easier to pull the very top thread of the lace, the one which makes a prominent scallop on the top of the lace. If you break that thread, go in and pull another one. Many laces have as many as 4 or 5 total threads which you can pull. Don't worry about that little pulled thread; when you zigzag the lace to the skirt or entredeux stitch it to the skirt, simply trim away that little pulled thread. The heaviness of the zigzag or the entredeux stitch will secure the lace to the skirt.

Step 8. Spray starch and press each scallop and miter after you finish shaping them.

Step 9. After finishing with the section of scallops you have room for on that one board, pin the laces flat to the skirt and begin another section of your skirt **(fig 15)**. You have the choice here of either zig zagging each section of the skirt as you complete it, or waiting until you finish the whole skirt.

Step 10. If you choose to use a decorative stitch on your sewing machine (entredeux stitch with a wing needle) you will need to stitch with some sort of stabilizer underneath the skirt. Stitch 'n Tear is an excellent one. Some use tissue paper, others prefer wax paper or adding machine paper. Actually, the paper you buy at a medical supply store that doctor's use for covering their examining tables is great also. As long as you are stitching using a wing needle and heavy decorative stitching, you really need a stabilizer.

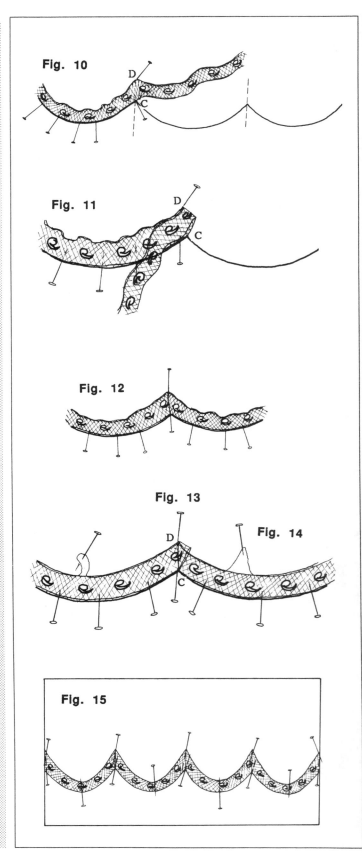

Fig. 10

Fig. 11

Fig. 12

Fig. 13

Fig. 14

Fig. 15

Step 11. If you have an entredeux stitch on your sewing machine, you can stitch entredeux at both the top and bottom of this scalloped skirt **(fig. 16)**. There are two methods of doing this:

Method Number One

Step 12. After you finish your entredeux/wing needle stitching on both the top and the bottom of the scalloped skirt, trim away the fabric from behind the lace scallop.

Step 13. Carefully trim the fabric from the bottom of the skirt also, leaving just a "hair" of seam allowance **(fig. 17)**.

Step 14. You are now ready to zigzag over the folded in miters **(fig. 18)**. Use a regular needle for this zigzag.

Step 15. Now zigzag the gathered laces to the bottom of this machine created entredeux.

Method Number Two

Step 12. Machine entredeux the top only of the scallop **(fig. 19a)**. Don't cut anything away.

Step 13. Butt your gathered lace edging, a few inches at a time, to the shaped bottom of the lace scallop. Machine entredeux stitch in between the flat scalloped lace and the gathered edging lace, thus attaching both laces at the same time you are stitching in the machine entredeux **(fig. 19b)**. Be sure you put more fullness in at the points of the scallop.

Step 14. After the gathered lace edging is completely stitched to the bottom of the skirt with your machine entredeux, cut away the bottom of the skirt fabric as closely to the stitching as possible **(fig. 20)**.

Step 15. Zigzag over your folded in miters **(fig. 20a)**. Please look at the section on machine entredeux stitching and ideas for more complete methods of stitching in your entredeux. I absolutely love machine stitched entredeux.

Step 16. If you are going to attach the lace to the fabric with just a plain zigzag stitch, you might try (Width=1-1/2 to 2, Length=1 to 1-1/2). You want the zigzag to be wide enough to completely go over the heading of the laces and short enough to be strong. If you are zigzagging the laces to the skirt, zigzag the **top only** of the lace scallops.

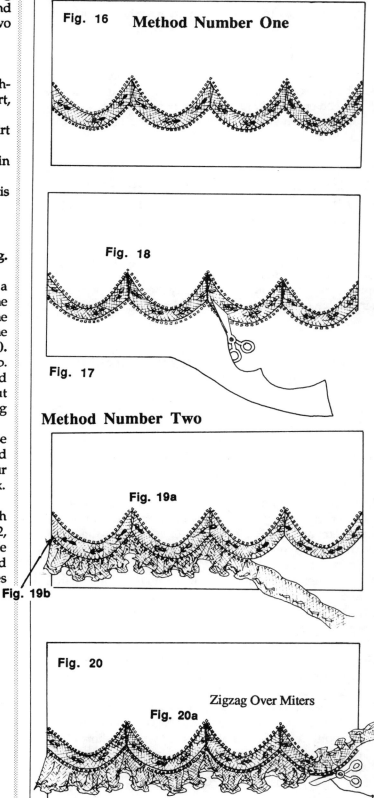

Fig. 16 **Method Number One**

Fig. 18

Fig. 17

Method Number Two

Fig. 19a

Fig. 19b

Fig. 20

Zigzag Over Miters

Fig. 20a

211

Step 17. After you zigzag the top only of this skirt, carefully trim away the bottom portion of the fabric skirt trimming all the way up to the stitches **(fig. 21)**.

Step 18. Now you have a scalloped skirt. Later you might want to add entredeux to the bottom of the scalloped skirt. It is perfectly alright just to add gathered laces to this lace scallop without either entredeux or machine stitched entredeux. Just treat the bottom of this lace scallop as a finished edge; gather your lace edging and zigzag to the bottom of the lace **(fig. 22)**.

■ FINISHING THE CENTER OF THE MITER
After Attaching It To The Skirt and Trimming Away The Fabric From Behind the Scallops

I always zigzag down the center of this folded miter. You can leave the folded lace portion in the miter to make the miter stronger or you can trim away the folded portion after you have zig zagged over the miter center. **(fig. 22)**.

■ SHAPING AND STITCHING PURCHASED ENTREDEUX TO SCALLOPS

Step 1. Trim off one side of the entredeux completely **(fig. 23)**.

Step 2. Slash the other side of the entredeux **(fig. 23)**.

Step 3. You must pin, starch, and press the entredeux before sewing it to the scallops. It won't hang right, otherwise.

Step 4. Here is a great trick. In order to pin the entredeux into the points of the scallops most effectively, trim entredeux about 1-1/2 inches on either side of the point. This allows you to see exactly where you are placing the entredeux **(fig. 24)**.

Step 5. After pinning the entredeux into the points, starch, and press the entredeux into its shape.

Step 6. Remove the pins from the skirt.

Step 7. Zigzag the lace to the entredeux trying to go into one hole and off onto the lace (W=3, L=1-1/2).

Step 8. As you go into the points with the entredeux, simply "smush" the entredeux into the point, stitch over it, and turn the corner **(fig. 25)**.

Step 9. There is an optional method for sewing entredeux on to scallops. Some people prefer to put entredeux on the bottom of a lace shaped skirt by using short pieces of entredeux which go only from top of the curve to top of the next curve **(fig. 26)**. Treat it exactly as you did in steps 1-6 in this section. Overlap the trimmed edges in each point. When you attach the gathered laces by zigzagging, these cut points will be zig zagged together.

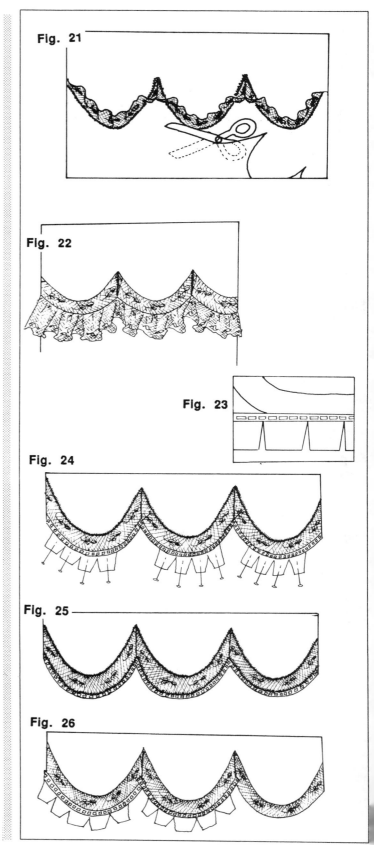

Fig. 21

Fig. 22

Fig. 23

Fig. 24

Fig. 25

Fig. 26

ADDING GATHERED LACE
To The Entredeux At the Bottom of Scallops

Step 1. Measure around the scalloped skirt to get your measurement for the gathered lace edging you are going to attach to finish the skirt bottom.

Step 2. Double that measurement for a 2-1 fullness. Remember that you can piece your laces if your piece of edging isn't long enough.

Step 3. Cut your lace edging.

Step 4. Using the technique "Sewing Hand-Gathered French Lace To Entredeux Edge" zigzag the gathered lace to the bottom of the entredeux **(fig. 27)**.

Step 5. You can also choose to use the method "Gathering French Lace By Machine, While Applying It To Trimmed Entredeux Edge" to attach this lace edging.

GATHERING FRENCH LACES BY HAND
Pull Thread In the Heading of Laces

On the straight sides of French or English cotton laces are several threads called the "heading." These threads serve as pull threads for lace shaping. Some laces have better pull threads than others. Before you begin dramatically-curved lace shaping, check to be sure your chosen lace has a good pull thread. The scallop on the top of most laces is the first pull thread that I pull. Most French and English laces have several good pull threads, so if you break the first one, pull another. If all the threads break, you could probably run a gathering thread in the top of the lace with your sewing machine.

Step 1. Cut a length of lace 2-3 times the finished length to have enough fullness to make a pretty lace ruffle.

Step 2. To gather the lace, pull one of the heavy threads that runs along the straight edge or heading of the lace **(fig. 28)**.

Step 3. Adjust gathers evenly before zigzagging.

SEWING HAND-GATHERED FRENCH LACE TO ENTREDEUX EDGE

Step 1. Gather lace by hand by pulling the thread in the heading of the lace. I prefer to use the scalloped outside thread of the heading first since I think it gathers better than the inside threads. Distribute gathers evenly.

Step 2. Trim the side of the entredeux to which the gathered lace is to be attached. Side by side, right sides up, zigzag the gathered lace to the trimmed entredeux (Width=1-1/2; Length=2). **Fig. 29.**

Step 3. Using a wooden shish kabob stick, push the gathers evenly into the sewing machine as you zigzag. You can also use a pick or long pin of some sort to push the gathers evenly into the sewing machine.

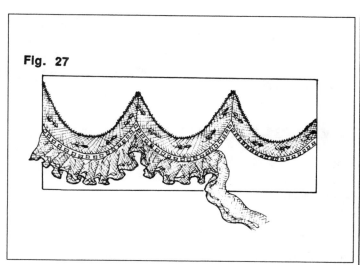

Fig. 27

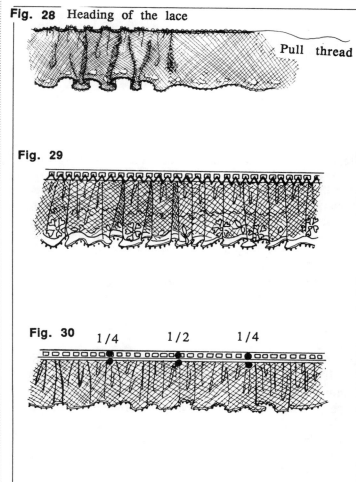

Fig. 28 Heading of the lace

Pull   thread

Fig. 29

Fig. 30   1/4   1/2   1/4

Note: If you want a more perfect match for your gathered lace to entredeux, fold and mark the quarter points on both. Then you have marked points to match.

MAKING LACE DIAMONDS - MARTHA'S NEW WAY

Lace diamonds can be used almost anywhere on heirloom garments. They are especially pretty at the point of a collar, on the skirt of a dress, at angles on the bodice of a garment, or all the way around a collar. The easiest way to make lace diamonds is to work on a fabric board with a diamond guide. You can make your diamonds as large or as small as you desire. I think you are really going to love this easy method of making diamonds with the fold back miter. Now, you don't have to remove those diamonds from the board to have perfect diamonds every time.

▧ MAKING LACE DIAMONDS

Materials Needed
1. Spray starch, iron, pins, fabric board
2. Lace insertion
3. Diamond guide

Step 1. Draw the diamond guide or template **(fig. 1)**.

Step 2. Tear both skirt pieces. French seam or serge one side only of the skirt.
Step 3. Working from the center seam you just made, draw diamonds all the way around the skirt. This way you can make any sized diamonds you want without worrying if they will fit the skirt perfectly. When you get all the way around both sides of the skirt you will have the same amount of skirt left over on both sides.
Step 4. Simply trim the excess skirt away. Later you will French seam or serge the skirt on the other side to complete your skirt. This is the easy way to make any type of lace shaping on any skirt and it will always fit perfectly **(fig. 2)**.
Step 5. The guide or template, which you have just drawn, will be the outside of the diamond **(fig. 3)**. Draw lines going into the diamond, bisecting each angle where the lace will be mitered. This is very important, since one of your critical pins will be placed exactly on this line. These bisecting lines need to be drawn about 2 inches long coming in from the angles of the diamonds. If you are making a diamond skirt, it is easier to draw your diamond larger and make your diamond shaping on the inside of the diamond. That way, the outside points of your diamond can touch when you are drawing all of your diamonds on the skirt.

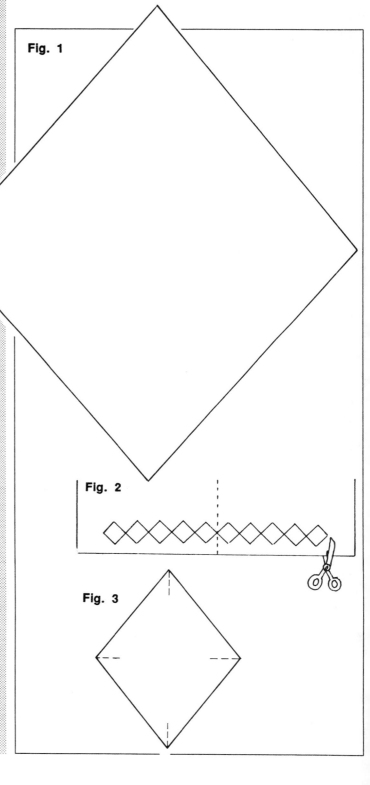

Fig. 1

Fig. 2

Fig. 3

Step 6. As I said earlier, you can shape the laces for diamonds on either the outside or the inside of the template. I actually think it is easier to shape your laces on the inside of the template.

Step 7. Place your skirt with the drawn diamonds on a fabric board.

Step 8. Place the lace flat and guiding it along the inside of the drawn template, put a pin at **point A** and one at **Point B** where the bisecting line goes to the inside **(fig. 4a)**. The pin goes through both the lace and the fabric into the fabric board.

Step 9. Guiding the edge of the lace along the drawn template line, place another pin into the fabric board through the lace (and the fabric skirt) at **point C** and another one at **point D** on the bisecting line **(fig. 4b)**.

Step 10. Fold back the lace right on top of itself. Remove the pin from the fabric board at **point D**, replacing it this time to go through both layers of lace rather than just one. Of course, the pin will not only go through both layers of lace but also through the skirt and into fabric board **(fig. 5)**.

Step 11. Take the lace piece and bring it around to once again follow the outside line. You magically have a folded miter already in place **(fig. 6)**.

Step 12. Guiding further, the edge of the lace along the inside of the drawn template line, place another pin into the fabric board through the lace at **point E** and another at **point F** on the bisecting line **(fig. 6)**.

Step 13. Fold the lace right back on top of itself. Remove the pin at **point F**, replacing it this time to go through both layers of lace rather than just one **(fig. 7)**.

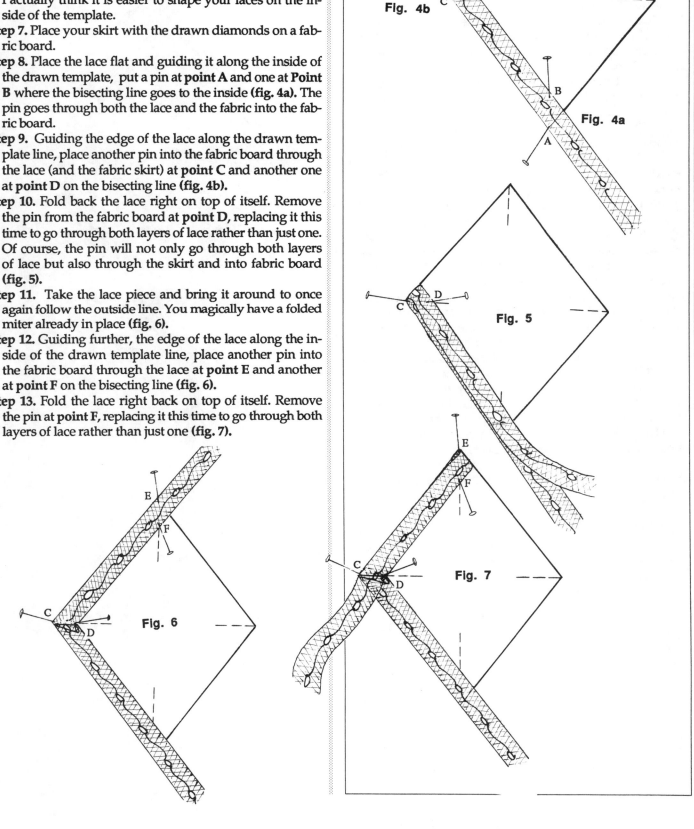

Fig. 4b

Fig. 4a

Fig. 5

Fig. 6

Fig. 7

MAKING LACE DIAMONDS - MARTHA'S NEW WAY

Step 14. Take the lace piece and bring it around to once again follow the outside line. You magically have a folded miter already in place **(fig. 8)**.

Step 15. Guiding further, the edge of the lace along the inside of the drawn template line, place another pin into the lace at **point G** and another pin at **point H** on the bisecting line.

Step 16. Fold the lace right back on top of itself. Remove the pin at **point H**, replace it this time to go through both layers of lace rather than just one.

Step 17. Take the lace piece and bring it around to once again follow the outside line. You magically have a folded miter already in place **(fig. 9)**.

Step 18. At the bottom of the lace diamond, let the laces cross at the bottom. Remove the pin at **point B** and replace it into the fabric board through both pieces of lace. Remove the pin completely at **point A (fig. 10)**.

Step 19. Taking the top piece of lace, and leaving in the pin at **point B** only, fold under and back the lace where it lays on top of the other piece of lace. You now have a folded in miter for the bottom of the lace.

Step 20. Put a pin in, now, at **point B (fig. 11.)**. Of course you are going to have to cut away this long tail of lace. I think the best time to do that is before you begin your final stitching to attach the diamonds to the garment. It is perfectly alright to leave those tails of lace until your final stitching is done and then trim them.

Step 21. You are now ready to spray starch and press the whole diamond shape. After spray starching and pressing the diamonds to the skirt, remove the pins from the fabric board and flat pin the lace shape to the skirt bottom. You are now ready to zigzag the diamond or machine entredeux stitch the diamond to the garments. Suggested zigzag settings are Width=2 to 3, Length=1 to 1-1/2.

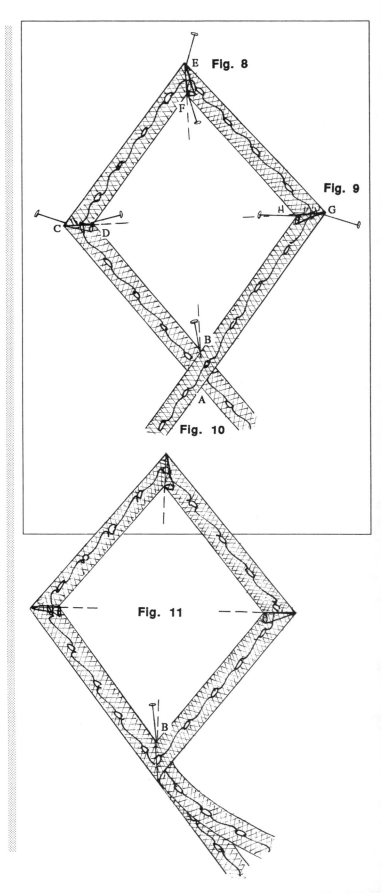

Fig. 8

Fig. 9

Fig. 10

Fig. 11

▨ FINISHING THE BOTTOM OF THE SKIRT

These techniques are for finishing the bottom of a Diamond Skirt, a Heart Skirt, a Bow Skirt, or any other lace shaped skirt where the figures travel all the way around the bottom touching each other.

Method One
Using Plain Zigzag To Attach Diamonds (Or Other Shapes) To The Skirt.

Step 1. First, zigzag across the top of the diamond pattern, stitching from **point A** to **point B** again to **point A** and finish the entire skirt **(fig. 12)**. Your lace is now attached to the skirt all the way across the skirt on the top. If your fabric and diamonds have been spray starched well, you don't have to use a stabilizer when zigzagging these lace shapes to the fabric. The width stitch will be wide enough to cover the heading of the lace and go off onto the fabric on the other side. The length will be from 1/2 to 1, depending on the look that you prefer.

Step 2. Zigzag all the diamonds, on the skirt, on the inside of the diamonds only **(fig. 13)**.

Step 3. You are now ready to trim away the fabric of the skirt from behind the diamonds. Trim the fabric carefully from behind the lace shapes. The rest of the skirt fabric will now fall away leaving a diamond shaped bottom of the skirt **(fig. 14)**. The lace will also be see through at the top of the diamonds also.

Step 4. If you are going to just gather lace and attach it at this point, then gather the lace and zigzag it to the bottom of the lace shapes being careful to put extra fullness in the points of the diamonds **(fig. 15)**. If you lace isn't wide enough to be pretty, then zigzag a couple of pieces of insertion to your edging to make it wider **(fig. 16)**.

Step 5. If you are going to put entredeux on the bottom of the shapes before attaching gathered lace to finish it, follow the instructions on attaching entredeux to the bottom of a scalloped skirt given earlier in this lace shaping section. Work with short pieces of entredeux stitching from **point A** to **point B** on the skirt.

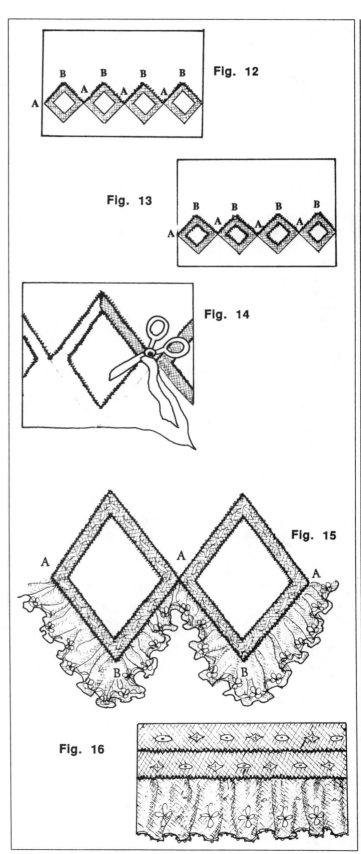

Fig. 12

Fig. 13

Fig. 14

Fig. 15

Fig. 16

MAKING LACE DIAMONDS - MARTHA'S NEW WAY

▓ FINISHING THE BOTTOM OF THE SKIRT

Method Two
Using A Wing Needle Machine Entredeux Stitch To Attach Diamonds (Or Other Lace Shapes) To The Skirt

Step 1. If you are going to use the wing needle/entredeux stitch on your sewing machine to attach your diamonds, or other lace shapes to the skirt, use the entredeux stitch for all attaching of the lace shapes to the skirt. Remember **you must use a stabilizer** when using the entredeux stitch/wing needle on any machine.

Step 2. Place your stabilizer underneath the skirt, behind the shapes to be stitched. You can use small pieces of stabilizer which are placed underneath only a few shapes rather than having to have a long piece of stabilizer. Just be sure that you have stabilizer underneath these lace shapes before you begin your entredeux/wing needle stitching.

Step 3. First, stitch the top side of the diamonds entredeux stitching from point A to point B all the way around the skirt. **(fig. 17).**

Step 4. Secondly, stitch the inside of the diamonds using the entredeux stitch **(fig. 18).** Do not cut any fabric away at this point. Remember to continue using stabilizer for all entredeux/wing needle stitching.

Step 5. You are now ready to gather your lace edging and machine entredeux it to the bottom of the skirt joining the bottom portions of the diamonds at the same time you attach the gathered lace edging. If your machine has an edge joining or edge stitching foot with a center blade for guiding, this is a great place for using it.

Step 6. Gather only a few inches of lace edging at a time. Butt the gathered lace edging to the flat bottom sides of the diamonds.

Step 7. Machine entredeux right between the gathered lace edging and the flat side of the diamond. Remember, you are stitching through your laces(which are butted together not overlapped), the fabric of the skirt and the stabilizer **(fig. 19).** Put a little extra lace gathered fullness at the upper and lower points of the diamonds.

Step 8. After you have stitched your machine entredeux all the way around the bottom of the skirt, you have attached the gathered lace edging to the bottom of the skirt with your entredeux stitch.

Step 9. Trim the fabric from behind the lace diamonds. Trim the fabric from underneath the gathered lace edging on the bottom of the skirt **(fig. 20).**

Step 10. Either zigzag your folded in miters in the angles of the diamonds or simply leave them folded in. I prefer to zigzag them **(fig. 21).** You also have the choice of cutting away the little folded back portions of the miters or leaving them for strength.

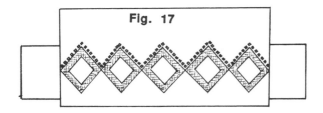

Fig. 17

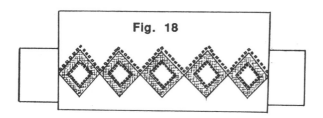

Fig. 18

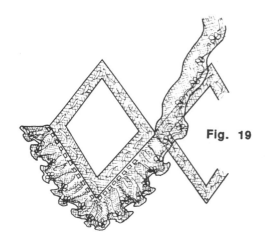

Fig. 19

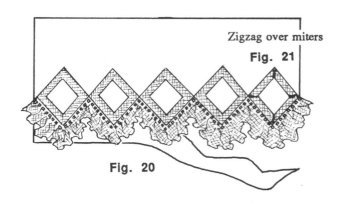

Zigzag over miters

Fig. 21

Fig. 20

218

LACE BOWS - FLIP-FLOPPING LACE

I make lace bows using a technique called "flip-flopping" lace — a relatively unsophisticated name for such a lovely trim. I first saw this technique on an antique teddy I bought at a local antique store. It had the most elegant flip-flopped lace bow. Upon careful examination, I noticed the lace was simply folded over at the corners, then continued down forming the outline of the bow. The corners were somewhat square. Certainly it was easier than mitering or pulling a

thread and curving. I found it not only looked easier, it was easier.

Follow the instructions for making a flip-flopped bow, using a bow template. This technique works just as well for lace angles up and down on a skirt. You can flip-flop any angle that traditionally would be mitered. It can be used to go around a square collar, around diamonds, and around any shape with an angle rather than a curve.

▨ FLIP-FLOPPING LACE

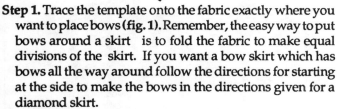

Fig. 1

Bow Template

Step 1. Trace the template onto the fabric exactly where you want to place bows **(fig. 1)**. Remember, the easy way to put bows around a skirt   is to fold the fabric to make equal divisions of the skirt. If you want a bow skirt which has bows all the way around follow the directions for starting at the side to make the bows in the directions given for a diamond skirt.

Step 2. Draw your bows on your garment or on a skirt, wherever you want this lace shape.

Step 3. Place your garment on your fabric board before you begin making your bow shapes. Beginning above the inside of one bow **(above E)**, place the lace along the angle. The template is the inside guide line of the bow **(fig. 2)**.

Step 4. At the first angle **(B)**, simply fold the lace where it will follow along the next line **(B-C) (Fig. 3)**. This is called flip flopping the lace.

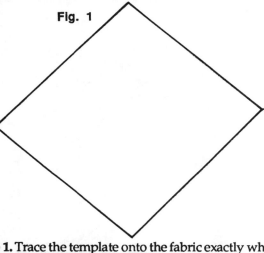

Fig. 2

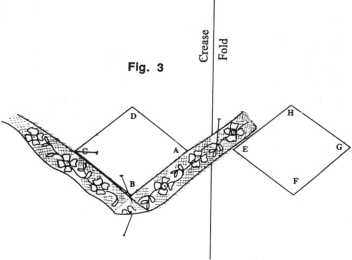

Fig. 3

LACE BOWS - FLIP-FLOPPING LACE

Step 5. Place pins sticking through the lace, the fabric, and into the shaping board. I like to place pins on both the inside edges and the outside edges. Remember to place your pins where they lay as flat a possible.

Step 6. The lines go as follows: A-B, B-C, C-D, D-A, A-E, E-F, F-G, G-H, H-E. Tuck your lace end under E, which is also where the first raw edge will end **(fig. 4)**.

Step 7. Cut a short bow tab of lace that is long enough to go around the whole tie area of the bow **(fig. 4)**. This will be the bow tie!

Step 8. Tuck in this lace tab to make the center of the bow **(fig. 5)**. Another way to attach this bow tie is to simply fold down a tab at the top and the bottom and place it right on top of the center of the bow. That is actually easier than tucking it under. Since you are going to zigzag all the way around the bow "tie" it really won't matter whether it is tucked in or not.

Step 9. Spray starch and press the bow, that is shaped with the pins still in the board, with its bow tie in place **(fig. 6)**. Remove pins from the board and pin the bow flat to the skirt or other garment. You are now ready to attach the shaped bow to the garment.

Step 10. This illustration gives you ideas for making a bow two ways. First, the "A" side of the bow has just the garment fabric peeking through the center of the bow. Second, the "B" side of the bow illustrates what the bow will look like if you put a pintucked strip in the center. Both are beautiful **(fig. 7)**.

Step 11. If you prefer the bow to look like side (A), which has the fabric of the garment showing through the middle of the bow, follow these steps for completing the bow. Zigzag around the total outside of the bow. Then, zigzag around the inside portions of both sides of the bow. Finally, zigzag around the finished bow "tie" portion **(fig. 8)**. The bows will be attached to the dress.

Step 12. If you prefer the bow to look like side (B), which will have pintucks (or anything else you choose) inside, follow the directions in this section. (These directions are when you have bows on areas other than the bottom of a skirt or sleeve or collar. If you have bows at the bottom of anything, then you have to follow the skirt directions given in the diamond skirt section.)

Step 13. Zigzag the outside only of the bows all the way around. Notice that your bow "tie" will be partially stitched since part of it is on the outside edges.

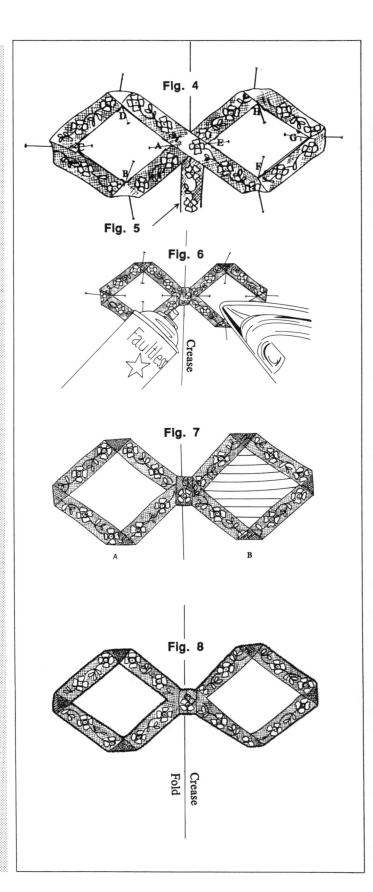

Fig. 4

Fig. 5

Fig. 6

Fig. 7

Fig. 8

Step 14. I suggest pintucking a larger piece of fabric and cutting small sections which are somewhat larger than the insides of the bows **(fig. 9)**.

Step 15. Cut away fabric from behind both center sections of the bow. I lovingly tell my students that now they can place their whole fists inside the holes in the centers of this bow.

Step 16. Place the pintucked section behind the center of the lace bows. Zigzag around the inside of the bows which will now attach the pintucked section. From the back, trim away the excess pintucked section. You now have pintucks in the center of each side of the bow **(fig. 10)**.

Step 17. Go back and stitch your sides of the bow "tie" down. After you have zig zagged all the way around your bow "tie" you can trim away excess laces which crossed under-neath the tie . This gives the bow tie a little neater look.

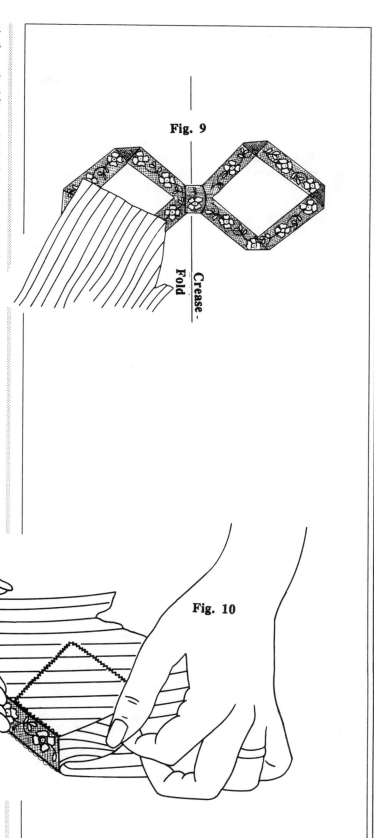

Fig. 9

Crease - Fold

Fig. 10

HEARTS – MARTHA'S NEW FOLD BACK MITER METHOD

CURVING LACE

Since many heirloom sewers are also incurable romantics, it's no wonder hearts are a popular lace shape. Hearts are the ultimate design for a wedding dress, wedding attendants' clothing, or on a ring bearer's pillow. As with the other lace shaping discussed in this chapter, begin with a template when making hearts. When using our heart template, we like to shape our laces inside the heart design. Of course, shaping along the outside of the heart design is permitted also. Whatever is easiest for you.

With the writing of the *Antique Clothing* book, I thought I had really figured out the easy way to make lace hearts. After two years of teaching heart making, I have totally changed my method of making hearts. This new method is so very easy that I just couldn't wait to write it in this book. After shaping your hearts, you don't even have to remove them from the skirt to finish the heart. What a relief and an improvement! Enjoy the new method of making hearts with the new fold back miters. It is so easy and you are going to have so much fun making hearts.

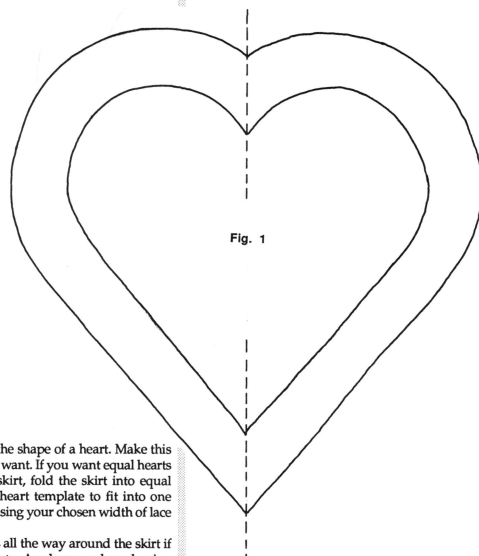

Fig. 1

Step 1. Draw a template in the shape of a heart. Make this as large or as small as you want. If you want equal hearts around the bottom of a skirt, fold the skirt into equal sections, and design the heart template to fit into one section of the skirt when using your chosen width of lace insertion.

Step 2. Draw on your hearts all the way around the skirt if you are using several hearts. As always, when shaping lace, draw the hearts onto the fabric where you will be stitching the laces.

Step 3. Draw a 2-inch bisecting line at the top into the center and at the bottom of the heart into the center **(fig. 1).**

NOTE: I would like to refresh your memory on lace shaping along the bottom of a skirt at this time. You make your hearts (or whatever else you wish to make) above the skirt while the skirt still has a straight bottom. Later after stitching your hearts (or whatever else) to the skirt, you cut away to make the shaped skirt bottom.

Step 4. Lay the fabric with the hearts drawn on top, on top of the fabric board. As always, pin the lace shaping through the lace, the fabric and into the fabric board.

Step 5. Cut one piece of lace which will be large enough to go all the way around one heart with about 4 inches extra. Before you begin shaping the lace, leave about 2 inches of lace on the outside of the bottom line.

Step 6. Place a pin at **point A.** Beginning at the bottom of the heart, pin the lace on the inside of the heart template. The pins will actually be on the outside of the lace insertion; however, you are shaping your laces on the inside of your drawn heart template.

Step 7. Work around the heart to **point C**, placing pins at 1/2-inch intervals. Notice that the outside will be pinned rather tightly and the inside will be curvy. **Note:** One of our math teacher students told me years ago, while I was teaching this lace shaping, a very important fact. She said, "Martha did you know that a curved line is just a bunch of straight lines placed in a funny way?" She said this as I was trying to explain that it was pretty easy to get the straight lace pinned into a curve. Since I remembered as little about my math classes as possible, I am sure that I didn't know this fact. It makes it a lot easier to explain taking that straight lace and making a curve out of it to know that fact.

Step 8. After finishing pinning around, to the center of the heart , place another pin at **point D (fig. 2).**

Step 9. Lay the lace back on itself curving it into the curve that you just pinned **(fig. 3).** Remove the pin from **Point D**, and repin it this time pinning through both layers of lace.

Step 10. Wrap the lace to the other side and begin pinning around the other side of the heart. Where you took the lace back on itself and repinned, there will be a miter which appears just like magic. This is the new fold-back miter which is just as wonderful on hearts as it is on diamonds and scalloped skirts.

Step 11. Pin the second side of the lace just like you pinned the first one. At the bottom of the heart lay the laces one over the other and put a pin at **point B (fig. 4).**

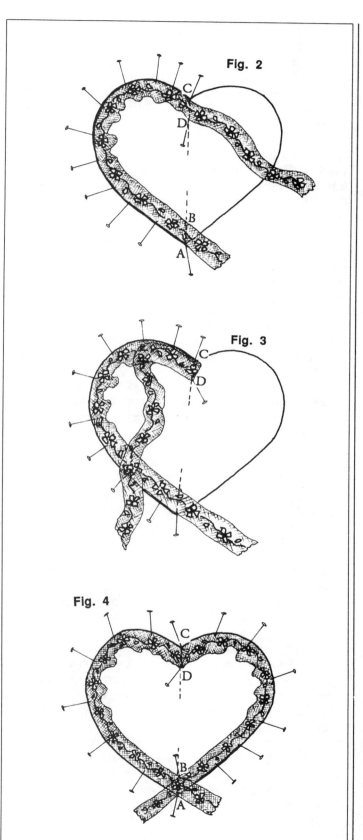

Fig. 2

Fig. 3

Fig. 4

Step 12. It is now time to pull the threads to make the curvy insides of the heart lay flat and become heart shaped. You can pull threads either from the bottom of the heart or threads from the center of each side of the heart.I prefer to pull the threads from the bottom of the heart. Pull the threads and watch the heart lay down flat and pretty. **(fig. 5).**

After teaching literally hundreds of students to make hearts, I think it is better to pull the thread from the bottom of the heart. You don't need to help the fullness lay down; simply pull the thread. On other lace shaped curves such as a scalloped skirt, loops, or ovals, you have to pull from the inside curve.

Step 13. Spray starch and press the curves into place.

Step 14. To make your magic miter at the bottom of the heart, remove the pin from **Point A**, fold back the lace so it lays on the other piece of lace, and repin **Point A**. You now have a folded back miter which completes the easy mitering on the heart **(fig. 6)**. You are now ready to pin the hearts flat onto the garment and remove the shaping from the fabric board.

Step 15. You can trim these bottom "tails" of lace away before you attach the heart to the garment or after you attach the heart to the garment. It probably looks better to trim them before you stitch **(Fig. 7).**

Step 16. You can attach the hearts just to the fabric or you can choose to put something else such as pintucks inside the hearts. If you have hearts which touch going all the way around a skirt, then follow the directions for zigzagging which were found in the diamond section

Step 17. If you have one heart on a collar or bodice of a dress, then zigzag the outside first. If you choose to put something on the inside of each heart, cut away the fabric from behind the shape after zig zagging it to the garment. Then, put whatever you want to insert in the heart behind the heart shape and zigzag around the center or inside of the heart. Refer to the directions on inserting pintucks or something else in the center of a lace shape in the flip flopped bow section.

Step 18. You can certainly use the entredeux/wing needle stitching for a beautiful look for attaching the hearts. Follow the directions for machine entredeux on the lace shaped skirt found in the diamond section of this lace shaping chapter.

Step 19. After you cut away the fabric from behind the hearts, go back and zigzag over each mitered point **(fig. 8)**. You then have the choice of either leaving the folded over section or of cutting it away. Personally, I usually leave the section because of the strength it adds to the miters. The choice is yours.

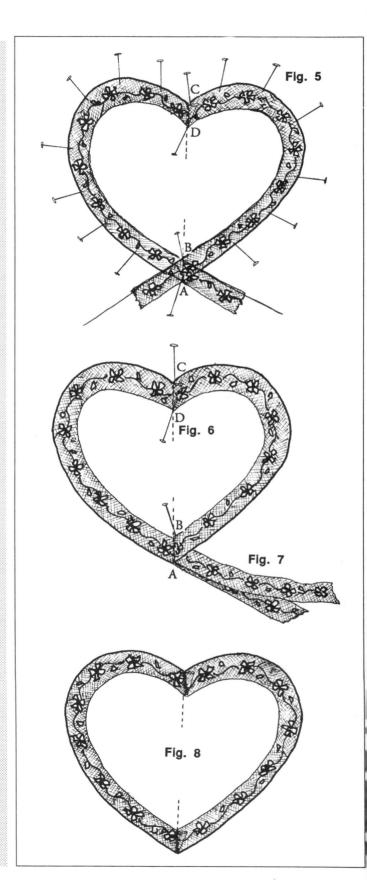

Fig. 5

Fig. 6

Fig. 7

Fig. 8

Geometric designs puzzled me until I began to experiment with them and discovered a surprisingly easy technique. Let me unravel the mystery of fancy squares, which are just as sweet on the bodice of a boy's suit as they are on a blouse or skirt! Start with a very long strip, and then cut it into little pieces. You can use embroidery, Swiss embroi-dered insertion, or pintucked fabrics for fancy squares. Let your imagination guide your journey! Two sets of fancy square instructions follow. The first set is for Swiss insertion, which is bi-directional; that is, it can be used either horizontally or vertically. The second set is for embroidery, which can only be used in one direction. Both are easy!

▨ METHOD I
Bi-Directional Swiss Insertion, A Fabric Strip, Or a Tucking Strip

Step 1. To determine how long to make your "strip," measure how wide each piece of fancy square will be. Each Swiss embroidered (insertion) strip will be approximately 2 inches wide and 2 inches long. With the addition of 2 inches of insertion, zigzagged together in between each 2-inch wide strip, you will need approximately 25 small sections (entredeux, embroidered square, entredeux, three pieces of lace insertion zigzagged together) to be sure you have enough to go around 90 inches of skirt. These little square sections will be approximately 4 inches wide. If you want to be much more careful and conservative in your measuring, make 23 before going on to 25.

Step 2. Using the technique "Entredeux To Flat Fabric," sew or serge the entredeux to both sides of the Swiss embroidered insertion. If you are using a tucking strip, do the same thing **(fig. 1)**. Trim the entredeux on both sides.

Step 3. Zigzag three pieces of lace insertion together, using the technique "Lace Straight Edge To Lace Straight Edge." Make the strip the same length as the strip of embroidered insertion and entredeux that you made in step 2 **(fig. 2)**.

Step 4. Butt the lace insertion to one side of the entredeux and zigzag together **(fig. 3)**.

Step 5. Divide the strip up evenly; cut between the strips **(fig. 4)**.

Step 6. Butt the lace insertion edge to the trimmed entredeux edge and zigzag the pieces into one strip **(fig. 5)**.

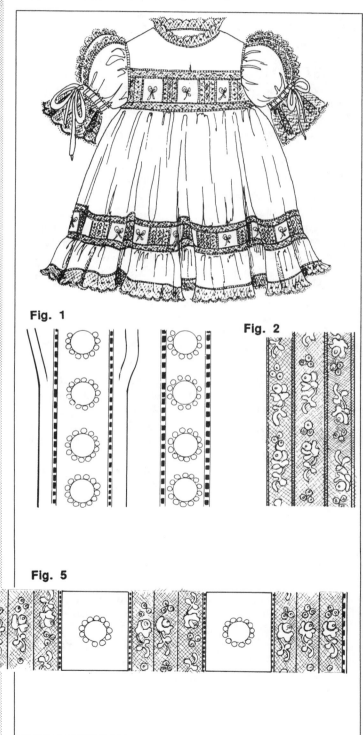

Fig. 1

Fig. 2

Fig. 3

Fig. 4

Fig. 5

MAKING FANCY SQUARE LACE SHAPES

Step 7. Using the technique "Entredeux To Flat Fabric," sew or serge entredeux to both sides of the strip you just made. You now have a fancy band to go around the skirt **(fig. 6)**.

Step 8. Look back at the dress in the illustration. You can see that another row of insertion plus another row of entredeux has been added before the fancy band was stitched into the dress. The same strips were repeated on the bodice of the dress.

▦ METHOD II
Swiss Insertion, Which Can Only Be Used In One Direction (fig. 7)

Step 9. To determine how long to make your "strip," measure how wide each piece of fancy square will be. Each Swiss embroidered (insertion) strip will be approximately 2 inches wide and 2 inches long. When adding 2 inches of insertion, zigzagged together between each 2-inch wide strip, you will need approximately 25 small sections (entredeux, embroidered square, entredeux, three pieces of lace insertion zigzagged together) to be sure you have enough to go around 90 inches of skirt. These little square sections will be approximately 4 inches wide. If you want to be much more careful and conservative in your measuring, make 23 before going on to 25.

Step 10. Cut apart your designs, in this case a bird flying with flowers **(fig. 8)**.

Step 11. Before applying the entredeux, it is a good idea to trim the seam allowance to 1/4 inch or 1/8 inch. The purpose for trimming the entredeux, is for the stitching of the entredeux to take off as little of the fabric square as possible. Using the technique "Entredeux To Flat Fabric," sew or serge the entredeux to both sides of the pieces of cut insertion. Trim away the seam allowance on both sides of the entredeux **(fig. 9)**.

Step 12. Butt two pieces of lace insertion to one side of the strip and one piece to the other side. Zigzag them to the entredeux as shown **(fig. 10)**.

Step 13. Cut apart the strips. Trim any excess lace and entredeux so that they will be even as shown **(fig. 11)**.

Step 14. Place the squares so that laces will make three pieces when butted together and zigzagged **(fig. 12)**.

Step 15. Using the technique "Entredeux To Flat Fabric," sew or serge entredeux to both sides of the strip that you just made. You now have your fancy band to go around the skirt.

Step 16. Look back at the dress in the illustration. You can see that another row of insertion plus another row of entredeux was added before the fancy band was stitched into the dress. The same strips were repeated on the bodice of the dress.

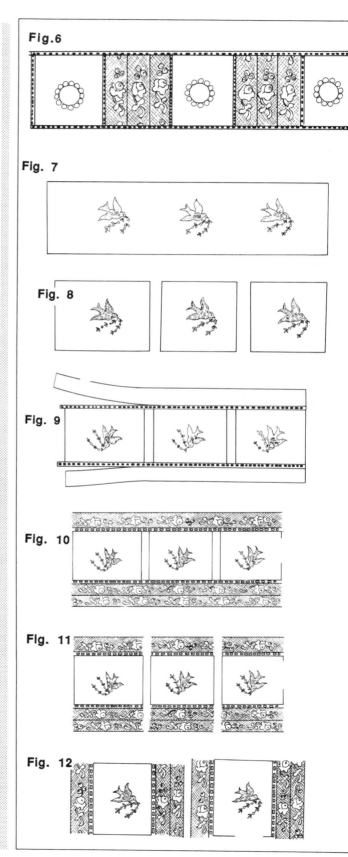

Fig.6

Fig. 7

Fig. 8

Fig. 9

Fig. 10

Fig. 11

Fig. 12

Grandmother's Hope Chest

MAKING A ROUND LACE PORTRAIT COLLAR

Materials Needed

- Sizes 4 and Under: 4 yards of 1/2-inch to 3/4-inch insertion; 2 yards of edging; 1-3/4 yards entredeux
- Sizes 5-12: 5 yards of 1/2-inch to 3/4-inch insertion; 2 yards of edging; 2 yards entredeux
- Adult: 6 or 7 yards of 1/2-inch to 3/4-inch insertion (This will depend on how wide you want to make your collar, of course.); 3 yards of edging; 2 1/2 yards entredeux
  NOTE: If you are using wider insertion, you need less yardage. If you are using narrow insertion, you need more yardage. You may want your collar wider than the shoulder/sleeve point. Get more lace. And vice versa. There is really no exact lace amount.
- Glass head pins or Iris Super Fine Nickel-Plated Steel Pins. **NOTE:** Do not use plastic head pins. They will melt when you press your laces into curves!
- Iron
- Magic Sizing or Spray Starch.
- Make a double-wide fabric board using the directions given earlier in this chapter. You can ask your fabric store to save two for you.
- Threads to match your laces
- A large piece of tissue paper like you use to wrap gifts
- Scissors

▓ MAKING YOUR FABRIC BOARD

Use the directions found earlier in this chapter.

▓ PREPARING THE PAPER GUIDE

Step 1. Trace your collar guide onto a piece of tissue paper.

Step 2. If your pattern doesn't have a collar guide, you can make one.

Step 3. Cut out the front yoke and the back yoke of your paper pattern (**fig. 1**). Put the shoulder seams of your paper pattern together to form the neckline. Be sure to overlap the seam allowance to get a true seam line at the shoulder (**fig. 2**). Subtract the seam allowance around the neckline. This is the neck guide to use for your paper pattern. Trace the neckline off. Mark the center-back lines, which will be evident from your pattern pieces (**fig. 3**). As you look at **Figure 3**, you will see that a large circle is on the outside of this pattern piece. You can draw this large circle on if you want to; however, you only need the neckline shape and the center back. You must draw the center back the length of your collar.

Step 4. Mark the fold-back line. To get your fold-back line, measure the width of the gathered lace that will be used around the bottom of the collar and up the center back on both sides. Take that measurement off of the center-back point and mark the fold-back line (**fig 3**).

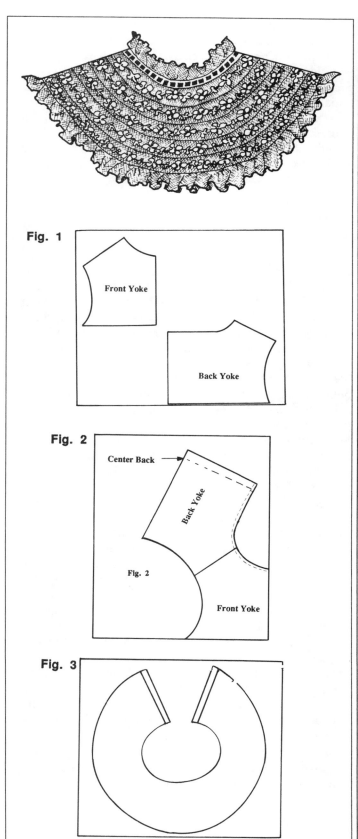

Fig. 1

Front Yoke

Back Yoke

Fig. 2

Center Back

Back Yoke

Fig. 2

Front Yoke

Fig. 3

Lace Shaping Techniques

227

MAKING A ROUND LACE PORTRAIT COLLAR

Step 6. You will probably notice that the neckline isn't really round, but oval shaped. That is the true neckline on any pattern, not an exact circle. Use that shaped neckline as your neckline guide.

Step 7. This neckline guide and the center-back line on the pattern are the only lines that you need to shape the circular laces around the collar. You will use the fold-back line after the lace shaping is done to finish the back of the collar. You only use the neckline guide for the first piece of lace. After that, you use the previously-shaped piece of rounded lace as your guide.

▓ MAKING THE FIRST TWO ROWS OF INSERTION

Step 1. Shape the neckline row first. Then work from the neckline down to complete the collar width you want.

Step 2. Cut your lace for the neckline or first row of your collar. **NOTE:** Cut extra. You will want to cut your laces longer than the center-back line of the collar you have marked. I suggest at least 3/4 inch to 1 inch longer than the exact center back.

Step 3. Place the tissue paper guide on the fabric board.

Step 4. Using your fabric board as your work base and your tissue paper collar guide, you are now ready to begin shaping your collar.

Step 5. Pin the outside of the lace where the inside will touch the neck guide when it is pressed down. The outside lace will have the pins jabbing through the lace and the tissue paper, right into the fabric board. This outside line is not gathered at all. The inside will be wavy. At this point, the inside has no pins in it **(fig. 4)**.

Step 6. After you have pinned the outside of the lace onto the fabric board, gently pull the gathering string in the heading of the INSIDE of the lace. The lace will pull flat **(fig. 5)**. Gently distribute the gathers by holding the lace down. Be certain that it is flat on the fabric board. You can pull your gathering rows from both ends. It is now time to put pins on the inside of the first row **(fig. 5)**. Jab them into the fabric board. Spray starch lightly and steam.

Step 7. Now that the first row is pretty and flat, you are ready to do the same thing with the second row. Pin the OUTSIDE edge to the board by jabbing the pins, just like you did on the first row. Be sure the inside of the lace touches the first row when you press it down with your fingers **(fig. 6)**. After you have gone all the way around with the second row of lace, pull from both ends to gather the inside row, just like you did the first row **(fig. 7)**.

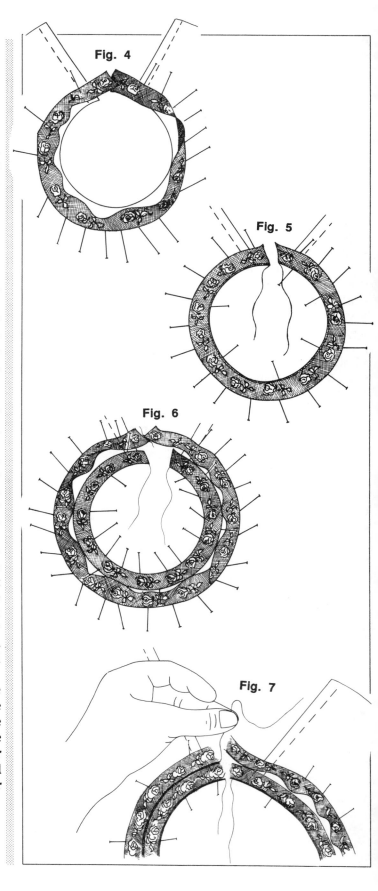

Fig. 4

Fig. 5

Fig. 6

Fig. 7

Grandmother's Hope Chest

Step 8. If you will remove the pins where the two rows butt (and where you will zigzag in a few minutes) and leave pins on the two outside rows, you will find it easier to press them.

Step 9. Spray starch the two rows **(fig. 8)**. Don't worry if spray starch gets on the tissue paper, because when you spray the two rows, it naturally gets on the tissue paper. It looks a little soggy; however, it will dry nicely with a hair dryer.

Step 10. Using a hair dryer, dry the starch and the tissue paper where the starch made it wet. If you do not dry the paper before you steam the laces, the paper will tear easily. If your tissue paper tears anytime during the process of making this collar, simply put another piece of tissue paper behind the whole collar and stitch through two pieces.

Step 11. After you have dried the starch, press and steam the laces right on the paper **(fig. 9)**.

Step 12. Remove the jabbed pins, one at a time, and flat pin the lace to the paper on both rows. Pin with the points toward the neckline. This makes it a lot easier when you stitch your collar, because when the pins are in this position, you can pull then out as you zigzag. If they are pinned the other way, it is difficult to remove the pins as you stitch. Never sew over pins, please! It is easier to remove the pin than it is to replace the needle **(fig. 10)**.

Step 13. (Stitch right through the tissue paper and the lace. Later, you will tear away the tissue paper.) Move to your sewing machine, and zigzag (Width=1-1/2 to 2, Length=1-1/2 to 2) **Fig. 10**. This width and length are just suggestions. Actually, the width and length will depend on the width of the laces in the heading of your particular lace. The length stitch will depend upon your preference. If you like a heavier, closer together look, make your stitch length shorter. If you like a looser, more delicate look, make your stitch length longer.

Step 14. The first two rows should now be zigzagged together.

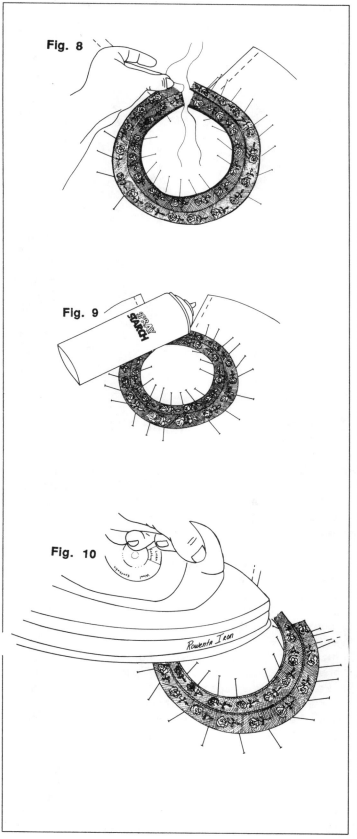

Fig. 8

Fig. 9

SPRAY STARCH

Fig. 10

Rowenta Iron

MAKING A ROUND LACE PORTRAIT COLLAR

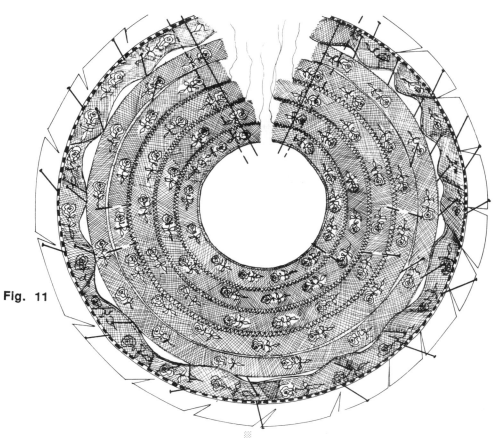

Fig. 11

▓ MAKING THE REST OF THE ROWS OF INSERTION

Step 1. Following the directions given for applying the second row, pin, and stitch the rest of the rows that you want to have on your collar. Make the collar as wide as you want it **(fig. 11)**.

Step 2. Here is a little trick that I have learned through experience. After you have pinned, pressed, starched, pressed, and zigzagged your first two rows together, the remaining rows can be made on the paper pattern at the same time. You don't have to stitch each row of insertion right after shaping it **(fig. 11)**. You might choose to stitch after each row of shaping. The choice is yours.

Step 3. Shape the laces on the rest of the collar by pinning, pressing, starching, pressing, and letting dry **(fig. 11)**.

Step 4. After all the lace rows are shaped and the tissue paper is completely dry, pin them flat, remembering to place the pins with the points toward the neckline and the heads away from the neckline **(fig. 11)**. Zigzag the laces together.

Step 5. Cut a piece of entredeux with enough length to go completely around the outside row of lace insertion, allowing for plenty of excess. You don't want to run out.

Step 6. Trim off one side of the entredeux completely and slash the other row so it will curve easily **(fig. 11)**.

Step 8. Pin the entredeux around the outside row of lace, jabbing pins into the holes of the entredeux about every 2 inches or so. After the entredeux is all the way around the curved lace collar, press, starch, press again, and allow to dry. You can always dry it with a hair dryer if you want to begin stitching immediately **(fig. 11)**.

Step 9. Pin the entredeux to the tissue paper at several places. You are now ready to begin stitching the first row of lace insertion that is not already stitched. Remember, if you have chosen to stitch each row of insertion after it was shaped, you might have already stitched all of your laces at this time.

Step 10. Stitch each row, starting with the unstitched one closest to the neckline. Move outward with each row for your stitching. Remove the pins, one at a time, as you are stitching.

Step 11. With each successive row, carefully remove the pins, and be sure to butt the lace edges exactly as you stitch around the collar.

Step 12. The entredeux to the last row of insertion may or may not be the last row that you will stitch, while the tissue paper is still on the collar. You will have to make a decision concerning whether you want to use Method I or Method II a little later on in the instructions.

USING THE CENTER BACK OF THE COLLAR
Check Your Fold Back Line

Step 1. The center back of a garment is just that - where the backs meet. This collar will not end at the center back point unless you are not putting laces up the center back of the collar.

Step 2. You can choose to put no laces and no entredeux up the center back. In this case, you will work on the center back line. The best way to finish the back of the collar, if you make this choice, is to serge or overlock the collar just outside of the center-back line **(fig. 1a)**. Then fold your serged seam to the back, and straight-stitch it to the collar **(fig. 1b)**. That leaves just a finished lace edge as the center back.

Step 3. If you are adding lace edging and entredeux up the back of the collar, you will have to use the fold-back line you made in the beginning on your pattern. Laces don't need to overlap at the center back, but meet instead. Check to be sure that your fold-back line is as wide as your lace edging is from the center-back line on your pattern.

METHOD I FOR ADDING ENTREDEUX

Step 1. Make a straight row of stitching on the fold-back line. You are still stitching through the tissue paper.

Step 2. Trim away the laces, leaving about 1/8 inch of raw lace edge **(fig. 2a)**.

Step 3. Zigzag very tightly (Width=1-1/2, Length=1/2) to finish the lace edge **(Fig. 2b)**. You can also serge the back of the collar to finish it.

Step 4. Butt the entredeux to the finished edge **(Fig. 3a)** and zigzag, going into the holes of the entredeux and off **(Fig. 3b)**.

METHOD II FOR ADDING ENTREDEUX

Step 1. Using the technique "Entredeux To Flat Fabric," attach the entredeux to the back of the collar. Stitch in the ditch **(fig. 1)**, trim **(fig. 2)**, and zigzag **(fig. 3)**.

Step 2. You have two options when finishing this straight line of stitching. Either serge or zigzag along this line. You will make the decision in the next section. For right now, don't trim away any laces along the fold-back line; just leave the collar like it is.

Step 3. Trim away the other side of the entredeux. It is now ready for gathered lace to be attached to it.

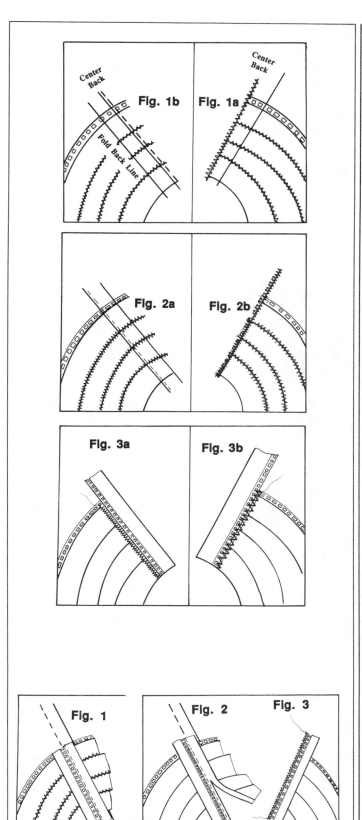

MAKING A ROUND LACE PORTRAIT COLLAR

METHOD I
For Attaching Gathered Lace To Entredeux On The Outside Edge of the Collar With Tissue Paper

Question: When would you use Method I?

For some, this method is the easiest for distributing lace evenly because you can put the quarter points exactly where you want them and control the fullness. If you have a machine which isn't up to par, stitching laces on tissue paper is easier than working without it. So, for some people the method of stitching the gathered lace on while tissue paper is still attached is the easiest.

Step 1. Cut lace edging to be gathered around the bottom and up the back of the collar. Use a 1-1/2 - 1 fullness or a 2 - 1 fullness, depending on the amount of lace desired.

Step 2. After cutting your lace, (allow about 2 inches to turn each back corner and about 10 inches to gather and go up each back of the collar) fold the rest of the lace in half, and mark the center of the lace. Fold once again, and mark the quarter points. This will allow you to distribute the fullness accurately.

Step 3. Pull the gathering thread in the top of the edging. Pin the center of the lace to the center of the entredeux edge of the collar. Pin the quarter points of the lace to the approximate quarter points of the collar. You should have about 12 inches of lace on each end to go around the corner of the collar and to gather it up the back of the collar. After figuring out these measurements, begin to distribute and pin the gathered lace to the bottom of the collar entredeux. Distribute the gathers carefully. Pin all the way around.

Step 4. Stitch the gathered lace (Width=1-1/2 to 2, Length=1/2) to the entredeux, still stitching through the tissue paper. You are only going to stitch around the bottom of the collar. Leave the laces unattached at this point, coming up the center back.

Step 5. Carefully tear away the tissue paper from collar.

Step 6. If you are not going to use a serger, trim away the lace ends 1/4 inch away from the fold-back line of the collar where you have stay-stitched. This 1/4 inch gives you a seam allowance to zigzag to finish. If you plan to serge the outside of this line, you do not have to trim away the lace since the serger does this for you.

Step 7. Zigzag tightly over this stay-stitched line (Width=1 to 2, Length=1/2).

Step 8. If you have a serger, serge this seam rather than zigzagging over it.

Step 9. If you serged this seam, fold back the serged edge, and straight-stitch it down.

Step 10. If you zigzagged over this seam, use this rolled and whipped edge as the finished edge of this seam.

FINISHING THE APPLICATION
Of Entredeux and Gathered Lace Edging

Step 1. Now that your fold-back line is finished, you are ready to finish gathering the lace edging and zigzag it to the back of the collar.

Step 2. Trim the other side of the entredeux up the back of the collar.

Step 3. Put extra gathers in the lace edging when going around the corner. This will keep it from folding under.

Step 4. After gathering the lace edging, butt the gathered laces to the trimmed entredeux and zigzag to the collar.

Step 5. Fold down the top of the lace edging before completely zigzagging to the top of the collar. That way you have a finished lace edge on the top of the collar.

METHOD II
For Attaching Gathered Lace To The Entredeux of the Collar Without Tissue Paper

Question: When would you use Method II?

If the tension is good on your sewing machine, use Method II. If you don't mind the laces not being exactly the same gathering all the way around, use Method II. By the way, the laces won't be distributed evenly using Method I either. I haven't found a way to perfectly distribute and gather laces and attach them using any method, including hand sewing! However, Method II is the easiest.

Step 1. Tear away the tissue paper from your collar.

Step 2. Cut the lace edging, which will be gathered around the bottom of the collar and up the back of the collar. You can use a 1-1/2 - 1 fullness or a 2 - 1 fullness. It really depends on how much lace you wish to use.

Step 3. Now that your fold-back line is finished, you are ready to finish gathering the lace edging and zigzag it to the back of the collar.

Step 4. Trim the other side of the entredeux.

Step 5. Using the techniques found in "Gathering French Lace By Machine, While Applying It To Trimmed Entredeux Edge," attach your lace to the bottom of the collar and up the back edges.

Grandmother's Hope Chest

ADDING A FABRIC NECKLINE PIECE

Portrait collars are lovely when they start with a fabric circular piece finished with entredeux at the bottom. After your entredeux is attached, then complete the portrait collar exactly as you would if the fabric weren't there. If you are adding a fabric neckline piece, **You must use the actual dress or blouse pattern to make your round portrait collar guide.** If you are making a lace only portrait collar, you can use a general neckline guide since lace can be shaped to go into many shapes. For the fabric neckline, you must make an exact pattern to fit the neckline of the garment.

Materials Needed
- Laces and entredeux for portrait collar given in the portrait collar section
- 1/3 yard batiste for adult collar
- 1/4 yard for infant or small child's collar
- 1 extra yard of entredeux for use at the bottom of the fabric portion of the collar (Optional if you have a machine which makes machine entredeux with a wing needle.)

Step 1. . Refer to the directions for Preparing The Paper Guide which tells you how to get your neckline curve for your actual garment. If you are putting in this fabric around the neckline, you must cut an actual pattern by the neckline of the garment to which it will be attached.

Step 2. Be certain when you cut the collar fabric piece that you mark in a seam allowance exactly like the one on the garment neck edge.

Step 3. Cut out a circular neckline piece extending beyond the center back neck edge. You're not going to use this excess, it is only for security in case you want to make the center backs a little wider after you try on the collar! Also, when you zigzag entredeux and laces together, sometimes the fabric shrinks up just a little because of all of that heavy stitching **(fig. 1).**

METHOD I
Purchased Entredeux Added To Bottom of Fabric Collar

Step 4. Cut enough entredeux to go around this curve with a little excess on either side. Trim one side only of the entredeux. Slash the other side so it will curve around the neckline edge.

Step 5. With the slashed side of the entredeux meeting the cut curved edge of the collar, pin , using the fabric board, the entredeux around the outside edge of this fabric neckline piece **(fig. 2).**

Step 6. Spray starch and press.

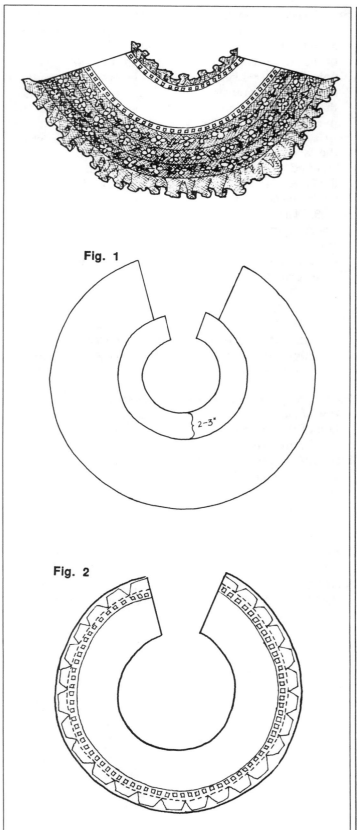

Fig. 1

Fig. 2

Step 7. Using the method, entredeux to flat fabric (stitch in the ditch, trim and zigzag or serge the whole thing with a rolled hem), stitch the entredeux to the outside edge of the curve. You can also serge this curved entredeux onto the collar. I suggest that first before you serge the entredeux on, you straight stitch in the ditch to be sure that it is perfectly placed. Then, using your rolled hemmer, serge it to the collar.

Step 8. Press the entredeux down. You now have completed the fabric circle with the trimmed entredeux already attached. You have a trimmed entredeux edge to shape the laces onto with the first row of shaped laces which will come next (**fig. 3**).

Step 9. Place this fabric/entredeux piece on the piece of tissue paper which you also drew to match this neckline edge. You are now ready to shape the laces and finish the collar following all directions in the Making A Round Lace Portrait Collar section.

▨ METHOD II
Stitching The First Row of Laces To The Collar Using Machine Entredeux Stitch and Wing Needle

Step 10. Skip the entredeux step altogether. Shape the first row of laces overlapping the raw edge of the fabric portion of the collar by about 1/4 inch; you can choose to overlap more if you want to (**fig. 4**).

Step 11. After pinning and shaping the first row of rounded laces to overlap this fabric collar, stitch a row of machine entredeux stitching at the seam line. Now, it looks as if you have entredeux on your collar and if was so much easier than actually applying entredeux. If you have excess fabric underneath your stitching, simply trim away this excess fabric from your collar after the whole collar is finished (**fig. 5**).

Step 12. To finish the collar, simply follow all directions in the Making A Round Lace Portrait Collar section.

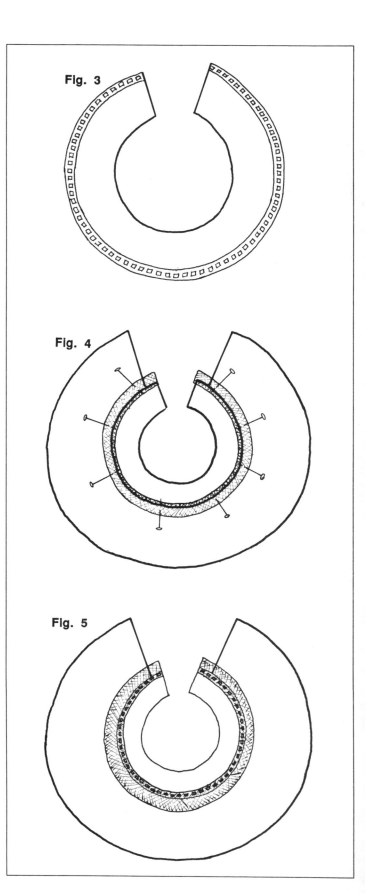

Fig. 3

Fig. 4

Fig. 5

PUFFING METHOD I
Gathering The Puffing Over A Quilting Thread Or Dental Floss

This method for making puffing simply rolls and whips the edges of the puffing strip by zig zagging over a quilting thread or dental floss. It has a finished edge which can be butted up to lace and zig zagged together. Although this is a good method for making puffing to curve around in a round portrait collar, I really do not believe that it is the easiest. Please read this method which is Puffing Method One. Then, if your machine has a gathering foot, read Puffing Method Two. Honestly, that is the easiest method. The choice is yours, of course.

Step 1. Cut your puffing strip at lest two times the length of the finished round portion of the collar to which it is to be attached.

Step 2. A suggested puffing length is to cut two strips of 45-inch fabric about 2 inches wide.

Step 3. Cut one of them in two pieces. Stitch these pieces to either end of the long strip. You can put in a French seam or serge these seams together **(fig. 1)**. You may press the puffing strip but **do not starch.** Starching will affect the gathers of the puffing.

Step 4. This puffing strip will probably be a little long for the collar. I like to have too much puffing and lace when I am working at portrait collars rather than too little. Since I like full puffing, I usually use the whole fullness. If it is fuller than you want, then simply put in the fullness you want and cut off the back at both sides after you have shaped your puffing.

Step 5. Mark the center of this puffing strip before you roll and whip the edge. The two quarter points are already marked with the two side strips **(fig. 2)**.

Step 6. Roll and whip the edges using quilting thread or dental floss. To do this, simply place the quilting thread or the dental floss on the very edge of both sides and zigzag it into place. Be careful not to catch the quilting thread or dental floss in the stitching **(fig. 3)**. Zigzag the edge of the fabric using approximately a 2 1/2 to 3 1/2 width and a 1-1 1/2 length. You should zig going into the fabric and zag going all the way off of the fabric. The fabric will roll into a seam as you zigzag. The quilting thread will be rolled into that seam. Later you will use the very strong quilting thread to pull the gathers in your puffing (fig. 4).

Step 7. Note: After you zigzag the quilting thread or dental floss into both sides of this puffing strip, you will probably see a few fuzzies and it may not look exactly perfect. This is normal because you used a relatively loose length (1- 1 1/2) for your zigzag. Using any tighter stitch tends to make the rolling and whipping too tight and makes the gathering of the puffing very difficult. Don't worry, when you zigzag your puffing to your lace, these fuzzies will go away.

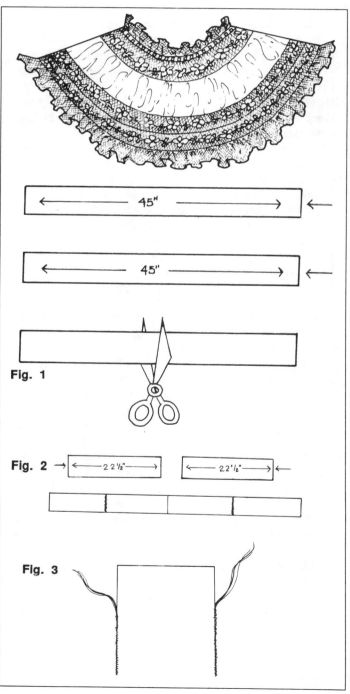

Fig. 1

Fig. 2

Fig. 3

235

Portrait Collar Variations

Step 8. Some sewing machines have a foot with a little hole in the center of the foot. If yours has this feature, put your quilting thread or dental floss in that little hole and your zig zagging will be perfectly in place and you won't have a chance of zig zagging through the quilting thread in the process of stitching.

Step 9. After you finish your rolling and whipping on both sides, pull the gathering threads on both sides from both ends until it is gathered up to look like puffing (**fig. 4**).

Step 10. Pin the puffing to the fabric board right through the tissue paper that you have already pinned your lace strips to, matching the center front of the collar with the center front of the puffing. Pin by "poking" the pins into your fabric board, on the bottom side of the puffing (**fig. 5**).

Step 11. Keep on playing with the gathers until you have them evenly distributed. Then, pin the top side (the smaller side) of the puffing. You treat the puffing exactly like you treated the laces. Pin the larger side first and then pin the smaller side (**fig. 6**).

Step 12. Press the puffing flat after spray starching it. **Note:** On any garment which will be washed, it is necessary to press the puffing flat because you will have to do this after it is washed anyway. A puffing iron is perfect for this job, depending on how wide the puffing is. I love flat pressed puffing and there really isn't much choice in leaving it unpressed unless it will go into a pillow to put on the bed and not wash for a very long time.

Step 13. Playing with and distributing your gathers carefully usually takes a long time. Don't become impatient. Just keep fiddling with the puffing to be sure you have distributed it carefully. This is a good project to save for evening t.v. watching so you can really make it perfect. After you have pinned your puffing where it looks beautiful, carefully remove the "poked" pins and pin it flat to the tissue paper where the edge of the puffing on the top exactly meets the bottom edge of the lace row above it (**fig. 7**). Width=1 1/2 to 2 1/2: Length=1 to 2

Step 14. You are now ready to take the tissue paper with its rows of lace insertion and rows of puffing over to the sewing machine to zigzag your row of puffing to the top row of lace. Stitch right through the tissue paper. Leave the pins in the puffing after you stitch around the top row because you are now ready to shape the next piece of lace to the collar just exactly like you did the others.

Step 15. Continue adding lace rows to the portrait collar to make it as wide as you wish it to be.

Step 16. If you choose, you can add more puffing rows in between the lace rows to put several puffing rows onto the collar.

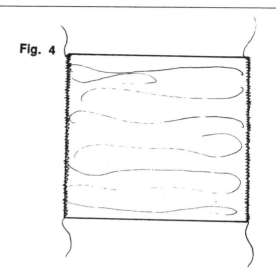

Fig. 4

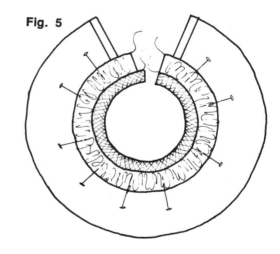

Fig. 5

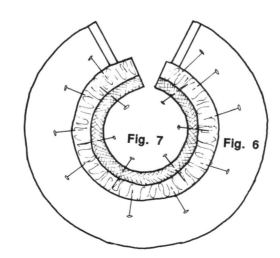

Fig. 7   Fig. 6

PUFFING METHOD II
Gathering The Puffing Using The Gathering Foot On Your Machine

Two years ago, I wouldn't have told you that this was the easiest method of applying puffing into a round portrait collar. The reason being I didn't know how to make perfect puffing using the gathering foot for the sewing machine. I thought you used the edge of the gathering foot to guide the fabric underneath the gathering foot. This left about a 1/4-inch seam allowance. It also made the gathers not perfect in some places with little "humps" and unevenness on some portions. Therefore, I wasn't happy with puffing made on the gathering foot. When I asked my friend, Sue Hausman, what might be wrong, she explained to me that to make perfect gathering, you had to move the fabric over so that you would have at least a 1/2-inch seam allowance. She further explained that there are two sides to the feed dogs; when you use the side of the gathering foot, then the fabric only catches on one side of the feed dogs. It works like magic to move your fabric over and guide it along one of the guide lines on the sewing machine. If your machine doesn't have these lines, simply put a piece of tape down to make a proper guide line.

Making Perfect Machine Puffing

Step 1. The speed of the sewing needs to be consistent. Sew either fast or slow but do not sew fast then slow then fast again. For the beginner, touch the "sew slow" button (if available on your machine). This will help to keep a constant speed.

Step 2. The puffing strip should be gathered with a 1/2 seam allowance, with an approximate straight stitch length of 3, right side up **(fig. 1)**. Remember that you can adjust your stitch length to make your puffing looser or fuller. Do not let the strings of the fabric wrap around the foot of the machine. This will cause to fabric to back up behind the foot causing an uneven seam allowance, as well as, uneven gathers. Leave the thread tails long in case adjustments are needed. One side of the gathering is now complete **(fig. 2)**.

Step 3. Begin gathering the second side of the strip, right side up. This row of gathering will be made from the bottom of the strip to the top of the strip. In other words, bi-directional sewing (first side sewn from the top to the bottom, second side sewn from the bottom to the top) is allowed. Gently unfold the ruffle with the left hand allowing flat fabric to feed under the foot. **Do not** apply any pressure to the fabric **(fig. 3)**.The feeding must remain constant. Leave the thread tails long in case adjustments are needed. The puffing strip in now complete.

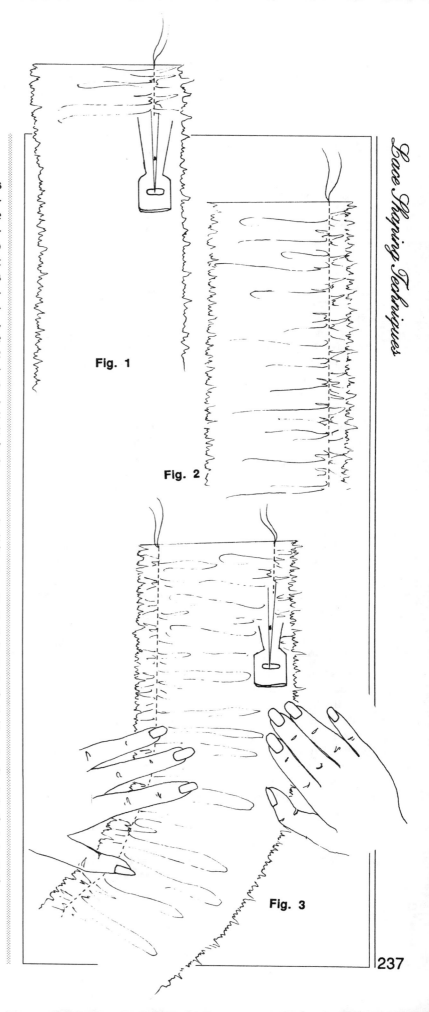

Fig. 1

Fig. 2

Fig. 3

PORTRAIT COLLAR VARIATIONS

▨ PLACING MACHINE GATHERED PUFFING INTO A COLLAR

Step 1. Cut your strips of fabric.

Step 2. Gather both sides of the puffing running the fabric under the gathering foot. Be sure you have at least a 1/2-inch seam allowance. When you use a gathering foot, the moveability of the puffing isn't as great as when you gather it the other way.

Step 3. You, of course, have two raw edges when you gather puffing with the gathering foot (fig. 8).

Step 4. Shape the puffing around the fabric board below the row of lace (or rows of lace) that you have already shaped into the rounded shape. Place the pins into the board through the outside edge of the puffing. Place the pins right into the place where the gathering row runs in the fabric (fig. 9).

Step 5. Pull the raw edge of the machine puffed strip up **underneath the finished edge of the curved lace,** so that your zig zagging to attach the puffing will be on the machine gathering line. Put the rounded lace edge on top of the puffing. Pin the bottom edge of the puffing first so you can "arrange" the top fullness" underneath the curved lace edge which is already in place (the top piece of lace) **fig. 9.**

Step 6. It will be necessary to "sort of" arrange the machine gathered puffing, especially on the top edge which will be gathered the fullest on your collar, and pin it where you want it since the machine gathering thread doesn't give too much. After you have pinned and poked the gathering into place where it looks pretty on the top and the bottom, flat pin it to the tissue paper and zigzag the puffing strip to the lace stitching right on top of the lace. **NOTE: You will have an unfinished fabric edge underneath the place where you stitched the lace to the puffing.** That is o.k. After you have zig zagged the puffing to the lace, then trim away the excess fabric underneath the lace edge. Be careful, of course, when you trim this excess fabric, not to accidentally cut the lace.

Step 7. If you have a machine entredeux/wing needle option on your sewing machine, you can stitch this beautiful stitch in place of the zig zagging. Since the fabric is gath-ered underneath the lace, you will have to be very careful stitching to get a pretty stitch.

Step 8. Shape another piece of lace around the bottom of this puffing bringing the inside piece of curved lace exactly to fit on top of the gathering line in the puffing. Once again, you will have unfinished fabric underneath the place where you will zigzag the lace to the puffing collar. After zig zagging the lace to the puffing collar, trim the excess fabric away.

Step 9. Continue curving the rest of the laces to make the collar as wide as you want it to be.

Fig. 8

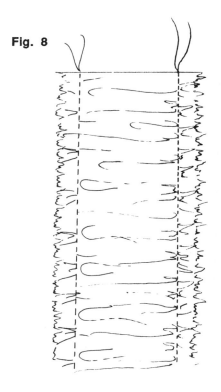

Fig. 9

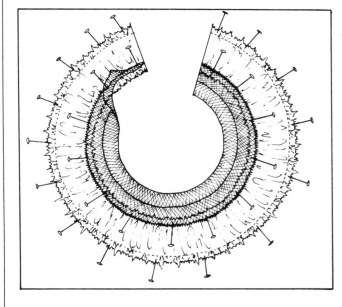

Grandmother's Hope Chest

▓ GATHERING FRENCH LACE
While Applying To Trimmed Entredeux Edge

NOTE: You must have a little extra lace when using this method. It may use more than the pattern requires. This method is easy and time saving. It can be used when attaching gathered lace around a collar that has entredeux at the bottom before the gathered lace. It is especially good when attaching gathered lace around a portrait collar. It is a great way to attach the gathered lace to an entredeux-trimmed neck edge. Actually, you can use this technique anytime you attach gathered lace to trimmed entredeux. It results in fairly even gathers, and saves you from having to pin, distribute, and straighten-out twisted lace.

Step 1. Trim off the outside edge of the entredeux, after the other edge has been attached to the garment.

Step 2. Press both the entredeux and the lace.

Step 3. Side by side, right sides up, begin to zigzag with lace still straight **(fig. 1).**

Step 4. About 6 inches out on the lace, pull one of the gathering threads. I find that using a little pick of some kind is effective. The same little pick that is used to pull a lace gathering thread, can also be used to push the gathers into the sewing machine. A pin will suffice if necessary **(fig. 2).**

Step 5. In order to get the gathers to move in the right direction (toward the foot of the sewing machine), you will need to pull on the side of the thread loop closest to the sewing machine. If you pull on the other side, the gathers will not go toward the sewing machine. Pull the thread, and push the gathers toward the sewing machine **(fig. 2).**

Step 6. Lift your pressure foot, and push a few gathers under it. Zigzag a few stitches (Width=3-1/2, Length=2). You may notice that the width is a little wider than usual for zigzagging lace to entredeux. I have found that with gathered lace, it is necessary to make the width wider in order to catch all of the heading of the gathered lace. As always, you should adjust the width and length, according to the width of your entredeux and your lace heading. They vary so much it is hard to give one exact width and length. Lift your pressure foot again, and push a few more gathers under it. Continue, until all of your gathers on that one section have been stitched in **(fig. 3).**

Step 7. Go out another 6 inches on your lace, and repeat the process. Continue, until all of the lace is gathered and stitched to the trimmed entredeux.

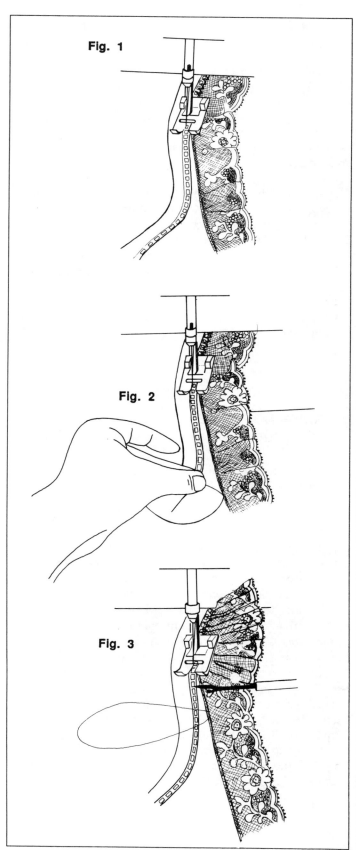

Fig. 1

Fig. 2

Fig. 3

MAKING AN ENTREDEUX AND LACE STRING

The method "Gathering French Lace A Little At A Time, While Applying It To Trimmed Entredeux Edge" is the perfect way to make an entredeux/gathered lace trim for the yoke of a French dress. This is the easy way to trim your yoke with entredeux and gathered lace. The hard way would be to apply your entredeux in the seams of the yokes and the sleeves.

Step 1. Follow the techniques found in the technique "Gathering French Lace By Machine, While Applying It To Trimmed Entredeux Edge."

Step 2. Make the entredeux and lace string as long as you need it to be to travel around the entire yoke (front and back) and over the shoulders of the dress. After making this long strip of entredeux and gathered lace, simply trim the other side of the entredeux. Pin into place, around the yoke edges, and zigzag the entredeux and lace string right onto the finished dress **(fig. 1)**.

FINISHING THE NECKLINE
With Entredeux/Gathered Lace

So many times, French dresses have an entredeux/gathered-lace nekline finish. Here is the technique I use.

Step 1. Check the seam allowance on the neckline of your pattern. This is important.

Step 2. Check the seam allowance on your entredeux. It is usually 1/2 inch; however, this is not always the case. Measure the seam allowance of your entredeux.

Step 3. If the seam allowance at the neck of the pattern and the seam allowance of your entredeux do not match, trim the seam allowance of the entredeux to match the seam allowance of the neckline of your garment.

Step 4. Using the techniques "Entredeux to Flat Fabric," attach the entredeux to the neckline of the garment.

Step 5. Stitch in the ditch **(fig. 1)**. Trim, leaving a 1/8-inch to 1/4-inch seam allowance **(fig. 2)**.

Step 6. Zigzag the seam allowance to finish **(fig. 3)**.

Step 7. Trim the remaining clipped seam allowance. Press the seam toward the body of the dress.

Step 8. Gather the lace edging. Butt it to the trimmed entredeux and zigzag **(fig. 4)**.

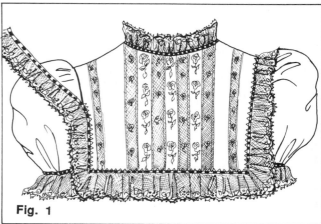

Fig. 1

Fig. 1

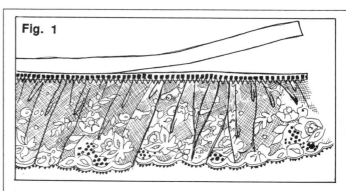

Fig. 1

Fig. 2

Fig. 3

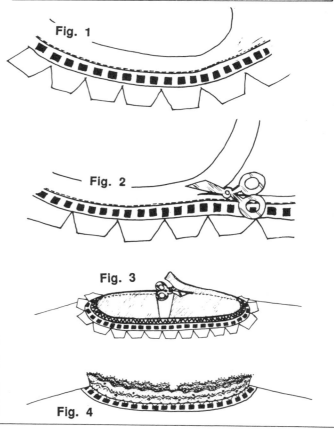

Fig. 4

I have a cute story to tell you about oval skirts. A few years ago, one of my *Sew Beautiful* readers made her daughter a magnificent French dress with oval-shaped lace and delicate embroidery on the skirt. When she brought the dress to a photo shoot for the magazine, she asked her little girl to tell me what was on the skirt of her dress. "Miss Martha, I have footballs on my dress," she answered. If that weren't the cutest thing. Since then I have referred to lace ovals as footballs.

▨ MAKING CONNECTING OVALS OR "FOOTBALLS"

Step 1. Tear both of your skirt strips. I suggest a width of 45 inches; this makes the total fullness of the skirt 90 inches. Make a French seam or serge the two skirt strips together on one side. Leave the skirt flat (**fig. 1**).

Step 2. You are now ready to measure to see approximately how many ovals you will need for your skirt. For example, if you elect to make your ovals 4 inches across, and your lace is 1/2 inch wide, you will need 20 ovals (4 inches wide each) plus 1/2-inch space between each oval. The 1/2-inch space is for the laces to cross between the exact oval shape and not distort your 4-inch oval.

Step 3. Pretend that you are using 1/2-inch insertion for this oval. Beginning from the seam you have just made, draw your ovals on the skirt leaving 1/2-inch space between each oval. If your lace is wider, say 3/4 inch, then, leave 3/4-inch space between each oval. Go ahead and draw on all of the ovals. If you have extra space left, you can quickly see that it is on the other side seam. You can just cut away any excess fabric before you put in the other side seam (**fig. 2**).

Step 4. You will need to work with two long pieces of lace insertion, long enough to go around either the top or bottom of your ovals around the whole skirt front and back. Measure around one oval and down to get the yardage you will need. Be sure to allow extra. Be sure you have two pieces of lace that are long enough. You could piece the lace by stitching it together (preferably at the overlap/mid point).

Step 5. Get your fabric board, since you will be pinning your laces into the board. Pin the insertion on the outside where the edge touches your traced oval similar to the other lace-shaping instructions in this chapter. At the mid points where you have your 1/2-inch space, pin the lace on each side, touching the edges of the oval. Follow around, pinning enough ovals to fit on one fabric board (**fig. 3**)

First you have to draw the oval shapes on your skirt. Margaret Taylor and I spent hours working on the easiest method to shape lace ovals or footballs. We tried everything and finally came back to my original thinking and the method I've always used. We align the outside edge of the lace to the drawn line, pin it, then pull the heading to shape the lace on the inside. The following technique is the one I recommend for shaping lace footballs.

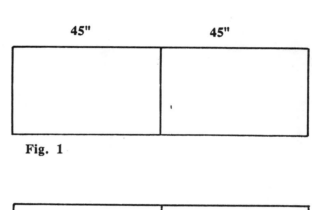

Fig. 1

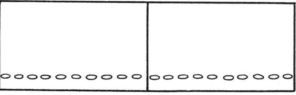

Fig. 2

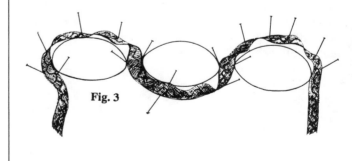

Fig. 3

OVALS

Step 6. Pull the threads in the center of the ovals to flatten the lace into the proper shape **(fig. 4)**.

Step 7. Pin the other side of the ovals on that same fabric board. After you have pinned both sides, pull the threads to flatten and shape the laces onto the board **(fig. 5)**.

Step 8. Press. Spray starch. When I say spray starch, I mean spray starch until the fabric and lace are glued together! This helps hold the laces to the fabric while you shape the rest of the ovals.

Step 9. One at a time, remove the jabbed pins from the fabric board. Pin the lace ovals flat to the fabric. This type of strong pinning is called pin basting. I very rarely baste anything (either by hand or machine); I do not think basting is necessary if you put in enough pins. If you want to baste by machine or baste by hand, feel free to do so. Remove from the fabric board and place another portion of the skirt on the board. Repeat the process until your whole skirt has been shaped. Remember to leave lots of pins in the skirt.

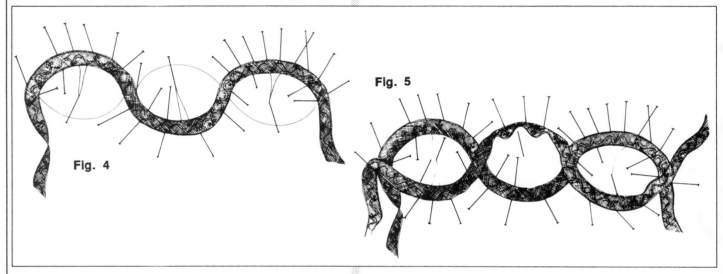

Fig. 4

Fig. 5

Step 10. After the entire skirt is shaped, starched, pressed, and pinned, you are ready to start zigzagging the ovals into place.

Step 11. Zigzag the top of each row of lace insertion. This first row of stitching will be in a scallop shape **(fig. 6)**. Notice that you do not stitch through the area where the laces cross each other.

Step 12. Zigzag around the inside of each oval shape **(fig. 7)**. Do not stitch through the places where the laces cross each other. By not stitching through this area, cutting away the fabric from behind these areas will be easier. Later, if you

want to, you can come back and zigzag over these pieces of lace. It is not necessary **(fig. 8)**. (If your oval shaping is not the bottom of a skirt but rather a decoration on the body of the skirt, it is now time to zigzag around the bottom part of the ovals.)

Step 13. Cut away the excess fabric if you are putting these scallops on the bottom of a dress. Trim away the fabric from behind the lace. As you trim the fabric from the bottom piece of lace, a large overall piece of fabric will fall away, leaving the ovals for a scalloped skirt.

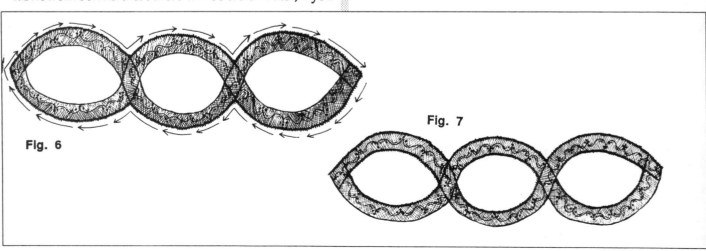

Fig. 6

Fig. 7

Lace loops have been one of the most beloved skirt trims since I have been involved in the heirloom sewing industry and for many years prior. Turn-of-the-century garments, blouses, skirts, and dresses were filled with loops of lace. Loops can be as large or as small as you want them to be; or, you might try a combination of large and small loops. One of

my favorite loop treatments is on the Sue Pennington christening dress Australian Window Pane Motifs where two different sizes of loops have been used with lots of heirloom machine work within the loops. A dress with even loops all the way around it, of course can be the beginning of a scalloped skirt, another lace shaping favorite of mine.

▩ PREPARING THE SKIRT

Step 1. Using the directions given for the skirt preparation for ovals, tear or cut two skirt pieces, stitch up one side of the skirt, and leave the whole skirt flat.

Step 2. It is now time to divide your skirt into sections. Fold your skirt lengthwise until you have it folded into the size fold that you want your ovals to be. Press. Open up and you will have the lines on which to place your ovals. (Refer to "Making A Scalloped Skirt.")

Step 3. After the skirt is folded and pressed into sections, make a loop guide **(fig. 1)**. You can use the one given **(fig. 2)** or make your own. Place the loop guide paper under the fold of the skirt. Measure up from the bottom to the place where the loop crosses. Be sure each loop is the same distance from the bottom when you make your loops. Trace (using a #2 lead pencil or a Dixon pencil) the first loop, centering it on the fold in the fabric that you made when you pressed your fabric. Repeat for the other fold lines on your skirt front and back. Trace all of the scallops onto your fabric before you begin shaping the lace.

Step 4. Place the fabric on the fabric board with as many of your drawn loops as possible on the board.

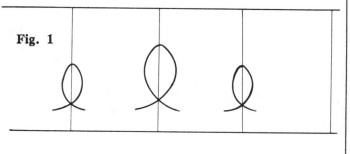

Fig. 1

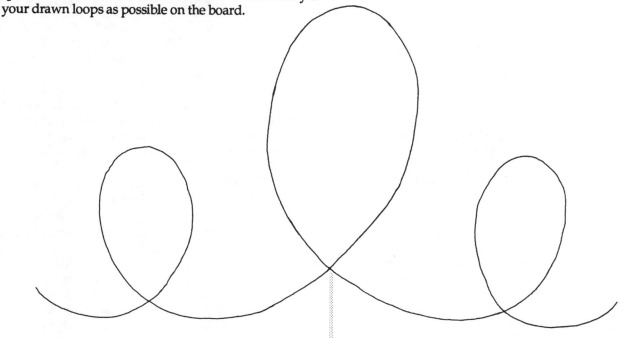

LOOPS OF LACE

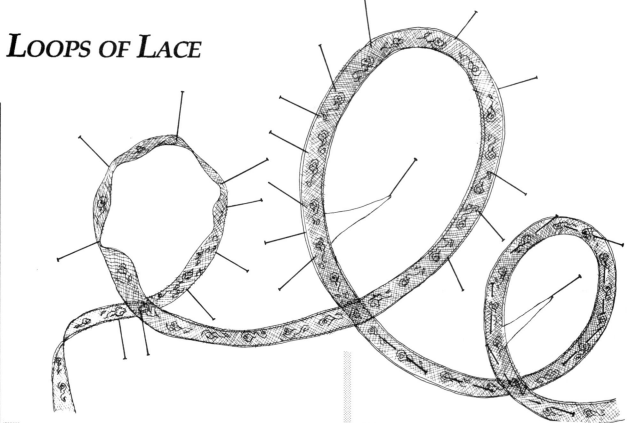

SHAPING THE LACE

Step 1. Start the lace at one of the points of the loop bottom. Using the guide line you just drew as the inside point of the lace, poke pins and curve the lace around the loop. Press down the inside of the lace to be sure that when it is pulled and shaped it will touch the drawn guide on the skirt. Push your pins in at an angle, pinning the outside edge all the way around.

Step 2. Complete the loop, and pin the lace along the bottom scallop, connecting the two loops. Continue this process until you completely run out of fabric board space to pin the laces.

Step 3. After you have pinned as many loops onto the board as possible, it is time to pull the threads and finish these loops before travelling on to the next set of loops.

Step 4. Pull a thread on the inside of one of the loops. Be sure that you pull the very top thread in the heading of the lace Pull it tightly enough that you can draw up the slack and shape the lace in loops flat to the fabric. Hold this thread tightly by sticking a pin into the board to hold it after you get the lace pulled into shape.

Step 5. Starch the laces. Press. Let them dry completely by using a hair dryer or by allowing time to dry naturally.

Step 6. Pin baste the lace loop to the fabric by removing the pins that are poked into the board and placing them through the laces and the fabric of the skirt.

Step 7. Remove this section of the looped lace from the board and move to the next section. Continue this process until the whole skirt has been shaped and pinned.

Step 8. When you run short of lace, end the lace under the loop cross point to hide the patched lace.

SEWING THE LACE LOOPS TO THE SKIRT

Step 1. After lace shaping has been made on the skirt, zigzag the laces to the skirt. Using a zigzag stitch (Width=1-1/2 to 2-1/2, length=1/2) stitch the top of the laces to the skirt.
NOTE: Never cross an intersection of lace with the zigzag stitches. The top loops are zigzagged in one continuous zigzag all around the skirt.

Step 2. Zigzag the loops in a circular shape to the skirt. Do not cross an intersection of the lace with the zigzag stitches.

Step 3. If this is the bottom of a skirt, you will not stitch the bottom of the lace insertion to the skirt at all.

Step 4. Trim away the fabric from behind the lace insertion. You will notice that the fabric falls away from the bottom of the skirt, leaving lace insertion shaped in a scallop for the bottom trim of the skirt.

Step 5. You can finish this skirt in several ways. If you are putting these loops on the bottom of a dress, cut away the excess fabric. Trim away the fabric from behind the lace. As you trim the fabric from the bottom piece of lace, a large overall piece of fabric will fall away, leaving the loops for a scalloped skirt.

Step 6. For a beautiful skirt bottom, trim away one side of a piece of entredeux. Slash the other side every 1 inch or so, so it will curve into the scalloped shapes. Go back to the fabric board and pin, starch, shape, and press this entredeux into the shape of the scallops. Let them dry stiff as a board. After your entredeux and lace skirt dry completely, zigzag the entredeux to the scalloped skirt edge by stitching into one hole and off on the lace.

Step 7. Trim away the slashed edge of the entredeux. You are now ready to gather your lace edging and zigzag it to the trimmed entredeux edge of your garment.

Quilting designs take on many different shapes and forms. Celtic quilting is the use of narrow bias strips of fabric used to create a design. These designs, inspired by Celtic art, are put in template form and traced on the fabric. The bias strips are then shaped over the template designs thus creating the Celtic quilting technique. Celtic lace shaping is simply replacing the bias strips of fabric with lace insertion. The lace insertion is shaped over the Celtic design template traced on the fabric. The lace is then stitched in place, creating a beautiful, intricate lace design. The fabric can then be cut away from the lace or the fabric can be left behind the lace.

An infinite number of Celtic designs would be possible for the person with the patience to imagine and draw them. In addition to Celtic designs, a lot of other quilting designs can be the inspiration for creative lace shaping.

CHOOSING A CELTIC LACE DESIGN

• Every line on the lace motif should be continuous.
• No more than two lines should cross at any intersection.

LACE REQUIREMENTS

Requirement 1. The insertion needs to be very narrow (3/8 inch or less) to be shaped into the tight curves and loops in these designs.

Requirement 2. The lace must be woven in an "over, under, over, under" (weaving) manner. There should not be two overs and two unders next to each other.

Requirement 3. Divide the template into sections or continuous loops (from one "under" to another "under"). The lace pieces will be easier to "weave" if the lace pieces are of shorter measure. Use a tape measure to determine the length of each continuous loop of lace, cut lace a few inches longer than these measurements.

CELTIC LACESHAPING RULES

Rule 1. Start at an "under."

Rule 2. Allow the raw end of the lace to extend 1/4 inch.

Rule 3. Patiently shape the lace directly onto the fabric, shaping all curves and mitering corners.

Rule 4. Follow the "over" and "under" markings, gently weaving the insertions under the sections of lace already pinned down at the appropriate points.

Rule 5. You should end each section at the same "under" at which you started. Shape and pin the lace on the entire motif before you do any sewing. Starch and press.

I think very narrow lace insertion(less than 1/2 inch wide) will be best in nearly all situations. As I look through quilting design books lots and lots of designs stand out in my mind as being lovely to interpret into lace shaping. I love the Hawaiian, shell, scallops, leaves, flowers, baskets, Virginia Reel, Grandmother's Flower Garden, hearts, gladioli, crazy quilt, wedding ring, lots of applique designs, tulips, sunflowers, daisies, forget-me-not, or wild rose. The possibilities are absolutely endless.

Several years ago I wouldn't have said that geometric designs are suitable for lace shaping. One summer at our school, a lady modeled the most beautiful linen dress with geometric quilting designs done in laces. It was very tailored and very lovely. So, the sky is really the limit when using quilting designs for lace shaping.

STITCHING CELTIC DESIGN IN PLACE

Step 1. Use a small pin stitch if possible to stitch if possible to stitch the insertion down, or a zigzag if you machine does not do a pinstitch.

Step 2. Begin stitching at an "under," and end the stitching by backstitching when you come to an "under."

Step 3. Continue in the manner until all the insertion is stitched down.

Step 4. Rinse the fabric in warm water to remove all the markings, and press to dry.

Step 5. Using a very small, very sharp scissors, carefully trim away all fabric from behind the insertion. Also trim away the lace on the underside of the intersections to enhance the woven appearance of this technique.

Machine Entredeux

▓ Making Entredeux (Or Hemstitching) On Today's Computer Sewing Machines

About eight years ago I was conned into purchasing a 1905 hemstitching machine for $1500. I was told that it had a perfect stitch and that stitch (about 2 inches) was demonstrated to me by the traveling salesman. I was very happy to finally have one of those wonderful machines. Guess how long that wonderful machine lasted before it broke down? I stitched about 10 inches more which looked great; at that point, the stitching was awful. I called several repairmen. It never made a decent hemstitch again.

The good news to follow this sad story is that today's new computer machines do an excellent job of making hemstitching and they work! I am going to give our favorite settings for our favorite sewing machines. Before you buy a new sewing machine, if you love heirloom sewing, please go try out each of these machines and see if you love these stitches as much as we do.

▓ Using A Stabilizer With Wing Needle Hemstitching or Pinstitching

Before you do any hemstitching or any decorative work with a wing needle which involves lots of stitching on these wonderful machines, first let me tell you that **you do have to have a stabilizer!** You can use stitch-n-tear, computer paper, tissue paper(not quite strong enough but o.k. in certain situations), wax paper, physician's examining table paper, typing paper, adding machine paper or almost any other type of paper. When you are doing heavy stitching such as a feather stitch, I recommend that type of paper which physicians spread out over their examining tables. You can get a roll of it at any medical supply place. If you use stitch-n-tear or adding machine paper in feather stitch type stitches, it is difficult to pull away all of the little pieces which remain when you take the paper from the back of the garment. This physician's paper seems to tear away pretty easily.

I do not like the thin, plastic looking, wash away stabilizers for heavy stitching with a wing needle because it doesn't have enough body. There is another type of wash away stabilizer which is absolutely wonderful. It is the paint on, liquid kind. In this country it is called Perfect Sew. You simply paint it on with a paint brush; let it dry, and stitch. You don't have to use any other stabilizer underneath it. It washes out after you have finished your stitching. It is available in this country from Pati Palmer, Palmer/Pletsch Publishing, Perfect Sew, P.O. Box 12046, Portland, OR 97212. 1-800-728-3784.

Make your own wash away stabilizer by using some water in a container and by dropping this wash away plastic looking sheet of stabilizer into the container. Some of the brand names are Solvy and Aqua Solve. Stir with a wooden spoon; keep adding the plastic looking wash away stabilizer sheets until it becomes the consistency of egg whites. Then, paint it on or brush it on with a sponge. Let it dry and then stitch. Both of the liquid, wash out stabilizers make batiste-type fabrics about as stiff as organdy which is wonderful for stitching. After stitching, simply wash the stabilizer away.

▓ Preparing Fabric Before You Begin Hemstitching or Pinstitching

Stiffen fabric with spray starch before lace shaping or decorative stitching with the hemstitches and wing needles. Use a hair dryer to dry the lace before you iron it if you have spray starched it too much. Also, if you wet your fabrics and laces too much with spray starch, place a piece of tissue paper on top of your work, and dry iron it dry. Hemstitching works best on natural fibers such as linen, cotton, cotton batiste, silk or cotton organdy. I don't advise hemstitching a fabric with a high polyester content. Polyester has a memory. If you punch a hole in polyester, it remembers the original positioning of the fibers, and the hole wants to close up.

▓ Threads To Use For Pinstitching or Hemstitching

Use all cotton thread, 50, 60, 70, 80 weight. If you have a thread breaking problem, you can also use a high quality polyester thread or a cotton covered polyester thread, like the Coats and Clark for machine lingerie and embroidery. Personally, I like to press needle down on all of the entredeux and pin stitch settings.

▓ Pinstitching or Point de Paris Stitch With A Sewing Machine

The pin stitch is another lovely "entredeux look" on my favorite machines. It is a little more delicate. Pin stitch looks similar to a ladder with **one of the long sides of the ladder missing**. Imagine the steps being fingers which reach over into the actual lace piece to grab the lace. The side of the ladder, the long side, will be stitched on the fabric right along side of the outside of the heading of the lace. The fingers reach into the lace to grab it. You need to look on all of the pinstitch settings given below and realize that you have to use reverse image on one of the sides of lace so that the fingers will grab into the lace while the straight side goes on the outside of the lace heading.

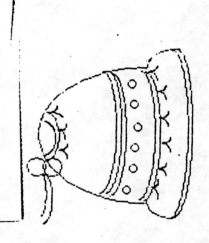

Martha Pullen's Little French Bonnet

MATERIALS NEEDED:

1. One piece of batiste 3 5/8" wide by 14" long.
2. Two pieces of lace insertion 14" long.
3. One piece of Swiss insertion 2" wide by 14" long.
4. One piece of Swiss entredeux 14" long.
5. One piece of batiste 2" wide by 21" long.
6. One piece lace edging 21" long.
7. Two pieces 1/2" ribbon, 18" long.
8. One piece 1/4" ribbon, 21" long.

CONSTRUCTION:

1. Fabric strips must be on grain. Pull a thread and straighten or tear strips.
2. Right sides up, butt lace insertion together (do not overlap) and zigzag. Zigzag wide enough to catch the headings of the lace on both pieces of the lace.
3. Pull threads and trim insertion to a width of 2". The dots should be directly in the middle of the insertion.
4. To sew the back batiste portion of the bonnet to the lace insertion, leave 1/8 to 3/16" of the fabric edge before placing the lace to be joined. Zigzag with a satin stitch going into the heading of the lace and all the way off the fabric edge. The exposed fabric edge will completely fold into the stitch when you are finished.
5. To sew the Swiss insertion to the lace insertion, follow the same steps as in #4.
6. To attach the lace edging to the 21" ruffle, follow the same steps as in #4.
7. To attach the entredeux to the flat fabric, follow the following steps:
   a. Do not trim entredeux!
   b. Press fabric and entredeux.
   c. Place batiste edge of untrimmed entredeux and edge of the fabric together.
   d. Sew a straight, short stitch along the right hand side of the entredeux. This is called "stitch in the ditch" because it is just that --- one stitches in the ditch beside the entredeux.

BONNET

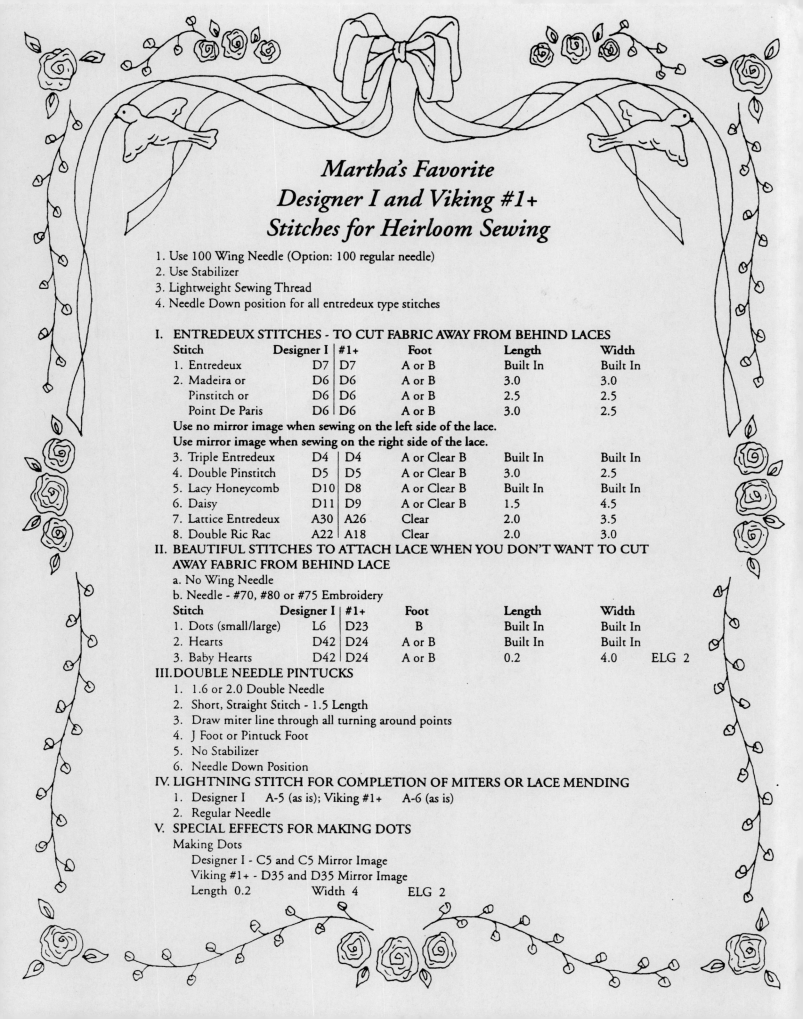

Martha's Favorite Designer I and Viking #1+ Stitches for Heirloom Sewing

1. Use 100 Wing Needle (Option: 100 regular needle)
2. Use Stabilizer
3. Lightweight Sewing Thread
4. Needle Down position for all entredeux type stitches

I. ENTREDEUX STITCHES - TO CUT FABRIC AWAY FROM BEHIND LACES

Stitch	Designer I	#1+	Foot	Length	Width	
1. Entredeux	D7	D7	A or B	Built In	Built In	
2. Madeira or	D6	D6	A or B	3.0	3.0	
Pinstitch or	D6	D6	A or B	2.5	2.5	
Point De Paris	D6	D6	A or B	3.0	2.5	

Use no mirror image when sewing on the left side of the lace.
Use mirror image when sewing on the right side of the lace.

Stitch	Designer I	#1+	Foot	Length	Width	
3. Triple Entredeux	D4	D4	A or Clear B	Built In	Built In	
4. Double Pinstitch	D5	D5	A or Clear B	3.0	2.5	
5. Lacy Honeycomb	D10	D8	A or Clear B	Built In	Built In	
6. Daisy	D11	D9	A or Clear B	1.5	4.5	
7. Lattice Entredeux	A30	A26	Clear	2.0	3.5	
8. Double Ric Rac	A22	A18	Clear	2.0	3.0	

II. BEAUTIFUL STITCHES TO ATTACH LACE WHEN YOU DON'T WANT TO CUT AWAY FABRIC FROM BEHIND LACE

a. No Wing Needle
b. Needle - #70, #80 or #75 Embroidery

Stitch	Designer I	#1+	Foot	Length	Width	
1. Dots (small/large)	L6	D23	B	Built In	Built In	
2. Hearts	D42	D24	A or B	Built In	Built In	
3. Baby Hearts	D42	D24	A or B	0.2	4.0	ELG 2

III. DOUBLE NEEDLE PINTUCKS

1. 1.6 or 2.0 Double Needle
2. Short, Straight Stitch - 1.5 Length
3. Draw miter line through all turning around points
4. J Foot or Pintuck Foot
5. No Stabilizer
6. Needle Down Position

IV. LIGHTNING STITCH FOR COMPLETION OF MITERS OR LACE MENDING

1. Designer I   A-5 (as is); Viking #1+   A-6 (as is)
2. Regular Needle

V. SPECIAL EFFECTS FOR MAKING DOTS

Making Dots
    Designer I - C5 and C5 Mirror Image
    Viking #1+ - D35 and D35 Mirror Image
    Length 0.2   Width 4   ELG 2

SETTINGS FOR ENTREDEUX (HEMSTITCH) AND PINSTITCH

Pfaff 1473-1475
-100 wing needle
-Pin Stitch-Stitch 165, tension 3, twin needle button, 4.0 width, 3.0 length
-Entredeux Program
  Stitch Number is followed by B(width) and L(Length).

1. 28, 00	13. 14, 12
2. 28, 12	14. 28, 12
3. 28, 00	15. 28, 14
4. 28, 12	16. 28, 12
5. 40, 12	17. 28, 14
6. 28, 12	18. 14, 12
7. 40, 12	19. 28, 12
8. 28, 00	20. 28, 24
9. 28, 12	21. 40, 12
10. 28, 00	22. 28, 12
11. 14, 12	23. 28, 24
12. 28, 12	24. 28, 12

Bernina 1530
Pinstitch
- 100 wing needle
- 1230   stitch #26, SW - 2.5, SL - 2
- 1530   menu H, pattern #10, SW - 2.5, SL - 2

Entredeux (Baby Daisy)
- 100 wing needle
- 1230   stitch #27, SW - 3, SL - 2.5
- 1530   menu G1, pattern #6, SW - 3, SL - 2.5

Entredeux
-100 wing needle
- 1230   stitch #18, long stitch, SW - 3, SL - 1.5
- 1530   menu H, pattern #2, long stitch, SW - 3, SL - 1.5

Viking #1, 1100, 1090
-100 wing needle
-Pinstitch-Stitch D6, width 2.5-3; length 2.5-3
-Entredeux-Stitch D7 (width and length are already set in)

Elna 9000
-100 wing needle
-Pinstitch-Stitch #120 (length and width are already set in)
-Entredeux-Stitch #121 (length and width are already set)

ATTACHING SHAPED LACE
To The Garment With Machine Entredeux Or Pinstitching and A Wing Needle

Probably my favorite place to use the machine entredeux/wing needle hemstitching is to attach shaped laces to a garment. Simply shape your laces in the desired shapes such as hearts, diamonds, ovals, loops, circles, or bows, and stitch the stitch. In addition to stitching this gorgeous decorative stitch, it also attaches the shaped lace to the garment **(fig. 1)**. Always use stabilizer when using this type of heavy hemstitching.

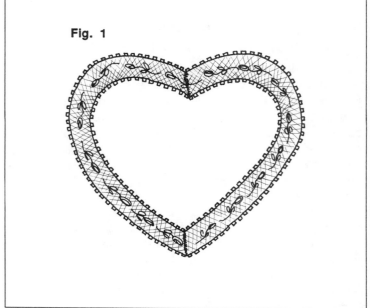

Fig. 1

ATTACHING TWO PIECES OF LACE WITH MACHINE ENTREDEUX

There is nothing prettier than a garment which has entredeux in between each layer of fabric and lace. That would take a million years to stitch with purchased entredeux, not to mention the cost. Here is how you can use your hemstitch/machine entredeux stitch and wing needle and make your laces look as if they had been joined with entredeux.

Step 1. Butt two pieces of lace insertion together. Since entredeux/hemstitching with a wing needle on your machine needs fabric underneath the stitching to hold the stitches perfectly, you need to put a narrow strip of batiste or other fabric underneath the place where these two laces will be joined.

Step 2. Put a strip of stabilizer underneath the butted laces and the fabric strip.

Step 3. Stitch using a wing needle and your hemstitching stitch. If your machine has an edge joining or edge stitching foot this is a great time to use it. It's little blade guides in between the two pieces of butted lace and makes it easy to stitch straight **(fig. 1)**. You can see that the entredeux stitching not only stitches in one of the most beautiful stitches, it also attaches the laces.

Step 4. When you have finished stitching, tear away the stabilizer and turn each side of the lace back to carefully trim away the excess fabric **(fig. 2)**.

Step 5. Now it looks as if you have two pieces of lace with purchased entredeux stitched in between them **(fig. 3)**.

MAKING MACHINE ENTREDEUX EMBROIDERY DESIGNS OR INITIALS

You can take almost any larger, plain embroidery design and stitch the entredeux stitch around it. You may find it necessary to put the design into an embroidery hoop for maximum effectiveness. I have some old handkerchiefs and some old tablecloths which actually look as if hemstitching has made the design. You can place several rows of entredeux stitching together to form a honeycomb effect which might be used to fill in embroidery designs.

Some of the prettiest monograms are those with hemstitching stitched around the letter. Once again, I think the liquid stabilizer and the embroidery hoop will be wonderful assets in doing this kind of wing needle work. Let your imagination be your guide when thinking of new and elegant things to do with these wonderful wing needle/entredeux stitches **(fig. 4)**.

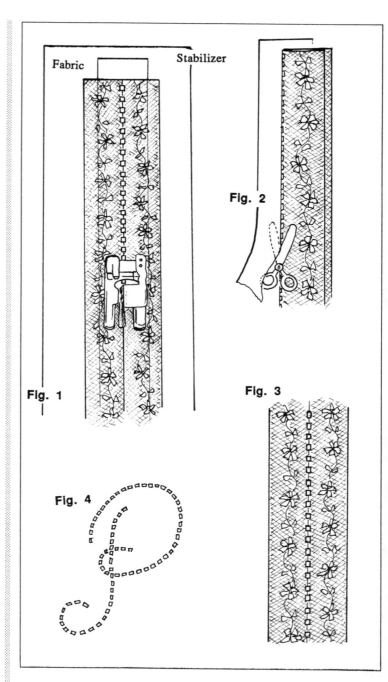

Fabric   Stabilizer

Fig. 1

Fig. 2

Fig. 3

Fig. 4

USING MACHINE ENTREDEUX FOR DECORATIVE WORK ON TAILORED CLOTHING

One of my favorite things to do with this entredeux stitch or pin stitch is simply to stitch it around cuffs, across yokes, around collars, down the center back or center front of a blouse. It is lovely stitched down both sides of the front placket of a very tailored woman's blouse. Some people love to machine entredeux in black thread on a black garment. The places you put this wing needling are endless. It is just as pretty stitched as a plain stitch as it is when it is used to stitch on laces.

Pintuck Fantasy

When I think about the addition of double needle pintucking to an heirloom garment I have to think about setting a table for dinner. I usually choose the everyday china and glasses, paper napkins, and ordinary cutlery. This can make a lovely table, of course. This type of table might be compared to a very pretty French garment. How might I add truly breathtaking elements to this same dinner setting without spending any money? Well, my best linen tablecloth and cloth napkins might begin the reconstruction. My yard usually has at least a green shrub, ivy or a tree with some leaves which might be picked for a centerpiece. During certain times of the year, perhaps flowers could be picked from my flower beds. Is there a green plant or a pot of blooming flowers such as violets in the house somewhere? Another lovely centerpiece might be a combination of apples and lemons, pulled from the refrigerator and placed in a bowl in the center of the table. Are there some candles in the dining room drawer from my last Christmas or dinner party extravaganza? It's O.K. if I relight them since candles can be any length. Several pretty figurines from your living room might be repositioned in the center of the table. What I am trying to say is that with a little imagination and no more money, I can make my family dinner table a lot more elegant.

Pintucks, both curved and straight, can have that very same effect on French garments. I love pintucks, especially when they are made this very easy and almost unbelievable way! The double needle magic is about to unravel! It really is as easy as the next section relates to you! Nobody every believes it until they stitch! The usual statement after curving and turning corners with this method is "Martha, I just can't believe it. This is magic."

Something very interesting has been happening over the last several years at the Martha Pullen School Of Art Fashion both in Huntsville and out around the world where we do the "Mini" schools. At least one person, sometimes several, will say after they have learned how easy it is to curve pintucks and turn those gorgeous corners with row after row of intricate pintucks, "Martha, I would have paid the whole tuition for the school just to have learned how easy it is to make these curved and squared off pintucks. I have thought that making these would be just physically impossible for me to do. IT IS SO EASY." Shaped pintucks are very delicate and pretty to look at, inexpensive to make and so easy that I am including a whole section on double needle pintucks. I have learned even easier methods for making these pintucks since writing my last book.

Traveling and teaching has been so much fun. One of the most enjoyable parts of this traveling has been learning new methods for doing almost everything. When we have made new discoveries, the ladies would laugh and say, "Now, you have to write a new book." Others would say, "Why wasn't this easy method in your *Antique Clothing* book?" I would respond to that by saying, "Life for me has been one big educational experience. I hope I never stop learning. My students are my very best teachers and sometimes we discover something absolutely by accident. Another reason for always learning something new is so I will be able to write new books, have new techniques for *Sew Beautiful* and be able to keep the doors of the business open for us all to enjoy." I always tease them by adding, "If Chrysler, Ford and General Motors can come up with new car models every year, then why can't we keep discovering new methods and writing new books?"

If I think about how many garments I made before I even knew about double needles and double needle pintucking, I might get a little embarrassed. Since my discovery of this very inexpensive and very precious way to embellish a French garment, I have gone crazy. By adding elaborate pintucking to a garment, you can really choose to make a budget garment. The pintucks are just as pretty as miles of lace insertion; they are really easier to make than shaping another row of lace onto the garment. The sky is the limit for your own creativity in shaping pintucks.

Heirloom sewing fanatics use pintucks to decorate everything from day gowns to ladies blouses to the insides of fancy lace shapes. There is nothing new about tucks and pintucks on clothing. Some of my most beautiful antique garments have tucks and pintucks on the skirt and nothing else for embellishment. That treatment is just as lovely today as it was 100 years ago. Nothing more than stitched folds of fabric, usually in rows of two or more, tucks have probably embellished clothing since the dawn of the needle. Portraits dating back to the fifteenth century indicate tucks were used on clothing at least as far back as the Italian Renaissance. Even doll clothes of yesteryear sported tucking. The Jules Nicholas Steiner (doll) Company, which was in operation for 1855 to 1891, used tucking extensively — primarily pintucking — on the sleeves, skirts, and yokes of the fancy doll dresses. These particular pintucks were so fine, they must have taken a seamstress days to complete since she had to make them by hand.

The good news for today's seamstress is that the pintucks can be made quickly and easily on the modern sewing machine. The even greater news is that you don't even have to have a pintuck foot to make double needle pintucks. That is a new discovery of ours. As a matter of fact, I prefer not using pintuck feet on curved pintucks around acute curves because I think the squared off pintuck foot doesn't turn curves as well as a regular zigzag

PINTUCKING

sewing foot. "Always use a pintuck foot for straight pintucks," seems to be my rule of thumb. It seems to me that it is easier to make straight pintucks using the grooved feet; however, it isn't necessary to use pintuck feet even for straight pintucks. Pintuck feet are available for nearly all models of sewing machines. Pintucks are made when two needle threads share one bobbin thread. The fabric between the needles is "pulled up" creating a tuck. Sometimes using the pintuck foot helps the pintuck pull up a little better than when using a regular foot. Pintucks are one of the most elegant treatments in heirloom clothing, and unlike yards of lace, they don't factor into the cost of a garment. Almost any fabric can be pintucked from Swiss batiste and delicate silk to wool and denim. For heirloom sewing, I suggest that you use Swiss batiste, Victorian batiste, American batiste, silk, or any lightweight fabric. Check with your sewing machine dealer about the pintuck feet and the corresponding needles that are available for your machine.

DOUBLE NEEDLES

Double needles come in different sizes. The first number on the double needle is the distance between the needles. The second number on the needle is the actual size of the needle. The chart below shows some of the double needle sizes. The size needle that you choose will depend on the weight of the fabric that you are pintucking (fig. 1).

Let me relate a little more information for any of you who haven't used the double needles yet. Some people have said to me, "Martha, I only have a place for one needle in my sewing machine." That is correct and on most sewing machines, you probably still can use a double needle. The double needle has only one stem which goes into the needle slot; the double needles join on a little bar below the needle slot. You use two spools of thread when you thread the double needles. If you don't have two spools of thread of the fine thread which you use for pintucking, then run an extra bobbin and use it as another spool of thread. For most shaped pintucking on heirloom garments, I prefer either the 1.6/70, the 1.6/80 or the 2.0/80 size needle.

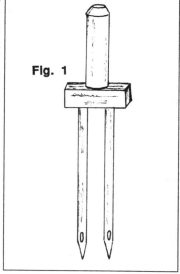

Fig. 1

Fabric
a. 1.6/70 - Light Weight
b. 1.6/80 - Light Weight
c. 2.0/80 - Light Weight
d. 2.5/80 - Light Weight
e. 3.0/90 - Medium Weight
f. 4.0/100 - Heavy Weight

PINTUCK FEET

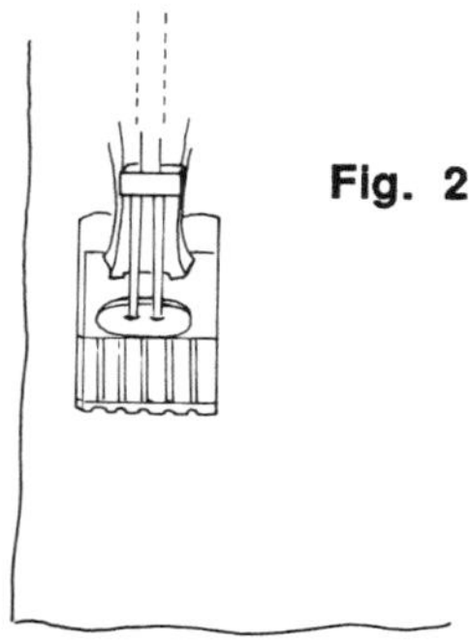

Pintuck feet are easy to use and they shave hours off pintucking time when you are making straight pintucks. They enable you to space straight pintucks perfectly. I might add here that some people also prefer a pintuck foot when making curved and angled pintucks. I prefer a regular zigzag sewing foot for curved pintucks. Pintuck feet correspond to the needle used with that pintuck foot; the needle used corresponds to the weight of fabric. The bottom of these feet have a certain number of grooves 3, 5, 7, or 9. The width of the groove matches the width between the two needles. When making straight pintucks, use a pintuck foot of your choice. The grooves enable one to make those pintucks as close or as far away as the distance on the foot allows (fig. 2).

Fig. 2

PREPARING FABRIC FOR PINTUCKING

Do I spray starch the fabric before I pintuck it? I usually do not spray starch fabric before pintucking it. Always press all-cotton fabric. A polyester/cotton blend won't need to be pressed unless it is very wrinkled. Tucks tend to lay flatter if you stiffen fabric with spray starch first; that is why I don't advise spray starching the fabric first in most cases. Pintuck a small piece of your chosen fabric with starch and one without starch, then make your own decision.

Circuit y Stores, Inc.

Store 3
S PORTL   ME 04106
(207) 7   433   21:50:44   08/31/98

Sold to   Ticket
                                                 310800519044

CUSTOME   PY   Orig Date 08/31/98

Salespe   Register   Cashier
A. J. MON   17   120985

Item Q	odel	Description	Tax	Amount
1 SL	AX XLII1003PLUS1	BLANK AUDIO TAPE	Y	7.59

Total Taxable	$	7.59
Sales Tax	$	0.46
TOTAL PURCHASE	$	8.05
CSH	$	20.05
CHA	$	12.00-
BALANCE	$	0.00

Item

CM NOW   NG - SALES, WAREHOUSE, CUSTOMER SERVICE
   POSI   S

For repair service call: (800) 677-8958

▦ STRAIGHT PINTUCKING WITH A PINTUCK FOOT

Some of my favorite places places for straight pintucks are on high yoke bodices of a dress and along the sleeves. On ladies blouses, straight pintucks are lovely running vertically on the front and back of the blouse, and so slenderizing! One of the prettiest treatments of straight pintucks on ladies blouses is stitching about three to five pintucks right down the center back of the blouse. Tuck a little shaped bow or heart on the center back of the blouse; stitch several tiny pintucks and top them off with a lace shape in the center back. Horizontally placed straight pintucks are lovely running across the back yoke of a tailored blouse. Tucks are always pretty running around the cuff of a blouse. I love pintucks just about anywhere.

Step 1. Put in your double needle. Thread machine with two spools of thread. Thread one spool at a time (including the needle). This will help keep the threads from becoming twisted while stitching the tucks. This would be a good time to look in the guide book, which came with your sewing machine, for directions on using pintuck feet and double needles. Some sewing machines have a special way of threading for use with double needles.

Step 2. The first tuck must be straight. To make this first tuck straight, do one of three things: **(a.)** Pull a thread all the way across the fabric and follow along that pulled line. **(b.)** Using a measuring stick, mark a straight line along the fabric. Stitch on that line. **(c.)** Fold the fabric in half and press that fold. Stitch along that folded line.

Step 3. Place the fabric under the foot for the first tuck and straight stitch the desired length of pintuck. (Length=1 to 2-1/2; Needle position is center) **Fig. 1.**

Step 4. Place your first tuck into one of the grooves in your pintuck foot. The space between each pintuck depends on the placement of the first pintuck **(Fig. 2)**.

Step 5. Continue pintucking by placing the last pintuck made into a groove in the foot.

▦ STRAIGHT PINTUCKING WITHOUT A PINTUCK FOOT

Step 1. Use a double needle. Use your regular zigzag foot.

Step 2. Thread your double needles.

Step 3. Draw the first line of pintucking. Pintuck along that line. At this point you can use the edge of your presser foot as a guide **(fig. 3)**.

NOTE: You might find a "generic" pintuck foot for your particular brand of machine.

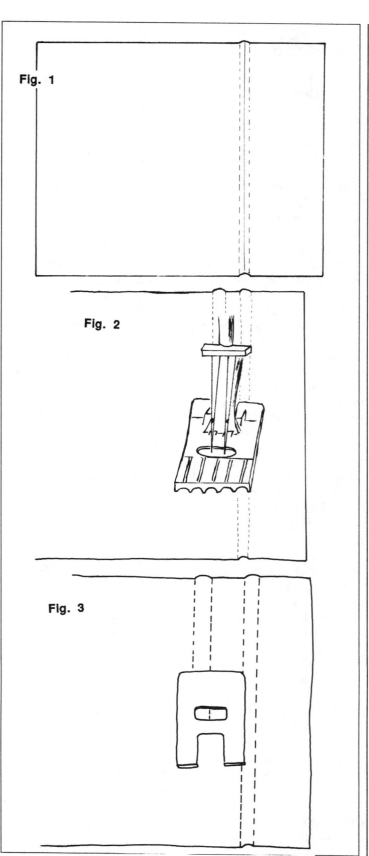

Fig. 1

Fig. 2

Fig. 3

PINTUCKING

▓ PROPERLY TYING OFF RELEASED PINTUCKS

A released pintuck is usually used to give fullness to a skirt. It is a perfectly elegant way to add detail to a garment which is easy to do using today's double needles. If you have a pintuck foot, please do use it for this treatment.

Straight pintucks that are made on a piece of fabric, cut out and stitched into the seams garment, do not have to be tied off. Why? When you sew the seam of the garment, the pintucks will be secured within that seam. Released pintucks stop at a designated point in the fabric. They are not caught in a seam and, therefore, have to be tied off. To make the most beautiful released pintuck possible, you must properly tie it off. If you want to take a short cut, then either back stitch on your machine or use the tie off feature that some of the modern machines offer. Please do not use a clear glue sold for tying off seams in sewing. One of my friends had a disastrous experience when making a lovely Susan York pattern featured in *Sew Beautiful* several years ago with over a hundred gorgeous released pintucks. She dabbed a little of this glue product at the end of each pintuck; when she washed and pressed the dress, each place on the Swiss batiste garment where that product had been touched on, turned absolutely brown. The dress with all of the money in Swiss batiste and French laces, had to be thrown away.

Properly tying off released pintucks is a lot of trouble. Remember, you can back stitch and cut the threads close to the fabric. The result isn't as pretty but it surely saves time. The choice, as always, is yours. If you are going to properly tie off those released pintucks, here are the directions.

Step 1. End your stitching at the designated stopping point (**fig. 1**).

Step 2. Pull out a reasonable length of thread before you cut the threads for this pintuck to go to the next pintuck. Five inches should be ample. You can use more or less.

Step 3. Pull the threads to the back of the fabric (**fig. 2**). Tie off each individual pintuck (**fig. 3**).

▓ BI-DIRECTIONAL STITCHING OF PIN-TUCKS

The general consensus, when stitching pintucks, is to stitch down one side and back up the other side instead of stitching pintucks all in the same direction.

To prevent pintucks from being lopsided, stitch down the length of one pintuck, pull your sewing machine threads several inches, and stitch back up in the opposite direction (**Fig. 4**).

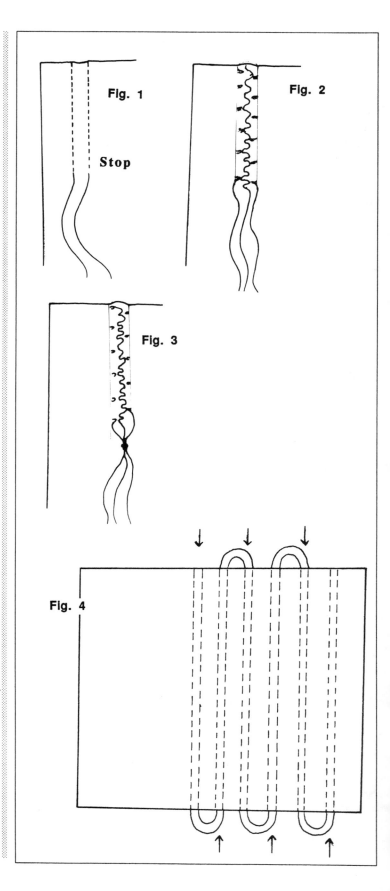

MAKING WAFFLE PINTUCKS

Step 1. Stitch pintucks all in the same direction to the width you desire.

Step 2. Stitch pintucks in the opposite direction (fig. 1).

CORDING PINTUCKS AND RAISING PINTUCKS

Cords make pintucks more prominent. Use Mettler gimp or #8 pearl cotton. Cording comes in handy when pintucks are being shaped. When pintucking across a bias with a double needle, you may get some distortion. The cord acts as a filler and will keep the fabric from distorting. Sometimes you might choose to use cording in order to add color to your pintucks. If you asked me, "Martha, do you usually cord pintucks? my answer would be no." However, just because I don't usually cord pintucks, doesn't mean that you won't prefer to cord them.

Some machines have a little device which sits in the base of the machine and sticks up just a little bit. That device tends to make the pintucks stand up a little more for a higher raised effect. Some people really like this feature.

Step 1. If your machine has a hole in the throat plate, run the cord up through that hole and it will be properly placed without another thought (fig. 2).

Step 2. If your machine does not have a hole in the throat plate, put the gimp or pearl cotton underneath the fabric, lining it up with the pintuck groove. Once you get the cording lined up under the proper groove, it will follow along for the whole pintuck.

Step 3. You can stitch pintucks without a pintuck foot at all. Some sewing machines have a foot with a little hole right in the middle of the foot underneath the foot. That is a perfectly proper place to place the cord for shadow pintucks. Remember, if you use a regular foot for pintucking, you must use the side of the foot for guiding your next pintuck.

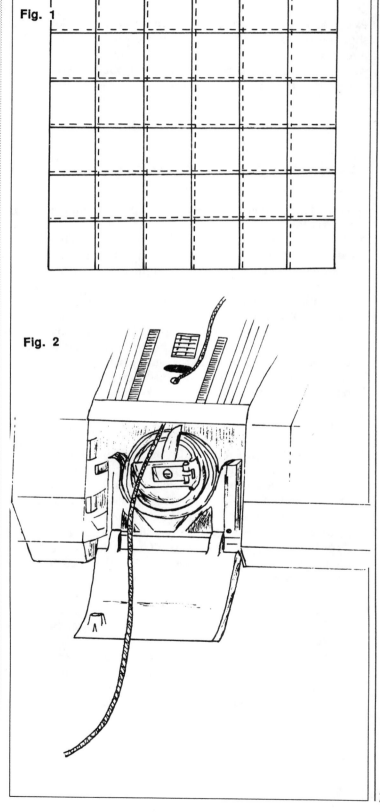

Fig. 1

Fig. 2

253

PINTUCKING QUESTIONS AND ANSWERS

▓ SHADOW PINTUCKS

Q. What is a shadow pintuck?
A. Shadow pintucks are pintucks with a touch of color showing through. Some people simply put a colored thread in the bobbin. You might want to try this to see if you like the effect. To properly shadow pintuck, you must use sheer fabric — batiste, organdy, or pastel silk.

▓ PINTUCKING ON THE SEWING MACHINE

Q. What do I do about puckering when I pintuck straight strips of fabric?
A. There are several things that you can try. Sewing machine pintucks tend to pucker slightly. You can shorten your stitch length. You can pull the fabric from the front and back as you sew. You can lightly starch your fabric before you pintuck. You can loosen your bobbin tension. If you do any or all of these things, you may prevent your fabric from puckering, but you will also change the look of the pintuck. Try various techniques on your particular sewing machine. Actually, I don't mind the tiny puckers. They add texture to the garment and make the pintucks stand out.

Q. Would I ever want to use a cord enclosed in my pintucks?
A. Cords will keep the fabric from puckering so much. They also keep the pintuck from smashing flat when you press it. Some people absolutely love cords in their pintucks. In fact, all of the students I met while teaching in Australia use cords within their pintucks.
Cords are also used decoratively with a darker color of cord under white or ecru batiste. One of the dresses in the first *Sew Beautiful* Sweepstakes, had dark peach cording under ecru batiste pintucks; it was fabulous.

Q. Can pintucks be run any way on your fabric, or do they have to run vertically or parallel with the straight of grain?
A. Pintucks can be run in any direction. Consider scalloped pintucks. The ease or difficulty of making pintucks depends on the fabric you use. When making straight pintucks, I prefer to make them on the straight of the grain, parallel to the selvage.

Step 1. Using the cording techniques found in this section, choose #8 pearl cotton in a color you would like to peek through the batiste or silk.
Step 2. Pintuck, using thread that matches your batiste in the regular sewing machine hook-up, and colored pearl cotton for the shadow. However, I have seen pintucks with colored thread for the regular sewing machine thread and color for the cording. The choice is certainly yours.

Q. Are there any fabrics to completely avoid for pintucking?
A. Yes. Dotted Swiss is terrible. Printed fabrics, on which the design has been stamped, does not pintuck well. Resulting pintucks are uneven. Stiff fabrics do not machine pintuck well. You will end up with parallel stitching lines with no fabric pulled up between the stitching lines.

Q. What happens when I put a pintuck in the wrong place or my pintuck is crooked? Can I take it out?
A. Yes. Pintucks are easy to take out. Turn your fabric to the wrong side, and slide your seam ripper underneath the bobbin thread, which looks like a zigzag on the underside. The parallel top-stitching lines will just come right out after you slice the under-side stitching.

Q. How do I press pintucks?
A. I prefer to spray starch a series of tucks before pressing it. Don't be afraid to starch and press pintucks. You might want to pin the edges of the pintucked fabric to the ironing board, stretching it out as far as you can. (This is nothing more than blocking your pintucked fabric.) Slide the iron in one direction to make all the pintucks lay in that one direction. Starch and press again. This will take out most of the puckers. Then, remove the pins from the ironing board. Flip over the pintucked piece you have just blocked and pressed, and press again. Not everyone prefers pintucks that lay in the same direction. For a less stringent appearance, lay your pintucked fabric piece face down on a terry cloth towel for the first and last pressing.

SHAPING CURVES AND ANGLES WITH PINTUCKS

Pintucks are inexpensive to make. They add texture and dimension without adding cost to the dress. They're rarely found on store-bought clothing. One of my favorite things in the whole world to do is to follow pintucked shapes with lace insertion or decorative stitches on your machine for an enchanting finish. Simply use your template and pintuck, then use the insertion like you would use any Swiss handloom. For threads, use white-on-white, ecru-on-ecru, or any pastel color on white or ecru.

The effect of shaped pintucks is so fabulous and so interesting. Virtually everybody is afraid that she doesn't know how to make those fabulous pintucks thus making a garment into a pintuck fantasy. It is so easy that I just can't wait to share with you the tricks. I promise, nobody in my schools all over the world ever believes me when I tell them this easiest way. Then, everybody, virtually everybody, has done these curved and angled pintucks with absolute perfection. They usually say, "This is really magic!

The big question here is, "What foot do I use for scalloped pintucks?" For straight pintucks, I use a pintuck foot with the grooves. That foot is fine for curved or scalloped pintucks also, but I prefer either the regular zigzag foot or the clear applique foot, which is plastic and allows easy "see through" of the turning points. Try your pintuck foot, your regular sewing foot, and your clear applique foot to see which one you like the best. Like all aspects of heirloom sewing, the "best" foot is really your personal preference. Listed below are my absolute recommendations for curved and angled pintucks.

▨ MARTHA'S GENERAL RULES OF CURVING AND ANGLING PINTUCKS

Step 1. Use a regular zigzag foot, not a pintuck foot **(fig. 1)**.

Step 2. Either draw on your pintuck shape, or zigzag your lace insertion to the garment. You can either draw on pintuck shapes or follow your lace shaping. My favorite way to make lots of pintucks is to follow lace shaping which has already been stitched to the garment.

Step 3. Using a ruler, draw straight lines with a fabric marker or washable pencil, bisecting each point where you will have to turn around with your pintuck. In other words, draw a line at all angles where you will have to turn your pintuck in order to keep stitching. This is the most important point to make with curved and angled pintucks. When you are going around curves, this bi-secting line is not necessary since you don't stop and pivot when you are turning curves. Everywhere you have to stop and pivot, these straight lines must be drawn **(fig. 2)**.

Step 4. Use a 1.6 or a 2.0 double needle. Any wider doesn't curve or turn well!

Step 5. Set your machine for straight sewing, W=1.5. Notice this is a **very short stitch.** When you turn angles, this short stitch is necessary for pretty turns.

Step 6. Press Needle Down on your sewing machine if your machine has this feature. This means that when you stop sewing at any time, your needle will remain in the fabric.

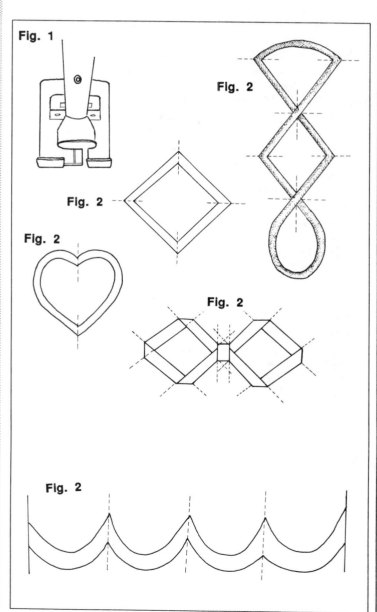

Fig. 1
Fig. 2
Fig. 2
Fig. 2
Fig. 2
Fig. 2

SHAPING CURVES AND ANGLES WITH PINTUCKS

Step 7. Stitch, using either the first line you drew or following around the lace shaping which you have already stitched to your garment. The edge of your presser foot will guide along the outside of the lace shape. When you go around curves, turn your fabric and keep stitching; do not pick up your foot and pivot. This makes the curves jumpy, not smooth (**fig. 3**).

Step 8. When you come to a pivot point, let your foot continue to travel until you can look into the hole of the foot, and see that your double needles have **straddled the line you drew on the fabric.** Remember your needles are **in the fabric (fig. 4).**

Step 9. Sometimes, the needles won't exactly straddle the line exactly the way they straddled the line on the last turn around. Lift the presser foot. (Remember, you needles are still in the fabric.) Turn your fabric where the edge of the presser foot properly begins in a new direction following your lace insertion lace shaping or your drawn line, lower the presser foot, and begin sewing again (**fig. 5**).

Step 10. Wait A Minute! Most of you are now thinking, "Martha You Are Crazy. There are two major problems with what you just said. You said to leave the double needles in the fabric, lift the presser foot , turn the fabric, lower the presser foot and begin sewing again. If I do that I will probably break my double needles, and there will be a big wad or hump of fabric where I twisted the fabric to turn around to go in a new directions. That will never work!" I know you are thinking these two things because everybody does. Neither one of these things will happen! It is really just like MAGIC. TRY THIS TECHNIQUE AND SEE WHAT I AM SAYING. Ladies all over the world absolutely adore this method and nobody believes how easy it is.

Step 11. After you get your first row of double needle pintucks, then you can use the edge of your regular zigzag sewing machine foot guiding along the just stitched pintuck row as the guide point for more rows. The only thing you have to remember, is to have made long enough lines to bisect each angle that you are going to turn. You must have these turn around lines drawn so you can know where to stop sewing, leave the needles in the fabric, turn around, and begin stitching again. These lines are the real key.

Fig. 3

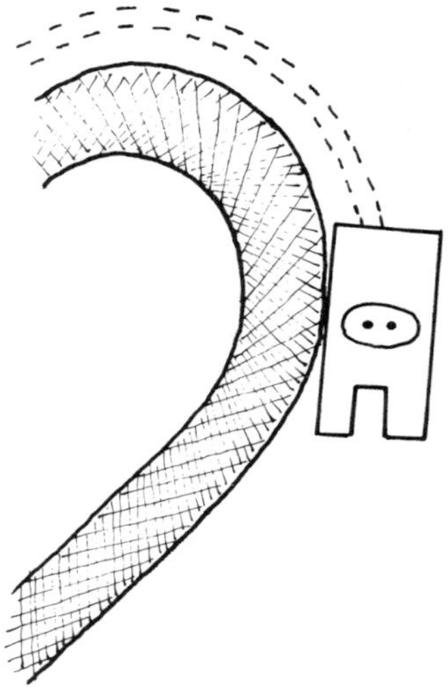

Fig. 4

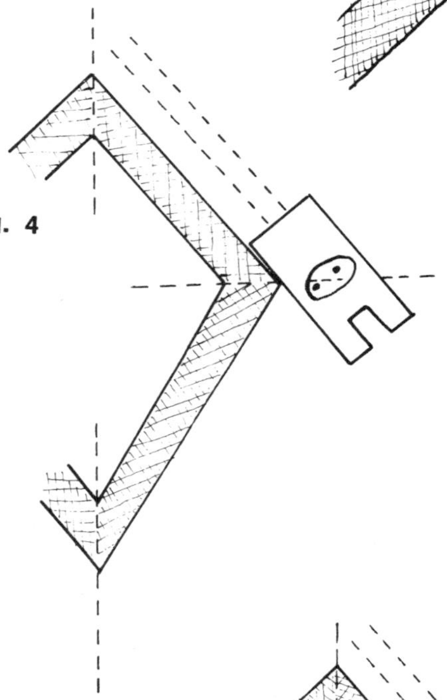

Fig. 5

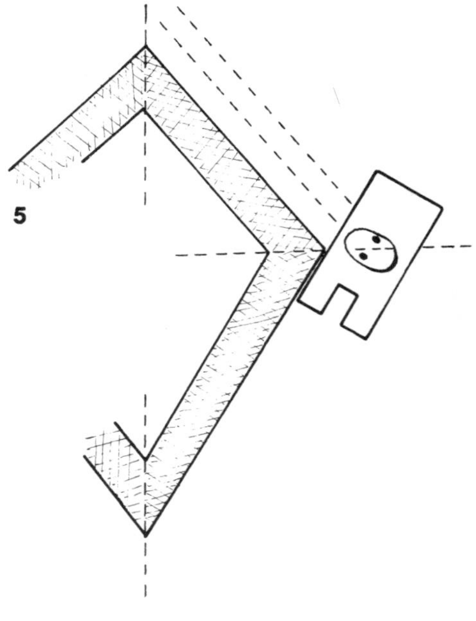

MARKING A SKIRT FOR CURVED PINTUCK SCALLOPS OR OTHER FANCY DESIGN

I always like to give the easiest way to do anything. Probably most of you know that by now! To divide any garment piece (skirt, bodice, collar or whatever) into equal parts, fold it in half. This marks the half-way point. Continue to fold in halves until the piece is divided the way you want it. If you are to mark the bottom of a skirt, seam (French seam, flat lock or rolled serger hem) one side seam first so that you can work on the entire skirt (fig. 1).

If you want to use this skirt for curved pintucks only, that is great. If you want to use the drawn scallop to make a scalloped piece of lace insertion, then you will guide your regular zigzag sewing machine foot with the double needles along the scalloped lace insertion later for your curved pintucks. Remember, those bisecting straight lines are the most significant part of making pintucks turn around properly at angles.

Step 1. Take your skirt, sleeve, bodice, or pattern part and fold it in half. Press **(fig. 2)**.

Step 2. Fold that in half again. Press. If you have a skirt with the front and back already stitched together on one side, you now have it folded in quarters. The seam will be on one side. Press on that seam line.

Step 3. Fold in half again. Press. Your piece is now divided into eighths **(fig. 3)**.

Step 4. Repeat this process as many times as necessary for you to have the divisions that you want.

Step 5. Open up your garment part. Use these fold lines as your measuring points and guide points **(fig. 4)**.

Step 6. It is now time to make one template which will fit between the scallops. Using this illustration make one template, only, with partial scallops on either side of this template. Use a piece of typing paper or notebook paper **(fig. 5)**. You can go to the cupboard and get a dinner plate, a saucer, or a coffee can or whatever to draw your one scallop which goes between the folds. Measure up evenly on each side of the scallop before you make this one pattern. Where the curve of the scallop meets the folded line of the skirt must be evenly placed on either side. After you have made your one pattern, you are ready to trace the first row of scallops on the skirt.

Step 7. Make the template pattern where the bottom of the piece of paper lines up with the bottom of the skirt. Each time you move the paper over to mark a new scallop you can always line up the bottom of this template with the bottom of the skirt. Draw the scallops and the dotted A-B lines also.

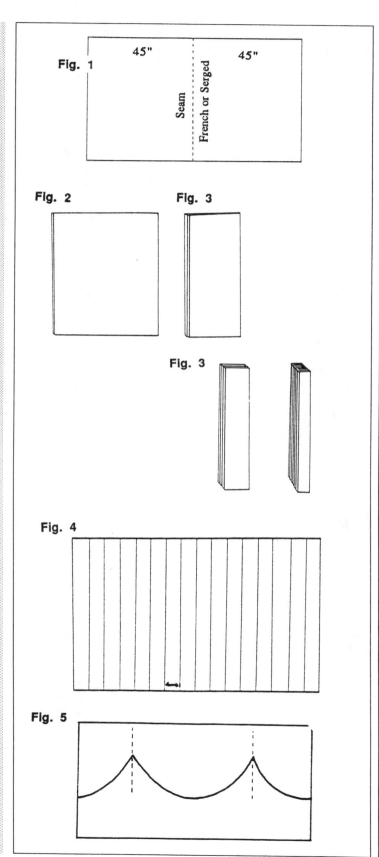

SHAPING CURVES AND ANGLES WITH PINTUCKS

Step 8. Draw dotted lines bisect the tops and bottoms of the scallops (**fig. 5**). Make these lines as tall as you want your pintuck sets to go. These lines serve as the turn around points for all of your pintucks. **They are absolutely necessary for correct turning around at the angles. These lines are the real keys to perfect sets of pintucks traveling in any angle and turning around at the proper point.**

Step 9. Trace with a fabric marker the scallops between the fold lines (**fig. 6**). Since you made your pattern where the bottom of the piece of paper follows along the bottom of the skirt, your scallops will be equally spaced and be properly aligned with the bottom of the fabric. You will move your template from fold to fold marking the whole scallop and a part of the next one. Mark the straight up and down lines bisecting each scallop. These lines will be along the fold lines. When you move your template over to the next fold to mark the next scallop you will line up three things: the last piece of the scallop which overlaps, the straight lines, and the bottom of your template along the bottom of the skirt.

Step 10. Use the curved lines for making only the first row of machine pintucks. After that you can use the edge of your sewing machine foot for guiding the next row of scallops.

Step 11. Follow directions from "Martha's General Rules Of Curving And Angling Pintucks," page 255.

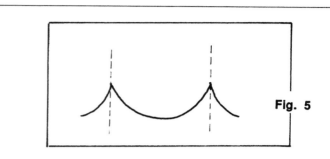

Fig. 5

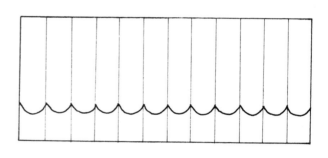

▨ MAKING STRIPS OF PINTUCKING TO INSERT IN CENTER OF LACE SHAPES

One of the prettiest things to do in lace shaping is to make a strip of double needle pintucks and insert these pintucks behind the center of a heart, a diamond, a bow, or an oval. There are several methods of inserting this pin-tucked strip behind a lace shape. I think the one below is the easiest.

Step 1. Make your heart, diamond, or bow and zigzag or machine entredeux stitch (**outside only**) to the garment skirt, collar, bodice, or whatever. In other words, make all of the shapes that you are going to make and zigzag the outside only to the garment (**fig. 1**). **Note:** If you are making a heart, diamond, oval or bow skirt, go ahead and stitch all the hearts around the skirt (**outside stitching only**) **fig. 2.** Trim away the inside fabric of the diamonds, several at a time. Stitch the pinstitching in each of those trimmed hearts before trimming the inside fabric of the next hearts.

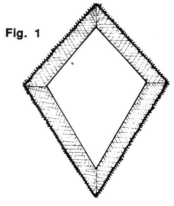

Fig. 1

Fig. 2

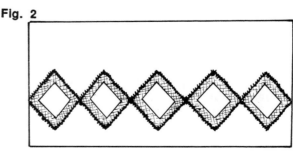

Step 2. Make a straight strip of machine pintucks longer that the actual insides of the shapes, and a little bit taller also **(fig. 3)**.

Step 3. After zig zagging or machine entredeux stitching the **outside only, of the lace shape** (diamond, heart, bow, loop or whatever) to the garment, cut away the whole fabric inside of the lace shape. It is alright to cut almost to the stitching since the heavy stitching of a heavy zigzag or the machine entredeux stitching has hundreds of stitches holding the shape to the garment **(fig. 3). Note:** If you are making a heart, diamond, oval or bow skirt, go ahead and stitch all the hearts around the skirt (outside stitching only). Trim away the inside of the hearts several at a time. Stitch the pinstitching in each of those trimmed hearts before trimming the inside fabric of the next hearts.

Step 4. Place the pintucked strip behind one shape at a time. Stitch around the inside of the shape attaching a portion of the pintucked strip **(fig. 4)**. You can either zigzag , machine entredeux stitch or machine pin stitch.

Step 5. Trim away the pintucked strip very close to the zigzag zagging from behind lace heart, diamond, bow or oval.

▧ STITCHING ONE OR TWO ROWS OF PINTUCKS INSIDE A FANCY LACE SHAPE

Unlike inserting a strip of pintucks into a lace shape, when you want to stitch only one or two rows of pintucks following the shape within a heart, bow, diamond, oval or whatever, you do not have to cut away the fabric. You will use your double needles, a regular zigzag foot , and the drawn lines bisecting each turn around point.

Step 1. Make your desired lace shape such as a heart, bow, diamond, oval or whatever. Attach to garment.

Step 2. After shaping your desired lace shape, simply draw the bisecting lines to intersect the turn around points. Draw the lines only to the inside of the shape if you are only going to put pintucks on the inside of the shape **(fig. 1)**.

Step 3. Using your regular zigzag foot and your 1.6 or 2.0 pintuck double needles, travel around the inside of the lace shape using the edge of the zigzag foot to guide alone your lace shapes. Use a needle down position and a straight stitch with a length=1.5.

Step 4. Using the directions for making curved and angled pintucks, stitch within the figure.

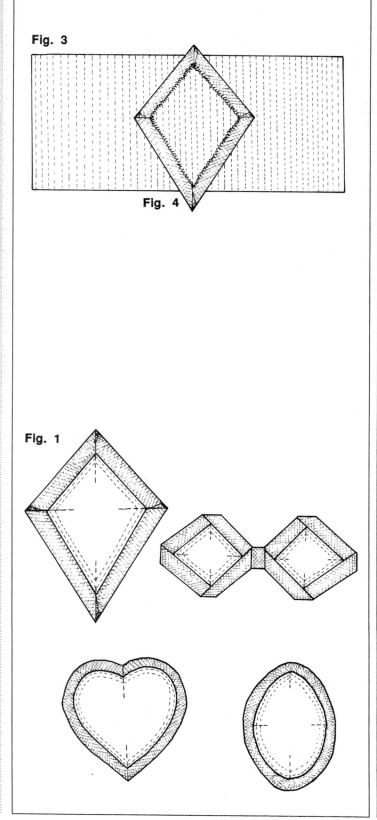

Fig. 3

Fig. 4

Fig. 1

SHAPING CURVES AND ANGLES WITH PINTUCKS

▨ MAKING DOUBLE NEEDLE SHADOW EMBROIDERY DESIGNS

When I was in Australia, one of my students who is a sewing teacher in New Zealand asked me if I had ever made shadow embroidered double needle designs. I replied that I hadn't but that I was certainly interested. She then painted on liquid stabilizer, let it dry and placed this piece of fabric in an embroidery hoop. She then drew a shadow work design from my shadow work embroidery book, put in 2.0 double needles, white thread, and proceeded to stitch all the away around that shadow work bow simply straight stitching with a short stitch (1.5 length) and made a perfectly acceptable looking shadow embroidered bow. She used a regular zigzag sewing foot not a pintuck foot with her double needles. Now, shadow work embroidery, it isn't; however, it is very lovely and very quick. You might want to try it **(fig. 1)**.

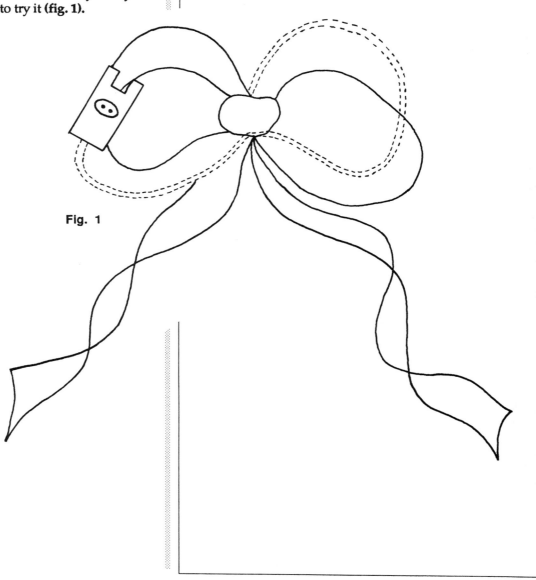

Fig. 1

Questions & Answers

FRENCH AND ENGLISH LACES AND SWISS EMBROIDERIES

TRIMS USED FOR FRENCH SEWING BY MACHINE

French or English Cotton Edging

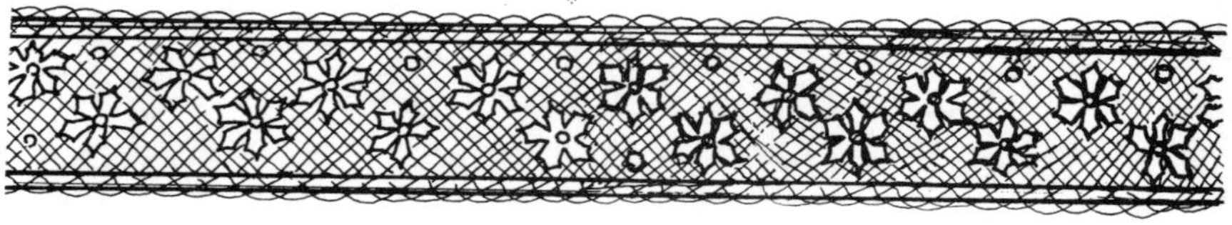

French or English Cotton Edging

French or English Cotton Beading

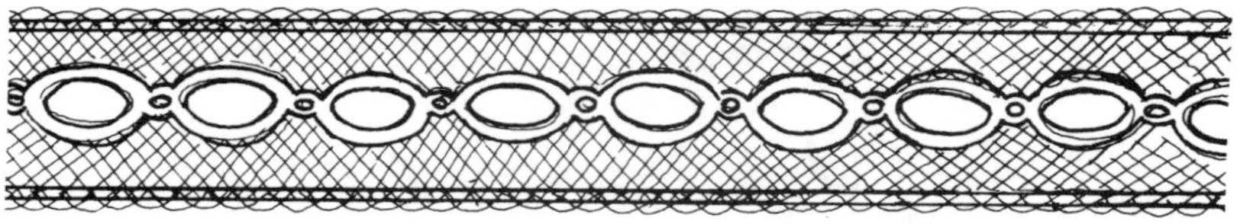

Swiss Entredeux

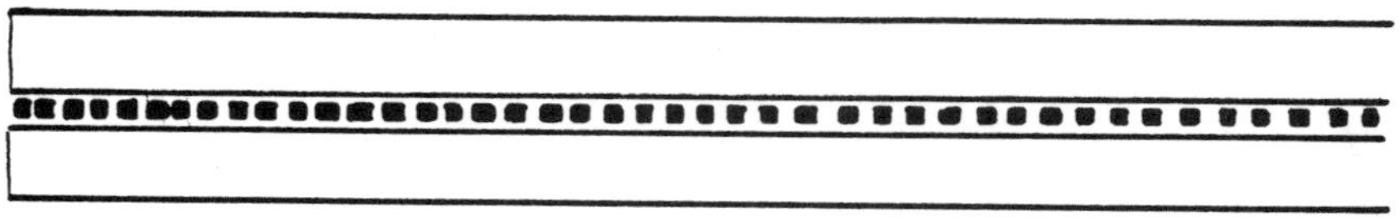

Swiss Handloom

Swiss Insertion with Entredeux Trim

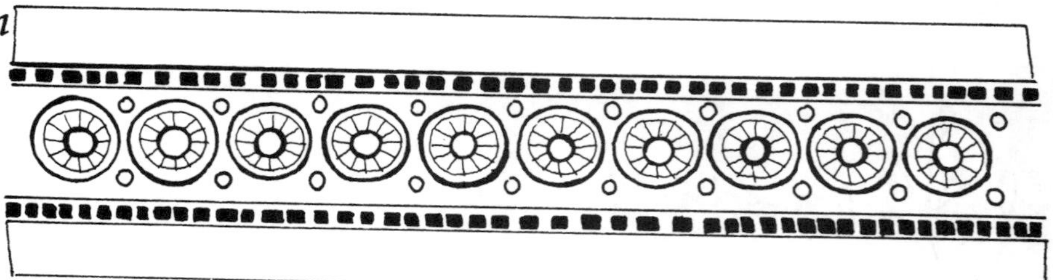

Swiss Beading

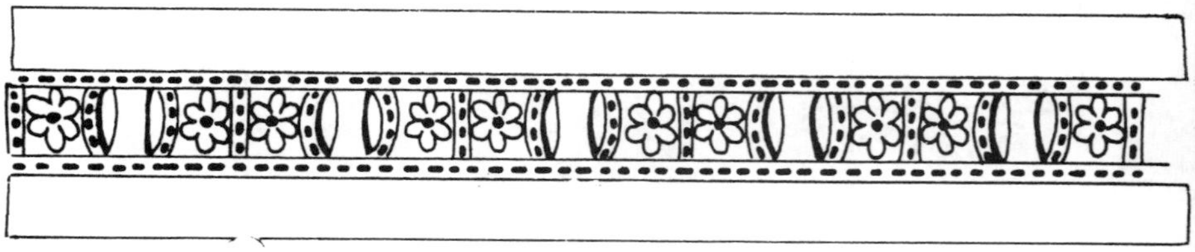

Q. What Is French Sewing By Machine?

A. French sewing by machine is another term for heirloom sewing. Heirloom is defined by Webster's as:

1. "A piece of property as a deed or character that is viewed by law or special custom or will or settlement as an inseparable part of an inheritance and is so inherited with the inheritance.

2. Something having special monetary or sentimental value or significance that is handed on either by or apart from formal inheritance from one generation to another."

I would call French sewing by machine "sewing machine constructed, delicate clothing, using primarily batiste and silk fabrics, cotton laces, and Swiss embroideries."

Q. Why Is This Type of Sewing Called French Sewing?

A. The first time I saw the little fluffy dresses which we call French dresses, was in a turn of the century pattern book. There were lovely names for all types of dresses; however, the ones which were described as having Swiss batiste, laces, and broderie anglaise were usually entitled "French Dresses." From there I think the term French sewing came. Of course since my French sewing of these little turn of the century French dresses is by machine, one can easily demise my sewing title, French Sewing By Machine.

Q. What Fabrics Are Best For French Sewing By Machine?

A. I prefer Swiss batiste, particularly Swiss batiste from the Nelo company in Switzerland, for most all my French sewing. It's the fabric I've been recommending and importing for nearly 10 years. If you want to be sure you have the real Martha Pullen imported Nelona, please look for the gold lettering "Made In Switzerland For Martha Pullen" in the selvage. This gold lettering washes out so don't worry about leaving it in the selvage while you sew. There are some fabrics labeled Nelona which certainly aren't Nelona. If you have ever felt, looked at, and stitched on Nelona you will know the difference between the Martha Pullen REAL Nelona and the fakes.

There are three weights of Swiss batiste: 1. Very thin, shiny, and delicate (Finella and Oriunda); 2. Thicker, non-shiny batiste (Finissima); 3. Nelona, which is a cross between the Finella and Finissima. My favorite Swiss batiste is Nelona, and nearly every dress that my daughter, Joanna, and my niece, Anna, have worn to church since their birth has been made of Nelona. It is a cross between the thinnest, or "tissue," batiste and the thicker batiste. Nelona is available in white, bridal white, pale pink, pale blue, pale peach, pale lemon yellow, pale robin's egg blue (turquoise), real robin's egg blue, lavender, pale peach, and dusty rose.

Silk is absolutely beautiful for French sewing by machine. We have the most beautiful silk batiste which we import from the Orient. It has enough body to handle beautifully and all of the French sewing techniques in this book work well on it including curved pintucks. I don't care for the very thin China silk. It doesn't work very well on a sewing machine and it is so flimsy that I doubt its holding up very well. This silk batiste which we are importing is gorgeous and really works well under the sewing machine even with wing needle stitching for machine entredeux. In Australia and New Zealand, the preferred silk for wedding, bridesmaid, wedding attendants, christening and special occasion dresses is Thai silk. This lovely silk has a tiny nub in its weave. It is heaver than silk batiste. It really is pretty. If I hadn't seen $10,000 wedding dresses made of this fabric in Australia, I would never have given this fabric a second thought. After seeing a silk ribbon hand embroidered christening dress of this fabric, I became a complete fan.

Q. Where Would I Use the Three Types of Swiss Batiste?

A. The thinnest batiste is lovely when you want to put several different colored slips under the dress for different looks and seasons. Colored slips show through the sheer dress. Make a white dress of Finella. Run red ribbons through the beading for Christmas, and use a white slip. For spring, run pink, blue, or peach ribbons and make a slip of a matching color. Choose pale green or dusty rose ribbons for fall, and make a matching slip of green or rose.

When I use the heaviest batiste, I prefer Swiss embroideries for the trim. Try heavy batiste with a Swiss smocked collar or unsmocked collar gathered around the neckline, Swiss trims in the fancy band of the skirt, and Swiss beading for the sleeves. Heavier batiste works well for ladies blouses and nightgowns, as well.

FRENCH SEWING QUESTIONS

Nelona is the best batiste for sewing machine enthusiasts. Don't let the sheer, delicate finish fool you. This is a strong batiste that doesn't tear easily and is perfect for machine sewing. My guess would be that it will hold up through the years quite well. Time will tell. Any 100 percent cotton should last, as long as it is washed before it is stored.

Q. I Hate To Iron. What Fabric Should I Use?

A. Try Imperial batiste. There are several other brands you might want to consider also. Domestic batiste is a blend of 65 percent polyester and 35 percent cotton, permanent pressed. The colors are absolutely gorgeous. You can use these polyester/cotton blends anywhere you would use 100 percent cotton Swiss batiste.

Q. I Love 100% Cotton, but Can't Afford Swiss Batiste. Are There Any Alternatives?

A. This year, I have some good news for you. We are purchasing from an American company a 100% cotton fabric which we are calling Victorian batiste. It is 75% as pretty as Swiss batiste and of course it holds the wing needle entredeux work beautifully since it is 100% cotton. Also, in this collection, I have designed some American embroideries, also 100% cotton, which are fabulous in price as well as looks. They, also, are 75% as pretty as Swiss embroideries and you will love the price. Actually, if I am smocking a collar, I prefer these Victorian embroideries to Swiss because they have a little more body for holding the smocking stitches. This Victorian batiste is a little heavier than Swiss batiste and doesn't have the shine of Swiss. It is really gorgeous and these two Victorian lines have been among our best selling items that we have ever had.

Q. What Laces and Other Trims Do You Use For French Sewing by Machine?

A. Always use 100 percent cotton laces and embroideries. Actually, few laces are true 100 percent cotton today. Even in France and England, where the best laces are made, the laces are 90 percent cotton and 10 percent nylon. This formula is still considered 100 percent cotton. Antique laces are 100 percent cotton.

Laces of 100 percent cotton come in a variety of widths and designs. Basically, French sewing calls for lace insertion, lace edging, and beading — referred to as "ribbon slot" in Europe. Insertion has two straight sides and is used between two other things. Edging usually is used on the edge of a garment for the final trim since is has one straight side and one scalloped or fancy finished side. Beading or "ribbon slot" is used where you want to run ribbon for trim or function; it has two straight sides.

Swiss, 100 percent cotton embroideries are used for heirloom sewing. Entredeux is an essential ingredient for strength and beauty. It means "between the two." Swiss insertions come either with entredeux on both sides or with an unfinished fabric finish on both sides. Swiss beading always comes with entredeux on both sides. Swiss edgings have an unfinished fabric side on one side and an embroidered finish on the other side. Swiss edgings range from very narrow to very wide; one common use of Swiss edgings is for a collar, smocked or gathered.

Swiss handlooms are one of the most beautiful additions to a child's or adult's garment. The delicate pinks, peaches, and blues offer a kiss of color; the white-on-white Swiss handlooms or ecru-on-ecru present a more subtle embellishment. One of my greatest pleasures in making children's garments is in choosing a Swiss handloom. I often repeat that color in ribbon at the sleeves. Although you can get away with a polyester blend

fabric for heirloom sewing, NEVER use polyester or nylon lace. They just won't do at all for French sewn garments. The sides of nylon lace aren't even, which detracts from the garment. The Victorian embroideries, which are 100% cotton, are a lovely cost cutting alternative to the Swiss embroideries. I keep hoping for a lovely line of laces made of polyester or a blend which would be less expensive. I haven't found it yet.

Q. Can You Silk In French Sewing by Machine?

A. Indeed, many christening robes or dresses are made of silk. My favorite silk for heirloom sewing is Martha Pullen silk batiste. It certainly is washable because I have many garments made of this silk and I wash them with regularity. To go one step further, I do wash them in the washing machine on the delicate cycle. Do I have to add that I don't wash them in the same wash as the blue jeans? It comes in bridal white, pink and blue. All silk is washable; however, some silks do have a "dry clean only" tag in the neck. Many of the newer silks are called "washable silk."

Speaking of silk christening dresses, I was looking in the infant department at a major department store in London, last fall, when I spotted a perfectly beautiful christening dress and bonnet made of ecru Thai silk and lovely English cotton laces. It was about 45 inches long and there was lace around the neckline, on the sleeves, and on the skirt. The skirt did not have lace shaping, only a little lace at various places. The dress probably had about 10 hours of lovely heirloom surface embroidery. Would you like to guess the price? Of course the price was in English pounds but it was an equivalent of $2300 U.S. dollars. If I were guessing I would think the total cost of materials would have been about $150 dollars. Since I have brought up the price of christening dresses, I might mention that several years ago in New York City I saw a christening dress with lots of French laces stitched in perfectly straight fancy bands on the skirt, no embroidery to speak of, and a very sweet bonnet which sported a price tag of $2000. My estimate of the goods in that dress would be about $180 since it had lots of French laces. By the way, the laces used weren't the expensive malines; they were the more reasonably priced French laces.

▒ Q.What Kind Of Sewing Machine Do I Need?

A. Your machine must make straight and zigzag stitches. There is all the difference in the world between old machines and the marvelous new computer machines. The tension on a computer machine is superior; the stitch capabilities seems endless. I guess the best reason for you to get a new machine is because of the wonderful machine entredeux and pin stitching you can do with a wing needle. The creativity that can be obtained with these new machines is something you will enjoy forever.

I probably shouldn't put this paragraph in; however, I'm going to anyway. If you need a new machine, I think perhaps, if you can possible swing it financially, you ought to go ahead and buy one. By the way, if you don't own a serger, you need that also. I asked Kathy McMakin if purchasing a top of the line serger was any better than a less expensive one. She replied that you pay for ease of operation and ease of threading. She said she would never consider anything but top of the line. Would I always purchase top of the line sewing machines? Yes, of course I would. I must add here very quickly that if your budget is really almost non-existent, I would get the finest brand machine with perfect tension and good buttonholes and not too many features before I would buy more glitz in a brand not known for its quality. If my budget were really slim, I would probably see if I couldn't teach enough smocking or French sewing lessons at a store, junior college, extension program for a school system or anywhere else, to earn the money to

get the top of the line. Many mothers smock and sew for other people in order to make extra money to save for that sewing machine that she wants.

It seems to me that mothers put every need and greed of other family members before their own needs. If you enjoy sewing, then a wonderful sewing machine is a need, not a greed in my opinion. Your time is your most valuable asset. An inferior sewing machine wastes your time. Sewing isn't expensive; store bought clothing is expensive. You can almost justify the total cost of a sewing machine if you make any clothing for you or your family. A precious child's dress which really looks right costs from $100 to $250. That dress price, by the way, is on garments which are made of $4 per yard fabric. Those made of Swiss batiste or Irish linen begin at about $400 and travel on upwards. Most ladies' three piece suits start at about $300 and go to around $500 in stores that I frequent. These prices are for off the rack nice brands of clothing, not the "crystal room" stuff. Your time is your most valuable asset. If you sew, you need a fine machine — for your pleasure and mainly for conserving your precious time.

▒ Q.Which Sewing Machine Should I Buy, If I Decide To Buy A New Machine?

A. There are a number of fine sewing machines on the market. All of them are manufactured outside of the United States. Please visit your sewing machine dealers — all of them — and take your laces and batiste with you. First ask the dealer for a demonstration. Then ask if you can sew on the machine, using your materials. Get the dealer to explain the proper adjustments for your fabrics and laces. One of the best tests of a sewing machine is to put two pieces of French lace under the presser foot and zigzag them together. Did they come through flat and pretty or did the machine gather it or eat it? Straight-stitch on Swiss batiste. Check the tension. Did you have to make a lot of adjustments, or did it come through

nice and flat? Remember, time is your most precious commodity. You don't want to fool with a sewing machine to get nice stitches. Look at the embroidery stitches and the monograms. Do you think they are pretty?

One of the best ways to have fun on a sewing machine is to make your own Swiss handlooms. Ask the dealer to demonstrate pintucks with the double needles. Ask him/her to show you entredeux or hemstitching with wing needles. Do you like this dealer? Ask about lessons on using the machine. Do these lessons come with the machine? One former dealer, who is a friend of mine, gave 12 hours of lessons with the purchase of each machine. I am a former sewing machine dealer; we gave six hours of free lessons with the purchase of a machine. You must feel comfortable with your dealer and your machine. Shop around.

The consumer, who has owned a machine for several years, will give you the most unbiased report on a machine's pluses and minuses. Call 10 people you know who love to sew. Ask them what kind of machine they have. If you belong to a sewing association, contact members of that association to talk about sewing machines.

▒ Q.Where would I ever use letters in French sewing by machine? Decorative stitches are beautiful also. Where would I embroider little flowers and leaves? What about those machines which make big flowers, leaves and alphabets?

A. I love those alphabets! Use them to sign your art work. "Art work?" you say. Your heirloom clothes, of course! Special occasion clothes should be permanently signed. Oh how I wish signatures were in these antique clothes in my collections. What a story they would tell. Please use the alphabets in the machine to put: 1. Name of child or person; 2. parents of child; 3. occasion for garment; 4. who made garment; 5. city in which person lives; 6. date of garment; 7. age of child. For example, "Joanna Emma Joyce Pullen, Christening Dress, First United Methodist Church, Huntsville, Alabama, September 13, 1976, Daughter of Dr. and Mrs. Joe Ross Pullen, Granddaughter of Mr. and Mrs. Paul Jones Campbell and Dr. and Mrs. Joyce Buren Pullen, Dress made by Martha Pullen." This information can be "stitched or signed" in the hem of the garment, on the ruffle, on the slip, on a "garment tag" to be stitched in the seam of the dress or suit. You can even do your stitching in the placket of the dress.

I would buy an "alphabet machine" for French sewing if only to do this one thing; sign my child's clothing. You could even take down a hem in a special-occasion dress that you purchased and put the information on this garment also. For smocked dresses, put the information on the hem before you hem the garment.

Where would I use those large alphabets which really look like cursive writing? I have a friend, Lynn Swanson, who told me about Susan's christening dress. She bought it at an Episcopal women's conference where vendors had booths set up to show liturgical garments. The dress was almost plain with the exception of a machine embroidered verse of scripture which goes around the skirt of the garment. When I first saw the larger alphabets on some machines, the first thing that popped into my head was to use this alphabet to embroider a verse of scripture around a christening dress or around a slip.

To answer the second question, "Where would I embroider little flowers and leaves?" these designs are lovely on a pleat down the front of a garment, on the collar, around the ruffle, or around the sleeves. My favorite for the lovely decorative stitches, however, is to make your own Swiss handlooms with your machine. Just think of the money that you will save and of the fun you will have designing your one-of-a-kind handloom.

On one of the patterns in the pattern envelope which accompanies this book, "French Daygown," there are eight tucks on the front. I use the decorative stitch on one of my machines to run a little green stem-like stitch down the center of each tuck. Then I make, by hand, little pink French knots down the center of my machine-stitched leaf/ stem combination. It is so sweet and it certainly takes less time than doing it all by hand. I must hasten to add that those decorative stitches aren't all just flowers and leaves. My favorite decorative stitch is perhaps the scallop. I scallop the edges of bonnets, sleeves of smocked and French dresses and skirts of several types. Use some of your decorative stitches to stitch over 1/16-inch and 1/8-inch ribbon. You can actually run decorative stitching down the center of a ribbon.

On the newer machines, you can make hemstitching and pin stitching with the wing needle and certain decorative stitches. In addition to this machine entredeux and pin stitching you can use that wing needle and make other stitches which sort of look like triple entredeux and double entredeux. Ask your sewing machine dealer to demonstrate all of these decorative stitches and edgings, and see for yourself what the newer machines will do.

Q. What Kind Of Machine Needles Do I Need For French Sewing?

A. For the basic zigzag and straight stitch, use a 60/8, 70/10, or 80/12. I prefer 60s or 70s. Double needles, 100 wing needles, and other types of needles such as 100 regular needles substituted for the 100 wing needles in hemstitching are all-important in French sewing for different stitches. You will learn more about them later.

Q. How Often Do I Change My Machine Needles?

A. Change your sewing machine needle after four or five hours of sewing. Yes, even if it isn't broken, change it anyway. Needles become burred and may damage the batiste or delicate lace. Needles are inexpensive; don't ruin your sewing by using bad needles. I heard many stories while I was a sewing machine dealer about how a certain brand of needle lasted for several years. That is ridiculous. Throw those needles away. I dread to think what a 4-year-old needle would do for French sewing. Trust me! Put in new needles! Now to be ecology minded, I would have to give suggestions on what to do with this needle which you are throwing away. Use them to hang pictures. They are very strong and the portion of the needle which goes into the wall is tiny and won't make a huge hole in the wall.

Q. What Kind Of Thread Do I Need?

A. There are several kinds of thread I recommend. The most fabulous thread for French sewing by machine is Madeira 80 weight. It is also the most beautiful thread available. The exact name of this thread is Madeira Tanne 80; 1,843 yards come on one spool. Another top thread is Coats and Clark. It is Dual Duty Plus-Extra Fine for Lightweight Fabrics and Machine Embroidery. It is cotton-covered polyester. D.M.C. 50 weight, Article 237 machine thread works as well. Mettler also makes a lovely, very fine 100% cotton thread. Do not use polyester or nylon thread. The only synthetic blend that will do is the Coats and Clark cotton-covered polyester mentioned above.

Grandmother's Hope Chest

Q. How Do I Match My Color Thread To My Dress Color?

A. It is not necessary to use any other color thread on heirloom sewing other than white or ecru, whichever matches your chosen laces.

Q. Do I Always Match The Pattern In My Laces When I Make A Garment?

A. When you are French sewing you have complete control over what to put in your garment. When a mother is making her first few garments, she nearly always matches her laces. In other words, if she uses daisy insertion, then she chooses daisy edging to go with it. The more garments she makes, the more adventurous she becomes in selecting laces and trims. If you are copying antique dresses, you will often find three or four different lace designs in the dresses. My theory is that back then, a woman was forced to use what she had to make her clothing. Perhaps she had several yards of tatting, which her aunt made for her. Maybe she had several yards of French laces, which she took off of an old petticoat of Aunt Bernice's. Maybe she could get a little Swiss insertion and a little entredeux. She would then combine the materials in a masterpiece of handwork.

I think I am ready to make a statement about mixing several patterns in one garment. It is probably a more exquisitely beautiful garment than if all the laces match. Please use more than one pattern! Experiment with your laces. Go to your fabric store and combine different designs. Be creative. Pull some laces you think wouldn't go at all and see if you find them pleasing after placing them side-by-side. This is the real design process.

Q. How Do I Dye White Laces To Ecru Or Cream? What About Dying 100 Percent Cotton Fabrics?

A. Ecru lace isn't always available in the patterns you want; however, any white cotton lace can be successfully dyed.

- **Step 1:** Add two tablespoons of vinegar to one cup of coffee, warm or cold. If you are dyeing a large piece of fabric (100% cotton only) or a large amount of lace, you will want to make more than one cup of the mixture. Use the same proportions, just make more.
- **Step 2:** NOTE: Thoroughly wet your fabric with water before placing it into the coffee.
- **Step 3:** Leave the fabric in the coffee mixture for several minutes.
- **Step 4:** Remove the fabric and rinse with water until the fabric or lace rinses clear.
- **Step 5:** Check your color. Do you want it darker? If so, repeat the procedure.
- **Step 6:** After getting the right color, let the laces or fabric dry before pressing it. When you press wet fabric, after dyeing it in this manner, you may get streaks.
- **Step 7:** Do not dry the fabric or laces in the dryer. Laces will tangle to the point of being ruined. Lay laces flat to dry, maybe on a towel. If you have one of those sweater stretcher dryers to lay over your tub, this is a good way to dry anything.
- **Step 8:** Do you want fabric which looks 100 years old? In this case, press it while it is still wet. It actually stains it in a very antique manner when pressed from a completely wet state. This technique does not work on laces, only fabrics. A very interesting effect can be obtained by coffee dyeing pastel-colored Swiss batiste. Try it.

Q. What Basic Sewing Supplies Do I Need For French Sewing By Machine?

A. Lightweight 100% cotton sewing thread, proper needles, fabric markers and pencils, fine scissors, hem gage, measuring tape, ruler, glass head pins or silk pins without plastic heads, good iron, extra feet for your sewing machine, which will make French sewing easier, stabilizer, tissue paper, #100 wing needles, either 1.6 or 2.0 double needles, gimp cord or #8 pearl cotton, and hand sewing needles.

Q. How Do You Make Knotted Rosettes or "froufrous"?

A. One of the most beautiful touches to a French dress is the addition of one or more rosettes. I love the knotted rosettes. Where did the tradition of ribbon flowers originate? My close friend, Margaret Boyles, told me that in the antique photographs we come across the child who had on a rosette was the birthday girl! That sounds like a lovely thing to do for a birthday — to single-out the special child with a ribbon rosette! I used to put rosettes on almost all of Joanna's French dresses.

Making rosettes can become very habit forming. Since French sewing by machine can be used for pillows, doll clothes, and other lovely things, you might want to start adding rosettes to other items. A ribbon rosette would be pretty on a diaper holder bag, on each corner of a baby crib canopy, or even a canopy for a bed for you. Small rosettes are pretty on doll clothes, bear clothes and on "Easter" purses.

Materials Needed:
- 5 yards 1/16-inch, 1/8-inch, or 1/4-inch double-face satin ribbon
- Ruler or tape measure
- Needle and thread; thimble (optional)

FRENCH SEWING QUESTIONS

░ Knotted Rosette

Step 1. Leave 12 inches to 15 inches of ribbon before making your first knot.

Step 2. Make one knot at either the 12-inch or the 15-inch point.

Step 3. Tie another knot **(fig. 1)**. Before tightening the knot, lay the first knot on the 2-1/2-inch mark on your ruler. Carefully slip the other, new knot, where it tightens on the 0-inch mark on your ruler **(fig. 2)**.

Step 4. Continue across the ribbon, making knots every 2-1/2 inches.

Step 5. Stop when you are 12 inches to 15 inches from the end.

Step 6. Tie a knot in the thread that is in your needle. It is best to use a double thread; this makes it stronger. You can also use quilting thread.

Step 7. Your needle will go between the knots for each stitch **(fig. 3)**.

Step 8. Keep your knots above the needle for each stitch **(fig. 4)**.

Step 9. When you make loops all the way across **(fig. 5)** to the other unknotted end, pull the loops up rather tightly and begin to stitch the rosette together at the bottom. Play with the rosette to distribute the loops. Finish stitching when you have it looking the way you want.

Step 10. If you want more than two streamers, add as many streamers to the back of the finished rosette as you wish. You may want to knot the streamers.

░ Unknotted Rosette

Step 1. Mark every 2 to 3 inches with a water-soluble marker.

Step 2. Pick up your loops, going into the marks. Follow the other instructions for making the knotted rosette.

Step 3. When you mark every 2 inches, you will have a small rosette, since your loops will only be 1 inch tall. This is great for christening dresses and for babies clothing.

Step 3. When you mark 2-1/2 inches, the loops are a little larger. Three-inch markings mean that each loop will be 1-1/2 inches. Your personal choice should be the only factor in your decision concerning the size of your rosette.

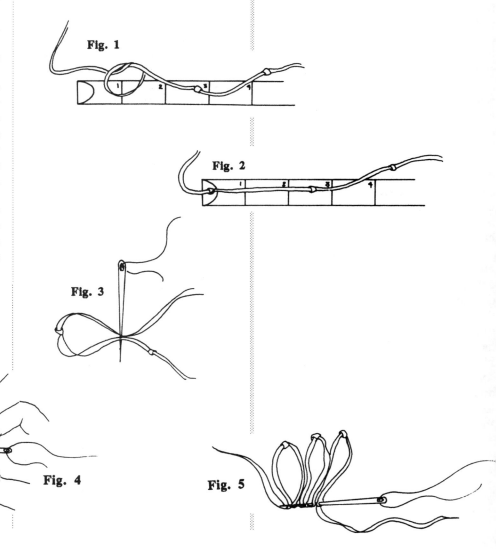

Fig. 1

Fig. 2

Fig. 3

Fig. 4

Fig. 5

Smocking

PREPARING TO SMOCK

▨ NEEDLES

Generally, a #8 crewel embroidery needle is used in smocking

For smockers with bad vision, it may not be comfortable to thread a #8 crewel needle with three or four strands of embroidery floss. If this is the case, use a #6 or #7 crewel needle.

Some needles work better for certain fabrics. For example:

a. for fine batiste or batiste blend, use a #8 or #9 crewel needle. Use a smaller size when using fewer strands of floss.

b. for fine to medium fabrics, such as broadcloth or quilting fabric, use a #7 or #8 crewel needle.

Personal preference for some smockers is to use milliner's needles. These needles are long and have a straight needle eye opening. Other smockers prefer to use #7 darners.

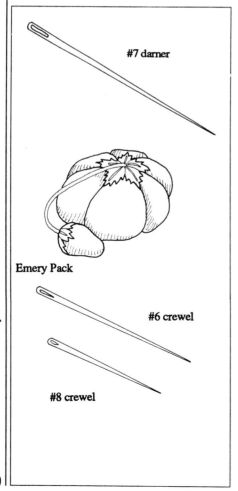

#7 darner

Emery Pack

#6 crewel

#8 crewel

▨ EMBROIDERY FLOSS

The general rule of thumb is to use three strands of embroidery floss when working with fine to medium fabrics. However, there are exceptions:

For a different look with fine fabrics, try using two strands. It is pretty and delicate.

For picture smocking, most designers recommend four strands.

For some heavier fabrics, such as corduroy and velveteen, use up to five or six strands. Experiment with heavier fabrics to find the right weight of floss for the desired look.

It is perfectly acceptable to use Pearl Cotton #8 for smocking.

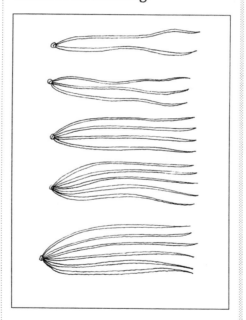

In order to prepare your embroidery floss for smocking, you must first make sure that it is put on grain properly. All thread has a grain. With DMC floss, it is easy to make sure the floss is on grain properly. Look at the two paper wraps on the embroidery floss. One has the round DMC symbol. The other has the color number and a picture of two hands pulling the floss out of the package. Follow these directions. Place your left hand on the floss, and with your right hand, pull the floss out of the package. Always knot the end that you cut. If I am smocking, I separate all

six strands, then I put three strands back together and knot those three strands. I put the other three strands back together and knot those at that time also.

If for some reason you forget which end you cut and therefore, which end to knot, here is a simple solution. One end of the floss "blooms" more than the other. The cut end of the floss does not fuzz out as much. The knot will go on the less fuzzy end.

Needles also have a right and wrong side. Think about sewing machine needles that only go in one way. If you have difficulty threading a needle, flip it to the other side. One side will usually thread more easily than the other.

▨ FABRIC

Some favorite fabrics to smock are the blends of 65 percent polyester and 35 percent cotton. Sometimes, a higher polyester count does not pleat well. However, using all of the half spaces of the Pullen Pleater, we have pleated lingerie - 100 percent nylon - without a pucker. Ginghams, Pima cottons, 100 percent cottons for quilting, challis, Swiss batiste, velveteen, soft corduroy, and silks are also good for smocking.

Fabrics, such as calico prints, which are 100 percent cotton, should be washed and dried before pleating. Fabrics with a polyester content generally do not shrink, and thus do not need to be washed prior to pleating. It is not necessary to pre-shrink Imperial batiste, Imperial broadcloth, 100 percent Swiss batiste (Nelona, Finella, Finissima), wool challis from Switzerland, and velveteen.

NOTE: When a 45-inch piece for the front and one for the back of a yoke dress is necessary, it is easier to tear those skirt lengths first and pre-shrink them separately. Then, pre-shrink the remaining fabric from which the bodice, sleeves, and collars will be cut. It is easier to pre-shrink and put fabric "on grain" in smaller pieces.

▦ FABRIC
Putting Fabric on Grain

Follow these directions for putting fabric on grain.

Tear both ends. Most fabric stores tear wovens (**fig. 1**).

Or, pull a thread and clip across from selvage to selvage. I always do this on Swiss batiste (**fig. 2**).

Fabric may be pre-shrunk after having "torn" or "pulled a thread" and cut the fabric.

Step 1. Fold right sides together.

Step 2. Machine-baste the selvage edges together, basting from point A to point B. Machine-baste both torn edges together, stitching from point A to point C, and from point B to point D (**fig. 3**).

Step 3. Fold the torn edges of the fabric to the halfway point. Keep folding until it is 6 - 8 inches wide (**fig. 4**).

Step 4. Carefully immerse the fabric in warm to hot water, and leave it until it is completely wet.

Step 5. Carefully bring the folded fabric out of the water. Pat it dry with towels. Do not twist or ring the fabric.

Step 6. Unfold the fabric and lay it flat. **Do not dry in the dryer, or hang on the clothesline.** Put a towel, sheet, or pillow case under the fabric as it dries flat. Gently pull on the fabric and press it with your hands to achieve 90 degree right angles on all four sides (**fig. 5**).

Step 7. After the fabric is dry, place it on an ironing board. Using a steam iron, press from torn edge downward about 11 or 12 inches (the width of the ironing board) all the way across. Always press with the up and down grain, which runs along the selvages. Do not press from right to left. Press only one, 12-inch section at a time (**fig. 6**).

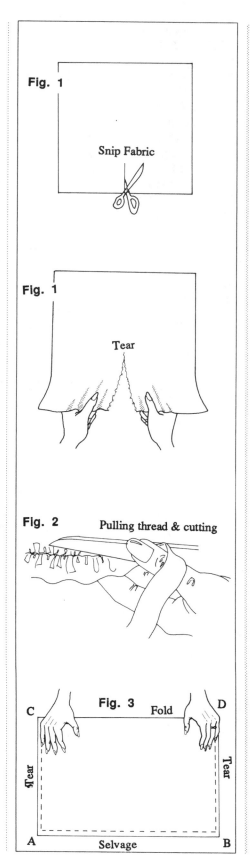

Fig. 1 Snip Fabric

Fig. 1 Tear

Fig. 2 Pulling thread & cutting

Fig. 3 Fold — C, D, Tear, Tear, A, Selvage, B

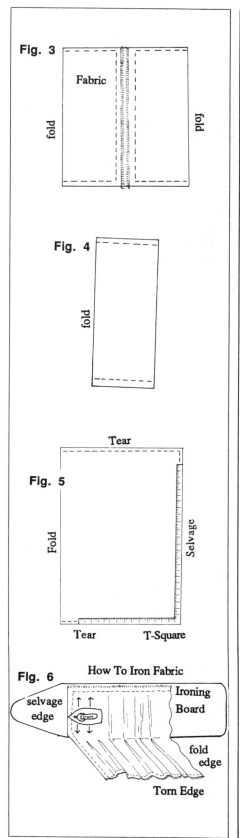

Fig. 3 Fabric, fold, fold

Fig. 4 fold

Fig. 5 Tear, Fold, Selvage, Tear, T-Square

Fig. 6 How To Iron Fabric — selvage edge, Ironing Board, fold edge, Torn Edge

PREPARING TO SMOCK

▦ Tying Off Pleating Threads Before Smocking

Much of the fitting is done before any smocking is done. Measure the piece to which the smocking is to be attached. The general rule is that the smocking is to be tied off 1 to 1-1/2 inches smaller than the finished piece will be.

Figure 7 is an example of where the whole skirt will be used in the smocked garment.

Figure 8 is a typical short yoke dress where a portion of the armhole curve must be cut away out of the skirt. Do not smock that portion. Do not count that portion when figuring the 1 to 1-1/2 inches rule of tying off.

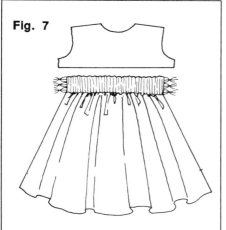

Fig. 7

This is a "longish" yoke dress where the whole 45" gathered skirt will be used in the garment. Tie off the skirt gathering threads **before smocking** where the total skirt is from 1" to 1-1/2" smaller than the yoke to which it will be attached after the smocking is completed.

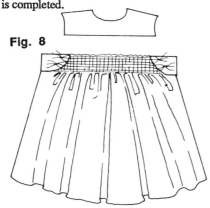

Fig. 8

This rule is sometimes called "smocking to size." It is a must to size the smocking before beginning to smock. The smocking will have to be stretched too much to fit the dress if this rule is not followed. This causes ripples and waves at the yoke after the dress is constructed. I suppose that the opposite could be true (smocking too loosely); however, I have never found beginning smockers to smock too loosely.

The width of fabric, before being pleated, should be three times as wide as the finished smocked piece will be. A little more or a little less fullness is acceptable.

Right and Wrong Side of Pleated Fabric

Pleated fabric has a right and wrong side. The secret to figuring out which side of the fabric to smock, assuming that the fabric does not already have a designated right or wrong side, is easy to remember - **Long is Wrong.**

Stretch out the pleated fabric **(fig. 9).** Look at the length of stitches on both sides. The flat stitches are longer on one side than they are on the other . This is the wrong side. The right side of the fabric, the side to be smocked, has the shorter stitches **(fig. 10).** Hence, the rule - **Long is Wrong.**

Another way to determine the right and wrong side of the pleated fabric is by the height of the pleats. Flip the pleated fabric back and forth to see which side has the tallest pleats from the gathering row up to the top of the pleat. The right side of the pleated fabric has the tallest pleats.

When running fabric through the pleater, the right side of the fabric should face the floor or the bottom of the pleater. If you are using a fabric with a designated right or wrong side (corduroy or printed fabric), run it through the pleater with the right side facing down to the floor.

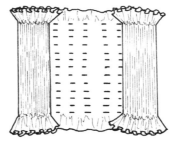

"Long Is Wrong"

"Pulling Pleating Apart So Stitches Can Be Seen"

Roll Down
Long Stitches

Short Stitches

▓ Tying Off Gathering Threads Before Smocking

After opening the pleated fabric to the desired width, it is time to tie off the excess gathering threads (fig. 11).

Tie off as many threads as is comfortable. I usually work with three threads (fig. 12).

It is not necessary to tie off gathering threads at all. Many smockers will work with them hanging long. As a beginner, you might find that the long hanging threads tangle. If so, tie them.

It is hard to keep the spongy quilting thread from coming untied. I find that a surgical knot does the trick.

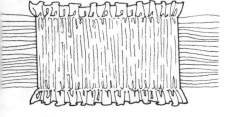

Fig. 11 How do you tie off?

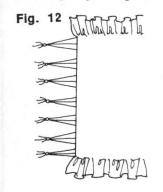

Tying off gathering threads.

Fig. 12

Step 1. Tie one knot. Do not take this first knot down to the fabric, but leave it about 1 inch away from the fabric edge (fig. 13).

Step 2.. Hold the knot with your right hand. Wrap the left hand strings around the knot one more time (figs. 14 and 15). Reverse if you are left handed.

Step 3. Tie one more knot, just like the first one (fig. 16). This last knot is pulled tightly for a very tight knot (fig. 17).

Step 4. Clip off the excess threads after tying each knot. Clip the threads to within 2 inches of the knot.

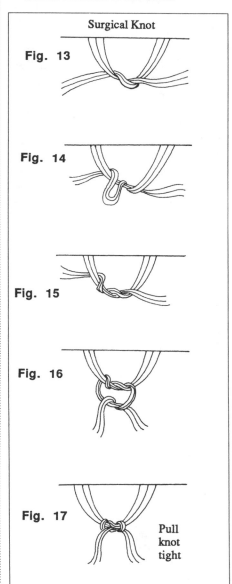

Surgical Knot

Fig. 13

Fig. 14

Fig. 15

Fig. 16

Fig. 17

Pull knot tight

▓ CENTERING SMOCKING DESIGN

The easiest way to mark the center of the fabric is to fold it in half and mark. Counting the pleats to determine the center will also work. There are two methods of centering the smocking.

• Method One
Step 1. Begin smocking in the exact center of the skirt or dress. Tie knots at this point, as if this were the left hand side of the smocking.
Step 2. Knot the floss. Bring it in on the left hand side of the middle pleat of the skirt. Smock half the skirt to the right side.
Step 3. Turn the work upside down. Smock the other side, working from the middle to the other side.

• Method Two
This method avoids the two knots on the center pleats (fig. 18).
Step 1. Leave a long thread with the first stitch.
Step 2. Take this first stitch from the front of the smocking. Do not bring the thread from the back. Leave your long, unknotted thread hanging on the front.
Step 3. Smock all the way over to the right and tie off.
Step 4. Turn the work upside down. Re-thread the long thread. Finish the first stitch you started. Smock the rest of the work to the other side.

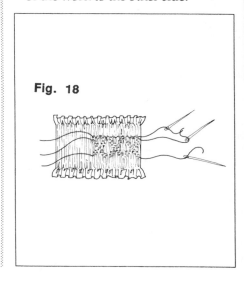

Fig. 18

Preparing To Smock

SMOCKING STITCHES
Crazy Cat and The Courthouse Story

Many beginner smockers get frustrated with the rule: When you move up, the thread is down, when you move down, the thread is up. For a beginner, this is the most difficult concept to learn. I made up a simple, and very silly, story to help beginners remember this principle. I was a little embarrassed the first time I told the story, but several years and smockers later, I can honestly say the story works.

Setting - A courthouse with lots of tall steps leading to the door.
Characters - A Tabby cat with a very long tail. Martha Pullen.
Time - During business hours.

Tabby Cat wants to drive a car and knows she must first have a driver's license. Martha Pullen drives Tabby Cat to the courthouse and parks at the side of the building to let Tabby Cat out. Tabby Cat climbs the long steps until she gets almost to the top. There, she remembers that you have to have money to pay for a license. Tabby Cat turns around, climbs down the long flight of steps and goes back to the car to get some money from her purse.

- **Important Points To This Story:**
Point A. Tabby Cat's tail is the thread.
Point B. When Tabby Cat climbs stairs, her tail points downward **(fig. 19)**. In smocking, when the needle is moving up, the tail of the thread is down.
Point C. When Tabby Cat climbs down steep stairs, her tail points upward **(fig. 20)**. In smocking, when you are moving to take a stitch downward, the tail of the thread is up
Point D. When Tabby Cat turns around at the top of stairs, at the landing, her tail swings around before she can begin to climb back down the stairs. This symbolizes a top cable before the wave or trellis moves downward. When Tabby Cat turns around at the bottom of the stairs to begin upward, this symbolizes a bottom cable before the climb back up.

Bringing In The Needle To Begin Smocking

There are two schools of thought on where to make the first stitch.

Method One
Step 1. Bring in the needle on the left hand side of the first pleat that begins your smocking **(fig. 21)**.
Step 2. Bring in the needle just above the gathering thread **(fig. 22)**.
Step 3. It is acceptable to bring in the needle in the same hole as the gathering thread, on this left side of the pleat.
Step 4. This method leaves the knot of the floss hidden within the first pleat on the back of the smocking.

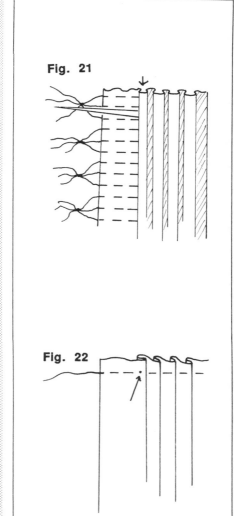

Fig. 21

Fig. 22

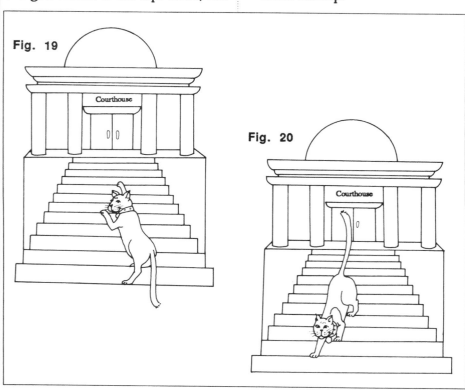

Fig. 19

Fig. 20

Method Two

Step 1. Bring in the needle on the left hand side of the second pleat, rather than on the left hand side of the first pleat (fig. 23).

Step 2. Go through the gathering holes of the first pleat to bring the needle out of the left hand side of the first pleat where smocking begins. This hides the knot in the second pleat and is stronger and more secure. The knot will less likely pull out with wear and washing since it is one pleat over from the edge of the smocking (fig. 24).

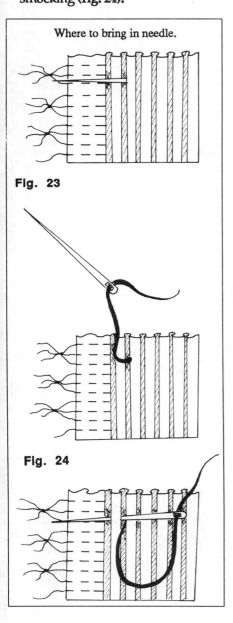

Where to bring in needle.

Fig. 23

Fig. 24

▓ Stitch Bite

Nearly all smocking books advise picking up from 1/3 to 1/2 of the pleat above the gathering threads (fig. 25).

I have tried my best to figure out how there is enough space using a #8 crewel embroidery needle to pick up 1/3 of the space above the gathering threads, when there is only about 1/16 of an inch in that distance. A #8 crewel needle is almost that wide.

I suggest picking up 5/8 to 7/8 of the distance from the gathering thread to the top of the pleat. Some people may pick up as little as 1/2 of the pleat above the gathering row.

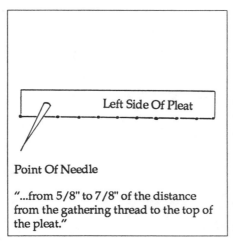

Left Side Of Pleat

Point Of Needle

"...from 5/8" to 7/8" of the distance from the gathering thread to the top of the pleat."

▓ Tangled Thread

Your thread may become tangled after making some stitches. There are several ways to fix this. Hold the smocking over, where the threaded needle can hang loose. Let the thread untangle by twirling around until it stops (fig. 26).

With the needle still threaded, push the needle all the way down to the fabric. Separate the strands of floss, untangling them all the way down to the needle which is slipped all the way down to the fabric. After separating the strands, carefully rub them together again, slip the needle up and begin to smock again (fig. 27).

Some people use beeswax for smocking. It does keep threads from tangling, somewhat. Be aware that beeswax may compress the threads more than you like (fig. 28).

I think a better substitute for beeswax is to run the threads (already threaded and knotted) over a dry bar of Ivory Soap. This gives a little lubrication (fig. 29)

Always remember to have floss running with the grain with the cut end knotted (fig. 30). Always remember to separate the floss, strand by strand, before knotting.

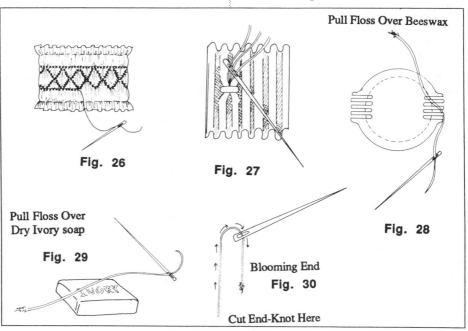

Fig. 26

Fig. 27

Pull Floss Over Beeswax

Fig. 28

Pull Floss Over Dry Ivory soap

Fig. 29

Blooming End

Fig. 30

Cut End-Knot Here

PREPARING TO SMOCK

▓ Slip-Snail Knot
Tying Off Your Thread

When you run out of thread in the middle of a row, when you change colors, or when you end a row of smocking, you must properly tie off your thread. I like to use a slip snail knot.

Step 1. Take the thread to the back of the smocking.

Step 2. Turn the work to the back and notice that the needle is in one pleat. This is the pleat on which you will want to put the knot.

Step 3. Make a stitch in that one pleat (fig. 31).

Step 4. Tighten that stitch but leave a little loop (fig. 32).

Step 5. Take the needle and slip it through the loop (fig. 33).

Step 6. Pull the thread to form a little knot (fig. 34). This is where the slip snail knot comes in. Slip the needle through the loop and slip a little knot in the thread. This knot should look like a snail.

Step 7. If you want to tie the second knot, follow the same instructions in the same pleat.

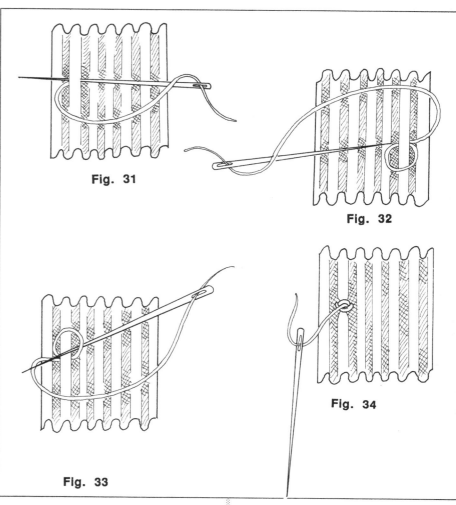

Fig. 31

Fig. 32

Fig. 33

Fig. 34

Tie-off, Re-thread, and Begin Again In Middle

Since smocking is best worked with 15- to 20-inch lengths of thread, tie off and begin again in the middle of the row. It is easiest to tie off on a level stitch, using the following technique.

Step 1. Take the smocking stitch, whatever that stitch may be.

Step 2. Take the needle to the back by going between the last two pleats involved in that last stitch. Slip the needle down very close to the stitch before taking the thread straight back to the back (fig. 35).

Step 3. Tie a slip snail knot. You may want to tie two.

Step 4. Re-thread. Tie a knot in the end of the thread.

Step 5. Bring the new thread in on the left hand side of the last pleat that already has smocking on it. It may be difficult to do, since the stitch will already be secured and tied off (fig. 36).

Step 6. Try to bring the needle in at exactly the same place that the smocking thread has travelled in the left hand side of that last pleat. The thread will appear as if it were not tied off at all, coming through the same hole as described.

NOTE: Try to bring the needle point in at exactly the same place that the smocking thread has already made a hole in the left hand side of that last pleat. If you can come in at that same hole, the thread will be as if it were not tied off at all.

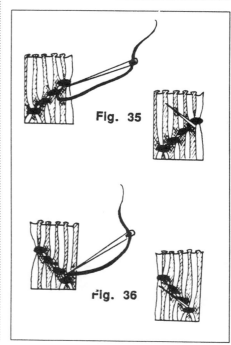

Fig. 35

Fig. 36

Specific Stitch Tie-Off Situations

Thread placement depends on whether the next stitch moves upward or downward.

• **Example A** You have just completed a two-step wave, coming down. You have made the down-cable, at the bottom. This is the turn-around stitch. Tie off the thread, and bring the new thread in the left hand side of the last pleat of the down-cable you just took. Bring the thread in on the top side of that down-cable because you are preparing to go back up in your two-step wave **(fig. 37)**.

• **Example B** You have just completed a two-step wave, going up. You have made the up-cable at the top of the wave. Tie off your thread and bring the new thread in on the left hand side of the last pleat of that up-cable you just took. Bring your thread in on the bottom side of that up-cable because you are preparing to go back down in your two-step wave **(fig. 38)**.

▓ SMOCKING COMPLETED
Blocking

Step 1. Always block your smocking before constructing the garment. After smocking is completed, carefully remove all gathering row threads except the top gathering thread.

Step 2. Set your steam iron on the lowest setting you can get and still have steam.

Step 3. Pin the smocked piece to the board at the top, middle, and sides **(fig. 39)**. Gently stretch it out to the exact measurement of the yoke to which it will be attached. I pin the smocking right side up to be sure the smocking design is straight.

Step 4. Hold the steam iron at least one or two inches above the smocking. Do not touch the smocking with the iron. Steam the piece **(fig. 40)**. Allow it to dry thoroughly before unpinning the piece from board

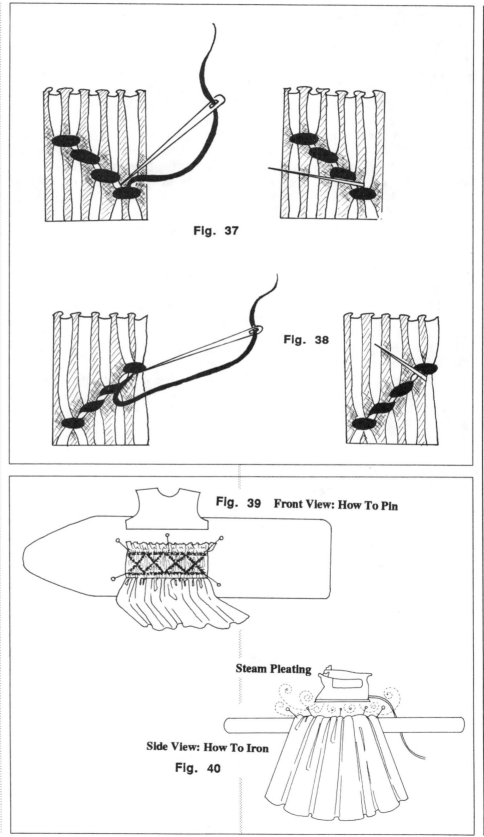

Fig. 37

Fig. 38

Fig. 39   Front View: How To Pin

Steam Pleating

Side View: How To Iron
Fig. 40

THE PULLEN PLEATER

I have taught beginning smocking to more than 1,000 people. The single largest problem for the beginners was guessing the location of the half spaces, between the two rows of pleats. Many beginners ended up with half-space smocking, which looks like a snake crawling through the rows. Needless to say, it was very frustrating.

Jerry and Ed (my partners in Smock Rite), soon took this challenge to their labs. About 10 months later, after much research and development, the Pullen Pleater, with its wonderful half spaces, was ready for the smocking world.

▨ PLEATER
Important Parts

1. Left hand end plate
2. Right hand end plate
3. Base of the machine
4. Needles inserted into the grooves
5. Drop-in roller
6. Keeper and keeper screw
7. Knob
8. Left hand groove for fabric to pass through.
9. Right hand groove for fabric to pass through in certain pleating instances.

▨ PLEATER NEEDLES
Replacing

Step 1. Loosen the keeper screw. Complete removal of the keeper and the screws is not necessary; just slide the keeper forward on the loosened screw (fig.1).

Step 2. Tilt the machine back and prop it on a book. Tilting the pleater keeps the needles from falling out.

Step 3. With the thumb, gently roll the small, drop-in roller up and off of the machine (fig. 2).

Step 4. Re-position the needles according to the specific pleating needs (fig. 3).

Step 5. Gently roll the drop-in roller back into place. Be sure to align the half spaces of the drop-in roller with the half space grooves on the pleater.

Step 6. Tighten the screw just until resistance is felt. Then turn just a tiny bit more. Do not over-tighten. Loosen the screws when pleating heavier fabrics; tighten them for sheer fabrics.

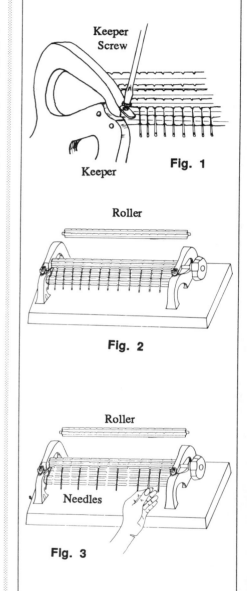

Keeper Screw

Keeper

Fig. 1

Roller

Fig. 2

Roller

Needles

Fig. 3

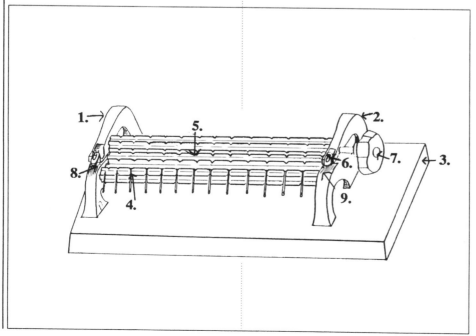

NOTE

To hold your pleater in place during pleating, try this.

Purchase a spool of 2-inch duck tape.

Cut enough of this tape to put across the back of the pleater. Put the pleater on a flat surface with the duck tape across the back of the pleater and on the flat surface.

Threading Needles So That One Side Is Already Tied

Step 1. Cut 72-inch pieces of quilting thread.

Step 2. Thread one end in one needle and the other end in the next needle. Leave about 6 inches for the short ends.

Step 3. Pleat as usual. Pull the piece off of the pleater. One side will not need tying off (**fig. 4**).

▓ FABRIC Preparing To Pleat

Step 1. Thread the required number of needles. I use a 36-inch long piece of quilting thread for each needle. Thread from the top. Pull 6 inches. Let the long end hang (**fig. 5**).

Step 2. Do not cut off the armholes of the dress until after the fabric has been pleated.

Step 3. The right side of the pleating should be downwards when going though the machine. The tallest pleats come from the bottom of the pleater (**fig. 6**).

Step 4. Lay the fabric flat with right sides down, and roll onto a dowel stick. Run the fabric through the pleater, right side down (**fig. 7**).

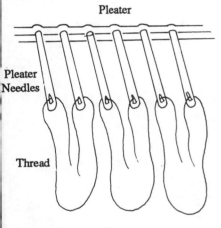

Fig. 4

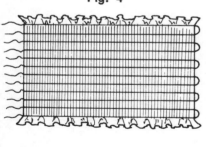

NOTE

If you are using a bobbin continuous feed holder or system, your quilting thread may become spongy. This may help.

Soak your spool of quilting thread in warm water. Place the spool in front of the refrigerator vent overnight to gently dry the thread. You may then wind it onto bobbins or put the spools into your smocking machine holder.

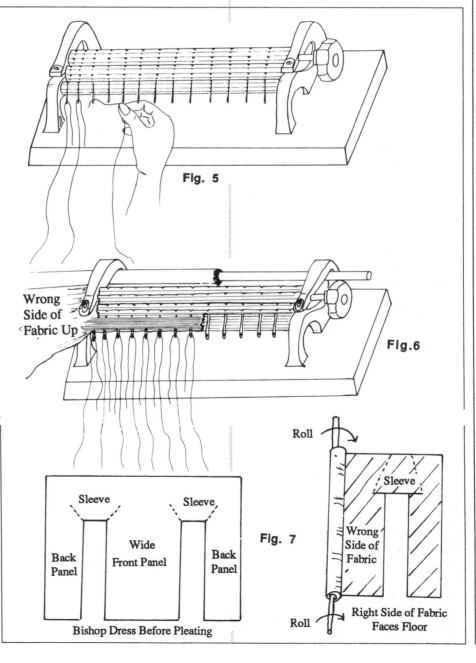

Fig. 5

Fig. 6

Fig. 7

Bishop Dress Before Pleating

THE PULLEN PLEATER

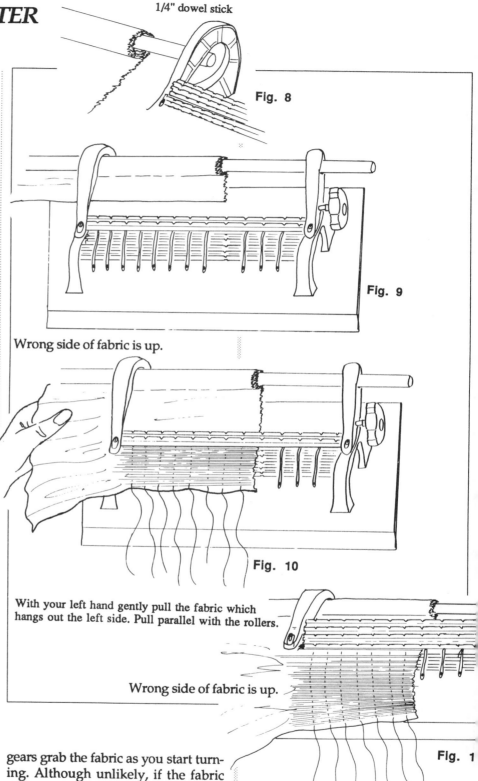

1/4" dowel stick

Fig. 8

Fig. 9

Wrong side of fabric is up.

Fig. 10

With your left hand gently pull the fabric which hangs out the left side. Pull parallel with the rollers.

Wrong side of fabric is up.

Fig. 1

DOWEL STICKS

Usually I use a 1/4-inch, wooden, craft-type dowel stick, about 36 inches long. However, some people like small, thin, steel rods which give some weight for holding the fabric and dowel in place while pleating. Others like a cafe curtain rod which opens or closes as much as needed for garments. The size of the dowel should be compatible with the type fabric used, no larger than 1 inch (fig. 8).

Step 1. Put the dowel stick, covered with the rolled fabric, through the left hand side of the pleater.

Step 2. Line up the exact rows to pleat. Eyeball the groove that you must use as a guideline in order to run the pleating through evenly (fig. 9).

tep 3. Leave one whole pleater space for the guideline (fig. 10).

Step 4. Hold the fabric and begin to guide it through.

Step 5. As your fabric goes through the pleater it is important to gently pull the fabric edge hanging out the left side. Gently pull parallel with the rollers. This will keep bumps from forming in the pleats. Let the rollers and the handle pull the fabric through (fig. 11).

Step 6. As the fabric comes onto the needles, stop and gently, gently, guide the fabric off of the needles. Do not force or jerk, since this could bend the needles.

PLEATER
General Instructions

The fabric edge to be fed into the machine should be cut straight and started evenly to avoid a crooked pleat and for pleating with ease. Gently "rocking" the fabric into the pleater may get it going.

Do not force or pull the fabric into the roller gears to get it started. Align the fabric straight into the gears and let the gears grab the fabric as you start turning. Although unlikely, if the fabric should jam and some of the needle start moving wildly, the pleater may become very difficult to turn. Remove the drop-in roller gear and remove the needles and fabric. "Cutting out the pleating" will be avoided this way.

Grandmother's Hope Chest

Always be sure to trim the selvage on heavier fabrics, such as corduroy and broadcloth. This is a good idea with any fabric, but especially with the heavier fabrics.

A strip of wax paper run through the pleater prior to pleating, will lubricate the needles and allow the fabric to pass more freely. If you are pleating over French seams, rub a bar of soap on the seams before pleating them. Rubbing the bar of soap over the edge of heavier fabric edge works well also (fig. 12).

Fabric may tend to pile up on the needles as it comes out of the pleater and make it hard to turn. If this occurs, gently slide the fabric along the needles onto the thread as it accumulates on the needles (fig. 13).

Always use the exact number of needles. Leaving excess needles in the pleater may cause wear and tear and even breakage of the needles.

To minimize dulling of the needles and machine wear, avoid turning the pleater without fabric in it.

Replace bent and dull needles. If not replaced, they can jam the cloth and break in the machine. A bent needle is easy to identify: it moves excessively while the pleater is turning, it has an unusual angle compared with the other needles, and it makes pleating more difficult.

From time to time, sharpen the needles by using an emery board. Needles do need to be changed after excess usage.

If the machine becomes stiff to operate, chances are that you have wound some threads into the machine or around the shaft of the roller. Pick these out carefully with a small needle and cut them.

Because the pleater's needles will rust when exposed to moisture, keep the pleater in a dry place.

Rub a bar of Ivory soap over French seams before pleating them.

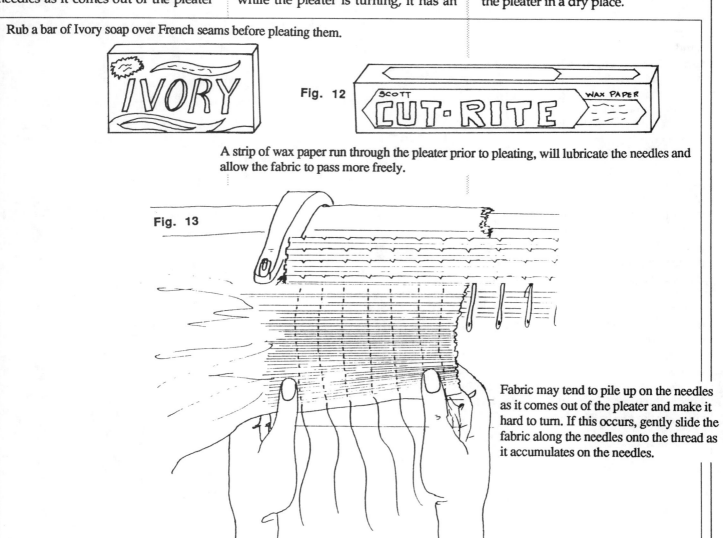

Fig. 12

A strip of wax paper run through the pleater prior to pleating, will lubricate the needles and allow the fabric to pass more freely.

Fig. 13

Fabric may tend to pile up on the needles as it comes out of the pleater and make it hard to turn. If this occurs, gently slide the fabric along the needles onto the thread as it accumulates on the needles.

281

SMOCKING STITCHES

CABLE STITCH

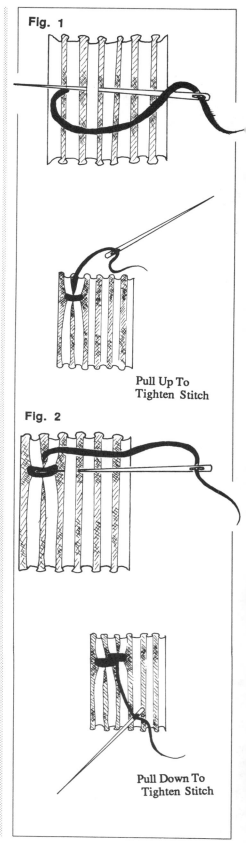

General Instructions

This stitch is worked from left to right. It consists of alternating up and down cables. Start the thread on the left hand side of the first pleat to smock (page 274 Bringing In The Needle To Begin Smocking).

Take every stitch with the needle running parallel to the gathering line, taking care to keep the needle parallel as you take the stitches.

The needles always "bite the fabric" exactly on top of the gathering row. It may appear that one stitch goes a tiny bit above the gathering thread and one stitch goes a tiny bit below. The up-cable (top cable) and down-cable (bottom cable) portions of the stitch gives this appearance. Be sure you keep each stitch exactly on top of the gathering thread.

A down cable is made by stitching into the pleat with the thread below the needle. An up cable is made by stitching into the pleat with the thread above the needle.

Take one cable stitch in every pleat. Throw the thread to the bottom in one stitch, to the top in the next.

NOTE
To make beautiful cable stitches, try this. After taking the stitch, begin to tighten by pulling upward on a down-cable and downward on an up-cable. Before actually pulling the final stitch to the fabric, place your thumbnail next to the stitch and guide the stitch into its exact position.

Directions

Step 1. Bring in the thread on the left hand side of the first pleat.

Step 2. Move to the second pleat and take a stitch there with the thread below the needle. This is a down cable (fig. 1).

Step 3. Move to the third pleat and take a stitch with the thread above the needle. This is an up cable (fig. 2).

Step 4. Move to the fourth pleat and take a stitch with the thread below the needle. This is another down cable.

Step 5. Move to the fifth pleat and take another stitch with the thread above the needle. This is another up cable.

Step 6. Every two to four stitches, with the needle or a fingernail, push the cable stitches together to be sure the fabric does not show through.

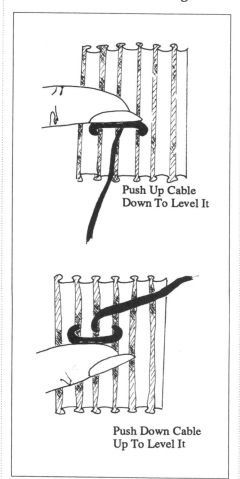

Push Up Cable
Down To Level It

Push Down Cable
Up To Level It

Fig. 1

Pull Up To
Tighten Stitch

Fig. 2

Pull Down To
Tighten Stitch

Grandmother's Hope Chest

OUTLINE STITCH

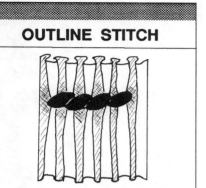

Directions

This stitch is worked from left to right.

Step 1. Bring the thread in on the left hand side of the first pleat **(fig. 4)**. See page 274 for needle placement.

Step 2. The outline stitch is a continuous row of up cables. The thread is thrown above the needle for every stitch **(fig. 5)**.

Step 3. Run the needle in parallel to the gathering row, on exactly the top of the gathering row. Tighten each up-cable by pulling down. Always tighten up cables in this manner. **(fig. 6)**.

Step 4. After tightening each stitch, gently pull upward to align the whole row with the gathering row **(fig. 7)**.

WHEAT STITCH

A wheat stitch derives its name because of the similarity in its looks to wheat. The wheat stitch is really two rows of stitching.

Directions

Step 1. The first row is the outline stitch **(fig. 8)**.

Step 2. Work a row of stem stitches (instructions on next page) directly under the outline stitch row **(fig. 9)**.

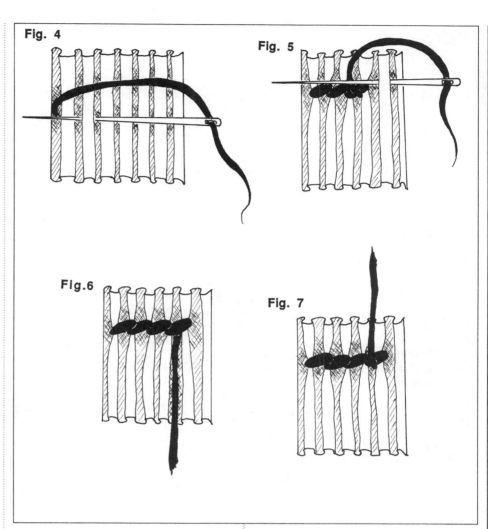

Fig. 4

Fig. 5

Fig.6

Fig. 7

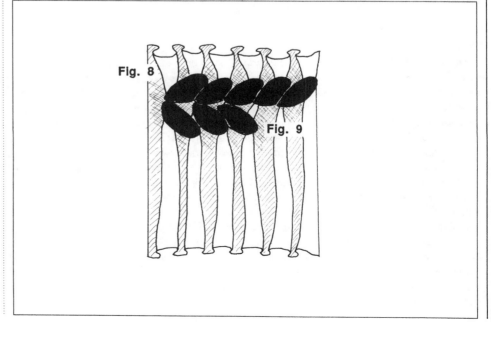

Fig. 8

Fig. 9

SMOCKING STITCHES

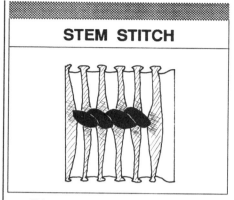

STEM STITCH

Directions

This stitch is worked from left to right.

Step 1. Bring the thread in on the left hand side of the first pleat **(fig. 10)**. Refer to page 247 for needle placement.

Step 2. The outline stitch is a continuous row of down cables. The thread is thrown down below the needle for each stitch **(fig.11)**.

Step 3. Take each stitch by running the needle in parallel to the gathering row on exactly the top of the gathering thread. Next, tighten each down cable by pulling up **(fig.12)**.

Step 4. After you do the up tighten on each stitch, gently pull downward to pull the whole row back in line with the gathering row **(fig. 13)**.

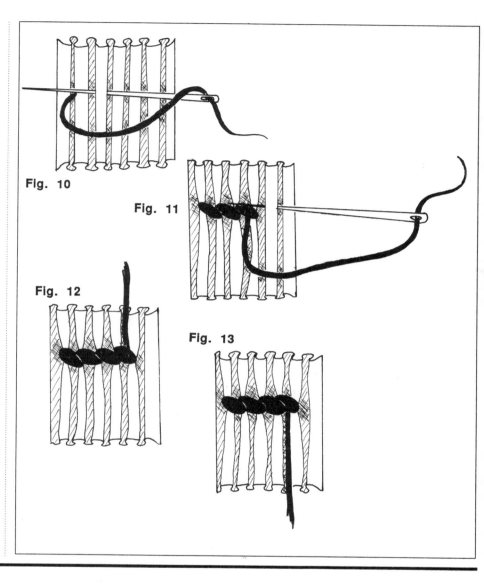

Fig. 10

Fig. 11

Fig. 12

Fig. 13

Reflections From Martha On Smocking

The very thought of the word, smocking, brings joy to my heart. The first smocking I ever stitched was begun in 1968 when I bought a soft coral fabric and a McCall's pattern with iron on dots. This lovely little bishop dress was lovingly constructed by me and then those dratted dots were ironed on. The commercial pattern instructed me to draw up each dot as I stitched a little wave design. My very nerves were shattered as I hunted among the stitches for the next dot to draw up. Actually, I gave up on completing the dress; however, I didn't throw it away. Years later, about 1978 to be exact, I found the little unfinished dress. Since I had begun my first smocking class at that time, I decided that it would be good to finish it for Joanna. The original plans for the dress were for a friend's little girl. Those plans fell through! I was so proud of my completing it, I even took Joanna for a picture in the dress which took 10 years to make!

I had a pleater ordered at that time and was very grateful for a teacher who would pleat for me until mine came. Back in the "olden days of smocking" (around 1978) you had to wait about a year for a smocking machine. Worse yet, the price was $165 for a small pleater. My pleater finally came and the rest is history, I suppose. Smocking has been one of the great joys of my life and smocking for grandchildren has brought the smocking bug back into my life in full swing. I'm even perfecting picture smocking.

I have a funny story to relate to you. About 1982, when I still had a smocking shop, the phone rang one day and a sweet sounding lady asked me to mail order her a smocking needle. Customarily, one ordered several needles for the pleater, but I figured that she had broken only one pleater needle and that she only wanted to spend $1. I wrapped a pleater needle carefully and mailed it to her. A few weeks later she wrote me a letter thanking me for this wonderful needle. She related that it had taken hours off of her smocking to have that interesting little crooked needle! Mortified, I picked up the phone and reconfirmed my fear that she had used that pleater needle to smock a whole dress. I apologized profusely, telling her that I thought she had wanted a pleater needle. Since she had never heard of a pleater, I sold her a pleater over the phone and she promised that she would never again use her crooked needle for hand smocking.

WAVE/CHEVRON STITCH or BABY WAVE

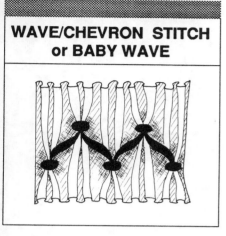

Directions

Step 1. Bring the thread in on the left hand side of the first pleat.

Step 2. Move to the second pleat and make a down cable **(fig. 10)**.

Step 3. Make another down cable at the half-space line (marked with a gathering thread on the Pullen Pleater). Remember the **Cat and the Courthouse** story. When the cat goes up the courthouse steps, the tail drops down **(fig. 11)**.

Step 4. Make an up cable on the half-space line also **(fig. 12)**. It may look as if the second stitch went in between the bottom row and the half-space row. Looks are deceiving. The second bottom cable and the top cable (the turn-around stitch) are placed on exactly the same line - the half-space line.

Step 5. Now move back down to the whole line. Make a top-cable at the starting line **(fig. 13)**. Remember the **Cat and the Courthouse** tale.

Step 6. At the same bottom row, make another down-cable. This is the turn-around stitch **(fig. 14)**.

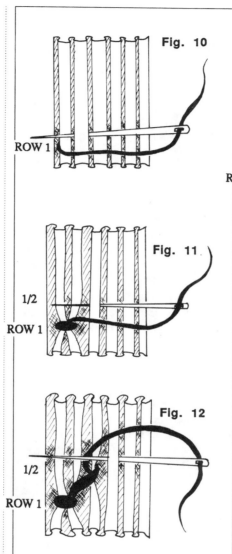

Sitting In Martha's Smocking Class

"Bring the thread in on the left hand side of the first pleat, on Row 1. Move over one pleat and make a down cable. Move over to the next pleat at the same time moving up to the 1/2 space and make another down cable. AT THE SAME 1/2 SPACE POINT, move over another pleat and make an up cable. This is your turn around stitch. Notice that two stitches were placed with your needle at the 1/2 space on your diagrams. Move over one pleat and make an up cable back at Row 1. Move over another pleat and make a down cable also at Row 1. That last stitch was your bottom turn around stitch."

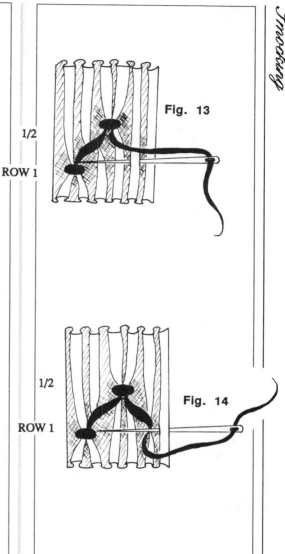

NOTE

Half-space chevrons end at the half space on the smocking rows. Whole-space chevrons are taller and go all the way to another row.

Half-space chevrons are easy if you own a Pullen pleater because the gathering thread is in the half spaces in addition to the whole spaces. Half-space refers to the fact that the stitch only goes from the main row to the halfway point and back again to its main row.

285

SMOCKING STITCHES

TWO-, THREE-, OR FOUR-STEP WAVE (TRELLIS)

My Misunderstanding

This stitch can be known as a wave or a trellis. Either is correct; I choose to call it a wave.

When I was a beginner, just learning to smock, one thing always confused me about waves. So, let's try to clear it up first. When looking at a two-step wave, I counted four stitches going up on one side and three stitches coming down on the other. How could this stitch be called a two-step wave with all these stitches. Each wave must have a cable at the bottom and a cable at the top. These are "level" or "turn-around" stitches. And counting these as steps to the two-step wave is where I got confused.

fig. 15
Stitch 1 is a bottom-cable working as a turn-around stitch.
Stitch 2 is moving up as **Step 1** in the two-step wave.
Stitch 3 is moving up as **Step 2** in the two-step wave.
Stitch 4 is a top-cable working as a turn-around stitch.

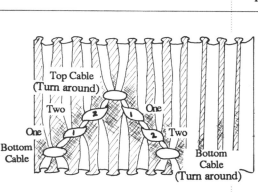

Correct Way To Count a Two-Step Wave

"Now, there is a common misunderstanding concerning 2 step waves. I will try to clear this up. Look at the illustration showing a completed 2 step wave. It appears that the two middle steps are stitched on the 1/3 and 2/3 points between the bottom cable and the top cable. That is only its appearance! In reality the two stitches are taken at the 1/4 point and at the 1/2 space itself. Look at figures 16 - 19."

TWO-STEP WAVE (TRELLIS)

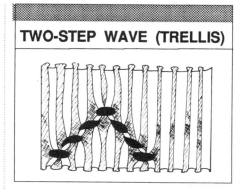

Directions

This is worked from left to right. Move over one pleat at a time as you move up and down between the rows.

A two-step wave can have various heights, depending on your design. **Example:** A two-step wave which goes from row 1 to row 1/2 above it (technically called a half-space, two-step wave) is done like this:

Step 1. Bring the needle in on the left side of the first pleat. Begin with a down-cable on Row1 **(fig. 16)**.
Step 2. Move up halfway between row 1 and row 1/2 (a 1/4 space) for the next stitch, a down cable **(fig. 17)**.
Step 3. Move up to the half-space for the next stitch, another down cable **(fig. 18)**.
Step 4. At this same half-space point, move over one pleat and do a top cable (turn-around stitch). **Fig. 19.**
Step 5. Move down 1/4 space, do a top cable.
Step 6. Move down to row 1 and do anther top cable
Step 7. Complete the stitch sequence with anotherturn-around stitch (a bottom cable).

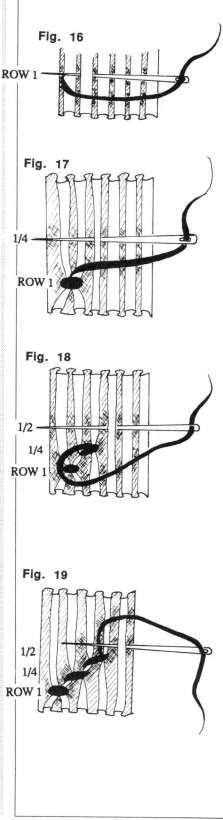

THREE-STEP WAVE (TRELLIS)

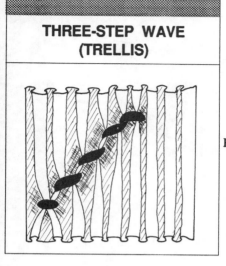

Directions

This is worked from left to right. Move over, one pleat at a time, as you move up and down between the rows.

A three-step wave can have various heights, depending on your design. **Example:** A three-step wave, which goes from one major gathering row to the next, for a distance of 3/8 inch (the usual distance between gathering rows on a pleater) is done like this:

Step 1. Row 1 begins with a down-cable on the gathering row **(fig. 20).**

Step 2. The second stitch, a down cable, will be placed 1/3 of the way up **(fig. 21).**

Step 3. The third stitch, a down cable, will be placed 2/3 of the way up **(fig. 22).**

Step 4. Row 2 is the fourth stitch, a down cable, placed on the next gathering row line **(fig. 23).**

Step 5. The fifth stitch, up cable, will be placed on the same gathering row (Row 2) as stitch number four **(fig. 24).** Look at the finished work. The fourth and fifth stitches will appear to be at different levels, with the fourth stitch slightly below the gathering row. However, the last down cable moving up the row is placed at the same level as the turn-around stitch, the up-cable at the top.

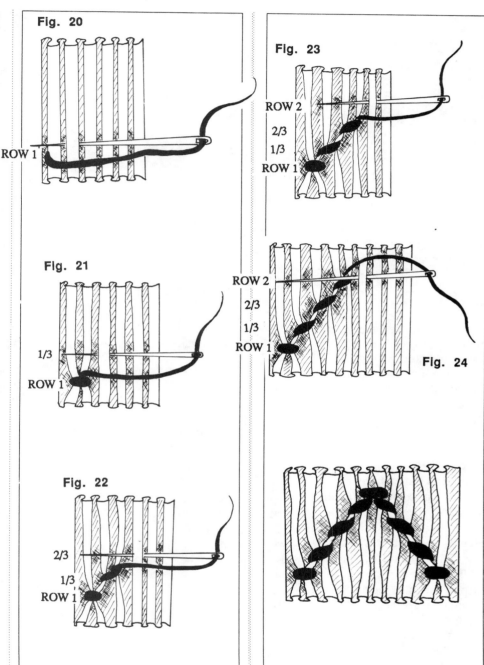

Fig. 20

ROW 1

Fig. 21

1/3

ROW 1

Fig. 22

2/3

1/3

ROW 1

Fig. 23

ROW 2

2/3

1/3

ROW 1

Fig. 24

ROW 2

2/3

1/3

ROW 1

Sitting In Martha's Smocking Class

"One of the things I like to do when I count my three step waves when going across a row is to say, 'Bottom cable, 1, 2, 3, top cable, 1, 2, 3, bottom cable, 1, 2, 3, top cable, 1, 2, 3.' Some people like to say, 'Turn around, 1, 2, 3, turn around, 1, 2, 3, turn around 1, 2, 3.' Always count by realizing that the three steps are in the middle with a cable at the top and a cable at the bottom."

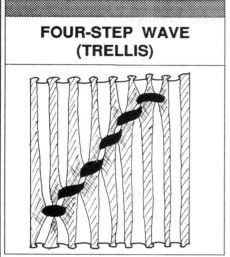

FOUR-STEP WAVE (TRELLIS)

Directions

This is worked from left to right. Move over, one pleat at a time, as you move up and down between the rows.

A four-step wave can have various heights, depending on your design. It goes from one major gathering row (Row 1) to the next gathering row (Row 2).

Step 1. Row 1 begins with a down-cable on the gathering row (**fig. 25**).

Step 2. The second stitch, a down cable, will be placed 1/4 of the way up (**fig. 26**).

Step 3 The third stitch, a down cable, will be placed on the half-space (**fig. 27**).

Step 4. The fourth stitch, a down cable, will be placed on the 3/4 space (**fig. 28**).

Step 5. The fifth stitch, a down cable, will be placed on the top gathering row, Row 2 (**fig. 29**).

Step 6. The sixth stitch, an up cable, is placed on the same gathering row (Row 2) as the fifth stitch (**fig. 30**). Look at the finished work. The fifth and sixth stitches will appear to be at different levels, with the fifth stitch slightly below the gathering row. However, the last down cable moving up the row is placed at the same level as the turn-around stitch, the up cable at the top.

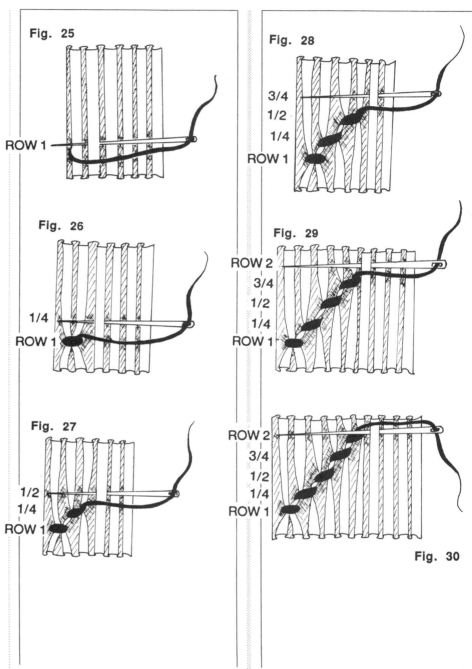

Grandmother's Hope Chest

Sitting In Martha's Smocking Class

"Just because we have stopped our instructions with a four step wave doesn't mean that you can make a five step wave or a six step wave or even more. Always remember that when you call a stitch a four step wave, that you have a bottom cable at the bottom before you make four stitches upward and that you have a top cable at the top before you make four stitches downward. Don't forget to count the four step wave as follows. Bottom cable, 1, 2, 3, 4, top cable, 1, 2, 3, 4, bottom cable, 1, 2, 3, 4, top cable."

DOUBLE WAVE or DIAMOND STITCH

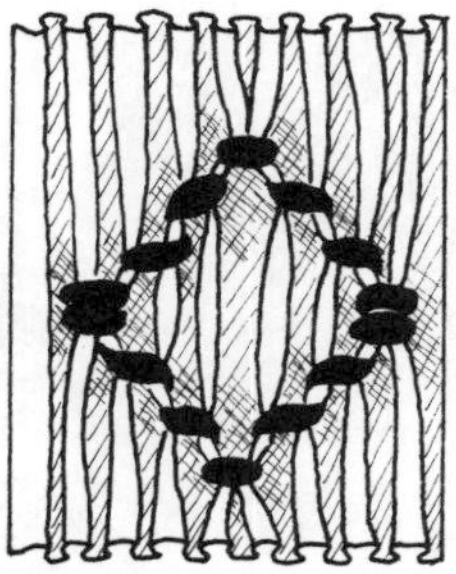

Directions

A double wave means that the second wave is worked in the opposite direction of the first, making a diamond shape.

Step 1. The top portion of the diamond wave (one-, two-, three-, four-wave) begins with a down-cable, and moves upward.

Step 2. The bottom portion of the diamond wave begins with a top cable and moves downward.

Step 3. Stack the cables that meet in the middle. A trick to matching the cables perfectly is to slip your needle between the pleats and slide it up. This will enable you to stitch very close to the first pleat.

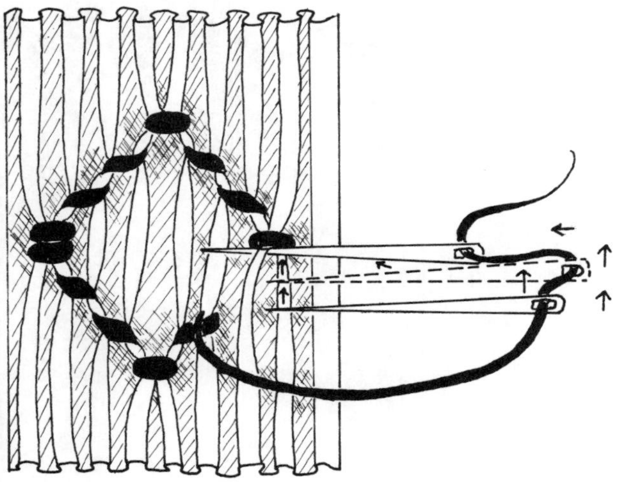

SIX-STEP FLOWERETTE

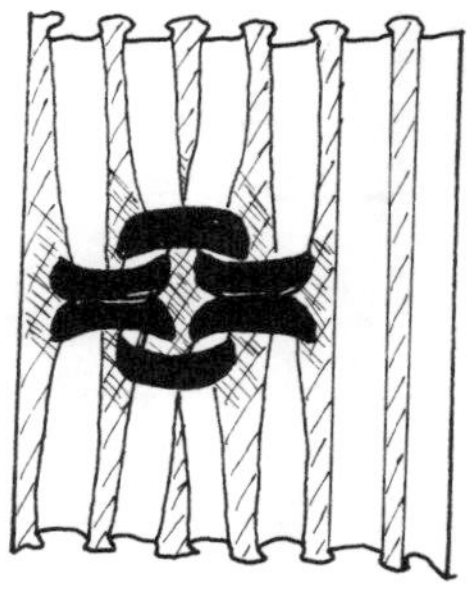

Directions

Work from left to right.

Step 1. Bring in the thread on the left hand side of the first pleat to be involved in the flowerette. Bring it in at X on pleat 1.

Step 2. Work a down cable **(stitch A - pleat 2).**

Step 3. Work an up cable **(stitch B - pleat 3).**

Step 4. Work a down cable **(stitch C - pleat 4).**

Step 5. Take the needle to the back of the work between the last two pleats **(pleat 3 and pleat 4).**

Step 6. Turn the work upside down, as well as the illustration.

Step 7. Bring the needle out on the left hand side of the half-finished flowerette. The needle should come out a tiny bit above the stitch showing on that left hand side of the pleat. It will be very, very close to the other stitch **(Point Z).**

Step 8. Now make another down cable **(stitch D - pleat 3).**

Step 9. Make an up cable **(stitch E - pleat 2).**

Step 10. Make another down cable **(stitch F - pleat 1).** When upside down, the needle comes out at this point, and it is also the left hand side where smocking begins.

Step 11. To finish, take the needle to the back by going between pleats 1 and 2. Tie the work off by making a slip-snail knot.

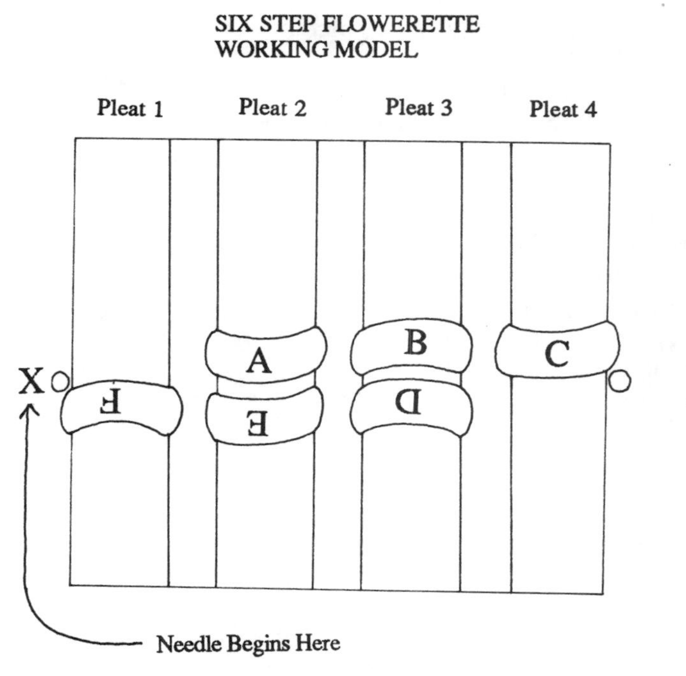

SMOCKING STITCHES

FOUR-STEP FLOWERETTE

Directions

Work from left to right, bringing the needle in on the left hand side of the first pleat **(fig. 31)**.

Step 1. Move over to the second pleat and make a down cable **(fig. 32)**.

Step 2. Move over to the third pleat, and make an up cable **(fig. 33)**.

Step 3. Move to the fourth pleat and make another up cable **(fig. 34)**.

Step 4. Look at the finished work. There are four pleats involved at this time with the floweret stitching **(fig. 35)**.

Step 5. Take the needle to the back of the garment, going between the first and second pleats. This will complete the flowerette stitching sequence **(fig. 36)**.

Step 7. Tie off each flowerette on the back of the garment by using the slip-snail knot instructions given earlier.

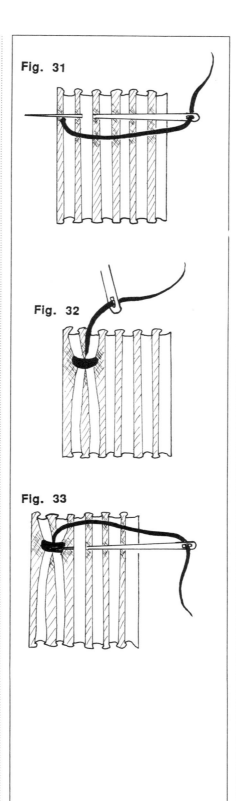

Fig. 31

Fig. 32

Fig. 33

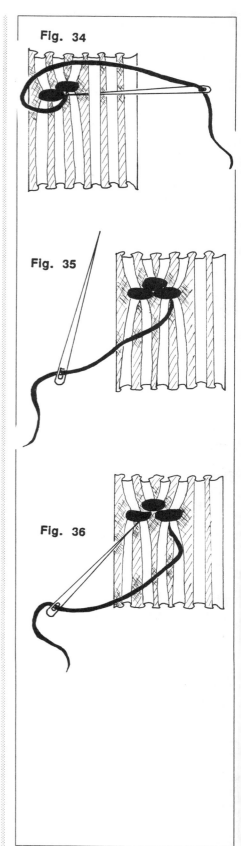

Fig. 34

Fig. 35

Fig. 36

SATIN STITCH FLOWERETTE

Directions

Satin-stitch flowerettes may be worked over two, three, or four pleats. I think two is usually prettiest.

Step 1. Bring the thread in on the left side of the first pleat of the satin stitch flowerette.

Step 2. Use the satin embroidery stitch. Stitch through the pleats as if making smocking stitches. Be sure the stitches lay close to each other.

Step 3. Use the needle tip or your thumb to place the stitches just right.

Step 4. After stitching the desired number of bars, take the needle to the back, on the right hand side of the smocked pleats. Continue at the point where another whole stitch would be taken if more bars were added to the floweretet.

Step 5. Tie off with a slip-snail knot on the back.

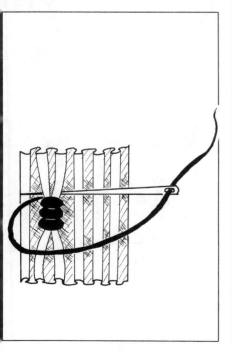

LAZY DAISY STITCH

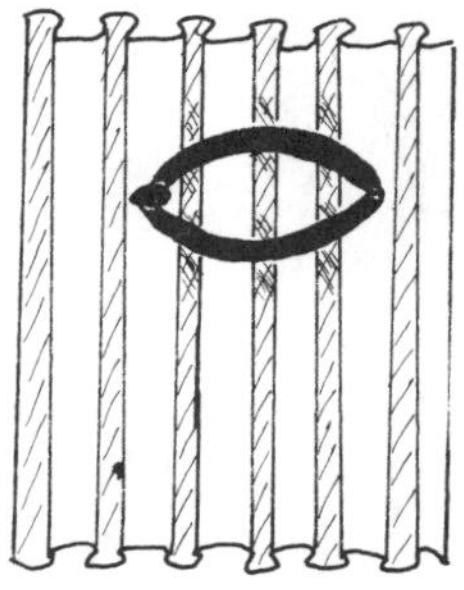

Directions

This is actually an embroidery stitch used to represent flower leaves or an actual daisy-type flower. It is a smocking embellishment technique.

Step 1. Knot the floss. Bring the threaded needle, from the back, up through the center of pleat (fig. 37).

Step 2. Insert the needle right above the hole you just came through, run it through two complete pleats, and up in the center of the third pleat (fig. 38). Make sure to involve four pleats in this stitch. A review: Bring the needle up through the back in the center of one pleat. Then, run the needle through the next two pleats. And finally, bring the needle through the center of the fourth pleat for the other side of the stitch. The thread should lay to the bottom of the needle while running the needle from the first pleat to the fourth.

Step 3. Before pulling the thread through, form a loop around the tip of the needle (fig. 38).

Step 4. Pull the thread, holding the loop carefully to shape it and place it with your fingers.

Step 5. Shape the loop as desired, and pull the thread through the smocking to tighten the loop.

Step 6. Take the tip of the needle through the same hole it came up out of in the fourth pleat (fig. 39). Do not pull too tightly.

Step 7. Tie off with a slip-snail knot after making all the lazy daisy stitches you want. When you move to another location for more lazy daisy stitches. Knot a new thread and start all over again.

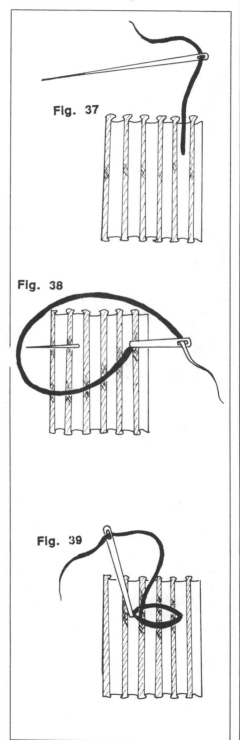

Fig. 37

Fig. 38

Fig. 39

291

WENDY LEE RAGAN DESIGNS

ABC

Baby

For more designs from Wendy Ragan, write or call:
Peter Pan & Wendy • Wendy Lee Ragan
P.O. Box 18714 • Anaheim Hills, CA 92817
714-970-5265

Grandmother's Hope Chest

Shadowwork Embroidery

QUESTIONS AND ANSWERS

▨ WHAT IS SHADOWWORK EMBROIDERY?

Shadowwork embroidery is "a closed herringbone stitch." Worked left to right between somewhat parallel lines, the color of the floss gives off a shadow effect through the fabric on which it is being stitched. The floss, crossed on the back of the fabric, can be stitched from either the front or the back of the piece. Directions will be given for both; however, my preference is to stitch from the back.

▨ WHERE CAN I USE THIS EMBROIDERY?

Shadowwork embroidery can be used anywhere. Try a white-on-white shadow work design trailing from the yoke to the bottom of the skirt of a christening gown. Yokes on little girl's dresses, collars of all types, even boudoir pillows are popular places for shadowwork. Embroider your own insertions. You can even choose to embellish a purchased outfit with shadowwork embroidery.

One of my favorite ideas for shadowwork is to smock a collar, leaving about 2 inches in the center front. Stitch shadowwork embroidery there. Something very pretty would be to stitch a few of the alphabet letters there. The finishing touch is a bullion rosebud nestled in each letter.

Shadowwork embroidery does not have to be fancy and lacy. It can be very tailored. In the Spring 1989 Sew Beautiful, Diane Zinser designed a small, navy blue anchor with gold metallic chain. This was placed on a very tailored collar of white linen; the blouse was worn with navy shorts. Several of the designers have taken story book ideas such as trains, rabbits, bears, houses, children, and other simple outlines and stitched them in shadow stitching. Of course, my very favorites are shadowworked bows, flowers, and monograms.

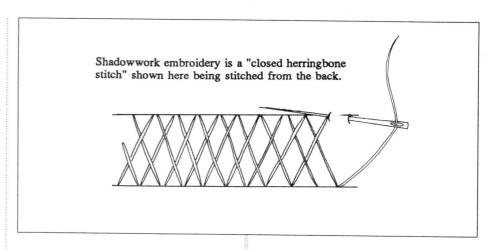

Shadowwork embroidery is a "closed herringbone stitch" shown here being stitched from the back.

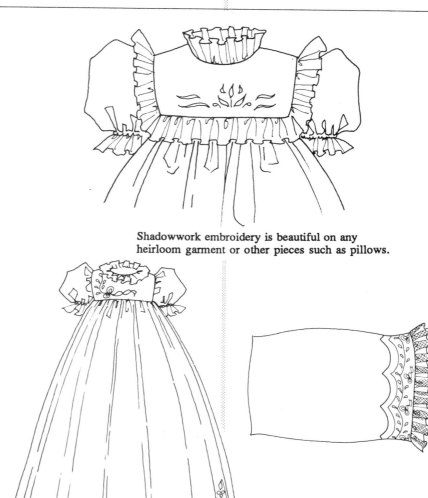

Shadowwork embroidery is beautiful on any heirloom garment or other pieces such as pillows.

▓ WHAT TYPE OF NEEDLE DO I NEED?

A #26 tapestry needle is preferred by most embroiderers. It is large enough to make a hole in the fabric which can be seen for the next stitch placement. The dull point of the tapestry needle is excellent for this stitch. If you prefer a needle with a point, try a #10 crewel needle. Many skilled embroiderers work with a #9 or a #10 crewel needles. Those who stitch shadowwork from the front sometimes use a #8 or a #10 sharps. Please don't waste your precious time with bad needles. Martha Pullen Company has a gorgeous package of needles called "Needles For Heirloom Sewing" which has over 100 fine English needles for smocking, picture smocking, shadowwork, shadowwork embroidery, general sewing, bullion roses, and duplicate stitch. The cost of the package of needles is $12.00.

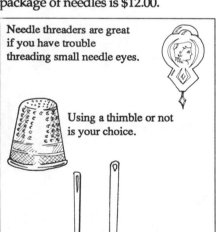

Needle threaders are great if you have trouble threading small needle eyes.

Using a thimble or not is your choice.

▓ NEEDLE TRICKS

Yes, they do. Have you ever wondered why sewing machine needles only go into the machine slot in one direction? Wonder no more. They do have a right and wrong side. It you have difficulty threading your needle before beginning your shadowwork embroidery, flip the needle to the other side.

There are several tricks for easier threading. One is to use a needle threader. The best trick I can share with you is to wet the back side of the needle before pushing the thread through the front. This works on hand sewing or on sewing machine needles. Another tip for threading a needle is to take the strand of floss in your hand and fold about an inch of one end over the thickest part of the needle. Pinch the strand tightly around the needle using your thumb and index finger. Pull the needle away from the floss. While you are still holding the pinched floss, push the eye of the needle toward it to pass the floss through.

▓ SHOULD I USE A THIMBLE?

This is entirely up to you. Before I began smocking, I used a thimble for all hand stitching. Since you are only using one strand of floss, you most likely won't poke holes in your fingers. Please try it both ways. Either way will be fine

Needles For Heirloom Sewing
Available through Martha Pullen Company

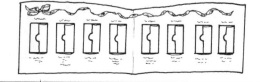

▓ WHICH HOOP IS THE BEST?

My preference is a 4-inch or 5-inch plastic hoop with a screw closing.

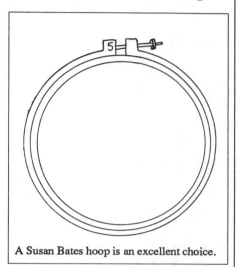

A Susan Bates hoop is an excellent choice.

▓ HOOP TRICK

Try wrapping the inner ring of the plastic hoop with medical gauze. This pads the hoop somewhat and helps keep the fabric from stretching. Just wrap the inner ring and place a few stitches to keep it from slipping off as you work.

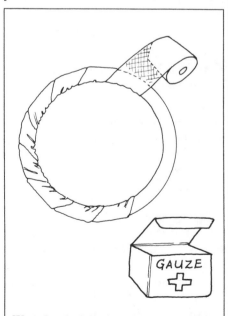

Wrapping the inner hoop keeps your fabric from stretching.

QUESTIONS AND ANSWERS

WHAT EMBROIDERY FLOSS SHOULD I USE?

DMC and Anchor floss are excellent choices for regular shadowwork embroidery.

Make your shadowwork embroidery unique by using variegated, 6-strand, cotton floss makes gorgeous shadowwork embroidery and also fabulous bullion rosebuds. The variegation is shorter than the usual variegated floss; the colors flow together in a very elegant manner. This imparts a very subtle shading to fine embroidery. The floss comes in a 20-yard skein for approximately $2. At present time there are twenty shades; more are expected shortly.

HOW MANY STRANDS OF FLOSS DO I USE?

The general rule of thumb is one strand (about 18 to 22 inches long. If you are doing shadowwork embroidery on a baby quilt, or on heavier fabric, such as broadcloth, you will need more. Heavier fabrics aren't as popular in shadowwork embroidery because the shadow effect is lost when you can't see through the fabric.

DOES FLOSS HAVE A GRAIN?

All thread has a grain. Thread for your sewing machine pulls off in only one direction. The grain comes off the spool in the correct manner. The same is true for DMC floss, if pulled from the package correctly. Look at the two paper wraps on the embroidery floss. One has the round DMC symbol. The other has the color number and a picture of two hands pulling the floss out of the package. Place your left hand on the floss as shown on the picture. With your right hand, pull the floss out of the package as instructed.

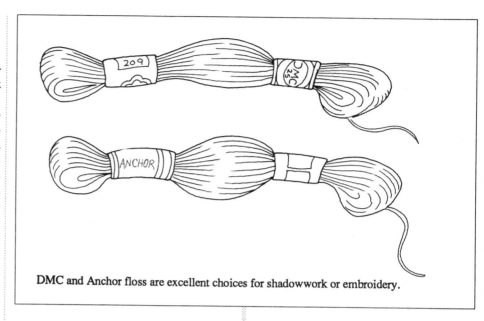

DMC and Anchor floss are excellent choices for shadowwork or embroidery.

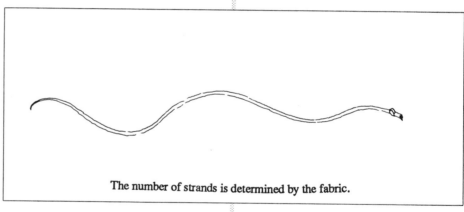

The number of strands is determined by the fabric.

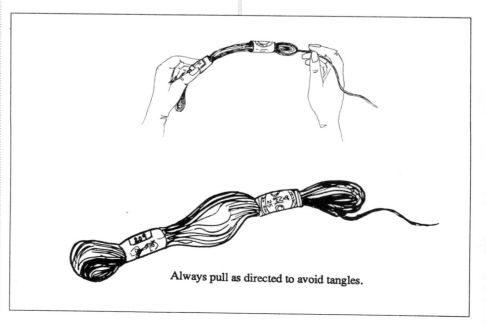

Always pull as directed to avoid tangles.

▓ HOW DO I PUT MY FLOSS ON GRAIN PROPERLY?

Always knot the floss at the end you cut. Since you don't knot thread for shadowwork embroidery, this will be the end you leave hanging before you begin your stitching.

Before shadow stitching, I separate all the strands and place a knot on the cut end. This way, I won't forget which end will be the "non-stitching" end. Since shadow embroidery uses lots of floss, you will be surprised how quickly you will have to thread up again.

If you forget which end of the thread to knot, remember this helpful tip. One end of the floss "blooms" more than the other end. The cut end of the floss (where you are going to place your knot) does not fuzz out as much as the other end of the floss. Place the knot on the less fuzzy end.

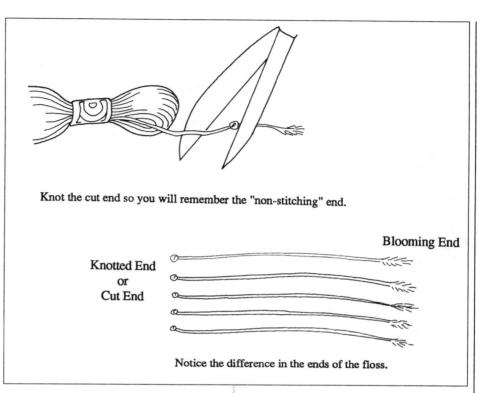

Knot the cut end so you will remember the "non-stitching" end.

Blooming End

Knotted End
or
Cut End

Notice the difference in the ends of the floss.

▓ CHOICES OF FABRIC FOR SHADOWWORK?

Swiss Nelona, known for its little bit of body, is especially wonderful for shadowwork embroidery. It is 100 percent, Swiss cotton batiste, available exclusively from Martha Pullen, Company, Inc.

Some Swiss batiste, such as Oriunda, is much thinner and big holes are left in the fabric where the needle travelled. While white seems to be everybody's favorite color for shadowwork embroidery, gorgeous work has been done on every pastel color of Nelona (ecru, lavender, pale robin's egg blue, pale blue, pale pink, gray and pale peach).

Ecru and white handkerchief linen are also nice. Imperial batiste or Wistful batiste are excellent choices in the poly/cotton domestic fabrics. Swiss organdy or Italian organdy are lovely also. When you work on organdy, you must be very careful to make your stitches precise. Each stitch really shows when you are working with this fabric.

QUESTIONS AND ANSWERS

▓ I WANT THE "ANTIQUE" LOOK TO MY FABRICS.

Step 1. Put two tablespoons of vinegar into one cup of warm or cold coffee. If you are dyeing a large piece of fabric, you will want to make more than one cup of the mixture.

Step 2. Very Important! Thoroughly wet your fabric with water before placing it into the coffee.

Step 3. Leave the fabric in the coffee mixture for several minutes.

Step 4. Remove the fabric and rinse with water until all of the coffee-colored mixture comes out.

Step 5. Check your color. Do you want it darker? If so, repeat the procedure.

Step 6. After getting the right color, let the fabric dry before pressing it. When you press wet fabric after dyeing it in this manner, you may get streaks.

Step 7. However, if you want your fabric to look 100 years old, press it while it is still wet. This will stain the fabric in an antique manner.

Experiment with Colors:
• Pale Peach Swiss Nelona dyes to a yellowish peach.
• Pale Robin's Egg Swiss Nelona dyes to a mint green.
• Pale Gray Swiss Nelona dyes to a darker gray.
• Pale Pink Swiss Nelona dyes to a pale pink.

▓ DO SOME HEIRLOOM FABRICS HAVE A RIGHT/ WRONG SIDE?

Technically they might in some cases. Some people say the sheen on Swiss Nelona and Imperial is prettier on one side. If you flip a fabric over several times and can't tell about the right and wrong side, it probably doesn't have one.

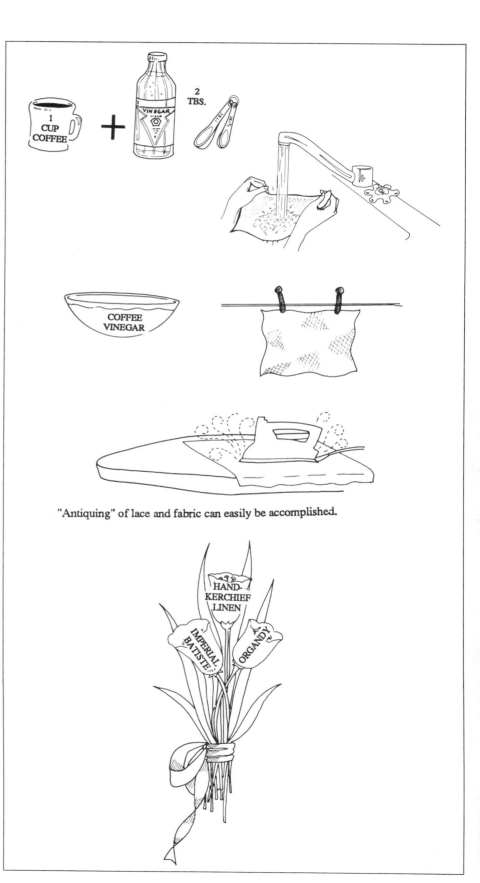

"Antiquing" of lace and fabric can easily be accomplished.

▓ TRACING AND TRANSFER-
RING THE DESIGN

A #2 , a Dixon pencil, or a quilter's pencil are my preferences for tracing. The water soluble pens do not work well because the lines are not exact enough. The Dixon pencil is exact, like a pencil, but it is water soluble.

If you are stitching from the back of the fabric, trace the design once onto the top of the fabric. Then, go to a light source, such as a window or a light box, and trace the design again through to the back of the fabric. If you use a window, just attach the pattern and your fabric to the window with a piece of masking tape. Often, you can use a copier to copy a design onto a thin paper; flip the paper and trace onto the back side of your fabric. Copy machines are also useful in reducing or enlarging your design. You might take color books, embroidery books, etc. to make a pattern out of something really large. The graph paper method will also work to change the size of a design. However, this method is tedious and time consuming.

Before you begin stitching, the outer portion of the hoop with the screw will be on the outside; the inner ring of the hoop (the one you have wrapped with gauze) will be on the inside of the fabric.

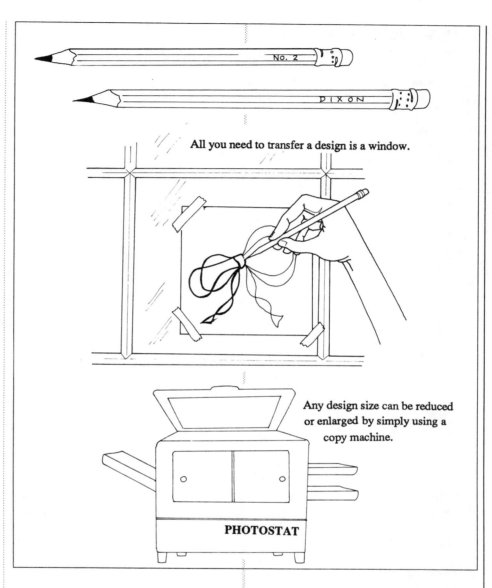

All you need to transfer a design is a window.

Any design size can be reduced or enlarged by simply using a copy machine.

PHOTOSTAT

▓ TRACING TIP

First, place your fabric in the hoop, right side up. Turn the hoop with the fabric over, so that the wrong side of the fabric is now showing up. Trace the design on this wrong side. Next, if you do the shadowwork from the wrong side, you need to take the fabric out of the hoop and turn it over. Place the fabric back in the hoop, with the wrong side and pencil drawing showing on the top surface of the embroidery hoop.

▓ HOW DO I FINISH MY WORK?

As with most needlework, do not put knots on the back of your work. When you have used your floss or finished a portion of the design, weave the floss along the outside edge of the design. Take care not to disturb the herringbone weave which makes the shadow peek through to the front.

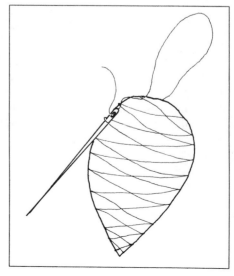

▨ I HAVE MADE A MISTAKE. WHAT SHOULD I DO?

Everyone makes mistakes. I don't care how perfect the shadowwork looks, I almost guarantee that one or more stitches will have to be pulled out for one reason or another. There are various reasons for ripping out, the most common: stitching in the wrong color and turning circles in a messy fashion.

When turning circles, beginners have the tendancy to make one side much larger than the other. If this is the case, carefully pull out the stitches and plan more carefully when to start increasing the stitches on the long side and decreasing the stitches on the short side. As with any needlework, practice. Try to establish some type of rhythm to your stitching. The stitches should be rather bouncy, not tight.

To take out shadowwork embroidery, unthread the needle before removing any unwanted stitches. Whenever possible use the eye rather than the point of the needle.

If you are working on fine batiste, little holes may show after taking out the stitches. Don't worry. Stitch over them. After removing your tracing lines, your fabric should still be damp. Steam the fabric with an iron, embroidery side down. This will close up any existing holes.

Before you begin, you might want to make some test stitches using your chosen colors and your chosen fabric. This is especially true if you are changing colors of a design or if you have made your own design. When you see changes you would like to make in your shadow embroidery, you will not have to pull out stitches and leave holes in your fabric.

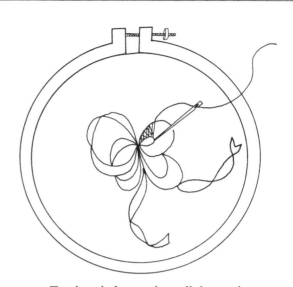

Turning circles requires a little practice.

Make longer stitches on the long side and shorter stitches on the short side.

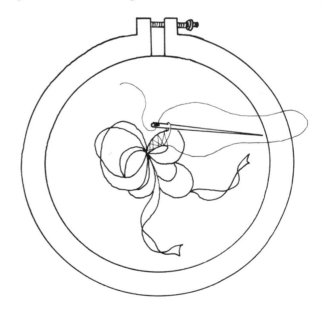

▓ FNISHING UP

Never, never, never, cut out your garment until your embroidery is completely finished. Complete your shadow embroidery, wash your work, dry and press it before cutting out your garment.

When pressing your work, never let the iron touch the surface of your shadowwork embroidery. After the stitching is completed, wash your work with Ivory soap or some other gentle brand. The pencil markings or Dixon pencil should be removed completely with this washing. Lay your work on a towel and batiste or other clean white fabric on top of the embroidery. Now you are ready to gently press your work.

▓ HOW SHOULD I CARE FOR MY HEIRLOOM GARMENT?

Heirloom garments should be washed by hand in a gentle soap such as Ivory Flakes. They should be laid flat to dry, not put in a dryer. Do Not Dry Clean Heirloom Garments. This tends to yellow fabrics and damage everything! Cleaners do not understand embroidery at all! Although the wonderful poly-cottons are great for permanent press, they do not clean as easily as 100% cotton. My preference is to use heirloom fabrics (100% Swiss Nelona) on garments which will have a lot of your hand work on them.

One hundred percent cotton will be just as beautiful 100 years from now if it is properly stored. First, thoroughly clean the garment to remove any soiled areas. Before storing an heirloom garment, do not iron or starch the garment. If the garment has plastic snaps or plastic buttons, remove them if the garment is to go into an attic or garage with excessive heat. Plastic sometimes melts. In a truly heirloom garment you should use pearl buttons and stainless steel snaps covered with batiste circles.

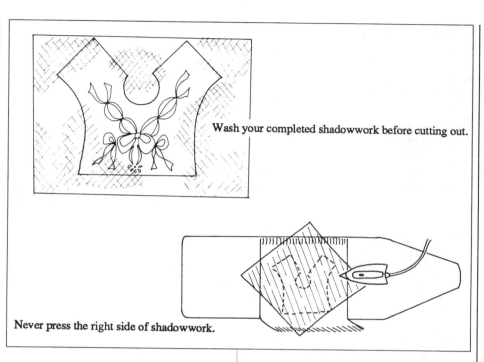

Wash your completed shadowwork before cutting out.

Never press the right side of shadowwork.

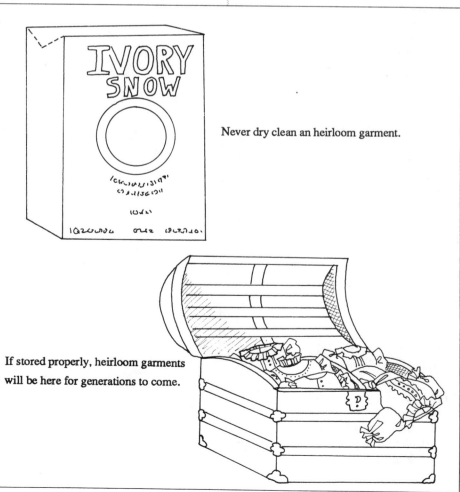

Never dry clean an heirloom garment.

If stored properly, heirloom garments will be here for generations to come.

SHADOWWORK EMBROIDERY - FROM THE BACK

With this method, you embroider from the wrong side of the fabric. When the fabric is loaded into the hoop, the wrong side of the fabric will be facing out. The design is traced onto that side. The stitches, a closed herringbone, are rather like "sewing" with a bite taken out of the top of the design and a bite taken out of the bottom. I prefer this method more than working from the front, because it is easiest.

Step. 1 Trace your design onto the wrong side of the fabric. If you are using an alphabet, be sure that the letters are properly reversed **(fig. 1)**. An easy way to reverse letters or a design onto the wrong side of the fabric is to use a photocopy machine. Copy the design onto a clear plastic sheet like you would use for an overhead projector. This is called a transparency. Flip the transparency over. Run a copy on paper this time. It will be reversed properly.

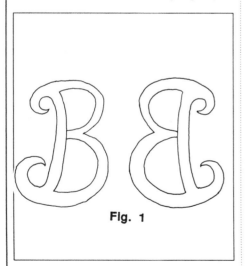

Fig. 1

Step 2. Insert the fabric into the embroidery hoop.

Step 3. Cut a piece of embroidery floss approximately 18 - 22 inches long **(fig. 2)**. Remember to knot the cut end, although you will later cut that knot away.

Step 4. There are two ways of placing the loose end (the knotted end of the floss) while you stitch your shadow embroidery.

    a. Lay the end of the floss (rather a long one) outside the embroidery hoop and close the hoop over it. This gives you plenty of floss to later weave into the completed design **(fig. 3)**.

    b. Bring your knot up through the circle of fabric as far away from your first stitch as possible. **Note:** Sometimes there is not enough embroidery floss "tail" to easily weave into the completed design.

Following the illustrations given, using the leaf shape **(fig. 4)**, begin your stitching.

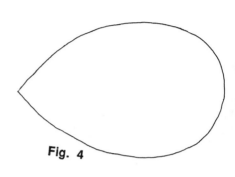

Fig. 4

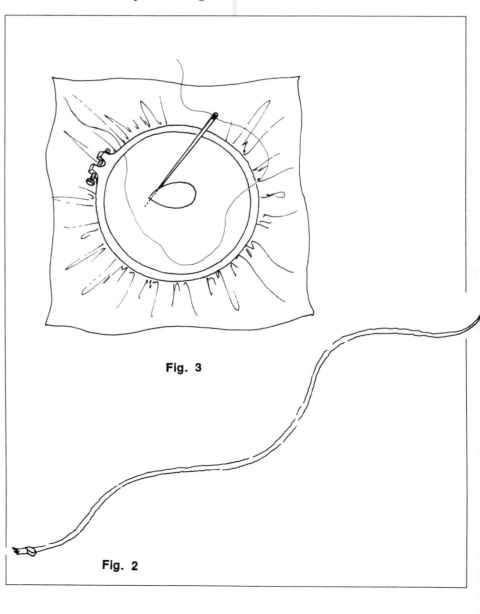

Fig. 3

Fig. 2

Grandmother's Hope Chest

SHADOWWORK EMBROIDERY - FROM THE BACK

Step 5. With the thread below the needle, bring the needle down at (A) **fig 5** and up at (B) **fig. 6.** Pull through.

Step 7. Move down. Thread above the needle, put your needle down at (C) **fig. 7** and up at (B) **fig. 8.** Move into the exact same hole as your needle made on the first bite at (B).

Note: In order to easily remember whether the thread is above or below the needle, see the "Cat And The Courthouse Story" in the *Smocking Techniques* chapter.

Step 8. With the thread below the needle, bring the needle down at (D) **fig. 9** and up at (A) **fig. 10.**

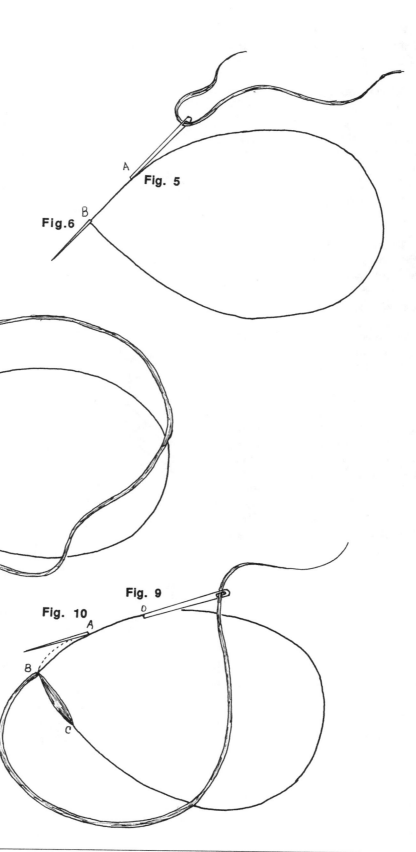

Fig. 5

Fig. 6

Fig. 8

Fig. 7

Fig. 9

Fig. 10

Step 9. With the thread above the needle, bring the needle down at (E) **fig. 11** and up at (C) **fig. 12.**

Step 10. When you come to a large curve, make your outside stitches (on the largest part of the curve) larger. Make the inside stitches closer together. You may find it necessary, sometimes, to go in one hole twice on the inside area. Finish the design according to **figures 13 - 30.**

Step 11. Keep turning your work so that the portion of the design you are currently working on is horizontally in front of you and so that you are working from left to right.

Step 12. When you have finished your work, weave the tail of the thread through the stitching on the sides. As with most needlework, never knot your thread. Just weave it.

Step 13. After you have finished with a design or with the amount of floss you have in your needle, weave that end into the design. Clip the knotted end which is either in the upper section of the fabric or held outside the embroidery hoop. Re-thread the needle with this end, and weave this end into the work as well.

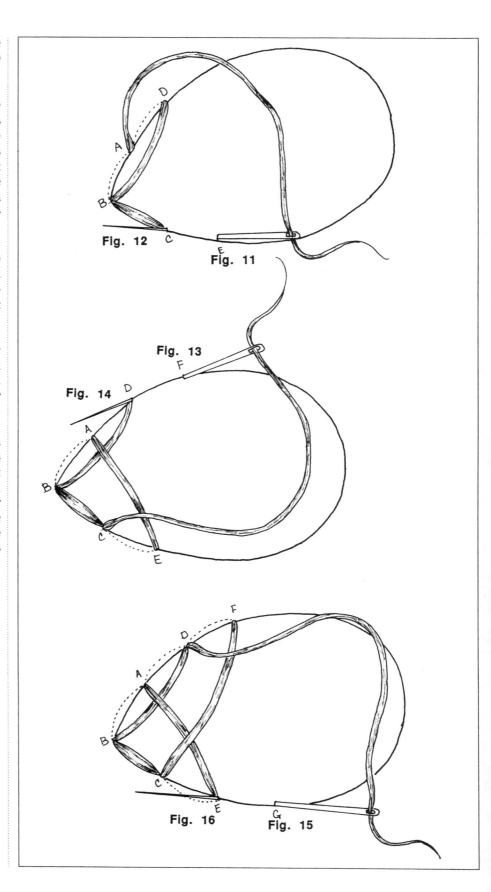

Fig. 12

Fig. 11

Fig. 13

Fig. 14

Fig. 16

Fig. 15

SHADOWWORK EMBROIDERY - FROM THE BACK

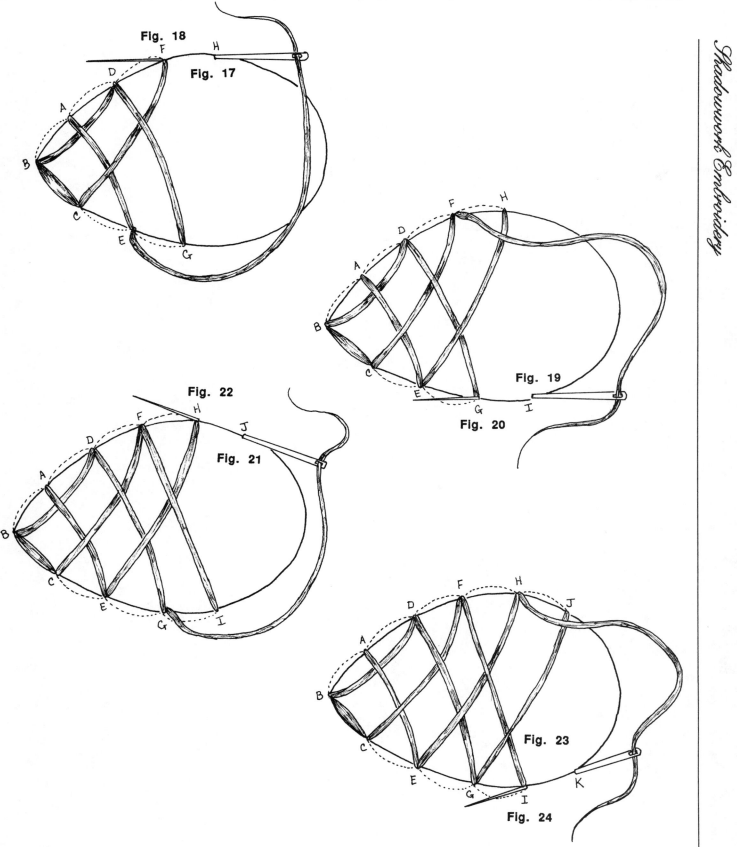

Fig. 18

Fig. 17

Fig. 19

Fig. 20

Fig. 22

Fig. 21

Fig. 23

Fig. 24

SHADOWWORK EMBROIDERY - FROM THE BACK

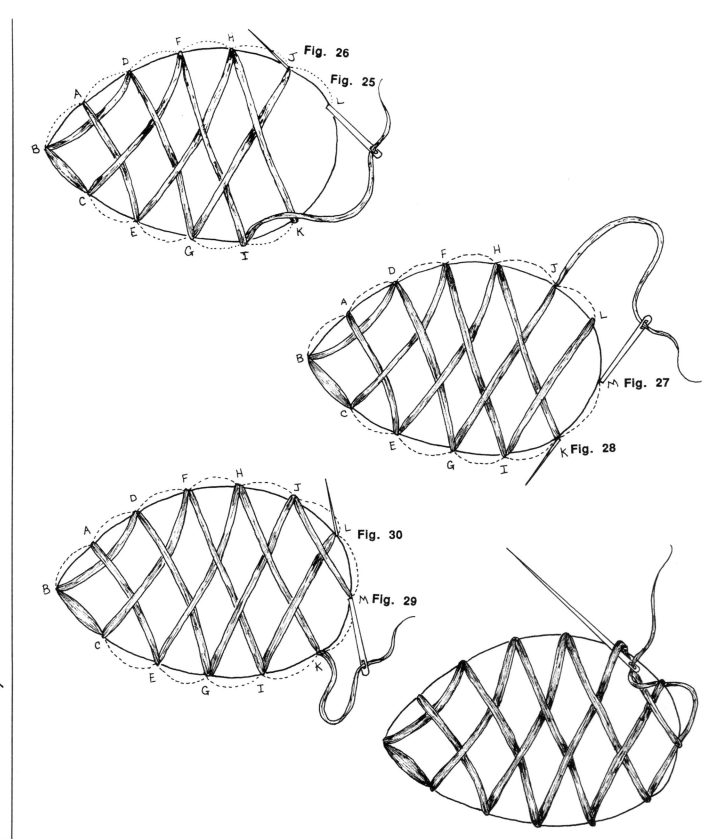

Fig. 25

Fig. 26

Fig. 27

Fig. 28

Fig. 29

Fig. 30

SHADOWWORK EMBROIDERY - FROM THE FRONT

Step 1. Trace the design you would like to shadowwork on the right side of the fabric **(fig. 1)**.

Step 2. Place the fabric into them embroidery hoop centering the design to be stitched. The right side of the fabric will be facing you.

Step 3. Cut a piece of embroidery floss aproximately 18 - 22 inches long. Separate the strands of floss. Thread one strand of floss through your favorite shadowwork needle. I suggest using a 10 sharp, 10 Crewels, or a 26 tapestry needle. Remember to knot the cut end of the floss, although you will later cut that knot away.

Step 4. Securing the thread.
Method 1. Place the knot on the wrong side of the fabric between the hoop and the fabric. Close the hoop **(fig. 2a)**.

Method 2. Place the needle in the right side of the fabric as far away from your first stitch as possible. The knot will end up on the right side of the fabric **(fig. 2b)**.

Either of these methods will put the needle/thread on the back side of the fabric. Note: This thread tail will need to be long enough to weave back through the stitching after the design is complete.

Step 5. Bring the needle to the right side of the fabric at the beginning point (A) **(fig. 3)**.

Step 6. To make the first stitch, take the needle down at point (B) to the wrong side of the fabric **(fig. 4)**.

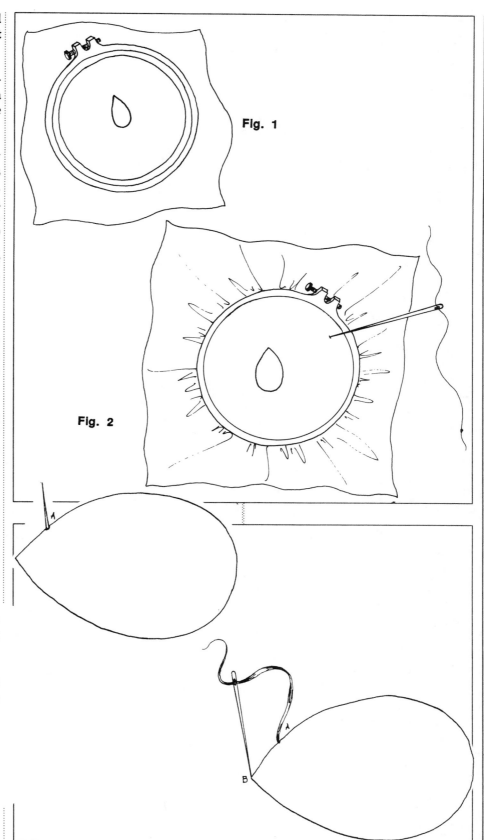

Fig. 1

Fig. 2

SHADOWWORK EMBROIDERY – FROM THE FRONT

Step 7. Move to the other side of the design and bring the needle up at (C) **fig. 5** and back down at (B) **fig. 6.** Pull gently.

Step 8. Bring the needle up from the backside at (D) **fig. 7** and back down at (A) **fig. 8.**

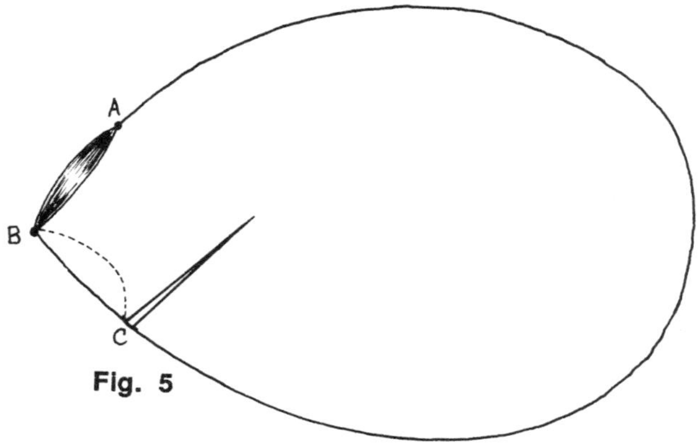

Fig. 5

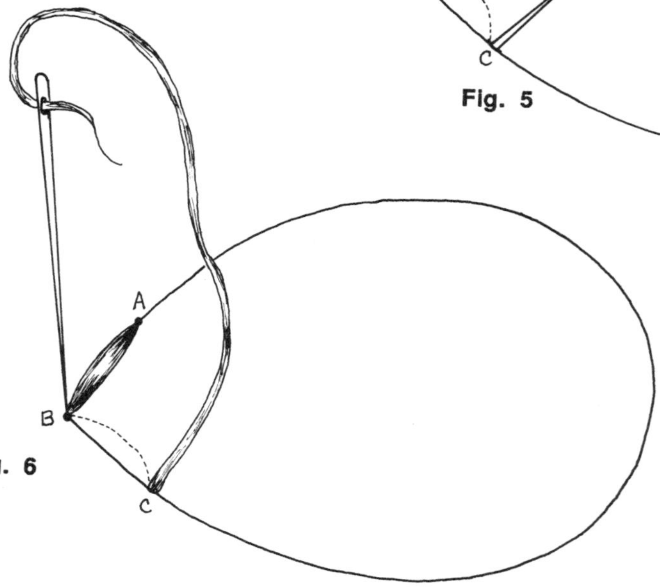

Fig. 6

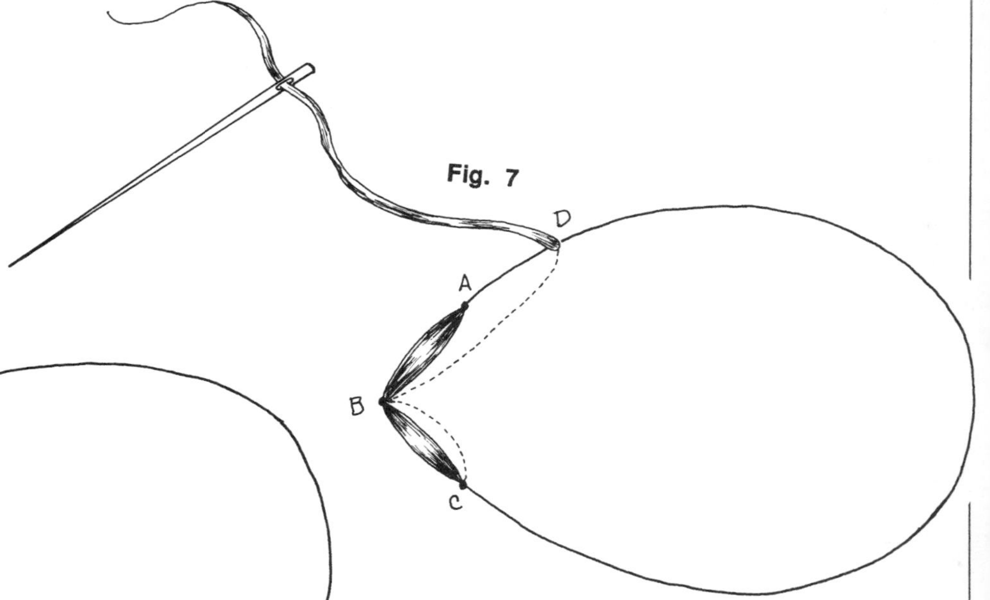

Fig. 7

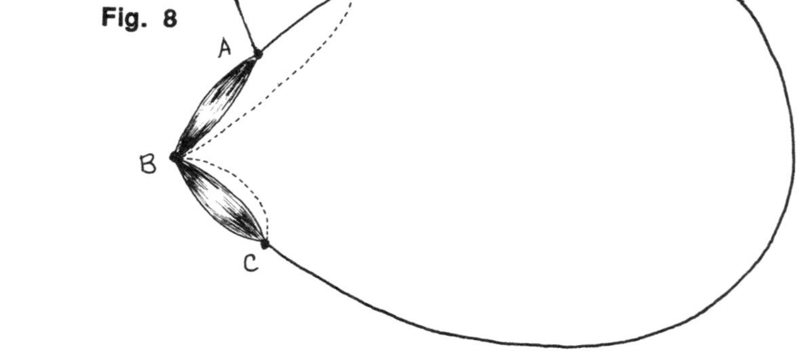

Fig. 8

SHADOWWORK EMBROIDERY - FROM THE FRONT

Step 9. Move down to the other side and come up through (E) **fig. 9** and go back down at (C) **fig. 10.**

Step 10. Move to the other side and come up at (F) and back down at (D) **fig. 11.**

Step 12. Move to the other side and come up through (G) and down at (E) **fig. 12.**

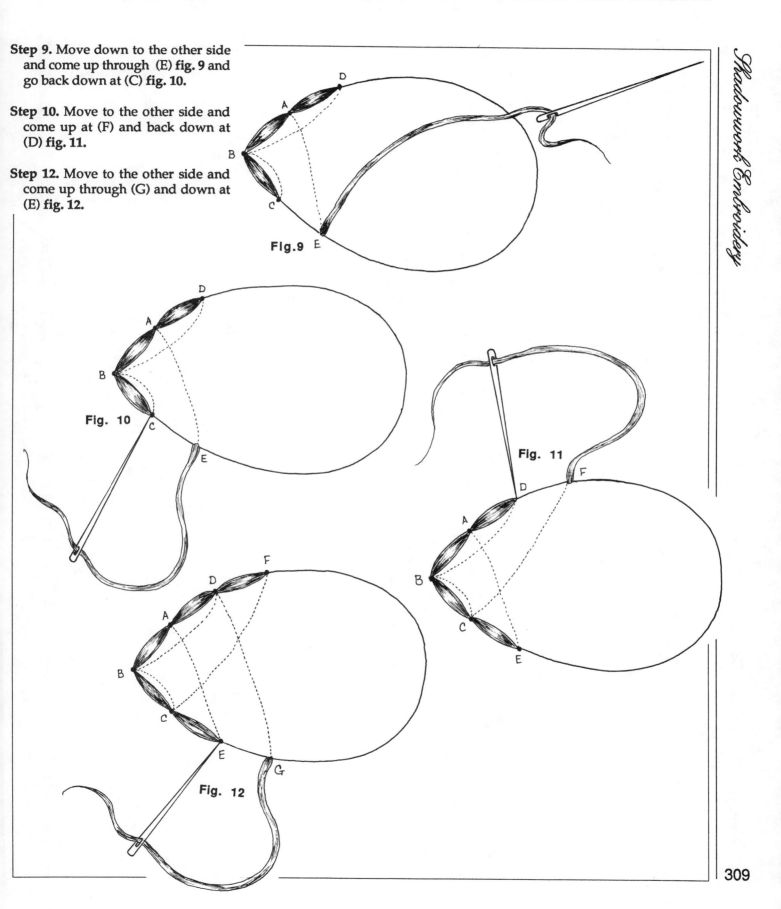

Fig.9

Fig. 10

Fig. 11

Fig. 12

Step 13. When you come to large curve, make your outside (on the largest part of the curve) larger. Make the inside stitches closer together. You may find it necessary to go in one hole twice on the inside area. Finish the design according to **figures 13 - 20.**

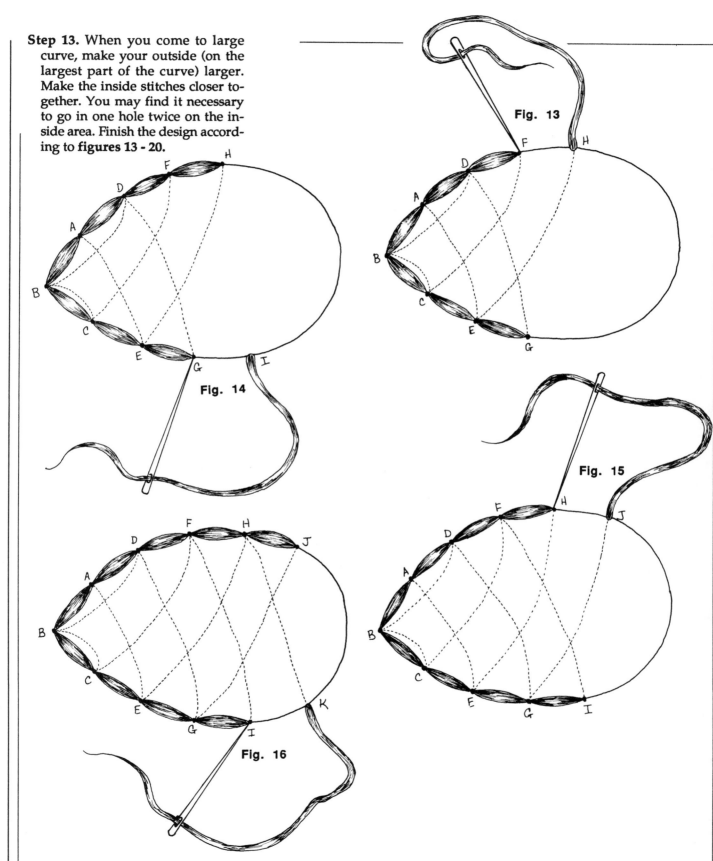

Fig. 13

Fig. 14

Fig. 15

Fig. 16

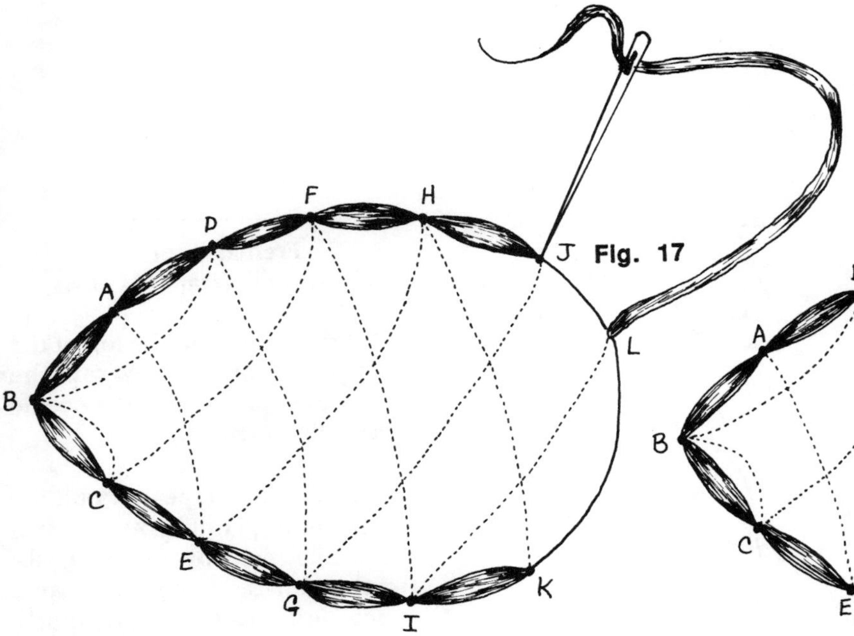

Fig. 17

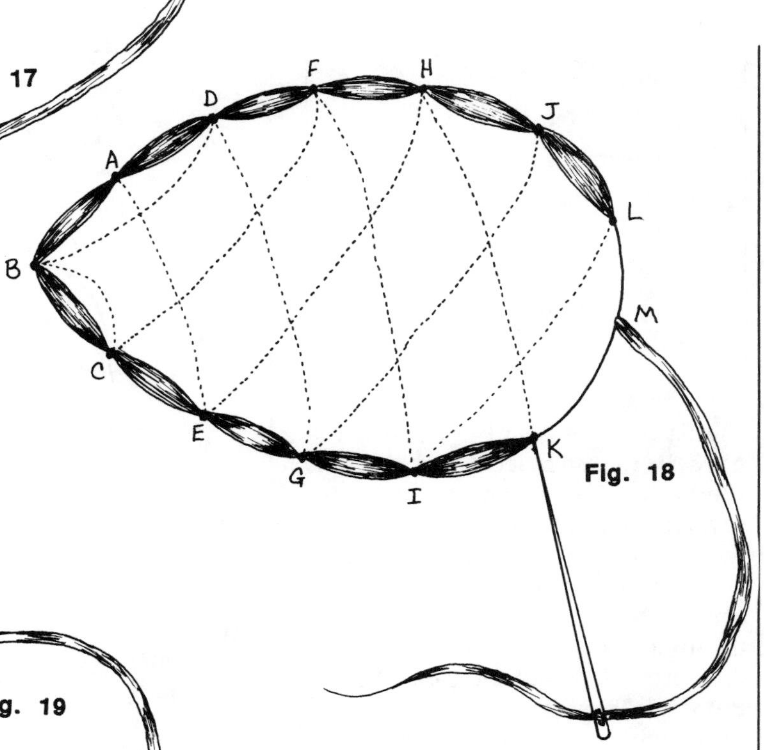

Fig. 18

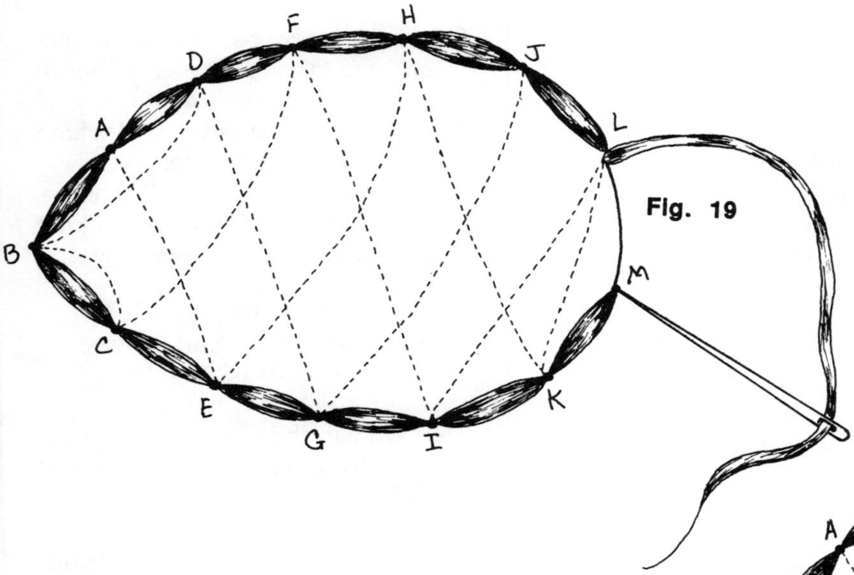

Fig. 19

Fig. 20

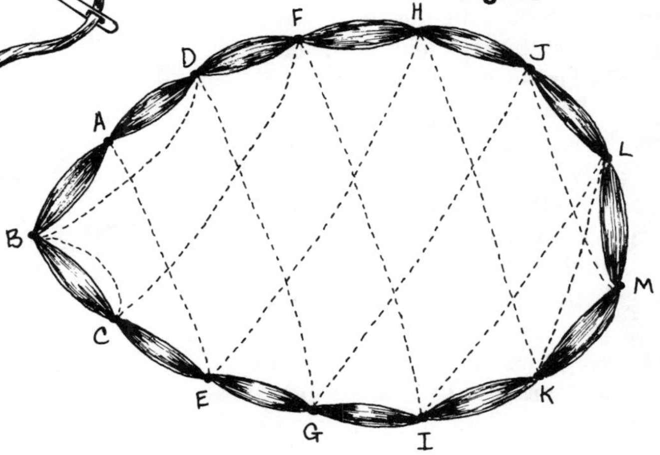

Fig. 21

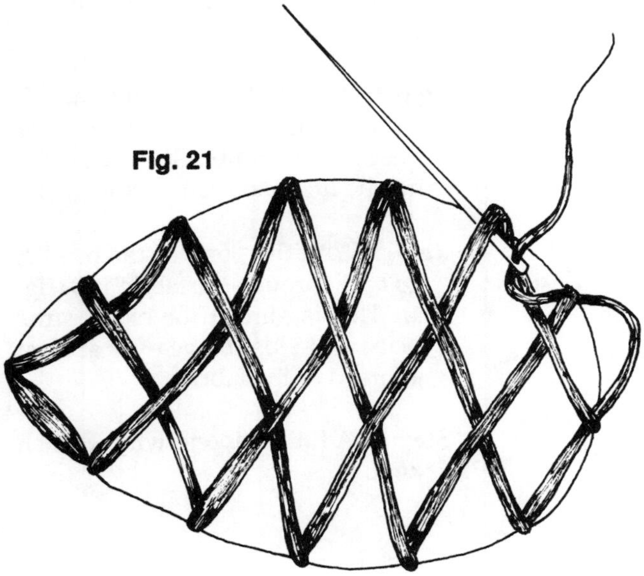

Step 14. After you have finished with a design or with the amount of floss you have in your needle, weave that end into the design. Clip the knotted end which is either in the upper section of the fabric or held outside the embroidery hoop. Rethread the needle with this end, and weave this end into the work as well **(fig. 21).**

EMBROIDERY STITCHES

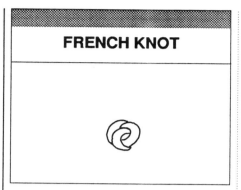

FRENCH KNOT

This delicate beauty of a stitch is used in many places to embellish shadowwork embroidery. There are several different theories concerning the French knot. Some say if you wrap the knot more than once, it becomes a bullion. After doing research through many embroidery books, I find that this is not the case. From a Butterick Transfer book dated 1917, I find the following description of a French knot.

"Bring the thread up and take an ordinary backstitch. Wind the thread once, twice, or three times around the needle, and draw it through, holding the coil down with the left thumb. Then, insert the needle over the edge of the coil in the same hole, thus making the knot secure. Do not cut the thread, but pass on to the next knot."

Please experiment with your French knots. After consulting with Margaret Boyles and Judith Dobson, I will share with you that they both prefer making a larger French knot by using more strands of floss and only wrapping once. They say that more than one wrap with one strand of floss makes the French knot topple over and become loose. You might want to try wrapping the needle just once and use more than one strand of floss. A little texture can be added with a few knots placed on the work. French knots can be used to fill in areas such as the center of flowers for a very lovely effect. Use a #10 sharp, a #8 sharp or a #7 milliner's (straw) needle.

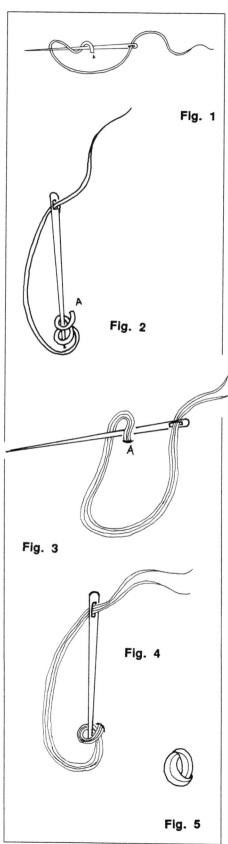

Fig. 1

Fig. 2

Fig. 3

Fig. 4

Fig. 5

French Knot With Several Wraps Of Floss

Step 1. Bring thread to the top of the work and out at A. Wrap the thread over and under the needle several times (fig. 1).

Step 2. Hold the wraps and pull the needle through until you can push the needle back down into the fabric at point B, almost the same place you came out originally (fig. 2).

Step 4. You may pass the thread behind the fabric to the next French knot if your fabric is not sheer. However, when you are stitching shadowwork embroidery, you will usually use a thin fabric. Therefore, it is best to tie off the French knot before passing to the next one.

French Knot With One Wrap And Several Strands of Floss

Step 1. Push the needle through the fabric from the back. Come out at A (fig. 3).

Step 2. Holding the needle in your right hand, place the needle in a horizontal position above the thread (fig. 3).

Step 3. Holding the floss in your left hand, wrap the floss around the needle one time. Go under the needle first and then over (fig. 3).

Step 4. With the point of the needle, go back through the fabric at B (fig. 4). This is almost the exact same place as A; just move over at least a thread of the fabric.

Step 5. A finished, one-wrap French knot.

BULLION KNOT

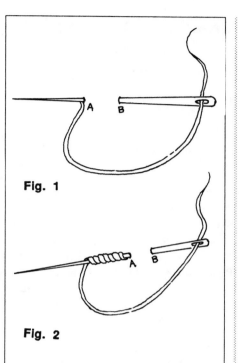

One of the favorite stitches for embellishing shadowwork embroidery is the bullion knot. It is exquisite for making roses, large or small. Some people seem to think that is it easier to make bullion knots while the hoop is in an embroidery frame so that you can use both hands to manipulate the needle and thread. Use a #10 crewel needle.

Step 1. Push the needle through the fabric from the back of your work. Come out at A **(fig. 1).**

Step 2. Bring the needle in at B, creating the length of the bullion that you want. Do not pull your floss through **(fig. 1).**

Step 3. Bring the needle out again into the same hole at A. Pass only three quarters of the needle through the fabric **(fig. 1).**

Step 4. With right hand holding the needle, left hand wrapping the floss, begin to wrap the loose floss in a counterclockwise direction around the needle **(fig. 2).**

Step 5. Wrap it the number of times you need for the length bullion you want. For a short bullion wrap about five times. For a longer bullion, wrap 13, 15, or even 19 times. Experiment at all levels.

Fig. 1

Fig. 2

Fig. 3

Fig. 4

Step 6. Slide the wraps down on the needle. Move the wraps close to the eye of the needle. Hold the wraps in place with your left thumb and index finger **(fig. 3).**

Step 7. Still holding the wraps with your left hand, carefully pull the needle up with your right hand. The rest of the floss will pass through the wraps **(fig. 3).**

Step 8. Arrange your bullion exactly right **(fig. 4).**

Step 9. Finish the bullion by pushing the needle into the back of the fabric near the last coil at B **(fig. 4).**

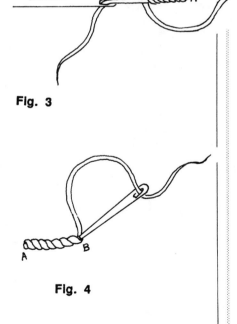

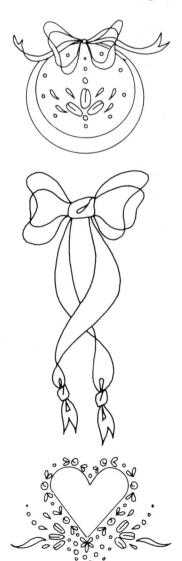

EMBROIDERY STITCHES

BACKSTITCH

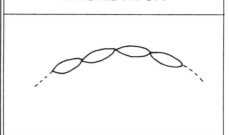

This technique makes a continuous line of stitches.

Step 1. Bring the thread through the fabric at A.

Step 2. Make a small backward stitch at B **(fig. 1)**.

Step 3. Bring the needle up again in front of the first stitch at C **(fig. 2)**, and take it back down again through the original insertion point at A **(fig. 3)**. The needle always emerges one stitch ahead, ready to make the next backstitch **(fig. 4)**.

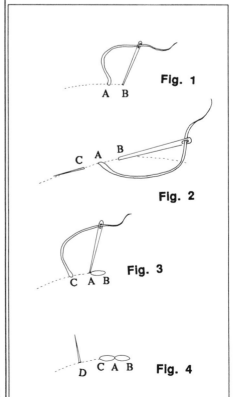

Fig. 1
A B

Fig. 2
C A B

Fig. 3
C A B

Fig. 4
D C A B

STEM/OUTLINE STITCH

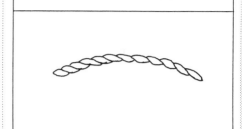

Worked from left to right, this stitch makes a line of slanting stitches. The thread is kept to the left and below the needle. Make small, even stitches. The needle is inserted just below the line to be followed, comes out to the left of it, and above the line, slightly.

Step 1. Come up from behind at A and go down into the fabric again at B **(fig. 1)**. This is a little above the line. Come back up at C **(fig. 1)**. This is a little above the line. Keep the thread below the needle.

Step 2. Go back down into fabric at D and come up a little above the line at B **(fig. 2)**.

Step 3. Continue working, always keeping the thread below the needle **(fig. 3)**.

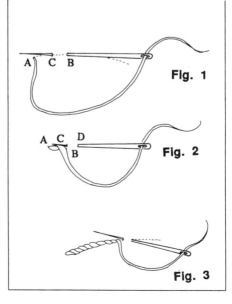

Fig. 1
A C B

Fig. 2
A C D
B

Fig. 3

LAZY DAISY STITCH

This little delicate stitch gets its name because it looks like a daisy.

Step 1. Bring the needle through the fabric at the inner point of the petal A. Insert again at almost the same point at B.

Step 2. Take a stitch toward the large loop of the daisy (the outside of the petal), with the thread looped under the needle **(fig. 1)**.

Step 3. Hold the loop with a small stitch at C **(fig. 2)**.

Step 4. Bring the needle back in again at the center of the inner point of the petal **(fig. 1)**.

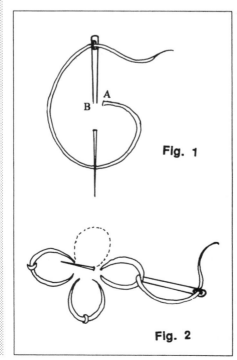

Fig. 1
B A

Fig. 2

OUTLINING STITCHES

The outlining of a pattern is very important before making a satin stitch.

Step 1. Use the directions for stem stitch found on the previous page. Make the stitches even and on the line **(fig. 1)**.

Step 2. Padding before satin stitching means just that. Fill in the outline in lengthwise stitches with uneven darning stitches, taking short stitches on the wrong side and longer stitches on the right side. Make them close together **(fig. 2)**.

Step 3. If a raised effect is desired, make three or four thicknesses of padding stitches. Keep the padding even, making it higher in the center and spreading the stitches more toward the edge. Several strands of darning cotton are used for padding.

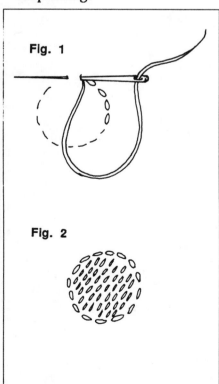

Fig. 1

Fig. 2

SATIN STITCH

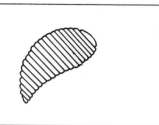

Basic satin stitch dates back for centuries. Satin stitch basically covers a whole shape. Use one or two strands of floss. This is a stitch which takes some practice to make pretty. You can work satin stitch either straight or on the diagonal.

Step 1. Bring the needle out at A. Go down at B **(fig. 1)**.

Step 2. Work the stitches over and over until the shape is covered **(fig. 2)**. The stitches should not overlap, but should be close together. Gradually, lengthen or shorten each stitch to conform to the shape you are making. The edges of the shape should be kept neat; the stitches at a reasonable length.

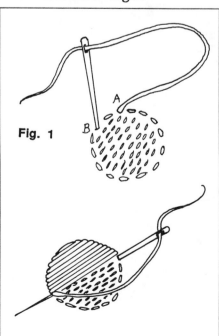

Fig. 1

EIGHT-STRAND STITCH

This pretty stitch is another form of a flower stitch. Use four strands of floss.

Step 1. Thread your needle with four strands of floss.

Step 2. Bring the needle up at A which is the inner part of the petal.

Step 3. Insert the needle down at B which is the outer end of the petal **(fig. 1)**.

Step 4. Bring the needle up in the inner end of the next petal.

Step 5. Do not pull too tightly. Spread the floss out a little bit with either your fingernail or the blunt end of your needle.

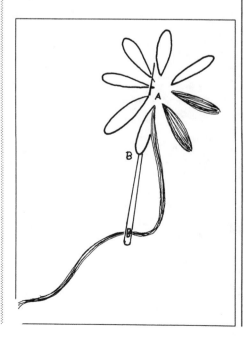

EMBROIDERY STITCHES

MILLE FLEUR STITCH

Use a single strand of floss. Experiment with a denser weight of floss which is more "rope like."

Step 1. Work from the inner point (A) to the outer point (B) **fig. 1.**

Step 2. Stitch from the inner point to the outer point.

Step 3. Come up again at the center point.

BUTTONHOLE STITCH

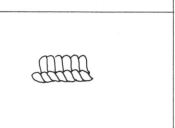

This stitch is worked from left to right and two lines are followed. It is especially pretty when you want to work a buttonhole scallop around the edge of a collar. Hold the work secure in a hoop or by basting onto an oilcloth if you do not like to use a hoop. The older embroidery books suggest filling in the scalloped areas with small stitches such as a running stitch. This would be done before you begin your buttonhole scallops.

Step 1. Work from left to right. Begin to buttonhole at the extreme left.

Step 2. Insert the needle at the lower edge at A **(fig. 1).**

Step 3. Insert the needle at B and bring in at C. The thread is held under the needle **(fig. 1).**

Step 4. Pass the thread under the point and draw the needle through **(fig. 2).**

Step 5. The needle is inserted a little to the right on the upper line, taken straight downwards behind the work to come out on the lower line over the thread. The thread is then pulled to form a loop **(fig. 2).**

Step 6. Keep them close together and curve them to make a scallop **(fig. 3).**

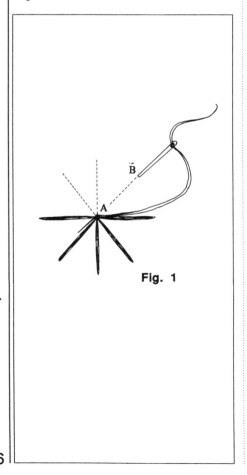

Fig. 1

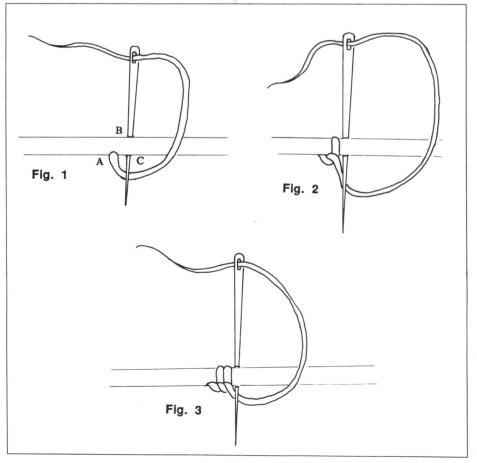

Fig. 1

Fig. 2

Fig. 3

Grandmother's Hope Chest

CHAIN STITCH

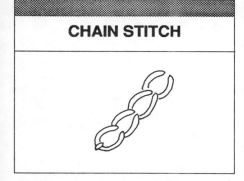

The chain stitch can be worked in a straight row, on a curve, or inside as a filler stitch. If the chain stitch is to be used as a filler stitch, work from the outside of the design to the inside. Place each row parallel to the other row of chain stitch beside it.

Step 1. Bring the thread from below the fabric at A **(fig. 1)**. Holding the thread to the left of the needle, go back into the same hole at A, forming a loop by holding the thread with your left thumb.

Step 2. Bring the needle out at B. Keep the thread under the needle. This forms a loop.

Step 3. For a curved chain stitch, take your needle to the right or left to form a curve **(fig. 2)**.

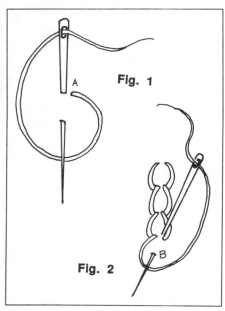

FEATHER STITCH

I used to think you could tell poor embroidery from excellent embroidery by the quality of a woman's feather stitch! I still put a great deal of faith in this stitch. It is lovely for borders, stems, branches and leaf fillings. I will give you a quick "cheat" trick at this time. If your sewing machine has a feather stitch on it, run the feather stitch, without any thread, anywhere you want your hand featherstitch. Then, just work your hand featherstitch in those holes.

Step 1. Bring your needle from behind your work at A **(fig. 1)**.

Step 2. Working at an angle, and holding the thread to make a loop, go down again at B and back up at C. Be sure you pass the needle over the thread. That is what forms the feather **(fig. 2)**.

Step 3. Move over at another angle at D and repeat **(fig. 3)**.

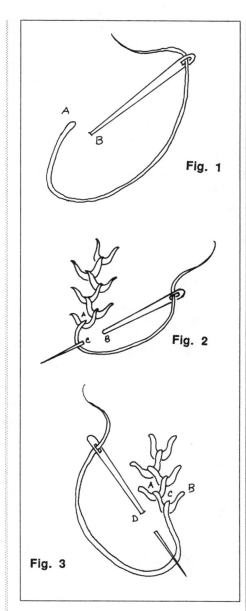

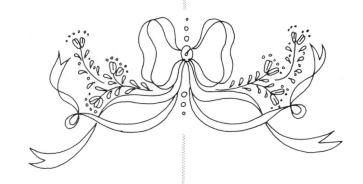

317

Note from Martha: Any of these shadowwork/embroidery designs can be reduced or enlarged to fit your spaces and garments. In larger sizes, they will be beautiful for adult clothing or pillows.

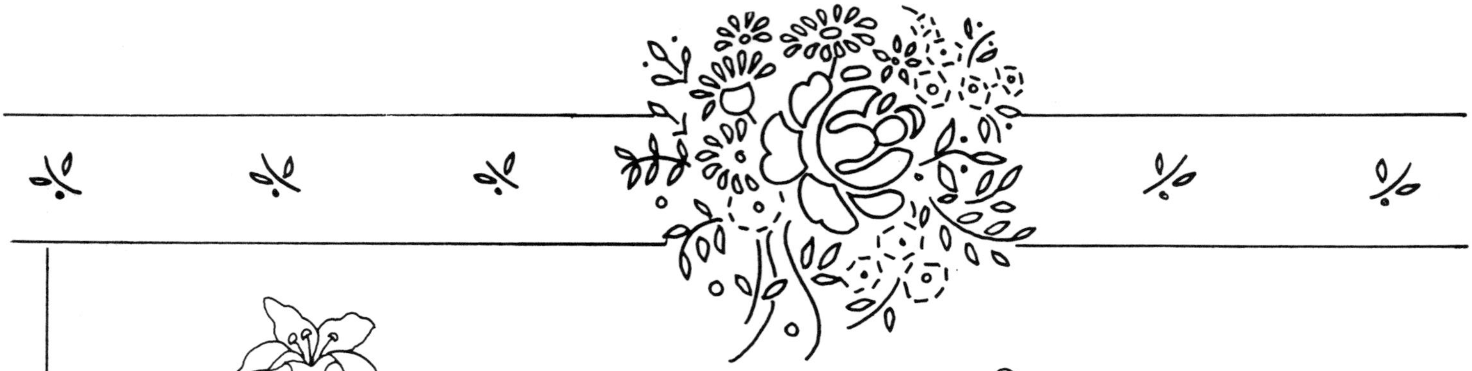

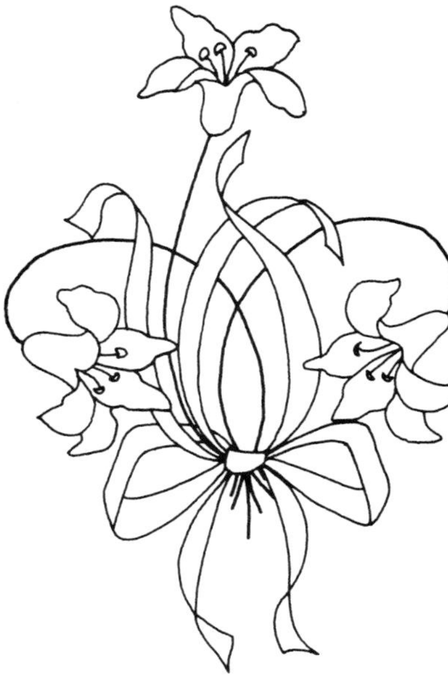

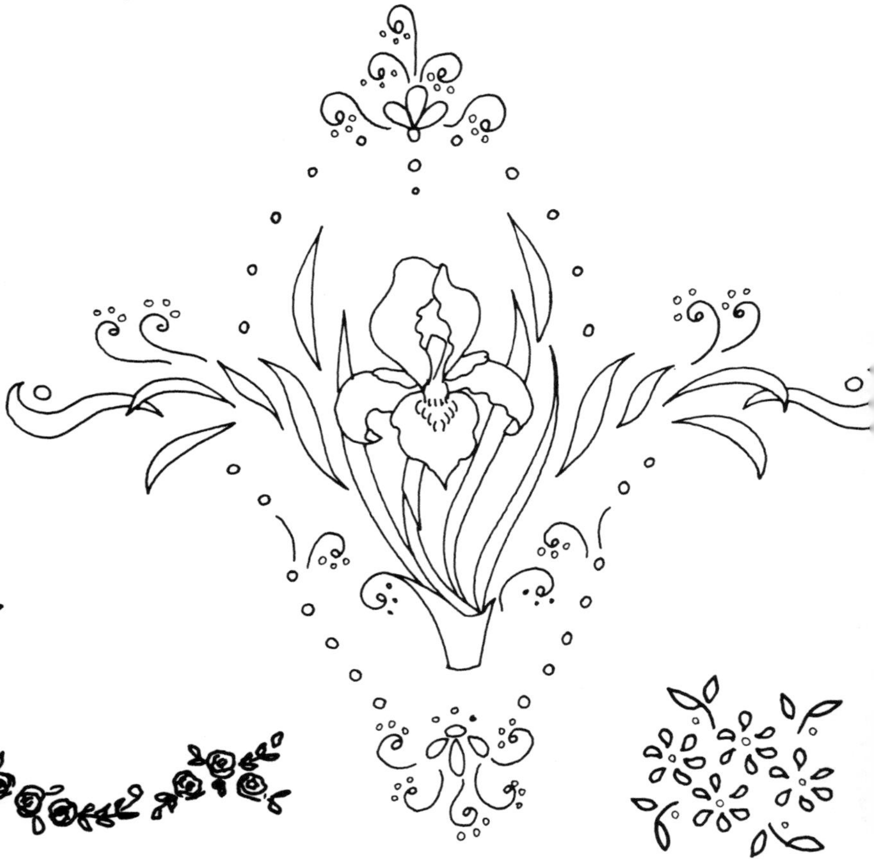

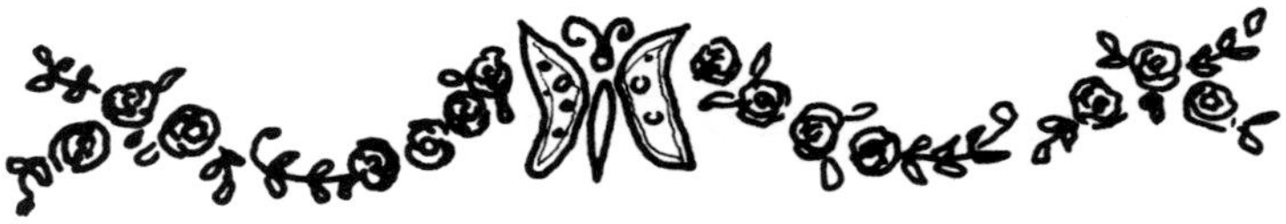

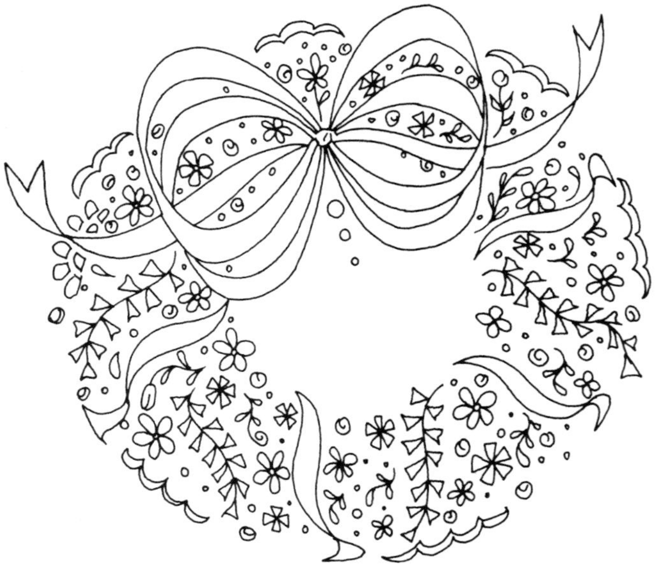

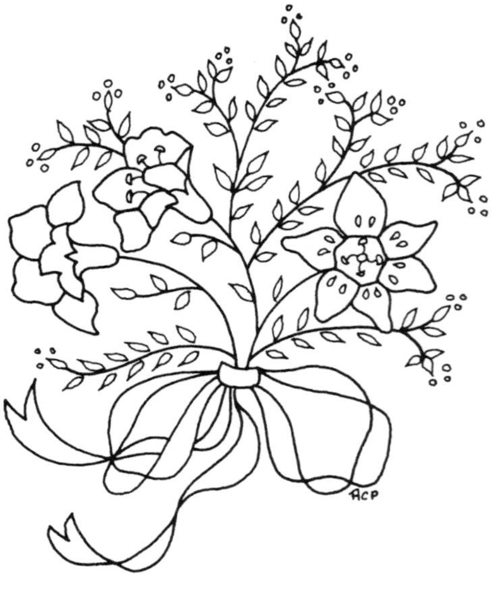
ACP

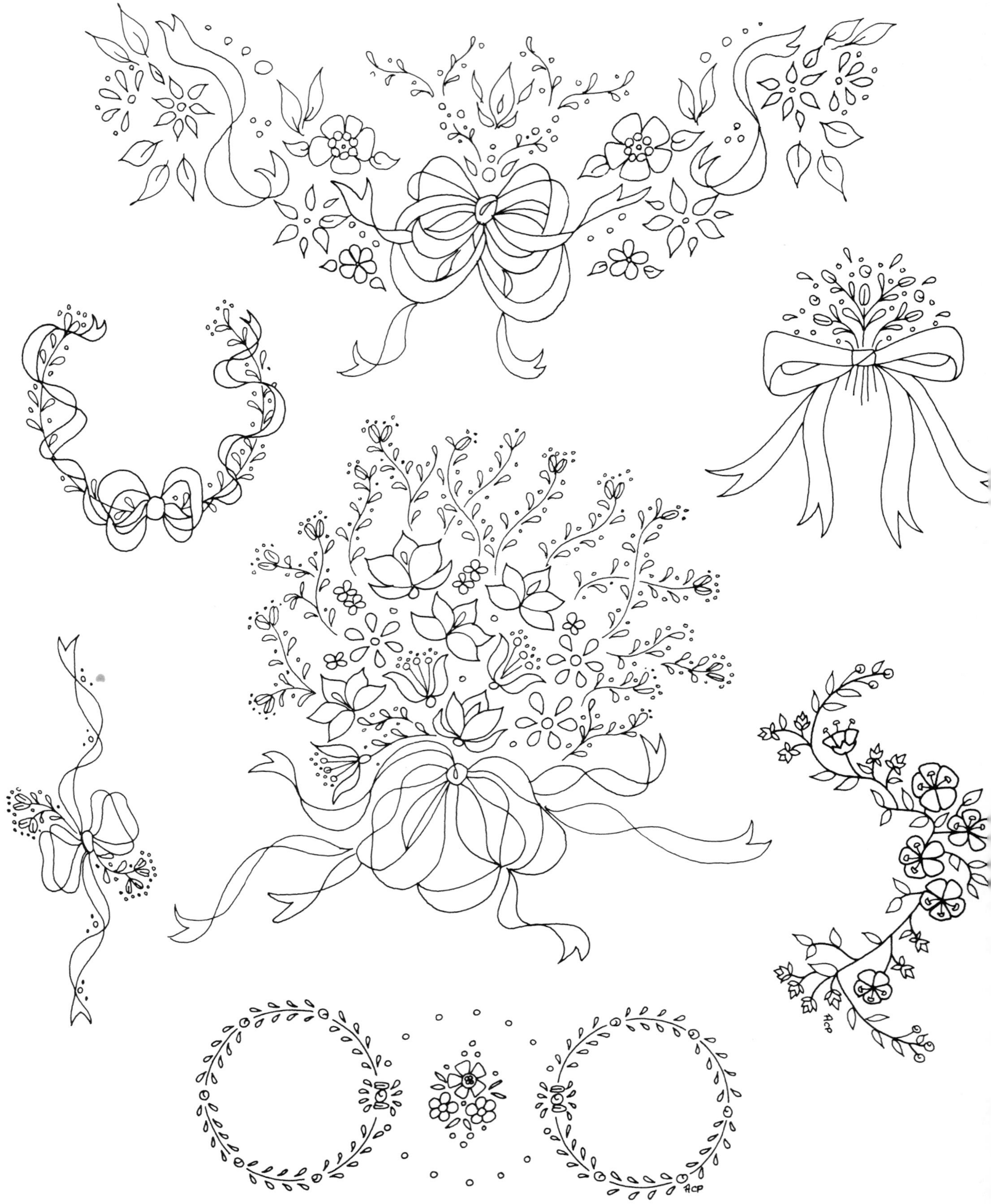

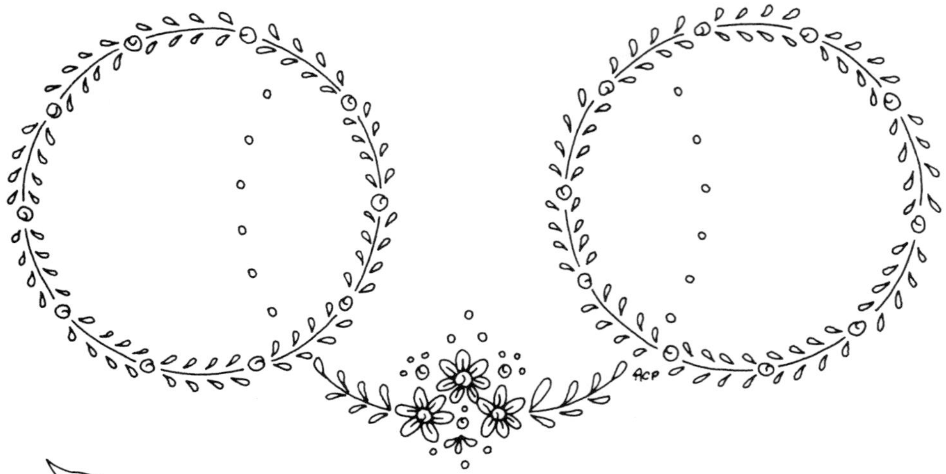

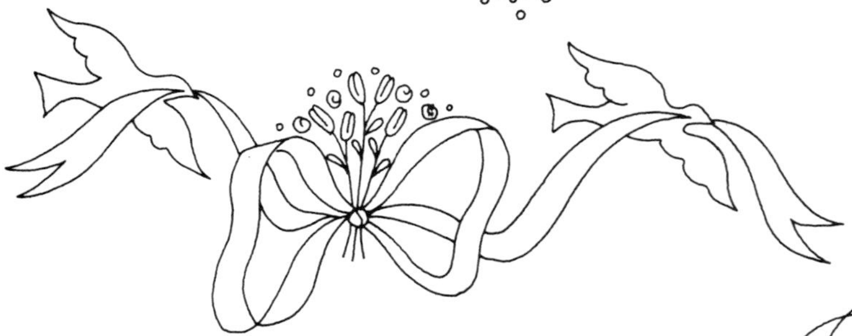

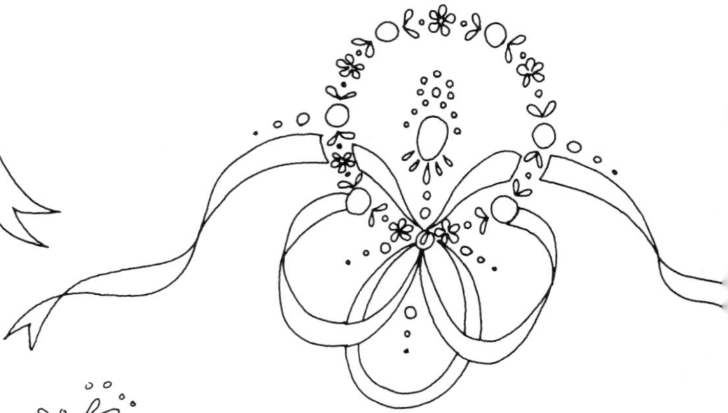

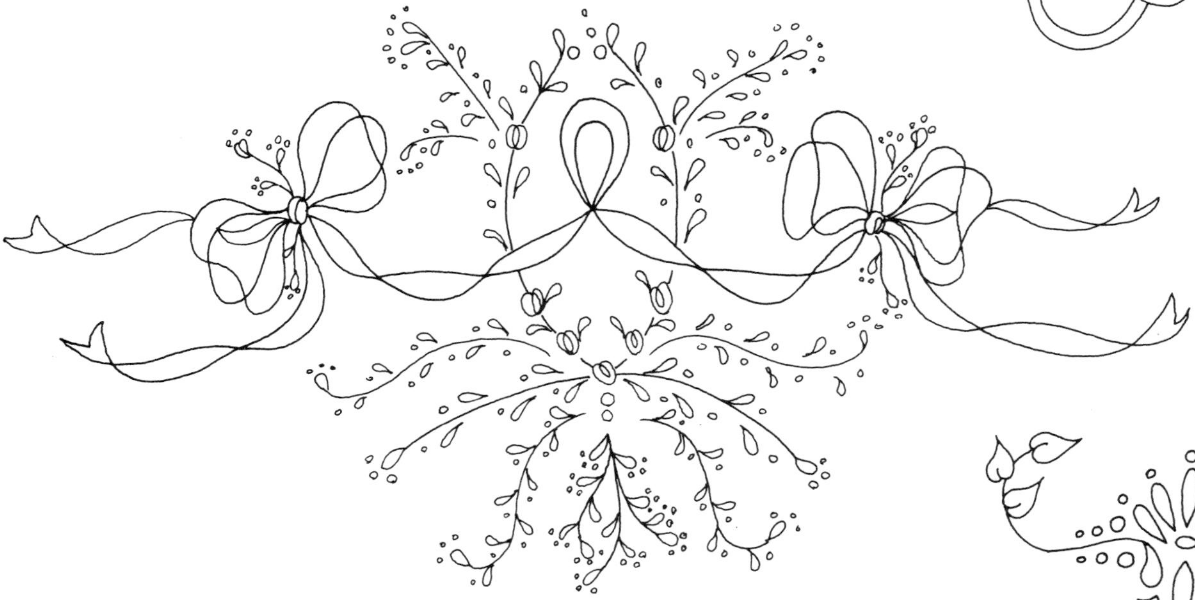

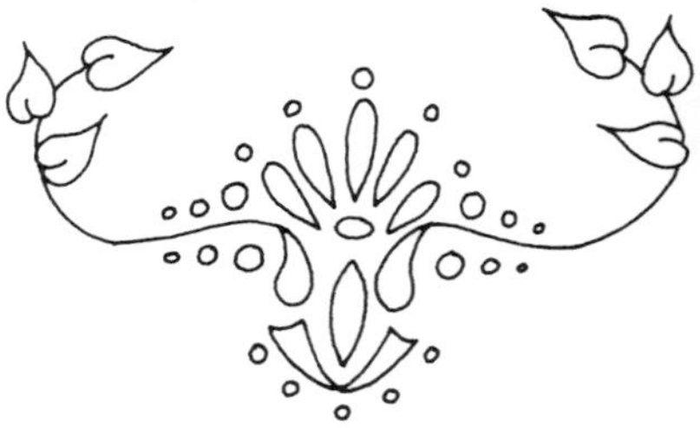

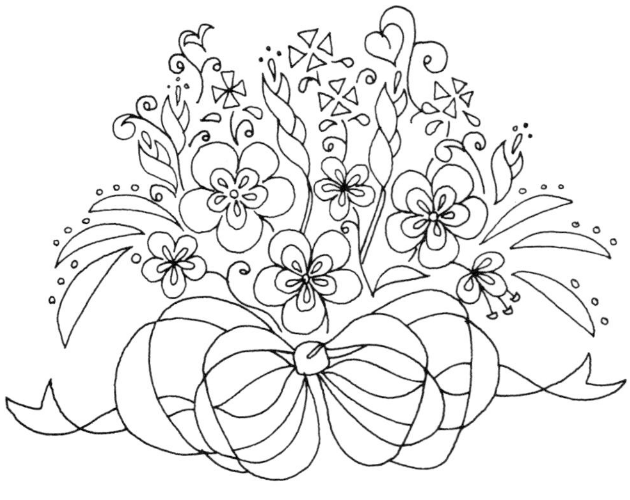

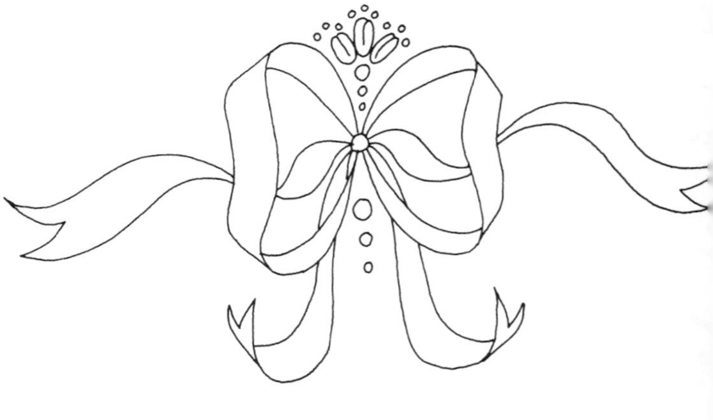

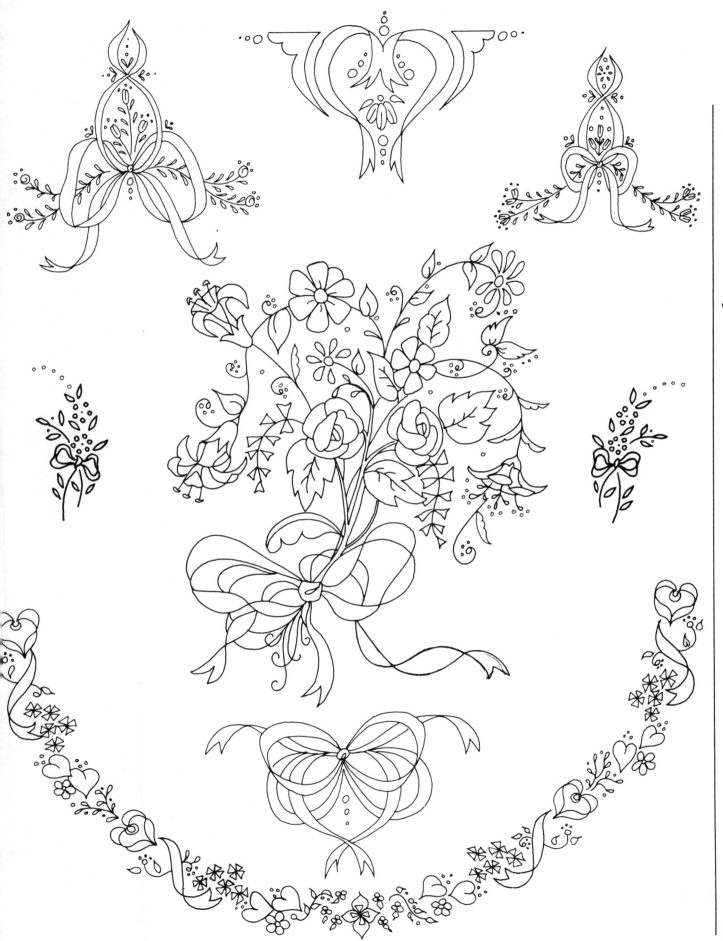

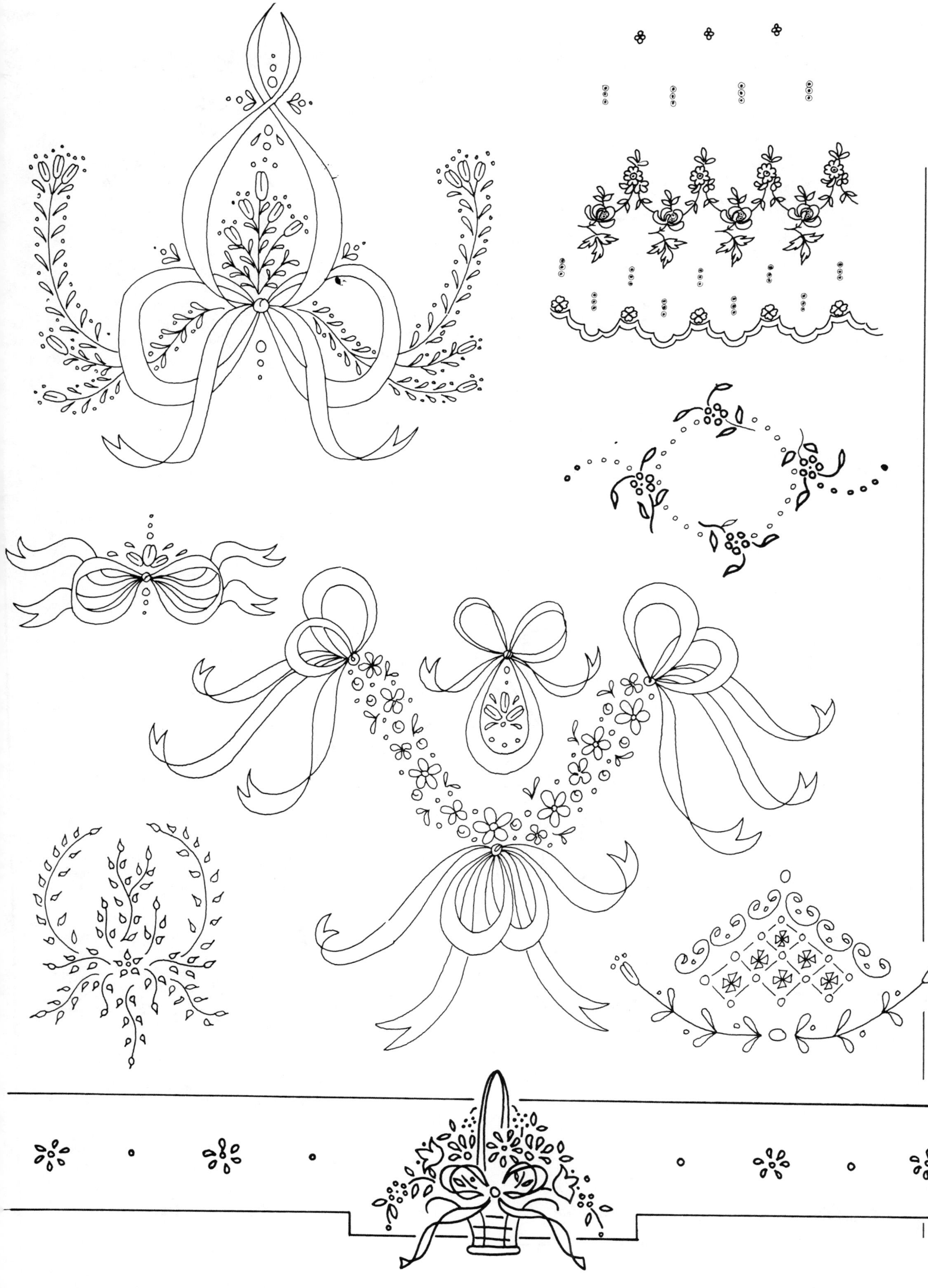

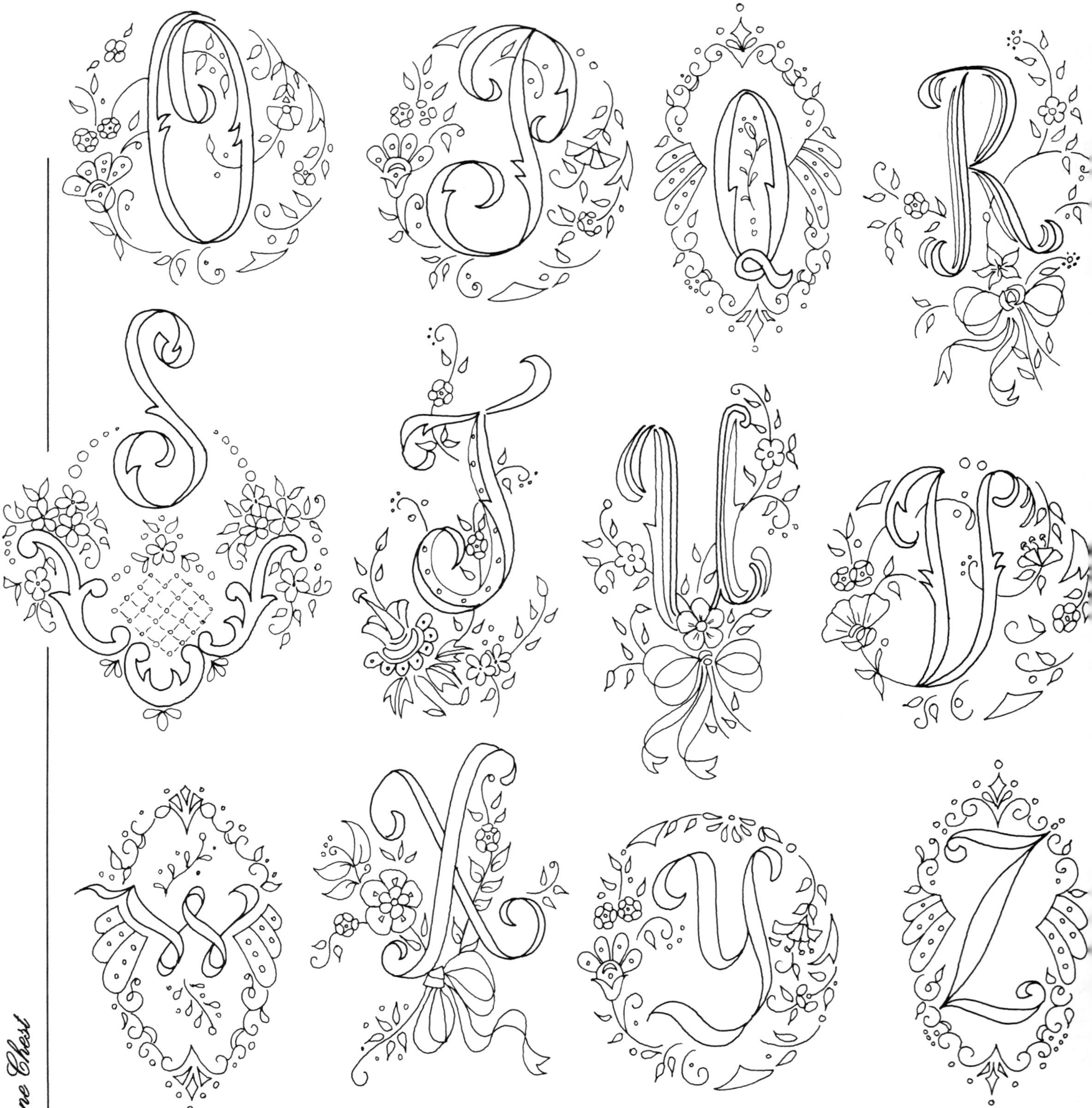

331

A B C D E F

G H I J K L

M N O P 2 R

S T U V W

X Y Z

French Knot Alphabet

French Knot Alphabet

Merry Christmas

SANTA

NOEL

Grandmother's Hope Chest

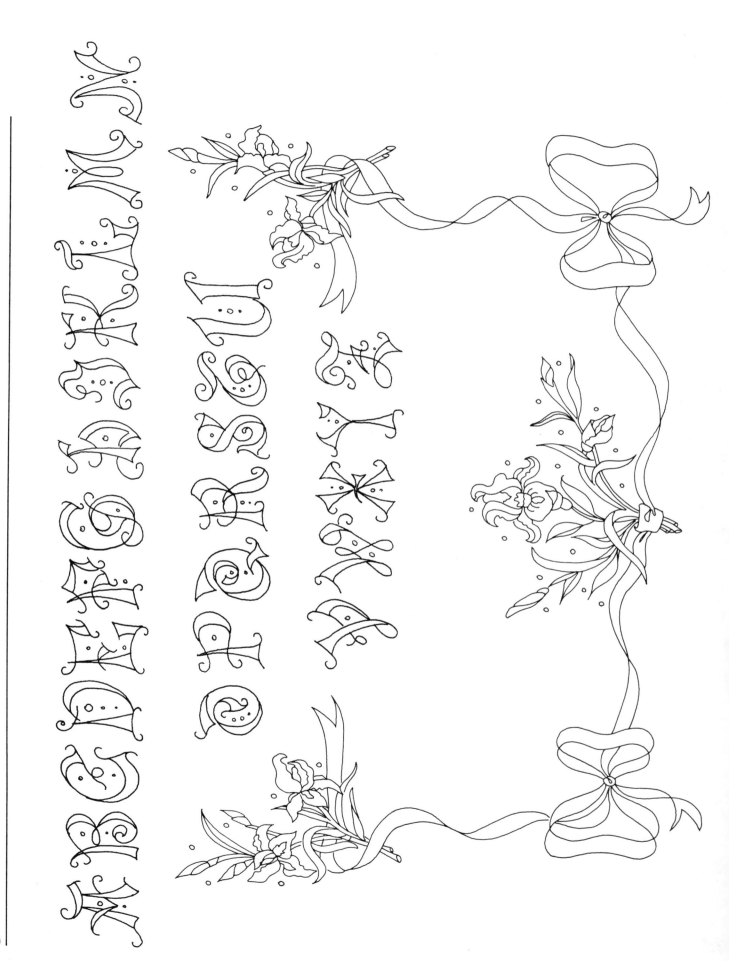

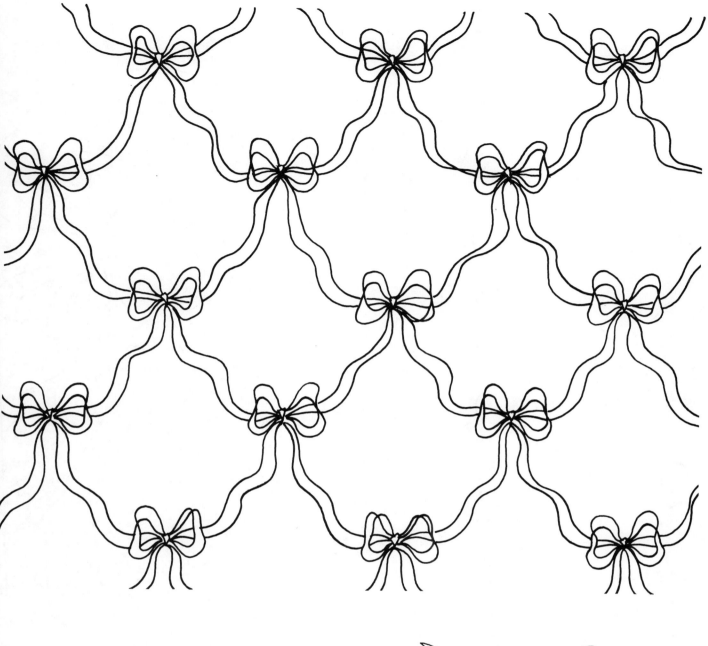

Example

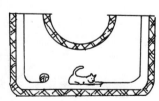

Extend line all the way around the collar.

A B C D E F
G H I J K L
M N O P Q R
S T U V W X
Y Z

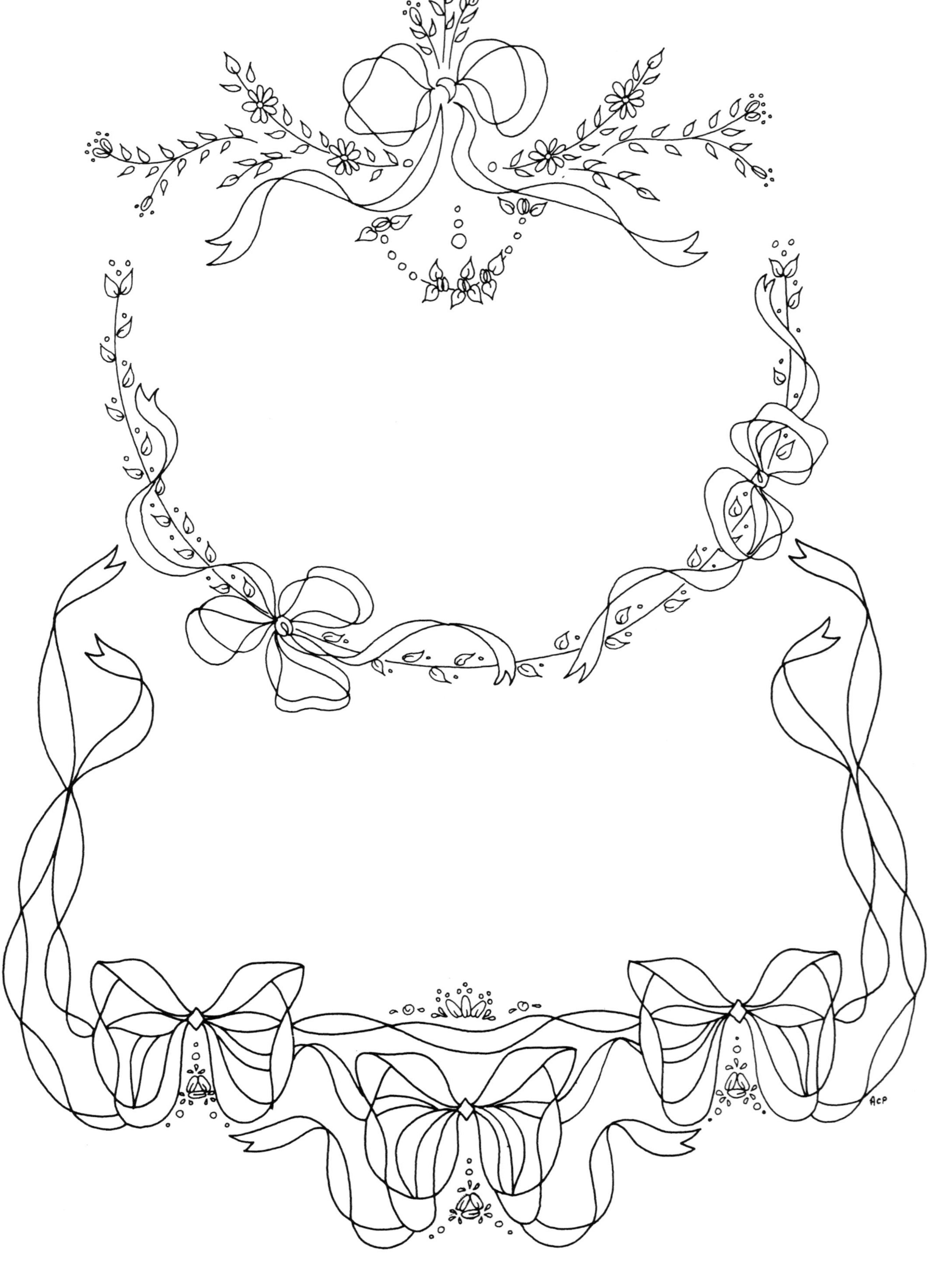
ACP

Spring Flowers

Pleat 18 rows

Rows 1 to 12 Back smock in cables.
Row 3 Stitch a 4 step flowerette with two straight stitch for leaves. Leave 19 pleats between flower leaves.

Row 5 Stitch flowerette centering flowerette on Row 3. Continue this pattern through to Row 11.
Row 13 Stitch 2 rows of cables. On first row of cable stitch 3 cables skipping 4 stitches between each set.

Row 15 Stitch flowerette with 8 pleat between each flower.
Row 16 Repeat Row 13 except stitch 3 cables below the two rows o cables.

Photographs of graphs are included in the color section in the middle of the book.

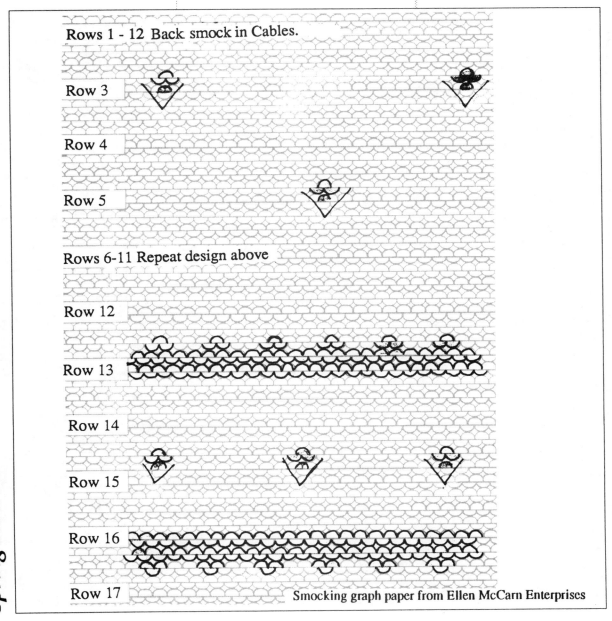

Rows 1 - 12 Back smock in Cables.

Row 3

Row 4

Row 5

Rows 6-11 Repeat design above

Row 12

Row 13

Row 14

Row 15

Row 16

Row 17

Spring Flowers

Smocking graph paper from Ellen McCarn Enterprises

345

SMOCKING DESIGNS

Sunshine Diamonds

Pleat 19 rows

Rows 1 to 8 Back smock with cables.

Rows 8-1/2 to 9-1/2 Stitch 3 step 1/2 space trellis.

Rows 10-1/2 to 15-1/2 Stitch 3 step 1/2 space waves forming diamonds.

Rows 16-1/2 to 17-1/2 Stitch 3 step 1/2 space trellis.

Flowerettes - Stitch 4 step flowerette inside the diamonds as shown on graph to form the proper design.

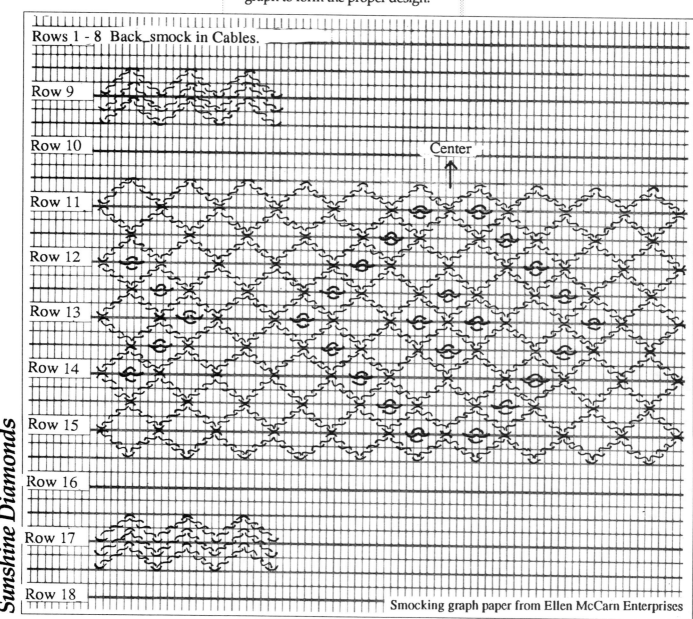

Rows 1 - 8 Back smock in Cables.

Row 9

Row 10   Center

Row 11

Row 12

Row 13

Row 14

Row 15

Row 16

Row 17

Row 18

Sunshine Diamonds

346

Smocking graph paper from Ellen McCarn Enterprises

Pink Fantasy

Pleat 19 rows

Rows 1 to 2 Stitch a 2 step 1/2 space trellis.
Repeat trellis for rows 3 to 4, 5 to 6, 7 to 8, and 9 to 10.
Rows 11 to 11-1/2 Stitch 3 cables, 2 step 1/2 space wave. Repeat.
Rows 11-3/4 to 11-1/4 Repeat Rows 11 to 11-1/2.
Rows 12 to 16 Stitch 2 step 1/2 space waves. These waves should form diamonds.
Rows 16-1/4 to 16-3/4 Repeat Rows 11 to 11-1/2.
Rows 16-1/2 to 17 Repeat Rows 11 to 11-1/2.

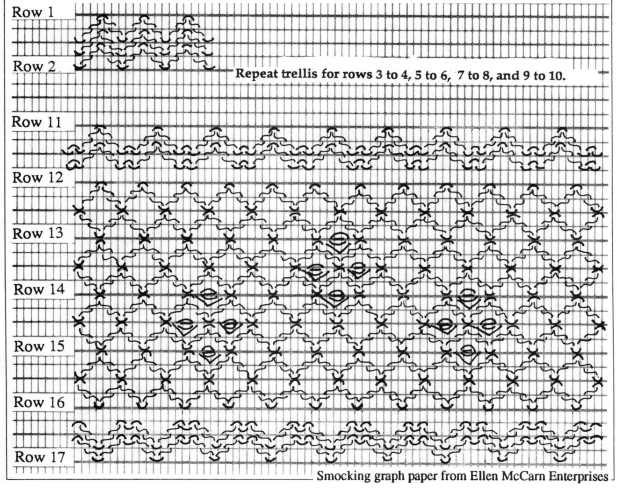

Row 1

Row 2   Repeat trellis for rows 3 to 4, 5 to 6, 7 to 8, and 9 to 10.

Row 11

Row 12

Row 13

Row 14

Row 15

Row 16

Row 17

Smocking graph paper from Ellen McCarn Enterprises

Pink Fantasy

347

Bullion Shamrocks

Pleat 16 rows

Rows 1 to 13 Back smock 3 step waves to form diamonds.

Rows 3, 5, 7, 9, 11, 13 Stitch 3 sets of bullion roses as shown on graph.

Rows 14 to 15 Stitch 2 step 1/2 space trellis wave.

Bullion Sailboats

Pleat 10 rows

Rows 3/4 to 1-1/2 Stitch a trellis wave with an outline stitch.

Rows 1-3/4 to Row 6 2 step 1/4 space waves.

Rows 6-1/2 to 7 Stitch outline wave.

Rows 7-1/2 to 7 Stitch outline wave.

Rows 8 to 7-1/2 Stitch outline wave.

Boats - Stitch 2 stitch bullion flower. Place inside diamonds as shown on graph. Be sure to center the boat.

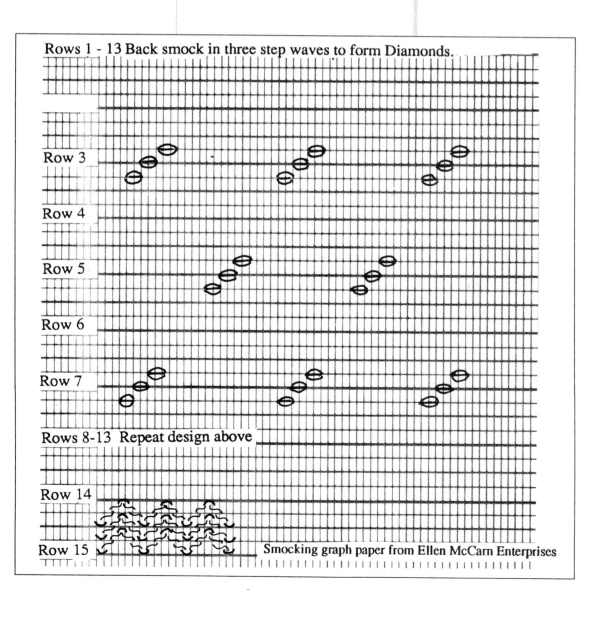

Rows 1 - 13 Back smock in three step waves to form Diamonds.

Row 3

Row 4

Row 5

Row 6

Row 7

Rows 8-13 Repeat design above

Row 14

Row 15   Smocking graph paper from Ellen McCarn Enterprises

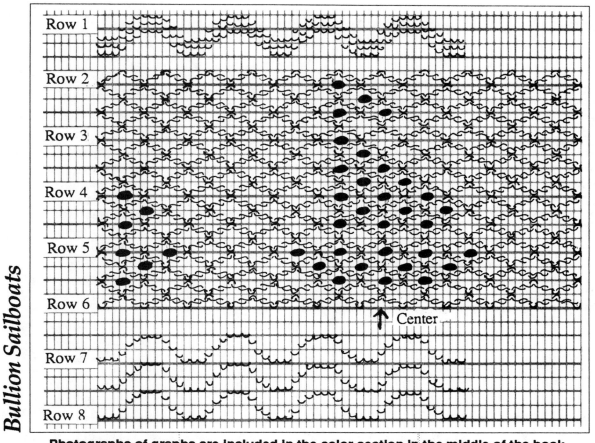

Row 1
Row 2
Row 3
Row 4
Row 5
Row 6
↑ Center
Row 7
Row 8

Bullion Sailboats

Photographs of graphs are included in the color section in the middle of the book.

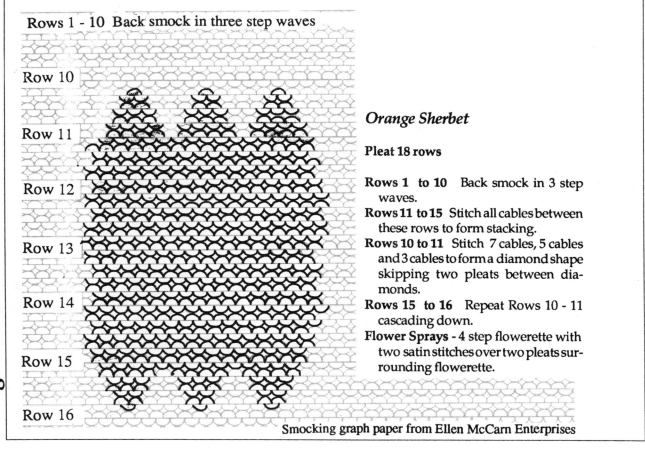

Rows 1 - 10 Back smock in three step waves

Row 10
Row 11
Row 12
Row 13
Row 14
Row 15
Row 16

Orange Sherbet

Orange Sherbet

Orange Sherbet

Pleat 18 rows

Rows 1 to 10 Back smock in 3 step waves.

Rows 11 to 15 Stitch all cables between these rows to form stacking.

Rows 10 to 11 Stitch 7 cables, 5 cables and 3 cables to form a diamond shape skipping two pleats between diamonds.

Rows 15 to 16 Repeat Rows 10 - 11 cascading down.

Flower Sprays - 4 step flowerette with two satin stitches over two pleats surrounding flowerette.

Smocking graph paper from Ellen McCarn Enterprises

349

INDEX

Grandmother's Hope Chest

ABOUT THE AUTHOR

Martha Campbell Pullen, a native of Scottsboro, Alabama, is an internationally-known lecturer and author in the heirloom sewing field. After graduating with a degree in speech and English from the University of Alabama, she taught those subjects at almost every level of middle school and high school. Later, her studies led to receiving a Ph. D. in educational administration and management from the University of Alabama. She has served on the faculties of the University of Florida and Athens State College. She was director of development for the University of Alabama in Huntsville. She completed post doctoral studies at Vanderbilt University, the University of Alabama in Huntsville, and Alabama A and M University.

Her love of sewing and children's clothing encouraged the opening of Martha Pullen's Heirloom Shop in Huntsville, Alabama, August 1, 1981. Two months later, she opened Martha Pullen Company, Inc., the wholesale division. She has served on the board of directors of the Smocking Arts Guild of America and has presented workshops on French sewing by machine throughout the United States, Australia, England, and New Zealand. She imports laces from France and England; Swiss batiste and embroideries from Switzerland. She has written books: French Hand Sewing by Machine, A Beginner's Guide; Heirloom Doll Clothes; Bearly Beginning Smocking; Shadowwork Embroidery; French Hand Sewing by Machine, The Second Book; and Antique Clothing, French Sewing by Machine. She has designed and published many garment patterns as well.

She conducts the Martha Pullen School of Art Fashion twice a year in Huntsville, Alabama. People come from all over the world for a fabulous five days of sewing, fellowship, food, and fun. Once a year, she teaches this same school in Australia and in New Zealand. Classes are planned for students who know absolutely nothing about French sewing and smocking to those who are already experts and who want more mastery!

She is the founder and publisher of a best-selling magazine, Sew Beautiful, which is dedicated to heirloom sewing. The publication charms over 55,000 readers worldwide. She loves people so much and wishes, "that I could travel home with everybody who buys a book and get to know them personally. We could have so much fun talking about antique clothing, sewing and our families."

She is the wife of Joseph Ross Pullen, an implant dentist. She is the mother of five of the most wonderful children in the world. She participates in many civic activities and is an active member of her church. She is a new grandmother!

Grandmother's Hope Chest